THE QUOTABLE WOMAN

WOMAN

From Eve to 1799

The Quotable Woman

From Eve to 1799

compiled and edited by

Elaine Partnow

assistant editor

Claudia B. Alexander

Facts On File Publications
New York, New York ● Bicester, England

The Quotable Woman: From Eve to 1799

Library of Congress Cataloging in Publication Data
Main entry under title:
The Quotable woman: From Eve to 1799.
  A companion volume to: The Quotable woman: 1800–1981.
  Bibliography: p.
  Includes index.
  1. Women–Quotations.   2. Quotations, English.
I. Partnow, Elaine.
PN6081.5.Q63 1984   082'.088042   82-15511
ISBN 0-87196-307-8

Printed in the United States of America
10 9 8 7 6 5 4 3 2 1

To Turner Browne
My dearest friend, my love—my husband. Thank you, cher. I couldn't have gotten through it without your support.

Contents

Preface

Many, many years ago a noted clairvoyant volunteered, unsolicited, that I was a medium. I scoffed, laughed and denied—and spent several sleepless nights. Self-protectively, I tucked the ghoulish prospect into a hidden corner of my mind. But light can reveal wonders in darkened caverns. A multifarious touch of women's words has revealed to me that I *am* a medium of sorts, for through me the voices of hundreds of women from the past speak to you today.

Since January 1974, when the idea for *The Quotable Woman* first crystallized in my mind, it has been my mission to document—at least in part—those voices. At first I envisioned a book encompassing all of written history. I had only the vaguest idea of the magnitude of work, and works, involved. Once exploration began, it became clear that the project was simply too vast for one compilation. Hence the first volume, *The Quotable Woman: 1800–1975* (later updated to 1981), and now the second, companion volume, including women born from biblical times to 1799. Ten years, off and on, spent on this project—ten years of entanglement in a web of women's words.

An inveterate quote plucker is what I have become; sometimes it comes back at me and I have a good laugh at myself, as on discovering Hannah More's caustic verse: "He liked those literary cooks/Who skim the cream of others' books;/And ruin half the author's graces/By plucking *bon-mots* from their places." But *The Quotable Woman* has been a fine excuse for indulging in my favorite sport—reading. However, there is much of what I call "mule's work" that went into making this book useful and educational as well as entertaining.

I have included a great number of footnotes, a feature missing from the first volume; in context, the quotations become more meaningful and contributors more quickly click into their historic place.

I have made what I believe is an even more comprehensive Subject Index than in the first volume, although again I opted for a classification system of careful distillation of meaning rather than the more traditional first- or key-word index. Emily Dickinson once wrote that "a poet can use but few words, and they must be the best words, the chiefest words..." It is the same with the indexer. While there is extensive cross-referencing in my index, it would be quite impossible, without a built-in thesaurus, to be complete in that regard. Not only should synonyms be considered when looking up things, but an exchange of subclassifications for classifications. To illustrate, under "death" there are various subcategories including " ~ of loved ones"; but for a quotation pertaining to the death of a specific relation it would be necessary to see, for example, "son, death of ~"; "child, death of ~"; "soldier, death of ~"; etc.

In compiling the index, it frequently seemed strange to apply contemporary terms and meanings to 5th- or 18th-century thought. Still, it seemed most useful to use today's terms; where the word "care," for instance, was used as we today use the word "worry," it is classified under "worry"; and although the term "blacks" was not at all in use, it is under that noun that quotations referring to for instance, "colored people" are to be found. I have also chosen terms without gender wherever it seemed comfortable to do so—"humankind" rather than "mankind" (one can also refer to "people," "individual," and "human nature").

The Biographical Index is, unfortunately, sometimes more vague than that in the first volume because lifespan is so often difficult to pin down with women who lived so long ago. We are today a record-keeping world; not so in the dawn and midday of history. And those few records that were maintained were too often lost or obscured. But I have added, when noting sisters, mothers, daughters and other female relatives, cross-references to those who are also contributors in this book.

During the Renaissance, women's voices grew in volume as well as numbers, but often they were distorted or off key. In response to Germaine de Staël's remark, "Oh, if I could make myself into a man! How I would settle accounts with those *antiphilosophes* once and for all!" J. Christopher Herold, in *Mistress to An Age*, his biography of de Staël, writes: "Had she been born a man, three quarters of her talents would not have been spent in combat to hold affection and to justify her right to be herself; the role she played and the work she left, though remarkable, are only a fraction of the potential she could have realized without the handicap of her sex." A comment applicable to too many of the women in this book. Of the backward evolution of her sex, Anna Maria Lenngren wrote: "The fairer sex possessed a mind/Of sturdy fabric, like her cloak./Now all is different in our lives—/Other fabrics, other mores!/Taffetas, indecent stories." Theirs was a narrow world—of fashion, social intrigue, the concerns of the distaff. Venturing outside that circle was not approved; as a 17th-century French proverb states, "Discreet women have neither eyes, nor ears." Such mores conditioned women to "keep their place," hold their tongue, conceal their brain. "I am a woman:—tell me not of fame,/The eagle's wing may sweep this stormy path,/And fling back arrows where the dove would die." (Landon, *Poems*)

Many of the quotations in this volume were plucked in the years I began the first collection. Fieldwork continued during the writing of my next two books. But the lion's share of the harvest began in the summer of 1981. I'd just moved to Louisiana and was living in a small travel trailer in the woods; we had no running water for too many months, and neither electricity nor a telephone for weeks on end. My "office" took up too much of our tiny living quarters, so my husband and I built an 8′ x 12′ hut to house *The Quotable Woman*. In their uninsulated space, my books had to be wiped down with Lysol every other week in summer to suppress mildew; winters found me wearing army-surplus gloves sans fingers to warm my hands enough to type. The exigencies of country life consumed huge quantities of time. My work slowed; deadlines were extended. My paperwork was soiled by the hens, walked on by the cats, drooled on by the dogs and eaten by the cockroaches. I thought of how many of our foremothers, who had to tolerate and overcome greater hardships than I was facing, managed, despite their overwhelming load of tasks, to write journals, letters, books and poems—how strong the impulse to communicate one's own experience of the world with others.

Those pioneer women wrote vividly of their lines. But they were not the prolific ones. The voluminous output of some of the women in these pages is astonishing—Jane Austen, Aphra Behn, Susan Centlivre, Marguerite Blessington, Sydney Owenson Morgan, Sarah Josepha

Hale (who didn't even begin to write till she'd reached her forties). . . . It is my opinion that women who wrote in times gone by were often more prolific than those of today because, for one thing, since they generally were educated, they were most often from the upper classes and thus had servants to care for their children and do all menial labor. Also, there were fewer distractions—no television, no telephone, husbands often away for weeks or months at a time. Further, they did not handle family finances, investments or properties. They had more time to sit at their writing than we do today. It has also struck me that more of what one had to say then might have seemed relevant because so relatively little had been committed to print.

As a consequence of this prolificacy I have taken a somewhat different approach here than in the first collection; each contributor, whenever possible, was more thoroughly investigated and so quoted more profusely. The number of quotations does not, however, necessarily reflect a contributor's importance in history, but simply the quotability of her words.

I have again chosen a chronological presentation of contributors for sociological and historical interest. I've also allowed the chronology to edge into the 19th century, limiting it to women whose years of birth are not known but who flourished no later than 1830. It did not seem farfetched to assume they were born no later than 1799.

Inspired, moved and provoked by much of what I've studied these past years, I'm frequently incensed to read, in books on 17th-century literature or in an encyclopedia, that certain poets or authors are "inferior." Why this denunciation? It comes not from a contemporary examination but merely mimics reputations established *in their own day*. And in their day women were resented, even frowned upon for daring to publish. In Jane Austen's *Persuasion* one character says: "...I do not think I ever opened a book in my life which had not something to say upon woman's inconstancy. Songs and proverbs all talk of woman's fickleness. But, perhaps, you will say, these were all written by men." He is answered: "Perhaps I shall. Yes, yes, if you please, no reference to examples in books...the pen has been in their hands. I will not allow books to prove anything." Unbiased, contemporary critics need to *re*-view these women's works without the prejudices of a more paternalistic age.

There seems to be a great difference between what occupied the minds of most pre-19th century women and what concerns contemporary women. Especially up through the 17th century, women did not seem so overtly concerned with their status, or with oppression and equality, as did later generations. Their interests were deep, yet narrow: the distaff side—love, children, the home, religion, social life.

As in my first collection, I have tried to remain objective and eclectic in my selections, plucking passages that were moving, persuasive or illuminating, whether or not I personally agreed with their viewpoint or sentiment. In fact, some of the quotations were chosen to elucidate the ignorance and closemindedness of the times. Witness Sarah Josepha Hale, whom I much admire but often disagree with, writing: "The belief in witchcraft was and is universal, where the spirit of Christianity has not shed its blessed light." That "blessed light" has caused inquisitions and crusades, has perpetrated the deaths of such as Joan of Arc, and more. And certainly it was not responsible for the enlightenment in the Far East.

The 804 women in these pages represent every quarter of the entire globe; contributors hail from exotic lands, Western lands, Latin places, and ancient city-states, the Far East and the Near, the Old World and the New. Freed slaves are quoted alongside Pompadour and Elizabeth; poets and painters, salonists and saints, soldiers and assassins alike are included. Titular rank, although included in the Biographical Index, is not included with the names in the Quotations section (except where necessary for identification). As representative voices of our past, each woman should share the stage equally.

I plowed through many collections of dull English letters describing the daily duties and harassments of running a proper upper-class English home. While much of this proved less than quotable, it occurred to me that many pseudonymous women whose real identities are untraceable—women such as Mary Tattlewell, Joan Hit-him-home, Esther Sournam—may have been those very same proper matrons.

Wherever it did not seem confusing, I have retained original spellings and punctuation, for flavor and interest. And while I had to accustom myself to *v*'s in place of *u*'s and *f*'s where we would have *s*'s, it struck me, nonetheless, how contemporary much of the language and humor of even the earliest writers can be, from Sappho to Murasaki Shikibu to Emily Eden.

As always, there are scores of notable women for whom there are no extant writings and who were, perforce, left out. For example, Elizabeth Timothy (d. 1757) was the first American woman (though born in Holland) to publish a newspaper. Information about her and her daughter-in-law Ann, who continued the paper after her husband's death, is available, but none of their words survive. Seventeenth-century painters Rachel Van Pool and Elisabetta Sirani, whose works can still be seen, left us no words of their own. The voice of the legendary Nefertiti remains silent. Translations were not included, as it has been my intention to quote original works; therefore, several notable translators do not appear. An exception is Mary Sidney Herbert, whose translations of the psalms are so far removed from any I've seen in several versions of the Bible in English that, in my opinion, they comprise original works.

Women speak a great deal in the 1980s of "networking." Nowhere have I found a greater example of this than among 17th- and 18th-century English and French women; the letter-writing, dedications, prefaces and journals were filled with references to one another. Readers will find throughout the Quotations section footnoted cross-references to other contributors who have been alluded to, as well as to women related to one another.

A word about alphabetization of names—particularly relevant when using the Biographical Index. A strict letter-by-letter method has been followed. All pseudonyms and *familiar* aka's (also known as) are cross-referenced. Please note that Germaine de Staël, for example, is alphabetized under S, and Madame de Fleury under F, not D; Marie de France is listed under M; Hroswitha of Gandersheim is under H. This kind of decision was not always apparent. The goal was to be distinct and clear and to stick with the most popular contemporary forms of listings. Japanese, Chinese, Korean and Vietnamese names are alphabetized under what appears to the Western eye as the Christian name, but what is, actually, the surname; thus Hŏ Nansŏrhŏn is listed under H, not N. It is interesting to note that women in these Eastern countries, by tradition, retain their surname when marrying, unlike their Western counterparts who lose theirs by assuming their husbands'.

I could not help noticing how many women in the Bible—and elsewhere in history, too, for that matter—have no names at all. How sad. It has reminded me of bit parts I played in my early acting days; I was given identifications, such as "guest at party." Like so many extras, these nameless women serve to advance the plot, but are not considered central enough to be entitled to individuality.

While many believe in the absolute veracity of the Bible, I have found it sensible, since much of it was written centuries after the history it documents, to keep separate from the other quotations those of biblical women. They may be considered more attributions than actual quotations, yet their importance in Western civilization is such that they could not be omitted from this volume.

It seemed more practical to present biblical women "in order of appearance," if you will, rather than chronologically, since there is often great disparity in experts' findings with respect to their lifespans. But I have attempted to identify that information as well as to find out the approximate years in which the various books of the Bible were written. I have arrived at as logical conclusions as possible, using the following resources: *Encyclopedia Britannica* (8th edition); *All the Women of the Bible* by Edith Deen; *Dictionary of the Bible* by James Hastings; *Encyclopedic Dictionary of Religion* by Paul Kevin Meager, et al; *Harper's Encyclopedia of Bible Life*, 3rd rev. ed., by Madeleine S. and J. Lane Miller; and *Women of the Bible* by H.V. Morton.

All biblical passages are from the King James version, with the exception of those books that do not appear in this translation: Judith, Tobit, Esther (lettered verses only), 2 Maccabees, and Daniel (chapter 13 only). These books are from the Jerusalem version.

During most of the making of this book, I lived a somewhat solitary life in the woods; therefore, it was more of a single-handed effort than the first *Quotable Woman*. Consequently, no one is more mindful than I of the omissions and shortcomings of this work. But there are a few people who were instrumental in its production and to whom I would like to express gratitude.

Foremost was my assistant editor, Claudia B. Alexander, who made the initial selection of quotations of all European Renaissance women, from which I culled more than 1,000 quotations; with the assistance of Catherine Plantego, she concluded the research on and did the organization of the Biographical Index; with the assistance of professors Carlo di Maio and Michael Fanning, she translated several poems from the Italian by writers whose works were not available in English; and she worked long hours with me on the arduous tasks of final checking of spellings, chronology, contributor numbers, etc. My friend Pat Jolly saved me miles of wandering through stacks in the library and did tedious clerical work without complaint. Friend and neighbor Arthur Charbonnet lent a sharp eye to some proofreading.

At my publisher's, copy editor Eleanor Wedge not only conquered a massive manuscript, but contributed her intelligence and knowledge by adding many footnotes and asking more questions than I care to remember. Finally, I wish to thank my editor, Gerard Helferich. Despite all the delays, the revisions, the missing pages, the revised revisions, the phone calls and letters and Express Mail packages and extended deadlines, he made it all seem smooth as silk. He supported and assisted me in helpful and meaningful ways, and his is the nicest telephone acquaintanceship I've ever been privileged to share.

As in my first collection, I must, finally, thank the women—the voices that have hovered about me these past ten years, echoing through the centuries, reverberating in my brain; it is they who have made this book possible. Thank you, sisters.

Elaine Partnow
Interlocken, at Hillsboro Upper
Village, New Hampshire
June 1984

How To Use This Book

The women quoted are presented in chronological order according to the year of their birth, then alphabetically within each year. Each contributor has been given a number; guides to these contributor numbers appear in the running heads throughout the Quotations section and are used, rather than page numbers, in the Biographical and Subject Indexes.

Where firm birth and/or death dates were not known, but it was possible to make a reasonable guess, dates are followed by a question mark; when guesses were more broadly based, dates are preceded by a "c.," for circa. Dates shown with a slash (e.g., 1734/35) indicate that birth or death was definitely in one of those two years. If neither year of birth nor of death can be surmised, flourished dates are given, indicated by "fl." In all instances it is the first year appearing that dictates the contributor's place in the chronology; thus (?–1301) places that contributor among women born or flourishing in 1301, even though she may have been born much earlier.

The quotations for each woman are presented chronologically according to the copyright or publication date of the source. If only an approximate year of publication is known, a circa date is given. Parenthetical dates within a source indicate the time at which the quotation was *originally* spoken or written or, when contained in a contemporary anthology, originally published. In some cases, no date of publication could be ascertained; these quotations follow the dated sources and, where the year should appear, are indicated by "n.d." (no date).

When possible, the location of a quotation within the source is given—that is, the part, chapter, stanza, act or scene. If, however, a quote was taken from something other than its original source—for example, from a critical review—and the precise location is not known, it precedes those quotations that are more specifically designated. Of course, many books have no chapter or part numbers or subheadings, and many poems are not separated into stanzas, and so locations cannot always be specified.

Abbreviations used in source citations are: Vol.—volume; Pt.—part; Bk.—book; Ch.—chapter; St.—stanza; Sec.—section; No.—number; Sc.—scene; l.—line; l.l.—last line(s); c.—circa; ed.—editor; tr.—translator.

When a quotation is taken from a book, an article, or any work by a writer other than the contributor, it is indicated by the words "Quoted in" followed by the source and its author. In the case of anthological works "Quoted in" is not used, but editors are indicated.

Quotation marks around a quotation indicate that it is dialogue spoken by a character in a work of fiction or that it appeared in quotations in the original work. Except for exchanges of dialogue, original paragraphing is not indicated in prose selections, whereas in poetry the integrity of form has been maintained.

For information concerning the use of the Biographical and Subject Indexes, see notes preceding each index.

Charm is deceitful, and beauty empty; the woman who is wise is the one to praise. Give her a share in what her hands have worked for, and let her works tell her praises at the city gates.

—*Proverbs 31:31*

Here dwell the true magicians. Nature is our servant. Man is our pupil. We change, we conquer, we create.

—*Anna Letitia Barbauld*

THE QUOTABLE WOMAN

WOMAN

From Eve to 1799

Quotations from the Bible

1. Eve
(pre-4000 B.C.)

1 We may eat of the fruit of the trees of the
garden: But of the fruit of the tree which is
in the midst of the garden, God hath said,
Ye shall not eat of it, neither shall ye touch
it, lest ye die.   Genesis, 3:2, 3
                            c.9th century B.C.

2 The serpent beguiled me, and I did eat.
                            Ibid., 3:13

3 I have gotten a man* from the Lord.
                            Ibid., 4:1
* Refers to birth of her son Seth.

2. Hagar
(c.2300–c.1850 B.C.)

1 Thou God seest me: . . . Have I also here
looked after him that seeth me?
                            Genesis, 16:13
                            c.9th century B.C.

2 Let me not see the death of the child.
                            Ibid., 21:16

3. Sarah
(c.1987–c.1860 B.C.)

1 After I am waxed old shall I have pleasure,
my lord being old also?   Genesis, 18:12
                            c.9th century B.C.

2 God hath made me to laugh, so that all that
hear will laugh with me.   Ibid., 21:6

3 Who would have said unto Abraham, that
Sarah should have given children suck? for
I have born him a son in his old age.
                            Ibid., 21:7

4. Lot's daughter (the elder)
(fl. c.18th century B.C.)

1 Our father is old, and there is not a man in
the earth to come in unto us after the manner of all the earth:
    Come, let us make our father drink wine,
and we will lie with him, that we may preserve seed of our father.
                            Genesis, 19:31, 32
                            c.9th century B.C.

5. Rebekah
(18th century B.C.)

1 Drink my lord:. . . .
I will draw water for thy camels also, until
they have done drinking.
                            Genesis, 24:18, 19
                            c.9th century B.C.

2 If it be so, why am I thus?
                            Ibid., 25:22

3 Upon me be thy curse, my son: only obey
my voice, and go fetch me them.
                            Ibid., 27:13

3

6. Leah
(18th century B.C.)

1 Surely the Lord hath looked upon my affliction; now therefore my husband will love.
Genesis, 29:32
c.9th century B.C.

2 Now this time will my husband be joined
unto me, because I have born him three
sons. . . . Ibid., 29:34

3 Happy am I, for the daughters will call me
blessed. . . . Ibid., 30:13

4 God hath endued me with a good dowry;
now will my husband dwell with me, because I have born his six sons. . . .
Ibid., 30:20

5   Is there yet any portion or inheritance for
us [Leah and Rachel] in our father's house?
    Are we not counted of him strangers?
For he hath sold us, and hath quite de-
voured also our money.
    For all the riches which God hath taken
from our father, that is ours, and our children's. . . . Ibid., 31:14–16
with Rachel

7. Rachel
(d. 1732 B.C.?)

1 Give me children, or else I die.
Genesis, 30:1
c.9th century B.C.

2 God hath judged me, and hath also heard
my voice, and hath given me a son. . . .
Ibid., 30:6

3 God hath taken away my reproach. . . .
Ibid., 30:23

Coauthor with Leah. See 6:5.

8. Pharaoh's daughter
(fl. c.1250 B.C.)

1 Because I drew him [Moses] out of the water. Exodus, 2:10
c.9th century B.C.

9. Zipporah
(fl. c.1230 B.C.)

1 Surely a bloody husband art thou to
me. . . .
A bloody husband thou art, because of the
circumcision. Exodus, 4:25, 26
c.9th century B.C.

10. Miriam
(fl. c.1250–1230 B.C.)

1 Sing ye to the Lord, for he hath triumphed
gloriously; the horse and his rider hath he
thrown into the sea. Exodus, 15:21
c.9th century B.C.

11. Five Daughters of Zelophehad: Mahlah, Noah, Hoglah, Milcah and Tirzah
(fl. 1240–1200 B.C.)

1 Our father died in the wilderness, and he
was not in the company of them that hath
gathered themselves together against the
Lord in the company of Kôr-ăh; but died in
his own sin, and had no sons.
    Why should the name of our father be
done away from among his family, because
he hath no son? Give unto us therefore a
possession among the brethren of our father. Numbers, 27:3, 4
c.9th century B.C.

12. Deborah
(fl. c.1070 B.C.)

1 Praise ye the Lord for the avenging of Israel, when the people willingly offered
themselves.
    Hear, O ye kings: give ear, O ye princes;
I, even I, will sing unto the Lord; I will sing
praise to the Lord God of Israel.
Judges, with Barak,* 5:2, 3
c.550 B.C.

* Leader who, with Deborah, delivered Israel from the
Canaanites.

2 The inhabitants of the villages ceased, they
ceased in Israel, until that I Deborah arose,
that I arose a mother in Israel.

> Ibid., 5:7

3 They chose new gods; then was war in the
gates: was there a shield or spear seen
among forty thousand in Israel?

> Ibid., 5:8

4 Speak, ye that ride on white asses, ye that
sit in judgment, and walk by the way.

> Ibid., 5:10

5 At her [Jael's] feet he bowed, he fell, he lay
down: at her feet he bowed, he fell: where
he bowed, there he fell down dead.

> Ibid., 5:27

6 So let all thine enemies perish, O Lord: but
let them that love him be as the sun when he
goeth forth in his might. And the land had
rest forty years.   Ibid., 5:31

13. Jael
(fl. 1070 B.C.)

1 Turn in, my Lord, turn in to me; fear not.

> Judges, 4:18
> c.550 B.C.

14. Daughter of Jephthah the Gileadite
(fl. 1140 B.C.)

1 Let this thing be done for me: let me alone
two months, that I may go up and down
upon the mountains, and bewail my vir-
ginity.   Judges, 11:37
                                          c.550 B.C.

15. Wife of Manoah
(fl. c.1080 B.C.)

1 If the Lord were pleased to kill us, he would
not have received a burnt offering and a
meat offering at our hands, neither would
he have shewed us all these things, nor
would as at this time have told us such
things as these.   Judges, 13:23
                          c.550 B.C.

16. First wife of Samson
(fl. c.1080 B.C.)

1 Thou dost but hate me, and lovest me not;
thou hast put forth a riddle unto the children of my people, and hast not told it me.

> Judges, 14:16
> c.550 B.C.

17. Delilah
(fl. 1080 B.C.)

1 Tell me, I pray thee, wherein thy great
strength lieth, and wherewith thou mightest be bound to afflict thee.

> Judges, 16:6
> c.550 B.C.

2 The Philistine be upon thee, Samson.

> Ibid., 16:9

3 How canst thou say, I love thee, when thine
heart is not with me? thou hast mocked me
these three times, and hast not told me
wherein thy great strength lieth.

> Ibid., 16:15

18. Naomi
(fl. c.1100 B.C.)

1 Go, return each to her mother's
house. . . . *   Ruth, 1:8
                          late 5th or 4th century B.C.

* Spoken to her daughters-in-law, Ruth and Orpah.

2 Call me not Naomi, call me Mara [bitter]:
for the Almighty hath dealt very bitterly
with me.

I went out full, and the Lord hath brough me home again empty: why then call me Naomi, seeing the Lord hath testified against me, and the Almighty hath afflicted me?   Ibid., 1:20, 21

19.   Ruth
(fl. c.1100 B.C.)

1 Intreat me not to leave thee,* or to return from following after thee: for whither thou goest, I will go; and where thou lodgest, I will lodge: thy people shall be my people, and thy God my God:

Where thou diest, will I die, and there will I be buried: the Lord do so to me, and more also, if ought but death part thee and me.   Ruth, 1:16, 17
      late 5th or 4th century B.C.

* Her mother-in-law, Naomi.

20.   Hannah
(c.1040 B.C.)

1 No, my lord, I am a woman of sorrowful spirit: I have drunk neither wine nor strong drink, but have poured out my soul before the Lord.

Count not thine handmaid for a daughter of Belial; for out of the abundance of my complaint and grief have I spoken hitherto.
      1 Samuel, 1:15, 16
      c.550 B.C.

2 My heart rejoiceth in the Lord, mine horn is exalted in the Lord: my mouth is enlarged over mine enemies; because I rejoice in thy salvation.

There is none holy as the Lord: for there is none beside thee: neither is there any rock like our God.

Talk no more so exceeding proudly; let not arrogancy come out of your mouth: for the Lord is a God of knowledge, and by him actions are weighed.

The bows of the mighty men are broken, and they that stumbled are girded with strength.

They that were full have hired out themselves for bread; and they that were hungry ceased: so that the barren hath born seven; and she that hath many children is waxed feeble.

The Lord killeth, and maketh alive: he bringeth down to the grave, and bringeth up.

The Lord maketh poor, and maketh rich: he bringeth low, and lifteth up.

He raiseth up the poor out of the dust, and lifteth up the beggar from the dunghill, to set them among princes, and to make them inherit the throne of glory: for the pillars of the earth are the Lord's, and he hath set the world upon them.

He will keep the feet of his saints, and the wicked shall be silent in darkness; for by strength shall no man prevail.

The adversaries of the Lord shall be broken to pieces; out of heaven shall he thunder upon them: the Lord shall judge the ends of the earth; and he shall give strength unto his king, and exalt the horn of his anointed.   Ibid., 2:1–10

21.   Wife of Phinehas
(c.1040–970 B.C.)

1 The glory is departed from Israel: for the ark of God is taken.   1 Samuel, 4:22
      c.550 B.C.

22.   Abigail
(fl. 990 B.C.)

1 I pray thee, forgive the trespass of thine handmaid: for the Lord will certainly make my lord a sure house; because my lord fighteth the battles of the Lord, and evil hath not been found in thee all thy days.

Yet a man is risen to pursue thee, and to seek thy soul: but the soul of my lord shall be bound in the bundle of life with the Lord thy God; and the souls of thine enemies, them shall he sling out, as out of the middle of a sling.   1 Samuel, 25:28, 29
      c.550 B.C.

2 Behold, let thine handmaid be a servant to wash the feet of the servants of my lord.
Ibid., 25:41

23. Michal
(fl. c.1010–970 B.C.)

1 If thou save not thy life tonight, tomorrow thou shalt be slain.   1 Samuel, 19:11
c.550 B.C.

2 How glorious was the king of Israel today, who uncovered himself today in the eyes of the handmaids of his servants, as one of the vain fellows shamelessly uncovereth himself!   2 Samuel, 6:20
c.550 B.C.

24. Tamar
(fl. c.990 B.C.)

1 Nay, my brother, do not force me; for no such thing ought to be done in Israel: do not thou this folly.   2 Samuel, 13:12
c.550 B.C.

25. Woman of Tekoa
(fl. c.940 B.C.)

1 For we must needs die, and are as water spilt on the ground, which cannot be gathered up again. . . .   2 Samuel, 14:14
c.550 B.C.

2 The word of my lord the king shall now be comfortable: for as an angel of God, so is my lord the king to discern good and bad: therefore the Lord thy God will be with thee.   Ibid., 14:17

26. Woman of Abel of Beth-maachah
(fl. c.1040–970 B.C.)

1 . . . why wilt thou swallow up the inheritance of the Lord?   2 Samuel, 20:19
c.550 B.C.

27. Bathsheba
(fl. c.1000–970 B.C.)

1 And thou, my lord, O king, the eyes of all Israel are upon thee, that thou shouldest tell them who shall sit on the throne of my lord the king after him.   1 Kings, 1:20
c.550 B.C.

28. Prostitute of Jerusalem (mother of the living child)
(fl. c.950 B.C.)

1 O my lord, give her the living child, and in no wise slay it: she is the mother thereof.
1 Kings, 3:26
c.550 B.C.

29. Prostitute of Jerusalem (mother of the dead child)
(fl. c.950 B.C.)

1 Let it be neither mine nor thine, but divide it.   1 Kings, 3:26
c.550 B.C.

30. Queen of Sheba
(fl. c.950 B.C.)

1 Howbeit I believed not the words, until I came, and mine eyes had seen it: and, behold, the half was not told me: thy wisdom and prosperity exceedeth the fame which I heard.   1 Kings, 10:7
c.550 B.C.

2 . . . because the Lord loved Israel for ever, therefore made he thee king, to do judgment and justice.   Ibid., 10:9

3 Happy are thy men, and happy are these thy servants, which stand continually before thee, and hear thy wisdom.
2 Chronicles, 9:7
c.350–300 B.C.

31.   Jezebel
(fl. c.874–853 B.C.)

1 So let the gods do to me, and more also, if I make not thy life as the life of one of them by tomorrow about this time.
                                                1 Kings, 19:2
                                                c.550 B.C.

2 ... arise, and eat bread, and let thine heart be merry....   Ibid., 21:7

3 Proclaim a fast....   Ibid., 21:9

32.   Huldah
(fl. c.586 B.C.)

1 Because they have forsaken me, and have burned incense unto other gods, that they might provoke me to anger with all the works of their hands; therefore my wrath shall be kindled against this place, and shall not be quenched.   2 Kings, 22:17
                                                c.550 B.C.

2 Behold therefore, I will gather thee unto thy fathers, and thou shalt be gathered into thy grave in peace; and thine eyes shall not see all the evil which I will bring upon this place.   Ibid., 22:20

33.   Judith
(fl. c.600–495 B.C.)

1 Who are you, to put God to the test today, you, out of all mankind, to set yourselves above him?

You of all people to put the Lord Almighty to the test! You do not understand anything, and never will.

If you cannot sound the depths of the heart of man or unravel the arguments of his mind, how can you fathom the God who made all things, or sound his mind or unravel his purposes?   Judith, 8:12–14
                                                c.150 B.C.

2 But you have no right to demand guarantees where the designs of the Lord our God are concerned. For God is not to be coerced as man is, nor is he, like mere man, to be cajoled.   Ibid., 8:16

3 ... you have made the past,
And what is happening now, and what will follow.
What is, what will be, you have planned;
What has been, you designed.
Your purposes stood forward;
"See, we are here!" they said.
For all of your ways are prepared
And your judgments delivered with foreknowledge.   Ibid., 9:5, 6

4 Break their price
by a woman's hand.   Ibid., 9:10

5 Give me a beguiling tongue
to wound and kill
those who have formed such cruel designs
against your covenant....
                                                Ibid., 9:13

6 My face seduced him, only to his own undoing....   Ibid., 13:16

7 For the Lord is a God who shatters war;
he has pitched his camp in the middle of his people
to deliver me from the hands of my enemies.   Ibid., 16:2

8 but the Lord Almighty has thwarted them
by a woman's hand   Ibid., 16:5

9 Her sandal ravished his eye,
her beauty took his soul prisoner ...
and the scimitar cut through his neck!
                                                Ibid., 16:9

10 May your whole creation serve you!
For you spoke and things came into being,
you sent your breath and they were put together,
and no one can resist your voice.
                                                Ibid., 16:14

11 A little thing indeed
is a sweetly smelling sacrifice, ...
                                                Ibid., 16:16

12 Woe to the nations

who rise against my race!

Ibid., 16:17

34. Sarah
(fl. c.724–722 B.C.)

1 I cannot cause my father a sorrow which would bring down his old age to the dwelling of the dead.   Tobit, 3:10
c.175–164 B.C.

2 I am my father's only daughter,
he has no other child as heir;
he has no brother at his side,
nor has he any kinsman left
for whom I ought to keep myself.

Ibid., 3:15

3 If it does not please you to take my life,
then look on me with pity;
I can hear myself traduced no longer.

Ibid.

35. Anna
(fl. c.724–722 B.C.)

1 Why must you send my child away? Is he not the staff of our hands, with his errands to and fro for us?   Tobit, 5:18
c.175–164 B.C.

2 Alas! I let you leave me, my child, you, the light of my eyes.   Ibid., 10:5

36. Edna
(fl. c.724–722 B.C.)

1 Courage, daughter! May the Lord of heaven turn your grief to joy! Courage, daughter!   Tobit, 7:16
c.175–164 B.C.

37. Esther
(fl. c.519–465 B.C.)

1 ... if I perish, I perish.   Esther, 4:16
c.199–150 B.C.

2 ... you, Lord, chose
Israel out of all the nations
and our ancestors out of all the people of old times
to be your heritage for ever;
and that you have treated them as you promised.   Ibid., 4:17

3 Never let men mock at our ruin.

Ibid., 4:17

4 ... I am alone
and have no one but you, Lord.

Ibid., 4:17

5 If I have found favour in thy sight, O king, and if it please the king, let my life be given me at my petition, and my people at my request:
For we are sold, I and my people, to be destroyed, to be slain, and to perish.

Ibid., 7:3, 4

6 The adversary and enemy is this wicked Ha-man.   Ibid., 7:6

7 For how can I endure to see the evil that shall come unto my people? or how can I endure to see the destruction of my kindred?   Ibid., 8:6

38. Mother of the Seven Brothers
(fl. c.164–161 B.C.)

1 I do not know how you appeared in my womb; it was not I who endowed you with breath and life, I had not the shaping of your every part.
It is the creator of the world, ordaining the process of man's birth and presiding over the origin of all things ...

2 Maccabees, 7:22, 23
c.A.D. 41–44

2 I implore you, my child, observe heaven and earth, consider all that is in them, and acknowledge that God made them out of what did not exist, and that mankind comes into being the same way.   Ibid., 7:28

39.   Wife of Job
(c.8th century B.C.)

1 Dost thou still retain thine integrity? curse God, and die.   Job, 2:9
c. early 5th century B.C.

40.   Susanna
(fl. c.587–538 B.C.)

1 But I prefer to fall innocent into your power than to sin in the eyes of the Lord.
Daniel, 13:23
c.167–164 B.C.

41.   Salome
(fl. c.A.D. 20)

1 I will that thou give me by and by in a charger the head of John the Baptist.
Mark, 6:25
A.D. 68

42.   Mary
(fl. c.7 B.C.–A.D. 25)

1 How shall this be, seeing I know not a man?
Luke, 1:34
c.A.D. 65–80

2 Behold the handmaid of the Lord; be it unto me according to thy word.
Ibid., 1:38

3 My soul doth magnify the Lord,
And my spirit hath rejoiced in God my Saviour.
For he hath regarded the low estate of his handmaiden; for, behold, from henceforth all generations shall call me blessed.
For he that is mighty hath done to me great things; and holy is his name.
And his mercy is on them that fear him from generation to generation.
He hath shewed strength with his arm; he hath scattered the proud in the imagination of their hearts.
He hath put down the mighty from their seats, and exalted them of low degree.

He hath filled the hungry with good things; and the rich he hath sent empty away.
He hath helped his servant Israel, in remembrance of his mercy;
As he spake to our fathers, to Abraham, and to his seed for ever.   Ibid., 1:46–55

43.   Elisabeth
(fl. c.20 B.C.–A.D. 1)

1 Blessed art thou [Mary] among women, and blessed is the fruit of thy womb.
And whence is this to me, that the mother of my Lord should come to me?
For, lo, as soon as the voice of thy salutation sounded in mine ears, the babe [John the Baptist] leaped in my womb for joy.
And blessed is she that believed: for there shall be a performance of those things which were told her from the Lord.
Luke, 1:42–45
c.A.D. 65–80

44.   Samaritan Woman
(fl. c.A.D. 25)

1 How is it that thou [Christ], being a Jew, askest drink of me, which am a woman of Samaria?. . . .   John, 4:9
A.D. 100

2 Sir, thou hast nothing to draw with, and the well is deep: from whence then hast thou that living water?   Ibid., 4:11

3 Sir, I perceive that thou art a prophet.
Our fathers worshipped in this mountain; and ye say, that in Jerusalem is the place where men ought to worship.
Ibid., 4:19, 20

4 I know that Messias cometh, which is called Christ: when he is come, he will tell us all things.   Ibid., 4:25

5 Come, see a man, which told me all things that ever I did: is not this the Christ?
Ibid., 4:29

45. Mary Magdalene
(fl. c.A.D. 25)

1 They have taken away the Lord out of the sepulchre, and we know not where they have laid him.   John, 20:2
                                    A.D. 100

2 Sir, if thou have borne him hence, tell me where thou hast laid him, and I will take him away.   Ibid., 20:15

46. Lydia
(fl. c.A.D. 50)

1 If ye have judged me to be faithful to the Lord, come into my house, and abide there.
                                    Acts, 16:15
                                    c.A.D. 85–95

47. Slave Girl Who Was a
Soothsayer
(fl. c.A.D. 50)

1 These men are the servants of the most high God, which shew unto us the way of salvation.   Acts, 16:17
                                    c.A.D. 85–95

Quotations from 2300 B.C.–A.D. 1799

48. Enheduanna
(b. c.2300 B.C.?)

1 O lady of all truths. . . .
                            "Inanna* and An,"
          adapted by Anne Draffkorn Kilmer;
                The Exaltation of Inanna by
                    William W. Hallo and
                    J. J. A. van Dijk   1968
*Sumerian goddess of love.

2 Like a dragon you have filled the land with venom.
Like thunder when you roar over the earth, trees and plants fall before you.

You are a flood descending from a mountain,
O primary one,
moon goddess Inanna of heaven and earth!
                    adapted by Aliki and Willis
                        Barnstone,
                        Ibid.

3 You are in all our great rites.
Who can understand you?
                        Ibid.

4 Your feet are filled with restlessness.
                    "Inanna and Ishkur,"
                    adapted by Aliki and Willis
                        Barnstone, op. cit.

5 Your furious heart   is past controlling. . . .   Ibid., adapted by Anne
                    Draffkorn Kilmer; op. cit.

6 You are lofty like Heaven.   Let the world know!
You are wide like the earth.   Let the world know!
You devastate the rebellious land.   Let the world know!
You roar over the land.   Let the world know!
You smash their heads.   Let the world know!
You devour corpses like a dog.   Let the world know!
Your glance is terrible.   Let the world know!
                    "Antiphonal Hymn in Praise of
                        Inanna,"
                    adapted by Aliki and Willis Barn-
                        stone, op. cit.

7 With cries of labor   I gave birth to this hymn. . . .   Ibid., adapted by Anne
                        Draffkorn Kilmer

8 The day was good for Enheduanna, for she was dressed in jewels.
She was dressed in womanly beauty.
Like the moon's first rays over the horizon,

11

how luxuriously she was dressed!
"The Restoration of
Enheduanna to Her Former
Station,"
adapted by Aliki and Willis
Barnstone, op. cit.

9 My Lady wrapped in beauty   Inanna be
praised!   Ibid.,
adapted by Anne Draffkorn
Kilmer

10 You of the eternal truths   O great queen
of queens
Born of the holy womb   now greater than
your mother
You the all-wise one   Lady of the lands
Faithful provider   of your truths I have
sung   Untitled,
adapted by Anne Draffkorn
Kilmer, op. cit.

11 My honeyed tongue   is tied with confu-
sion   Untitled,
adapted by Anne Draffkorn
Kilmer, op. cit.

49. Kubatum
(fl. c.2032 B.C.)

1 my sweet and darling one,
with whom I would speak honey—
youth, I am in love with you!
"Love Song to King Shu-Suen,"
St. 6, Thorkild Jacobsen, tr.;
Most Ancient Verse, Thorkild
Jacobsen and John A. Wilson, eds.
n.d.

50. Eristi-Aya
(c.1790–1745 B.C.)

1 even warriors seized as booty in war
are treated humanely.
At least, treat me like them!
"A Letter to Her Mother,"
Willis Barnstone, tr.; *A Book of
Women Poets*, Aliki and Willis
Barnstone, eds.   1980

51. Hatshepsut
(fl. 1503–1482 B.C.)

1 Now my heart turns to and fro,
In thinking what will the people say,
They who shall see my monument in after
years,
And shall speak of what I have done.
Quoted from her obelisk
inscription in *Ancient Egyptian
Literature,
Volume II; The New Kingdom,*
Miriam Lichtheim, ed. and tr.
1976

2 No one rebels against me in all lands.
Ibid.

3 He* gave it to him who came from him,
Knowing I would rule it for him.
I am his daughter in very truth,
Who serves him, who knows what he or-
dains.   Ibid.
*The Egyptian god Amun.

4 My command stands firm like the mountains and the sun's disk shines and spreads
rays over the titulary of my august person,
and my falcon rises high above the kingly
banner unto all eternity.   Quoted in *The
Remarkable Women of Ancient
Egypt*
by Barbara Lesko
1978

52. Ankhesenpaton
(fl. 1390s B.C.)

1 My husband, Nib-khuruia,* has recently
died, and I have no son. But thy sons, they
say, are many. If thou wilt send me a son of
thine, he shall become my husband.
Letter to Shuppululuiuma,
the Hittite king (62 B.C.),
Quoted in *When Egypt Ruled the East,*
Ch. 15, by George Steindorff and
Keith C. Seele   1942
*Official name of Tutankhamen, who ruled
c.1379–1362 B.C.

2 Why didst thou say, "They wish to deceive me?" If I had a son, would I of my own accord to the humiliation of my country write to another country? Dost thou not trust me now? 2nd letter to Shuppiluliuma, op. cit.

53. Penelope
(c.1214 B.C.–?)

1 Careless to please, with insolence ye woo!
Quoted in *The Odyssey* by
Homer   c.800 B.C.

2 When have I not been dreading dangers more grievous than the reality? Love is a thing replete with anxious fears.
Quoted in *Epistulae Heroidum*
[*Letters from Heroines*] by Ovid
c.20 B.C.

3 What to fear I know not; still, bewildered, I dread everything; and a wide field lies open for my apprehensions.   Ibid.

54. Semiramis
(8th century B.C.)

1 Nature gave me the form of a woman; my actions have raised me to the level of the most valiant of men. Quoted in *Women of Beauty and Heroism*
by Frank B. Goodrich   1858

55. Sappho
(fl. c.610–635 B.C.)

1 I am not of revengeful temper, but have a childlike mind. Untitled fragment, Quoted in *Women in the Golden Ages,*
by Amelia Gere Mason   1901

2 When anger spreads through the breast, guard thy tongue from barking idly.
Untitled fragment, op. cit.

3 ... death is an evil; the gods have so judged; had it been good, they would die.
Untitled fragment, op. cit.

4 ... dark-eyed sleep, child of night. ...
Untitled fragment, op. cit.

5 I flutter like a child after her mother. ...
Untitled fragment, op. cit.

6 I do not expect to touch the heavens with my two arms. ...   Untitled fragment,
Quoted in *Distinguished Women
Writers*
by Virginia Moore   1934

7 ... all lovely things are pure and holy.
Untitled fragment, op. cit.

8 If you had a desire of noble or beautiful things ... shame would not possess your eyes, but you would speak of it justly.
Untitled fragment, op. cit.

9 Gentle ladies, you will remember till old age what we did together in our brilliant youth!   Untitled fragment, op. cit.

10 It is not right that in the house of song there should be mourning; such things befit us not.   Untitled fragment, op. cit.

11 Those whom I treat well harm me most.
Untitled fragment, op. cit.

12 You swarthy she-dog, setting your ill-smelling snout to the ground, pursue other prey!   Untitled fragment, op. cit.

13 But the hearts of the doves became cold, and they dropped beside them their wings.
Untitled fragment, op. cit.

14 All-hearing night. ...   Untitled fragment,
op. cit.

15 Sleep streams down. ...   Untitled
fragment, op. cit.

16 Night's black sleep was shed upon their eyes.   Untitled fragment, op. cit.

17 Now Eros has shaken my thoughts, like a wind among highland oaks.
Untitled fragment, op. cit.

18 Love, fatal creature. ...   Untitled
fragment, op. cit.

19 Now love the limb-loosener sweeps me away. ...   Untitled fragment, op. cit.

20 I know not what to do; my thoughts are double.   Untitled fragment, op. cit.

21 Some say an army of horsemen
is the fairest sight
on this sluggish black earth,
others an army of foot-soldiers, and others
    a navy of ships,
but I say it is the one you love.
                    Untitled fragment, op. cit.

22 I have received true prosperity from the golden Muses, and when I die shall not be forgot.   Untitled fragment, op. cit.

23 Like a mountain whirlwind
punishing the oak trees,
love shattered my heart.   Untitled
          fragment, *Greek Lyric Poetry*,
          Willis Barnstone, ed. and
                              tr.   1962

24 . . . in her roundness she burns silver
about the world.   Untitled fragment,
                              op. cit.

25 In gold sandals
dawn like a thief
fell upon me.   Untitled fragment, op. cit.

26 Love—bittersweet, irrepressible—
loosens my limbs and I tremble.
          Untitled fragment, St. 1, op. cit.

27   Labor
for my mad heart, and be
my ally.   Untitled, St. 7, op. cit.

28 Like a hyacinth crushed in the mountains
by shepherds; lying trampled on the earth
yet blooming purple.   Untitled, St. 2,
                              op. cit.

29 . . . the confusion of sweet flutes and crash-
ing cymbals. . . .   "Andromache's
                    Wedding," St. 4, op. cit.

30 all my flesh is wrinkled with age,
my black hair has faded to white,

my legs can no longer carry me,
once nimble like a fawn's,

but what can I do?
It cannot be undone,

no more than can pink-armed Dawn

not end in darkness on earth.
                    Untitled, Sts. 2-5, op. cit.

31 yet I love refinement, and beauty and light
are for me the same as desire for the sun.
                              Ibid., St. 7

32 but age dries my flesh with a thousand
wrinkles, and love is in no hurry
to seize my body with the gifts
of pleasant pain.   Untitled, St. 2, op. cit.

33 Now in my
heart I
see clearly

a beautiful
face
shining,

etched
by love.   Untitled, in toto, op. cit.

34   incense
smokes on the altar, cold
streams murmur through thee

apple branches, a young
rose thicket shades the ground
and quivering leaves pour

down deep sleep   Untitled, Sts. 3–5, *The
          Penguin Book of Women Poets*,
          Carol Cosman, Joan Keefe and
          Kathleen Weaver, eds.   1978

35   If I meet
you suddenly, I can't

speak—my tongue is broken;
a thin flame runs under
my skin; seeing nothing,

hearing only my own ears
drumming, I drip with sweat;
trembling shakes my body

and I turn paler than
dry grass. At such times
death isn't far from me.   Untitled, op. cit.

36 Don't ask me what to wear

I have no embroidered
headband from Sardis to
give you. . . .   Untitled, op. cit.

37 I hear that Andromeda–

that hayseed in her hay-
seed finery—has put
a torch to your heart

and she without even
the art of lifting her
skirt over her ankles.   Untitled, op. cit.

38 The angel of spring, the mellow-throated
nightingale.   No. 39, *Fragments*
n.d.

39 Art thou the topmost apple
  The gatherers could not reach,
  Reddening on the bough?
  Shall I not take thee?   Ibid., No. 53

40 The moon has set, and the Pleiades; it is
midnight, and time passes, and I sleep
alone.   Ibid., No. 94

41 What is beautiful is good, and who is good
will soon also be beautiful.
          Ibid., No. 101

42 Sweet mother, I cannot play the loom, vanquished by desire for a youth through the
work of soft Aphrodite.   Ibid., No. 114

43 Hesperus, you bring all things which the
bright dawn has scattered: you bring the
sheep, you bring the goat, you bring the
child back to its mother.   Ibid., No. 120

56. Erinna
(fl. 610–595 B.C.)

1 Little trails through my heart that are
Still warm—my remembrances of you.
          "The Distaff," Marylin Bentley
          Arthur, tr.; *Women Poets of the*
          World, Joanna Bankier and
          Deirdre Lashgari, eds.   1983

57. Corinna
(ca.520–420 B.C.)

1 When he sailed into the harbor

his ship became a snorting horse.
          Untitled, St. 1,
          Greek Lyric Poetry,
          Willis Barnstone, ed. and
          tr.   1962

2 . . . the wind like a nightingale
sang with its whirling war axe.
          Ibid., St. 3

3 . . . and the city rejoices mightily
at the keen melody of my voice.
          Untitled, John Dillon, tr.; *The*
          Penguin Book of Women Poets,
          Carol Cosman, Joan Keefe and
          Kathleen Weaver, eds.   1978

4 will you sleep forever?
you were not like that, Corinna,
in the old days.   Ibid.

58. Telesilla
(5th century B.C.)

1 Run swiftly to escape
the rape of the hunter Alpheus.
          Untitled, *Greek Lyric Poetry*,
          Willis Barnstone, ed. and tr.
          1962

59. Artemisia
(fl. 480 B.C.)

1 I was not the least brave of those who
fought at Euboea, nor were my achievements there among the meanest. . . .
          Remark to King Xerxes, Quoted
          in *The Persian Wars*, Bk. VIII,
          by Herodotus   c.450 B.C.

2 Spare your ships, and do not risk a battle;
for these people [the Greeks] are as much
superior to your people in seamanship, as
men to women.   Ibid.

3 This, too, you should remember, O king;
good masters are apt to have bad servants,
and bad masters good ones.
          Ibid.

60. Praxilla
(fl. c.451 B.C.)

1 You gaze at me teasingly through the window:
a virgin—and below—a woman's thighs.
Untitled, *Greek Lyric Poetry*,
Willis Barnstone, ed. and
tr.   1962

2 Loveliest of what I leave
is the sun himself
Next to that the bright stars
and the face of mother moon
Oh yes, and cucumbers in season,
and apples, and pears.
"Adonis, Dying," John Dillon, tr.;
The Penguin Book of Women Poets,
Carol Cosman, Joan Keefe and
Kathleen Weaver, eds.   1978

3 Watch out, my dear,
there's a scorpion under every stone.
Untitled fragment, op. cit.

61. Aspasia
(fl. c.420s B.C.)

1 . . . if you don't endeavor that there be not
a better husband and wife in the world than
yourselves, you will always be wishing for
that which you shall think best.
Quoted by Socrates
in *Dialogue of Aeschines* by
Plato   c.A.D. 360–386

2 Your great glory is not to be inferior to
what God has made you, and the greatest
glory of a woman is to be least talked about
by men, whether they are praising you or
criticizing you.   Quoted in *History of the
Peloponnesian War* by
Thucydides   c.A.D. 413

62. Theano
(fl. c.420s B.C.)

1 Put off your shame with your clothes when
you go in to your husband, and put it on
again when you come out.
Quoted in *Lives, Teachings, and
Sayings of Famous Philosophers;
Pythagoras*, Bk. VIII, Sec. 43, by
Diogenes Laertius
c.300 B.C.

2 The gods could not be honored by lies.
Quoted in *Biography of
Distinguished Women*,
by Sarah Josepha Hale
rev. ed., 1879

63. Ambapali
(4th century B.C.)

1 Such was my body once. Now it is weary
and tottering,
the home of many ills, an old house with
flaking plaster.
Not otherwise is the word of the truthful.
Untitled, St. 9,
The Wonder That Was India,
A. L. Basham, ed. and
tr.   1959

64. Phyrne
(4th century B.C.)

1 He* is not a man but a statue.
Quoted in *Lives, Teachings, and
Sayings of Famous Philosophers*
by Diogenes Laertius
c.300 B.C.

*The Greek philosopher Xenocrates.

65. Lais
(?–340 B.C.)

1 I do not understand what is meant by the austerity of philosophers, for with this fine name, they are as much in my power as the rest of the Athenians.　　Quoted in
Biography of Distinguished Women
by Sarah Josepha Hale
rev. ed., 1879

66. Lady Ho
(fl. 300 B.C.)

1 When a pair of magpies fly together
They do not envy the pair of phoenixes.
"A Song of Magpies,"
The Orchid Boat, Women Poets of China,
Kenneth Rexroth and Ling
Chung, eds. and trs.　　1972

67. Mother of Sumangala
(c.3rd–1st century B.C.)

1 A free woman. At last free!
Free from slavery in the kitchen
where I walked back and forth stained
and squalid among cooking pots.
Untitled, Willis Barnstone, tr.;
A Book of Women Poets, Aliki
and Willis Barnstone,
eds.　　1980

68. Sibyl, the Jewish
(fl. c.199– c.165 B.C.)

1 . . . here is a city, Chaldean Ur,
Whence come the race of most upright men,
Who are ever right-minded and their works good.
They are neither concerned for the sun's course,
Nor the moon's, nor for monstrosities on earth,
Nor for satisfaction from ocean's depths,

Nor for signs of sneezing and the augury from birds;
Nor for soothsaying, nor sorcery, nor incantations;
Nor for deceitful follies of ventriloquists.
They do not, Chaldean fashion, astrologize,
Nor watch the stars. . . .
But they are concerned about rightness and virtue.　　*The Fourth Book of Sibylline Oracles*
c.100 B.C.

69. Chuo Wên-chün
(179?–117 B.C.)

1 Why should marriage bring only tears?
All I wanted was a man
With a single heart,
And we would stay together
As our hair turned white,
Not somebody always after wriggling fish
With his big bamboo rod.
"A Song of White Hair," *The Orchid Boat, Women Poets of China*, Kenneth Rexroth and Ling Chung,
eds. and trs.　　1972

70. Cornelia
(fl. 160–140 B.C.)

1 These* are all the jewels of which I can boast.　　Quoted in *Biography of Distinguished Women*
by Sarah Josepha Hale　　1876
*Her sons, Tiberius and Caius Gracchi.

71. Hsi-chün
(fl. c.105 B.C.)

1 Would I were a yellow stork
And could fly to my old home!
"Lament of Hsi-Chün,"
Translations from the Chinese,
Arthur Waley, tr.　　1919

17

72. Wife of Ch'in Chia
(1st century B.C.)

1 I stood on tiptoe gazing into the distance, Interminably gazing at the road that had taken you.   "Ch'in Chia's Wife's Reply," *Translations from the Chinese*, Arthur Waley, tr.   1919

73. Hortensia
(85 B.C.–?)

1 . . . you assume the glorious title of reformers of the state, a title which will turn to your eternal infamy, if, without the least regard to the laws of equity, you persist in your wicked resolution of plundering those [women] of their lives and fortunes, who have given you no just cause of offence.
(c.45 B.C.), Quoted in *Civil Wars*, Vol. IV, by Appian of Alexandria   A.D. 32–34

74. Cleopatra VII
(69 B.C.–A.D. 30)

1 Leave the fishing-rod, Great General, to us sovereigns of Pharos and Canopus. Your game is cities and kings and continents.
Remark to Marc Antony, Quoted in *Cleopatra of Egypt*, Ch. 9, by Philip W. Sergeant   1909

2 As surely as one day I shall administer justice on the Capitol. . . . *   Ibid., Ch. XIII
*Her favorite oath, referring to the capital of the Roman Empire.

3 Fool! Don't you see now that I could have poisoned you a hundred times had I been able to live without you! Remark to Marc Antony, Quoted in *Cleopatra's Daughter, The Queen of Mauretania*, Ch. 5, by Beatrice Chanler   1934

4 Thirty-six hours spent in a continuous drinking bout with his friends is not likely to improve the temper of "the old fellow."*
Ibid., Ch. 20
*"The old fellow" was the nickname given to the Roman emperor Tiberius (42 B.C.–A.D. 37).

5 I *will not* be exhibited in his Triumph.*
Remark concerning Octavian's victory, Quoted in *The Life and Times of Cleopatra*, Ch. 20, by Arthur Weigall   1968
*Formal celebration in Rome honoring victorious generals.

6 You know how much I was with your father, [Julius Caesar] and you are aware that it was he who placed the crown of Egypt upon my head. . . .   Remark to Octavian, op. cit.

7 Nothing could part us while we lived, but death seems to threaten to divide us. You, a Roman born, have found a grave in Egypt. I, an Egyptian, am to seek that favour, and none but that, in your country.
Spoken over Marc Antony's tombstone, op. cit.

8 But if the gods below, with whom you now are dwelling, can or will do anything for me, since those above have betrayed us, do not allow your living wife to be abandoned, let me not be led in triumph to your shame; but hide me, hide me; bury me here with you. For amongst all my bitter misfortunes, nothing has been so terrible as this brief time that I have lived away from you.*
Ibid.
*The source for all her remarks can be found in the work of Plutarch, who probably derived this last speech from the diary of her doctor, Olympus.

75. Sulpicia
(fl. 63 B.C.–A.D. 14)

1 Drat my hateful birthday

to be spent in the boring old country.
Untitled, John Dillon, tr.; *The Penguin Book of Women Poets*, Carol Cosman, Joan Keefe and Kathleen Weaver, eds.   1978

2 If I'm to be snatched away
I'll leave heart and soul behind here,
Since I'm not to be granted
license to run my life.
Ibid.

3 I'm grateful, really grateful
for the favour you've just done me.
You've saved me from being a fool
and rushing into your arms.
Untitled, John Dillon, tr., op. cit.

4 I left you yesterday night,
ran off and left you alone–
Honestly, love, it was only
that I didn't dare show my passion.
Untitled, John Dillon, tr., op. cit.

5 At last love has come. I would be more ashamed
to hide it in cloth than leave it naked.
Untitled, *A Book of Women Poets*, Aliki and Willis Barnstone, eds. and trs.   1980

6 I delight in sinning and hate to compose a mask
for gossip.
Ibid.

7 Friends worry about me and are upset that somehow
I might tumble into bed with a nobody.
Untitled, op. cit.

8 Trips are often poorly timed.
Untitled, op. cit.

76. Lady Pan
(fl. 48–46 B.C.)

1 I took a piece of the rare cloth of Ch'i,
White silk glowing and pure as frost on snow,
And made you a fan of harmony and joy,

As flawlessly round as the full moon.
"A Present from the Emperor's New Concubine," *Love and the Turning Year. One Hundred More Poems from the Chinese*, Kenneth Rexroth, ed. and tr.   1970

77. Porcia
(?–42 B.C.)

1 Brutus, I am Cato's daughter, and I was brought into thy house, not, like a mere concubine, to share thy bed and board merely, but to be a partner in thy troubles. Thou, indeed, art faultless as a husband; but how can I show thee any grateful service if I am to share neither thy secret suffering nor the anxiety which craves a loyal confidant? I know that woman's nature is thought too weak to endure a secret; but good rearing and excellent companionship go far towards strengthening the character, and it is my happy lot to be both the daughter of Cato and the wife of Brutus. Before this I put less confidence in these advantages, but now I know that I am superior even to pain.*   from *Parallel Lives* by Plutarch (c.A.D. 100), Quoted in *Plutarch's Lives*, Vol. VI, B. Perrin, tr.   1914–1926

*Spoken shortly before Ceasar's murder, when she sensed Brutus' troubled mind; she wounded her thigh with a small knife just before making the above speech.

78. Okkur Macatti
(c.1st–3rd century A.D.)

1 In Jasmine country, it is evening
for the hovering bees,
but look, he hasn't come back.

He left me and went in search
of wealth.   "What She Said," *Speaking of Siva*, A. K. Ramanujan, ed. and tr.   1973

79. Myrta
(fl. 1st century)

1 Paul the servant of the Lord will save many in Rome and will nourish many with the word . . . so that there will be great grace in Rome.
Quoted in "Word, Spirit and Power: Women in Early Christian Communities" by Elisabeth Schüssler Fiorenza, *Women of Spirit*, Rosemary Reuther and Eleanor McLaughlin, eds. 1979

80. Venmanippūṭi
(c.1st–3rd century)

1 my arms grow beautiful
in the coupling
and grow lean
as they come away.
    What shall I make of this?
"What She Said to her Girl-friend," St. 2, *Interior Landscape: Love Poems from a Classical Tamil Anthology*, A. K. Ramanujan, ed. and tr. 1967

81. Agrippina the Younger
(c.14–59)

1 No philosophy, my son [Nero]; it is of no use to an emperor.
Quoted in *The Great Empress, A Portrait*, Ch. 8, by Maximilian Schele de Vere 1870

2 Let him [Nero] slay me, so he reign!
Ibid., Ch. 11

3 Do you too desert me? Ibid., Remark to a slave

4 If you [Anicetus] come to inquire after my well-being, you may tell the emperor, my son, that I am well; if you come to murder me, I will not believe that you come from him: the guilt of parricide is unknown to his heart.
Ibid.

5 Strike the womb that bore a monster!
Ibid.

6 The reign of Nero has begun as that of Augustus ended; but when I am gone, it will end as that of Augustus began.
Quoted in *Biography of Distinguished Women* by Sarah Josepha Hale 1876

82. Boadicea
(fl. c.40–65)

1 It will not be the first time, Britons, that you have been victorious under the conduct of your queen. For my part, I come not here as one descended of royal blood, not to fight for empire or riches, but as one of the common people, to avenge the loss of their liberty, the wrongs of myself and children.
Speech, Quoted in *Biography of Distinguished Women* by Sarah Josepha Hale 1876

2 Is it not much better to fall honourably in defence of liberty, than be again exposed to the outrages of the Romans? Such, at least, is my resolution; as for you men, you may, if you please, live and be slaves!
Ibid.

3 Roman lust has gone so far that not even our own persons remain unpolluted. If you weigh well the strengths of our armies, you will see that in this battle we must conquer or die. This is a woman's resolve. As for the men, they may live or be slaves.
Quoted in *The Dinner Party, A Symbol of Our Heritage* by Judy Chicago 1979

83. Arria, the Elder
(d.42)

1 It does not hurt, my Paetus.*
Quoted in *Epistles*, Bk. III,
epistle 16, by Pliny the Younger
c.100–109

*Remark to her husband, who had been ordered to commit suicide, after she had stabbed herself.

84. Pan Chao
(c.45–c.115)

1 The virtues of women are not brilliant talent, nor distinction and elegance. The virtues of women are reserve, quiet, chastity, orderliness, governing herself to maintain a sense of shame, and conducting herself according to the rules of Confucian etiquette.
from *Nü Chieh*
[*Precepts for Women*],
quoted in *Chinese Women:
Yesterday and Today*
by Florence Ayscough   1936

2 Only needle-and-thread's delicate footsteps are truly broad-ranging yet without beginning!   "Needle and Thread," St. 3,
Richard Mather and Rob
Swigart, trs.; *Women Poets of the
World*, Joanna Bankier and
Deirdre Lashgari, eds.
1983

3 How can those who count pennies calculate their worth?
They may carve monuments yet lack all understanding.   Ibid., St. 5

85. Poppæa Sabina
(fl. 50–60)

1 Rather die than see my beauty pass away!
Quoted in *The Great Empress,
A Portrait*,
Ch. 9, by Maximilian Schele
de Vere   1870

2 You* an emperor! and you are not even a free man yet!   Ibid.

*Her husband Nero.

86. Pompeia Plotina
(c.80–122)

1 May the gods send me forth from this august palace, whenever I may be destined to leave it, even as I now enter it; and may the high destiny to which fortune now raises me leave me in possession of the same qualities with which I this day assume it.
Speech (99), Quoted in
Biography of Distinguished Women
by Sarah Josepha Hale   1876

87. Sulpicia
(fl. 80–99)

1 Tell me, O Calliope,* what is it the great father of the gods purposes to do? Does he revert to earth, and his father's age; and wrest from us in death the arts that once he gave; and bid us, in silence, nay, bereft of reason too, just as when we arose in the primaeval age, stoop again to acorns, and the pure stream?   *Satire*
c.90

*The muse of epic poetry.

2 Then as the victor, who, left alone in the Grecian stadium, droops, and though with valour undaunted, feels his heart sink within him—just so the Roman race, when it had ceased from its struggles, and had bridled peace in lasting trammels. . . .
Ibid.

3 . . . Priscus Cato* held it of such deep import to determine whether the Roman stock would better be upheld by prosperity or adversity.—By adversity, doubtless; for when the love of country urges them to defend themselves by arms, and their wife held prisoner together with their household goods, they combine just like wasps, (a bristling band, with weapons all unsheathed along their yellow bodies,). . . .
Ibid.

*Probably the same as Publius Valerius Cato, the first-century A.D. Roman poet and grammarian.

21

4 ... when care-dispelling peace has returned, forgetful of labour, commons and fathers together lie buried in lethargic sleep.
Ibid.

5 ... kind Muse [Calliope], without whom life is no pleasure to me. ...
Ibid.

88. Ts'ai Yen
(162?–239?)

1 Heaven was pitiless.
It sent down confusion and separation.
Earth was pitiless.
It brought me to birth in such a time.
War was everywhere.
Every road was dangerous.
Soldiers and civilians everywhere
Fleeing death and suffering.
"Eighteen Verses Sung to A Tatar Reed Whistle," I:2, *The Orchid Boat, Women Poets of China*, Kenneth Rexroth and Ling Chung, eds. and trs. 1972

2 I can never learn the ways of the barbarians.
Ibid.

3 Men here are as savage as giant vipers,
And strut about in armour, snapping their bows.
Ibid., II:1

4 Will broken, heart broken, I sing to myself.
Ibid.

5 I have no desire to live, but I am afraid of death.
I cannot kill my body, for my heart still has hope
Ibid., XI

6 No one can know
The sorrow which tears my bowels.
Ibid., XIII:2

89. Vivia Perpetua
(183?–205)

1 Continue firm in the faith, love one another, and be not offended at our sufferings.
Quoted in *Biography of Distinguished Women* by Sarah Josepha Hale 1876

90. Auvaiyar
(3rd century?)

1 It knows nothing, and sleeps
through all my agony, my sleeplessness,
and the swirls of this swaying south wind.
Untitled, St. 3, *Interior Landscape: Love Poems from a Classical Tamil Anthology*, A. K. Ramanujan, ed. and tr. 1967

2 This is the womb that carried him,
like a stone cave
lived in by a tiger and now abondoned.
Untitled, George Hart, tr.; *Women Poets of the World*, Joanna Bankier and Deirdre Lashgari, eds. 1983

91. Kaccipēṭṭu Nannākaiyār
(3rd century?)

1 ... a dream
that lied like truth. "What She Said," St. 1, *Interior Landscape: Love Poems from a Classical Tamil Anthology*, A. K. Ramanujan, ed. and tr. 1967

2 I grow lean
in loneliness,
like a water lily
gnawed by a beetle.
Ibid., St. 3

92. Tzŭ Yeh
(c.3rd–4th century)

1 I let down my silken hair
Over my shoulders
And open my thighs

Over my lover.
"Tell me, is there any part of me
That is not lovable?" "Song," II,
The Orchid Boat,
Women Poets of China,
Kenneth Rexroth and Ling
Chung, eds. and trs. 1972

2 Your sun-like heart
Goes East in the morning
And West in the evening.
Ibid., V

93. Zenobia of Palmyra
(240–300)

1 By valor alone, by the force of arms only,
can wars be brought to a close.
Letter to Aurelian Augustus* (272),
Quoted in *Women of Beauty*
and Heroism
by Frank B. Goodrich 1858

2 It is not by writing, but by arms, that the
submission you require from me can be obtained. "Zenobia,
Queen of the East,
to Aurelian Augustus,"
Epistle,* Quoted in *Biography of*
Distinguished Women
by Sarah Josepha Hale 1876

*Both quotations probably from same document, pos-
sibly different translations (EP).

94. Monica
(fl. 340–395)

1 Son, what I should here, and why I am
here, I know not; the hope of this life is now
quite spent. Quoted in *Biography of*
Distinguished Women
by Sarah Josepha Hale 1876

2 Nothing is far from God; and I do not fear
that he will not know where to find me at
the resurrection. Ibid.

95. Iwa no Hime
(?–347)

1 In the autumn field,
Over the rice ears,
The morning mist trails,
Vanishing somewhere. . . .
Can my love fade too? "Longing for the
Emperor," *The Penguin Book of*
Japanese Verse, Geoffrey Bownas
and Anthony Thwaite, eds. and
trs. 1964

96. Hypatia
(c.370–d. 415)

1 Neo-Platonism is a progressive philosophy,
and does not expect to state final conditions
to men whose minds are finite. Life is an un-
foldment, and the further we travel the
more truth we can comprehend. To understand the things that are at our door is the
best preparation for understanding those
that lie beyond. Quoted in *Little Journeys*
to the Homes of Great Teachers,
"Hypatia," by Elbert
Hubbard 1908

2 Fables should be taught as fables, myths as
myths, and miracles as poetic fancies. To
teach superstitions as truths is a most terrible thing. The child mind accepts and believes them, and only through great pain
and perhaps tragedy can he be in after years
relieved of them. Ibid.

3 Men will fight for a superstition quite as
quickly as for a living truth—often more so,
since a superstition is so intangible you cannot get at it to refute it, but truth is a point
of view, and so is changeable.
Ibid.

4 He who influences the thought of his times,
influences all the times that follow. He has
made his impress on eternity.
Ibid.

5 Let's keep the windows open to the East, be
worthy, and sometime we shall know.
Ibid.

6 At the last, no man who does his own thinking is an "ite." Outwardly he may subscribe to this creed or that, and if he is very discreet he may make his language conform, but inwardly his belief is never pigeonholed, nor is his soul labeled. Ibid.

7 In theology the great man recoils at thought of dogmatism, for he knows its vanity; and all algebraic formulae in his sublime moments are cast away. Ibid.

8 It does not make much difference what a person studies—all knowledge is related, and the man who studies anything, if he keeps at it, will become learned. Ibid.

9 Had there been no Plato there would have been no Plotinus, and although Plotinus surpassed Plato, yet it is plain that Plato, the inspirer of Plotinus and so many more, is the one man whom philosophy cannot spare. Hail Plato! Ibid.

10 The Mintage of Wisdom is to know that rest is rust, and that Real Life lies in Love, Laughter and Work. Ibid.

11 To rule by fettering the mind through fear of punishment in another world, is just as base as to use force. Ibid.

97. Egeria
(fl. 381–384)

1 I saw many holy monks from those parts when they came to Jerusalem on pilgrimage to the holy places, and all they told me about Uz* made me eager to take the trouble to make a further journey to visit it—if one can really speak of trouble when one sees one's wishes fulfilled.
from *Travels*, Quoted in *Egeria: Diary of a Pilgrimage*, George E. Gingras, ed. and tr. 1970

*The Land of Uz was probably near Damascus, although there is little evidence of its actual location.

98. Pulcheria Aelia
(399–454)

1 The more princes abstain from touching the wealth of their people, the greater will be their resources in the wants of the state.
Quoted in *Biography of Distinguished Women* by Sarah Josepha Hale 1876

99. Brigid of Kildare
(453–523)

1 I should like a great lake of ale
For the King of kings
"The Feast of St. Brigid of Kildare," n.d.

100. Maximilla
(c.465–1465)

1 I am pursued like a wolf out of the sheep fold; I am no wolf: I am word and spirit and power.
Quoted in "Word, Spirit and Power: Women in Early Christian Communities" by Elisabeth Schüssler Fiorenza, *Women of Spirit*, Rosemary Reuther and Eleanor McLaughlin, eds. 1979

101. Basine
(fl. c.467)

1 Had I known a more valiant hero than yourself [Childeric] I should have fled over the seas to his arms.
Remark to Childeric [Merovingian king], Quoted in *Biography of Distinguished Women* by Sarah Josepha Hale 1876

102. Ita
(480–570)

1 Jesu, more than angel aid,

Fosterling not formed to fade,
Nursed by me in desert wild,
Jesu, Child of Judas' Maid.
> "Jesukin," *The Catholic
> Anthology*, Thomas Walsh,
> ed.   1927

103.   Baudonivia
(6th century)

1 I am but the least among the least, small is my understanding and timid my heart.
> Letter to her abbess, Dedimia,
> Quoted in
> *Women and Their Letters in the
> Early Middle Ages*
> by Eleanor Shipley
> Duckett   1965

104.   Caesaria
(c.6th century)

1 . . . you cannot fight lust if you do not flee from the presence of men.
> Quoted in *Women in Frankish
> Society, Marriage and the
> Cloister, 500–900*, Ch. 6,
> by Suzanne Fonay
> Wemple   1981

2 . . . read and hear assiduously the divine lessons . . . to gather from them precious daisies for your ears and make from them rings and bracelets.   Ibid., Ch. 8

105.   Theodora
(c.508–d. 547/48)

1 For a King, death is better than dethronement and exile.   Attributed, n.d.

106.   Radegunda
(c.518–587)

1 If you refuse to consecrate me, fearing more a man than God, you will be held responsible for the soul of one of your sheep, O Pastor!   Quoted in *Vita Radegundis* [*Life of
> Radegunda*]
> by Fortunatus   c.580–600

2 If you do not understand what is read, it is because you do not ask solicitously for a mirror of the soul.   Ibid.

107.   Bertegund
(fl. 530s)

1 Go home and govern our children. I will not return to you [her husband], for the married will not see the kingdom of heaven.
> Quoted in *Histoire Française*,
> Ch. 6,
> by Gregory of Tours
> c.538

108.   Al-Khansa
(575–646)

1 He is dead, who was the buckler of our tribe
> "For Her Brother," St. 3, E.
> Powys Mathers, tr.; *The Penguin
> Book of Women Poets*,
> Carol Cosman,
> Joan Keefe and Kathleen
> Weaver, eds.
> 1978

2 Your captives were as troupes of antelopes Whose beauty troubles the first drops of rain. . . .   Ibid., St. 9

3 While you have tears, O daughters of the Solamides,
Weep! Weep! Weep!   Ibid., St. 14

4   ... he kindled wars on the morning of
fear.   "On Her Brother Sakhr,"
                St. 5, Willis Barnstone, tr.;
                A Book of Women Poets, Aliki
                    and Willis Barnstone, eds.
                                        1980

5 My eye cried and woke me.
The night was pain. "The Night," in toto,
        Willis Barnstone, tr., op. cit.

6 ... every tribe is a journey to ruin

and every treaty is erased by time.
        "In Death's Field," Sts. 12, 13,
        Willis Barnstone, tr., op. cit.

7 He protects angrily,

scattering his iron-armored men over the
earth
like dust in the noses of mangled warriors.
        "Rain to the Tribe," Sts. 4, 5,
        Willis Barnstone and Tony
        Nawfal, trs., op. cit.

8 Stream sorrow, eyes:
    wailing-weary
coursing streamlets.   "Elegy for Her
        Brother, Sakhr," St. 1,
        Bridget Connelly, tr.; *Women
        Poets of the World*, Joanna
        Bankier and Deirdre Lashgari,
            eds.   1983

109.   Liadan
(7th century)

1 Not vain,
    it seemed, our choice,
    to seek Paradise through pain.
        "Liadan Laments Cuirithir,"* St.
                                        3,
        *The Penguin Book of Women
        Poets*, Carol Cosman,
        Joan Keefe and Kathleen
        Weaver, eds.   1978

*Her lover who, after she became a nun, unknown to
Liadan became a monk.

2 Gain without gladness

Is in the bargain I have struck
Untitled, St. 1, Frank O'Connor, tr.;
        The Penguin Book of Irish Verse,
        Brendan Kennelly, ed.
                                        1981

3 A furnace blast
Of love has melted down my heart,
Without his love it cannot last.
                        Ibid., St. 9

110.   Herchenfreda
(fl. c.600)

1 What shall I, an unfortunate mother, do
now that I have lost your brothers? If you
were also to die, I would have no children
left! But you, my most pious son, my sweetest, you must constantly guard yourself
against murder, for now that I have lost
your brothers, I cannot lose you too!
        Quoted in *Women in Frankish
        Society, Marriage and the
        Cloister, 500–900*, Ch. 3,
        by Suzanne Fonay
        Wemple   1981

111.   Hind bint Utba
(fl. 600–635)

1 Rrrrrrrraaarghr
We have paid you back
Battle feeds battle
and war that follows war is always violent.
        "Fury Against the Moslems at
                                Uhud,"
        St. 1, Bridget Connelly and
        Deirdre Lashgari, trs.; *Women
        Poets of the World*, Joanna
        Bankier and Deirdre Lashgari,
            eds.   1983

2 War will hit you hard
coming at you like lions raging.
                        Ibid., St. 4

112. Wu Tse-t'ien
(624–705)

1 My thoughts are many and tumultuous,
As troubled as the tossing branches,
All for thinking of you. "A Love Song of
the Empress Wu,"
The Orchid Boat,
Women Poets of China,
Kenneth Rexroth and Ling
Chung, eds. and trs.   1972

113. Oku
(661–701)

1 How will you cross
the autumn mountain
alone?
It was hard
for us,
even when we went
together.   Untitled, Willis Barnstone, tr.;
A Book of Women Poets,
Aliki and Willis Barnstone, eds.
1980

114. Laila Akhyaliyya
(fl. 665–699)

1 If a man has not lived shamefully,
there is no shame in dying.
"Lamenting Tauba,"
St. 2, Willis Barnstone, tr.;
A Book of Women Poets,
Aliki and Willis Barnstone,
eds.   1980

2 No life is favored,
nor corpse reborn.
Every youth passes through destruction
to Allah.   Ibid., St. 3

3 Our lungs are strong
when we wail with the first knives
of dawn.   "Laila Boasting,"
Willis Barnstone, tr., op. cit.

115. Nukada
(fl. 665–699)

1 When, loosened from the winter's bond,
The spring appears,
The birds that were silent
Come out and sing,
The flowers that were prisoned
Come out and bloom;
But the hills are so rank with trees
We cannot seek the flowers,
And the flowers are so tangled with weeds
We cannot take them in our hands.
Untitled, from *Manyō-Shū*
[*Collection of Ten Thousand
Leaves*]   mid-8th century

2 Here we have waited at Nigitazu*
For the rise of the moon, to put to sea.
The moon is up, the tide is high;
Away! let us row out speedily.
"The Tide Too Is Up,"
from *Manyō-Shū*, Vol. I,
An Anthology of Japanese Poems,
Miyamori Asatarō, ed. and
tr.   1938

*Ancient name of Mitsugahama, a seacoast town in
Iyo Province, Japan.

116. Yamatohime
(fl. 671)

1 Others may forget you, but not I.
I am haunted by your beautiful ghost.
Untitled, *One Hundred Poems
from the Japanese,*
Kenneth Rexroth, tr.   1964

117. Safiya bint Musafir
(fl. 674)

1 Emptied with weeping
my eyes are
two buckets of the waterman

as he walks among the orchard trees
"At the Badr Trench,"*
St. 1, Bridget Connelly and
Deirdre Lashgari, trs.;
Women Poets of the World,
Joanna Bankier and Deirdre
Lashgari, eds.   1983
*Burial place for 14 Muslim martyrs killed at Battle of Badr at Medina (now in Saudi Arabia) in 674.

118.   Chao Luan-luan
(8th century)

1 Small cherries sip delicately
At the edge of the wine cup.
"Red Sandalwood Mouth,"
The Orchid Boat,
Women Poets of China,
Kenneth Rexroth and Ling
Chung, eds. and trs.   1972

2 I am too pretty to bother with an eyebrow
pencil.
Spring hills paint themselves
With their own personality.
"Willow Eyebrows," op. cit.

3 Fragrant with powder, moist with perspira-
tion,
They are the pegs of a jade inlaid harp.
"Creamy Breasts," op. cit.

4 Slender, delicate, soft jade,
Fresh peeled spring onions—
They are always hidden in emerald
Sleeves of perfumed silk.   "Slender
Fingers," op. cit.

119.   Egburg
(8th century)

1 No sailor tossed by the tempest hopes so
keenly for the harbour, not thus does the
thirsty field wait for the rain, not so eagerly
does the anxious mother look from the
curving shore for the coming of her son, as,
My Father, I long for the sight of you.
Letter to St. Boniface (c.716–726),
Quoted in *Women and Letters in
the Early Middle Ages*
by Eleanor Shipley
Duckett   1965

120.   Kasa no Iratsume
(8th century)

1 To love someone
Who does not return that love
Is like offering prayers
Back behind a starving god
Within a Buddhist temple.
Untitled, from *Manyō-Shū*
[*Collection of Ten Thousand
Leaves*],
Harold P. Wright,
tr.   c.mid-8th century

2 Although the bell has tolled,
Warning all to "Go to sleep!"
My great longings after you
My eyelids wakeful keep.
"A Verse Sent to Otomo no
Yakamochi,"
in toto, from *Manyō-Shū*, Vol. IV,
An Anthology of Japanese Poems,
Miyamori Asatarō, ed. and
tr.   1938

3 I dreamed I held
A sword against my flesh.
What does it mean?
It means I shall see you soon.
Untitled, in toto, *One Hundred
Poems from the Japanese,*
Kenneth Rexroth, ed. and tr.
1964

4 I love and fear him
Steadily as the surf

Roars on the coast at Ise.
Untitled, op. cit.

121. Lady Kii
(8th century)

1 ... the idle ways
of the beach.   Untitled, *The Burning
Heart: Women Poets of Japan*,
Kenneth Rexroth and Ikuko
Atsumi, eds. and trs.   1977

122. Li Yeh
(8th century)

1 It is good to get drunk once in a while.
What else is there to do? "A Greeting to
Lu Hung-Chien,"
*The Orchid Boat, Women Poets
of China*,
Kenneth Rexroth and Ling
Chung, eds. and trs.   1972

123. Sahakdoukht Siunetsi
(8th century)

1 And spiritual orchard, bright flower,
you conceived from God, as from rains
flowing through the soul, the word,
and with the shield of your body
made it apparent to men.
"Acrostic," St. 2,
Anthology of Armenian Poetry,
Diana Der Hovanessian and
Marzbed Margossian, eds. and
trs.   1978

124. Mahodahi
(c.700–1050)

1 The sun's charioteer is lost. . . .
Untitled, Willis Barnstone, tr.;
A Book of Women Poets,
Aliki and Willis Barnstone, eds.
1980

125. Ōtomo no Sakano-e no Iratsume
(c.700–750)

1 Ah! I have handed over
The jewel to its owner;
So from henceforth, my dear pillow,
Let us two sleep together.
"On the Marriage of a
Daughter," in toto,
from *Manyō-Shū*, Vol. IV,
An Anthology of Japanese Poems,
Miyamori Asatarō, ed. and. tr.
1938

2 Do not smile to yourself
Like a green mountain
With a cloud drifting across it.
People will know we are in love.
Untitled, *One Hundred Poems
from the Japanese*,
Kenneth Rexroth, ed. and
tr.   1964

3 You say, "I will come."
And you do not come.
Now you say, "I will not come."
So I shall expect you.
Have I learned to understand you?
Untitled, op. cit.

4 Since we parted,
Like a spreading vine
Your eyebrows, pencil-arched,
Like waves about to break
Have flitted before my eyes,
Bobbing like tiny boats.   "Sent from the
Capital to her Elder Daughter,"
St. 2, *The Penguin Book of
Japanese Verse*,
Geoffrey Bownas and Anthony
Thwaite, eds. and trs.   1964

5 Had I only known
My longing would be so great,
Like a clear mirror
I'd have looked on you. . . .
Ibid., St. 3

6 My heart, thinking
"How beautiful he is"
Is like a swift river
Which though one dams it and dams it

Will still break through.   Untitled, from
*Manyō-Shū, Japanese Poetry:
The Uta,*
Arthur Waley, ed. and tr.
1976

7 Unknown love
is bitter
as a virgin lily
on the summer
meadow,
blooming in bushes.
Untitled, in toto,
Willis Barnstone, tr.;
A Book of Women Poets,
Aliki and Willis Barnstone, eds.
1980

126.   Sila
(c.700–1050)

1 We knew long evenings wet with the moon.
Untitled, Willis Barnstone, tr.;
The Book of Women Poets,
Aliki and Willis Barnstone, eds.
1980

127.   Śilabhlaṭṭarikā
(c.700–1050)

1 I too am still the same;
and yet with all my heart I yearn for the
reedbeds by the stream
which knew our happy, graceful
unending bouts of love.
"The Wanton,"
from *Treasury of Well-Turned Verse*
comp. by Vidya Kara (c.1100),
Quoted in *Sanskrit Poetry,*
Daniel H. H. Ingalls, ed. and
tr.   1955

2 ... winds just coming of age....
Ibid.

128.   Vidya
(c.700–1050)

1 I praise the disc of the rising sun
red as a parrot's beak, sharp-rayed,
friend of the lotus grove,
an earring for the goddess of the east.
"The Sun," from *Treasury of
Well-Turned Verse*
comp. by Vidya Kara (c.1100),
Quoted in *Sanskrit Poetry,*
Daniel H. H. Ingalls, ed. and
tr.   1955

2 One born to hardship in his place and station
does well enough to keep himself alive.
"Substantiations," op. cit.

3 Friends,
you are lucky you can talk
about what you did as lovers:
the tricks, laughter, the words,
the ecstasy.
After my darling put his hand on the knot
of my dress,
I swear I remember nothing.
Untitled, in toto,
Willis Barnstone, tr.;
A Book of Women Poets,
Aliki and Willis Barnstone,
eds.   1980

129.   Sanu Chigami
(fl. 710–784)

1 These are the garments
I, a helpless woman, sewed
with troubled longings
as a token of the day
when we two shall meet again.
Untitled,
from the *Manyō-Shū* (c.800),
Quoted in *Land of the Reed Plains,*
Kenneth Yashuda, ed. and tr.   1972

130.   Rabi'a the Mystic
(712–801)

1 My Lord

if I worship Thee from fear of Hell
burn me in Hell

and if I worship Thee from hope of Paradise
exclude me thence

but if I worship Thee
for Thine own sake alone
do not withhold from me Thine Eternal
Beauty   "A Prayer,"
Sts. 1-3.
Quoted in *Rabi'a the Mystic and
Her Fellow Saints in Islam*,
Margaret Smith   1928

2 O my Lord, the stars glitter and eyes of men
are closed,
kings have shut their doors
and each lover is alone with his love.
Here, I am alone with you.
Untitled, Willis Barnstone, tr.;
A Book of Women Poets,
Aliki and Willis Barnstone, eds.
1980

131. Young Woman of Harima
(fl. c.715–719)

1 If you go away,
why should I adorn myself?
Untitled, from the Manyōshū,
Quoted in *Land of the Reed Plains*,
Kenneth Yashuda, ed. & tr.
1972

132. Khosrovidoukht Koghtnatsi
(?–737)

1 More astonishing to me
than the lyrics made for you,
more amazing than the music composed
for your death,
is the sound of the sobbing mourning
"More Astonishing,"
St. 1 (737), *Anthology of
Armenian Poetry*,
Diana Der Hovanessian and
Marzbed Margossian, eds. and
trs.   1978

133. Rabi'a bint Isma'il of Syria
(?–755)

1 But if You consume me in fire, goal of my
longing,
where then lies my hope of You, and where
my fear?   "Sufi Quatrain,"
St. 2, Deirdre Lashgari, tr.;
Women Poets of the World,
Joanna Bankier and Deirdre
Lashgari, eds.   1983

134. Hsüeh T'ao
(768–831)

1 Blossoms crowd the branches: too beautiful
to endure.
Thinking of you, I break into bloom again.
"Spring-Gazing Song,"
Carolyn Kizer, tr.;
A Book of Women Poets,
Aliki and Willis Barnstone,
eds.   1980

2 Happiness, long-deferred, is deferred again.
"Weaving Love-Knots;"
Carolyn Kizer; tr., op. cit.

3 He is gone, who knew the music of my soul.
"Weaving Love Knots" 2,
op. cit.

135. Lady Ishikawa
(fl. 780–800)

1 You were soaked, my lord,
with the drops of mountain dew:
how I wish that I were they!
Untitled, from the Manyōshū,
Quoted in *Land of the Reed Plains*,
Kenneth Yashuda, ed. and tr.
1972

136. Ono no Komachi
(834–880)

1 I once saw my beloved one
For a moment in a nap;
Since then I have begun

To look to dreams with hope.
"Dreams,"
in toto, from *Kokin Shū, Vol. XIL,
An Anthology of Japanese Poems,*
Miyamori Asatarō, ed. and tr.
1938

2 Alas! the colours of the flowers
Have faded in the long continued rain;
My beauty aging, too, as in this world
I gazed, engrossed, on things that were
but vain.   "The Colours of Flowers,"
in toto, Ibid., Vol. II, op. cit.

3 So lonely am I
My body is a floating weed
Severed at the roots.
Were there water to entice me,
I would follow it, I think.
Untitled, in toto,
from *Kokinshū* (905),
Anthology of Japanese Literature,
Donald Keene, ed. and tr.
1955

4 As certain as color
Passes from the petal,
Irrevocable as flesh,
The gazing eye falls through the world.
Untitled,
One Hundred Poems from the Japanese,
Kenneth Rexroth, ed. and tr.
1964

5 A thing which fades
With no outward sign—
Is the flower
Of the heart of man
In this world!   Untitled,
Japanese Poetry: The Uta,
Arthur Waley, ed. and tr.
1976

6 Doesn't he realize
that I am not
like the swaying kelp
in the surf,
where the seaweed gatherer

can come as often as he wants.
Untitled, in toto,
*The Burning Heart:
Women Poets of Japan,*
Kenneth Rexroth and Ikuko
Atsumi, eds. and trs.   1977

7 On fire with longing,
A running fire in my breast
That turns my heart to ashes.
Untitled, Rob Swigart, tr.;
Women Poets of the World,
Joanna Bankier and Deirdre
Lashgari, eds.   1983

8 . . . like the drifting duckweed
Give in to the water's will.
Untitled, Rob Swigart, tr.,
op. cit.

137. Kassia
(fl. c.840)

1 You meet your friend, your face
brightens—you have struck gold.
Untitled, Patrick Diehl, tr.; *The
Penguin Book of Women Poets,*
Carol Cosman, Joan Keefe and
Kathleen Weaver   1978

2 Poverty? wealth? seek neither—
One causes swollen heads,
The other, swollen bellies.
Untitled, Patrick Diehl, tr.,
op. cit.

3 Better unborn than fool.
If born, spare earth your tread.
Don't wait. Go straight to hell.
Untitled, Patrick Diehl, tr.,
op. cit.

4 No remedy for fools,
No helping them, but death.
In office? puffed and strutting.
Acclaimed? beyond endurance.
Columns of stone will kneel
Before you change a fool.
Untitled, Patrick Diehl, tr.,
op. cit.

5 A nun—a door unopened.
> Untitled, Patrick Diehl, tr.,
> op. cit.

6 "O what a night what a night I've had!
Extravagant frenzy in a moonless gloom,
craving the body." "Mary Magdalene,"
> Aliki and Willis Barnstone and
> Elene Kolb, trs.;
> *A Book of Women Poets*,
> Aliki and Willis Barnstone, eds.
> 1980

7 Accept this spring of tears,
> you who empty seawater from the
clouds. Ibid.

8 A woman working hard and wisely
Has misfortune at her will;
A woman living soft and idly
Sees misfortune bring the bill.
> Untitled, Patrick Diehl, tr.;
> *Women Poets of the World*,
> Joanna Bankier and Deirdre
> Lashgari, eds. 1983

9 Wealth covers sin—the poor
Are naked as a pin Untitled, Patrick
> Diehl, tr., op. cit.

10 Hold my tears in Your heart
Weaver of clouds
> "Sticheron [hymn] for Matins,
> Wednesday of Holy Week"

138. The Empress of Nijo
(842–910)

1 Spring has already come round
> While on the ground lies snow;
The frozen tears of *uguisu**
> Soon in the soft warm breeze will
thaw. "The Tears of *Uguisu*,"
> in toto, from *Kokin Shū*, Vol. I,
> *An Anthology of Japanese Poems*,
> Miyamori Asatarō, ed. and
> tr. 1938

*A bird similar to a nightingale.

139. Yü Hsüan-chi
(c.843–868)

1 I have moved to this home of Immortals.
> "Living in the Summer
> Mountains,"
> *The Orchid Boat*,
> *Women Poets of China*,
> Kenneth Rexroth and Ling
> Chung, eds. and trs. 1972

2 How I hate this silk dress
That conceals a poet. "On A Visit to
> Ch'ung Chên Taoist Temple
> I see In the South Hall the List
> of Successful Candidates in the
> Imperial Examinations," op. cit.

3 I lift my head and read their names
In powerless envy. Ibid.

4 Spring flowers and autumn moon enter poems.
Bright days and clear nights are fit for idle
> gods. "For Hidden Mist Pavilion,"
> St. 1,*
> *A Book of Women Poets*,
> Aliki and Willis Barnstone, eds.
> 1980

*Quotations 4–17 tr. by Geoffrey Waters.

5 To find a rare jewel is easy.
To get a good man is harder.
> "For a Neighbor Girl,"
> op. cit.

6 How do we get the life we want?
I am a loosed boat floating a thousand
miles. "At the End of Spring,"
> St. 2, op. cit.

7 For now, in happy times like these,
Even small talents live at ease.
> "To the Minister Liu,"
> St. 6, op. cit.

8 Evening, page by page, I hum beneath my
quilt. "Rhyming a Friend's Poem,"
> St. 3, op. cit.

9 Then: the wind's whistle on a rainy night
Invades my dream. I awake to grief.
> to the tune "Riverbank Willows,"
> St. 4, op. cit.

10 Noisy politicians confuse the world
I sing to the moon alone.
> "Rhyming with a Friend,"
> St. 1, op. cit.

11 Thinking hard, hunting rhymes, humming
by my lamp,
Awake all night, I fear the cold quilt.
> "Sent to Wen T'ing
> on a Winter Night,"
> St. 1, op. cit.

12 But life's changes are nothing to a sage's
heart.   Ibid., St. 3

13 The mountain road is steep, the stone steps
are dangerous;
The hard climb hurts me less than thoughts
of you.   "Spring Thoughts
> Sent to Tzu-an,"
> St. 1. op. cit.

14 The sun falls into West Mountain, the
moon rises in the east.
From mourning, there is no relief.
> "Elegy for the Wife of a
> Friend,"
> St. 4, op. cit.

15 Spring comes, fall goes, love stays.
Fall goes, spring comes, messages are rare.
> "Boudoir Lament,"
> St. 3, op. cit.

16 Unmoved by heartless friends,
I go within, beyond the bitter sea.
> "Regretful Thoughts," I,
> St. 2, op. cit.

17 In dark rooms, I hear the watch sound,
Every night, by my lamp, hair turning
white.   Ibid., II, St. 2

140.   Han Ts'ui-p'in
(fl. 850s)

1 Red leaf, I order you—
Go find someone

In the world of men.   "A Poem Written
On A Floating Red Leaf,"
The Orchid Boat,
Women Poets of China,
Kenneth Rexroth and Ling
Chung, eds. and trs.   1972

141.   Ukon
(fl. 865–899)

1 It does not matter
That I am forgotten,
But I pity
His foresworn life.
> Untitled, *One Hundred*
> *Poems from the Japanese,*
> Kenneth Rexroth, tr.   1964

2 You gave me your solemn word, and I was
sure you would be constant.
I am moved to call down on you the penalty
of death for abandoning me!
> *Waga,* n.d.

142.   Lady Ise
(875?–938?)

1 Not even in dreams
Can I meet him anymore. . . .
> Untitled,
> *Japanese Literature: An*
> *Introduction for*
> *Western Readers,*
> Donald Keene, ed. and
> tr.   1955

2 Can I hope, though I am burnt,
That spring will come again?
> Untitled, op. cit.

3 . . . my reputation
reaches to the skies
like a dust storm.   Untitled,
> *The Burning Heart: Women*
> *Poets of Japan,*
> Kenneth Rexroth and Ikuko
> Atsumi, eds. and trs.   1977

4 . . . the spring rain
is a

thread of pearls.   Untitled, Willis
Barnstone, tr.;
A Book of Women Poets,
Aliki and Willis Barnstone, eds.
1980

5 Soon there will be nothing left
with which to compare myself.
Untitled,
Etsuko Terasaki with Irma
Brandeis, tr., op. cit.

6 And like the maple leaves
of autumn, when members
of the household
have scattered
in their own ways,
uncertainty
fills the air.   "Elegy: Ise Lamenting the
Death of Empress Onshi,"
Etsuko Terasaki with Irma
Brandeis, tr., op. cit.

143. Andal
(c.10th century)

1 Sing,
but not too loudly, so he will come.
Untitled,
Willis Barnstone, tr.;
A Book of Women Poets,
Aliki and Willis Barnstone, eds.
1980

2 we will do good things,
use good words,
give away our possessions and live for him.
Untitled,
Willis Barnstone, tr., op. cit.

3 Is it true that black birds infinitely dispersed
wake the dawn,
sing to the god
and welcome the sun?   "To Krishna
Haunting the Hills,"
Willis Barnstone, tr., op. cit.

144. Gormley
(10th century)

1 though I have loved twenty men
this is not what women seek.
"Gormley's Laments,"
St. 1, Joan Keefe, tr.; *The
Penguin Book of Women Poets*,
Carol Cosman, Joan Keefe and
Kathleen Weaver, eds.   1978

2 his full tide of fortune ebbed,
each in its turn has fled.   Ibid., St. 4

3 I paid poets for their words
before God took my riches.
Ibid., St. 14

145. Rabi'a of Balkh
(10th century)

1 My wish for you
that God should make your love
fall on a heart as cold and stony as
your own   Untitled,
Deirdre Lashgari, tr.;
Women Poets of the World,
Joanna Bankier and Deirdre
Lashgari, eds.   1983

146. Qernertoq
(c.900–1400)

1 It seems as if
I'll never get beyond
the foot-prints that I made
"The Widow's Song," St. 2,
*Eskimo Poets of Canada and
Greenland*,
Tom Lowenstein, ed. and tr.
1973

147. Vallana
(c.900–1100)

1 who could save me from plunging into a sea
of shame
but the love god

who teaches us how to faint?

> Untitled,
> Willis Barnstone, tr.;
> *A Book of Women Poets*,
> Aliki and Willis Barnstone, eds.
> 1980

148.   Hroswitha of Gandersheim
(c.935–1000)

1 One thing has all the same embarrassed me and often brought a blush to my cheek. It is that I have been compelled through the nature of this work to apply my mind and pen to depicting the dreadful frenzy of those possessed by unlawful love, and the insidious sweetness of passion—things which should not even be named among us.

> "Preface to the Plays of Hroswitha,
> German Religious and Virgin of
> the Saxon Race" (c.960),
> *The Plays of Roswitha*,
> Christopher St. John, tr.
> 1923

2 To think that you who have been nurtured in the most profound philosophical studies and have attained knowledge in perfection, should have deigned to approve the humble work of an obscure woman! You have, however, not praised me but the Giver of the grace which works in me, by sending me your paternal congratulations and admitting that I possess some little knowledge of those arts the subtleties of which exceed the grasp of my woman's mind.

> "Epistle of the Same to Certain
> Learned Patrons of this Book,"
> op. cit.

3 I know that it is as wrong to deny a divine gift as to pretend falsely that we have received it. So I will not deny that through the grace of the Creator I have acquired some knowledge of the arts. He has given me the ability to learn—I am a teachable creature—yet of myself I should know nothing. He has given me a perspicacious mind, but one that lies fallow and idle when it is not cultivated.   Ibid.

4 Unknown to all round me, I have toiled in secret, often destroying what seemed to me to be ill written, and rewriting it . . . I was eager that the talent given me by Heaven should not grow rusty from neglect, and remain silent in my heart from apathy, but under the hammer of assiduous devotion should sound a chord of divine praise. If I have achieved nothing else, this alone should make my work of some value.

> "Preface to Her Poetical
> Works,"
> op. cit.

5 CONSTANCE. But a heart which trusts in God's goodness is armed against sorrow.

> *Gallicanus*,
> Pt. I, Sc. 2, op. cit.

6 GALLICANUS. It is said that the face is the mirror of the soul.   Ibid., Sc. 3

7 PAUL. That is natural, for, as the saying goes, "The friends of our friends are our friends."   Ibid., Sc. 7

8 JOHN. How much more powerful is one fervent prayer than all the pride of man!

> Ibid., Sc. 9

9 GALLICANUS. What temptation is to be feared more than the lust of the eyes?

> Ibid., Sc. 13

10 JULIAN. Do you deny that I am Augustus? PAUL. No, but we say you are Augustus with a difference.   Ibid., Pt. II, Sc. 5

11 IRENA. A God who can be bought cheap in the market-place, what is he but a slave?

> *Dulcitius*,
> Sc. 1, op. cit.

12 IRENA. Better far that my body should suffer outrage than my soul.

> Ibid., Sc. 12

13 FRIENDS. When a man tells his friends of his sufferings it is only fair that they should try to share them.   *Callimachus*,
> Sc. 2, op. cit.

14 FRIENDS. We should be poor friends if we consoled and flattered you at the expense of the truth.   Ibid.

15 JOHN. Human wisdom cannot grasp the subtlety of the divine judgment.
Ibid., Sc. 9

16 ANDRONICUS. . . . it is not in our power to attain a precise knowledge of the causes of things. *Ibid.*

17 JOHN. Nothing is more terrible than envy, nothing more evil than pride. . . . The proud are envious, and the envious are proud. A jealous man cannot endure to hear others praised, and seeks to belittle those who are more perfect. He disdains to take a lower place, and arrogantly seeks to be put above his equals. *Ibid.*

18 EPHREM. Out of the mouths of babes and sucklings! *Abraham*, Sc. 1, op. cit.

19 ABRAHAM. It is human to sin, but it is devilish to remain in sin. *Ibid.*, Sc. 7

20 MARY. Everything is easy when we put our hearts into it. *Ibid.*, Sc. 8

21 PAPHNUTIUS. You know that the greater world is composed of four elements which are contraries, yet by the will of the Creator these contraries are adjusted in harmonious arrangement . . . [and] as low and high sounds harmoniously united produce a certain music, so discordant elements rightly adjusted make one world.
Paphnutius, Sc. 1, op. cit.

22 DISCIPLES. It is better to know nothing than to be bewildered. *Ibid.*

23 PAPHNUTIUS. The more a man realizes the wonderful way in which God has set all things in number and measure and weight, the more ardent his love. *Ibid.*

24 THAIS. Remorse has killed everything.
Ibid., Sc. 3

25 THAIS. Rumour never delays.
Ibid., Sc. 6

26 THAIS. I have been so long accustomed to pleasure and distraction. My mind is still a slave to the senses. *Ibid.*

27 ANTONY. What pleasures God sends us, when we resign ourselves to have none!
Ibid., Sc. 10

28 ANTONY. Hard words are necessary when natures have grown soft and can no longer distinguish between good and evil.
Ibid.

29 PAPHNUTIUS. Grace is the free gift of God and does not depend on our merits. If it did, it could not be called grace.
Ibid., Sc. 12

30 SAPIENTIA. . . . the Author of the world, Who in the beginning created the world out of nothing, and set everything in number, measure, and weight, and then, in time and the age of man, formulated a science which reveals fresh wonders the more we study it.
Sapientia, Sc. 3, op. cit.

31 Look now, bride of God,
what splendour on earth awaits you,
what glories, too, in Heaven–
Look now, bride of God!
"In Praise of Virginity,"
St. 1, John Dillon, tr.;
The Penguin Book of Women Poets,
Carol Cosman, Joan Keefe and
Kathleen Weaver, eds. 1978

149. Daughter of Ki no Tsurayuki
(fl. 947-967)

1 But if the *uguisu** inquire
For their home, oh! what shall I say?
"The *Uguisu's* Home,"**
from *Go Shūi Shū*, Vol. IX,
An Anthology of Japanese Poems,
Miyamori Asatarō, ed. and tr.
1938

*A bird similar to a nightingale. **Poem in response to Emperor Murakami's order to transplant a plum tree from the poet's garden to his own.

150. Mother of Michitsuna
(fl. 954–974)

1 Every day he promises that it shall be to-morrow. And when tomorrow comes, it is to be the day after. Of course I do not believe him; yet each time that this happens I begin imagining that he has repented,— that all has come right again. So day after day goes by.   Diary entry (970), *Kagero Nikki [Gossamer Diary]* 954–974

2 Have you any idea
How long a night can last, spent
Lying alone and sobbing?
     Untitled, *One Hundred Poems from the Japanese*, Kenneth Rexroth, tr.   1964

151. Nieh Sheng-ch'iung
(c.960–1279)

1 I try to dream good dreams
But it is hard to do   "Farewell To Li," *The Orchid Boat, Women Poets of China*, Kenneth Rexroth & Ling Chung, eds. and trs.   1972

152. 'Aisha bint Ahmad al-Qurtubiyya
(fl. 965–999)

1 I am a lioness
and will never allow my body
to be anyone's resting place.
     Untitled, Elene Margot Kolb, tr.; *Women Poets of the World*, Joanna Bankier and Deirdre Lashgari, eds.   1983

153. Sei Shonagon
(966/67–1013?)

1 One writes a letter, taking particular trouble to get it up as prettily as possible; then waits for the answer, making sure every moment that it cannot be much longer before something comes. At last, frightfully late, is brought in—one's own note, still folded or tied exactly as one sent it, but so fingermarked and smudged that even the address is barely legible. "The family is not in residence," the messenger says, giving one back the note. *Makura no Soshi [The Pillow-Book of Sei Shonagon]*, (991–1100), Arthur Waley, tr.   1928

2 Among five thousand arrogants, you too will surely find a place.   *Ibid.*

3 If, whenever there is a question of poetry, you turn upon me and ask me to compose, I shall stay in your service no longer. When I am called upon like that, I can't even count the syllables, still less think whether I am writing a winter song in spring. . . .   *Ibid.*

4 A Court lady, when she is on holiday . . . will get on best in a house where people are always going in and out, where there is a great deal of conversation always going on in the back rooms, and where at the gate there is a continual clatter of horsemen. Indeed, she would far rather have too much noise than too little.   *Ibid.*

5 But step-parents can be a nuisance. One is always wondering how they will take things. . . .   *Ibid.*

6 Small children and babies ought to be fat. So ought provincial governors, or one suspects them of being bad-tempered.   *Ibid.*

7 For secret meetings summer is best. It is true that the nights are terribly short and it begins to grow light before one has had a wink of sleep. But it is delightful to have all the shutters open, so that the cool air comes in and one can see into the garden.
Ibid.

8 Very Tiresome Things: When a poem of one's own, that one has allowed someone else to use as his, is singled out for praise.
Ibid.

9 There is nothing in the whole world so painful as feeling that one is not liked. It always seems to me that people who hate me must be suffering from some strange form of lunacy.
Ibid.

10 Writing is an ordinary enough thing; yet how precious it is! When someone is in a far corner of the world and one is terribly anxious about him, suddenly there comes a letter, and one feels as though the person were actually in the room. It is really very amazing.
Ibid.

11 Strangely enough, to put down one's thoughts in a letter, even if one knows that it will probably never reach its destination, is an immense comfort.
Ibid.

12 If writing did not exist, what terrible depressions we should suffer from!
Ibid.

13 . . . it is no exaggeration to say that the arrival of an answer [letter] can sometimes work like a real Elixir of Life!
Ibid.

14 If someone with whom one is having an affair keeps on mentioning some woman whom he knew in the past, however long ago it is since they separated, one is always irritated.
Ibid.

15 Though you can tell me
You heard a cock crow
In the middle of the night,
The guard at Ōsaka Gate*

Will not believe you.   Untitled,
*One Hundred Poems
from the Japanese,*
Kenneth Rexroth, ed. and tr.
1964

154. Nakatsukasa
(fl. c.970)

1 Before they bloomed I longed for them;
  After they bloomed, I mourned that
they must fade;
The mountain cherry-flowers
  Sorrow alone for my poor heart have
made.   "Pining for a Dead Child,"
*in toto,
from Go Shūi Shū, Vol. I,
An Anthology of Japanese Poems,*
Miyamori Asatarō, ed. and tr.
1938

155. Izumi Shikibu
(974?–c.1030)

1 If in my gardens only, nowhere else,
  The flowers of spring should bloom,
Even the man who has neglected me
  To gaze on them would surely come.
"Flowers of Spring,"
*in toto,
from Go Shūi Shū, Vol. I,
An Anthology of Japanese Poems,*
Miyamori Asatarō, ed. and tr.
1938

2 Ah, when I count the years still left,
  I find them quickly told;
In all the world is nought so sad
  As growing old.
"At the Close of the Year,"
*in toto, from Shin Kokin Shū,
Vol. VI, op. cit.*

3 Will I cease to be,
  Or will I remember
Beyond the world,

Our last meeting together?
Untitled,
*One Hundred Poems
from the Japanese*,
Kenneth Rexroth, ed. and tr.
1964

4 I go out of the darkness
Onto a road of darkness
Lit only by the far off
Moon on the edge of the mountains.
Ibid.

5 Perhaps
A heart in love
Becomes a deep ravine? Untitled,
Edwin A. Cranston, tr.;
*The Penguin Book
of Women Poets*,
Carol Cosman, Joan Keefe and
Kathleen Weaver, eds. 1978

6 You told me it was
because of me
you gazed at the moon.
I've come to see
if this is true. Untitled, in toto, from *The
Diary of Izumi Shikibu*,
Willis Barnstone, tr.;
A Book of Women Poets,
Aliki and Willis Barnstone,
eds. 1980

7 When you broke from me
I thought I let the thread
of my life break Untitled,
Willis Barnstone, tr., op. cit.

8 I wore out the darkness
until lazy dawn. Untitled,
Willis Barnstone, tr., op. cit.

156. Murasaki Shikibu
(974–1031?)

1 ... so quick was I at picking up the language [Chinese] that I was soon able to prompt my brother whenever he got stuck. At this my father used to sigh and say to me: "If only you were a boy how proud and happy I should be." But it was not long before I repented of having thus distinguished myself; for person after person assured me that even boys generally become very unpopular if it is discovered that they are fond of their books. For a girl, of course, it would be even worse....
*Murasaki Shikibu Nikki [The
Diary of Murasaki Shikibu]*,
Hakubunkwan text
c.994–1010

2 There [at Princess Senshi's Court] I should be allowed to live buried in my own thoughts like a tree-stump in the earth....
Ibid.

3 If these* beyond other flowers are fair, 'tis but because the dew hath picked them out and by its power made them sweeter than the rest. Ibid.
**Ominabeshi*, or lady-flowers.*

4 Who has told you that the fruit belies the flower? For the fruit you have not tasted, and the flower you know but by report.*
Ibid.
*Addressing Michinaga, the prime minister, and implying that he has neither read her book, The Tale of Genji, nor won her love.

5 I have never seen her [a friend] so handsome. So it often is; even those whom we at all times admire will, upon some occasion, suddenly seem to us ten times more lovely than ever before. Ibid.

6 Today I picked up a romance which I used to think quite entertaining, and found to my astonishment that it no longer amused me at all. And it is the same with my friends.
Ibid.

7 The truth is I now find that I have not the slightest pleasure in the society of any but a few indispensable friends. They must be people who really interest me, with whom I can talk seriously on serious subjects, and with whom I am brought into contact without effort on my side in the natural course of everyday existence. Ibid.

8 That I am very vain, reserved, unsociable, wanting always to keep people at a distance—that I am wrapped up in the study of ancient stories, conceited, living all the time in a poetical world of my own and scarcely realizing the existence of other people, save occasionally to make spiteful and depreciatory comments upon them—such is the opinion of me that most strangers hold, and they are prepared to dislike me accordingly. But when they get to know me, they find to their extreme surprise that I am kind and gentle—in fact, quite a different person from the monster they had imagined.... Ibid.

9 Sad is any parting at the red of dawn; but never since the world began, gleamed day so tragically in the autumn sky.
Genji Monogatari [*The Tale of Genji*], (1001–1015) Vol. II, "The Sacred Tree," Ch. 1, Arthur Waley, tr. 1925–1933

10 Sad enough already is this autumn parting; add not your dismal song O pine-crickets of the moor. Ibid.

11 It was as though she had never till that moment fully realized the desolation and misery into which an intrigue, undertaken originally in a reckless and frivolous spirit, had at last plunged her. Ibid.

12 "We are told," answered Genji, "that everything which happens to us in this life is the result of our conduct in some previous existence. If this is to be taken literally I suppose I must now accept the fact that in a previous incarnation I must have misbehaved myself in some way."
Ibid., Ch. 3

13 "But when the Government has shown that it mistrusts a man, he is generally considered much to blame if he continues to flaunt himself at Court as though nothing were amiss." Ibid.

14 "My conscience is of course perfectly clear; but I see that it would be very dangerous to sit down and await events."
Ibid.

15 As a rule provincial governors seem to think that there are no reputable families in the land except those of other provincial governors.... Ibid.

16 "What is all this about criminals?" he growled. "Surely you know that some of the most distinguished men in history both here and in China have been forced at one time or another to retire from Court. There is nothing disgraceful about it."
Ibid.

17 But there are many instances in foreign history of people saving a whole country from peril by obeying an apparently senseless dream. Ibid., Ch. 4

18 "It is only as a background to music that the sound of the sea is tolerable."
Ibid.

19 "O thou, my milk-white pony, whose coat is as the moon-beams of this autumn night, carry me like a bird through the air that though it be but for a moment I may look upon the lady whom I love!"
Ibid.

20 "A night of endless dreams, inconsequent and wild, is this my life; none more worth telling than the rest." Ibid.

21 "You are inventing all sorts of feelings for me such as I have never really had at all, and then getting cross with me for having them. That is not a very amiable proceeding, is it?" Ibid., Ch. 5

22 "You had best be quick, if you are ever going to forgive me at all; life does not last forever." Ibid.

41

23 One cannot enjoy beautiful scenery or works of art in the company of any but the right person. . . .   Ibid.

24 Would that like the snow-flakes when they are weary of falling I might sink down upon the earth and end my days.
                                                                Ibid.

25 In fact he was a saint, and consequently very unlikely to notice that the whole place was overgrown with weeds and bushes. . . .
                                                        Ibid., Ch. 6

26 Solitary people with a great deal of time on their hands seem to turn to old ballads and romances for amusement and distraction. . . .   Ibid.

27 "To the tears I shed in longing for him that is no more, are added the ceaseless drippings that patter from my broken roof!"
                                                                Ibid.

28 "Better had it been for me when I was alone to look at pictures of the realms where fishes dwell, than stare at nothing, as I did all day long!"   Ibid., Ch. 7

29 "Upon the topmost regions of the sky* our hero's heart is set; with scorn he views your shoals, upon which, heavy as a thousand watery fathoms, the ages rest."
                                                                Ibid.

*The allusion is to a promotion at court; courtiers were called "men above the clouds."

30 But though he [Prince Genji] was a spectator of their lives rather than a participator in them, his casual exits and entrances had become the rock in which her whole existance was rooted. . . .   Ibid., Ch. 9

31 The child was brought in, its infant beauty shining like a jewel in the greyness of the dawn.   Ibid.

32 Princes are the lamps that light this world. . . .   Ibid.

33 "Though the snow-drifts of Yoshino were heaped across his path, doubt not that whither his heart is set, his footsteps shall tread out their way."   Ibid., Vol. III, "A Wreath of Cloud," Ch. 1

34 . . . she had died suddenly like a candle blown out by the wind. . . .
                                                                Ibid.

35 "Is it for me to change, for me who hear on every wind some tale that proves you, though the years go by, not other than you were?"   Ibid., Ch. 2

36 Indeed, she had seen enough of the world to know that in few people is discretion stronger than the desire to tell a good story. . . .   Ibid.

37 "Beauty without colour seems somehow to belong to another world."
                                                                Ibid.

38 "How little do I agree with the proverb that calls the moon in winter a dismal sight!"
                                                                Ibid.

39 "I have noticed that children of good families, assured of such titles and emoluments as they desire, and used to receive the homage of the world however little they do to deserve it, see no advantage in fatiguing themselves by arduous and exacting studies."   Ibid., Ch. 3

40 "Unbroken is my misery as this dull sky that day on day has bound the waters of the earth in ice and snow."   Ibid.

41 "A man ought to bear himself with pride even if he knows that he deserves a higher rank than that which for the moment has been accorded to him."   Ibid.

42 There was indeed an undeniable difference between this splendid princess and the shy girl from Tsukushi. But it was only the difference between obscurity and success; a single turn of fortune would quickly redress the balance.   Ibid., Ch. 4

43 "It shows not from afar; but seek and you shall find it, the marsh-flower of the island. For from the ancient stem new shoots for ever spring."   Ibid.

44 "Alas," she wrote, "your present serves but to remind me of your absence. What pleasure can I take in a dress that you will never see me wear?" With this was the poem: "Was ever gift more heartless? Behold, I send it back to you, your Chinese dress,— worn but an instant, yet discoloured with the brine of tears."   Ibid.

45 "In the soft spring sunshine even the spray that falls from the rower's oars, sinks soft as scattered petals on to the waveless waters of the lake."   Ibid., Ch. 6

46 "Of my love perchance you know not, for like a stream that is buried under the ground, a moment it springs into the sunlight; then sinks into the cavern whence it sprang."   Ibid.

47 "You cannot simply disappear while people are talking to you."   Ibid., Ch. 7

48 "Far deeper is the glow-worm's love that speaks in silent points of flame, than all the passions idle courtiers prate with facile tongue."   Ibid.

49 "But I have a theory of my own about what this art of the novel is, and how it came into being. To begin with, it does not simply consist in the author's telling a story about the adventures of some other person. On the contrary it happens because the storyteller's own experience of men and things, whether for good or ill—not only what he has passed through himself, but even events which he has only witnessed or been told of—has moved him to an emotion so passionate that he can no longer keep it shut up in his heart."   Ibid.

50 "Some people have taken exception on moral grounds to an art [storytelling] in which the perfect and imperfect are set side by side. But even in the discourses which Buddha in his bounty allowed to be recorded, certain passages contain what the learned call Upāya or 'Adapted Truth' . . . ."   Ibid.

51 " . . . the art of fiction must not lose our allegiance because . . . it sets virtue by the side of vice, or mingles wisdom with folly. Viewed in this light the novel is seen to be not, as is usually supposed, a mixture of useful truth with idle invention, but something which at every stage and in every part has a definite and serious purpose."   Ibid.

52 "I have never thought there was much to be said in favour of dragging on long after all one's friends were dead. . . . "   Ibid., Vol. IV, "Blue Trousers," Ch. 1

53 "It would be fatal, for example, if this situation were suddenly sprung upon the world in all its details. But allowed to leak out piecemeal, it will do very little harm. What matters is that people should have plenty of time to get used to one part of a scandal before the next is allowed to leak out."   Ibid.

54 At this last moment many a tree, never noticed before, seemed the one place where it would be pleasant to seek shade when the summer-time came round. . . .   Ibid., Ch. 3

55 "Like the man who lost his rudder said, when he found himself at the same place where he started: 'It all comes to the same thing in the end,' " she added encouragingly.   Ibid.

56 "Now faithlessness, that once was held a crime, rules all the world, and he a half-wit is accounted whose heart is steadfast for an hour."   Ibid., Ch. 4

57 "Though loath to pile the years about my head, not lightly shall I quit the field where Spring by Spring these pines spread wider shade."   Ibid., Ch. 6

58 . . . it is far easier to learn ancient Chinese tunes, though every note has to be played exactly as it is handed down, than to improvise upon the Japanese zithern, where one has complete freedom, save for the necessity of giving scope to the accompanying players.   Ibid.

59 But unfortunately, Genji reflected, people who do not get into scrapes are a great deal less interesting than those who do.
                                                   Ibid.

60 Now came the news (disconcerting to gossip of either kind) that perfect harmony prevailed between the two ladies, and to these outside observers the situation lost all further interest.   Ibid.

61 The most unsociable cat, when it finds itself wrapped up in some one's coat and put to sleep upon his bed—stroked, fed and tended with every imaginable care—soon ceases to stand upon its dignity. . . .
                                                   Ibid.

62 "Though the body moves, the soul may stay behind."   Ibid., Ch. 7

63 There is in many high-born women an abundance of natural appetite that the good manners instilled into them from childhood render invisible to the common eye. But upon the mildest provocation this tendency will manifest itself in the most surprising ways.   Ibid.

64 The soothsayers and diviners . . . [a] motley crowd of clerics and healers. "How I hate this noise!" cried Kashiwagi at last. "It may be because of my sins—I do not know—but so far from giving me any comfort this jangle of holy words dismays me, and I feel I should live longer were it utterly to cease."
                                                   Ibid., Ch. 8

65 "I have lived long enough myself to know that loss and sorrow are what we must expect as our portion in this life. If happiness comes in, it is only by the way."
                                                   Ibid.

66 "For surely the position of a woman who stands first among many rivals is far more distinguished than that of one who stands alone? Moreover, the affection of the husband is far more likely to be permanent if he is allowed a certain amount of variety and diversion. You would not set much store by my admiration, if it merely meant I were too dull to see the beauty of other women."
                                                   Ibid., Ch. 10

67 "Think not that I have come in quest of common flowers; but rather to bemoan the loss of one whose scent has vanished from the air."   Ibid., Ch. 12

68 Someone passes,
And while I wonder
If it is he,
The midnight moon
Is covered with clouds.   Untitled, in toto,
                            *One Hundred Poems
                             from the Japanese,*
                        Kenneth Rexroth, ed. and tr.
                                              1964

69 The memories of long love
gather like drifting snow,
poignant as the mandarin ducks
who float side by side in sleep.
                              Untitled, in toto,
                            *The Burning Heart:
                             Women Poets of Japan,*
                        Kenneth Rexroth & Ikuko
                        Atsumi, eds. and trs.   1977

157.   Akazome Emon
(c.11th century)

1 I should not have waited.
It would have been better
To have slept and dreamed,
Than to have watched night pass,
And this slow moon sink.
                            *One Hundred Poems
                             from the Japanese,*
                        Kenneth Rexroth, ed. and tr.
                                              1964

2 Why do I still long
for the floating world?   Untitled,
                            *The Burning Heart:
                             Women Poets of Japan,*
                        Kenneth Rexroth and Ikuko
                        Atsumi, eds. and trs.   1977

158.   Ise Tayu
(11th century)

1 . . . the long May rains
that fall without cease,

from a sky with never a rift in the clouds.
Untitled,
The Burning Heart:
Women Poets of Japan,
Kenneth Rexroth and Ikuko
Atsumi, eds. and trs.   1977

159.   Maryam bint Abi Ya'qub al-Ansari
(fl. 1000–1035)

1 What can you expect
from a woman with seventy-seven years,
frail as the web of a spider?
Untitled,
Elene Margot Kolb, tr.;
Women Poets of the World,
Joanna Bankier and Deirdre
Lashgari, eds.   1983

160.   Wallada
(fl. 1000–1035)

1 Expect my visit when the darkness comes.
The night I think is best for hiding all.
If the full moon felt like me she wouldn't
rise;
if the star, it wouldn't move;
if the night, it wouldn't fall.
Untitled,
Quoted in *The Troubadours and*
Their World of the Twelfth and
Thirteenth Centuries,
by Jack Lindsay   1976

2 Time passes, yet I see no end to your long
absence,
Nor does patience free me from the bond-
age of yearning! "A Correspondence to
Ibn Zaidun:* #4,"
A. R. Nykl, tr.;
The Penguin Book
of Women Poets,
Carol Cosman, Joan Keefe and
Kathleen Weaver, eds.   1978

*Her lover, an Andalusian writer of classical Arabic
poetry.

3 Leaving aside the bough that produced
beauty's fruit,
Inclining toward a bough that no such fruit
does show.   Ibid., #2

4 In winter with you near
no need for coals—
our passion blazed.   "To Ibn Zaidun,"
St. 2, James Monroe and Deirdre
Lashgari, trs.;
Women Poets of the World,
Joanna Bankier and Deirdre
Lashgari, eds.   1983

5 Longing chains me.   Ibid., St. 4

6 The sun if it loved as I do
would hide its light,
full moon not come into view
stars not journey by night.
Untitled,*
St. 2, James Monroe and Deirdre
Lashgari, trs., op. cit.

*Possible variant of quotation no. 1, above.

161.   Suo
(fl. 1035–1065)

1 That spring night I spent
Pillowed on your arm
Never really happened
Except in a dream.
Unfortunately I am
Talked about anyway.   Untitled,
One Hundred Poems
from the Japanese,
Kenneth Rexroth, ed. and tr.
1964

162.   Li Ch'ing-chao
(1084–1151)

1 My body is a prisoner
In this room above the misty
River, the jade green river,
That is the only companion

of my endless days.   Untitled, St. 2,
Love and the Turning Year:
One Hundred More Poems
from the Chinese,
Kenneth Rexroth, ed. and tr.
1970

2 Who can
Take a letter beyond the clouds?
Untitled, op. cit.

3 Search. Search. Seek. Seek.
Cold. Cold. Clear. Clear.
Sorrow. Sorrow. Pain. Pain.
Hot flashes. Sudden chills.
Stabbing pains. Slow agonies.
"A Weary Song
to a Slow Sad Tune,"
op. cit.

4 I bought a spray of Spring in bud,
All moist as if with tears,
Still holding the pink clouds of dawn
And traces of morning dew.
to the tune "The Magnolias,"
The Orchid Boat,
Women Poets of China,
Kenneth Rexroth and Ling
Chung, eds. and trs.   1972

5 But I am startled by the breaking cup of
Spring.   to the tune "A Hilly Garden,"
op. cit.

6 Nothing is left of Spring but fragrant dust.
"Spring Ends," op. cit.

7 The huge roc bird is flying
On a ninety thousand mile wind.
to the tune "The Honor of a
Fisherman," op. cit.

8 Multitudinous dew
On thin flower
a mist of sweat
dampens

her light dress through
to the tune "Crimson Lips
Adorned,"
C. H. Kwôck and Vincent
McHugh, trs.;
The Penguin Book
of Women Poets,
Carol Cosman, Joan Keefe and
Kathleen Weaver, eds.   1978

9   O flower! flower!
don't make fun of me
Have pity!
Spring
like all men living
will soon
grow old   to the tune "The
Butterfly Woos the Blossoms,"
op. cit.

10   joyful days
in my room
much
time to myself
to the tune "Endless Union,"
op. cit.

11 Too diffident
to venture among flowers
I loiter
under the window screen
eavesdropping
on the talk
and laughter
of others   Ibid.

12 The jade
burner
is cold,
a companion
to
my
feelings,
which
are
water.   Untitled,
St. 3, Willis Barnstone
and Sun Chu-chin, trs.;
A Book of Women Poets,
Aliki and Willis Barnstone, eds.
1980

13 My chest

is
broken.
On whom
can I
lean?   Ibid., St. 9

14 Alone
I hug
dense
pain,
with no
good dreams.   Untitled,
                                  St. 9, op. cit.

15 eagerly   hearing   As
asking: heaven's   if
Where   voice,   in dream
am I   my soul
going   returns
back   to god's
to?   home.
                                       Untitled,
                                       Sts. 3–5
                    (Note: read down, right to left),
                                       op. cit.

16 Dense
sleep
doesn't
fade
a wine
hangover.   Untitled,
                                  St. 2, op.cit.

17 There is no way to banish this feeling.
As it leaves the eyebrows,
it enters the heart. to the tune "Yi chian
                                       mei,"
                      St. 3, Marsha Wagner, tr.;
                      Women Poets of the World,
                      Joanna Bankier and Deirdre
                      Lashgari, eds.   1983

163.   Hildegarde von Bingen
(1098–1179)

1 ... when in my forty-third year, attentive,
yet trembling in great fear, I worshipped a
heavenly vision, I saw in it a mighty brilliance through which came to me a voice
from heaven crying out "You frail creature,
ash from ashes, dust from dust, say and
write what you see and hear."
                                       Scivias
                                       1147

2 You beautiful faces
Beholding God and building in the dawn
How noble you are. Song 38, "Antiphon
                      about the Virgins,"
              *Symphony of the Harmony of
                   Heavenly Relations*
                      1151–1158

3 You most glorious greenness,
You take root in the sun,
And in clear day-brightness
You shine forth in a wheel
Which no earthly excellence comprehends
              Song 39, "Responsory about the
                      Virgins,"
                      op. cit.

4 Greetings, greenest branch
              Song 71, "About the Blessed
                      Virgin Mary,"
                      St. 1, op. cit.

5 In you has blossomed the beautiful flower
Which has given fragrance to all the spices.
                                       Ibid., St. 3

6 At last is there food made for humanity
And great joy for the banqueters.
                                       Ibid., St. 5

7 I am that supreme and fiery force that sends forth all living sparks. Death hath no part in me, yet I bestow death, wherefore I am girt about with wisdom as with wings. I am that living and fiery essence of the divine substance that glows in the beauty of the fields, and in the shining water, and in the burning sun and the moon and the stars, and in the force of the invisible wind, the breath of all living things, I breathe in the green grass and in the flowers, and in the living waters.... All these live and do not die because I am in them ... I am the source of the thundered word by which all creatures were made, I permeate all things that they may not die. I am life.
Book of Divine Works
c.1167

8 ... there may be only one love between man and woman, and no other is to come between them. Man's love with its glowing heat compared with the love of woman is as the fire of burning mountains, hard to extinguish, to the fire of burning wood that can easily be put out. Woman's love resembles the mild warmth of the sun producing fruit, so different from the burning of wood, because she too is mild and produces fruit: her offspring. Quoted in *Women in the Middle Ages*
by Sibylle Harksen 1975

9 ... man ... rushes to woman like the stag to the spring, and the woman to him like the threshing floor of the barn, shaken and heated by the many blows of the flail when the grain is threshed. Ibid.

10 Take care that the Highest King does not strike you down because of the blindness which prevents you from governing justly. See that God does not withdraw His grace from you. Letter to Frederick Barbarossa, Quoted in *Women in the Middle Ages*
by Frances and Joseph Gies 1978

11 From my infancy up to the present time, when I am more than seventy years of age, I have always seen this light in my spirit.... The light which I see ... is more brilliant than the sun ... and I name it the cloud of living light. And as the sun, moon, and stars are reflected in the water, so the scripture and sermons, and virtues, and works of men shine in it before me....
But sometimes I see within this light another light which I call the Living Light itself.... And when I look upon it every sadness and pain is erased from my memory, so that I am once more as a simple maid and not as an old woman.
Remark (c.1171), op. cit.

12 The body is truly the garment of the soul, which has a living voice; for that reason it is fitting that the body simultaneously with the soul repeatedly sing praises to God through the voice. Letter to the Prelates of Mainz (c.1178), Quoted in *Women in Music*, Carol Neuls-Bates 1982

13 The prophetic spirit orders that God be praised with cymbals of jubilation and with the rest of the musical instruments which the wise and studious have created, since all of the arts (whose purpose is to fill uses and needs of man) are brought to life by that breath of life which God breathed into the body of man: and therefore it is just that God be praised in all things.
Ibid.

14 ... let sound the cithara whose purpose on earth is to train the body; let sound the psaltery which gives back the sound from the heavenly realm above for expanding the spirit; let sound the ten-string harp for contemplation of the law. Ibid.

15 ... those of the Church who have imposed silence on the singing of the chants for the praise of God without well-considered weight of reason ... have unustly stripped God of the grace and comeliness of His own praise, [and] unless they will have freed themselves from their errors here on earth, will be without company of the angelic songs of praise in heaven.
Ibid.

16 You are the flower
The winter-storm the serpent breathes
Has never withered. "O Crimson Blood," from *Carmina* [Songs], Patrick Diehl, tr.; *Women Poets of the World,* Joanna Bankier and Deirdre Lashgari, eds. 1983

164. Héloise
(c.1098–1164)

1 Only tell me, if you can, why, since the retirement from the world which you yourself enjoined upon me, you have neglected me. Tell me, I say, or I will say what I think, and what is on everybody's lips. Ah! it was lust rather than love which attracted you to me ... Letter to Peter Abelard, Quoted in *Women of Medieval France* by Pierce Butler. 1907

2 Under all circumstances, God knows, I have feared offending you more than I have feared offending Him; and it is you far more than God whom I wish to please.
Ibid.

3 Can it be said, in fact, that one is truly penitent, whatever be the bodily penances submitted to, when the soul still harbors the thought of sin and burns with the same passions as of old?
Ibid.

4 They praise me for purity of life; it is only because they do not know of my hypocrisy. The purity of the flesh is set down to the credit of virtue; but true virtue is of the soul, not of the body. Ibid.

5 The blessings promised us by Christ were not promised to those alone who were priests; woe unto the world, indeed, if all that deserved the name of virtue were shut up in a cloister. Ibid.

6 With thee I suffered the rigor of destiny;
With thee shall I, weary, sleep;
With thee shall I enter Sion.
Dirge (attributed), op. cit.

7 Riches and power are but gifts of blind fate, whereas goodness is the result of one's own merits. Letter to Peter Abelard, #2, *The Letters of Abelard and Heloise,* C. K. Scott Moncrieff, tr. 1925

8 At thy command I would change, not merely my costume, but my very soul, so entirely art thou the sole possessor of my body and my spirit. Never, God is my witness, have I sought anything in thee but thyself; I have sought thee, and not thy gifts. I have not looked to the marriage-bond or dowry. Ibid.

9 Prosperity seldom chooses the side of the virtuous.... First letter to Abelard (c.1122), *The World's Great Letters,* M. Lincoln Schuster, ed. 1940

10 If a picture, which is but a mute representation of an object, can give such pleasure, what cannot letters inspire? They have souls; they can speak; they have in them all that force which expresses the transports of the heart.... Ibid.

11 ... I was more pleased with possessing your heart than with any other happiness ... the man was the thing I least valued in you. Ibid.

12 Riches and pomp are not the charm of love. True tenderness makes us separate the lover from all that is external to him.... Ibid.

13 These martyrs of marriage pine always for larger fortunes which they think they have missed. Ibid.

14 If there is anything that may properly be
called happiness here below, I am persuaded it is the union of two persons who
love each other with perfect liberty, who are
united by a secret inclination, and satisfied
with each other's merits.   Ibid.

15 . . . it is natural to avoid those to whom we
have been too much obliged . . . uncommon
generosity causes neglect rather than ingratitude.   Ibid.

16 Among those who are wedded to God I am
wedded to a man; among the heroic sup-
porters of the Cross I am the slave of a human desire; at the head of a religious community I am devoted to Abelard alone.
                                   Ibid.

17 We fluctuate long between love and hatred
before we can arrive at tranquillity.
                                   Ibid.

18 God has a peculiar right over the hearts of
great men He has created. When He pleases
to touch them He ravishes them, and lets
them not speak nor breathe but for His
glory.   Ibid.

19 To my lord / no / my father
my husband / no / my brother
his servant / no / his daughter
his wife / no / his sister
To my Abelard his Heloise.
                           Untitled,
                           Quoted in
          Women in the Middle Ages
                  by Sibylle Harksen
                               1975

20 When my self is not with you, it is
   nowhere . . .   Letter to Peter Abelard,
                               op. cit.

21 I need not say any more about the basic impossibility of combining matrimony and
scholarship; but think of the details of a
good burgher's marriage. . . . The spinning
wheel charmingly combined with books
and copy-books, style and pen with the
spindle. You are immersed in your theolog-
ical or philosophical ideas, and at that moment the infants begin to squall; the wet
nurses try to quieten them with their
monotonous singsong . . . can then your attention remain uninterrupted?
          Quoted in Abelard's *Historia
          Calamitatum [History of My
                          Troubles]*,
                           op. cit.

165.   Alais
(12th century)

1 . . . shall I stay unwed? that would please
   me,
for making babies doesn't seem so good,
and it's too anguishing to be a wife.
                           Untitled,
          St. 1, with Iselda and Carenza,
                The Women Troubadours,
                   Meg Bodin   1976

2 Lady Carenza, I'd like to have a husband,
but making babies I think is a huge penitence:
your breasts hang way down
and it's too anguishing to be a wife
                           Ibid., St. 2

166.   Carenza
(12th century)

Co-author with Alais. See 165:1, 2.

167.   Domna H.
(12th century)

1 for when a man is in love's grip
it's wrong for him to knowingly

ignore his lady's orders. Untitled, St. 2,
The Women Troubadours,
Meg Bodin 1976

2 . . . for shared bed and lovely sight
make true love burn so bright
that he can't hear or see or know
if he does wrong or right.
Ibid., St. 3

168. Iselda
(12th century)

Co-author with Alais. See 165:1.

169. Kasmuneh
(12th–13th century)

1 In only thee, my timid, fleet gazelle,
Dark-eyed like thee, I see my counterpart;
We both live lone, without companion
dwell,
Accepting fate's decree with patient heart.
"The Timid Gazelle,"
in toto,
A Treasury of Jewish Poetry,
Nathan and Maryann Ausubel,
eds. 1957

2 A vine I see, and though 'tis time to glean,
No hand is yet stretched forth to cull the
fruit. "Overripe Fruit,"
op. cit.

170. Mahādēviyakka
(12th century)

1 husband, inside,
lover outside.
I can't manage them both.
Untitled,
Speaking of Siva,
A. K. Ramanujan, ed. and tr.
1973

2 You can confiscate
money in hand;
can you confiscate

the body's glory? Untitled,
op. cit.

3 When all the world is the eye of the lord,
onlooking everywhere, what can you
cover and conceal? Untitled,
op. cit.

4 Like
treasure hidden in the ground
taste in the fruit
gold in the rock
oil in the seed Untitled,
St. 1, op. cit.

5 She has no strength of limb,
has lost the world,
lost power of will,
turned devotee,
she has lain down
with the lord, white as jasmine,*
and has lost caste. Untitled,
op. cit.

*Another name for the god Siva.

6 Like a silkworm weaving
her house with love
from her marrow Untitled,
op. cit.

7 Till you know and lose this knowing
you've no way
of knowing
my lord white as jasmine.
Untitled,
op. cit.

171. Mahsati
(12th century)

1 Better to live as a rogue and a bum,
a lover all treat as a joke
to hang out with a crowd of comfortable
drunks,
than crouch in a hypocrite's cloak.
Selected Quatrains, #1,
Deirdre Lashgari, tr.;
Women Poets of the World,
Joanna Bankier and Deirdre Lashgari,
eds. 1983

2 Gone are the games we played all night,

gone the pearls my lashes strung.
You were my comfort and my friend.
You've left, with all the songs I'd sung.
Ibid., #4

172.   Stewardess of the Empress Kōka
(fl. 12th century)

1 For the sake of a night
Short as the nodes
Of the reeds of Naniwa
Must I live on,
My flesh wasted with longing?
Untitled,
One Hundred Poems
from the Japanese,
Kenneth Rexroth, tr.   1964

2 For the sake of a joint of reed of Naniwa
     Bay,
shall I wade past the depth-measuring
     gauge.   Ibid. (variation)

173.   T'ang Wan
(c.12th century)

1 The world's love runs thin.
to the tune "The Phoenix
Hairpin,"
The Orchid Boat,
Women Poets of China,
Kenneth Rexroth and Ling
Chung, eds. and trs.   1972

2 Today is not yesterday.
My troubled mind sways
Like the rope of a swing.   Ibid.

174.   Sun Tao-hüsan
(fl.1100–1135)

1 The wind blows down from the emerald sky
A song like a string of pearls.
But the singer is invisible

Hidden behind her embroidered curtains.
to the tune "A Dream Song,"
The Orchid Boat,
Women Poets of China,
Kenneth Rexroth and Ling
Chung, eds. and trs.   1972

175.   Eleanor of Aquitaine
(1122–1204)

1 The kings and princes of the earth have
conspired against my son [Richard I Coeur
de Lion], the anointed of the Lord. One
keeps him in chains while another ravages
his lands; one holds him by the heels while
the other flays him. And while this goes on,
the sword of Saint Peter reposes in its scabbard. Letter to Pope Celestine III (1192),
Quoted in *Eleanor of Aquitaine*
by Amy Kelly   1950

2 Trees are not known by their leaves, nor
even by their blossoms, but by their fruits.
In this wise we have known your cardinals.
Ibid.

3 The fateful moment is at hand when the tunic of Christ shall be rent again, when the
bonds of Saint Peter shall be broken, the
catholic unity dissolved.   Ibid.

4 My posterity has been snatched from
me. . . . The young king and the Count of
Brittany sleep in the dust. Their unhappy
mother is forced to live on, ceaselessly tormented by their memory.
Ibid.

5 I have lost the staff of my age, the light of
my eyes.   Comment on the death of
her son, Richard I (1199),
op. cit.

176.   Frau Ava
(?–1127)

1 I am yours,
you are mine.
Of this we are certain.
You are lodged

in my heart,
the small key
is lost.
You must stay there
forever.

Attributed, attached to a letter
to a cleric (c.1160),
Willis Barnstone, tr.;
A Book of Women Poets,
Willis and Aliki Barnstone,
eds.   1980

177.   Tibors
(c.1130–1182)

1 nor did it ever come to pass, if you went off angry,
that I felt joy until you had come back

Untitled,
from *Die Provenzalischen Dichterinnen*
by Oscar Schultz-Gora (1888),
Quoted in *The Women Troubadours*,
Meg Bodin, tr.   1976

178.   Horikawa
(fl. 1135–1165)

1 Will he always love me?
I cannot read his heart.
This morning my thoughts
Are as disordered
As my black hair.

Untitled,
One Hundred Poems from the Japanese,
Kenneth Rexroth and
Ikuko Atsumi, eds. and
trs.   1964

179.   Almucs de Castelnau
(c.1140–?)

1 but if you want him dead let him receive the sacraments, to guarantee

that he'll refrain from doing further injury.

Untitled,
St. 1, with Iseut de Capio,
Quoted in
The Women Troubadours,
Meg Bodin, tr.   1976

2 Still, if you can get him to repent his perfidy
you'll have no trouble in converting me.

Ibid., St. 2

180.   Azalais de Porcairages
(c.1140–?)

1 Now we are come to the cold time

Untitled, St. 1,
Quoted in
The Women Troubadours,
Meg Bodin, tr.   1976

2 My heart is so disordered
that I'm rude to everyone

Ibid., St. 2

3 A lady's love is badly placed
who argues with a wealthy man

Ibid., St. 3

4 Handsome friend, I'll gladly stay
forever in your service—
such noble mien and such fine looks—
so long as you don't ask too much

Ibid., St. 5

181.   Beatritz de Dia
(c.1140–post-1189?)

1 For times to come, I tell the plight
I've earned through loving in excess.

Untitled,
The Troubadours and Their World of the Twelfth and Thirteenth Centuries,
Jack Lindsay   1976

2 He in my heart alone has place;
for him my soul, my life is spread.

Ibid.

3 I'll sing what I would never wish to sing.

Ibid.

4 Tell me, dear, gentle friend, why I'm de-
    nied,
  why you're so cruelly harsh in all you do.
  Is it from malice that you act, or pride?
                                        Ibid.

5 If all the pangs are mine, I say
  unequal parts in love we play.
                                    Untitled,
                                    op. cit.

6 What you lose is merely sand beside the
    good that I am losing.   Ibid.

7 I thrive on youth and joy.
                                    Untitled,
                                    St. 1,
                                    Quoted in
                        The Women Troubadours,
                        Meg Bodin, tr.   1976

8 and she should dare to love him face to face;
  for courteous and worthy men
  can only speak with great esteem
  of a lady who loves openly.
                                    Ibid., St. 3

9 Why did you become a lover,
  since you leave the suffering to me?
  Why don't we split it evenly?
                                    Untitled,
                        St. 1 (attributed), op. cit.

10 Lady, such is love's nature
   when it links two friends together
   that whatever grief or joy they have
   each feels according to his way.
                                    Ibid., St. 2

11 I don't lie: out of envy
   evil men insult my name.
                                    Ibid., St. 8

12 I sing a song reluctantly,
   A complaint about my friend; for
   I love him more than all the world
   Yet he cares not for me   Untitled,
                        St. 1, Carol Cosman and
                            Howard Bloch, trs.;
                            The Penguin Book
                                of Women Poets,
                        Carol Cosman, Joan Keefe and
                        Kathleen Weaver, eds.   1978

13 Remember our love's blossoming!
                                    Ibid., St. 3

14 I must find strength and solace
   In my merits and my birth,
   In my beauty and my heart's devotion
                                    Ibid., St. 5

15 Excess of pride can bring the greatest misery.   Ibid., St. 6

16 I'd give him crazy joy—that harms
   no one—a cushion of delight.
                                    Untitled,
                        St. 2, Willis Barnstone, tr.;
                            A Book of Women Poets,
                        Aliki and Willis Barnstone, eds.
                                                1980

17 Those bad-talking gossips
   No one who counts
   Pays any attention to them.
   They are a fog that rises
   Against the sunlight.   Untitled,
                        St. 2, Doris Earnshaw, tr.;
                            Women Poets of the World,
                        Joanna Bankier and Deirdre
                            Lashgari, eds.   1983

18 beware, or grief will bring you low.
                                    Ibid., St. 3

182.   Iseut de Capio
(c.1140–?)

Co-author with Almucs de Castelnau. See
179:1.

183.   Marula
(fl. c.1156)

1 She was troubled with indescribable love.
                        "Meeting after Separation,"
                                    Tambimuttu and
                                G. V. Vaidya, trs.;
                                    Indian Love Poems,
                        Tambimuttu, ed.   n.d.

184. Marie de France
(1160?–1215?)

1 Whoever has received knowledge
and eloquence in speech from God
should not be silent or secretive
but demonstrate it willingly.
When a great good is widely heard of,
then, and only then, does it bloom,
and when that good is praised by man,
it has spread its blossoms.

Prologue, ll. 1–8,
The Lais of Marie de France,
Robert Hannings and Joan
Ferrante. trs. 1978

2 He who would guard himself from vice
should study and understand
and begin a weighty work
by which he might keep vice at a distance,
and free himself from great sorrow.

Ibid., ll. 23–27

3 Whoever deals with good material
feels pain if it's treated improperly.

"Guigemar,"
ll. 1, 2, op. cit.

4 People should praise anyone
who wins admiring comments for herself.

Ibid., ll. 5, 6

5 But anywhere there is
a man or a woman of great worth,
people who envy their good fortune
often say evil things about them;
they want to ruin their reputations.
Thus they act like
vicious, cowardly dogs
who bite people treacherously.

Ibid., ll. 7–14

6 But in forming him nature had so badly
erred
that he never gave any thought to love.

Ibid., ll. 57, 58

7 It was fit and ready to go,
caulked outside and in—
no one could discover a seam in its hull.
Every deck rail and peg
was solid ebony;

no gold under the sun could be worth more.

Ibid., ll. 153–158

8 (All folk are jealous;
every one of them hates the thought of being cuckholded,
such is the perversity of age.)

Ibid., ll. 215–217

9 you have to endure what you can't change.

Ibid., l. 410

10 But he who hides his sickness
can hardly be brought back to health;
love is a wound in the body,
and yet nothing appears on the outside.

Ibid., ll. 481–484

11 It's appropriate for an inconstant woman
to make some one plead with her a long
time
to enhance her worth; that way he won't
think
she's used to such sport.
But a woman of good character,
sensible as well as virtuous,
if she finds a man to her liking,
oughtn't to treat him too disdainfully.

Ibid., ll. 515–522

12 But Fortune, who never forgets her duty,
turns her wheel suddenly.

Ibid., ll. 538, 539

13 Whoever indulges in love without sense or
moderation
recklessly endangers his life;
such is the nature of love
that no one involved with it can keep his
head. "Equitan,"
ll. 17–20, op. cit.

14 What would become of her finer qualities
if she didn't nourish them by a secret love?

Ibid., ll. 81, 82

15 Love is worthless if it's not mutual.

Ibid., l. 137

16 Anyone who aims higher in love
than his own wealth entitles him to
will be frightened by every little thing that
occurs. Ibid., ll. 143–145

17 Whoever is inconstant in love

and gives himself up to treachery
is mocked and deceived in the end
Ibid., ll. 163–165

18 he who plans evil for another
may have that evil rebound back on him.
Ibid., ll. 309, 310

19 indeed, I condemned myself
when I slandered all womankind.
"Le Fresne [The Ash Tree],"
ll. 79, 80, op. cit.

20 This beast is rational—he has a mind.
"Bisclavret [The Werewolf],"
l. 157, op. cit.

21 a strange man, without friends,
is very sad in another land,
when he doesn't know where to look for
help.   "Lanval,"
ll. 35–38, op. cit.

22 whether it makes you weep or sing
justice must be carried out.
Ibid., ll. 435, 436

23 Her body was elegant, her hips slim,
her neck whiter than snow on a branch,
her eyes bright, her face white,
a beautiful mouth, a well-set nose,
dark eyebrows and an elegant forehead,
her hair curly and rather blond;
golden wire does not shine
like her hair in the light.   Ibid., ll.
563–570

24 Alas, how hard it is to protect yourself
from someone who wants to trap you,
to betray and deceive you!
"Yonec,"
ll. 254–256, op. cit.

25 Whoever wants to tell a variety of stories
ought to have a variety of beginnings
"Milun,"
ll. 1, 2, op. cit.

26 "A man oughtn't to think he's worth much,
being born in such a manner
and having such a famous father,
if he doesn't seek out even greater renown
away from home, in foreign lands."
Ibid., ll. 308–312

27 She didn't want to lose three in order to
have one,
so she was nice to each of them;
she gave them all tokens of love,
she sent them all messages.
"Chaitivel
[The Unfortunate One],"
ll. 55–58, op. cit.

28 With the two of them it was just
as it is with the honeysuckle
that attaches itself to the hazel tree:
when it has wound and attached
and worked itself around the trunk,
the two can survive together;
but if someone tries to separate them,
the hazel dies quickly
and the honeysuckle with it.
"Sweet love, so it is with us:
You cannot live without me, nor I without
you."   "Chevrefoil [The Honeysuckle],"
ll. 68–78, op. cit.

29 The peasant proverb says,
when it admonishes the ploughman,
that the love of a lord is not a fief:
he is wise and clever
who gives loyalty to his lord,
and love to his good neighbors.
"Eliduc,"
ll. 61–66, op. cit.

30 "Whoever believes in a man is very foolish."   Ibid., l. 1084

31 . . . it is neither good nor fitting
to keep two wives,
nor should the law consent to it.
Ibid., ll. 1128–1130

185.   Alamanda
(fl. 1165–1199)

1 I'm so angry that my body's
all but bursting into flame.
Untitled, St. 1,
Quoted in
The Women Troubadours,
Meg Bodin, tr.   1976

2 . . . if one partner fails
the other should keep up appearances

so that their trouble doesn't spread or grow.
Ibid., St. 2

186.   Marie de Ventadorn
(c.1165–?)

1 . . . the lady
ought to do exactly for her lover
as he does for her, without regard to rank;
for between two friends neither one should
rule.   Untitled, St. 2,
Quoted in
The Woman Troubadours,
Meg Bodin, tr.   1976

2 . . . she should honor him the way
she would a friend, but never as a lord.
Ibid., St. 3

3 . . . to me it's nothing short of treason
if a man says he's her equal *and* her servant.
Ibid., St. 5

187.   Garsenda de Forcalquier
(c.1170–?)

1 . . . it's you who stands to lose
if you're not brave enough to state your case
Untitled, St. 1,
Quoted in
The Women Troubadours,
Meg Bodin, tr.   1976

2 If only deeds were messengers to you,
and you accepted *them* in wooing's place:
for noble deeds, as much as words, deserve
your grace.   Ibid., St. 2

188.   Aldrude
(fl. 1170s)

1 It is by those only who are truly great, that
virtue is esteemed more than riches or honours, or that virtuous actions can be duly
appreciated. (1172), Quoted in *Biography*
of Distinguished Women
by Sarah Josepha Hale, ed.
1876

2 Courage is relaxed by delay.
Ibid.

189.   Isabella
(c.1180–?)

1 . . . if I sang your praises
it wasn't out of love
but for the profit I might get from it
Untitled, St. 2,
Quoted in
The Women Troubadours,
Meg Bodin, tr.   1976

2 Elias Cairel,* you're a phoney
if I ever saw one,
like a man who says he's sick
when he hasn't got the slightest pain.
Ibid., St. 5

*Troubadour from Périgord.

190.   Chu Shu-chên
(fl. c.1182–1200)

1 I write poems, change and correct them,
And finally throw them away.
"Sorrow,"
Love and the Turning Year:
One Hundred More Poems
from the Chinese,
Kenneth Rexroth, ed. and tr.
1970

2 All alone by my window
Hidden in my empty room,
All alone, I burn incense,
And dream in the smoke, all alone.
Ibid.

3 Like a flight of arrows the wind
Pierces my curtain.
"Stormy Night in Autumn,"
One Hundred Poems
from the Chinese,
Kenneth Rexroth, ed. and tr.
1971

4 Alone in the dark, I am
Going mad, counting my sorrow.
Ibid.

5 The oriole is not to blame
For a broken dream of a
Bygone Spring.   "The Old Anguish,"
op. cit.

6 Enveloped in this puzzling scented wind,
Who can appreciate such a subtle joy?
"Plum Blossoms,"
The Orchid Boat,
Women Poets of China,
Kenneth Rexroth and Ling
Chung, eds. and trs.   1972

7 It is easier to see Heaven
Than to see you.   "Spring Joy,"
(1182)   op. cit.

191.   Lombarda
(c.1190–?)

1 but then when I remember what my name
records,
all my thoughts unite in one accord.
Untitled, St. 3,
Quoted in
The Women Troubadours,
Meg Bodin, tr.   1976

192.   Clare of Assisi
(1193/94–1253)

1 . . . sisters beware of all pride, vain ambition, envy, greed, and of taking part in the
cares and busy ways of the world . . .
Rule and Testament
1253

2 . . . have no fear of poverty, toil, tribula-
tion, reviling, and the world's scorn, but
rather . . . hold them as delectable things.
Ibid.

193.   Mistress of Albrecht of Johannsdorf
(13th century)

1 How can you combine two unlike things, to
cross the sea and bide with me? You leave
the tenderness of my heart, then how can
you cherish it also?   Quoted in
Saint Elizabeth
by Elisabeth von Schmidt-Pauli;
Olga Marx, tr.   1932

194.   Mukta Bai
(13th century)

1 What is beyond the mind,
has no boundary,
In it our senses end.   Untitled,
Willis Barnstone, tr.;
A Book of Women Poets,
Aliki and Willis Barnstone, eds.
1980

2 Mukta says: Words cannot contain him,
yet in him all words are.   Ibid.

195.   La Compiuta Donzella
(13th century)

1 To leave the world serve God
make my escape from all pretension . . .
That is my wish.

For what I see flourish and ascend
the stalk is only
insanity, low acts and lies of men.
Untitled, Sts. 1 and 2,
Laura Stortoni, tr.;
Women Poets of the World,
Joanna Bankier
and Deirdre Lashgari, eds.
1983

2 . . . all men find evil
a proper ornament   Ibid., St. 3

196.   Duchess of Lorraine
(13th century)

1 . . . would that I could die even as she did
whose example I would follow, Dido slain
for love of Aeneas.   "Elegy," St. 1,
Quoted in
Medieval Lyrics of Europe
by Willard R. Trask, tr.   1969

2 Churl Death, who wars on all mankind,
you have taken from me what I most loved.
Now I am the Phoenix, alas! alone and bereft, the single bird of which they tell.
Ibid., St. 3

3 Would that I could change, but love has dominion over me.   Ibid., St. 4

197.   Wang Ch'ing-hui
(13th century)

1 Suddenly, one day, war drums on
horseback
Came like thunder, tearing off the sky,
And all glorious flowery days were gone
forever.   Untitled,
The Orchid Boat,
Women Poets of China,
Kenneth Rexroth and Ling
Chung, eds. and trs.   1972

198.   Clara d'Anduza
(fl. 1200–1235)

1 for the love that has me in its spell
wants me to lock you up and guard you
well;
and I will . . .   Untitled, St. 3,
Quoted in
The Women Troubadours,
Meg Bodin, tr.   1976

199.   Bieiris de Romans
(fl. 1200–1235)

1 don't grant your love to a deceitful suitor.
Untitled, St. 3,
Quoted in
The Women Troubadours,
Meg Bodin, tr.   1976

200.   Castelloza
(c.1200–?)

1 My love of you is censored all in vain.
No oath could change my heart, I surely
know,
no, nor my love, which cannot cease to
grow,
nor my desire, my longing sweet with pain.
Untitled, Quoted in
The Troubadours and Their
World of the Twelfth and
Thirteenth Centuries,
by Jack Lindsay   1976

2 I won't consider you a decent man
nor love you fully nor with trust
until I see if it would help me more
to make my heart turn mean or treacherous.   Untitled, St. 2,
Quoted in
The Women Troubadours,
Meg Bodin, tr.   1976

3 It greatly pleases me
when people say that it's unseemly
for a lady to approach a man she likes
and hold him deep in conversation,
but whoever says that isn't very bright
Ibid., St. 3

4 . . . at any moment I might
rediscover reason to rejoice
Ibid., St. 4

5 I don't know why you're always on my
mind,
for I've searched and searched from good to
evil
your hard heart, and yet my own's un-
swerving.   Ibid., St. 6

6 the more I sing

the worse I fare in love   Untitled, St. 1,
                                                          op. cit.

7 And if you left me now,
I wouldn't feel a thing,
for since no joy sustains me
a little pain won't drive me mad.
                                              Ibid., St. 4

201. Shikishi
(?–1201)

1 The double cherry glowing near the eaves
Already nearly overblown I find.
Oh, how I hope someone will call on me
   Before the flowers are visited by the
wind!   "The Cherry Flowers,"
                                                  in toto,
                     from *Shin Kokin Shū*, Vol. II,
                     An Anthology of Japanese Poems,
                     Miyamori Asatarō, ed. and tr.
                                                      1938

2 The blossoms have fallen.
I stare blankly at a world
Bereft of color.   Untitled,
               Anthology of Japanese Literature,
               Donald Keene, ed. and tr.
                                                      1955

3 There has been no change
but I am no longer young.
Autumn wind blows and
I am as disturbed as before.
                              "Autumn,"
               in toto, from *Shin Kokin Shū*,
                              Hiroaki Sato, tr.;
                              *The Penguin Book
                                of Women Poets*,
               Carol Cosman, Joan Keefe and
               Kathleen Weaver, eds.   1978

202. Elizabeth of Thuringia
(1206/07–1231)

1 We must not sadden God with sullen looks.
                     Quoted in *Saint Elizabeth*
                     by Elisabeth von Schmidt-Pauli;
                     Olga Marx, tr.   1932

2 Praise be to Thee, O Lord, through the sun
and the moon, the wind and the stars and
all the glorious things of earth.
                                              Ibid.

3 We are made loveless by our possessions.
                                              Ibid.

4 We women were allowed to stand at the
Cross. We saw His wounds bleed and His
eyes grow dim. As He was dying Jesus put
His faith in us, we were to carry His love
through the whole world and here we sit
and have forgotten Him.   Ibid.

5 . . . the world is indifferent to me . . .
                                              Ibid.

6 I have always told you that we must give
joy to the people.   Ibid.

7 O dear Lord Jesus, to Thee and to Thy
Holy Mother, I do offer this fruit of my
body. . . . Receive among Thy servants and
friends this little child bathed in my tears.
                     Prayer upon the birth of her
                     first child, Herman (1221/22),
                                                  op. cit.

203. Beruriah
(fl. 1210–1280)

1 How do you make out [that such a prayer
should be permitted]? Because it is written
"Let *hattaim* [sins] cease"? Is it written *hot-
tim* [sinners]? It is written *hattaim*! Further,
look to the end of the verse "and let the
wicked men be no more." Since the sins will
cease, there will be no more wicked men!
Rather pray for them that they should repent, and there will be no more wicked.
                     Quoted in *The Jewish Woman:
                     New Perspectives*,
                     Elizabeth Koltun, ed.   1976

204. Mechtild von Magdeburg
(c.1212–1283)

1 The writing of this book is seen and heard and felt in every limb. I see it with the eyes of my soul, and hear it with the ears of my eternal spirit, and feel in every part of my body the power of the Holy Ghost.

> Introduction, *Das fliessende Licht der Gottheit [The Flowering Light of God]* 1344

2 This book began with love, and with love it shall end; for there is not anything as wise, as holy, as beautiful, as strong, or as perfect as love. Ibid.

3 O thou God, out-pouring in thy gift!
O thou God, o'erflowing in thy love!
O thou God, all burning in thy desire!
O thou God, melting in union with thy body!
O thou God, reposing on my breast!
Without Thee, never could I live.
Ibid.

4 I come to my Beloved
Like dew upon the flowers.
Ibid.

5 The fish cannot drown in the water, the bird cannot sink in the air, gold cannot perish in the fire, where it gains its clear and shining worth. God has granted to each creature to cherish its own nature. How can I withstand my nature? Ibid.

6 ...a hungry man can do no deep study, and thus must God, through such default, lose the best prayers. Ibid.

7 Those who would know much, and love little, will ever remain at but the beginning of a godly life. Ibid.

8 Simple love, with but little knowledge, can do great things. Ibid.

9 What most of all hinders the spiritually minded from full perfection is, that they pay so little heed to small sins.
Ibid.

10 It [prayer] makes a sour heart sweet, a sad heart merry, a poor heart rich, a dull heart wise, a timid heart bold, a weak heart strong, a blind heart seeing, a cold heart burning. It draws the great God down into the small heart, it drives the hungry soul out to the full God, it brings together the two lovers, God and the soul, into a blissful place, where they speak much of love.
Ibid.

11 I cannot dance, Oh, Lord, unless Thou lead me.
If Thou wilt that I leap joyfully
Then must Thou Thyself first dance and sing!
Then will I leap for love,
From Love to Knowledge,
From Knowledge to Fruition,
From Fruition to beyond all human sense
There will I remain and circle evermore.
Ibid.

12 Of the heavenly things God has shown me, I can speak but a little word, not more than a honey bee can carry away on its feet from an overflowing jar. Ibid.

13 Love flows from God to man without effort
As a bird glides through the air
Without moving its wings

> "Love Flows From God," Lucy Menzies, tr.; *Women Poets of the World*, Joanna Bankier and Deirdre Lashgari, eds. 1983

14 The Holy Spirit is the harpist
And all the strings must sound
Which are strung in love.

> Ibid.

205. Guillelma de Rosers
(fl.1235–1265)

1 a man who keeps his word is worth much more

than one whose plans are constantly re-
vised.   Untitled, St. 2,
Quoted in
The Women Troubadours,
Meg Bodin, tr.   1976

2 . . . there's no such thing
as chivalry that doesn't spring from love
Ibid., St. 3

3 but if you want to teach a horse to joust,
you have to guide it with intelligence and
care,
and since you urge them on so hard, the
lovers
lose their strength, and you end up enraged.
Ibid., St. 5

206.   Hadewijch
(fl. 1235–1265)

1 All things
Crowd me in!
I am so wide!   "All things Confine,"
St. 1, Frans van Rosevelt, tr.;
*The Penguin Book
of Women Poets,*
Carol Cosman, Joan Keefe and
Kathleen Weaver, eds.   1978

2 After the unshapen
Have I grasped
In everlasting time.

I have caught it.
It has cast me
Wider than wide!   Ibid., Sts. 2 and 3

3 How tight and strong love's fettering
Untitled,
Frans van Rosevelt, tr., op. cit.

4 Love bridled me so forcefully
What good is now my reining in?
Ibid.

5 . . . had I given me to love
Entire, for efforts lent and spent
I'd have received for what was spent what
lent
A bond of life and love.

Then might I dwell with all above.
Untitled,
Frans van Rosevelt, tr., op. cit.

6 Love appears every day
for one who offers love,
That wisdom is enough.   "Poem on the
Seven Names of Love,"
St. 2, Willis Barnstone
and Elene Kolb, trs.;
A Book of Women Poets,
Aliki and Willis Barnstone, eds.
1980

7 Love is a ROPE, for it ties
and holds us in its yoke.
It can do all, nothing snaps it.
You who love must know.
Ibid., St. 4

8 HELL (I feel its torture)
damns, covering the world.
Nothing escapes. No one has grace
to see a way out.   Ibid., St. 9

9 Take care, you who wish
to deal with names
for love. Behind their sweetness
and wrath, nothing endures.
Nothing but wounds and kisses.
Ibid., St. 10

207.   Gertrude the Great
(fl. 1256–1302)

1 . . . conscious of thy grace, I flow back to
be joined to Thee like water . . .
from *Legacy of Divine Piety,*
Quoted in *Women in the Middle
Ages: Religion, Marriage, and
Letters*
by Angela M. Lucas   1983

2 . . . growing in the knowledge of virtue like
unto these trees, I flower in the greenness of
good deeds . . .   Ibid.

3 . . . looking down on things earthly in free
flight like these doves, I approach heaven,
and with my bodily senses removed from
external turmoil, apprehend thee with my
whole mind . . .   Ibid.

4 . . . in joyfulness my heart will make for thee a habitation.   Ibid.

208. Kuan Tao-shêng
(1262–1319)

1 I am your clay.
You are my clay.
In life we share a single quilt.
In death we will share one coffin.
                    "Married Love,"
                    The Orchid Boat,
                    Women Poets of China,
                    Kenneth Rexroth and Ling
                    Chung, eds. and trs.   1972

209. Empress Eifuku
(1271–1342)

1   we
Were caught in bed by the dawn
                    Untitled,
                    One Hundred More Poems
                    from the Japanese,
                    Kenneth Rexroth, ed. and tr.
                    1974

210. Jeanne of Navarre
(1271–1307-9)

1 When you kill these Flemish boars, do not spare the sows; them I would have spitted.
                    Attributed comment about
                    revolt of Flanders (1302),
                    Quoted in *Women*
                    of Medieval France
                    by Pierce Butler   1907

211. Abutsu
(?–c.1283)

1 Between the pines of the shore hills on the eastern road,

Even the waves rise in the image of flowers.
                    "The Diary of
                    the Waning Loon,"
                    Edwin O. Reischauer, tr.;
                    The Penguin Book
                    of Women Poets,
                    Carol Cosman, Joan Keefe and
                    Kathleen Weaver, eds.   1978

212. Mahaut d'Artois
(fl. 1285–1319)

1 . . . have pity upon me, a poor widow driven from her heritage, and here without counsel! You see how your people besiege me, one barking on my right, another at my left, till I know not what to answer, in the great trouble of my mind.
                    Plea before the Duke de Noirs
                    (1319),
                    Quoted in
                    Women of Medieval France
                    by Pierce Butler   1907

213. Padeshah Khatun
(14th century)

1 Two yards of veil won't make any woman a lady
  nor a hat make any head worthy of command   "Sovereign Queen,"
                    Deirdre Lashgari, tr.;
                    Women Poets of the World,
                    Joanna Bankier and Deirdre
                    Lashgari, eds.   1983

214. Bridget of Sweden
(1303–1373)

1 . . . I went forth in the wild forest of this world, in misery and labour and prepared the way in my blood and the sweat of my toil.   *Revelations*, Vol. II
                    1344–1349

2 I have a few friends, but they fly like little birds timidly from bush to bush, and are ashamed to serve me.   Ibid.

3 If any man love the world, the charity of the Father is not in him. For all that is in the world is the concupiscence of the flesh, and the concupiscence of the eyes and the pride of life . . .   Ibid.

4 Because my way has grown narrow, and the path of the world is wide and broad, I am not crying in the wilderness to my friends, that they must uproot the thorns and thistles and prepare the way for those who will walk in it.   Ibid.

5 Mary is the lily in God's garden . . .
                                   Ibid., Vol. III

6 Wine is wholesome, gives health to the sick, joy to the sorrowful, courage and bravery to those who are well.   Ibid., Vol. IV

7 I am like the rainbow, standing in the cloud, but touching the earth at both ends—thus do I also stoop over the world with my prayer.   Ibid.,
                     "Written of the Virgin Mary"

8 MONK. Why have You given us feelings, if we cannot use them freely at our own will? JUDGE. My friend, man's feelings are not to be used just for a good diversion; they are created in him to serve the good of his soul.
                                   Ibid., Vol. V,
                              "Book of Questions"

9 Pride alienates man from heaven; humility leads to heaven.   Ibid.

10 The source of justice is not vengeance but charity.   Ibid.

11 Man is endowed with intelligence to guide his appetites and emotions along the path of righteousness and to keep them from the path of self-destruction. Food supports and strengthens man's powers, but taken in excess, it exhausts them.   Ibid.

12 JUDGE. The man who is wise according to the world is blind according to God; one must search humbly after the divine wisdom.   Ibid.

13 JUDGE. Free will deprived of divine guidance can be nothing but a source of license and sin.   Ibid.

14 JUDGE. If the nobleman is superior to the commoner, the nobleman should fear that his ultimate Judgment will be the more severe, because God has given him more.
                                   Ibid.

15 To write well and speak well is mere vanity if one does not live well.   Ibid.

16 Man, the author of evil, must bear it.
                                   Ibid.

17 The time will come when . . . there shall be one flock, and One Shepherd, one faith and one clear knowledge of God. Then many who were called shall be rejected, but the wilderness shall blossom, and the heathens shall sing.   Ibid., Vol. VI

18 I beheld a Virgin of extreme beauty wrapped in a white mantle and a delicate tunic . . . with her beautiful golden hair falling loosely down her shoulders. . . . She stood with uplifted hands, her eyes fixed on heaven, rapt, as it were, in an ecstasy of contemplation, in a rapture of divine sweetness. And while she stood in prayer, I beheld her Child move in her womb and . . . she brought forth her Son, from Whom such ineffable light and splendor radiated that the sun could not be compared to it. . . . And then I heard the wonderful singing of many angels.*   Ibid., Vol. VII
*Her vision of the nativity has become the standard, "influencing Western art, music, literature and even the decisions at the Council of Trent." (Anthony Butkovich, *Revelations*, 1972).

19 Some women behave like harlots; when they feel the life of a child in their wombs, they induce herbs or other means to cause miscarriage, only to perpetuate their amusement and unchastity. Therefore I shall deprive them from everlasting life and send them to everlasting death.
                                   Ibid.

20 . . . it happens at times that from a black furnace issues a fair flame, with which many beautiful things may be wrought. Yet the black furnace should not be praised for this, but He who bestows upon mankind the perfect will to do what is good.
                                   Ibid.

21 You stab me with your anger and I will pierce you with my malice.
> Ibid., Vol. VIII,
> "Written of the Devil"

22 Woe is me, I have become like a newborn whelp that cannot see, and cannot find the paps of its mother. Woe is me, for in my blindness I see that I shall never see God.
> Ibid.

23 Prick up your ears and hear how from the rising of the sun until its setting the heart of man is hardened and he thinks of nothing but of shedding the blood of his neighbor. See how all adorn their bodies with vain ornaments, see how the desires of man are as senseless as those of the beasts. Open your mouths and ask where are those men to be found who fight against the enemies of God, where are they who will venture their lives for their Lord? Look diligently and you will find that I have very few friends.
> *Extravagantes,*
> Ch. 51   c.1373

24 When I buried my husband I buried all my earthly love with him, for though I loved him as my own soul, I would not for a penny buy back his life against the will of God.
> Ibid., Ch. XCIII

25 O sweet Jesus, wound my heart, that tears of penitence and love may be my food night and day, and bring me entirely to thee.
> Prayer, "In Honor of our Lord
> Jesus Christ,"
> Quoted in *Revelations*
> by Anthony Butkovich   1972

26 The world would have peace if the men of politics would only follow the Gospel.
> Ibid.

215. Juliana of Norwich
(c.1342–1417?)

1 He is to us all-thing that is good and comfortable for our help. He is our clothing, for love; He enwraps us and envelops us, embraces and encloses us; He hovers over us for tender love, that He may never leave us.
> *Revelations of Divine Love,*
> Ch. 4   1373

2 He shewed me a little thing, the quantity of a hazel nut, lying in the palm of my hand.... I looked thereupon and thought: "What may this be?" And I was answered ... thus: "It is all that is made.... It lasts and ever shall last because God loves it, and hath all-things its being through the love of God."
> Ibid.

3 They that are preoccupied wilfully with earthly business and ever more seek after worldly weal are not His in heart and in soul here: they love and seek their rest in this thing that is so little, wherein is no rest, and know not God who is All-Mighty, All-Good. For He is very rest.
> Ibid.

4 Thou hast now great busy-ness. If thou wouldst now from this time ever more be so busy to keep thee from sin, this were a sovereign and a good occupation.
> Ibid., Ch. 23

5 In my folly often I wondered why by the great foresaid wisdom of God, the beginning of sin was not letted, for then thought me that all should have been well.
> Ibid., Ch. 27

6 I saw not sin; for I believe that it had no manner of substance, nor no part of being, nor it might not be known but by the pain that is caused thereof. And this pain ... maketh us to know our self, and ask mercy.
> Ibid.

7 And then our good Lord opened my ghostly eye, and shewed me my soul in the midst of my heart. I saw the soul so large as it were an endless world, and also as it were a blessed kingdom. And by the conditions that I saw therein, I understood that it is a worshipful city.   Ibid., Ch. 68

8 The place that Jesu taketh in our soul He shall never remove without end . . . for in us is His homeliest home, and His endless dwelling.   Ibid.

9 He said not, "thou shalt not be troubled, thou shalt not be travailed, thou shalt not be diseased;" but He said, "Thou shalt not be overcome."   Ibid.

216. Catherine of Siena
(1347–1380)

1 Every evil, harm, and suffering in this life or in the next comes from the love of riches.
The Dialogue of the Seraphic Virgin Catherine of Siena, Algar Thorold, ed. and tr. 1896

2 . . . if you were to ask me which is more meritorious, those who are in a religious order or those who are outside I should reply that the merit of obedience is not measured by the act or the place . . . but according to the measure of love which the obedient one has . . .   Ibid.

3 Merit consists in the virtue of love alone, flavoured with the light of true discretion . . .   Ibid., Ch. 11

4 Oh, how blind is the human generation in that it considers not its own dignity! From being great thou hast become small, from a ruler thou hast become a slave . . .
Ibid., Ch. 35

5 . . . the Devil invites men to the water of death . . . and blinding them with the pleasures and conditions of the world, he catches them with the hook of pleasure . . .
Ibid., Ch. 44

6 How great is the pain of the prick of conscience! How great is his pain who thirsts for revenge, which pain continually gnaws him and causes him to die, before he has killed his enemy with the knife of hatred! How much pain the miser endures, who through avarice cuts down his needs! How much torment the envious man endures, for envy always gnaws his heart, and does not allow him to take delight in the well-being of his neighbour!   Ibid., Ch. 48

7 The Devil often places himself upon the tongues of creatures, causing them to chatter nonsensically . . .   Ibid., Ch. 66

8 Abandon judgment, which is Mine [God's], and take up rather compassion . . .
Ibid., Ch. 103

9 Knowledge in itself is good and perfect when a learned person is also good, honourable, and humble in life. But if knowledge be joined with a proud, dishonourable, and wicked life it is a poison . . .
Ibid., Ch. 127

10 Thy miseries are not hid from thee now, for the worm of conscience sleeps no longer . . .   Ibid., Ch. 132

11 . . . charity, the mother of patience, has given her as a sister to obedience, and so closely united them together that one cannot be lost without the other. Either thou hast them both or thou hast neither.
Ibid., Ch. 135

12 . . . if thou wish to reach the perfection of love, it befits thee to set thy life in order.
Letter to Monna Alessa dei Saracini, *Saint Catherine of Siena as Seen in her Letters,* Vida D. Scudder, ed. and tr. 1906

13 Make two homes for thyself, my daughter. One actual home . . . and another spiritual home, which thou art to carry with thee always. . . .   Ibid.

14 ... without light we shall not be able to walk in the way of truth, but shall walk in shadows. Two lights are necessary. First, we must be illumined to know the transitory things of the world, which all pass like the wind. But these are not rightly known if we do not know our own frailty. ...
Letter to Brother William of England,
op. cit.

15 ... perfection does not consist in macerating or killing the body, but in killing our perverse self-will. Letter to Daniella of Orvieto,
op. cit.

16 ... love tenderly every rational being.
Letter to Monna Agnese,
op. cit.

17 ... from knowledge of self the soul draws true humility. Letter to Brother Matteo di Francesco Tolomei,
op. cit.

18 ... through charity to God we conceive virtues, and through charity toward our neighbours they are brought to the birth.
Letter to Catarina di Scetto,
op. cit.

19 ... virtue is the only thing that makes us gentlefolk ... Letter to Monna Colomba of Lucca,
op. cit.

20 O daughter mine, thou has begun to put thy hand to the plough of virtue ... bridle its youth, that it may not run to be a member of the devil. Letter to Catarina and Giovanna di Capo,
op. cit.

21 Oh, how the man should be ashamed who follows the teaching of the devil and his own lower nature. ... Surely he is foolish and blind, for he does not see that with the sword of hate to his neighbour he is killing himself. Letter to Charles V of France,
op. cit.

22 ... sometimes God works through rascally men, in order that they may execute justice on His enemy. Letter to Giovanna, Queen of Naples,
op. cit.

23 O sheep, return to your fold; let you be governed by the Shepherd: else the wolf of hell shall devour you! Ibid.

24 O God, give me the grace to be ever the lover and herald of truth, and for this truth I shall gladly give my life.
Quoted in *Catherine of Siena: Fire and Blood*
by Igino Giordani;
Thomas J. Tobin, tr.
1959

25 My nature is a flame. Ibid.

26 *Vidi arcana Dei* [I have seen the hidden things of God]. Ibid.

27 I trust only in the goodness of God; I have no confidence in myself. Letter to Bianco di Santi,
op. cit.

28 Sleeping, eating, speaking, and in every other thing we do, we are marching toward death. ... Letter to Piero Canigiani of Florence,
op. cit.

29 ... we are all pilgrims and wayfarers in this life. ... Arise then, pilgrim, shake off sleep for this is not the hour for sleeping. ... Ibid.

30 Sin is the only thing of which we should grow weary. ... Letter to Nicolo Soderini,
op. cit.

31 The moment that is past you have no more; you are not sure of any future moment; you have only the present moment, nothing more ... Letter to Stefano Maconi,
op. cit.

32 . . . if our neighbor injures us and we bear the injury with patience, the poisoned thrust boomerangs upon the offender. If the world assails us with its pleasures, its delights and its promises and we reject them, the world is weakened even as it hates us. And if the demon grives us with his many and varied temptations, we overcome him with the force of our will, remaining firm, constant and persevering until death. . . .
Letter to Ristoro Canigiani,
op. cit.

33 My soul . . . can see no other remedy pleasing to God than peace. Peace, peace, therefore, for the love of Christ crucified!
Letter to Pope Gregory XI,
op. cit.

34 Is there anything more beautiful than peace?   *Letter to Nicolo Soderini,*
op. cit.

35 This regal Babe
Of Bethlehem town
Is not too small
To wear a crown.   "Christmas Canticle,"
Sister Madeleva, C.S.C., tr.,
op. cit.

217.   Jefimija
(c.1348–c.1405)

1 The sorrow for him is burning steadily in my heart
And I am overcome by my motherly ways.
"The Lament Over the Dead Son Overcome by Her Motherly Ways," St. 3
An Anthology of Medieval Serbian Literature in English,
Mateja Matejic and Dragan Milivojevic, eds.   1978

2 I did not offer you praise according to your dignity, but according to the power of my limited mind. . . .   "The Encomium to Prince Lazar"* (1402),
op. cit.
*Prince Lazar Hrebeljanović (1371–1389).

3 I have been already judged by my conscience   "Prayer to Lord Jesus Christ" (1405),
op. cit.

218.   Jevgenija
(c.1353–1405)

1 O God, who as the Holy Trinity
has been hymned with awe
by bodiless powers
before all ages "Mother's Prayers" (1397),
An Anthology of Medieval Serbian Literature in English,
Mateja Matejic and Dragan Milivojevic, eds.   1978

2 Who is this one?
Whisper into my ears!
Is this the one for whom I used to long . . . ?
"Who Is This One?,"
St. 1, op. cit.

3 Blessed are you, indeed, Lazar;*
bless me, the one who blesses you.
There is no praise of which you would not be worthy,
but my wit is getting tired . . . ,
Ibid., St. 3
*Prince Lazar Hrebeljanović (1371–1389).

219.   Margherita Datini
(1360–1423)

1 You say, always sermonizing, that we will have a fine life, and every month and every week will be the one. You have told me this for ten years, and today it seems more timely than ever to reply: it is your fault. . . .

If you delay so much, you will never seize this "fine life," and if you say, "Look at the hardships that I undergo every day, never can one live in this world without them:" that is no excuse for not living a fine life for the soul and the body.

Letter to [her husband]
Francesco di Marco Datini
(January 1386),
Quoted in Women
in the Middle Ages,
by Frances and Joseph Gies
1978

2 I have found companions in my female friends; sad would be the woman who had to depend on you!   Ibid. (1386), op. cit.

3 If I'm sad, they say I'm jealous; if I'm happy, they say I am cured of Francesco di Marco.   Ibid.

4 I would like to know whether you are sleeping alone or not; if you are not sleeping alone, I would like to know who is sleeping with you.   Ibid.

5 To my mind, only two things are needful: the first, to do what is pleasing to God, and the second, to spend the little time that is left to you so that you may give back to God what He, in His goodness, has lent you.

Ibid. (c.1399), op. cit.

220.   Christine de Pisan
(1363/64–1430/31)

1 You ask whether woman possesses any natural intelligence. Yes. It can be developed to become wisdom, and then it is most beautiful.   Prologue,

La Cité des Dames
[The City of Women]   1404

2 This woman in love with scholarship intends, to be sure, that woman should acquire learning; but it must be for the purpose of developing her intelligence, or raising her heart to higher things, not of widening her field of ambitions, dethroning man and reigning in his stead.

Ibid.

3 If it were customary to send little girls to school and to teach them the same subjects as are taught to boys, they would learn just as fully and would understand the subtleties of all arts and sciences. Indeed, maybe they would understand them better . . . for just as women's bodies are softer than men's, so their understanding is sharper.

Ibid.

4 . . . some there are . . . who will tell you that the fairest ladies in the land have honored them with love. Good Lord! what gentility! How ill it becomes a noble man to lie and tell false tales of women! Such fellows are but villains, pure and simple.

Quoted in Women
of Medieval France
by Pierce Butler   1907

5 He loved me, and 'twas right that he should, for I had come to him as a girl-bride; we two had made such wise provision in all our love that our two hearts were moved in all things, whether of joy or of sorrow, by a common wish, more united in love than the hearts of brother and sister.

Prose translation of untitled
poem written after
death of her husband,
op. cit.

6 O Thou! ordained Maid of very God!
Joanna!* born in Fortune's golden hour

Untitled,
St. 1 (1429),
Quoted in
Of Six Medieval Women
by Alice Kemp-Welch,
tr.   1913

7 Until a Woman* came to show the way

Ibid., St. 2

8 Honour to Womankind! It needs must be
That God loves Woman, since He fashioned Thee.*   Ibid.

9 She* seemeth fed by that same armour's touch,
Nurtured on iron—   Untitled poem,

St. 1 (1429), op. cit.

*All references to Joan of Arc.

10 Learn to know what people are,
And so, by seeing what they're like,
Protect yourself from gross mistake.
                    "Christine to Her Son,"
                    St. 2, Barbara Howes, tr.;
                        Poems from France,
            William Jay Smith, ed.   1967

11 No one can have too many friends,
There is no minor enemy.
                            Ibid., St. 3

12 It is a month today
Since my friend departed.
Sad and silent my heart has been,
It is a month today.
"Goodbye," he said, "I am going away."
And spoke to me no more;
It is a month today.   Untitled, in toto,
                            Quoted in
                Women of the Middle Ages
                by Sibylle Harksen   1975

13 No one knows the labor my poor heart en-
    dures
To dissimulate my grief when I find no pity.
The less sympathy in friendship, the more
    cause for tears.
So I make no plaint of my piteous mourn-
    ing,
But laugh when I would rather weep,
And without rhyme or rhythm make my
    songs
To conceal my heart.   Untitled, in toto,
                Quoted in *A Distant Mirror*
                by Barbara Tuchman   1978

14 . . . upon constance set thy mind and heart,
And then will nobleness to thee-ward start.
                    "The Epistle of Othea to
                            Hector,"
                            St. 10,
                        *The Penguin Book
                        of Women Poets,*
                Carol Cosman, Joan Keefe and
                Kathleen Weaver, eds.   1978

15 Where true love is, it showeth; it will not
feign.   Ibid., St. 27

16 He is too unwise that, for default of one,
will therefore despise woman everyone.
                            Ibid., St. 45

17 Trust not on fortune, called the great god-
dess;
. . . .
Before men's eyes she casteth a great mist.
When they find her favourable, they think
they be well;
And yet is it feeble hold on a slipper eel.
                            Ibid., St. 74

18 I will not stay when you behave
harshly, insult me like a cur,
for things have changed. I won't concur
and won't reveal my sorrow, save
I'll always dress in black and rave.
                        Untitled, St. 3,
                    Willis Barnstone, tr.;
                A Book of Women Poets,
            Aliki and Willis Barnstone, eds.
                                    1980

19 With poison herbs my hard terrain is sewn.
I am a widow, robed in black, alone.
                        Untitled, St. 3,
                Willis Barnstone, tr., op. cit.

20 Alone am I, menaced by mourning,
Alone am I, dyed deeper than dark brown,
Alone am I, my love no longer living.
                        Untitled, St. 4,
                    Julie Allen, tr., op. cit.

21 Marriage is a lovely thing
                        Untitled, St. 1,
                    Joanna Bankier, tr.;
                Women Poets of the World,
                Joanna Bankier and Deirdre
                    Lashgari, eds.   1983

22 Fountain of tears, river of grief
torrent of pain, sea brimful with bitterness
I am submerged, I drown in deep misery
for my heart is too easily moved.
                        Untitled, St. 1,
                Joanna Bankier, tr., op. cit.

221.   Lalleswari
(fl. 1365–1399)

1 I set forth hopeful—cotton-blossom Lal.
Untitled,
George Grierson, tr., adapted by
Deirdre Lashgari;
Women Poets of the World,
Joanna Bankier and Deirdre
Lashgari, eds.   1983

2 With the fire of love, I parched my heart
like seeds.   Untitled,
George Grierson, tr., op. cit.

3 Good repute is water carried in a sieve.
Untitled,
George Grierson, tr., op. cit.

222.   Margaret of Nassau
(fl. 1367)

1 Know, my love, that I should like to call
you a thief, because you have stolen my
heart....   Letter to Matilda of Cleves
(1367),
Quoted in
Women in the Middle Ages
by Sibylle Harksen   1975

223.   Chao Li-hua
(fl. c.1368–1644)

1 my boat goes west, yours east
heaven's a wind for both journeys
"Farewell,"
J. P. Seaton, tr.;
A Book of Women Poets,
Aliki and Willis Barnstone, eds.
1980

224.   Margery Kempe
(1373–1438?)

1 She thought that she loved God more than
He did her. She was smitten with the deadly
wound of vainglory, and felt it not, for she
many times desired that the crucifix should
loosen His hands from the Cross, and embrace her in token of love.
The Book of Margery Kempe
c.1435

2 For, no dread, our ghostly enemy sleepeth
not, but he full busily searcheth our com-
plexions and dispositions and where he fin-
deth us most frail, there, by Our Lord's suf-
ferance, he layeth his snare, which no man
may escape by his own power.
Ibid.

3 "For I tell thee, daughter, that they who are
great fasters, and great doers of penance,
they would that it should be held the best
life; also they that are given to saying many
devotions, they would have that the best
life; and they that give much alms, they
would that that were held the best life."
Ibid.

4 "I have oftentimes told thee, daughter, that
thinking, weeping, and high comtemplation
is the best life on earth, and thou shalt have
more merit in Heaven for one year of thinking in thy mind than for a hundred years of
praying with thy mouth...."
Ibid.

5 She saw, as she thought, devils opening
their mouths all inflamed with burning
waves of fire, as if they would have swallowed her in, sometimes ramping at her,
sometimes threatening her, pulling her and
hauling her, night and day.... Also the
devils cried upon her with great threaten-
ings, and bade her that she should forsake
Christendom, her faith, and deny her
God.... And so she did.
Ibid., Ch. 1

6 All her desire was to be worshipped by the people. She would not take heed of any chastisement, nor be content with the goods that God had sent her . . . but ever desired more and more. Ibid.

7 . . . her husband asked his wife this question:—
"Margery, if there came a man with a sword, who would strike off my head, unless I should commune naturally with you as I have done before, tell me on your conscience—for ye say ye will not lie—whether ye would suffer my head to be smitten off, or whether ye would suffer me to meddle with you again, as I did at one time?". . . . And then she said with great sorrow:—"Forsooth, I would rather see you being slain, than that we should turn again to our uncleanness." And he replied:—"Ye are no good wife." Ibid., Ch. 11

8 . . . for He may give His gifts where He will. . . . Ibid., Ch. 18

9 He that is ever doubting is like the flood of the sea which is moved and borne about with the wind, and that man is not likely to receive the gifts of God. Ibid.

10 . . . fear not the language of the world, for the more despite, shame and reproof that ye have in the world, the more is your merit in the sight of God. Ibid.

11 "Patience is necessary to you, for in that shall ye keep your soul." Ibid.

12 And sometimes those that men think were revelations, are deceits and illusions, and therefore it is not expedient to give readily credence to every stirring, but soberly abide . . . Ibid., Ch. 89

13 Sometimes she was in a great gloom for her feelings. . . . For sometimes, what she understood bodily was to be understood ghostly, and the dread that she had of her feelings was the greatest scourge that she had on earth. Ibid.

225. Juliana Berners
(1388?–?)

1 Lysten to your dame and she shall you lere.
Four manere of bestis of venere there are:
The fyrste of theym is the harte: the seconde is the hare
The boore is one of tho; the wulfe and not one mo. *Boke of Saint Albans* 1486

2 A faythfulle frende wold I fayne finde,
to fynde hym where he myghte be founde.
But now is the worlde wext so unkynde,
Yet frenship is fall to the grounde;
(Now a Frende I have Founde)
That I woll nother banne ne curse,
But of all frendes in felde or towne
Ever, gramercy, myn own purse.
Ibid., "Song," St. 1

226. A Northern Mother*
(fl. 1390s?)

1 Laugh not to scorne nodir [neither] olde ne young,
Be of good bering and have a good tongue
The Good Wife Taught her Daughter, St. 2 1350

*This is the only name this author is known by. We *assume* she lived about the time of the date of her book but it may well have been earlier.

2 What man that shall wed the fore God with a ring,
Looke thou love him best of any earthly thing,
And meekly him answere and not to snatching;*
So may thou slake his ire and be his darling
Ibid., St. 4

*Captious arguing.

3 . . . keepe the ever daughter fro velony [villainy] and shame
That men for thy doing speake the no blame:
Good life ends wele,
Be true ever as the stele.
Ibid., St. 5

4 Laugh not too loud ne gape not too wide,

Maydens should laugh softlye
                              Ibid., St. 6

5 Go not to the wrastling, ne shoting the
   cock,
As it were a strumpet or a giglot*:
Be at home doughter and thy things tend,
For thine owne profit at the latter end
                              Ibid., St. 10
*Wanton woman.

6 ... good name is worth gold. . . .
                              Ibid., St. 13

7 Huswifely shall thou go on the werk-day,
Pride, rest and idlenes put hem cleane away
                              Ibid., St. 16

8 ... God will love the,
More for worship of our lord
Than for pride of the world.
                              Ibid.

9 ... their thrift wexis thin
That spend more than they win
                              Ibid., St. 17

10 ... better it is a childe to be unborne,
Than for unteaching to be forlorne.
                              Ibid., St. 24

11 He that woll a good house keepe
Must ofte-times breake asleepe
                              Ibid., St. 25

227. Valentine Visconti
(fl. 1392–1405)

1 There is nothing more for me, nothing matters more. [*Rien ne m'est plus, plus ne m'est
rien*]. Motto, adopted after her husband's
                              death (c.1405),
                              Quoted in
         Women of Medieval France
         by Pierce Butler   1907

228. Nahabed Kouchak
(15th century)

1 My heart is turned into a wailing child,
In vain with sweets I seek to still its cries;
Sweet love, it calls for thee in sobbings wild

All day and night, with longing and with
sighs.
What solace can I give it?
         "My Heart Is Turned into a
                  Wailing Child,"
                              St. 1,
         Armenian Legends and Poems,
         Zabelle C. Boyajian, ed.   1916

2 O Night, be long—long as an endless year!
                  "O Night, Be Long,"
                              St. 1, op. cit.

3 On the morning of thy birth
We were glad but thou wert wailing,
See that when thou leav'st the earth
Thou art glad and we bewailing.
                  "Birthday Song,"
                              St. 1, op. cit.

4 Keep thyself from fools apart,
All their flatteries withstanding.
For the fool, like fire and heat,
Scorcheth everything, and burneth;
But the wise, like water sweet,
Deserts into gardens turneth.
                              Ibid., St. 2

229. Mehri
(c.1404–1447)

1 The king has bound the silver-limbed tree
and women and men cry loud for me.
Alas that this hand should waste to a grave
which was pillory once to both knight and
knave.   Untitled (written from prison),
                  Deirdre Lashgari, tr.;
         Women Poets of the World,
         Joanna Bankier and Deirdre
         Lashgari, eds.   1983

2 Each subtlety hard for the pedant to solve
I found a drop of wine would dissolve.
                  "Coming Across,"
         Deirdre Lashgari, tr., op. cit.

230.   Alessandra de' Machingi Strozzi
(1406–1471)

1 One has nothing to do now but to pay taxes.... It is miraculous how much money they extort from us, and yet we seem to gain no advantage.   Letter to her son,
Lorenzo (1452),
Quoted in
Famous Women of Florence
by Edgecumbe Staley, tr.
1909

2 Let me remind you of the need we have of a slave, for so far we have always had one. If you give orders to have one bought, ask for a Tartar, for they are the best for hard work, and are simple in their ways. The Russians are more delicate and prettier, but, according to my judgment, a Tartar would be best.
Letter to her son, Filippo (1452),
op. cit.

3 ... in time we all see many strange things ...   Letter (c.1458),
op. cit.

4 Those who have no money are bound to go down ...   Letter to her son, Filippo
(1464),
op. cit.

5 Let everyone kiss the ground the Medici walks upon ... I care not; I am but a woman, and I don't understand your political matters like a man. Whoever will restore me my sons, to him I wish well!
Ibid.

6 To have a good mate comforts and ennobles the man both in body and soul.
Letter (c.1466),
op. cit.

7 A man, when he is a man indeed, makes woman a woman.   Ibid.

8 I am old, you know, now, and instead of getting better, I grow worse.
Letter (1469),
op. cit.

231.   Joan of Arc
(c.1412–1431)

1 Messire, I am but a poor village girl; I cannot ride on horseback nor lead men to battle.   Attributed response to vision of St.
Michael (c.1425),
Quoted in
Women of Beauty and Heroism,
by Frank B. Goodrich   1858

2 Fear not for me. God guides me on my way, and will bring me to the king; I was born for that.   Remark, op. cit.

3 My brothers in Paradise tell me what to do.
Ibid.

4 The soldiers will fight, and God will give the victory.   Ibid.

5 I know neither A nor B; but I come from God to deliver Orleans and consecrate the king.   Ibid.

6 Children say that people are hung sometimes for speaking the truth.
Defense at her tribunal
(February 23, 1431),
op. cit.

7 If I am not [in a state of grace], God bring me there; if I am, God keep me there!
Ibid.

8 Do you think that the King of Heaven has no glory wherewith to clothe his saints!
Ibid.

9 Of the love or hate of God for the English, or of what He does with their souls, I know nothing: but I know that the English will be driven out of France, except those who perish in it.   Ibid.

10 Alas! alas! that I should be so horribly and cruelly treated, that my body, pure and unstained by corruption, should be consumed and reduced to ashes! Oh! I would rather be beheaded seven times over than be burned! I appeal to God, the judge of all, against the wrongs and outrages they inflict upon me!
(May 1431), op. cit.

11 They must needs get me to the Dauphin before Mid-Lent, were I to wear out my legs to the knees walking there; . . . there is for him no other help save in me.
Quoted in
Women of Medieval France
by Pierce Butler   1907

12 I should far rather stay beside my poor mother and spin, for these things do not belong to my station, yet it is necessary that I should go . . . since God wishes that I should do them.   Ibid.

13 Deliver the keys of all the good towns you have taken and violated in France to the Maid who has been sent by God the King of Heaven! Go away, for God's sake, back to your own country; otherwise, await news of the Maid, who will soon visit you to your great detriment.
Letter to the English (1429),
Quoted in *Saint Joan of Arc*
by Vita Sackville-West   1935

14 I was in my thirteenth year when God sent a voice to guide me. At first, I was very much frightened. The voice came towards the hour of noon, in summer, in my father's garden.   Spoken at her tribunal (1431), op. cit.

232.   Isotta Nogarola
(1418–1466)

1 There are already so many women in the world! Why then . . . was I born a woman, to be scorned by men in words and deeds?
Letter to Guarino Veronese,
Quoted in "Book-Lined Cells"
by Margaret King, tr.;
Beyond Their Sex,
Patricia Labalme, ed.   1980

2 . . . they jeer at me throughout the city, the women mock me. I cannot find a quiet stable to hide in, and the donkeys tear me with their teeth, the oxen stab me with their horns.   Ibid.

233.   Lucrezia de Medici
(1425–1482)

1   Here is the mighty king
He has conquered the evil
Which has lasted many years,
And makes the earth tremble
Removing sorrows from it
Thus filling the seats of paradise
To restore his court.
"Here is the Mighty King,"
Claudia Alexander with
Carlo Di Maio, trs.;
from *Laude,* Quoted in *Poesia
italiana: Il quatrocento,*
Giulio Ferroni, ed.   1978

2 The promise is fulfilled.
The Redeemer comes.   Ibid.

3 Come! Without delay.
Don't lose sight of them
In the eternal chorus.   Ibid.

234.   Costanza Varano Sforza
(1426–1447)

1 Even the wisest and most famous men would fear to attempt to praise you adequately. What then can I, an ignorant, unlettered, and inexperienced girl hope to do?
"Oration to
Bianca Maria Visconti,*
Quoted in "Book-Lined Cells"
by Margaret King, tr.;
Beyond Their Sex,
Patricia Labalme, ed.   1980
*Last surviving member of the Visconti family of Milan, who dominated the history of northern Italy in the 14th and 15th centuries.

235.   Sister Bertken
(c.1427–c.1514)

1 I must sow lilies by the light of the dawn,

And start my work early as the new day is born. "A Ditty,"
St. 8 (1518), Jonathan Crewe, tr.;
Women Poets of the World,
Joanne Bankier and Deirdre
Lashgari, eds.   1983

2 Red roses unfurl.
In their calices burns the pearl.
Ibid., St. 11,
Willis Barnstone, tr.;
A Book of Women Poets,
Aliki and Willis Barnstone, eds.
1980

236. Margaret of Anjou
(1429–1482)

1 You have in your hands what may be easily made the foundation of the noblest realm in Europe. . . . if you would take the government of it into your own hands.
Remark to Henry VI,
her husband,
Quoted in *The History of
Marguerite d'Anjou,*
Ch. 9, by Jacob Abbott   1861

2 The world is always disposed to consider what is done by a great and powerful monarch as of course right, and even when it would seem to them wrong they believe that its having that appearance is only because they are not in a position to form a just judgment on the question, not being fully acquainted with the facts, or not seeing all the bearings of them.   Ibid.

237. Macuilxochitl
(1435–1499?)

1 Will my songs
be borne to his house
where he dwells in mystery?
Or do thy flowers bloom
here only?

Let the dance begin!   "Battle Song,"
St. 2, Miguel León-Portilla and
Catherine Rodriguez-Nieto, trs.;
Trece poetas del mundo azteca
[*Thirteen Poets of the Aztec World*],
Miguel León-Portilla, ed.
1967

2 there on the plains
there where war is burning
Ibid., St. 4

238. Elizabeth Woodville Grey
(1437?–1492)

1 . . . I dare put no person earthly in trust of his* keeping. . . . The law of nature will the mother to keep her child, God's law privilegeth the sanctuary, and the sanctuary my son. . . .   Speech to the Archbishop of
Canterbury (1483),
Quoted in *Chronicles*
by Raphael Holinshed   1577
*Her son, Richard, Duke of York.

2 . . . desire of kingdom knoweth no kindred . . .   Ibid.

3 . . . for as ye think I fear too much, be you well ware that you fear not as far too little.
Ibid.

4 Farewell, mine own sweet son. God send you good keeping; let me kiss you yet once ere you go, for God knoweth when we shall kiss together again.   Final leave-taking of
her son, Richard, Duke of
York** (1483),
op. cit.

**He disappeared and is presumed to have been murdered, along with his older brother Edward V, in the Tower of London, during the reign of Richard III.

239. Philipa of Avis and Lancaster
(1437–1497)

1 I lack in service, lack in love,
Yet never cease in my desire
"To Holy Jesus,"
The Catholic Anthology,
Thomas Walsh, ed.   1927

240. Margaret Mautby Paston
(1441–1484)

1 I would that ye should not be too hasty to be married till ye were more sure of your livelode, for ye must remember what charge ye shall have; and if ye have not [the means] to maintain it it will be a great rebuke. And therefore labour that ye . . . be more in surety of your land ere than ye be married.
Letter to her son, John Paston II (1469),
The Paston Letters and Papers of the Fifteenth Century,
Pt. II, Norman Davis, ed.
1976

2 God for his mercy send us a good world.
Letter to her husband, John Paston I,
op. cit.

241. Catherine of Genoa
(1447–1510)

1 I am so washed in the tide of His measureless love that I seem to be below the surface of a sea and cannot touch or see or feel anything around me except its water.
La Vita della B. Caterina Fiesca Adorna Dama Genouese
1681

2 My Me is God, nor do I recognize any other Me except my God himself.
Quoted in
The Perennial Philosophy
by Aldous Huxley   1945

242. Elizabeth Clere
(fl. 1450)

1 Cousin, think on this matter, for sorrow oftentime causeth women to beset them otherwise than they should do.
Letter to John Paston I (c.1450),
The Paston Letters and Papers of the Fifteenth Century,
Pt. II, Norman Davis, ed.
1976

243. Isabella I
(1451–1504)

1 Whosoever hath a good presence and a good fashion, carries continual letters of recommandation.
Quoted in
Apophthagmes New and Old,
#99, Francis Bacon, ed.
1625

2 God, the witness of hearts, knows that before my own affection I look first to the welfare of these kingdoms.
Remark, (c.1468),
Quoted in *Isabella of Spain*
by William Thomas Walsh
1930

3 . . . hear the prayer of Thy servant, and show forth the truth, and manifest Thy will with Thy marvellous works: so that if my cause is not just, I may not be allowed to sin through ignorance, and if it is just, Thou give me wisdom and courage to sustain it with the aid of Thine arm. . . .
Remark concerning her campaign for the right of succession to the kingdom of Castile (1475),
op. cit.

4 . . . kings who wish to reign have to labor. . . .   (1476), op. cit.

5 . . . in all human affairs there are things both certain and doubtful, and both are equally in the hands of God.
Ibid.

6 . . . tell him that if he will surrender Trujillo peacefully, I will reward him with money and honors. If not, I will put the walls down about his ears.
Message to the alcaide [commander] of Trujillo (1476),
op. cit.

7 . . . let our only thought be how to extend our glorious conquest. Statement after the taking of the Alhambra (1482/83),
op. cit.

8 Since . . . kings, like other men, are exposed to mortal accidents . . . they should be prepared for death. . . . Letter* to Archbishop of Granada, (1492/93), op. cit.

*Occasioned by the attempted assassination of her husband, King Ferdinand V of Aragon.

9 Although I have never doubted it . . . the distance is great from the firm belief to the realization from concrete experience. Ibid.

10 As for the bullfights . . . after I had consented to them, I had the fullest determination never to attend them again in my life nor to be where they were held. Letter to Archbishop Talavera, her confessor (March 1493), op. cit.

11 In addition to being the daughters of such monarchs as we [the daughters of Castile] are, respect is likewise had to the fact that in Spain daughters inherit, which is not the case in France. . . . Letter to Duke of Estrada, from Bergenroth (1503), op. cit.

12 It would not be consonant either with reason, or with right, human or divine, but would, on the contrary, be a most barbarous and dishonest proceeding, if the King of England [Henry VII], provided he could, were to keep by force that which the Princess of Wales* took with her, and which belongs to her. Ibid.

*Catherine of Aragon, her daughter.

13 Should the King,* my lord, prefer a sepulchre in some other place, then my will is that my body be transported there and laid by his side, that the union we have enjoyed in this world, and through the mercy of God may hope again for our souls in heaven, may be represented by our bodies in the earth. Last will and testament (October 12, 1504), op. cit.

* King Ferdinand V of Aragon, her husband.

244. Gwerfyl Mechain
(c.1460–1500)

1 The moon in its robes of snow clouds
welcomes you
and your silver coins.
"Lady of the Ferry Inn,"
St. 1, Willis Barnstone, tr.;
A Book of Women Poets,
Aliki and Willis Barnstone, eds.
1980

2 Before the men who drink here, I offer
a perfect world.
I want nothing more.
I walk among men, faultlessly,
sing intimate songs
and pour the mead. Ibid., St. 2

3 Tiny snow of the stunningly cold black day
is white flour,
is flesh of the earth,
cold lamb fleece on the mountain
"In the Snowfall,"
St. 1, Willis Barnstone, tr.,
op. cit.

245. Caterina Sforza
(1462–1509)

1 Could I write all, the world would turn to stone. Letter to her Dominican confessor (c.1501–1509),* Quoted in The Medici by G. F. Young 1930
*From her prison in the Castel Sant'Angelo, Rome.

2 War is not for ladies and children like mine. Letter to her uncle, Ludovico Sforza il Moro (August 27, 1498), Quoted in Caterina Sforza by Ernst Breisach 1967

3 . . . nobody believes me . . . being just a lady and timid, too. Letter to her uncle (September 24, 1498), op. cit.

4 One cannot defend a state with mere words.
Letter to her uncle
(November 14, 1498),
op. cit.

246.   Clemence Isaure
(1464–1515/16)

1 In the shelter of the woods the amorous
dove
Peacefully murmurs her long and sweet ac-
cents;
On our hills, the heartiest wrens
Will celebrate the return of spring!
Untitled,
St. 1, Michael Fanning, tr.;
*Dictats de Dona Clamenza
Isaure*   1505

2 ... I, alas, plaintive and solitary,
I who have known only that I love, and that
I suffer,
I must—a stranger to the world, to happi-
ness—
Weep ... and die.   Ibid., St. 2

247.   Elizabeth of York
(1465/66–1503)

1 Delivered from sorrow, annexed to pleas-
ance,
Of all comfort having abundance.
This joy and I, I trust, shall never twin—
My heart is set upon a lusty pin.
"My Heart Is Set
Upon a Lusty Pin,"
St. 1,
The Women Poets in English,
Ann Stanford, ed.   1972

2 My joys be double where other's are but
thin,
For I am stably set in such a place,
Where beauty 'creaseth and ever willeth
grace. ...   Ibid., St. 6

248.   Cassandra Fedele
(1465–1558)

1 Do that for which nature has suited
you. ...   "Letter to Alessandra Scala,"
from *Clarissimae feminae
Cassandrae Fidelis benetae
epistolae et orationes posthumae*
(1636),
Quoted in "Book-Lined Cells"
by Margaret King, tr.;
Beyond Their Sex,
Patricia Labalme, ed.   1980

2 I must put an end to my timidity. ...
"Oration delivered in Padua,"
op. cit.

3 ... many of you no doubt will see it as
audacious, that I, a maiden ... haven come
forth to speak in this radiance of learned
men. ...   Ibid.

249.   Florencia del Pinar
(fl. 1465–1499)

1   These birds were born
singing for joy;
such softness imprisoned
gives me much sorrow—
yet no one weeps for me.   "To Some
Partridges, Sent to Her Alive"
(c.1511), Julie Allen, tr.;
A Book of Women Poets,
Aliki and Willis Barnstone, eds.
1980

250.   Laura Cereta
(1469–1499)

1 I cannot bear these babbling and chattering
women who, aflame with wine and drunkenness, do injury by their impudent words
not only to the [female] sex but above all to
themselves. Quoted in "Book-Lined Cells"
by Margaret King, tr.;
Beyond Their Sex,
Patricia Labalme, ed.   1980

2 Burning with the fires of hatred, the more they gnaw others, spewing forth words, the more are they worldless, gnawed within.
From *Epistolae*,
op. cit.

3 Knowledge is not given as gift, but through study. . . .   Ibid.

4 The free mind, not afraid to labor, presses on to attain the good.   Ibid.

251. Elisabetta Gonzago
(1471–1526)

1 Who is there among us whose conduct is so perfect as to close the mouth of slanderers? . . . trouble yourself no more on the subject, but . . . allow the wrong to recoil on the heads of those who invent these slanders, and who, in my judgment, are sufficiently punished by seeing how hateful they become in the eyes of all virtuous and honest persons.   Letter to Isabella d'Este
(1513),
Quoted in *Isabella d'Este*,
Vol. II, by Julia Cartwright
1903

252. Isabella D'Este
(1474–1530)

1 This [Milan] is the school of the Master and of those who know, the home of art and understanding.
(1492), Quoted in *Beatrice d'Este*
by Julia Cartwright   1899

2 . . . the treasure [state treasury] . . . which has lately received the addition of two large chests full of ducats, and another full of gold quartz about two and a half feet square. Would to God that we, who are so fond of spending money, possessed as much!   Letter to her husband (1492),
op. cit.

3 . . . the discontent of the people is more dangerous to a monarch than all the might of his enemies on the battlefield.
Letter to her husband (February 1495), from Milan,
op. cit.

4 . . . bring me the latest novelties . . . [but] if it is only as good as those which I see other people wear, I had rather be without it!
Letter to Ziliolo (April, 1491),
Quoted in *Isabella d'Este*,
Vol. I, by Julia Cartwright
1903

5 Since we have learnt by experience that you are as slow in finishing your work as you are in everything else, we send this to remind you that for once you must change your nature . . .   Letter to [the artist] Luca Liombeni (November 6, 1491),
op. cit.

6 Let Your Highness, I beg of you, keep a tranquil mind, and attend wholly to military affairs, for I intend to govern the State, with the help of these magnificent gentlemen and officials, in such a manner that you will suffer no wrong, and all that is possible will be done for the good of your subjects. And if any one should write or tell you of disorders of which you have not heard from me, you may be certain that it is a lie.
Letter to her husband
(June 29, 1495),
op. cit.

7 Your Excellency owes me as much gratitude as ever any husband owed his wife, and even if you loved and honored me as much as possible you could never repay my faithfulness. . . . But even if you should always treat me badly, I would never cease to do what is right, and the less love you show me, the more I shall always love you, because, in truth, this love is part of myself, and I became your wife so young that I can never remember having been without it.
Letter to her husband (c.1513),
op. cit., Vol. II

8 I am here in Mantua, but all my heart is in Rome. Letter to Cardinal Bibbiena (1515), op. cit.

9 Our portrait by the hand of Titian pleases us so much that we doubt if we were ever as beautiful as this, even at the age at which he has represented us. Letter to Ambassador Agnello (1536), op. cit.

10 Neither hope nor fear. (*Nec spe nec metu.*) Personal motto, Quoted in *Great Ages of Man: The Renaissance* by John R. Hale   1964

11 ... resolve to think of nothing but ... health in the first place and ... honor and comfort in the second, because in this fickle world we can do nothing else, and those who do not know how to spend their time profitably allow their lives to slip away with much sorrow and little praise. Letter to Elisabetta of Urbino (1492), Quoted in *Lucrezia Borgia* by Rachel Erlanger   1978

253.   Beatrice D'Este
(1475–1497)

1 I cannot say much of the perils of the chase, since game is so plentiful here that hares are to be seen jumping out at every corner—so much so, that often we hardly know which way to turn to find the best sport. Letter to Isabella d'Este (1491), Quoted in *Beatrice D'Este* by Julia Cartwright   1899

2 I must tell you that I have had a whole field of garlic planted for your benefit, so that when you come, we may be able to have plenty of your favourite dishes! Ibid.

3 ... I cannot deny that, now I am without your company I feel not only that I am deprived of a very dear sister, but that I have lost half of myself. Letter to Isabella d'Este (c.1491), op. cit.

4 Wherever I turn, in the house or out-of-doors, I seem to see your face before my eyes, and when I find myself deceived, and realize that you are really gone, you will understand how sore my distress has been— nay, how great it still is. Letter to Isabella d'Este (1495), op. cit.

254.   Barbara Torelli
(1475–1533)

1 Would that my fire might warm this frigid ice
And turn with tears, this dust to living flesh Poem on the death of her husband* (1508), Quoted in *Lucrezia Borgia* by Rachel Erlanger   1978

*Her second husband was murdered by the Bentivoglio, the family of her first husband.

2 ... then would I boldly, ardently confront The man who snapped our dearest bond and cry
Cruel monster, see what love can do. Ibid.

255.   Giulia Farnese
(1476?–?)

1 We look as if we had despoiled Florence [Italy] of brocade. Letter to Pope Alexander VI, Quoted in *Lucrezia Borgia* by Rachel Erlanger   1978

256. Elizabeth Brews
(fl. 1477)

1 Cousin, it is but a simple oak that [is] cut down at the first stroke.   Letter to John Paston III, her son-in-law (February 1477), *Paston Letters, 1422–1509,* James Gairdner, ed.   1904

257. Agnes Paston
(?–1479)

1 Dispose yourself as much as ye may to have less to do in the world . . . In little business lyeth much rest.
Letter to her son John (c.1444), *The Paston Letters and Papers of the Fifteenth Century,* Pt. II, Norman Davis, ed.   1976

2 This world is but a thoroughfare, and full of woe; and when we depart therefrom, right nought bear with us but our good deeds and ill.   Ibid.

3 There knoweth no man how soon God will call him; and therefore it is good for every creature to be ready. Whom God visiteth, he he loveth.   Ibid.

258. Lucrezia Borgia
(1480–1519)

1 . . . my husbands have been very unlucky.
Remark to her father after the murder of her second husband, Quoted in *Lucrezia Borgia,* Rachel Erlanger   1978

2 [This is] almost as one of those proofs God occasionally gives of His Kindness to those who love him. Remark upon birth of her first daughter, op. cit.

3 The more I try to do God's will the more he visits me with misfortune.
Remark upon hearing of the death of her brother, op. cit.

4 So great is the favor which our merciful Creator has shown me, that I approach the end of my life with pleasure, knowing that in a few hours, after receiving for the last time all the holy sacraments of the Church, I shall be released. Having arrived at this moment, I desire as a Christian, although I am a sinner, to ask your Holiness in your mercy to give me all possible spiritual consolation and your Holiness' blessing for my soul. Letter at her death (June 22, 1519), op. cit.

259. Margaret of Austria
(1480–1530)

1 The time is troubled, but the time will clear; After the rain one awaits fair weather.
Untitled roundelay, St. 1, Quoted in *Margaret of Austria: Regent of the Netherlands* by Jane de Iongh; M. D. Herter-Norton, tr.   1953

2 Peace will arrive, misfortune will cease

But meanwhile how much evil one suffers!
Ibid., Sts. 1, 2

3 All goes awry and lawless in the land, Where power takes the place of justice.
Untitled roundelay, St. 1, op. cit.

4 Quite possibly there will be whisperings; Nevertheless they'll not disturb my courage Long as I live.   Untitled, St. 2, op. cit.

5 . . . my life is nothing but pining And in the end I shall die of it.
Untitled roundelay, St. 1, op. cit.

6 To those presumptuous charmers Who counterfeit like lovers

By fine pretense and otherwise
Give no credence. . . .   Untitled,
Sts. 1, 2, op. cit.

7 . . . unpleasing thoughts
Drive me about, whence I am much
harassed,
And can repeat it to you even now:
Time is long to me.   Untitled,
St. 3, op. cit.

8 God wills, certainly, that we remain
In fortune good or sinister,
Always loyal.   Untitled,
St. 2, op. cit.

9 Here lies Margot, the nice young girl
Who had two husbands and is virgin still.
Epitaph composed for herself
during a storm at sea (1497),
op. cit.

10 *Fortune. Infortune. Fort. Une.* (Fortune
persecutes one harshly.)   Motto (1506),
op. cit.

11 Because we are women, we have a heart of a
different nature, and cannot do good to
those who harm us.   Letter to Duke of
Savoy, adviser to Charles III
(c.1515),
op. cit.

12 I am prepared and at rest in my conscience,
and in all ways resolved to receive what it
pleases God to send me: I have no
regrets. . . . Letter to her nephew, Charles
V (November 30, 1530)*,
op. cit.

*This was her last letter, written on the day of her
death.

260.   Catherine of Aragon
(1485–1536)

1 . . . I am in debt in London. . . . So that,
my lord, I am in the greatest trouble and
anguish in the world. . . . I have now sold
some bracelets to get a dress of black velvet,
for I was all but naked; . . . certainly I shall
not be able to live in this manner.
Letter to King Ferdinand of
Spain (1505),
Quoted in *Letters of Royal and
Illustrious Ladies
of Great Britain,*
Vol. I, Mary Anne Everett
Wood Green, ed.   1846

2 I do not understand the English language,
nor know how to speak it; and I have no
confessor.   Ibid.

3 Our time is ever passed in continual feasts.
Letter to King Ferdinand of
Spain (1509),
op. cit.

4 I confess to you that I am consumed by a
very great desire to be able to die, either together with you or before you . . . and
would purchase [death] by any amount of
the most heavy and infinite torments
. . . provided it were not a thing repugnant
to the Divine will.   Letter to Dr. John
Forest, her confessor (1535),
op. cit., Vol. II

5 When you have fought the battle and obtained the crown, I shall expect you to receive more abundant grace from heaven by
your means.   Ibid.

6 They tell me nothing but lies here, and they
think they can break my spirit. But I believe
what I choose and say nothing. I am not so
simple as I seem.   Letter to King
Ferdinand of Spain (1508),
Quoted in *Catherine of Aragon*
by Garrett Mattingly   1941

7 And when ye [Henry VIII] had me at the first, I take God to be my judge, I was a true maid, without touch of man. And whether this be true or no, I put it to your conscience. Court testimony (June 18, 1529), op. cit.

8 I trust so much in the natural goodness and virtue of the King [Henry VIII], my lord, that if I could only have him with me two months as he used to be, I alone should be powerful enough to make him forget the past.   Letter (c.1531), op. cit.

9 I came not into this realm as merchandise, nor yet to be married to any merchant.
Letter replying to request she acquiesce to the marriage of Henry VIII and Anne Boleyn (1533), op. cit.

10 . . . there is no punishment from God except for neglected duty. Letter to Eustace Chapuys, Catholic ambassador of Charles V, Holy Roman Emperor (1533), op. cit.

11 If a remedy be not applied shortly, there will be no end to ruined souls and martyred saints. The good will be firm and suffer. The lukewarm will fail if they find none to help them, and the greater part will stray away like sheep without a shepherd. . . .
Letter to Pope Paul III (October 15, 1534)

12 Speak you few words and meddle nothing.
Letter to [her daughter] Mary Tudor (1535), op. cit.

13 I beg you speak to the King, and desire him from me to be so charitable as to send his daughter and mine [Mary Tudor] where I am, because if I care for her with my own hands and by the advice of my own and other physicians, and God still pleases to take her from this world, my heart be at peace, otherwise in great pain.
Letter to Chapuys (1535), op. cit.

14 Lastly I make this vow that mine eyes desire you above all things. Farewell.
Last letter, to Henry VIII (January 7, 1535), op. cit.

261.   Elisabeth of Brandenburg
(1485–1545)

1 I believe in Him who made the sun and the moon and all the stars. . . . May he not tarry to fetch me. . . . I am so weary of life.
Last words (1545), Quoted in Women of the Reformation, Vol. I: Germany and Italy, by Roland H. Bainton   1971

262.   Veronica Gambara
(1485–1550)

1 How brief is this miserable mortal life!
Even this meadow now green and blossoming
Before was full of snow. . . .
Untitled, Brenda Webster, tr., from Rime (1759); The Penguin Book of Women Poets, Carol Cosman, Joan Keefe and Kathleen Weaver, eds.   1978

2 . . . time flees and with its fleeing
Bears off the years together with our life!
Ibid.

3 . . . we . . . lack all hope,

Sure of nothing but our dying.
         Ibid.

4 ... blissful in heaven you see dawn appear
And under your feet you see the stars. ...
        Sonnet on the death of an
        unidentified poet,
        Claudia Alexander with Carlo
        DiMaio, trs.;
        from *Rime* (1759),
        Poesia italiana: il cinquecento,
        Giulio Ferroni, ed.   1978

5 Eyes bright and beautiful
How can you instantly
Encompass so many moods?
You seem, at the same moment, joyful, excited,
proud, humble, haughty; you fill
Me with waves of hope and fear
        "Madrigal for Marriage,"
        Claudia Alexander, tr., op. cit.

263.   Vittoria da Colonna
(1490–1549)

1 Your virtue may raise you above the glory
of being king. The sort of honour that goes
down to our children with real lustre is
derived from our deeds and qualities, not
from power or titles. Letter to Francesco,
        Marquis of Pescara, her
        husband,
        Quoted in *Biography of*
        Distinguished Women
        by Sarah Josepha Hale   1876

2 ... it is not riches, titles, and kingdoms,
which can give true glory, infinite praise,
and perpetual renown to noble spirits desirous of eternal fame, but faith, sincerity, and
other virtues of the soul. ...
        Letter to Francesco, Marquis of
        Pescara (1509),
        Quoted in *A Princess of the*
        Italian Reformation:
        Giulia Gonzaga
        by Christopher Hare*   1912

*Pseudonym of Marian Andrews.

3 I only write to vent that inward pain

On which my heart doth feed itself. ...
        First sonnet, in memory of her
        husband (c.1525–1529),
        op. cit.

4 Thou knowest, Love, I never sought to flee
From thy sweet prison, nor impatient threw
Thy dear yoke from my neck; nor e'er
withdrew
What, that first day, my soul bestowed on
thee. ...   Untitled sonnet (c.1525-1529),
        op. cit.

5 My soul, the Lord appears; disperse
The clouds that gather round thy heart,
And clear thee from the mist of earthly
love,
Lest it o'ershade thy heavenly light.
        Untitled sonnet (c.1546),
        op. cit.

6 ... the swaggering knights prepare to ride.
The war begins. They gloat and cannot
wait.
They think they are masters of their fate
        Untitled sonnet (c.1529–1549),
        Quoted in
        Women of the Reformation,
        Vol. I: *Germany and Italy,*
        by Roland H. Bainton,
        tr.   1971

7 Father Noah, from whose good seed God
graced
To populate the ancient world anew

· ·
If our age, not less impure, were faced
By the holy eye of him who knew,
With what holy ire would he then spew
A second flood. ...   Untitled sonnet
        (c.1529–1549),
        op. cit.

8 Credit to the women goes by right.
They have the open heart and unaffrighted
face.
        Untitled sonnet on Mary Magdalene
        (c.1529–1549),
        op. cit.

9 By true humility we reach the light
And know the sacred writings to be true.

Read little, then, and believe the more.
Untitled sonnet (c.1529–1549),
op. cit.

10 One cannot have a lively faith, I trow,
Of God's eternal promises if fear
Has left the warm heart chilled and sear
And placed a veil between the I and Thou.
Untitled sonnet (c.1529–1549),
op. cit.

11 You, Noah, were delivered in the ark, but
why?
And you became the father of the race.
Why God should have conferred on you
such grace
Is something you cannot explain, nor I.
Untitled sonnet (c.1529–1549),
op. cit.

12 Our surcease from war, within, wherever,
Comes from Him, the author of our peace.
He is the sun whose brilliance blinds our
eyes.
The Father's secrets, how He will release,
To whom and where and when, none can
surmise.
Enough for us to know He cannot err.
Untitled sonnet (c.1529–1549),
op. cit.

13 The glorious Lady is above the arch-
angels . . . above the cherubim . . . above
the seraphim. She rises to the light which is
one and three.   Letters,
op. cit.

14 . . . if, at times, desire's gale
attempts new war, I race to land
and with a knot of love intertwined with
faith
I tie my bark to that in which I trust.
Untitled sonnet (c.1529–1549),
tr. Brenda Webster;
The Penguin Book
of Women Poets,
Carol Cosman, Joan Keefe and
Kathleen Weaver, eds.   1978

15 How must one fear who happily proceeds!—

for the end is not always like the beginning.
Untitled sonnet (c.1529–1549),
tr. Lynne Lawner, op. cit.

16 I live on this depraved and lonely cliff
like a sad bird abhorring a green tree
Untitled sonnet (c.1525–1549),
tr. Willis Barnstone;
A Book of Women Poets,
Aliki and Willis Barnstone, eds.
1980

17 . . . these first cares that sleep had gently
lessened, again grow heavy
and all my pleasures sink in shadows
just when the shadows vanish from every
side.   "When the Orient is lit,"
St. 2 (c.1525–1549),
tr. Brenda Webster;
Women Poets of the World,
Johanna Bankier and Deirdre
Lashgari, eds.   1983

18   That which dims other eyes, brightens
mine,
for, closing them, the door is opened
to sleep which brings me to my sun.
Ibid., St. 4

19   so I, when the hot and live ray
of the heavenly sun, whence I nourish my
heart,
more clear than usual shines,
move my pen urged by love
"As a Hungry Fledgling,"
Sts. 3, 4, tr. Brenda Webster,
op. cit.

264.   Argula von Grumbach
(1492–post-1563)

1 Where do you read in the Bible that Christ,
the apostles, and the prophets imprisoned,
banished, burned or murdered anyone?
Letter of protest to the faculty of
the University of Ingolstadt
(1523),
Quoted in Women of the
Reformation, Vol. I:
Germany and Italy,
by Roland H. Bainton   1971

2 You need not think you can pull God, the prophets and the apostles out of heaven with papal decretals drawn from Aristotle, who was not a Christian.   Ibid.

3 You have the key of knowledge and you close the kingdom of Heaven. But you are defeating yourselves.   Ibid.

4 Have regard, gracious princes, to the flock of the Lord Jesus Christ, purchased not with silver and gold but with his rose red blood.   Letter to Duke William (1523), op. cit.

5 To obey my man indeed is fitting,
But if he drives me from God's Word
In Matthew ten it is declared
Home and child we must forsake
When God's honor is at stake.
     Untitled,
     op. cit.

6 Be not surprised that I confess God, for he who does not confess God is no Christian, though he has been baptized a thousand times.   Letter to her cousin, Adam von Torring, op. cit.

7 I am distressed that our princes take the Word of God no more seriously than a cow does a game of chess.   Ibid.

8 I have even heard some say, "if my father and mother were in hell, I wouldn't want to be in heaven." Not me, not if all my friends were down there.   Ibid.

265. Margaret of Navarre
(1492–1549)

1 A father will have compassion on his son. A mother will never forget her child. A brother will cover the sin of his sister. But what husband ever forgave the faithlessness of his wife?   *Mirror of the Sinful Soul* 1531

2 Make me blind that I may see,
Crippled and bound to walk and run,

Drown me in nothingness that I may be

Whole and complete and all in Thee.
     "The Paradox of Mortification,"
     Sts. 1, 2,
     Les Marguerites de la marguerite
     des princesses [The Pearls of the
     Pearl of Princesses]
     1547

3 Assuage my streaming eyes
And hear my sigh.
And may I have a gentle sleep
When I shall die.   Untitled poem,
     op. cit.

4 He honours with his virtues, and finally crowns with His glory, those whom He has elected; and often He chooses low and despised things to confound those which the world esteems high and honourable.
     "Novel II, the first day,"
     The Heptameron, or Novels of the
     Queen of Navarre
     1558

5 Let us not rejoice in our virtues, as Jesus Christ says, but let us rejoice for that we are enrolled in the Book of life.
     Ibid.

6 ... spite will make a woman do more than love. ...   Ibid.,
     "Novel III, the first day"

7 ... without love, all the merits and power of man are nothing.   Ibid.,
     "Novel IV, the first day"

8 "These good fathers ... preach chastity to us, and want to foul our wives. They dare not touch money ... but they are ready enough to handle women's thighs, which are far more dangerous."   Ibid.,
     "Novel VI, the first day"

9 I have heard much of these languishing lovers, but I never yet saw one of them die for love.   Ibid.,
     "Novel VIII, the first day"

10 ... chastity in an enamored heart is a thing more divine than human.   Ibid.,
     "Novel IX, the first day"

11 Were all mankind to condemn me, whilst my conscience was free from all reproach, I should derive a sort of pleasure from calumny, so true it is that virtue is never wholly unhappy.　　　　　Ibid., "Novel X, the first day"

12 ... the guilty are easily susceptible of the contagion of fear. ...　　　　　Ibid., "Novel XII, the Second Day"

13 Princes and those who are in authority ought to fear to outrage their inferiors. There is no man so insignificant but he can do mischief when it is God's will to inflict vengeance on the sinner, nor any so great that he can do hurt to one whom God chooses to protect.　　　　　Ibid.

14 To me it seems much better to love a woman as a woman, than to make her one's idol, as many do. For my part, I am convinced that it is better to use than to abuse.　　　　　Ibid., "Novel XIII, the Second Day"

15 ... all the lovers I have had have invariably begun by talking of my interests, and telling me that they loved my life, my welfare, and my honor, and the upshot of it all has no less invariably been their own interest, their own pleasure, and their own vanity.　　　　　Ibid., "Novel XIV, the Second Day"

16 Everyone knows that ... a woman ought not to let it appear that she understands, still less that she believes, the declaration made to her by a lover. ...　　　　　Ibid.

17 ... the ill one thinks to do to another often recoils upon the doer.　　　　　Ibid., "Novel XV, the Second Day"

18 ... ladies, if you are wise, you will be on your guard against us [men] as the stag would be against the hunter ... for our felicity, our glory, and delight, is to see you captured, and to despoil you of what ought to be dearer to you than life.　　　　　Ibid., "Novel XVII, the Second Day"

19 ... one cannot arrive at the temple of Fame without passing through that of Virtue.　　　　　Ibid., "Novel XVIII, the Second Day"

20 ... no one ever perfectly loved God who did not perfectly love some of His creatures in this world.　　　　　Ibid., "Novel XIX, the Second Day"

21 ... the soul rushes forth, and thinks to find in outward beauty, in visible graces, and in moral virtues, the supreme beauty, grace, and virtue. But after having sought and proved them, and not found what it loves, the soul lets them go, and passes on its way, like the child who loves apples, pears, dolls, and ... thinks that to amass pebbles is to be wealthy; but as it grows up loves living dolls, and amasses things necessary to human life.　　　　　Ibid.

22 Man is a whimsical mixture of good and evil, and a perpetual contradiction.　　　　　Ibid., "Novel XXI, the Third Day"

23 ... there is no greater ninny than a man who thinks himself cunning, nor any one wiser than he who knows that he is not so.　　　　　Ibid., "Novel XXIX, the Third Day"

24 He who knows his own incapacity, knows something, after all. ...　　　　　Ibid.

25 ... the first step man takes in self-confidence, removes him so far from the confidence he ought to have in God.　　　　　Ibid., "Novel XXX, the Third Day"

26 Man is wise ... when he recognizes no greater enemy than himself. ...　　　　　Ibid.

27 A vicious love perishes and has no long abode in a good heart; but decorous love has bonds of silk so fine and delicate that one is caught in them before one perceives them.　　　　　Ibid., "Novel XXXVI, the Fourth Day"

28 ... true love is a ladder by which to ascend to the perfect love which we owe to God. No one can ascend to it except through the afflictions and calamities of this world. ...
Ibid.,
"Novel XXXVII, the Fourth Day"

29 There are few husbands, ladies, whom the wife does not win in the long run by patience and love, unless they are harder than the rocks which yet the weak and soft water pierces in time. Ibid.,
"Novel XXXVIII, the Fourth Day"

30 ... God always helps madmen, lovers, and drunkards. ... Ibid.

31 ... fools live longer than the wise, unless someone kills them ... for ... fools do not dissemble their passions. If they are angry they strike; if they are merry they laugh; but those who deem themselves wise hide their defects with so much care that their hearts are all poisoned with them.
Ibid.

32 When one has one good day in the year, one is not wholly unfortunate.
Ibid.,
"Novel XL, the Fourth Day"

33 A prison is never narrow when the imagination can range in it as it will.
Ibid.

34 Blessed ... is he who has it in his power to do evil, yet does it not. Ibid., "Novel XLIII, the Fifth Day"

35 ... for as trusting a friend is the greatest honor one can do him, so doubting him is the greatest dishonor. ...
Ibid.,
"Novel XLVI, the Fifth Day"

36 I have never known a woman to have been beguiled for having been slow to believe men; but I have known many a one who has been beguiled for too easily believing their falsehoods. Ibid.,
"Novel XLVII, the Fifth Day"

37 Though jealousy be produced by love, as ashes are by fire, yet jealousy extinguishes love as ashes smother the flame.
Ibid., "Novel XLVIII, the Fifth Day"

38 There is no hunter who does not take pleasure in blowing his horn over his quarry, or lover who is not very glad to proclaim the glory of his victory. Ibid.,
"Novel XLIX, the Fifth Day"

39 When one loves well, one knows no other bread than the glances and the words of the beloved. ... Ibid.,
"Novel L, the Sixth Day"

40 I never knew a mocker who was not mocked ... a deceiver who was not deceived, or a proud man who was not humbled. Ibid.,
"Novel LI, the Sixth Day"

41 ... the ambition of women is so great, that they never content themselves with one lover. I have heard that the best of them like to have three—one for honor, one for interest, and the third for pleasure. ...
Ibid.,
"Novel LIII, the Sixth Day"

42 People pretend ... not to like grapes when they are too high for them to reach.
Ibid.

43 Truly I have often wondered ... how they think to make their peace with God by means of things which He himself reprobated when He was on earth, such as great buildings, gildings, painting, and decorations ... if they have rightly understood what God has said ... they would have taken pains to adorn their consciences. ...
Ibid.,
"Novel LVI, the Sixth Day"

44 ... some there are who are much more ashamed of confessing a sin than of committing it. Ibid.,
"Novel LX, the Sixth Day"

45 ... to give men a taste for going into foreign parts, and not loitering by their own
firesides, nothing more need be done than
to marry them.   *Ibid.*,
                    "Novel LXX, the Seventh Day"

46 Perfect love—would that it were known!—
Bestows a pleasure that can never end,
And every breath of bitterness is blown.
                    "The Rapture of Divine Love,"
                                        St. 1,
                                  Quoted in
                    Women of the Reformation,
                    Vol. II: *France and England,*
                    by Roland H. Bainton   1973

47 "Paradise is this," I say to me,
"Chants melodious, organs with holy glee
Reverent priests with sermons that console
To bring the seeker to his cherished goal.
I am in rapture, Lord, my altar Thou."
                              Ibid., St. 3

48 O my God, that death is fair
Which takes me from this fetid air,
By death I'm victor in the race.
By death I look upon Thy face.
                              Untitled poem,
                                    op. cit.

49 I did not know that love could grow
through death. But now I know.
                    Dialogue on the death of her
                    brother, King Francis I
                    (c.1547/48),
                                    op. cit.

50 ... my brother, I know that you are sitting
at the banquet of the Lord, but I am not
there. I ought to rejoice in the spirit, but my
frail clay cannot rejoice when yours is
ashes.   *Ibid.*

51 Churches entrance me with their ancient
towers
Triumphant portals and chimes that mark
the hours
Altars within, with silver marked and gold,
Given lavishly by those of old.
                    "Prisons" (post-1547),
                                    op. cit.

52 If someone insults you,
Endure him lightheartedly;

And if all slander you,
Give no heed to them:
    Tis nothing new
To hear such frequent talk:
Autant en emporte le vent
                    "Autant en Emporte le Vente"
                    [It All Will Vanish
                              into Thin Air],
                    St. 1 (c.1547), Aline Allard, tr.;
                    *The Penguin Book
                    of Women Poets,*
                    Carol Cosman, Joan Keefe and
                    Kathleen Weaver, eds.   1978

53 If you are told of a place
(Not God's) where can be found
Solace and true salvation,
It is to murder your soul.
    Be a rebel.
Belie the most learned:
Autant en emporte le vent
                              Ibid., St. 5

266.   Margery Brews Paston
(?–c.1495)

1 ... right well-beloved Valentine ... if that
ye could be content with ... my poor person, I would be the merriest maiden on
ground. And if ye think not yourself so satisfied, or that ye might have much more
good ... take no such labour upon you as
to come more.... Letter to John Paston
                              III (February 1477),
                    *The Paston Letters and Papers of
                    the Fifteenth Century,*
                    Pt. II, Norman Davis, ed.
                                            1976

267.   Mary of France
(1496–1533)

1 God's will sufficeth me. (*La Volonté de
Dieu me suffit.*)   Personal motto (1514),
                    Quoted in *Mary Tudor: The
                    White Queen*
                    by Walter C. Richardson
                                            1970

2 Sir, your Grace knoweth well that I did marry for your pleasure . . . and now I trust you will suffer me to marry as me liketh for to do. Letter to her brother, Henry VIII
(c.1514/15),
op. cit.

268. Katherine Zell
(1497/98–1562)

1 You remind me that the Apostle Paul told women to be silent in church. I would remind you of the word of this same apostle that in Christ there is no longer male nor female. "Entschuldigung [Apology of] Katharina Schutzinn" (1524),
Quoted in
Women of the Reformation,
Vol. I: *Germany and Italy,*
by Roland H. Bainton   1971

2 I do not pretend to be John the Baptist rebuking the Pharisees. I do not claim to be Nathan upbraiding David. I aspire only to be Balaam's ass, castigating his master.
Ibid.

3 Faith is not faith which is not tried.
"Den Leydenden Christgläubigen" [To Suffering Believers in Christ] (1524),
op. cit.

4 Save us from murmuring against any cross laid upon us. "Den Psalmen Misere"
(1558),
op. cit.

5 Save us from resentment when we are maligned and scorned, like Christ who as a sheep before the shearers was dumb and opened not his mouth. Ibid.

6 Lead us not into the temptation of believing that we have truly forgiven, while rancor lingers. . . . Ibid.

7 God is glad when the craftsman at his bench . . . the farmer at the plough . . . the mother at the cradle break forth in hymns of prayer, praise and instruction.
Preface to her collection of
hymns (1534),
op. cit.

8 A disturber of the peace am I? Yes indeed, of my own peace. Do you call this disturbing the peace that instead of spending my time in frivolous amusements I have visited the plague infested and carried out the dead? . . . I have never mounted the pulpit, but I have done more than any minister in visiting those in misery. Is this disturbing the peace of the church?"Ein Brief an die genze Bürgerschaft der Stadt Strassburg" [A Letter to the Citizency of the City of Strassburg] (1557),
op. cit.

9 The Good Samaritan, when he came upon the man who had fallen among thieves, did not ask him to what denomination he belonged, but put him on his ass and took him to an inn. Ibid.

269. Mira Bai
(1498–1547)

1 O King, I know you gave me poison.
But I emerged
just as gold burned in fire
comes out bright as a dozen suns.
Untitled,
Usha Nilsson, tr.;
*The Penguin Book
of Women Poets,*
Carol Cosman, Joan Keefe and
Kathleen Weaver, eds.   1978

2 In my servanthood I shall get his vision,
the remembrance would be my pay.
And my estate, the devotion and love,
all three are pleasing to me.
Untitled,
Usha Nilsson, tr.; op. cit.

3 She drinks the honey of her vision.
                              Untitled,
                    St. 4, Willis Barnstone
                    and Usha Nilsson, trs.;
                    A Book of Women Poets,
                    Aliki and Willis Barnstone, eds.
                                          1980

4 My hope is in your glance
  no other place.   Untitled,
                    Willis Barnstone and Usha
                    Nilsson, trs., op. cit.

5 Hari is an ocean,
  my eyes touch him.
  Mira is an ocean of joy.
  She takes him inside.   Untitled, op. cit.

6 This pain of separation
  cannot be understood.
  I am like the rainbird calling for clouds,
  like fish craving water.   Untitled,
                    Willis Barnstone and Usha
                    Nilsson, trs., op. cit.

7 The energy that holds up mountains is the
  one Mirabai bows down to, He lives century after century, and the test I set for him
  he has passed.   "The Clouds,"
                    News of the Universe,
                    Robert Bly, ed. and adapter
                                          1980

8 Making love with Krishna and eating little—those are my pearls and my carneli-
  ans.*   "Why Mira Can't Go Back to her
                              Old House,"
                                       op. cit.
*A translucent variety of quartz with a variegated red-
dish color.

9   My teacher taught me this.
          Approve me or disapprove me; I
  praise the Mountain Energy night and day.
  I take the path that ecstatic human beings
  have taken for centuries.   Ibid.

10 I have felt the swaying of the elephant's
   shoulders . . .
          and now you want me to climb on a
   jackass? Try to be serious!
                                       Ibid.

11 Get up, dear child, the dawn has come,

outside the door wait gods and men.
                              Untitled,
                    Usha Nilsson, tr.;
                    Women Poets of the World,
                    Joanna Bankier and Deirdre
                    Lashgari, eds.   1983

270.   Huang O
(1498–1569)

1   Once more I will shyly
  Let you undress me and gently
  Unlock my sealed jewel.   "A Farewell to
                              A Southern Melody,"
                    The Orchid Boat,
                    Women Poets of China,
                    Kenneth Rexroth and Ling
                    Chung, eds. and trs.   1972

2 My slender waist and thighs
  Are exhausted and weak
  From a night of cloud dancing.
          To the tune "A Floating Cloud
                    Crosses Enchanted Mountain,"
                                       op. cit.

3   I will allow only
  My lord to possess my sacred
  Lotus pond, and every night
  You can make blossom in me
  Flowers of fire.   To the tune "Soaring
                                       Clouds,"
                                       op. cit.

4 If you don't know how, why pretend?
          To the tune "Red Embroidered
                                   Shoes,"
                                       op. cit.

5 Maybe you can fool some girls,
  But you can't fool Heaven.
                                       Ibid.

6 Go and make somebody else
  Unsatisfied.   Ibid.

271. Diane de Poitiers
(1499–1566)

1 Let my enemies know that I fear them not;
when the king dies, I shall be too much occupied in my grief at his loss to pay heed to
the insults which they may heap upon me.
Remark on the day of Henry II's
death (July 21, 1559),
Quoted in
Women of Beauty and Heroism
by Frank B. Goodrich   1858

2 Farewell sweet kisses, pigeon-wise,
With lip and tongue; farewell again
The secret sports betwixt us twain
"To Henry II Upon His Leaving
for a Trip" (c.1552),
Quoted in *The Life and Times of
Catherine de Medici*
by Francis Watson   1935

3 O! Louis de Breze, Diane de Poitiers,
stricken by the death of her husband, has
raised this sepulchre to thee. She was thy
inseparable and very faithful wife in the
marriage bed; she will be the same in the
tomb. Inscription on tomb of her husband
(1531),
Quoted in *Women of Power*
by Mark Strage   1976

4 The years that a woman subtracts from her
age are not lost. They are added to the
ages of other women.   Attributed, n.d.

272. Lal Ded
(16th century?)

1 Like water in goblets of unbaked clay
I drip out slowly,
and dry.   Untitled,
Willis Barnstone, tr.;
A Book of Women Poets,
Aliki and Willis Barnstone,
eds.   1980

2 I came by the way
but didn't go back by the way.
Untitled,
Willis Barnstone, tr., op. cit.

273. Agnes the Martyr
(fl. 1500–1535)

1 O Eternall Governour, vouchsafe to open
the gates of heaven once shut up against all
the inhabitants of the earth. . . .
"The praier of Agnes the Martyr
at hir death,"
*The Monument of Matrones
conteining seven severall Lamps
of Virginitie, or distinct
treatises . . . ,*
Vol. I, Thomas Bentley,
ed.   1582

274. Honor Lisle
(c.1500–1550)

1 Pity moveth me to write.
Letter to
Thomas Cromwell (1533),
Quoted in *Letters of Royal and
Illustrious Ladies of Great Britain*,
Vol. II, Mary Everett Wood
Green, ed.   1846

2 I was . . . sorry for your departing, and that
you would tarry no longer at my desire; but
my lord of Winchester and you will do
nothing after a woman's advice.
Letter to Thomas Thirlby (1538),
op. cit., Vol. III

3 . . . his grace [Edward VI] is the goodliest
babe that ever I set mine eye upon. I pray
God make him an old man, for I think I
should never be weary of looking on him.
Letter to Arthur Plantagenet
(1538),
op. cit.

4 If I be driven to it, I must and will not fail to
speak that which shall stand with
reason. . . .   Ibid.

5 My lord, you will me to be plain with my
Lord Privy Seal [Cromwell] . . . the truth is
so have [I] been, but how he handled me
and shook me up, I will not now write, nor
it is not to be written.   Ibid.

6 My Lord, I beseech you keep my letters close, or burn them; for though I have sorrows, I would no creature should be partaker, nor of knowledge with me.
Ibid.

7 Good my lord, whereas in my former letters I have written to you that you should write to me with your own hand, whereof two lines should be more comfort to me than a hundred of another man's hand. . . .
Letter to Arthur Plantagenet (1539), op. cit.

8 . . . use and behave yourself towards his majesty that it may be for the increase of your honour and profit. For now is your time or never.
Ibid.

275.   Caterina Cibo
(1501–1557)

1 . . . all creatures are flames of love.
Quoted in *Seven Dialogues* by Bernardino Orchino (n.d.); cited in *Women of the Reformation,* Vol. I: *Germany and Italy,* by Roland H. Bainton   1971

2 We have but a little knowledge of God. . . . We are like bats who cannot look upon the light of the sun. God is infinite, immense, uncircumscribed, but our intellect is finite, limited, imprisoned in this body of darkness, tainted with primal sin.
Ibid.

3 I will live without love of any created thing . . . I will cast myself wholly into the arms of the crucified . . . I will place my reliance on the merits and glory of all the angels, the saints in paradise, the Madonna in glory . . . I will rejoice in the divine perfections.
Ibid.

4 I will flee evil and seek good and, even though I should suffer an infinite number of indignities, every instant I will forgive them all in Christ into whom I am transformed.
Ibid.

276.   Maria of Hungary and Bohemia
(1505–1558)

1 Full well I know
God is my sword,
And of my Lord
None is me relieving.   Untitled, St. 1 (1529), *Women of the Reformation,* Vol. III: *From Spain to Scandinavia,* by Roland H. Bainton   1977

2 As one and one must equal twice
So sure is Jesus Christ.   Ibid., St. 4

3 World take the field.
God is my shield.   Ibid., St. 5

277.   Mihri Hatun
(?–1506)

1 At one glance
I love you
With a thousand hearts   Untitled, St. 1, Tâlat S. Halman, tr.; *The Penguin Book of Women Poets,* Carol Cosman, Joan Keefe and Kathleen Weaver, eds.   1978

2 Let the zealots think
Loving is sinful
Never mind
Let me burn in the hellfire
Of that sin   Ibid., St. 3

278.   Hwang Chin-i
(c.1506–1544)

1 I cut in two
A long November night   Untitled, Peter H. Lee, tr.; *The Penguin Book of Women Poets,* Carol Cosman, Joan Keefe and Kathleen Weaver, eds.   1978

2 Mountains are steadfast but the mountain
  streams
Go by, go by,
And yesterdays are like the rushing
  streams,
They fly, they fly,
And the great heroes, famous for a day,
They die, they die.   Untitled,
                    Peter H. Lee, tr., op. cit.

279. Ann Boleyn
(1507–1536)

1 Commend me to the king, and tell him he is
constant in his course of advancing me;
from a private gentlewoman he made me a
marquise, and from a marquise a queen;
and now, as he had left no higher degree of
earthly honour, he hath made me a martyr.
                    (May 19, 1536),
                    Quoted in
                    Apophthagmes New and Old,
                    No. 9, Francis Bacon   1625

2 I will rather lose my life than my virtue,
which will be the greatest and best part of
the dowry I shall bring my husband.
                    Letter to Henry VIII,
                    Quoted in
                    Women of Beauty and Heroism
                    by Frank B. Goodrich   1858

3 Your wife I cannot be, both in respect of
mine own unworthiness, and also because
you have a queen already; your mistress I
will not be.   Ibid.

4 Try me, good king, but let me have a lawful
trial, and let not my sworn enemies sit as
my accusers and judges; yea, let me receive
an open trial, for my truth shall fear no
open shame. . . .   Letter to Henry VIII
                    from the Tower of London
                    (May 6, 1536),
                    op. cit.

5 Oh, Father! oh, Creator! Thou who art the
way, the life and the truth, thou knowest
whether I have deserved this death!
                    Spoken at her trial
                    (May 16, 1536),
                    op. cit.

6 Farewell my pleasures past,
Welcome my present pain,
I feel my torments so increase,
That life cannot remain.   Untitled
                    (May 17, 1536),
                    op. cit.

7 I have heard say the executioner is very
good, and I have a little neck.
                    Ibid. (May 19, 1536),
                    op. cit.

8 Alas! poor head, in a very brief space thou
wilt roll in the dust upon the scaffold; and
as in life thou didst not merit to wear the
crown of a queen, so in death thou deservest
not better doom than this.*
                    Spoken at her execution
                    (May 19, 1536),
                    op. cit.

*The linen cap she placed over her head before submitting to the executioner.

9 Inexhaustible as is the treasury of your
majesty's bounties, I pray you to consider
that it cannot be sufficient to your
generosity; for if you recompense so slight a
conversation by gifts so great, what will you
be able to do for those who are ready to
consecrate their entire obedience to your
desires.
                    Letter to Henry VIII (1527),
                    Quoted in *Letters of Royal and
                    Illustrious Ladies of Great Britain*,
                    Vol. II, Mary Anne Everett
                    Wood Green, ed.   1846

10 For the future, I shall rely on nothing but the protection of Heaven and the love of my dear king, which alone will be able to set right again those plans which you have broken and spoiled, and to place me in that happy station which God wills, the king so much wishes, and which will be entirely to the advantage of the kingdom.
Letter to Cardinal Wolsey (1529), op. cit.

11 Did I not tell you that whenever you disputed with the Queen she was sure to have the upper hand? I see that some fine morning you will succumb to her reasoning, and that you will cast me off . . . alas! farewell to my time and youth spent to no purpose at all.   Letter to Henry VIII (1529),
Quoted in *Anne Boleyn* by Marie Louise Bruce   1972

12 I wish all Spaniards were at the bottom of the sea.
Letter to Henry VIII (c.1530/31), op. cit.

13 What will be, will be, grumble who may. (*Ainsi sera, groigne qui groigne.*)
Motto embroidered on servants' livery (c.1530/31), op. cit.

14 You should be more bound to me than man can be to woman. Have I not extricated you from a state of sin?
Letter to Henry VIII (1535), op. cit.

15 The King will marry again [and] he will do with me as with the dead Queen.
Reported in dispatches of Chapuys* (1536), op. cit.

*See 260:10.

16 I am her death, as she is mine.
Said of Catherine of Aragon's death (January 1536), op. cit.

17 The people will have no difficulty in finding a nickname for me, I shall be Queen Anne Lack-Head.
Spoken at her execution (May 19, 1536), op. cit.

18 Defiled is my name full sore
  Through cruel spite and false report,
That I may say for evermore,
  Farewell, my joy! adieu comfort!
For wrongfully ye judge of me
  Unto my fame a mortal wound,
Say what ye list, it will not be,
  Ye seek for that can not be found.
"Defiled Is My Name Full Sore," in toto, *The Women Poets in English*, Ann Stanford, ed.   1972

19 O Death, rock me asleep,
  Bring me to quiet rest,
Let pass my weary guiltless ghost
  Out of my careful breast.
"O Death, Rock Me Asleep," St. 1, op. cit.

20 Death doth draw nigh;
There is no remedy.   Ibid., St. 2

280.   Elisabeth of Braunschweig
(1510–1558)

1 Obey God, the emperor, and your mother.
Treatise on government written for her son, Erich II, Quoted in *Women of the Reformation*, Vol. I: *Germany and Italy*, by Roland H. Bainton   1971

2 O Lord God, to whom have I given birth? Whom have I reared? . . . My son has brought me to bed. If he keeps on, he will bring me to the grave. Letter to Antonius Corvinus, op. cit.

3 Woe, woe, woe and again woe to you if you do not change.   Letter to her son, op. cit.

4 Better be hurt than to hurt.

> Hymn,
> op. cit.

5 To Thee O God alone be praise
And thanks to Thee for grace,
That Thou hast vouchsafed to me
To look on Katherine's face.

The jewels she wears are godliness.
She helps me bear my cross.
She will have reward of thee.
She counts the world but dross.

> Poem on her daughter,
> Katherine,
> Sts. 1, 2, op. cit.

6 No one without the experience knows the anguish which children can cause and yet be loved.

> From *Book of Consolation for Widows*,
> op. cit.

281. Marina de Guevara
(c.1510–1559)

1 Better than the castigation of the flesh is the overcoming of pride and anger.

> Testimony before the Inquisition
> (1558/59),
> *Women of the Reformation*,
> Vol. III: *From Spain to Scandinavia*,
> by Roland H. Bainton 1977

2 To bring the heart into tune with God is better than audible prayer.

> Ibid.

3 When a sister was upset over losing her rosary, I said maybe God had hidden it from her to keep her from interminable babbling.

> Ibid.

282. Renée de France
(1510–1575)

1 . . . Satan is the father of lies and God of the truth. . . .

> Letter to John Calvin
> (1564),
> Quoted in *Queen of Navarre:
> Jeanne d'Albret*
> by Nancy Lyman
> Roelker 1968

2 Had I had a beard I would have been the King of France. I have been defrauded by that confounded Salic law.*

> Quoted in *Women of the Reformation*,
> Vol. I: *Germany and Italy*,
> by Roland H. Bainton 1971

*European law of succession (derived from a 5th-century Frankish code) preventing women from succeeding to a throne.

3 If there are any on earth rejected by God, it is those who pervert the truth with their insolent lies.

> Letter to John Calvin (1563),
> op. cit.

283. Giulia Gonzaga
(1513–1566)

1 What mad credulity is ours! How infinite is the cupidity of mortals!

> Letter to Livia
> Negra,
> Quoted in *A Princess of the
> Italian Reformation:
> Giulia Gonzaga*
> by Christopher Hare* 1912

*Pseudonym of Marian Andrews.

2 . . . what should we do if we had to remain in this world perpetually? We cannot inhabit a house for three days in this miserable world without being dissatisfied.

> Ibid.

3 Truly, we are like drunkards, who, the more they drink, the more their thirst grows . . . we cannot remember that we are mortal, and that we have one day to leave all things behind us. . . .

> Ibid.

4 That which is acquired by evil means is no gain, but a great and dangerous loss.

           Ibid.

5 The promises of the alchemist are like those of the astrologers, who boast that they can foretell future things, and do not even know the present or the past. . . . I do not know whether their fraud is more shameful, or our folly in believing, as we do. . . .

           Ibid.

284. Catherine Parr
(1513–1548)

1 He as a loving father, of most abundant and high goodness, hath heaped upon me, innumerable benefits: and I contrary, have heaped manifold sins, despising that which was good, holy, pleasant, and acceptable in His sight, and choosing that which was delicious, pleasant, and acceptable to my sight. "The Lamentation on or Complaint
of a Sinner,"
The Lamentation of a Sinner
1545

2 A goodly example and lesson for us to follow at all times and seasons, as well in prosperity as in adversity, to have no will but God's will. . . . But we be yet so carnal and fleshly, that we run headlong like unbridled colts, without snaffle or bit.

If we had the love of God printed in our hearts, it would keep us back from running astray. And until such time as it pleases God to send us this bit to hold us in, we shall never run the right way, although we speak and talk never so much of God and His word.   *Ibid.*

3 Verily if all sorts of people would look to their own vocation and ordain the same according to Christ's doctrine, we should not have so many eyes and ears to other men's faults as we have.   *Ibid.*

4 We be so busy and glad to find and espy out other men's doings that we forget and can have no time to weigh and ponder our own.

           Ibid.

5 We ought first to reform, and then we shall the better help another with the straw out of his eyes.   *Ibid.*

6 I know the world to be a blind Judge, and the praises thereof vain, and of little moment.   *Ibid.*

7 We humbly beseech thee (O Lord God of Hosts) so to turn the hearts of our enemies to the desire of peace, that no Christian blood be spilt, or else grant (O Lord) that with small effusion of blood, and to the little hurt and damage of innocents, we may to thy glory obtain victory and that the wars being soon ended, we may all with one heart and mind knit together in concord and unity. "A Prayer for Men to Say
Entering into Battle,"
Prayers and Meditations
1545

285. Chiara Cantarini Matraini
(1514–post-1597)

1 Left without you my sweet life
Lost in the perilous waves
Of the ocean of my tears
I cannot reach the shore. Untitled sonnet,
Claudia Alexander with Carlo
DiMaio, trs.;
from *Poemas* (1560),
Poesia italiana: il cinquecento,
Giulio Ferroni, ed. 1978

2 Return soul of the sky, candid moon
To the first sphere, shining and beautiful,
And with your customary brilliance restore
The crown of silver to the darkened sky
Untitled sonnet,
op. cit.

3 Destroy with firm and righteous scorn
Every impious and vile mist which desires
to darken
Your lucid sky, clear and serene.

           Ibid.

4 . . . contrary and fierce winds
That drive the waves against these cliffs
Seem to me like strong and haughty enemies

To my serene and noble thoughts.
Untitled sonnet,
op. cit.

5 . . . that weak and tired vessel finding
Itself with broken mast and sail
Bereft of helmsman, tossed by monstrous
waves,
Seems like my soul deprived of light, bereft
of every hope.   Ibid.

286.   Teresa of Avila
(1515–1582)

1 . . . how great was the vanity of the world
[which] would shortly end.
Quoted in
Distinguished Women Writers
by Virginia Moore   1934

2 The hour I have long wished for is now
come.   Last words (1582),
op. cit.

3 We are not angels and we have bodies. To
want to become angels while we are still on
earth . . . is ridiculous.
"Life" (1562),
*The Complete Works of
Saint Teresa of Jesus*,
Vol. I, E. Allison Peers, ed. and tr.
1946

4 How is it that there are not many who are
led by sermons to forsake open sin? Do you
know what I think? That is because preach-
ers have too much worldly wisdom. They
are not like the Apostles, flinging it all aside
and catching fire with love of God; and so
their flame gives little heat.   . Ibid.

5 Oh, God help me! What a miserable life is
this! There is no happiness that is secure
and nothing that does not change.
Ibid.

6 . . . to those who love God in truth and
have put aside the things of this world
death must come very gently.
Ibid.

7 Everything I see is like a dream and what I
see with my bodily eyes is a mockery.
Ibid.

8 I only wish I could write with both hands,
so as not to forget one thing while I am saying another. "Way of Perfection," Ch. 20
(1579),
op. cit., Vol. II

9 . . . I believe that honour and money nearly
always go together . . . seldom or *never* is a
poor man honoured by the world; however
worthy of honour he may be, he is apt
rather to be despised by it.
Ibid., Ch. 22

10 When that sweet Huntsman from above
First wounded me and left me prone,
Into the very arms of Love
My stricken soul forthwith was thrown.
"Yo toda me entregué y di . . . ,"
St. 1, op. cit., Vol. III

11 Happy the heart where love has come to
birth   "Dichoso el corazon
enamorado . . . ,"
op. cit.

12 Life has no beginning
Till to Heaven we go.
Grant me, O my Saviour,
Thither soon to fly
"Cuan triste es, Dios mio . . . ,"
St. 5, op. cit.

13 "Oh, why do those who ask for Him
Resist Him when He deigns to come?"
"Ah, pastores que velais . . . ,"
St. 4, op. cit.

14 "My shepherd-boy, go, see who's calling."
" 'Tis angels, and the day is dawning." '
"Mi gallejo, mira quien llama,"
refrain, op. cit.

15 Must His cruel torments
At his birth begin?
Yes, for He is dying
To remove our sin.
What a mighty Shepherd
Have we, by my fay!

Dominguillo, eh!   "Vertiendo esta
                              sangre . . . ,"
                            St. 2, op. cit.

16 The Cross is like an olive-tree,
Fair to the sight,
Whereof the holy oil provides
Healing and light.   "En la cruz esta la
                            vida . . . ,"
                            St. 3, op. cit.

17 Let the timorous coward
Gaze upon this maid,*
Blind to wealth and beauty,
When he is afraid.
Persecutions met her,
War was everywhere,
But she suffered bravely
With a courage rare.   "O gran amadora,"
                            St. 3, op. cit.

*The Virgin Mary.

18 My laurel wreath is wov'n of scorn;
In sorrows all my joys reside;
I'm noblest when I'm flung aside;
In solitude my joy is born.
         "Sea mi gozo en el llanto,"
                            St. 8, op. cit.

19 Drive away whate'er molests you
With fervent prayer;
Nothing else so surely tests you
If love is there.   "Pues nos dais vestido
                            nuevo,"
                            St. 2, op. cit.

20 I live, yet no true life I know,
And, living thus expectantly,
I die because I do not die.
             "Vivo sin vivir el mi,"
      prefatory stanza (1571), op. cit.

21 Until this present life be o'er
We cannot savour life at all.
                         Ibid., St. 7

22 How is it, Lord, that we are cowards in everything save in opposing Thee?
        "Exclamations of Soul to God"
                       (1569),
                Selected Writings of
                 St. Teresa of Avila,
      E. Allison Peers, tr.; William J.
           Doheny, ed.   1950

23 O incomprehensible Wisdom! In truth Thou needest all the love which Thou hast for Thy creatures to enable Thee to endure such folly and to await our recovery. . . .
                               Ibid.

24 Oh, what incurable madness, my God, that we should use what Thou givest us for serving the devil!   Ibid.

25 It is true that we cannot be free from sin, but at least let our sins not be always the same. . . .   "Conception of Love of God"
                         (1571),
                         op. cit.

26 If we plant a flower or a shrub and water it daily it will grow so tall that in time we shall need a spade and a hoe to uproot it. It is just so, I think, when we commit a fault, however small, each day, and do not cure ourselves of it.   Ibid.

27 In speaking of the soul we must always think of it as spacious, ample, and lofty. . . . Since God has given it such dignity, it must be allowed to roam. . . . It must not be compelled to remain for a long time in one single room—not, at least, unless it is in the room of self-knowledge. "Interior Castle"
                         (1577),
                         op. cit.

28 Humility must always be doing its work like a bee making its honey in the hive: without humility all will be lost.
                               Ibid.

29 There seem to me a great many blessings which come from true poverty and I should be sorry to be deprived of them.
              "Spiritual Relations"
                 (1560–1582),
                         op. cit.

30 I used to think I needed other people and I had more confidence in worldly aids, but now I clearly realize that they are none of them of any more use than dry rosemary twigs and that we shall get no safety by leaning on them, for at the least breath of opposition or slander they break.
                               Ibid.

31 Oh, whatever will become of the poor souls who are in hell and will never get out of it? For if a person does no more than pass from one trial to another there seems to be some relief even in the very change.
      "The Book of Foundations"
      (1573–1582),
      op. cit.

32 Untilled soil, however fertile it may be, will bear thistles and thorns; and so it is with man's mind.   "Maxims for Her Nuns,"
      op. cit.

33 Never be importunate, especially about things of little moment.   Ibid.

34 Accustom yourself continually to make many acts of love, for they enkindle and melt the soul.   Ibid.

35 Be gentle to all and stern with yourself.
      Ibid.

36 Remember that you have only one soul; that you have only one death to die; that you have only one life, which is short and has to be lived by you alone; and there is only one glory, which is eternal. If you do this, there will be many things about which you care nothing.   Ibid.

37 My Lord, it is time to set out; may the journey be a propitious one and may Thy will be done.   Quoted by Sister Ana de San Bartoleme (two days before St. Teresa's death),
      op. cit.

38 O King of glory, Lord of Lords, Emperor of Emperors, holy of the holiest, power above all wisdoms. Truth itself art Thou and riches. Of thy reign there is no end. Thy perfections cease not. Infinite are they above all understanding, a bottomless ocean of wonders, a loveliness comprising all beauties and strength.   Letter,
      Quoted in *Women of the Reformation*,
      Vol. III: *From Spain to Scandinavia*,
      by Roland H. Bainton   1977

39 . . . about the injunction of the Apostle Paul that women should keep silent in church? Don't go by one text only.
      Ibid.

40 Let nothing disturb thee,
Nothing affright thee;
All things are passing;
God never changeth.
Patient endurance
Attaineth to all things;
Who God possesseth
In nothing is wanting;
Alone God sufficeth.   "Nada te turbe"
      ("Nothing disturbs thee"; aka
      "Saint Teresa's Bookmark"),
      in toto, Henry Wadsworth
      Longfellow, tr.;
      An Anthology of Spanish Poetry,
      John A. Crow, ed.   1979

41 If, Lord, Thy love for me is strong
As this which binds me unto Thee,
What holds me from Thee, Lord, so long,
What holds Thee, Lord, so long from me?
      "Si el amor que me teneis" ("If,
      Lord, thy love for me is strong"),
      St. 1, Arthur Symons, tr., op. cit.

42 Lord, make my soul Thine own abode,
And I will build a nest so sweet
It may not be too poor for God.
      Ibid., St. 3

43 A soul in God hidden from sin
What more desires for thee remain,
Save but to love, and love again,
And, all on flame with love within,
Love on, and turn to love again?
      Ibid., St. 4

44 God walks among the pots and pipkins.
      Attributed, n.d.

287.   Mary I of England
(1516–1558)

1 When I am dead and opened, you shall find "Calais" lying in my heart.
      Quoted in *Chronicles*,
      Vol. III, by Raphael
      Holinshed   1585

2 I confess the frailty of my youth to be such, that by negligence I may forget myself, without good counsel.　Letter to Thomas Cromwell (1538), Quoted in *Letters of Royal and Illustrious Ladies,* Vol. II, Mary Anne Everett Wood Green, ed.　1846

3 I have been often minded to have written to your highness before this time, which to do mine old diseased rheumatic head would by no means let me, nor presently scarce will.　Letter to her brother, Edward VI (1549), op. cit.

4 The well bringing up of the youth and company of the same is, to the increase of thy service of God, and the common wealth of our *whole* realm.　Letter (1558), op. cit.

5 . . . as for your new books,* I thank God I never read any of them. I never did, nor ever will do.　Letter to the Bishop of London (c.1551),* Quoted in *Catherine of Aragon* by Garrett Mattingly　1942

*In reply to being asked about her refusal to give up the mass and adopt the new Protestant prayer book.

6 . . . there are two things only, soul and body, My soul I offer to God, and my body to your Majesty's service.　Letter to Edward VI (c.1552), op. cit.

7 May it please you to take away my life rather than the old religion.　Ibid.

288.　Catherine de Medici
(1519–1589)

1 Ah, sentiments of mercy are in unison with a woman's heart.　Quoted in *The Huguenots in France and America,* Vol. I, Ch. 3, by Hannah Farnham Lee　1843

2 . . . suppress this violence of emotion. I have always found it best *to appear to yield.* Assume a seeming conformity to your husband's will, even attend mass, and you will more easily get the reins into your own hands.　Remark to Queen of Navarre, Op. cit., Ch. 7

3 The King of Navarre was resolved to have nut for nut, but mine is the better kernelled.　Op. cit., Ch. 14

4 Whenever that period arrives, how gladly shall we exchange the cannon's roar, and the shrill voice of the trumpet, for the soft music of the harp.　Op. cit., ch. 17

5 Man cannot judge your motives; God alone sees the heart. Though now of a different faith, we are still children of the same family. There is but one God and one Saviour, and at the throne of heaven our prayers must meet.　Letter to Henry IV, op. cit., Ch. 19

6 The true grandeur and excellence of a prince, my very dear sister, does not consist in honors, in gold, in purple, and other luxuries of fortune, but in prudence, wisdom, and knowledge. And by so much as the prince wishes to differ from his people in his mode and fashion of living, by so much should he be removed from the foolish opinions of the vulgar.　Letter to Mary, Queen of Scots (c.1554), Quoted in *The Medici* by G. F. Young　1930

7 *Lachrymae hinc, hinc dolor.* (Tears henceforth, henceforth sadness.)　Motto (1559), op. cit.

8 When I see these poor people burnt, beaten, and tormented, not for thieving or marauding, but simply for upholding their religious opinions, when I see some of them suffer cheerfully, with a glad heart, I am forced to believe that there is something is this which transcendeth human understanding.　Letter regarding persecution of Protestants (1559/60), op. cit.

9 The ashes of the fire which has gone out are still so hot that the least spark will make them leap up into bigger flames than we have ever seen.   Letter to Ambassador of Spain (1561), op. cit.

10 If things were even worse than they are after all this war they might have laid the blame upon the rule of a woman; but if such persons are honest they should blame only the rule of men who desire to play the part of kings. In future, if I am not any more hampered, I hope to show that women have a more sincere determination to preserve the country than those who have plunged it into the miserable condition to which it has been brought.   Letter to Ambassador of Spain (1570), op. cit.

11 ... my daughter ... do not trust so much in the love which you bear your husband and in the honor and the ease which you have at this present moment, as to forget to recommend yourself to Him, who can continue your happiness. ...
Letter to Elizabeth,
Quoted in *Women of Power*
by Mark Strage   1976

12 Although I am oppressed by the natural sorrow of a mother over the loss of the most dear and precious thing in the world—a sorrow which makes me desire to leave all public affairs to find some tranquillity of life—nevertheless, persuaded by the pressing request which my son made to me in his last words to take up the office of Regent for the good of this Crown ... I feel constrained to accept this office.
Acceptance letter (1574), op. cit.

13 ... never did woman who loved her husband succeed in loving his whore. One must call a spade a spade, though the term is an ugly one on the lips.   Letter (1583), op. cit.

289.   Laura Terracina
(c.1519–1577?)

1 ... alas, who has taken you from me?
Who has torn you from my breast so brazenly
And locked such beauty in a little grave?
Untitled sonnet,
Claudia Alexander with Carlo
DiMaio, trs.;
Poesia italiana: il cinquecento,
Giulio Ferroni, ed.   1978

2 ... nothing awaits but further pain;
Tears in my eyes, in my breast ardent fire.
O heaven, how unjust, how wrong, you were.   Ibid.

3 ... I see virtue abondoned
and the Muses enslaved by such baseness
that my brain is nearly overwhelmed.
"Sonnett to Marcantonio
Passero,"
Claudia Alexander, tr., op. cit.

290.   Catherine Willoughby
(1519/20–1580)

1 And now ... marrying by our orders, and without their consents ... I cannot tell what more unkindness one of us might show one another, or wherein we might work more wickedly, than to bring our children into so miserable a state as not to choose, by their own likings. ...
Letter to William Cecil (1550),
Quoted in *Letters of Royal and
Illustrious Ladies
of Great Britain*,
Vol. III, Mary Anne Everett
Wood Green, ed.   1846

2 Undoubtedly the greatest wisdom is not to be too wise. ...
Letter to William Cecil (1559),
Quoted in
Women of the Tudor Age
by Cecilie Goff   1930

3 ... though God wink ... He sleepeth not. ...   Ibid.

4 . . . there is no exception by man's law that may serve against God's.　　Ibid.

5 . . . it is to be feared men have so long worn the Gospel slopewise that they will not gladly have it straight to their legs.　　Ibid.

6 Christ's plain coat without a seam is fairer to the older eyes than all the jaggs* of Germany.　　Ibid.

*A slash made in a garment to show a different color beneath.

7 . . . all creatures embrace liberty and fly servitude. . . .　　Letter to Elizabeth I (1558), Quoted in *My Lady Suffolk* by Evelyn Read　1963

8 . . . I remembered that though men might fail me yet God would be merciful to me. . . .　　Letter to William Cecil (1571), op. cit.

9 . . . my Lady* loves wine, who knows her that knows not that. . . .　　Letter to William Cecil (1578), op. cit.

*Her daughter-in-law, Mary Vere.

10 God is a marvellous man.　　Quoted by Catherine Parr in a letter to Thomas Seymour (c.1548), Cited in *Tudor Women* by Alison Plowdon　1979

291. Anne Askew
(1520–1546)

1 . . . unadvised hasty judgment is a token apparent of a very slender wit.　　Testimony at inquisition (1545), Quoted in *Actes and monuments of these latter and perillous dayes* (aka *The Book of Martyrs*) by John Foxe　1563

2 God has given me the bread of adversity and the water of trouble.　　Letter to King Henry VIII (1546), op. cit.

3 . . . as I am by the law condemned for an evil doer, here I take heaven and earth to record, that I shall die in my innocency. . . .　　Ibid.

4 . . . what God hath charged me with his mouth, that have I shut up in my heart.　　Ibid.

5 Lord open the eyes of their blind hearts, that the truth may take place.　　Remark after being condemned and tortured (1546), op. cit.

6 Farewell, dear friend, and pray, pray, pray!　　Ibid.

7 O friend . . . I marvel not a little what should move you to judge in me so slender a faith as to fear death, which is the end of all misery.　　Letter to John Lacel (1546), op. cit.

8 O Lord! I have more enemies now, than there be hairs on my head: yet Lord, let them never overcome me with vain words, but fight thou, Lord, in my stead, for on thee cast I my care.　　Prayer of Anne Askew (1546), op. cit.

9 Like as the armed knight
Appointed to the field,
With this world will I fight,
And faith shall be my shield.　　"The Ballad Which Anne Askew Made and Sang When She Was in Newgate," St. 1 (1547p), *The Women Poets in English*, Ann Stanford, ed.　1972

10 I am not she that list
My anchor to let fall,
For every drizzling mist,
My ship substantial.　　Ibid., St. 9

11 . . . Lord, I thee desire
For that they do to me,
Let them not taste the hire
Of their iniquity.　　Ibid., St. 14

292.   Madeleine Fradonnet
(c.1520–1587)

1 Distaff, my pride and care, I vow to thee
That I shall love thee ever nor exchange
Thy homely virtue for a pleasure strange
    "To My Distaff,"
    with Catherine Fradonnet,
    Anthology of European Poetry,
    13th to 17th century,
    William Stirling, tr.; Mervyn
    Savill, ed.   1947

2 . . . dear distaff it doth not behove
That I prove to thee my faithful love
Should set aside this honest task of mine:

For when I write, then can I write of thee.
    Ibid.

293.   Pernette du Guillet
(c.1520–1545?)

1 True love, to whom my heart is prey,
How dost thou hold me in thy sway,
That in each day I find no fault
But daily wait for love's assault
    "Song,"
    St. 1, William Stirling, tr. (1947);
    Rymes de Gentille et Vertueuse
    Dame de Pernette due Guillet,
    Lyonaisse (1545)

2 Alas, my friend, when thou art gone,
I have no love to lean upon.
    Ibid., St. 3

3 . . . aid me in this restless ease,
And cure me of love's rare disease.
    Ibid.

4 If they say I love too many,
Passing the time for joy,
Taking my pleasure here and there:
    How should I know?
    "Chanson,"
    St. 2, Joan Keefe with Richard
    Terdiman, trs. (1978), op. cit.

5 . . . if they say that Virtue
Which cloaks you richly
Shines through to me in love:

This I do know

And if they say that Holy Love
Hits me cleanly in the heart,
Never wounding honour:
    This I do know!   Ibid., Sts. 5, 6

6 As the body denies the means to look
Into the spirit or know its force,
Likewise Error for me drew
Around my eyes the blindfold of ignorance
    "Epigram",
    Joan Keefe with Richard
    Terdiman, trs. (1978), op. cit.

7 . . . the closer Good, the less my chance to
see.   Ibid.

8 I no longer need be concerned
whether daylight goes or night comes,
  . . . because my Day,* with tender brilliance,
enlightens me through and through.
    "Epigram 8,"
    Ann Rosalind Jones, tr. (1981),
    op. cit.

*Allusion to the poet Maurice Scève, with whom she had a liaison.

9 The happy outcome of my woe, enflaming
desire, distills two hearts into one. . . .
    "Epigram 13,"
    Ann Rosalind Jones, tr. (1981),
    op. cit.

10 Take it as given that as I am yours, (and
want to be), you are entirely mine.
Certainly, according to our shared good,
You would owe me the same right
    "Epigram 26,"
    Ann Rosalind Jones, tr. (1981),
    op. cit.

11 If I am no longer as I used to be, blame time
for it, which has taught me that by treating
me harshly, as a master, you will never win
the upper hand. . . .   "Epigram 28,"
    Ann Rosalind Jones, tr. (1981),
    op. cit.

12 O blessed Day, she whom you deigned to set afire must value you highly, always careful as you are to bring back to the light those whom dark night has led astray.

> "Chanson 9,"
> Ann Rosalind Jones, tr. (1981),
> op. cit.

13 Not that I wish to drive him left and right,
Command him like a workman in my hire;
But I would wish, to both our hearts' delight,
For his will to be joined with my desire.

> "Not that I Wish to Take the
> Liberty,"
> Raymond Oliver, tr. (1983),
> op. cit.

294.   Isabella da Morra
(1520–1546)

1 Once more, O arid valley
O wild river, O wretched, barbarous stones
You shall hear my eternal pain and weeping.

> Untitled sonnet,
> Claudia Alexander with Carlo
> DiMaio, trs.;
> *Poesia italiana: il cinquecento*,
> Giulio Ferroni, ed.   1978

2 . . . eternal fortune never rests. . . .

> Ibid.

3 Turbid Siri,* now that my bitter end is here, proclaim my sorrow. . . .

. . . .

Tumultuously incite your waves
And say, "Not merely tears, but the copious weeping
Of Isabella increased me while she lived.

> Untitled poem,
> Claudia Alexander with Carlo
> DiMaio, trs., op. cit.

*A river running between Calabria and Basilicata in southern Italy.

295.   Lucia dall'Oro Bertana
(1521–1567)

1 . . . bless me Muse and I will go
Through thick woods and over pleasant hills

. . . .

To bright fountains where I will find mercy.

> Sonnet on her marriage,
> Claudia Alexander, tr.;
> Quoted in *Women's Record*
> by Sarah Josepha Hale   1855

296.   Ippolita Castiglione
(?–1521)

1 Alas, alas! how different flows,
With thee and me, the time away!
Not that I wish thee sad, heaven knows;
    Still, if thou canst be light and gay,
I only know that without thee,
The sun himself is dark to me.

> Untitled, to her husband, St. 2,
> Quoted in *Biography of
> Distinguished Women*
> by Sarah Josepha Hale   1876

2 My dear Lord, —I have got a little daughter, of which I think you will not be sorry. I have been much worse than I was last time, and have had three attacks of high fever, but to-day I feel better, and hope to have no more trouble. I will not try to write more, lest I overdo myself, but commend myself to you with all my heart— Your wife who is a little tired out with pain, your Ippolita.

> Letter to Baldassare Castiglione,
> her husband (August 24, 1521;
> four days before her death),
> Quoted in *Isabella D'Este*
> by Julia Cartwright   1903

297. Lucrezia Gonzaga
(1522–pre-1552)

1 . . . a poor man's life is like sailing near the coast, whereas that of a rich man resembles the condition of those who are in the main sea. The former can easily throw a cable on the shore, and bring their ship safe into a harbour; whereas the latter cannot do it without much danger and difficulty.
Letter to Hortensio Lando,
Quoted in *Women's Record*
by Sarah Josepha Hale 1855

2 . . . all things are good which are according to nature, and what is there more natural to all men than death? Letter to Ippolita Gonzaga (c.1552),
Quoted in *A Princess of the Italian Reformation: Giulia Gonzaga*
by Christopher Hare* 1912
*Pseudonym of Marian Andrews.

3 This world . . . is a very deep and dark vale of tears, full of troubles, and it is a fortunate adventure to leave it happily.
Ibid.

4 Ah, how many times have I smiled at those who do not know that to lament for the irreparable is rather a sign of folly than of true grief. . . . Ibid.

5 . . . he alone acts wisely who, being mortal, expects nothing from this life of ours but mortal things. Ibid.

298. Luisa Sigea
(1522–1560)

1 You have written me a letter which . . . exudes the fragrance of a life unspotted, which I would inhale were I not so spoiled by the stench of the human as to be incapable of the divine. . . . Letter to a friend (n.d.),
Women of the Reformation,
Vol. III: *From Spain to Scandinavia,*
by Roland H. Bainton 1977

2 If you have for virtue a passionate love—a simple love is not enough—you must be willing to die for it—then will it bring naught but blessedness and felicity.
"Dialogue of Blesilla and Flaminia,"
op. cit.

3 We have our wings . . . withdraw from the throng with a few elect spirits . . . certain figures against whom to measure yourself.
Ibid.

4 Blaze with the fire that is never extinguished. Ibid.

5 Love is the way, love by which all is brought into existence. By such fervent love we are upheld. Ibid.

299. Gaspara Stampa
(1523–1554)

1 Love made me such that I live in fire
like a new salamander on earth
or like that other rare creature, the Phoenix,
who expires and rises at the same time.
Untitled sonnet,
Lynne Lawner, tr.;
The Penguin Book of Women Poets,
Carol Cosman, Joan Keefe and
Kathleen Weaver, eds. 1978

2 I hate who loves me, love who scorns me.
Untitled sonnet,
Lynne Lawner, tr., op. cit.

3 . . . Love, in your school one learns
to do the opposite of what seems right
Ibid.

4 If I could believe that death
would put an end to all this suffering,
then certainly I'd seek it. . . .
Untitled sonnet,
Lynne Lawner, tr., op. cit.

5 You surpass my rejoicing only in these ways:
your glory is eternal and fixed in space,

while mine can pass by in a few days.
> Untitled sonnet,
> J. Vitiello, tr.;
> *A Book of Women Poets*,
> Aliki and Willis Barnstone, eds.
> 1980

6   Often when alone I liken my lord
to the cosmos: his lovely brow the sun,
his eyes the stars, the sound of his words
one
harmony, Lord Apollo's concord
> Untitled sonnet,
> J. Vitiello, tr., op. cit.

7   O love, what strange and wonderful fits:
one sole thing, one beauty alone,
can give me life and deprive me of wits.
> Untitled sonnet,
> J. Vitiello, tr., op. cit.

8 ultimately perfect in word and deed,
except, alas! in love, all lies and spite.
> Untitled sonnet,
> J. Vitiello, tr., op. cit.

9 Before the bitter parting,
my soul, invited to so cruel a fast,
craves better nourishment
to sustain such absence   "Hunger,"
> Brenda Webster, tr.;
> *Women Poets of the World*,
> Joanna Bankier and Deirdre
> Lashgari, eds.   1983

10 . . . the words whose harmonies are sweeter
than those of Paradise.   Ibid.

11 Deeply repentant of my sinful ways
And of my trivial, manifold desires,
Of squandering, alas, these few brief days
Of fugitive life in tending love's vain fires
> Untitled sonnet,
> Lorna de'Lucchi, tr., op. cit.

12 And from this whirlpool rescue me, for I
Without Thine aid could never reach the
land   Ibid.

300.   Louise Labé
(1524/25–1566)

1 Of thee do I complain whose myriad fires

Have every way possessed my whole
desires,
Though thou impervious to flame hast
stayed.   Untitled sonnet,
> *Anthology of European Poetry*,
> Vol. I: *13th to 17th centuries*,
> William Stirling, tr., Mervyn
> Savill, ed.   1947

2 O terrible fate! Suffering the scorpion to
feast
on me, I seek protection from the pain
of poison by appealing to the beast
that stings me.   Sonnet I,
> *Oeuvres* (1555),
> Willis Barnstone, tr.;
> *A Book of Women Poets*,
> Aliki and Willis Barnstone, eds.
> 1980

3 O lamentations, O obstinate desires,
O wasted time, O grief scattered about,
O thousand deaths. . . .   Sonnet II,
> Willis Barnstone, tr., op. cit.

4 A woman's heart always has a burned
mark.   Ibid.

5 However much Love tries to batter us
our force congeals at every impetus,
becoming fresh with each attacking prong.
> Sonnet IV,
> Willis Barnstone, tr., op. cit.

6 But people have a feeble spirit. They need
to lie down, fade away, and deeply feed
on sleep.   Sonnet V,
> Aliki and Willis Barnstone, trs.,
> op. cit.

7 Where are you soul I love and sanctify?
> Sonnet VII,
> Willis Barnstone, tr., op. cit.

8 I live, I die, I burn myself and drown.
> Sonnet VIII,
> Willis Barnstone, tr., op. cit.

9 Let each night be an agent that will tie
me to my dream.   Sonnet IX,
> Willis Barnstone, tr., op. cit.

10 small gardens filled with amorous blossoms
where

felonious darts of Love spin through the air.
Sonnet XI,
Willis Barnstone, tr., op. cit.

11　... my arms ... sleeping on the nape
of his neck, like ivy circling a tree
Sonnet XIII,
Aliki and Willis Barnstone, trs.,
op. cit.

12　Now birds and trees perform their books
of wonder, passersby hear wondrous news
and are less sad.　　　　　Sonnet XV,
Willis Barnstone, tr., op. cit.

13　Games, masques, tournaments bore me and
I sigh
and dream no beauty that is not of you.
Sonnet XVII,*
op. cit.

*Quotations 13–21 tr. by Willis Barnstone.

14　Only outside my body can I live
or else in exile like a fugitive.
Ibid.

15　Kiss me again, rekiss me, kiss me more,
give me your most consuming, tasty one,
give me your sensual kiss, a savory one,
I'll give you back four burning at the core.
Sonnet XVIII,
op. cit.

16　Love, please allow a little madness.
Ibid.

17　Who would have ever dreamed that something born
of destiny and heaven could be bad?
Sonnet XX,
op. cit.

18　I think that powers out of hell have torn
the world and schemed the shipwreck of my
life.　　　　　　　　　　　　Ibid.

19　What grandeur makes a man seem venerable?
What hair? What color of his skin? What
size?
What kind of glance is best? What honeyed
eyes?　　　　　　　　Sonnet XXI,
op. cit.

20　Your brutal goal was to make *me* a slave

beneath the ruse of being served by you.
Pardon me, friend, and for once hear me
through:
I am outrage with anger and I rave.
Sonnet XXIII,
op. cit.

21　Don't blame me, ladies, if I've loved. No
sneers
if I have felt a thousand torches burn
Sonnet XXIV,
op. cit.

301.　Cicely Ormes
(c.1525–1557)

1　... this my death is and shall be a witness
of my faith unto you all here present. Good
People! as many of you as believe as I believe, pray for me.　　　　Spoken at her
execution (September 23, 1557),
Quoted in *Actes and monuments
of these latter and perillous dayes*
(aka *The Book of Martyrs*)
by John Foxe　　　1563

2　Welcome the sweet cross of Christ.
Ibid.

302.　Olimpia Morata
(1526–1555)

1　Never does the same desire enlist us all.
Tastes are not conferred by Zeus on all
alike.　　　　　　　　Untitled (c.1542),
Jules Bonnet and Roland H.
Bainton, trs.;
Women of the Reformation,
Vol. I: *Germany and Italy*,
by Roland H. Bainton　　　1971

2　I, a woman, have dropped the symbols of
my sex,
Yarn, shuttle, basket, thread
Ibid.

3　King of kings and Lord of lords, creator of
male and female
Thou has given to the first man a mate that
the race perish not.

Thou hast willed that fallen humanity be
the mystical bride of thy Son,
Who for her has given his life,
Spread now harmony and peace over those
united in this hour,
For of thine ordinance is the nuptial couch.
Untitled (1550),
op. cit.

4 Love is full of solicitous fear.
Letter to her husband (1550),
op. cit.

5 Do you think that God can lie? Why would
he make so many promises to all who call
upon his name if he did not intend to fulfill
them? Letter (c.1552),
op. cit.

6 It is not enough to know the history of
Christ. The devil knows that. It must be the
sort of faith which is active in love.
Letter to Anne, Duchess of
Guise (c.1552),
op. cit.

7 Remembering that the span of our life is but
toil and trouble and we soon fly away, may
I give myself to the contemplation of things
eternal. Letter to her sister, Vittoria
(c.1553),
op. cit.

8 God is a light to our feet. Let us not be troubled by men, for what is man if not a fleeting shadow, a windblown leaf, a fading
flower, and vanishing smoke!
Last letter, to Lavinia della
Rovere (1555),
op. cit.

9 OLIMPIA. I do indeed immerse myself in
books that I may not waste the time which
God has given me. Untitled dialogue
between Olimpia and Lavinia
della Rovere,
op. cit.

10 OLIMPIA. I have been lauded to the skies because I read so many authors, but I know
my ignorance. Ibid.

11 OLIMPIA. I have been in danger of forgetting
God. Ibid.

12 LAVINIA. Oh God. . . . Our feeble human
nature cannot ascend to things divine unless thy Spirit come on the wings of the
wind to bestow thy wisdom.
Ibid.

13 PHILOTINA. As a young girl . . . I thought
there would be no greater blessing in life
than to have a loving husband. That is why
I married, but it has not worked out that
way and I am grieving. Dialogue between
Philotina and Theophila,
op. cit.

14 THEOPHILA. God gives to some and with-
holds from others, and it is not for us to
judge. . . . I can give you no better counsel
than to endure with patience. Remember
there is no thirst which shall not be as-
suaged. Ibid.

303.   Jeanne d'Albret
(1528–1572)

1 . . . arms once taken up should never be
laid down, but upon one of three conditions—a safe peace, a complete victory, or
an honourable death.
Quoted in Biography
of Distinguished Women
by Sarah Josepha Hale   1876

2 It is the nature of love to be very cruel, I
speak from much experience. . . .
Letter to Marguerite de Navarre,
her mother (c.1549),
Quoted in Queen of Navarre:
Jeanne d'Albret
by Nancy Lyman
Roelker   1968

3 I well know that I am serving God, whose
grace surrounds my lands more surely than
the great ocean England. Letter to
George, Cardinal d'Armagnac
(1563),
op. cit.

4 I forgive you the past, hoping that my clemency will produce fruits worthy of good and faithful subjects.   Speech to leaders of Basse-Nevarre revolt (1568), op. cit.

5 ... I am sufficiently accustomed ... to resist things so vile and unworthy of a generous heart as ambition and avarice.
From *Mémoires* (November 1568), op. cit.

6 ... the task of women and men who do not bear arms ... is to fight for peace ... do your part, for God's sake. As for me I will spare nothing.   Letter to Cardinal de Bourbon (1568), op. cit.

7 ... if religion separates us, does our common blood then separate? do friendship and natural duty cease to exist? *Non, mon frère.*
Ibid.

8 ... the affairs of the immortal soul admit not of the same latitude as temporal concerns. There is only one road to obtain eternal salvation.   Letter to Catherine de Medici (1569), op. cit.

9 ... I am a proud little woman and I desire to receive ... the honor and favor I think I deserve.   Letter to Catherine de Medici (January 3, 1571), op. cit.

10 ... in this world ... I see nothing but vanity.   Spoken during her last illness, op. cit.

11 Here [at the French court] it is the women who made advances to the men, rather than the other way around. If you were here you would never escape without special intervention from God.   Letter to Henry IV, her son (March 8, 1572), Quoted in *Women of Power* by Mark Strage   1976

12 Nothing is impossible to a valiant heart. (*À coeur vaillant rien d'impossible.*)
Motto (adopted by her son, Henry IV), n.d.

304.   Anne Cooke Bacon
(c.1528–1610?)

1 Ignorance, especially of the heavenly things is the greatest lack that can be seen in man.
Sermons ... concerning the predestination and election of God: very expedient to the setting forth of his glory among creatures,
15th sermon   c.1570

2 ... we must of force reput him a very ydeote [idiot] that denieth God.
Ibid.

3 ... our wits are drowned in the bodie, occupied of fantasies, and shadowed by the dark vaynes of things created.
Ibid.

4 ... it behoveth him that will know what thing God is to study in the schole of simplicitie.   Ibid.

5 Simple ignoraunce hath not so much confused ... wisdom, as Philosophie, which maketh men bold, unshamefaced, hot, lyers, proud, contentious, frenticke, foolysh, and wicked.   Ibid., 17th sermon

6 I do perceive that the old proverb be not always true, for I do find that the absence of my Nath. doth breed in me the more continual rememberance of him.
Letter to Lady Jane Cornwallis (1613), *Private Correspondence of Lady Cornwallis,* n.d.

305.   Elizabeth Hoby Russell
(1528–post-1603)

1 No one need honor me with tears, or lament my burial! This is why! I go through the stars to God! (*Nemo me lachrymis decoret, neque funera fletio! Faxit cur! Vado perastra deo*!) Composed for and inscribed on
her monument in Bisham
Church, near Great Marlow,
England, John Williams, tr.;
Quoted in *Society Women of Shakespeare's Time*
by Violet A. Wilson   1924

2 I beseech your Majesty, let me have Justice, and I will then trust the law.
Spoken to King James I (1603),
Quoted in *Diary of Lady Margaret Hoby*,
Dorothy M. Meads, ed.   1930

3 The certain fruits daily found of young men's travel nowadays [are] nothing but pride . . . and vanity in deeming better of their own conceits than wisdom would.
Ibid.,
Letter to [William Cecil, Lord]
Burghley (n.d.),
op. cit.

4 Though I will never be found unnatural, yet will I not, while I live, beggar myself for my cradle,* if I may prevent it.
Ibid.

*I.e., her children.

5 Though I be not so bad a bird as to defile mine own nest, yet I know my children. . . .
Ibid.

306.   Maria Cazalla
(fl. 1530s)

1 Why do you need to torture me? I have told the truth and can say no more.
Testimony before the Inquisition
(c.1531–1534),
Women of the Reformation,
Vol. III: *From Spain to Scandinavia*,
by Roland H. Bainton   1977

2 You do this to a woman? I dread more the affront than the pain.   Ibid.

3 O Thou who suppliest strength in need, I confess Thee, I adore Thee. Give me strength in my trial.   Ibid.

307.   Catherine Killigrew
(1530?–1583)

1 In thee my soul shall own combined
The sister and the friend.

If from my eyes by thee detained
The wanderer cross the seas,
No more thy love shall soothe, as friend,
No more as sister please.
Untitled, Sts. 2, 3,
Women of the Reformation,
Vol. III: *From Spain to Scandinavia*,
by Roland H. Bainton   1977

308.   Anne d'Este
(1531–post-1563)

1 My sweet God, so much blood, surely some of it will fall upon our house.
Comment on the mass execution
of conspirators
(March 22, 1560),
Quoted in *Women of Power*
by Mark Strage   1976

309.   Elizabeth I of England
(1533–1603)

1 As the saying is, So many heads, so many wits. "Godly Meditation of the Christian Soul"
1548

2 Much suspected of me,
  Nothing proved can be,
    Quoth Elizabeth, prisoner.
      Scratched with a Diamond on her Window at Woodstock Prison (c.1554–1555),
Actes and monuments of these later and perillous dayes (aka *The Book of Martyrs*) by John Foxe   1563

3 The [use of the] sea and air is common to all; neither can a title to the ocean belong to any people or private persons, for as much as neither nature nor public use and custom permit any possession thereof.
Letter to the Spanish Ambassador   1580

4 As for me, I see no such great cause why I should either be fond to live or fear to die. I have had good experience of this world, and I know what it is to be a subject and what to be a sovereign.   Speech to Parliament
1586

5 I know I have the body of a weak and feeble woman, but I have the heart and stomach of a king, and of a king of England too. . . .
Speech to the Troops at Tilbury on the Approach of the Armada
1588

6 For falsehood now doth flow, and subjects' faith doth ebb,
Which should not be if reason ruled or wisdom weaved the webb. "The Doubt of Future Foes" (c. 1570),
Art of English Poesy by George Puttenham   1589

7 Though God hath raised me high, yet this I count the glory of my crown: that I have reigned with your loves.
"The Golden Speech"   1601

8 If thy heart fails thee, climb not at all.*
Quoted in *History of the Worthies of England*, Vol. I, by Thomas Fuller   1662
*Response to Walter Raleigh's line: "Fain would I climb, yet fear I to fall."

9 I am and not, I freeze and yet am burned, Since from myself another self I turned.
"On Messieur's Departure" (c.1582),
Quoted in *Progresses of Queen Elizabeth* by John Nichols   1823

10 Must! Is *must* a word to be addressed to princes? Little man, little man! thy father, if he had been alive, durst not have used that word. To Robert Cecil [on her deathbed] (1603),
Quoted in *Short History of the English People*, Ch. 7, by John Richard Green   1874

11 . . . I know they are most deceived that trusteth most in themselves. . . .
Letter to Edward Seymour, Lord Protector (February 21, 1549),
The Sayings of Queen Elizabeth, Frederick Chamberlain, ed.   1923

12 For, what is a family without a steward, a ship without a pilot, a flock without a shepherd, a body without a head, the same, I think, is a kingdom without the health and safety of a good monarch.
Letter to King Edward VI (c.1551), op. cit.

13 I walk many times into the pleasant fields of the Holy Scriptures, where I pluck of the goodsome herbes of sentences by pruning, eat them by reading, chew them by musing, and lay them up at length in the high seat memorie, by gathering them together, that so having tasted their sweetness I may the less perceive the bitterness of this miserable life.   Journal entry (August 1554), op. cit.

14 I care not for myself; my life is not dear to me. My care is for my people. I pray God, whoever succeedeth me, be as careful of them as I am.   To her judges upon their assumption of office (1559), op. cit.

15 I have the heart of a man, not a woman, and I am not afraid of anything.
To the Swedish ambassador (n.d.), op. cit.

16 Do not suppose that I am seeking what belongs to others. God forbid. I seek only that which is mine own. But be sure that I will take good heed of the sword which threatens me with destruction, nor think that I am so craven-spirited as to endure a wrong, or to place myself at the mercy of my enemy.   To the Prince of Parma (c.1586), op. cit.

17 I am more afraid of making a fault in my Latin, than of the Kings of Spain, France, Scotland, the whole House of Guise, and all of their confederates.
To the Archbishop of St. Andrews (n.d.), op. cit.

18 I am your anointed Queen. I will never be by violence constrained to do anything. I thank God I am endued with such qualities that if I were turned out of the Realm in my petticoat I were able to live in any place in Christendom.   Remark (n.d.), op. cit.

19 I will make you [Chamberlin] shorter by the head.   Remark (n.d.), op. cit.

20 The daughter of debate,* that eke discord doth sow.   Remark (n.d.), op. cit.

*Her cousin, Mary, Queen of Scots.

21 ... I know I have a soul to save, as well as other folks have, wherefore I will above all things have respect unto the same.
Letter to Edward Seymour, Lord Protector (January 28, 1549), *The Letters of Queen Elizabeth the First,* G. B. Harrison, ed.   1935

22 For the face, I grant, I might well blush to offer, but the mind I shall never be ashamed to present. For though from the grace of the picture the colours may fade by time, may give by weather, may be spotted by chance; yet the other nor time with her swift wings shall overtake, nor the misty clouds with their lowerings may darken, nor chance with her slippery foot may overthrow.
Letter to King Edward VI (May 15, 1549–1553?), op. cit.

23 The king's word is more than another man's oath.   Letter (1554), op. cit.

24 ... I cannot but muse for my part, and blush for theirs, to see the rebellious hearts and devilish intents of Christians in name, but Jews in deed....   Letter to Mary, Queen of Scots (August 2, 1556), op. cit.

25 And among earthly things I chiefly wish this one, that there were as good surgeons for making anatomies of hearts that might show my thoughts to your Majesty, as there are expert physicians of the bodies, able to express the inward griefs of their maladies to their patients.   Ibid.

26 But since wishes are vain and desires oft fail, I must crave that my deeds may supply what my thoughts cannot declare....
Ibid.

27 Make some difference twixt tried, just and false friend.   Letter to Sir Henry Sidney (1565), op. cit.

28 You know a kingdom knows no kindred....   Ibid.

29 A strength to harm is perilous in the hand of an ambitious head. Ibid.

30 Where might is mixed with wit, there is too good an accord. Ibid.

31 It has always been held for a special principle in friendship that prosperity provideth but adversity proveth friends. . . .
Letter to Mary, Queen of Scots
(June 23, 1567),
op. cit.

32 . . . free we ought to be from the calumniation of certain persons that will never be content to say well of us, how well soever we do. Letter to Sir Francis Walsingham, Ambassador to France (September 2, 1571), op. cit.

33 . . . I thought . . . to move you to stay or qualify your passions, and to consider that it is not the manner to obtain good things with evil speeches, nor benefits with injurious challenges, nor to conclude, all in one word, good to yourself, with doing evil to myself. Letter to Mary, Queen of Scots (February 1, 1572), op. cit.

34 Methinks that I am more beholden to the hinder part of my head, than well dare trust the forewards side of the same. . . .
Letter to William Cecil, Lord Burghley (April 11, 1572), op. cit.

35 You be put there to be grave and sage advisors, to temper such sudden affections either the one way or the other, of love or of hatred . . . and to have regard to God first, and then to our honour and the surety and good government of our realm.
Letter to Sir William Fitzwilliams, Lord Deputy, and the Council of Ireland (June 29, 1573), op. cit.

36 . . . there is no debt more lawful than the word of a just man nor anything which binds our actions more than a promise. . . .
Letter to Francis, Duke of Anjou (December 1579/January 1580)

37 I . . . believe that you have too much distrust in a woman's silence, or else I should learn less by other means and more by you. Ibid.

38 . . . when I make collection of sundry kinds of discontentments, all tied in a bundle, I suppose the faggot will be harder altogether to be broken.
Letter to Sir Edward Stafford (c.August 1580), op. cit.

39 Let him never procure her harm whose love he seeks to win. Ibid.

40 My mortal [foe can] wish me no greater loss than England's hate; neither should death be less welcome unto me, than such a mishap betide me. Ibid.

41 God keep the innocent from enduring the evil that ill-founded agreements merit.
Letter to "the Monk" (c.1581), op. cit.

42 Brass shines as fair to the ignorant as gold to the goldsmith. Ibid.

43 . . . if the imperfections of this declining age we live in be truly weighed, and the sundry miseries that we are daily subject unto be duly looked into, we shall then find more cause to judge them unhappy that live, than to bewail those as unfortunate that are dead. Letter to George Talbot, Earl of Shrewsbury (c.September 5, 1582), op. cit.

44 Serve God, fear the King, and be a good fellow to the rest. Letter to William Cecil, Lord Burghley (May 8, 1583), op. cit.

45 I hope you will remember that who seeketh two strings to one bow, he may shoot strong but never straight. Letter to James VI [of Scotland] (1585), op. cit.

46 Give not the rein in God's name to wild horses, lest they should shake you from your saddle. Letter to Henry III, King of France (January 1587), op. cit.

47 ... there can be no folly greater than by fearing that which is not, nor by overgrieving for that which needs not, to overthrow at one instant the health of mind and body, which once being lost, the rest of our life is labour and sorrow, a work to God unacceptable, and to our friends discomfortable.
Letter to Frances, Countess of Hertford (November 5, 1595), op. cit.

48 Eyes of youth have sharp sight, but commonly not so deep as those of elder age. ...
Letter to Robert Devereux, Earl of Essex (July 8, 1597), op. cit.

49 We were loathe to have written at all because in such accidents (for the most part) the offering of comfort is but the presenting of fresh occasion of sorrow.
Letter to Lord Henry and Lady Norris [on the death of their son] (September 6, 1599), op. cit.

50 To trust this traitor upon oath is to trust a devil upon his religion.   Letter to Robert Devereux, Lord of Essex (September 17, 1599), op. cit.

51 ... in all government nothing giveth greater encouragement for practise nor more weakeneth for defence than when there is either dissensions in deed or opinion of which there is no great notice there of late. ...   Letter to Peregrine, Lord Willoughby (March 21, 1601), op. cit.

52 In upright demeanour there's ever more poise than all disguised shows of good can do.   Letter to James VI, King of Scotland (April 6, 1601), op. cit.

53 My care is like a shadow in the sun—

Follows me flying, flies when I pursue it.
"On the Departure of the Duke d'Alençon" (1582), *The Poems of Queen Elizabeth I,* Leicester Bradner, ed.   1964

54 Never think you fortune can bear the sway
Where virtue's force can cause her to obey.
"On Fortune," op. cit.

55 No crooked leg, no bleared eye,
    No part deformed out of kind,
Nor yet so ugly half can be
    As is the inward suspicious mind.
Written in her French psalter, op. cit.

56 'Twas God the word that spake it,
He took the Bread and brake it;
And what the word did make it;
That I believe, and take it.
Answer on being asked her opinion of Christ's presence in the Sacrament, op. cit.

57 *Semper eadem* [Ever the same].
Motto, n.d.

58 There was never promise made, but it was broken or kept.   Quoted by John Dee in his *Diary,* n.d.

59 All my possessions for a moment of time.
Attributed, n.d.

60 I am no lover of pompous title, but only desire that my name be recorded in a line or two, which shall briefly express my name, my virginity, the years of my reign, the reformation of religion under it, and my preservation of peace.   To her ladies, discussing her epitaph, n.d.

310.   Sofonisba Anguissola
(c.1535-1540–1625)

1 It will be a great pleasure to me if I have gratified your Holiness's wish, but I must add that, if the brush could represent the beauties of the queen's [Isabel of Valois] soul to your eyes, they would be marvelous. However, I have used the utmost diligence to present what art can show, to tell your Holiness the truth. Letter to Pope Pius IV (September 16, 1561),
Quoted in The Lives of the Painters, Sculptors, and Architects,
Vol. III, by Giorgio Vasari; A. B. Hinds, tr.   1927

311.   Jane Grey
(1537–1554)

1 I am charged and esteemed guilty more than I have deserved.   Statement written to Queen Mary I (1553),
Letters of Royal and Illustrious Ladies of Great Britain,
Vol. III, Mary Anne Everett Wood Green, ed.   1846

2 Think not, O mortal, vainly gay,
That thou from human woes art free;
The bitter cup I drink today,
Tomorrow may be drunk by thee.
Lines written on prison wall at the Tower of London (1554),
Quoted in Woman's Record
by Sarah Josepha Hale   1855

3 Harmless all malice if our God is nigh;
Fruitless all pains, if he his help deny.
Patient I pass these gloomy hours away,
And wait the morning of eternal day.
Ibid.

4 My book hath been so much pleasure and more, that in respect of it, all other pleasures in very deed be but trifles and troubles unto me.   "The Scholemaster" (1569),
The English Works of Roger Ascham,
William Aldis Wright, ed. 1904

5 One of the greatest benefits that ever God gave me is, that he sent me so sharp and severe parents and so gentle a schoolmaster.
Ibid.

312.   Margaret Bryan
(fl. c.1539)

1 The minstrels played, and his grace [Edward VI] danced ... so wantonly that he could not stand still, and was as full of pretty toys as ever I saw child in my life.
Letter to [Thomas] Cromwell (1539),
Letter of Royal and Illustrious Ladies,
Vol. III, Mary Anne Everett Wood Green, ed.   1846

313.   Anna Maria of Braunschweig
(fl. 1540s)

1 I'd rather marry a wise old man than a young fool.   Quoted in *Women of the Reformation,*
Vol. I: *Germany and Italy,*
by Roland H. Bainton   1971

314.   Lettice Knollys
(1540–1634)

1 ... country life is fittest for disgraced persons. Letter to her son, the Earl of Essex (c. 1595–1598),
Quoted in *Queen Elizabeth's Maids of Honour*
by Violet A. Wilson, n.d.

2 ... I doubt not but you are wise and politic enough to countermine with your enemies, whose devilish practises can no way hurt you but one.   Letter to her son, the Earl of Essex (c.1599), op. cit.

3 Well, if it be men's matters I know you have courage enough; if women's you have meetly well passed the pikes already, and therein should be skilful.   Ibid.

315. Countess de Marcelle
(fl. c.1540s)

1 By compelling us to return to the world, it is not liberty the Calvinists offer us, but bondage.*   Quoted in *The Huguenots in France and America*, Vol. II, Ch. 26, by Hannah Farnham Lee   1843

*The Calvinists attempted to abolish monasteries and convents in France.

316. Isabella de'Medici Orsini
(1542–1576)

1 Make yourself happy where you are adored, and on no account seek another abode.
Letter to her sister-in-law, Bianca Capello (September 24, 1572), Quoted in *Famous Women of Florence* by Edgecumbe Staley   1909

317. Mary, Queen of Scots
(1542–1587)

1 Farewell, France! farewell beloved country, which I shall never more behold!
(August 1559), Quoted in *Women of Beauty and Heroism* by Frank B. Goodrich   1858

2 I am no subject to Elizabeth, but an independent queen as well as she; and I will consent to nothing unbecoming the majesty of a crowned head.   Remark (October 11, 1586), op. cit.

3 I would disdain to purchase all that is most valuable upon earth by the assassination of the meanest of the human race....
At her trial (October 13, 1586), op. cit.

4 If ever I have given consent by my words, or even by my thoughts, to any attempt against the life of the Queen of England, far from declining the judgment of men, I shall not even pray for the mercy of God.
Ibid.

5 Here the sun can never penetrate, neither does any pure air ever visit this habitation, on which descend drizzling damps and eternal fogs, to such excess that not an article of furniture can be placed beneath the roof, but in four days it becomes covered with green mould.
Remark (1586/87) from her prison cell, op. cit.

6 Oh Lord, in thee have I hoped, and into thy hands I commit my spirit.
Last words (February 8, 1587), op. cit.

7 I will that you do nothing by which any spot may be laid on my honor or conscience; but wait till God of His goodness shall put a remedy to it.   Ibid.

8 No more tears now; I will think upon revenge.   Remarking on the murder of her servant, David Riccio (1566), Quoted in *Memorials of Mary Stewart*, J. Stevenson, ed.   1883

9 ... the world is not that what we do make of it, nor yet are they most happy that continue longest in it.   Remark to Lord Randolph (c.1551), *Calendar of State Papers Relating to Scottish Affairs*, J. Bain, ed.   1898

10 Look to your consciences and remember that the theater of the world is wider than the realm of England.
Remark at her trial (1586), Quoted in *The Tragedy of Fotheringhay* by Mrs. Maxwell-Scot   1905

11 Ah! here are many counsellors, but not one for me.   Ibid.

12 ... perchance a passing note of pain
Speaks sometimes to thy heart of days gone by   Untitled poem to the poet Ronsard (c.1565), *Queen Mary's Book*, P. Steward-Mackenzie, ed. and tr. 1905

13 Time than fortune should be held more precious
For Fortune is as false as she is specious.
"Book of Hours" (1579), op. cit.

14 Give me, dear Lord, the true humility
And strengthen my too feeble halting faith;
Let but Thy Spirit shed his light on me—
Checking my fever with His purer breath.
"Book of Hours" (c.1581), op. cit.

15 O Lord my God, I have trusted in thee;
O Jesu my dearest one, now set me free.
In prison's oppression, in sorrow's obsession,
I weary for thee.
With sighing and crying bowed down as dying,
I adore thee, I implore thee, set me free!
"Book of Devotion" (February 1587), Algernon Swinburne, tr., op. cit.

16 Whatever the hour of day

Be it dawn or the eventide
My heart still feels it yet
The eternal regret.   "The Absent One" [poem on the death of Francis II, her first husband] (1561), Antonia Fraser, tr., Quoted in *Mary, Queen of Scots* by Antonia Fraser   1969

17 As a sinner I am truly conscious of having often offended my Creator and I beg him to forgive me, but as a Queen and Sovereign, I am aware of no fault or offence for which I have to render account to anyone here below.
To Sir Amyas Paulet (October 1586), op. cit.

18 I do not aspire to any public position, especially when I consider the pain and desperance which meet those who wish to do right, and act with justice and dignity in the midst of so perverse a generation, and when a whole world is full of crimes and troubles.
Remark at her trial (1586), op. cit.

19 I do not desire vengeance.... I would rather pray with Esther than take the sword with Judith.   Ibid.

20 In my end is my beginning. (*En ma fin est mon commencement.*)   Motto, op. cit.

21 Constancy does become all folks well, but none better than princes, and such as have rule over realms. Quoted in *Women of the Reformation*, Vol. III: *From Spain to Scandinavia*, by Roland H. Bainton   1977

22 I mean to constrain none of my subjects; and I trust they should have no support to constrain me.   Ibid.

23 I will defend the Kirk of Rome, for it is, I think, the true Kirk of God.
Reported by John Knox, op. cit.

24 There is much ado in my realm about matter of religion.   Recorded by John Knox
(c.1561),
op. cit.

318. Mary Grey
(1543/44–1578)

1 ... the princes favor is not so soon gotten
agayn, and ... to be without it is such a
greff to any true subjectes harte, as no tur-
ment can be greater. ....   Letter to
William Cecil, Lord Burghley,
written from prison (1566),
*Original Letters Illustrative of
English History,*
Vol. II, Henry Ellis, ed.
1824–1846

319. Veronica Franco
(1546–1591)

1 Now that my mind is bent upon revenge,
my disrespectful, my rebellious lover,
step up and arm yourself with what you
will.

What battlefield do you prefer? this place?
this secret hideaway where I have sam-
pled—
unwarily—so many bitter sweets?
Untitled, Sts. 10, 11,
Lynne Lawner, tr.;
*The Penguin Book
of Women Poets,*
Carol Cosman, Joan Keefe and
Kathleen Weaver, eds.   1978

2 Alas! I say now and always will say
That to live without you is cruel death to
me
And pleasures to me are cruel torments.
"Lontana dall'Amante e da
Venezia" ["Far from My Lover
and from Venice"],
Claudia Alexander with Carlo
Dimaio, trs.;
Poesia italiana: il cinquecento,
Giulio Ferroni, ed.   1978

3 The fresh roses, the fleur-de-lys, and the
violets
Are wilted with the heat of my sighs
And I see the sun pale piteously.
Ibid.

4 Because of the swirling tears in my eyes, the
rivers stopped, and the sea was stilled
With sweet pity for my torment.
Ibid.

5 ... with my knee to the earth I bow
To my Apollo in wisdom and beauty
To the victor in the war of love
Ibid.

320. Catherine Fradonnet
(1547–1587)

Co-author with Madeline Fradonnet, See
292:1.

321. Idelette de Bure Calvin
(?–1549)

1 O glorious resurrection! God of Abraham
and of all our fathers! The faithful have is so
many ages hoped in Thee, and not one has
been disappointed! I will also hope!
Dying words (1549),
Quoted in *The Huguenots in
France and America,*
Vol. I, Ch. 3, by Hannah
Farnham Lee   1843

322. Elizabeth Bowes
(fl. 1550)

1 Alas, wretched woman that I am, for the
self-same sins that reigned in Sodom and
Gomorrah reign in me!   Letter to John
Knox (c.1550),
Women of the Reformation,
Vol. III: *From Spain to
Scandinavia,*
by Roland H. Bainton   1977

323.   Renée de Chateauneuf Rieux
(1550-1587)

1 Marriage is a lottery in which men stake their liberty and women their happiness.

         Attributed, n.d.

324.   Grace Sherrington
(c.1552–1620)

1 She [her governess] scoffed at all dalliance, idle talk, and wanton behaviour appertayning thereto. . . . She counselled us when we were alone so to behave ourselves as if all the worlde did looke upon us, and to doe nothing in secret whereof our conscience might accus us. . . .   Quoted in *Diary of Lady Margaret Hoby*, Dorothy M. Meads, ed.   1930

2 Deal truly and faithfully in all things, both in small matters and in greate . . . beware of all lies and oathes reporting of newes; . . . heare much and . . . speake little. . . .   Ibid.

3 If all fathers and mothers were . . . provident and careful, and governors and governesses put in trust by them were diligent and faithfull in performing their trust, so many parents should not be discomfited as they are in their age by the wickedness and misfortunes of their children.

         Ibid.

4 I spent the best part of my youth in solitarinesse, shunning all opportunities to remove into company, lest I might be inticed and drawn away by evil suggestion.

         Ibid.

5 Every day I spent some tyme in works of myne owne invention, without sample or pattern before me. . . . And, though I was but meanly furnished to be excellent in any of those exercises, yet they did me good, inasmuch as I found myselfe that God wrought with me in all.   Ibid.

325.   Marguerite of Valois
(1553–1615)

1 Joy takes far away from us the thoughts of our actions; sorrow it is that awakens the soul.   *Memoirs* (1594–1600)   1628

2 I have no ambition and I have no need of it, being who and what I am.

         Ibid.

3 It is the usual frailty of our sex to be fond of flattery. I blame this in other women, and should wish not to be chargeable with it myself.   Ibid., Letter I

4 I had no ambition of any kind, and had been so strictly brought up under the Queen my mother [Catherine de Medici] that I scarcely durst speak before her; and if she chanced to turn her eyes towards me I trembled. . . .   Ibid., Letter II

5 Her son became the god of her idolatry, at the shrine of whose will she sacrificed everything.   Ibid., Letter III

6 . . . mistrust is the sure forerunner of hatred.   Ibid., Letter IX

7 Adversity is solitary, while prosperity dwells in a crowd.   Ibid., Letter XII

8 Science conducts us, step by step, through the whole range of creation, until we arrive, at length, at God.   Ibid.

9 . . . reading in this beautiful universal book of nature . . . the soul comes to realize the ladder of which God is the last and highest rung, and in ecstasy adores the wondrous light and splendour of this incomprehensible Being.   Ibid.

10 In my sadness and solitude, I rediscovered the great gifts of study and devotion—gifts which, among the vanities and magnificence of my former good fortune, I had never truly tasted.   Ibid.

11 . . . fame and happiness always arouse envy. . . .   Ibid., Letter XXI

12 ... the sight of you ... is as necessary for me as is the sun for the spring flowers.
Letter to Jacques de Harlay, Marquess of Chanvallon (1582), Quoted in *A Daughter of the Medicis* by Jean H. Mariejol; John Peile, tr.   1929

13 ... let no one ever say that marriages are made in Heaven; the gods would not commit so great an injustice! Letter to Jacques de Harlay (1582), Quoted in *Queen of Hearts* by Charlotte Haldane   1968

14 Adieu, source of my eternal sufferings! If I could only say the same to my life. ...
Letter to Jacques de Harlay (Spring 1583), op. cit.

15 ... by the loss of your beautiful eyes my life and beauty lose their lustre and their strength.   Letter to Jacques de Harlay (Summer 1583), op. cit.

16 ... to my inferiors, to whom I owe nothing, I will surrender nothing.
Letter to her former husband, Henry IV (November 9, 1603), op. cit.

326.   Margaret Clitherow
(1556?–1586)

1 They that think much and are not willing to do such base things [as housework], have little regard of well-doing or knowledge of themselves.   Quoted in *A True Report of the Life and Martyrdom of Mrs. Margaret Clitherow* by Fr. John Mush   1586

2 God forbid that I should will any to do that in my house which I would not willingly do myself. ...   Ibid.

3 This is a time of war and trial in God's Church, and therefore if I cannot do my duty without peril and dangers, yet by God's grace I will not be slacker for them.   Ibid.

4 Children ... with an apple and a rod you may make to say what you will.
Testimony to her judges, op. cit.

5 I have deserved death for mine offences to God, but not for anything that I am accused of.   Ibid.

6 ... I have care over my children as a mother ought to have; I trust I have done my duty to them to bring them up in the fear of God, and so I trust now I am discharged of them. And for this cause I am willing to offer them freely to God that sent them to me, rather than I will yield one jot from my faith.   Ibid.

7 ... bear me company this night, not for any fear of death, for it is my comfort, but the flesh is frail.   Remark to a friend before her execution, op. cit.

8 I mind by God's assistance to spend my blood in this faith [Catholicism], as willing as ever I put my paps to my children's mouths.   Ibid.

327.   Zofia Olesnicka
(fl. 1556)

1 Better to safeguard Thy treasure,
Which neither moth nor rust can corrupt
Than enmeshed in the ways of the world
To forfeit Thy favor forever.
Hymn, St. 5 (1556), Quoted in *Women of the Reformation*, Vol. III: *From Spain to Scandinavia*, by Roland H. Bainton   1977

2 Lord of heaven, sustain us,
For vain else is all our endeavor,
Be we not drawn by Thy Love

And fainting upheld by Thy spirit.
Ibid., St. 6

3 For He will work for us wonders
While foul maggots receive not forgiveness.
Ibid., St. 8

328. Anne Dacre Howard
(1557–1630)

1 In sad and ashy weeds I sigh. . . .
Elegy on the Death of Her
Husband, l. 1 (1595),
The Women Poets in English,
Ann Stanford, ed.   1972

2 I envy aire because it dare
Still breathe, and he not so;
Hate earthe, that doth entomb his youth,
And who can blame my woe?
Ibid., St. 3

329. Joyce Lewes
(?–1557)

1 When I behold the amiable countenance of
Christ my dear Saviour, the . . . face of
death doth not greatly trouble me.
At her execution (1557),
Quoted in *Actes and monuments
of these latter and perillous dayes*
(aka *The Book of Martyrs*),
Vol. VIII, by John
Foxe   1563

2 I thank my God that he will make me
worthy to adventure my life in his quarrel.
Ibid.

330. Mother Benet
(fl. 1558)

1 O man! be content, and let us be thankful;
for God hath given us enough, if we can see
it.   Quoted in *Actes and monuments of
these latter and perillous dayes*
(aka *The Book of Martyrs*)
by John Foxe   1563

2 I cannot firkin [store] up my butter, and
keep my cheese in the chamber and wait a
great price, and let the poor want, and so
displease God.   Ibid.

3 . . . let us be rich in good works, and so
shall we please the Lord, and have all good
things given us.   Ibid.

331. Prest's Wife
(?–1558)

1 . . . in the cause of Christ and his truth,
where I must either forsake Christ or my
husband, I am contented to stick only to
Christ my heavenly spouse, and renounce
the other. Testimony to examining bishop,
Quoted in *Actes and monuments
of these latter and perillous dayes*
(aka *The Book of Martyrs*)
by John Foxe   1563

2 How save you souls, when you preach nothing but damnable lies. . . .
Ibid.

3 Farewell you with your salvation.
Ibid.

4 God forbid that I should lose the life eternal, for this carnal and short life.
At her execution (1558),
op. cit.

332. Elizabeth Young
(fl. 1558)

1 . . . I had rather all the world should accuse
me, than mine own conscience.
Testimony at her first
examination,
Quoted in *Actes and monuments
of these latter and perillous dayes*
(aka *The Book of Martyrs*)
by John Foxe   1563

2 If ye take away my meat, I trust God will
take my hunger.   Ibid., Second
examination

3 Here is my carcase: do with it what you will . . . ye can have no more but my blood.
Ibid.

4 . . . I was a body before I had a soul; which body God has created, and yet it could not live, till God had breathed life into me, and by that life doth my body live.
Ibid., Fifth examination (1558)

5 . . . ye have not touched my conscience; but beware ye hurt not your own.
Ibid., Sixth examination

6 No man can be the head of Christ's church; for Christ himself is the head, and his word is the governor of all.   Ibid., Seventh examination

7 I will not go . . . to mass or matins, till I may hear it in a tongue [English] that I can understand: for I will be fed no longer in a strange language [Latin].   Ibid.

333.   Catherine de Bourbon
(1559–1604)

1 . . . [King Henry of] Navarre can ill brook words when *deeds* are so much wanted.
Remark to Count de Soissons, Quoted in *The Huguenots in France and America*, Vol. I, Ch. 15, by Hannah Farnham Lee   1843

2 For God's sake, my King, make clear that you are a good King and a good brother. If I were the meanest woman in the kingdom, you would not deny me justice.
Letter to her brother, Henry IV of France (1592), Quoted in *Queen of Navarre: Jeanne d'Albret* by Nancy Lyman Roelker, tr.   1968

3 Command me, my King, to make you a little page, for I fear that unless you command it yourself, he will not consent to lodge in my body. Letter to Henry IV (August 18, 1599), op. cit.

334.   Anne Locke
(fl. 1560s)

1 . . . why (casting off all impediments that presseth down) do we not run on our course with cheerfulness and Hope, having Christ so mighty a King, for our captain and Guide?   Preface to her translation of *The Markes of the Children of God* by J. Taffin   1590

2 Because great things by reason of my sexe, I may not doe, and that which I may, I ought to doe, I have according to my duety, brought my poore basket of stones to the strengthening of the walls of that Jerusalem, wherof (by Grace) we are all both Citizens and members.   Ibid.

3 What perfect help can they give to a diseased mind, that understand not, or believe not the only thing that must of needful necessity be put into all medicines that may serve for a tormented soul, that is to say, the determined providence of almighty God. . . .   Preface to her translation of John Calvin's sermon on Hezikiah's song of thanksgiving, Quoted in *Women of the Reformation*, Vol. III: *From Spain to Scandinavia*, by Roland H. Bainton   1977

4 He that cureth the sick mind . . . cureth or preserveth not only mind but body also.
Ibid.

335.   Blanche Parry
(fl. 1560s)

1 . . . madam . . . if you ever marry without the Queen's [Elizabeth I] writing, you and your husband will be undone, and your fate worse than that of my Lady Jane.*
Letter to Lady Catherine Grey (c.1560), Quoted in *Queen Elizabeth's Maids of Honour* by Violet A. Wilson, n.d.

*Sister of Lady Catherine; subsequently, Catherine was imprisoned after her secret marriage to the Earl of Hertford.

336. Frances Walsingham
(c.1560–post-1603)

1 I will have more care of my self for your little one's sake.   Letter to her husband, the
Earl of Essex (c.1599),
Quoted in *Society Women of
Shakespeare's Time*
by Violet A. Wilson   1924

2 . . . the joy which I took in receiving news from you did deliver me out of a fever.
Letter to her husband
(August 1599),
op. cit.

3 Simple thankes is a slender recompens. . . .
Letter to Robert Cecil
(December 1599),
op. cit.

4 . . . as you desire of God that your own son never be made orphan by the untimely or unnatural death of his dear father, vouchsafe a relenting*. . . .   Letter to Robert
Cecil (February 1600),
op. cit.

*Plea for reversal of order of execution of her husband, the Earl of Essex.

5 . . . that fatal warrant for execution . . . if it be once signed, I shall never wish to breathe one hour after.   Ibid.

337. Mary Sidney Herbert
(1561–1621)

1   My fellow, my companion, held most dear,
My soul, my other self, my inward friend
The Psalmes of David (c.1593),
Psalm LV, "Exaudi, Deus,"
St. 4, C. Whittingham,
ed.   1823

2 There is a God that carves to each his own.
Ibid., Psalm LVIII,
"Si Vere Utique," St. 4

3   To thee I cry,
          My crying hear.
To thee my praying voice doth fly:
   Lord lend my voice a listening ear.
Ibid., Psalm LXI, St. 1

4 Witnesse this waterlesse, this weary waste
Ibid., Psalm LXIII, St. 1

5 How thou hast been the target of my head
Ibid., St. 3

6 When lying mouthes shall stopped lye no more   Ibid., St. 4

7 Know first that he is God; and after know
This God did us, not we our selves create   Ibid., Psalm C, St. 1

8 O Sun, whom light nor flight can match,
   Suppose thy lightful flightful wings
      Thou lend to me,
      And I could flee
As far as thee the ev'ning brings
Ibid., Psalm CXXXIX,
"Domine, Probasti,"
St. 5

9 Do thou thy best, O secret night,
   In sable veil to cover me
Ibid., St. 6

10 Each inmost piece in me is thine:
   While yet I in my mother dwelt,
   All that me clad
   From thee I had.   Ibid., St. 7

11 Make trumpet's noise in shrillest notes ascend,
Make lute and lyre His loved fame express
Ibid., Psalm CL, St. 1

12 What Heavenly powers thee highest throne assigned,
assigned thee goodness suiting that Degree:
and by thy strength thy burth so designed,

To others toil, is Exercise to thee.
"To the Thrice Sacred Queen
Elizabeth,"
St. 2 (1599),
*Two Poems by
the Countess of Pembroke,*
Bent Juel-Jensen, ed.   1962

13 Cares though still great, cannot be greatest
still,
Business must ebb, though Leisure never
flow   Ibid., St. 3

14 If ever hapless woman had a cause
    To breathe her plaints into the open
air,
And never suffer inward grief to pause,
    Or seek her sorrow-shaken soul's re-
pair:
Then I, for I have lost my only brother,*
Whose like this age can scarcely yield
another. "If Ever Hapless Woman Had a
Cause,"
St. 1 (c. 1599),
The Woman Poets in English,
Ann Stanford, ed.   1972

*The poet Sir Philip Sidney (1554–1586), who, in their
joint translation of the Psalms, translated the first 43.

15 Ay me, can so divine a thing be dead?
Ah! no: it is not dead, ne can it die,
But lives for aie, in blissfull Paradise:
Where like a new-borne babe it soft doth lie
"The Dolefull Lay of
Clorinda,"*
Sts. 11, 12 (1599),
The World Split Open,
Louise Bernikow, ed.   1974

*Elegy on the death of her brother.

16 Three thousands birds all of celestial brood,
To him do sweetly caroll day and night;
And with straunge notes, of him well un-
derstood,
Lull him a sleep in angelick delight
Ibid., St. 13

17 But live thou there, still happie, happie
Spirit,
And give us leave thee here thus to lament
Not thee that doest thy heavens joy inherit,
But our owne selves that here in dole are
drent.   Ibid., St. 16

338.   Penelope Devereaux Rich
(1562/63–post-1605)

1 Early did I hope this morning to have had
myne eyes blessed with your Majestie's
butyes, but seeing the sonne desappere into
a cloud, and meeting with spiritts that did
presage by the wheeles of theyr chariotts
some thunder in the ayr, I must complayn
and express my feares. . . .
Letter to Queen Elizabeth I
(1599),*
Quoted in *Society Women of
Shakespeare's Time*
by Violet A. Wilson   1924

*Requesting permission to visit her brother, the Earl
of Essex, during his imprisonment.

2 . . . they will seem . . . such crafty workmen as will not only pull downe all the obstacles of theyr greatnes, but when they are
in theyr full strengths (like gyants) make
warr agaynst Heaven.   Ibid.

3 Faction . . . careth not upon whose neck
they buyld the walles of theyr owne fortunes. . . .   Ibid.

4 . . . so strangely have I been wronged, as
may well be an argument to make one despise the world, finding the smoke of envy
where affection should be clearest.
Letter (c.1600),
op. cit.

339.   Elizabeth Grymeston
(1563?–1603)

1 . . . there is nothing so strong as the force of
love; there is no love so forcible as the love
of an affectionate mother to her natural
child. Dedicatory letter to her son, Bernye
Grymeston,
*Miscelanea: Prayer, Meditations,
Memoratives*   1604

2 I resolved to break the barren soil of my
fruitless brain.   Ibid.

3 I have prayed for thee, that thou mightest be fortunate in two hours of thy life time: in the hour of thy marriage, and at the hour of thy death.   Ibid.

4 Defer not thy marriage till thou comest to be saluted with a "God speed you, Sir," as a man going out of the world after forty; neither yet to the time of "God keep you, Sir," whilst thou are in thy best strength after thirty; but marry in the time of "You are welcome, Sir," when thou are coming into the world: for seldom shalt thou see a woman out of her own love to pull a rose that is full blown, deeming them always sweetest at the first opening of the bud.   Ibid.

5 . . . he seldom dies well that liveth ill.   Ibid.

6 Let thy thoughts be examined . . . if bad, forbid them entrance: for once admitted, they straightways fortify; and are expelled with more difficulty, than not admitted.   Ibid.

7 Crush the serpent in the head,
Break ill eggs ere they be hatched.
Kill bad chickens in the tread,
Fledged they hardly can be catched.
In the rising stifle ill,
Lest it grow against thy will.   Ibid.

8 . . . because God hath endued thee with so violent a spirit, as that *quicquid vis valdè vis**; therefore by so much the more it behooveth thee to deliberate what thou undertakest.   Ibid.
*Whatever you want, you want very strongly.

9 . . . be a bridle to thy self, to restrain thee from doing that which indeed thou mayest do. . . .   Ibid.

10 Sweet . . . is the end of the laborers: . . . the woman great with child will often muse of her delivery: and he that knows his life is but a way to death, will sit upon the threshold with the poor prisoner, expecting to have the door open to be let out of so loathsome a prison, looking for death without fear, desiring it without delight, and accepting it with devotion.   Ibid., Ch. 4

11 It is . . . the good man that did sow in tears [who] by death shall reap in joy; . . . what doth he lose, but frail and fickle life, a vapor that vanisheth, a dry leaf carried with every wind, a sleep fed with imaginary dreams, a tragedy of transitory things and disguised persons, that pass away like a post in the night, like a ship in the sea, like a bird in the air, whose tract the air closeth?   Ibid.

12 Who can sit in his study and look on his hourglass, and say not to himself . . . That thy life is spent with the hour? Who can walk in the sun, and look on his shadow, and not say with Pindar . . . Man is but a dream of a shadow? . . . Canst thou feel the wind beat on thy face, and canst thou forget that thou holdest thy tenement by a puff of wind? Canst thou sit by the river side, and not remember that as the river runneth, and doth not return, so is the life of man? Canst thou shoot in the fields, and not call to mind that as the arrow flieth in the air, so swiftly do thy days pass? Or canst thou walk in the fields, and see how some grass is coming, some newly withered, and some already come, and dost not remember that all flesh is grass?   Ibid.

13 Miserable man, why dost thou not dispose thyself to death, since thou are sure thou canst not live?   Ibid.

14 Our best life is to die well: for living here we enjoy nothing: things past are dead and gone: things present are always ending: things future always beginning: while we live we die; and we leave dying when we leave living.   Ibid.

15 Our life was a smoke, and a vanished; was a shadow and is passed; was a bubble and is dissolved.   Ibid.

16 The darts of lust are in the eyes; and therefore fix not thy eye on that which thou mayest not desire.   Ibid., Ch. 20, "Memoratives"

17 Epicurism is the fuel of lust; the more thou addest, the more she is enflamed.
                                                  Ibid.

18 Think from whence thou camest, and blush; where thou art, and sigh; and tremble to remember whither thou shalt go.
                                                  Ibid.

19 The whole world is as an house of exchange, in which Fortune is the nurse that breeds alteration.   Ibid.

20 If thou givest a benefit, keep it close; but if thou receivest one, publish it, for that invites another.   Ibid.

21 On the anvil of upbraiding is forged the office of unthankfulness.   Ibid.

22 Be not at any time idle. Alexander's soldiers should scale molehills rather than rest unoccupied; it is the woman that sitteth still that imagineth mischief; it is the rolling stone that riseth clean, and the running water that remaineth clear.   Ibid.

23 There be four good mothers have four bad daughters: Truth hath Hatred; Prosperity hath Pride; Security hath Peril, and Familiarity hath Contempt.
                                                  Ibid.

24 A fair woman is a paradise to the eye, a purgatory to the purse, and a hell to the soul.
                                                  Ibid.

340. Hŏ Nansŏrhŏn
(1563–1589)

1 Yesterday I fancied I was young;

But already, alas, I am aging.
                          "A Woman's Sorrow,"
                              Peter H. Lee, tr.;
                          The Penguin Book
                              of Woman Poets,
            Carol Cosman, Joan Keefe and
            Kathleen Weaver, eds.   1978

2 Spring breezes and autumn rains,
Alas, they flew like a shuttle.
And my face that once was beautiful,
Where did it go? Who disgraced it so?
                                                  Ibid.

3 Numberless are the sorrowful.
                    Untitled, Peter H. Lee, tr.,
                                          op.cit.

341. Marie de Jars
(1565–1645)

1 Concern for individual well-being is for private citizens . . . but Princes, who enjoy public possessions, should be concerned with the public good. *Proumenoir* (1594),
                Quoted in *A Daughter of the
                                    Renaissance*
                            by Marjorie Henry
                              Ilsley   1963

2 He must enter friendship through the portals of virtue who would be assured of leaving it only through those of death.
                                                  Ibid.

3 The common man believes that in order to be chaste a woman must not be clever: in truth it is doing chastity too little honor to believe it can be found beautiful only by the blind.   Ibid.

4 . . . even if a woman has only the name of being educated she will be evilly spoken of.
                                                  Ibid.

5 I am on the side of those who believe that vice comes from stupidity and consequently that the nearer one draws to wisdom the farther one gets from vice.
                            Preface to *Essais*
                              by Montaigne
                              (1595), op. cit.

6 Pierre, your life is condemned
By the crime of a single moment:
While you believe that you are just for a whole year
Because you are good for a single day.
"Illusions Bigottes"
(1626), op. cit.

7 No one can say that he loves God if he disdains one of His principal commandments . . . charity toward our neighbors.
"Des Fauces Devotions"
(1626), op. cit.

8 . . . although children are good and well born,
Vice will blight them if they are not well educated.   "Advis"
(1634), op. cit.

9 . . . a seed . . . can be profitably sown only in a soul first well cultivated by the art of reason and fortified by that of virtue.
Ibid.

10 Knowledge not based on ethics cannot . . . bring real honor nor profit to its master. . . .   Ibid.

11 Since language and speech are the cement of human society whoever falsifies them should be punished for counterfeit or for poisoning the public water well.
Ibid.

12 What are our efforts but a flood-gate of reeds against the roaring torrent of fortune?
Ibid.

13 How shall we know the strength of a mind if it makes no effort? . . . No one can claim to be a master Pilot who has not battled against a bitter tempest.   Ibid.

14 One sees the sky at a glance but we need time to envisage a mind.   Ibid.

15 Society is a cage of idiots
"A Lenten"
(1634), op. cit.

16 Among the good things that man possesses
Honor holds the highest place;

. . . .

He then who damages one's reputation

Slays us with more bitter death
Than if he sent us to the grave
By the thrust of a bloody sword.
Ibid.

342.   Elizabeth Joceline
(1566–1622)

1 . . . sometimes women have greater portions of learning than wisdom. . . .
"Epistle,"
*The Mothers Legacie to her
Unborne Childe*   1624

2 . . . delight not to have a bold childe: modesty and humility are the sweetest ground-works of all vertue.
Ibid.

3 . . . all the delight a Parent may take in a child is honey mingled with gall.
Ibid., Introduction

4 The Lord will not despise a contrite heart.
Ibid., Ch. 3

5 . . . the rules of selfe-conceit are . . . contrary; they stand on tiptoes, reckoning their vertues like the proud Pharisie.
Ibid., Ch. 5

6 . . . shunne multiplicity of words . . . for it is a grating to the eare to heare a man talk at randome.   Ibid., Ch. 8

7 How hatefull is obscene speech in rude people! But it makes one of gentle birth odious to all people.   Ibid.

8 Drunkennesse . . . is the highway to hell. . . .   Ibid., Ch. 9

9 I must exhort thee from a sinne, that I cannot name, thou must search thine owne heart for it. It is thy darling sin, that which to enjoy, thou couldst resist all others, at least thou thinkest so.   Ibid.

10 . . . there is nothing more contrary to our wicked nature then this loving our neibour as our selves. Wee can with ease envie him if hee be rich, or scorne him if he be poore; but love him?   Ibid., Ch. 10

11 I desire her bringing up to bee learning the
Bible, good huswifery, and good workes;
other learning a woman needs not. I desired
not much my owne, having seen that a
woman hath no greater use for learning
than a mainsaile to a flyeboat, which runs
under water. Ibid.

343. Isabella Whitney
(fl. 1567–1573)

1 The present day we cannot spend
as we the same should do
Except to count it as our last
we frame our selves unto.
"The 85. Flower,"
*A Sweet Nosegay or Pleasant
Posye Containing a Hundred and
Ten Phylosophicall
Flowers* 1573

2 Gold savours well, though it be got
with occupations vile:
If thou hast gold, thou welcome art,
though virtue thou exile. Ibid.,
"The 103. Flower"

3 Such poor folk as to law do go
are driven oft to curse:
But in mean while, the Lawyer thrives,
the money in his purse. Ibid.,
"The 104. Flower"

4 Seek not man to please, for that
is more than God bids do:
Please thou the best and never care,
what wicked say thereto. Ibid.,
"The 108. Flower"

344. Emilia Lanier
(1569/70–c.1640-45)

1 . . . nine fair virgins sat upon the ground,
With harps and viols in their lily hands
"The Author's Dream"
St. 3,
*Salve Deus Rex
Judeorum* 1611

2 He [fame] trailed along the woods in wan-
ton wise,
With sweet delight to entertain them all;
Inviting them to sit and to devise
On holy hymns Ibid., St. 29

3 While saints like swans about this silver
brook
Should Hallelujah sing continually
Ibid., St. 32

4 But thou [sleep], base cunning thief, that
robs our spirits
Of half that span of life which years doth
give Ibid., St. 45

5 In Slumber's bower thou sealest away our
breath,
Yet none there is that thy base stealths con-
trols. Ibid., St. 46

6 That very Night our Saviour was betrayed,
Oh night! exceeding all the nights of sorrow
"The Passion of Christ,"
St. 1, op. cit.

7 Open thine eyes, that thou the truth mayest
see,
Do not the thing that goes against thy heart
Ibid.

8 But surely Adam can not be excused,
Her fault though great, yet he was most to
blame;
What Weakness offered, Strength might
have refused,
Being Lord of all, the greater was his shame
"Eve's Apology",
op. cit.

9 If Eve did err, it was for knowledge sake,
No subtle Serpent's falsehood did betray
him,
If he would eat it, who had power to stay
him?
Not Eve, whose fault was only too much
love,
Which made her give this present to her
Dear,
That what she tasted, he likewise might
prove,
Whereby his knowledge might become
more clear Ibid.

10 Then let us [women] have our Liberty
again,
And challenge to your selves no Sover-
eignty;
You came not in the world without our
pain,
Make that a bar against your cruelty;
Your fault being greater, why should you
disdain
Our being your equals, free from tyranny?
Ibid.

345. Mairi MacLeod
(1569–1674?)

1 I will go to my home

. . . .

To Ullinish
with its white-hoofed herds,

Where once in childhood
I was nourished

On breast-milk
of smooth-skinned women
"A Complaint About Exile,"
ll. 8–16, Joan Keefe, tr.,
*The Penguin Book
of Women Poets,*
Carol Cosman, Joan Keefe and
Kathleen Weaver, eds.   1978

2 I have known indulgence

Danced with abandon
on spreading floors

Fiddle music
putting me to sleep

Pipes stirring
me in the morning   Ibid., ll. 24–30

346. Antoinette de Pons Guercheville
(1570–1632)

1 If I am not noble enough to be your wife, I
am too much so to be your mistress.
Remark to Henry IV,
Quoted in *Biography of
Distinguished Women*
by Sarah Josepha Hale   1876

2 A king, wherever he is, should always be
master. As to myself, I also choose to be
free.   Message to Henry IV,
op. cit.

347. Margaret Hoby
(1570–1633)

1 It is the Lord, and not the physician, who
both ordains the medicine for our health
and ordereth the ministering of it for the
good of His children . . . therefore let every
one, physician and patient, call upon the
Lord for a blessing.   (August 31, 1599),
Diary of Lady Margaret Hoby,
Dorothy M. Meads, ed.   1930

2 . . . it is not sufficient only to have
faith . . . but I must likewise pray especially
for that virtue which is opposed to that vice
whereunto I am then tempted.
Ibid. (December 10, 1599)

3 Though faith be the fundamental cause of
overcoming sin, yet operatively the several
graces of God work.   Ibid.

4 They are unworthy of God's benefits and
special favors that can find no time to make
a thankful record of them.
Ibid. (April 1, 1605)

348. Katherine Stubbes
(1571–1591/92)

1 I would rather be a door keeper in the house of my God, than to dwell in the tents of the wicked.   Spoken during her final illness (1591/92),
*Quoted in Women of the Reformation,
Vol. III: From Spain to Scandinavia,
by Roland H. Bainton   1977*

2 Christ is to me life, and death to me advantage.   *Ibid.*

3 Yea, the day of death is the day of everlasting life, and I cannot enter into life but by death ... O my God, why not now? why not now?   *Ibid.*

4 O my good God, I am ready for thee. .... O send thy messenger of death to fetch me. Send thy Sargeant to arrest me, thy Pursevant to attach me, thy Herald to summon me. O send thy Jailer to deliver my soul out of prison.   *Ibid.*

349. Elizabeth Clinton
(1574–1630?)

1 ... it is the express ordinance of God that mothers should nurse their own children, and, being his ordinance, they are bound to it in conscience. *The Countess of Lincoln's Nurserie   1622*

2 Now who shall deny the own mother's suckling of their own children to be their duty, since every godly matron hath walked in these steps before them: Eve, the mother of all the living; Sarah, the mother of all the faithful; Hannah, so graciously heard of God; Mary, blessed among women, and called blessed of all ages.   *Ibid.*

3 Whatsoever things are true, whatsoever things are honest ... whatsoever things are just, whatsoever things are pure, whatsoever things are of good report ... think on these things; these things do, and the God of peace shall be with you.   *Ibid.*

4 Trust not other women whom wages hire ... better than yourselves whom God and nature tie. ....   *Ibid.*

5 Indeed, I see some, if the weather be wet, or cold; if the way be foul, if the church be far off, I see they are so coy, so nice, so lukewarm, they will not take pains for their own souls.   *Ibid.*

6 ... think always that, having the child at your breast, and having it in your arms, you have God's blessing there.   *Ibid.*

7 ... you may consider that, when your child is at your breast, it is a fit occasion to move your heart to pray for a blessing upon that work, and to give thanks for your child, and for ability and freedom unto that which many a mother would have done and could not; who have tried and ventured their health, and taken much pains, and yet not obtained their desire.   *Ibid.*

350. Beatrice Cenci
(1577–1599)

1 I am no Turk and no dog that I should wish to shed my own blood.
Testimony at her trial (1599),
Quoted in Beatrice Cenci
by Morris Bishop and Henry
Longan Stuart   1925*
*Quotations 1–5 tr. by Corrado Ricci.

2 If a thousand witnesses should come, I say that all would tell lies and perjury.   *Ibid.*

3 I no longer know what to do in order not to fall from one evil into another, and even though I slew myself, I would fall under the curse of the Holy Father.
> Letter to her defense lawyer,
> Prospero Farinaccio (1599),
> op. cit.

4 Alas! Alas! O Madonna *santissima*, aid me! . . . Let me down! I will tell the truth.
> Remark during torture on the
> rack (1599),
> op. cit.

5 . . . she was always saying: "This father of yours will hold us here forever, and he will abuse you and rob you of your honour and do you a thousand ills." . . . she often exhorted me to hasten on the death of my father. Testimony against her step-mother, Lucrezia Cenci (1599),
> op. cit.

351.   Frances Abergavenny
(fl. 1580s)

1 The Praiers made by the right Honourable Ladie Frances Aburguaennie, and committed at the houre of hir death, to the right Worshipfull Ladie Marie Fane (hir onlie daughter) as a Jewel of health for the soule, and a perfect path to Paradise, verie profitable to be used of everie Christian man and woman.   Title of work   1582

2 . . . my soule thirsteth to rest, even as vehementlie as the hart longeth after the water brookes. . . . "A fruitfull praier to be said in the Morning,"
> op. cit.

3 . . . grant, good Lord, that my soule may continually keepe watch and ward: let not the enemie find me slumbering & sleeping. . . . "A fruitfull praier to be said at the going to bed of everie Christian,"
> op. cit.

4 No thought let there arise in me

Contrarie to thy precepts ten.
> "The Precious Perles of perfect
> Godliness" (c.1581),
> *The Monument of Matrones*
> *conteining seven severall Lamps*
> *of Virginitie, or Distinct*
> *Treatises . . . ,*
> Vol. I, Thomas Bentley, ed.
> 1582

352.   Alice Harvey
(fl. 1580–1600)

1 All the speed is in the morning.
> Quoted in *Commonplace Book*
> by Gabriel Harvey   c.1580

353.   Elizabeth Vernon
(c.1580–post-1647)

1 . . . ever you like best I should be, that place shall be most pleasing to me. . . .
> Letter to her husband, Henry
> Wriothesley, 3rd Earl of
> Southampton (July 8, 1599),
> Quoted in *Society Women of*
> *Shakespeare's Time*
> by Violet A. Wilson   1924

2 . . . I read in a letter from London that Sir John Falstaf is by his Mrs. Dame Pintpot made father of godly miller's thumb, a boye that's all heade and verie litel body; but this is a secrit.   Ibid.

354.   Lucy Harington
(1581–1627)

1 Death be not proud, thy hand gave not this blow. . . .
> "Elegy," l. 1,
> *Women Poets in English,*
> Ann Stanford, ed.   1972

2 And teach this hymn of her with joy, and sing,
> *The grave no conquest gets, Death hath no*
> *sting.*   Ibid., last ll.

355. Mistress Bradford
(fl. 1582)

1 As Hanna did applie, dedicate, and give her first child and sonne Samuel unto thee: even so doo J deere Father; beseeching thee, for Christ's sake, to accept this my gift.

> "The praier that maister Bradford's mother said and offered unto God in his* behalfe, a little before his martyrdome,"
> *The Monument of Matrones conteining seven severall Lamps of Virginitie, or Distinct Treatises . . . ,*
> Thomas Bentley, ed.   1582

*Her son, John Bradford, executed c. 1582 for heresy.

356. Elizabeth Tyrwhit
(fl. 1582)

1 . . . from Sathan deliver me, with the bread of Angels feede me, from fleshlie lusts purge me, from sudden death and deadlie sinne, O Lord take me.

> "Another praier at our uprising,"
> *Morning and Evening praiers, with divers Psalmes, Hymnes, and Meditations, made and set forth by the Ladie Elizabeth Tyrwhit*   1582

2 The beamie sun large light doth give, & chase away the night. Ibid., "The Hymne or praier to the sonne of God"

3 Sweets dews from heven to earth God grant, of peace & quiet mind,
That we may serve the living God, as his statutes doo bind.
> Ibid.

4 . . . conscience pricketh me to crie to thee my Lord for a heavenly cordiall of comfort. . . .   Ibid.,
> "A praier to God the father to be used before Morning praier"

5 Almightie God, teach me to doo thy will, take my right hand, and leade me in the true waie . . . bind my mouth with snaffle and bridle, when I will not drawe unto thee.
> Ibid.,
> "A praier to the blessed Trinitie"

6 Set little by the judgement of man: but feare the judgement of God.   Ibid.,
> "Certaine godlie sentences written by the Ladie E. T."

7 Harbour a harmlesse hart.
> Ibid.

8 Once you were not heere.
Awaie you must, and turne to dust.
> Ibid.

357. Ann Wheathill
(fl. 1584)

1 Give me . . . that most precious jewel of faith.   Prayer 7,
> *A Handfull of holesome (though homelie) Hearbs, gathered out of the Godlie Garden of Gods most Holie Word: for the common Benefit and comfortable Exercise of all such as are Devoutlie disposed*   1584

2 . . . humilitie . . . the beautiful flowre of vertue that groweth in the garden of man's soule. . . .   Ibid.,
> Prayer 9

3 [God's] love is like the evening and morning raine upon the earth. . . .
> Ibid.,
> Prayer 11

4 The house of our bodies is environed with enemies, but Thy providence will defend us out of all dangers.   Ibid.,
> Prayer 15

5 The yong chickens, when the kite striketh at them, have no other refuge but to run dickering under the wings of the hen: no more hath mankind any other defense against his enemies, but onelie the covering of Thy grace, and the shaddowe of Thy most precious passion. . . .
Ibid.,
Prayer 28

6 . . . to the wicked and carnall man Thou appeerest as a flaming fire, but unto them that be drawne with thy holie spirit, thou art like a plesant saphir. Ibid.,
Prayer 33

7 Thou are the well of pleasant waters, wherewith whoever is filled, they shall never be athirst. Ibid.,
Prayer 49

358. Elizabeth Carew
(1585?–1639)

1 MARIAM. Excuse too rash a judgment in a woman:
My sex pleads pardon, pardon then afford,
Mistaking is with us but too too common.
The Tragedie of Mariam the Faire Queene of Jewry,
Act I, Sc. 1 1613

2 Tis not enough for one that is a wife
To keep her spotless from an act of ill:
But from suspicion she should free her life,
And bare herself of power as well as will.
Ibid., Act III

3 For in a wife it is no worse to find
A common body, than a common mind.
Ibid.

4 HEROD. The hours are so increased by discontent,
Deep sorrow, Joshua-like the season stays.
But when I am with Mariam, time runs on,
Her sight can make months, minutes, days of weeks;
An hour is then no sooner come than gone,
When in her face mine eye for wonders seeks. Ibid., Act IV, Sc. 1

5 CHORUS. The fairest action of our human life,
Is scorning to revenge an injury;
For who forgives without a further strife,
His adversary's heart to him doth tie:
And 't is a firmer conquest, truly said,
To win the heart, and overthrow the head.
Ibid.

6 When she hath spacious ground to walk upon,
Why on the ridge should she desire to go?
Ibid.

7 Great hearts are tasked beyond their power. . . . Ibid.

8 In base revenge there is no honour won.
Who would a worthy courage overthrow,
And Who would wrestle with a worthless foe? Ibid., Sc. 2

9 We say our hearts are great, and cannot yield;
Because they cannot yield, it proves them poor Ibid., Sc. 3

10 CHORUS. A noble heart doth teach a virtuous scorn
To scorn to owe a duty over long;
To scorn to be for benefits forborne;
To scorn to lie, to scorn to do a wrong.
To scorn to bear an injury in mind;
To scorn a free-born heart slave-like to bind. Ibid., Sc. 4

11 CHORUS. What can 'gainst him a greater vengeance be,
Then make his foe more worthy far than he? Ibid., Sc. 5

12 HEROD. Oh do not with thy words my life destroy,
I prithee tell no dying-tale.
Ibid., Act V, Sc. 1

13 . . . benefit upbraided, forfeits thanks.
Ibid.

14 A bounteous act hath glory following it,
They cause the glory, that the act desire.
Ibid.

15 Oh, how you wrong our friendship, valiant
youth
With friends there is not such a word as
debts:
Where amity is ty'd with band of truth,
All benefits are therein common set.
Ibid.

359. Catalina de Erauso
(1585–post-1624)

1 I went out of the convent; I found myself in
the street, without knowing where to go;
that was no matter; all I wanted was liberty.
Quoted in *Biography of*
Distinguished Women
by Sarah Josepha Hale   1876

2 In this attempt [to cross the deserts of the
Andes] I *may* find death; by remaining here
[in this sanctuary] I shall certainly find it.
Ibid.

360. Mary Ward
(1585–1645)

1 Fervour is not placed in feelings but in will
to do well, which women may have as well
as men. There is no such difference between
men and women that women may not do
great things as we have seen by example of
many saints who have done great things.
Quoted in
The Life of Mary Ward
by Mary Catherine Elizabeth
Chambers   1884

361. Mary Sidney Wroth
(1586?–1640?)

1 . . . wounds still cureless, must my rulers
be.   "Morea's Sonnet,"
St. 2,
The Countess of Montgomeries
Urania   c.1615

2 . . . out-live me, and testify my woes.
Ibid., St. 3

3 Had I not happy been, I had not known
So great a loss; a king deposed feels
most
The torment of a throne-like-want
when lost. . . . "Pamphilia's Sonnet,"
St. 3, op. cit.

4 O Memory, could I but loose thee now . . .
"Lindamira's Complaint,"
l. 1, op. cit.

5 Those blessed hours, the only time of bliss,
When we feared nothing but we time
might miss
Long enough to enjoy what's now off
cast.   Ibid., St. 4

6 Press me with love, rather than lightly
fly. . . .   "The Verses of the Talkative
Knight,"
St. 4, op. cit.

7 Who thought such fair eyes could shine,
and dissemble?
Who thought such sweet breath could poison love's shame? "The Duke's Song,"
St. 2, op. cit.

8 When every one to pleasing pastime hies,
Some hunt, some hawk, some play
while some delight
In sweet discourse, and music shows
joy's might:
Yet I my thought do far above these
prize. "Pamphilia to Amphilanthus,"
St. 1, op. cit.

9 Who can blame me if I love,
Since Love before the world did move?
'Song,"
St. 1, op. cit.

10 Love in chaos did appear;
When nothing was, yet he seem'd clear
Ibid., St. 3

11 Love, a child, is ever crying;
Please him, and he straight is flying;
Give him, he the more is craving,
Never satisfied with having.
"Song,"
St. 1, op. cit.

362. Anna of Saxony
(fl. c.1587)

1 ... many pregnant women in confinement and small children of noble as well as of common rank are often miserably neglected, injured, harmed and crippled at the time of the birth or in the following six weeks, all through the clumsiness, arrogance, and rashness of the midwives and assisting women; few sensible midwives are to be found in this country [Germany].

(c.1587),
Quoted in
Women in the Middle Ages
by Sibylle Harksen   1975

363. Francesca Caccini
(1587–1640?)

1 I would rather lose my life before the desire to study and the affection I have always had for virtue, because this is worth more than all treasure and all grandeur.

Letter to Michaelangelo
Buonarroti the Younger, from
Genoa (May 26, 1617),
Quoted in *Women in Music*
by Carol Neuls-Bates   1982

364. Margaret Lambrun
(fl. 1587)

1 I confess to you, that I suffered many struggles within my breast, and have made all possible efforts to divert my resolution from so pernicious a design, but all in vain; I found myself necessitated to prove by experience the certain truth of that maxim, that neither reason nor force can hinder a woman from vengeance, when she is impelled thereto by love. Remark to Queen Elizabeth I when caught attempting to assassinate her

(1587),
Quoted in *Biography of
Distinguished Women*
by Sarah Josepha Hale   1876

2 Your majesty ought to grant me a pardon [without assurances from me].... A favour given under ... restraint is no more a favour; and, in so doing, your majesty would act against me as a judge.

Ibid.

365. Jane Anger
(fl. 1589)

1 Fie on the falsehood of men, whose minds go oft a madding, and whose tongues can not so soon be wagging, but straight they fall a railing. Was there ever any so abused, so slandered, so railed upon, or so wickedly handled undeservedly as are we women?

Protection for Women   1589

2 We are the grief of man, in that we take all the grief from man: we languish when they laugh, we lie sighing when they sit singing, and sit sobbing when they lie slugging and sleeping.

Ibid.

3 The lion rages when he is hungry, but man rails when he is glutted.

Ibid.

4 Wealth makes them lavish, wit knavish, beauty effeminate, poverty deceitful, and deformity ugly. Therefore, of me take this counsel:
Esteem of men as of a broken reed,
Mistrust them still, and then you well shall speed.

Ibid.

366. Anne Dowriche
(fl. 1589)

1 As winde disperse the wavring chaffe, and
toss it quite away,
All worldly pompe shall so consume, and pass without delay.   "Dedicatory poem to her brother,"

The French Historie   1589

2 Where is thy mirth become? where is thy smiling cheere?
Where is thy joyful peace, that erst did make thee shine so cleer?

Ibid., recto, p.1

3 What shall become of thee thou blinde and
  bloodie land?
  How dost thou think for to escape Gods
  just revenging hand?   Ibid., verso, p. 2

4 Be strong therefore my friends, make sharp
  the fatal knife;
  For of the Rebels ere the day not one shall
  scape with life.*   Ibid., recto, p. 25
  *Refers to Charles IX's plotting the massacre of
  Huguenots on St. Bartholomew's Day.

5 From Seate supernall of celestiall Jove
  Descended Truth, devoid of worldlie weed;
  And with the brightnesse of her beames she
  strove
  Gainst Sathan, Sinne, & Adams fleshlie
  Seed   Epilogue: "Veritie purtraied by the
                          French Pilgrime,"
                                St. 1, op. cit.

6 Who thinke they swim in wealth (blinded
  by guile):
  Yet wanting Truth; are wretched, poore &
  vile.   Ibid.

7 . . . malicious Men devise
  Torments for Truth. . . .   Ibid., St. 2

367.   Anne Clifford
(1590–1676)

1 I am like an owl in the desert.
                  Diary entry (May 1616),
                            The Diary of
                       the Lady Anne Clifford,
  Vita Sackville-West, ed.   1923

2 I . . . strived to sit as merry a face as I could
  upon a discontented heart . . . knowing that
  God often brings things to pass by contrary
  means.   Ibid. (March 1617)

3 She was naturally of a high spirit, though
  she tempered it by grace.   Portrait of her
          mother, Margaret, Countess of
                              Cumberland,
              Quoted in Society Women of
                      Shakespeare's Time
                      by Violet A. Wilson
                                      1924

4 . . . there were few things worthy of knowledge but that she had some insight into
  them . . . whereby that excellent mind of
  hers was much enriched, which even by nature was endowed with the seeks of the four
  moral virtues, Prudence, Justice, Fortitude,
  and Temperance. . . .   Ibid.

5 I was born a happy Creature in Mind, body,
  fortune.   Quoted in Diary of Lady
                          Margaret Hoby,
          Dorothy M. Meads, ed.   1930

6 . . . I gave myself wholly to retiredness as
  much as I could . . . and made good books
  and virtuous thoughts my Companions.
                                      Ibid.

368.   Mary Harding
(fl. c.1591)

1 . . . how weary my lady of the courte, and
  what littel gayne there is gotten in this
  tyme.   Letter to Countess of Rutland
                                    (1594),
              Quoted in Queen Elizabeth's
                          Maids of Honour
                    by Violet A. Wilson, n. d.

369.   Anne Hutchinson
(1591–1643)

1 Give me Christ, I seeke not for graces, but
  for Christ, I seeke not for promises, but for
  Christ, I seeke not for sanctification, but for
  Christ, tell not me of meditation and duties,
  but tell me of Christ.   Quoted in "Short
          Story by John Winthrop"*
                                  (c.1636),
          in Antinomianism in the Colony
            of Massachusetts Bay, 1636–1638,
              Charles Francis Adams, ed.
                                      1894
  *Governor of Massachusetts, who opposed her reli-
  gious views.

2 An oath, sir, is an end of all strife, and it is
  God's ordinance.   Spoken at her trial in
              Boston (November 1, 1637),
                                  op. cit.

3 I thinke the soule to be nothing but Light.
Ibid.

4 What from the Church at Boston? I know
no such church, neither will I own it. Call it
the whore and strumpet of Boston, no
Church of Christ!   Remark (c.1638),
op. cit.

370.   Margaret Winthrop
(c.1591–1647)

1 I have many reasons to make me love thee,
whereof I will name two, first because thou
lovest God, and secondly because that thou
lovest me.   Letter to John Winthrop,
The Winthrop Papers,
Samuel E. Morison et al., eds.
1929

371.   Sarah Copia Sullam
(1592–1641)

1 The lying tongue's deceit with silence
blight,
Protect me from its venom, you, my Rock,
And show the spiteful sland'rer by this sign
That you will shield me with your endless
might.   "My Inmost Hope,"
A Treasury of Jewish Poetry,
Nathan and Marynn Ausubel,
eds.
1957

372.   Artemisia Gentileschi
(1593–1652/53)

1 I have no wish to stay here [Naples] longer
because of the tumults of war as well as the
uncomfortable life and high prices.
Letter to patron (c.1630),
Quoted in "Artemisia
Gentileschi—A New
Documented Chronology"
by R. Ward Bissell,
Art Bulletin,
Vol. L, pp. 153–168.   1968

2 I have the greatest sympathy for your lordship, because the name of a woman makes
one doubtful until one has seen the work.
Letter to Don Antonio Ruffo, a
patron (January 30, 1649),
Quoted in *Women Artists:
1550–1950*
by Ann Sutherland Harris and
Linda Nochlin   1976

3 As long as I live, I will have control over my
being. . . .   Letter to Ruffo (March 1649),
op. cit.

4 This* will show your Lordship what a
woman can do.   Letter to Ruffo
(August 7, 1649),
op. cit.
*Her painting entitled *Venus and Adonis*.

5 Thanks to the grace of God and of the most
glorious Virgin, one woman at least has
been given that gift, namely to vary the subjects of my paintings, and no one has ever
found the same design repeated, not even
one hand.   Letter to Ruffo
(November 1649),
op. cit.

6 You will find the spirit of Caesar in the soul
of this woman.   Ibid.

373.   Gabrielle de Coignard
(?–d.1594)

1 I'm dust and ashes, Lord; remember this.

You are the wind and I am straw, or less,
For you can sweep me into nothingness.
Ah, do not let me fall in the abyss!
"Prayer,"
Sts. 3 , 4, Raymond Oliver, tr.;
Women Poets of the World,
Joanna Bankier and Deirdre
Lashgari, eds.   1983

374. Elizabeth Compton
(fl. 1595)

1 I would have two gentlewomen, lest one should be sick. . . . It is an indecent thing for a gentlewoman to stand mumping alone when God hath blessed their Lord and Lady with a great estate.
> Letter to her husband
> [William, Earl of Northampton],
> Quoted in *Court of King James*
> by Goodman, n.d.

2 . . . my desire is that you would pay your debts . . . purchase lands, and lend no money, as you Love God. . . .
> *Ibid.*

3 Lord Walden, what entertainment he gave me when you were at the tilt yard. If you were dead, he said he would be a husband, a father, a brother, and said he would marry me.
> *Ibid.*

375. Pocahontas
(1595/96–1616/17)

1 You promised my father [Chief Powhatan] that whatever was yours should be his, and that you and he would be all one. Being a stranger in our country, you called Powhatan father; and I for the same reason will now call you so.
> Remark to Captain John Smith (c.1616),
> Quoted in
> *Women of Beauty and Heroism*
> by Frank B. Goodrich   1858

2 I tell you then I *will* call you father and you *shall* call me child; and so I will forever be of your kindred and country.
> *Ibid.*

376. Rachel Speght
(1597–?)

1 . . . if fire, though but with a small sparke kindled, bee not at the first quenced, it may worke great mischiefe and dammage: So likewise may the scandals and defamations of the malevolent in time prove pernitious if they bee not nipt in the head. . . .
> "Epistle Dedicatorie,"
> *A Mouzell for Melastomus, the*
> *Cynicall Bayter of, and foule*
> *mouthed Barker against Evahs*
> *Sex. Or an apologeticall Answere*
> *to that Irreligious and Illiterate*
> *Pamphlet made by Jo[seph]*
> *Sw[etnam] and by him intituled,*
> *The Arraignement of*
> *Women*   1617

2 Some dogs barke more upon custome then curstnesse; and some speake evill of others, not that the defamed deserve it, but because through custom and corruption of their hearts they cannot speake well of any.
> *Ibid.*

3 If Reason had but curb'd thy witless will, Or feare of God restrain'd thy raving quill, Such venime foule thou would'st have blush to spue
> *Ibid.,*
> "Poem to Joseph Swetnam,"
> St. 1

4 Nefarious fiends thy sence heerein deluded, And from thee all humanitie excluded, Monster of men, worthie no other name
> *Ibid.,* St. 2

5 . . . God extracting a rib from his side, thereof made . . . Woman; shewing thereby, that man was as an unperfect building afore woman was made. . . .
> *Ibid.,*
> "Essay"

6 . . . man was created of the dust of the earth, but woman was made of a part of man, after that he was a living soule: yet was shee not produced from Adam's foote, to be his too low inferiour; nor from his head to be his superiour, but from his side, neare his heart, to be his equall. . . .
> *Ibid.*

7 ... men ought to love their wives as themselves, because hee that loves his wife, loves himself: And never man hated his owne flesh (which the woman is) unlesse a monster in nature.   Ibid.

8 ... then are those husbands to be blamed, which lay the whole burthen of domesticall affaires and maintenance on the shoulder of their wives. For, as yoake-fellowes they are to sustayne part of each others cares, griefs, and calamities. ...   Ibid.

9 ... if two Oxen be put in one yoke, the one being bigger then the other, the greater beares most weight; so the Husband being the stronger vessell is to beare a greater burthen then his wife.   Ibid.

10 For as Christ turned water into wine, a farre more excellent liquor ... So the single man is by marriage changed from a Batchelour to a Husband, a farre more excellent title: from a solitarie life unto a joyfull union. ...   Ibid.

11 Marriage is a merri-age, and this world's Paradise, where there is mutuall love.
      Ibid.

12 ... husbands should not account their wives as their vassals, but as those that are heires together of the grace of life. ...
      Ibid.

13 Great ... is the ingratitude of those men toward God, that dare presume to speake and exclaime against Woman. ...
      Ibid., Epilogue

14 ... where Ingratitude is harbored, there Love is banished.   Ibid.

15 Let men therefore beware ... it had been better for them to have been borne dumbe and lame,then to have used their tonges writing against God's handie worke, their owne flesh, women I meane, whom God hath made equall with themselves in dignity, both temporally and eternally.
      Ibid.

16 Upon a sudden, as I gazing stood, Thought came to me and asked me of my state.

. . . .
To whose demand, I thus again replied, I as a stranger in this place abide.
      "A Dream,"
      St. 1,
Mortalitie's Memorandum, with a Dreame Prefixed, imaginarie in manner, reall in matter   1621

17 My grief, quoth I, is called Ignorance, Which makes me differ little from a brute. ...   Ibid., St. 3

18 And from the soul three faculties arise, The mind, the will, the power; then wherefore shall
A woman have her intellect in vain, Or not endeavor Knowledge to attain.
      Ibid., St. 14

19 All parts and faculties were made for use; The God of Knowledge nothing gave in vain.   Ibid., St. 15

377.   Lucy Hay
(1599–1660)

1 Spell well, if you can.   *Thoughts*, n.d.

378.   Marie de L'Incarnation
(1599–1672)

1 We were within a hair's bredth of shipwreck,* but the One that commands the winds and the seas preserved us with his all-powerful finger.   Letter to her brother
      (1639),
      Quoted in
      Word from New France
      by Joyce Marshall   1967
*Written en route across the Atlantic from France to Canada.

2 The air is excellent and in consequence this [Quebec] is an earthly paradise where crosses and thorns grow so lovingly that the more one is pricked by them, the more filled with tenderness is the heart.
      Letter to Mother Marie-Gillette
      Roland (1640), op. cit.

3 God expects great things from you if you let
him govern your heart. . . .
                    Letter to Mlle. De Luynes
                              (1642),
                              op. cit.

4 Is it not painful to see the demons hold so
absolute an empire over so many peoples?
      Letter to her son (1644), op. cit.

5 I had to yield to the strength of divine love
and suffer that division* that was more sensible to me than I can tell you, but this has
not prevented my considering myself an in-
finity of times as the most cruel of all mothers. I ask your pardon for this, my very dear
son, for I am the reason for your suffering
many afflictions.*   Ibid.
*Refers to her decision to leave her son and found the
Ursuline Mission in Quebec.

6 Wretched as we may be, we are not forsaken by God.   Ibid., Letter to her son
                              (1647),
                              op. cit.

7 It is He that nourishes the birds of the air. It
is He that feeds the beasts of the forests. Is
His goodness then not great enough to extend to me that believes and trusts in Him?
                              Ibid.

8 We see nothing, we walk gropingly,
and . . . ordinarily things do not come
about as they have been foreseen and advised. One falls and, just when one thinks
oneself at the bottom of an abyss, one finds
oneself on one's feet.   Letter to her son
                              (1652),
                              op. cit.

9 Everything is savage here [Quebec], the
flowers as well as the men.
            Ibid., Letter to her sister (1653),
                              op. cit.

10 I run incessantly towards death, and such a
poor sinner as I am has need of help for the
passage to eternity.   Ibid.

11 . . . if God strikes us with one hand, he con-
soles us with another.   Letter to her son
                          (1665), op. cit.

12 Everything seems good to him that is hungry.   Letter to her son (1667),
                              op. cit.

13 The divine Spirit, which saw my struggles,
was pitiless to my feelings, saying in the
depths of my heart, "Quick, quick, it is
time, you must no longer delay, there is no
more for you in the world." Then it opened
the door to religion for me, its voice continuing to urge me with a holy im-
petuousity, which gave me no rest either by
day or by night.*
              Letter to her son (1669),
                              op. cit.
*Refers to her decision to leave her twelve-year-old
son and join the Ursulines.

14 If practical affairs . . . cause some objects to
pass through my imagination, these are but
little clouds, like those that pass across the
sun and remove it from our sight for a brief
moment, leaving it bright as before.
              Letter to Father Poncet, S.J.
                              (1670),
                              op. cit.

15 Writing teaches us our mysteries. . . .
              Letter to her son (1670),
                              op. cit.

379.   Kshetrayya
(17th century)

1 He set my heart floating on the honey
  stream of his words,
With his amorous kiss he burnt my lips,
And left me utterly alone, and unfulfilled.
                    "Dancing-Girl's Song,"
                              St. 2,
                    Indian Love Poems,
                    Tambimuttu and R.
                    Appalaswamy, eds. and trs.
                              n.d.

2 The playful youngster* with cloud-blue
  skin and garment of yellow silk,
Boasted to me he rules the hearts of sixteen
  thousand shepherdesses,
And walked proudly away
                              Ibid., St. 3
*The god Krishna.

380.   Marchioness de Tibergeau
(17th century)

1 No, it isn't the point of poetry to write of
the tenderness of love:
To pick away at it, finding just the right
words,
Arranging all in perfect measure and
rhyme,
Stripping the heart to feed the mind.
Untitled,
Elaine Partnow, tr.,
Quoted in *Biography of*
Distinguished Women
by Sarah Josepha Hale   1876

381.   Wang Wei
(17th century)

1 A traveller's thoughts in the night
Wander in a thousand miles of dreams.
"Seeking A Mooring,"
The Orchid Boat,
Women Poets of China,
Kenneth Rexroth and Ling
Chung, eds. and trs.   1972

382.   Brilliana Harley
(1600–1643)

1 . . . that is the evil in [those who are] melancholy; it acts most, inwardly; full of
thoughts they are, but not active in expressions. Many times they are so long in studying what is fit for them to do, that the opportunity is past.   Letter to her son,
Edward (January 4, 1638),
Letters of the
Lady Brilliana Harley,
Thomas Taylor Lewis, ed.
1854

2 Do exercise; for health can no more be had
without it. . . .   Letter to her son
(January 26, 1638),
op. cit.

3 If we could be so wise, we should find much
more sweetness in our lives than we do: for
certainly there is some good in all conditions (but that of sin), if we had the art to
distract the sweet and leave the rest.
Letter to her son
(November 2, 1638),
op.cit.

4 . . . I earnestly desire you may have that
wisdom, that from all the flowers of learning you may draw the honey and leave the
rest.   Letter to her son
(November 13, 1638),
op. cit.

5 . . . as to the body, those things do most
hurt which are of a deadly quality as poison, so nothing hurts the soul like that
deadly poison of sin; therefore . . . be
watchful against those great and subtile and
vigilent enemies of your precious soul.
Letter to her son (July 5, 1639),
op. cit.

6 . . . if Satan surprise us, he takes us at his
will, and if we turn our backs and run away,
O! he will pursue us till we be taken.
Ibid.

7 . . . tie yourself to a daily self-examination. . . .   Letter to her son (November 2,
1639),
op. cit.

8 . . . man is so forgetful of his God, that all,
and most of all great men, live in prosperity
as if they were lords of what they had, forgetting that they are but tenants at will.
Letter to her son (November 29,
1639),
op. cit.

9 . . . as some sharpness give a better relish to
sweet meats, so some sense of sickness
makes us taste the benefit of health.
Letter to her son (1639),
op. cit.

10 ... it is a most tedious thing to be served by a child without you had other servants that might help out his defects; they want wit and discretion and have their passions unbridled ... take my word; boys are troublesome servants. Letter to her son (May 22, 1641), op. cit.

11 ... keep your heart above the world, and then you will not be troubled at the changes in it. Letter to her son (July 15, 1642), op. cit.

383. Lucrezia Marinella
(fl. 1600)

1 It is an amazing thing to see in our city [Venice] the wife of a shoemaker, or a butcher, or a porter dressed in silk with chains of gold at the throat, with pearls and a ring of good value ... and then in contrast to see her husband cutting the meat, all smeared with cow's blood, poorly dressed, or burdened like an ass, clothed with the stuff from which sacks are made ... but whoever considers this carefully will find it reasonable, because it is necessary that the lady, even if low-born and humble, be draped with such clothes for her natural excellence and dignity, and that the man less adorned as if a slave, or a little ass, born to her service.
The Nobility and Excellence of Women together with the Defects and Deficiences of Men 1600

384. Ann Sutcliffe
(fl. 1600–1630)

1 ... remember thy dayes of Darknes, for they are many. *Meditations of Man's Mortalitie. Or, a Way to true Blessednesse,* 2nd ed. 1634

2 How soone alas, is thy span grasped, thy minute wasted, thy flower dead, thy vapor of life gone. ... Ibid.

3 ... the Glory of this World, is but the singing of Syrens, sweet, but a deadly poison. Ibid.

4 ... if the World fawne upon thee, it doth it that it may deceive thee, if it Exalt thee, it doth it that thy fall may bee the greater. ... Ibid.

5 ... take heed, lest thou by looking backe upon the vanities of this life, forget the care of thy Soule. ... Ibid.

6 Sathan's deceipts are covered, all with smiles. ... Ibid.

7 Pride, in it selfe doth beare a poyson'd breath. ... Ibid.

8 Sinne will increase, though creeping like a Snaile.
And if unto a Custome, it doth com,
He feeles it not, his soule is now growne numb. Ibid.

9 ... why should man ... wast his precious time
And triflingly let slip his golden dayes. ... Ibid.

10 Boast not of youth, or honours, wealth, or strength,
Who trust to them upon a reede doth leane Ibid.

11 ... feare not Death it brings with it no rod:
With care attend that sure uncertainty. ... Ibid.

385. Anne of Austria
(1601–1666)

1 God does not pay at the end of every week, but He pays. Letter to Cardinal Mazarin, *Letters,* n.d.

386. Elizabeth Raleigh
(fl. 1601)

1 I wish she would be as ambitious to do good
as she is apt to the contrary.
*Letter to Sir Robert Cecil
(c.1601),
Quoted in Society Women of
Shakespeare's Time
by Violet A. Wilson   1924*

387. Priscilla Alden
(1602?–pre-1687)

1 John, why do you not speak for yourself?*
*Quoted in Collections of
American Epitaphs and
Inscriptions with Original Notes,
Vol. III, Rev. Timothy Alden,
ed.
1814*

*Reply to John Alden's intervention for Miles Standish.

388. María de Agreda
(1602–1664/65)

1 Earth has 2,502 leagues, and up to the half
of it, which is the place or seat of Hell, there
are 1,251 leagues of profundity. In this center or middle of the Earth are the Purgatory
and the Limbo. Hell has many caverns and
mansions of punishment, and everything in
there forms a big infernal cavern with a
mouth in it, and is a proven fact that there is
a big stone, bigger than the mouth, to cover
it, when Hell will be sealed with all the sinners inside of it, where they have to suffer
for all the eternities to come.
*Quoted in
Women in Myth and History
by Violeta Miqueli   1962*

389. Violante do Céu
(1602?–1693)

1 You fool yourself and live a crazy day
or year, dizzy with adventures, and bent
solely on pleasures! Know the argument
of rigid doom and find a wiser way.
*"Voice of a Dissipated Woman
Inside a Tomb, Talking to
Another Woman Who Presumed
to Enter a Church with the
Purpose of Being Seen and
Praised by Everyone, Who Sat
Down Near a Sepulchar
Containing This Epitaph, Which
Curiously Reads,"
Rimas Varias   1646*

2 . . . the end which ends with no way out.
Ibid.

3 "From that world to bring to this
Peace, which, of all earthly blisses,
Is the brightest, purest bliss."
*"While to Bethlehem We Are
Going,"
St. 2, op. cit.*

4 A God—a God! becomes a man!
A mortal man becomes a god!
*"The Night of Marvels,"
St. 9, op. cit.*

390. Anna Maria Marchocka
(1603–1652)

1 Be Thou to me a physician and buoy that
my words may have purpose and profit.
*Prayer found in her
Autobiography,
Quoted in Women of the
Reformation,
Vol. III: From Spain to
Scandinavia,
by Roland H. Bainton   1977*

2 Humbly I beseech Thee, my Father. Cover
me with Thy pinions, enlighten mine eyes
that I wander not in a haze, knowing not
what to write nor where.   *Ibid.*

391. Elizabeth Melvill
(fl. 1603)

1 Through moss and mire, through ditches
deep we passed,
Through pricking thorns, through water
and through fire,
Through dreadful dens which made my
heart aghast,
He bare me up when I began to tire.
*Ane Godlie Dreame Complit in
Scottish Meter be M.M.,
Gentilwoman in Cul Ross, at the
Request of her Freindes,*
St. 1   1606

2 The brain of man most surely did invent
That purging place, he answer'd me again:
For greediness together they consent
To say that souls in torment may remain,
Till gold and goods relieve them of their
pain.   Ibid.

3 Weary I was, and thought to sit at rest,
But he said no, thou may not sit nor stand;
Hold on thy course, and thou shalt find it
best
If thou desirest to see that pleasant land.
Ibid., St. 7

4 The fire was great, the heat did pierce me
sore;
My faith was weak, my grip was wondrous
small,
I trembled fast, my fear grew more and
more. . . .   Ibid., St. 8

5 Away vaine world, bewitcher of my heart.
"A Verie Comfortable Song,"
St. 1, op. cit.

6 What shall I doe, are all my pleasures
passed,
Shall wordly lustes now take their leave at
last?   Ibid.

392. Marcela de Carpio de San Feliz
(1605–1688)

1 Love giving gifts
Is suspicous and cold;

I have all, my Belovèd,
When thee I hold.   "Amor Mysticus,"
St. 3,
The Catholic Anthology,
Thomas Walsh, ed.   1927

2 But in Thy chastising
Is joy and peace.
O Master and Love,
Let Thy blows not cease.   Ibid., St. 8

393. A. M. Bigot de Cornuel
(c.1605-14–1694)

1 Turenne's small change. (*La monnaie de M.
Turenne.*)*   Remark,
Quoted in *Nouvelle Biographie
Universelle*   1853–1866
*I.e., The eight generals appointed to take the place of
the great French marshal Henri de La Tour
d'Auvergne, vicomte de Turenne (1611–1675).

2 No man is a hero to his valet. (*Il n'y a point
de héros pour son valet de chambre.*)
Letter (August 13, 1728),
Lettres de Mlle. Aissé, n.d.

394. Anna van Schurman
(1607–1678)

1 Woman has the same erect countenance* as
man, the same ideals, the same love of
beauty, honor, truth, the same wish for self-
development, the same longing after righteousness, and yet she is to be imprisoned in
an empty soul of which the very windows
are shuttered.   Quoted in *The Dinner
Party, A Symbol of our Heritage*
by Judy Chicago   1979
*Probably a faulty translation; more likely, "stance"
or "posture."

395. Madeleine de Scudéry
(1607–1701)

1 Since we cannot be knowledgeable except for what others teach us, and since those that come last must follow what has come before, I decided that in drawing up the plan for this work, it was necessary to consult the Greeks, who have been our first masters.   Preface,
Ibrahim or the Illustrious Bassa,
an Excellent New
Romance   1652

2 In order to represent the heroic spirit it is undoubtedly necessary to have the hero do something extraordinary, as in a moment of heroic rapture, but this should not continue too long or it will degenerate into something ridiculous and will not have any good effect on the reader.   Ibid.

3 Since the body and the mind are so closely linked that one cannot suffer without the other, I fell ill.   Ibid., Vol. I

4 There are no husbands who take pleasure in wearing a bracelet of their wife's hair, who ask of them only little favors, who are delighted to kiss just the tip of their gloved hands, or to say gallant things to them. . . . Does it not seem strange that these husbands, who do not love, and yet completely possess their women, would deprive us, who truly love them, of the little things that in no way compromise their virtue?   Ibid., Vol. II

5 It is certain that I am inconstant, but at the same time I am not troublesome. I never contradict anyone's opinions or stand in the way of his pleasures. I give to others the freedom that I would have them accord me. I do not find fault with constancy, although I myself am happier with change, and my soul is so passionate that I could never condemn anything connected with love.   Ibid.

6 The cheerfulness and the joy that come from one's own nature are not easily affected by external matters.   Ibid.

7 "I am leaving then, Madame, or perhaps it is better to say that I am being separated from myself in being separated from you."   Ibid.

8 Any road that can take us where we want to go is the right one. Don't trouble yourself in asking if what you do is just, but only if it is advantageous.   Ibid.

9 . . . among private citizens it is prudent not to rise above the average.   Ibid., Vol. III

10 "I know how to love properly and I respect you."
"Respect can be considered a sign of admiration and not necessarily a mark of love."
"If I no longer respected you, I would stop trusting you. Then I would be worried and jealous."
"If you stopped being so indifferent, you would learn how to really love."   Ibid., Vol. IV

11 He who imposes unnecessary problems upon himself cannot complain because he is the sole cause of whatever ills befall him.   Ibid.

12 Repentance, which was an unknown feeling to me, is now ridding my heart of its love for Isabelle. . . . Reason is taking its place again in my heart.   Ibid.

13 When we know the truth in our own consciences it is unncessary to be troubled about anything else.   *Artamenes, or The*
Grand Cyrus, an Excellent New
Romance,
Vol. I   1653–1655

14 I want to learn from traveling. I want the opportunity to prove myself. I want to learn about myself, and, if possible, I want the whole world to know my name.   Ibid.

15 "I do not know if you have won without peril, but I know well that you have not triumphed without glory."   Ibid.

16 He loved Parthénie for her beauty alone, and when his eyes became accustomed to the sight of her, his passion diminished. His feelings slowly went from mild affection to indifference and from indifference to contempt. *Ibid., Vol. VI*

17 I find nothing more extravagant than to see a husband who is still in love with his wife. *Ibid.*

18 I do not think that she has ever been indisposed on a day when there was a party to attend. *Ibid., Vol. VII*

19 One cannot change mistresses without giving the reason why, and mistresses are bound to do the same if they wish to change. *Ibid., Vol. X*

20 ... the conquerer of all Asia is a foreigner nowhere. *Ibid.*

21 ... by staying in Babylon during the autumn and winter, in Susa during the spring, and in Ecbatana during the summer, he was able to live in an eternal springtime, feeling neither the great discomfort of the cold nor that of the heat. *Ibid.*

22 No one enters my heart the very first day.... *Ibid.*

23 Sapho* also has such admirable hands that in truth they are hands made for the taking of hearts, or, if you wish to consider her as a girl dearly loved by the Muses, hands worthy to pluck the loveliest flowers of Parnassus. *Ibid.*

*Scudéry referred to herself as Sappho.

24 She can so well draw the anatomy of the heart in love, if one may be permitted to say so, that she knows how to describe all kinds of jealousy, anxiety, impatience, joy, repulsion ... and all the tumultuous sentiments which are never understood but by those who feel them. *Ibid.*

25 If a feeling of glory had not placed in her heart the necessary strength to rise above herself, she doubtlessly would have acted in a different manner. *Clelia, An Excellent New Romance, Vol. I   1656–1661*

26 I would, without a doubt, rather be a simple soldier than be a woman, because to be truthful, a soldier can become king, but a woman can never become free. *Ibid.*

27 ... I believe that one is guilty only when committing useless crimes.... I am equally persuaded that any crime can be justified if followed by a great success. *Ibid., Vol. II*

28 Do not stop. There is no road to the throne that is not beautiful! *Ibid.*

29 This passion that I create for myself without troubling my heart, and this amorous disposition, which causes me neither great pain nor great joy, allows me a most pleasant reverie. *Ibid., Vol. III*

30 Glory is something that is the result of a virtuous action as much as light is a result of the sun that produces it, and, like the light from the sun, does not depend on any external stimuli. Since a virtuous action does not need to be witnessed in order to be what it is, it necessarily follows that glory, which is born of this action, will infallibly follow even though the action has not been publicized. It is better to find glory in one's own merit. In fact it is more important to have self-respect than to gain respect from others, and it is better to earn glory than to publicize it. *Ibid.*

31 He is not without some good sense, but is also incapable of a precise understanding of things. If he is not at all guilty of having any vice worth mentioning, he also does not have any virtues that could distinguish him from any other man, and if he has not been guilty of cowardice, he also has not given any indication of great courage. Finally, he is one of those men who never says anything that has not already been said, is never blamed or praised for anything he has done, and who during his whole life is spoken of only in reference to someone else.
Ibid.

32 In losing a husband one loses a master who is often an obstacle to the enjoyment of many things.   Ibid., Vol. IV

33 ... the familiarity of married life does not encourage love to grow.   Ibid., Vol. VI

34 An *honnête homme* must marry for the good of his family but should love as he pleases.   Ibid., Vol. VIII

35 ... one always admires her at first but inevitably comes to the point of despising her.   Ibid., Vol. IX

36 One should never reproach a person for a lack of beauty or for being unfortunate if one does not wish to seem cowardly or taunting. If unpleasant things are called for they must be said of those who are villains, scandal-mongers, slanderers, swindlers, and those envious of other persons' glory.
Ibid.

37 In fashioning a good portrait of an evil man one can sometimes instill a loathing for vice.   Ibid.

38 I could no longer summon up in my heart, even if I wanted to, this kind of love, filled as it is with an uneasy tenderness. The resentment I felt has chased it away and my good sense, having become stronger, will not allow it to return.   Ibid., Vol. X

39 Victory follows me, and all things follow victory. (*La victoire me suit, et tout suit la victoire.*)   "Tyrannic Love," n.d.

396. Henrietta Maria
(1609–1666)

1 Queens of England are never drowned.
Written during storm at sea
(February 1642),
Letters of Queen Henrietta Maria,
Mary Anne Everett Wood
Green, ed.   1857

397. Jane Owen
(fl. 1610–d. 1633?)

1 Among all the Passions of the mind, there is not any, which hath so great a sovereignty, and command over man, as the Passion of Feare. *An Antidote against Purgatory. Or Discourse, wherein is shewed that Good Workes, and Almes-Deeds, are a meanes for the preventing, or mitigating the Torments of Purgatory*   1634

398. Anne Bradstreet
(1612?–1672)

1 If at any time you are chastened of God, take it as thankfully and Joyfully as in greatest mercyes, for if yee bee His yee shall reap the greatest benefitt by it.
"To My Dear Children:
Religious Experience and
Occasional Pieces,"
Dedication to *The Tenth Muse
Lately Sprung Up in
America*   1650

2 That there is a God my Reason would soon tell me by the wondrous workes that I see, the vast frame of the Heaven and the Earth, the order of all things, night and day, Summer and Winter, Spring and Autumn, the dayly providing for this great household upon the Earth, the preserving and directing of All to its proper end.
Ibid.

3 Base World, I trample on thy face,
Thy Glory I despise,
No gain I find in ought below,

For God hath made me wise.
"Joy in God,"
op. cit.

4 I am obnoxious to each carping tongue
Who says my hand a needle better fits,
A Poet's pen all scorn I should thus wrong,
For such despite they cast on Female wits:
If what I do prove well, it won't advance,
They'll say it's stoln, or else it was by
chance.   Prologue, St. 5,
*Several Poems Compiled with
Great Variety of Wit and
Learning*   1678

5 Ye Cooks, your Kitchen implements I
frame
Your Spits, Pots, Jacks, what else I need
not name
Your dayly food I wholsome make, I warm
Your shrinking Limbs, which winter's cold
doth harm. "The Four Elements; Fire,"
op. cit.

6 Remember Sons, your mould is of my dust
And after death whether interr'd or burn'd
As Earth at first so into Earth return'd.
"Earth,"
op. cit.

7 But thou art bound to me, above the rest
Who am thy drink, thy blood, thy sap and
best. . . .   "Water,"
op. cit.

8 Nay what are words which do reveal the
mind,
Speak who or what they will they are but
wind.   "Air,"
op. cit.

9 But all admire our perfect Amity
Nor be descern'd, here's water, earth, air,
fire,
But here a compact body, whole intire.
"The Four Humours of Man:
Flegme,"
op. cit.

10 Ah me! conceiv'd in sin and born with sorrow,
A nothing, here to day and gone to morrow,
Whose mean beginning blushing can't reveal,

But night and darkness must with shame
conceal. "Of the Four Ages of Man:
Childhood,"
op. cit.

11 My silliness did only take delight
In that which riper age did scorn and slight.
Ibid.

12 For he that loveth wine, wanteth no woes.
Ibid.,
"Youth"

13 Man at his best estate is vanity.
Ibid.,
"Middle Age"

14 Each Season hath his fruit, so hath each
Clime:
Each man his own peculiar excellence,
But none in all that hath preheminence.
"The Four Seasons of the Year:
Spring,"
op. cit.

15 Blessed be thy Commons, who for common
good,
And thy infringed Laws have boldly stood.
"A Dialogue Between Old
England and New: New
England" (1642), op. cit.

16 Who was so good, so just, so learn'd, so
wise,
From all the Kings on earth she won the
prize.
Nor say I more than duly is her due,
Millions will testify that this is true.
She hath wip'd off th' aspersion of her Sex,
That women wisdome lack to play the Rex.
"In Honour of that High and
Mighty Princess, Queen
Elizabeth,"
op. cit.

17 Now say, have women worth? or have they
none?
Or had they some, but with our queen is't
gone?
Nay Masculines, you have thus taxt us
long,
But she, though dead, will vindicate our
wrong.
Let such as say our Sex is void of Reason,

Know 'tis a Slander now, but once was
   Treason.   Ibid.

18 And he that knowes the most, doth still bemoan
   He knows not all that here is to be known.
           "The Vanity of All Worldly
                       Things,"
                      op. cit.

19 Thou ill-form'd offspring of my feeble
   brain. . . .   "From the Author to her
                        Book,"
                      op. cit.

20 If for thy Father askt, say, thou hast none:
   And for thy Mother, she alas is poor,
   Which caus'd her thus to send thee out of
   doors.   Ibid.

21 Then when that knot's untyd that made us
   one,
   I may seem thine, who in effect am none.
            "Before the Birth of one of her
                    Children,"
                    op. cit.

22 If ever two were one, than surely we.
   If ever man were lov'd by wife, than thee.
            "To my Dear and loving
                    Husband,"
                    op. cit.

23 I had eight birds hatcht in one nest,
   Four Cocks there were, and Hens the rest,
   I nurst them up with pain and care,
   Nor cost nor labour did I spare
          "In reference to her Children"
           (June 23, 1656?), op. cit.

24 More fool than I to look on that was lent,
   As if mine own, when thus impermanent.
          "In Memory of my dear Child,
               Anne Bradstreet"
           (June 20, 1669), op. cit.

25 No sooner come, but gone, and fal'n asleep,
   Acquaintance short, yet parting caus'd us
   weep   "On my dear Grandchild, Simon
                  Bradstreet"
        (November 16, 1669), op. cit.

26 And if the sun would ever shine, there
   would I dwell.   "Contemplations,"
                    op. cit.

27 Children do natureally rather follow the
   failings than the virtues of their predecessors, but I am persuaded better things of
   you.   Letter to Simon Bradstreet (March
                  20, 1664),
       *The Works of Anne Bradstreet in
               Prose and Verse,*
       John Harvard Ellis, ed.   1867

28 There is no object that we see; no action
   that we do; no good that we enjoy; no evill
   that we feel, or fear, but we may make some
   spiritual advantage of all: and he that
   makes such improvement is wise, as well as
   pious.   "Meditations Devine and Moral,"
                  I, op. cit.

29 A prosperous state makes a secure Christian, but adversity makes him Consider.
                  Ibid., VIII

30 . . . those parents are wise that can fit their
   nurture according to their Nature.
                  Ibid., X

31 Authority without wisdom is like a heavy
   axe without an edg[e], fitter to bruise than
   polish.   Ibid., XII

32 The skillfull fisher hath his severall baits for
   severall fish, but there is a hooke under all;
   Satain, that great angler, hath his sundry
   baits for sundry tempers of men. . . .
                  Ibid., XXIII

33 A shadow in the parching sun, and a shelter
   in a blustering storme, are of all seasons the
   most welcom; so a faithfull friend in time of
   adversity, is of all other most comfortable.
                Ibid., XLVII

399.   Bathsua Makin
(1612?–1674?)

1 ... imprisonment of all other afflictions is one of the heaviest, oftentimes worse than death, for thereby a man is kept in lingering death, and is continually dying....
The Malady ... and Remedy of Vexations and Unjust Arrests and Actions   1646

2 ... these men of Law and their confederates ... the caterpillars of this Kingdom, who with their uncontrolled exactions and extortions, eat up the free-born people of this Nation....   Ibid.

3 Pass not, but wonder, and amazed stand
At this sad tomb; for here enclosed lie
Such rare perfections that no tongue or hand
Can speak them or portray them to the eye;
Such was her body, such her soul divine!
"Upon the much lamented death of the Right Honourable, the Lady Elizabeth Langham," ll. 1-5   1664

4 Recount her parts? her memory speaks more
Than what can be, or hath been said before:
It asks a volume, rather than a verse
Ibid., ll. 30-33

5 A learned woman is thought to be a comet, that bodes mischeif whenever it appears.
An Essay to Revive the Ancient Education of Gentlewomen 1673

6 To offer the world the liberal education of women is to deface the image of God in man; it will make women so high and men so low; like the fire in the house-top, it will set the whole world in a flame.
These things and worse than these are commonly talked of and verily believed by many who think themselves wise men.
Ibid.

7 To ask too much is the way to be denied all.
Ibid.

8 One generation passeth away and another cometh, but the earth, the theatre on which we act, abideth forever.   Ibid.

9 The harvest of bliss or woe will be according to the seed-time of this life.... A cask will long preserve the flavor with which, when new, it was once impregnated.
Ibid.

10 Merely to teach gentlewomen to frisk and dance, to paint their faces, to curl their hair, to put on a whisk,* to wear gay clothes, is not truly to adorn, but to adulterate their bodies; yea, (what is worse) to defile their souls.   Ibid.
*A woman's scarf, worn around the neck.

11 Had God intended women only as a finer sort of cattle, He would not have made them reasonable. Brutes, a few degrees higher than ... monkeys ... might have better fitted some men's lust, pride, and pleasure; especially those that desire to keep them ignorant to be tyrannized over.
Ibid.

12 If any desire distinctly to know what they should be instructed in?
I answer: I cannot tell where to begin to admit women, nor from what part of learning to exclude them, in regard of their capacities. The whole encyclopaedia of learning may be useful some way or other.
Ibid.

13 ... there is no pleasure greater, nor more suitable to an ingenious mind, than what is founded in knowledge; it is the first fruits of heaven and a glimpse of that glory we afterwards expect.   Ibid.

14 We cannot be so stupid as to imagine that God give ladies great estates merely that they may eat, drink, sleep, and rise up to play.... God, that will take an account for every idle thought, will certainly reckon with those persons that shall spend their whole lives in idle play and chat.
Ibid.

15 . . . women are not such silly giddy creatures as many proud men would make them. . . . Let such but look into history, they will find examples of illustrious women to confute them.   Ibid.

16 Objection: If we bring up our daughters to learning, no persons will adventure to marry them.
    Answer: . . . Many men, silly enough (God knows), think themselves wise, and will not dare marry a wise woman, lest they should be overtopped. . . . Learned men, to be sure, will choose such the rather, because they are suitable.   Ibid.

17 . . . a little philosophy, carries a man from God, but a great deal brings him back again.   Ibid.

18 . . . a little knowledge, like windy bladders, puffs up, but a good measure of true knowledge, like ballast in a ship, settles down and makes a person move more even in his station; 'tis not knowing too much, but too little that causes irregularity.
    Ibid.

19 Objection: Women do not desire learning.
    Answer: Neither do many boys . . . yet I suppose you do not intend to lay fallow all children that will not bring forth fruit of themselves.   Ibid.

20 Objection: Women are of low parts.
    Answer: . . . if this be true . . . there is the more need they should by all convenient means be improved. Crutches are for infirm persons.   Ibid.

21 Bad customs . . . ought to be broken, or else good customs can never come into use.
    Ibid.

22 Let women be fools, and then you may easily make them slaves.   Ibid.

400.   Henriette de Coligny
(1613?–1673)

1 His cleverness in the art of love is unequaled.

He knows how to draw the soul out by the ear.   Untitled sonnet (c.1725), Quoted in *Precious Women* by Dorothy Backer   1974

2 My heart opened to the poison which is killing me.   Ibid.

401.   Dorothy Leigh
(?–c.1616)

1 . . . gather hony of each flowre,
    as doth the labrous Bee.
Shee lookes not who did place the Plant,
    nor how the flowre did grow;
Whether so stately up aloft,
    or neere the ground below.

But where she finds it, there she workes,
    and gets the wholsome food,
And beares it home, and layes it up,
    to doe her Countrey good.
       "Counsell to my Children," prefatory poem, *The Mother's Blessing*   1616

2 . . . Feare not to be poore with Lazarus, but feare a thousand times to be rich with Dives.*   Ibid., Ch. 6
*Latin for rich; traditionally used as the name for the unnamed rich man in Luke 16:19 ff.

3 For before, man might say: The Woman beguiled me, and I did eate the poisoned fruit of disobedience, and I dye. But now man may say, if he say truely: The Woman brought me a Saviour, and I feede of him by Faith and live.   Ibid., Ch. 9

4 Children may be taught to reade, beginning at four yeeres old or before, and let them learn til ten, in which time they are not able to do any good in the Commonwealth, but to learne how to serve God, their King and Country by reading.   Ibid., Ch. 11

5 . . . have your Children brought up with much gentlenesse and patience . . . for forwardnes and curstnesse doth harden the heart of a child, and maketh him weary of vertue.   Ibid.

6 If a man hasn't enough wit to choose a woman he can love always, he should have wit enough to conceal his folly. . . .
Ibid., Ch. 13

7 . . . a woman fit to be a man's wife is too good to be his servant.   Ibid.

8 Take heede of idleness and slothfulnesses, which is a great hindrance.
Ibid., Ch. 18

402.   Costantia Munda
(fl. 1617)

1 Woman the crowne, perfection, and the meanes
Of all men's being

. . . .

Is the propagation of all humane kind,
Wherein the bodies frame, the intellect and mind
With all their operations doe first finde
Their Essence and beginning. . . .
Prefatory poem,
The Worming of a Mad Dogge
1617

2 . . . things simply good
Keep still their essence, though they be withstood
By all the compices of hell. . . .
Ibid.

3 Virtue oppos'd is stronger, and the foe
That's queld and foyld, addeth but more
Triumph to the conquest. . . .
Ibid.

4 . . . printing that was invented to be the store-house of famous wits, the treasure of Divine literature . . . is become . . . the nursery and hospitall of every spurious and pernicious brat, which proceeds from base phreneticall braine-sicke bablers.
Ibid. [Text]

5 . . . Woman, the greatest part of the lesser world, is generally become the subject of every pendanticall goose-quill. Every fantasticke Poetaster which . . . can but patch a hobling verse together, will strive to represent figments imputed to our sex. . . .
Ibid.

6 A man should give himself either to virtuous speech, or prudent silence.
Ibid.

7 . . . you lay open your imperfections . . . by heaping together the . . . fragments . . . of diverse english phrases . . . by scraping together the glaunder and . . . the refuse of idle-headed Authors and making a minglemangle gallimauphrie of them . . . let every bird take his owne feathers, and you would be as naked as Aesop's jay.
Answer to Joseph Swetnam's
"The Arraignment of Lewd, Idle,
Forward and Unconstant
Women"
(1615), op. cit.

8 . . . your booke being but the howling of a night bird shall circumscribe thy name in the dungeon of perpetual infamy.
Ibid.

403.   Joane Sharp
(fl. 1617)

1 Any answere may serve an impudent lyar,
Any mangie scab'd horse doth fit a scab'd
Squire "Epilogue: A Defence of Women,
against the Author of the
Arraignment of Women,"
Quoted in *Ester Hath Hang'd
Haman: or An Answere to a lewd
Pamphlet, entituled, The
Arraignment of Women** by
Ester Sowernam   1617
*Written by Joseph Swetnam in 1617.

2 If you ask how it happens some women prove naught,
By men turn'd to Serpents they are overwrought,

What the Serpent began, men follow that
still,
They tempt what they may to make women
do ill. Ibid.

3 To make a poore Maden or woman a
whore,
They care not how much they spend of
their store.
But where is there a man that will any thing
give
That woman or maide may with honestie
live? Ibid.

4 For a woman that's honest they care not a
whit,
Theyle say she is honest because she lackes
wit. Ibid.

5 The humors of men, see how forward they
bee;
We know not to please them in any degree:
For if we goe plaine we are sluts they doe
say,
They doubt of our honesty if we goe gay
Ibid.

6 Let Women and Maides whatsoever they
be,
Come follow my counsell, be warned by
me.
Trust not men's suites, their love proveth
lust,
Both hearts, tongues, and pens, doe all
prove unjust. Ibid.

7 Let women alone, and seeke not their
shame.
You shall have no cause then women to
blame. Ibid.

404. Ester Sowernam
(fl. 1617)

1 You are women; in creation, noble; in Re-
demption, gracious; in use, most blessed; be
not forgetfull of yourselves....
"Epistle Dedicatory,"
*Ester Hath Hang'd Haman: or
An Answere to a lewd Pamphlet,
entituled, The Arraignment of
Women** 1617

*Written by Joseph Swetnam in 1617.

2 The world is a large field, and it is full of
brambles, bryers, and weedes.
Ibid.,
"To the Reader"

3 There can be no love betwixt a man and his
wife, but where there is a respective estimate the one towards the other.
Ibid.

4 Eve was a good woman before she met with
the serpent, her daughters are good Virgins,
if they meet with good Tutors.
Ibid.

5 In all dangers, troubles, and extremities,
which fell to our Saviour, when all men fled
from Him, living or dead, women never for-
sook Him. Ibid., Ch. 3

6 I will not say that women are better than
men, but I will say that men are not so wise
as I would wish them to be....
Ibid., Ch. 4

7 ... it is apparant, yong men which are unmarried ... may serve an apprentiship to
honesty, but they are never free-men, nor
ever called honest men, till they be married:
for that is the portion which they get by
their wives. Ibid.

8 ... recollect your wits, write out of deliber-
ation, not out of furie; write out of advice,
not out of idlenesse.... Ibid., Ch. 7

9 ... forbeare to charge women with faults
which come from the contagion of Masculine serpents. Ibid.

405. Charlotte Bregy
(1619?–1693)

1 I never oppose the opinions of any; but I
must own that I never adopt them to the
prejudice of my own. Letters (1688),
Quoted in *Biography of
Distinguished Women*
by Sarah Josepha Hale 1876

2 I am indolent; I never seek pleasure and diversions, but when my friends take more pains than I do to procure them for me, I feel myself obliged to appear very gay at them, though I am not so in fact.
Ibid.

3 I am constant, even to obstinacy, and secret to excess.   Ibid.

406.   Lucy Hutchinson
(1620–1671)

1 If he esteemed her at a higher rate then she deserved, he was himself the author of the virtue he doated on; for she was but a faithful mirror, reflecting truly, but dimly, his own glories upon him.   "Address to her Children,"
The Life of Colonel Hutchinson,
by his widow Lucy   post-1664

2 Never was there a passion more ardent and less idolatrous; he loved her better than his life; with inexpressible tenderness and kindness; had a most high, obliging esteem of her; yet still considered honour, religion and duty, above her....   Ibid.

3 ... I was very attentive to all, and gathered up things that I would utter again to the great admiration of many that took my memory and imitation for wit.
Journal entry,
Quoted in
Leading Women of the
Restoration
by Grace Johnstone   1891

4 The greatest excellency she had was the power of apprehending and the virtue of loving him; so, as his shadow, she waited on him everywhere, till he was taken into that region of light which admits of none, and then she vanished into nothing.
Ibid.

5 'Twas not her face he loved, her honour and her virtue were his mistresses....
Ibid.

6 ... if he had erred, it was the inexperience of his age and the defect of his judgment, and not the malice of his heart, which had prompted him to pursue the general advantage of his country more than his own.
(c.1660), op. cit.

407.   Ninon de Lenclos
(1620–1705)

1 Old age is woman's hell. (*La vieillesse est l'enfer des femmes.*)
La Coquette vengée   1659

2 The joy of the mind marks its strength.
Letter to St. Évremond,
Lettres de Ninon de Lenclos au
marquis de Sévigné ... de la
correspondance de
cette femme célèbre avec
Saint-Évremond....   1806

3 Ah! the days pass in idleness and ignorance, and these same days destroy us and rob us of all that we have loved.
Letter to St. Évremond (1690),
op. cit.

4 If any one had proposed such a life to me [of chastity], I should have hanged myself.
Ibid.

5 We should take care to lay in a stock of provisions, but not of pleasures: these should be gathered day by day.
Correspondance authentique
de Ninon de Lenclos,
Émile Colombey, ed.   1886

6 The joy of a soul is the measure of its force. (*La joie de de l'esprit en marque la force.*)
Ibid.

7 I believe that I go further than most people do in everything that touches the heart.
Ibid.

8 What you priests tell us is sheer nonsense. I don't believe a single word of it.
Quoted in *The Immortal Ninon*
by Cecil Austin   1927

9 I put your consolations by,

And care not for the hopes you give:
Since I am old enough to die,
Why should I longer wish to live?
Untitled, op. cit.

10 ... I will keep my word ... and upon all occasions shall speak the truth, though I sometimes tell it at my own expense.
Letter to Marquis de Sévigné
(pre-1651),
The World's Great Letters,
M. Lincoln Schuster,
ed.   1940

11 ... please to remember that I have only the outside of a woman, and that my heart and mind are wholly masculine.
Ibid.

12 ... love, considered as a passion, is merely a blind instinct. ... It is an appetite, which inclines us to one object, rather than another, without being able to account for our taste.   Ibid.

13 Love never dies of starvation, but often of indigestion.   *L'Esprit des autres*,
Ch. 3, n.d.

408.   Jane Cavendish
(1621–1669)

1 LUCENAY. My distruction is that when I marry Courtly I shall bee condemn'd to looke upon my Nose, whenever I walke and when I sitt at meate confin'd by his grave winke to looke upon the Salt, and if it bee but the paireing of his Nales to admire him.
The Concealed Fansyes,
with Elizabeth Brackley
c.1644-1646

409.   Leonora Christina
(1621–1685)

1 Who can have any care for a child when one does not love its father? "A Record of the Sufferings of the Imprisoned Countess Leonora Christina"
(1674-1685),
Memoirs of Leonora Christina,
F. E. Bunnet, tr.   1929

2 ... it is not a disgrace to die for an honourable deed. ...   Ibid.

3 ... in the twinkling of an eye much may change; the hand of God, in whom are the hearts of kings, can change everything.
Preface, op. cit.

4 Many a one has acquired great learning in captivity, and has gained a knowledge of things which he could not master before. Yes, imprisonment leads to heaven. I have often said to myself: "Comfort thyself, thou captive one, thou art happy."
Ibid.

5 The past is rarely remembered without sorrow, for it has been either better or worse than the present.   Ibid.

6 He who rejoices to-day, cannot know that he may not weep to-morrow. ...
Ibid.

7 ... cultivate now in your youth what your parents taught you in childhood; now, while trouble visits you less severely, so that when it comes, you may be ready to receive it. ...   Ibid.

8 Thanks to Thee, fount of good!
Thou canst no evil brood
Thy blows are fatherly   "Song in
Remembrance of God's
Goodness,"
St. 6 (1674), op. cit.

9 What is all our labour here,
The servitude and yoke we bear?
Are they aught but vanity?
Art and learning what are ye?
Like a vapour all we see   Spiritual song,
St. 1 (1682), op. cit.

10 Naked to the world I came,
And I leave it just the same;
The Lord has given and He takes;
It is well whate'er He makes.
                    Ibid., St. 3

11 [Power is] like to Fortune, changeful the
course she flies,
And both, oh earthly pilgrim, are but vain
    fraud and lies.   "To Myself"
                    (January 1, 1683), op. cit.

12 . . . Fortune frolics ever, now under, now
above,
Emerging here and there her varied powers
to prove.
All that is earthly comes and vanishes again
                    Ibid.

13 True is the sentence we are sometimes told:
A friend is worth far more than bags of
gold.   Untitled poem (1683),
                    op. cit.

14 The vanished hours can ne'er come back
again,
Still may the old their youthful joys retain;
The past may yet within our memory live,
And courage vigor to the old may give.
            "Contemplation on Memory and
            Courage, recorded to the honour
            of God by the suffering Christian
            woman in the sixty-third year of
            her life, and the almost
            completed 21st year of her
            captivity"
                    (1684), op. cit.

15 Far oftener is it that the youth will lie
Helpless, when Fortune's favours from him
fly,
Than that the old man should inactive stay,
Who knows full well how Fortune loves to
play.   Ibid.

16 I am but dust and ashes,
    Yet one request I crave:
Let me not go unawares
    Into the silent grave.
            "A Morning Hymn,"
                    St. 6, op. cit.

17 Reason speaketh to my soul:
Fret not Soul,

Thou hast a better goal! Untitled Hymn,
                    St. 1, op. cit.

18 Loss of earthly gain
    Bringeth pain;
Fresh courage seek to obtain!
Much was still superfluous
Ceded,
    Nature's call
    After all
Makes but little needed.
                    Ibid., St. 3

410.   Margareta Ruarowna
(fl. 1621)

1 Riches exceeding and wealth without mea-
sure
God has conserved, safe in His keeping.
Abundant for flesh, abundant for spirit.
Radiant joy and resolute courage.
            From *Prayer Book* (1621),
            Quoted in *Women of the
                    Reformation,*
            Vol. III: *From Spain to
                    Scandinavia,*
            by Roland R. Bainton   1977

2 O King . . . The nations in Thy sight are as
nothing and are esteemed as vain and
empty. The world before Thee is as the
quivering of the balance, as the drop of the
morning dew when it lights upon the earth.
                    Ibid.

3 Chasten not Thy people because of those
who assist not in dispelling errors, but
rather for the sake of Thy children among
them extend Thy mercy.   Ibid.

411.   Elizabeth Brackley
(c.1623–1663)

Co-author with Jane Cavendish. See 408.

412. Margaret Cavendish
(1623/24–1673/74)

1 Great Nature clothes the soul, which is but
thin,
With fleshly garments, which the Fates do
spin,
And when these garments are grown old
and bare,
With sickness torn, Death takes them off
with care,
And folds them up in peace and quiet rest,
And lays them safe within an earthly chest:
Then scours them well and makes them
sweet and clean,
Fit for the soul to wear those clothes again.
"The Soul's Garment," in toto,
Poems & Fancies   1653

2 My cabinets are oyster-shells,
In which I keep my orient pearls;
To open them I use the tide,
As keys to locks, which opens wide
The oyster-shells
"The Convent of Pleasure,"
op. cit.

3 Mirth laughing came, and running to me,
flung
Her fat white arms about my neck. . . .
"Mirth and Melancholy,"
Mirth, op. cit.

4 Let you and I in Mirth and Pleasure swell,
And drink long lusty draughts from Bac-
chus' bowl,
Until our brains on vaporous waves do roll
Ibid.

5 Mirth good for nothing is, like weeds doth
grow,
Or such plants as cause madness, reason's
foe.
Her face with laughter crumples on a heap,
Which makes great wrinkles, and ploughs
furrows deep   Ibid.,
Melancholy

6 My music is the buzzing of a fly.
Ibid.,
Her Dwelling

7 Thus am I solitary, live alone,

Yet better loved, the more that I am known;
And though my face ill-favoured at first
sight,
After acquaintaince it will give delight.
Ibid.

8 I have not read much history to inform me
of the past ages; indeed I dare not examine
the former times, for fear I should meet
with such of my sex that have outdone all
the glory I can aim at, or hope to attain; for
I confess my ambition is restless, and not
ordinary; because it would have an extraordinary fame.
"An Epistle to My Readers,"
*Nature's Pictures, Drawn by
Fancies Pencil to the Life*
1656

9 Since all heroic actions, public employments, powerful governments, and eloquent pleadings are denied our sex in this
age, or at least would be condemned for
want of custom . . . I write.
Ibid.

10 Fare well, my dearest husband, die I must,
Yet do not you forget me in the dust.
"A diagram of Diverted Grief,"
op. cit.

11 A man awalking did a lady spy;
To her he went, and when he came hard by,
Fair Lady, said he, why walk you alone?
Because, said she, my thoughts are then my
own   "The Effeminate Description,"
op. cit.

12 We seem to love to death, but 'tis not so,
Because our passion moveth to and fro;
They are not fixed, but do run all about;
Every new object thrusts the former out
Ibid.

13 For I perceive the world is evil bent,
Judging the worst, although it good was
meant "Her Excellencies Tales in Verse,"
Bk. I, op. cit.

14 I love extraordinarily and constantly, yet not fondly, but soberly and observingly, not to hang about them as a trouble, but to wait upon them as a servant. . . .
The True Relation of my Birth, Breeding, and Life   1656

15 I never received a courtesy—but I am impatient and troubled until I can return it.
Ibid.

16 I think it no crime to wish myself the exactest of Nature's works, my thread of life the longest, my chain of destiny the strongest, my mind the peacablest, my life the pleasantest, my death the easiest, and the greatest saint in heaven; also to do my endeavour, so far as honour and honesty doth allow of, to be the highest on Fortune's wheel and to hold the wheel from turning, if I can.   Ibid.

17 I am very ambitious; yet 'tis neither for beauty, wit, titles, wealth, or power, but as they are steps to raise me to Fame's tower, which is to live by remembrance in afterages.   Ibid.

18 . . . I verily believe some censuring readers will scornfully say, why hath this Lady writ her own life? since none cares to know whose daughter she was or whose wife she is, or how she was bred, or what fortunes she had, or how she lived or what humour or disposition she was of. I answer that it is true, that 'tis to no purpose to the readers, but it is to the authoress, because I write it for my own sake, not theirs.
Ibid.

19 I am chaste, both by nature, and education, inasmuch as I do abhor an unchaste thought.   Ibid.

20 For had my brain as many fancies in 't
To fill the world, I'd put them all *in print*:
No matter whether they be well or ill exprest,
My *will* is done, and that please woman best.   Ibid.

21 It is an old saying that Ill News hath wings and Good News no legs.
Sociable Companions,
Act I, Sc. 1   c.1660

22 Many times married women desire children, as maids do husbands, more for honour than for comfort or happiness, thinking it a disgrace to live old maids, and so likewise to be barren.
Sociable Letters   1664

23 Women's minds are like shops of smallwares, wherein some have pretty toys, but nothing of any great value.
Ibid.

24 . . . it is no commendation to give them [women] courage and confidence, if I cannot give them wit.   Ibid.

25 . . . one may be my very good friend, and yet not of my opinion.   Ibid., Letter XVI

26 Everyone's conscience in religion is between God and themselves, and it belongs to none other.   Ibid.

27 And if we be not citizens in the commonwealth, I know no reason we should be subjects to the commonwealth.
Ibid.

28 But nature be thanked, she has been so bountiful to us as we oftener enslave men than men enslave us. They seem to govern the world, but we really govern the world in that we govern men. For what man is he that is not governed by a woman, more or less?   Ibid.

29 For like as women take a greater pride in their beauty than pleasure or content in their virtue, so they take more pride in being with child than in having a child.
Ibid., Letter XLVII

30 For though it be the part of every good wife to desire children to keep alive the memory of their husband's name and family by posterity, yet a woman has no such reason to desire children for her own sake. For first her name is lost as to her particular in marrying, for she quits her own and is named as her husband; also, her family, for neither name nor estate goest to her family according to the laws and customs of this country. Also, she hazards her life by bringing them into the world, and has the greatest share of trouble in bringing them up. Neither can women assure themselves of comfort or happiness by them when they are grown to be men, for their name only lives in sons, who continue the line of succession, whereas daughters are but branches which by marriage are broken off from the root from whence they sprange and engrafted into the stock of another family, so that daughters are to be accounted but as moveable goods or furnitures that wear out . . . for the line, name, and life of a family ends with the male issue.

Ibid., Letter XCIII

31 . . . I think a bad husband is far worse than no husband, and to have unnatural children is more unhappy than to have no children. And where one husband proves good, as loving and prudent, a thousand prove bad, as cross and spendthrifts, and where one child proves good, as dutiful and wise, a thousand prove disobedient and fools, as to do actions both to the dishonor and ruin of their families. Ibid.

32 I had rather die in the adventure of noble achievements, than live in obscure and sluggish security. *The Description of a New World Called the Blazing World* 1666

33 The shortest-lived Fame lasts longer than the longest life of Man. Ibid.

34 Every humane Creature can create an Immaterial World fully inhabited by immaterial Creatures, and populous of immaterial subjects, such as we are, and all this within the compass of the head or scull; nay, not onely so, but he may create a World of what fashion and Government he will, and give the Creatures thereof such motions, figures, forms, colours, perceptions, etc. as he pleases, and make Whirlpools, Lights, Pressures and Reactions . . . also he may alter that world as often as he pleases, or change it from a natural world, to an artificial; he may make a world of Ideas, a world of Atomes, a world of Lights, or whatsoever his fancy leads him to. And since it is in your power to create such a world, What need you to venture life, reputation and tranquility, to conquer a gross material world?

Ibid.

35 The truth is, a Sovereign Monarch has the general trouble; but the Subjects enjoy all the delights and pleasures.

Ibid.

36 Women make poems? burn them, burn them,
Let them make bone-lace, let them make bone-lace (1662), Quoted in *Reconstructing Aphra*, by Angeline Goreau 1980

37 . . . for all the Brothers were Valiant, and all the Sisters virtuous. Epitaph, Westminster Abbey, n.d.

38 True it is, our sex make great complaints that men from their first creation usurped a supremacy to themselves, although we were made equal by nature, which tyrannical government they have kept ever since, so that we could never come to be free, but rather more and more enslaved, using us either like children, fools, or subjects, that is, to flatter or threaten us, to allure or force us to obey, and will not let us divide the world equally with them, as to govern and command, to direct and dispose as they do; which slavery has so dejected our spirits, as we are become so stupid that beasts are but a degree below us, and men use us but a degree above beasts.

> "The Preface to the Reader,"
> *The World's Olio*, n.d.

39 Whereas in nature we have as clear an understanding as men, if we were bred in schools to mature our brains and to manure our understandings, that we might bring forth the fruits of knowledge.

> Ibid.

40 ... we have more wit than judgment, more active than industrious, we have more courage than conduct, more will than strength, more curiosity than secrecy, more vanity than good housewifery, more complaints than pains, more jealousy than love, more tears than sorrow, more stupidity than patience, more pride than affability, more beauty than constancy, more ill nature than good.

> Ibid.

413.   Hannah Woolley
(1623–c.1675)

1 ... blows are fitter for beasts than for rational creatures.

> *The Gentlewoman's Companion*   1675

2 ... a woman in this age is considered learned enough if she can distinguish her husband's bed from that of another.

> (c.1675), Quoted in
> *The Stuarts in Love*
> by Maurice Ashely   1964

414.   Mary of Warwick
(1624–1678)

1 O Lord, from my soul I bless Thee for making me again remember the wormwood and the gall I had met with from all my worldly enjoyments, to which I had too much let out my heart, and from which I did foolishly expect too much comfort.

> Diary (December 2, 1672),
> Quoted in
> *Leading Women of the Restoration*
> by Grace Johnstone   1891

2 I will begin my first rule of advice to your lordship, with desiring you not to turn the day into night ... by sleeping so long in the morning. ...

> Letter to George, Earl of Berkeley,
> "Rules for a Holy Life,"
> op. cit.

3 This sweet river, which I looked upon with so much pleasure and delight, while it was smooth, serene, and calm, when a sudden tempest rose unexpectedly, and made it rough and troubled, proved rather frightful than delightful to me, and made me shut my window, and cease looking on it.

> "Upon looking out of my window at Chelsea, upon the Thames,"
> op. cit.

415.   Eleanor Audeley
(fl. 1625–1651)

1 ... poore Beasts who hath bewitched you; why lye yee still ... arise, choose not Death rather then life. ...

> *A Warning to the Dragon and all his Angels*   1625

2 ... Awake yee Drunkards, weepe and howle all yee drinkers of Wine. ...

> Ibid.

3 POPE. Kings I Depose, and all their Race, to Raigne.

DIVELL. And Popes to Friers I can turne againe. Ibid.

4 Behold the Lord is at the Dore, as a man come from a farre journey; All that sleepe in the Dust of the Earth, shall heare his voyce and awake, and come forth. . . . Ibid.

5 No man so well knowes his owne frailtie, as the Lord your God knowes how prone Devotion is to Superstition. Ibid.

6 . . . as holy as Scarcrowes in a Garden of Cowcumbers. . . . Ibid.

416.   Bessie Clarkstone
(?–1625)

1 O for absolution! O for a drop to coole my tormented soule. Quoted in *The Conflict in Conscience of a deare Christian, named Bessie Clarkstone, in the Parish of Lanark, which she lay under threee yeare & an half* by John Wreittoun   1631

2 I am the most miserable and wretched creature in the world, for my sinnes are hid to my selfe, and knowne to God. Ibid.

3 Alas, I have long to live, and a wretched life . . . sighes helpe not, sobs helpe not, groanes helpe not, and prayer is faint. Ibid.

417.   Ann Fanshawe
(1625–1680)

1 Endeavour to be innocent as a dove, but as wise as a serpent. *Memoirs of Ann, Lady Fanshawe*   c.1670

2 Hate idleness, and curb all passions. Ibid.

3 Be true in all words and actions; and unnecessarily deliver not your opinion, but when you do, let it be just, and considered, and plain. Ibid.

4 . . . it was never seen that a vicious youth terminated in a contented, cheerful old age. . . . Ibid.

5 . . . reserve some hours daily to examine yourself and fortune; for if you embark yourself in perpetual conversation or recreation, you will certainly shipwreck your mind and fortune. Ibid.

6 Pardon me, O God, forgive whatsoever is amiss in me; break not a bruised reed. Ibid.

7 My glory and my guide, all my comfort in this life, is taken from me.* See me staggering in my path, because I expected a temporal blessing as a reward for the great innocence and integrity of his whole life. Ibid.

*Referring to the death of her husband, Sir Richard Fanshawe (1608–1666), diplomat and author.

8 Do with me, and for me, what thou pleasest; for I do wholly rely on thy promises to the widow and the fatherless. . . . Ibid.

9 Sometimes I thought to quit the world . . . and to shut myself up in a house for ever from all people; but upon the consideration of my children, who were all young and unprovided for, I resolved to suffer, as long as it pleased God, the storms and blows of fortune. Ibid.

418.   Christina of Sweden
(1626–1689)

1 There is a star above us which unites souls of the first order, though worlds and ages separate them. *Maxims* (1660–1680), cited in toto in *Pensées de Christine, reine de Suède*   1825

2 Life becomes useless and insipid when we have no longer either friends or enemies. Ibid.

3 Fools are more to be feared than the wicked. Ibid.

4 We read for instruction, for correction, and for consolation.   Ibid.

5 We grow old more through indolence, than through age.   Ibid.

6 This life is like an inn, in which the soul spends a few moments on its journey.
                                     Ibid.

7 I love men, not because they are men, but because they are not women.
                                     Ibid.

8 Confessors of princes are like men engaged in taming tigers and lions: they can induce the beasts to perform hundreds of movements and thousands of actions, so that on seeing them one might believe they were completely tamed; but when the confessor least expects it, he is knocked over by one blow of the animal's paw, which shows that such beasts can never be completely tamed.
                                     Ibid.

9 All that is visible and tangible has a bitter taste which some notice earlier, others later.   Ibid.

10 All that has an end can be borne, the insignificant duration of our life can and should help us through all the evil that this world has in store for us.   Ibid.

11 Man is an abyss of unhappiness and ignorance; he knows neither his body nor his soul, he is aware of being truly Nothing, clothed in a little life; but this knowledge does not make him wise, only unhappy, for philosophy can neither change him nor make him better.   Ibid.

12 The philosophers may say what they like, I believe that poverty, illness and physical pain are really evil things which reason cannot conjure away from us. Only religion assures us of acceptable consolation in the midst of all the evil of this life.
                                     Ibid.

13 Our true worth and our blessedness depend wholly on the last moment of our life: all the rest vanishes like smoke that disperses and is scattered by the wind. But in this last terrible or happy moment, God lets us know what we were and shall remain for all eternity, before the whole universe, and in God's own sight.   Ibid.

14 Nuns and married women are equally unhappy, if in different ways.
                                     Ibid.

15 All these dream-pictures of fatherland, freedom, honor, happiness amd pride, which have inspired so many outstanding men to perform great and noble deeds, are in truth no more than human day-dreams.
                          Ibid., last maxim

16 As you know, no one over thirty years of age is afraid of tittle-tattle. I myself find it much less difficult to strangle a man than to fear him.   Letter (1657),
                   Quoted in Christina of Sweden
                        by Sven Stolpe   1960

17 I shall never be virtuous enough to be a saint, nor infamous enough to pretend to be one.   Letter to Cardinal Azzolino
                                (c.1666–1668),
                                     op. cit.

18 Believe me—I would rather live on bread and water in Rome and have only one chambermaid to wait on me, than be elsewhere and possess all the kingdoms and treasures of the world.   Letter to Cardinal
                                Azzolino (c.1666),
                                     op. cit.

19 God has neither form nor shape under which we can know Him; when he speaks of Himself in metaphors and similes, He is adapting Himself to our foolishness, our limited capacity.   Marginal notes (c.1684),
                                     op. cit.

419. Marie de Sévigné
(1626–1696)

1 I love you so passionately that I hide a great part of my love not to oppress you with it.
Letter to Françoise Marguerite,
the Comtesse de Grignan,
her daughter,
*Letters of Madame de Sévigné to
her daughter and
friends* 1811

2 ... the most astonishing, the most surprising, the most marvelous, the most miraculous, the most magnificent, the most confounding, the most unheard of, the most singular, the most extraordinary, the most incredible, the most unforeseen, the greatest, the least, the rarest, the most common, the most public, the most private till today ... I cannot bring myself to tell you: guess what it is. Letter to M. de
Coulanges,
op. cit.

3 Everything unreasonable vexes me, and want of sincerity offends me.
From letters to her daughter,
op. cit.

4 There is nothing I have greater aversion and contempt for than idle stories.
Ibid.

5 If I inflict wounds, I heal them.
Ibid.

6 An inquiry after truth does not distract the brain half so much as numberless compliments and nothings. Ibid.

7 I am embarked in life without my own consent, and I know I must leave it again: that distracts me; for how shall I leave it? in what manner? by what door? at what time? in what disposition?.... I am frequently buried in thoughts of this nature, and then death appears so dreadful to me, that I hate life more for leading to it, than for all the thorns that strew its way.
Ibid.

8 There is no real evil in life, except great pain; all the rest is imaginary, and depends on the light in which we view things.
Ibid.

9 I am not the devil's because I fear God, and have at the bottom a principle of religion; then, on the other hand, I am not properly God's, because his law appears hard and irksome to me. Ibid.

10 Ah, how few are there of the really *true*! Consider the word a little, and you will like it. Ibid.

11 ...we must have fortitude, and make a merit of the impossibility of doing better.
Ibid.

12 There is no person who is not dangerous for someone. (*Il n'y a personne qui ne soit dangereux pour quelqu'un.*) Ibid.

13 In these woods reveries sometimes fall upon me so black that I come out of them as if I had had a touch of fever.
Ibid.

14 ... the singing woods....
Ibid.

15 ... lonely as a violet, easy to be hid....
Ibid.

16 When I step into this library, I cannot understand why I ever step out of it.
Ibid.

17 Racine has outdone himself; he loves God as he loved his mistresses; he enters into sacred things as he did into profane.
Ibid.

18 You can only thank God for such a man* and pray to have nothing to do with him.
Ibid.

*The French poet Jean de La Fontaine (1621–1695).

19 I feel about infections as you do about precipices, there are people with whom I have no fear of them. Ibid.

20 Ah, how easy it really is to live with me! A little gentleness, a little social impulse, a little confidence, even superficial, will lead me such a long way. Ibid.

21 We like so much to hear people talk of us and of our motives, that we are charmed even when they abuse us.
Ibid.

22 The desire to be singular and to astonish by ways out of the common seems to me to be the source of many virtues.
Ibid.

23 There is nothing so lovely as to be beautiful. Beauty is a gift of God and we should cherish it as such. Ibid.

24 I went to the marriage of Mademoiselle de Louvois. What shall I say about it? Magnificence, gorgeousness, all France, garments loaded and slashed with gold, jewels, a blaze of fires and flowers, a jam of coaches, cries in the street, torches flaring, poor folk thrust back and run over; in short, the usual whirlwind of nothing, questions not answered, compliments not meant, civilities addressed to no one in particular, everybody's feet tangled up in everybody's train.
Ibid.

25 I have seen the Abbé de la Vergne; we talked about my soul; he says that unless he can lock me up, not stir a step from me, take me to and from church himself, and neither let me read, speak, nor hear a single thing, he will have nothing to do with me whatever. Ibid.

26 It is sometimes best to slip over thoughts and not go to the bottom of them. (*Il faut glisser sur les pensées et ne pas les approfondir.*) Ibid.

27 The mind should be at peace but the heart debauches it perpetually. Ibid.

28 In the midst of all my moralizing, I keep a good share of the frailty of humanity.
Ibid.

29 I know nothing but you, and beyond you everything is nothing to me.
Ibid.

30 ... long journeys are strange things: if we were always to continue in the same mind we are in at the end of a journey, we should never stir from the place we were then in; but Providence in kindness to us causes us to forget it. It is much the same with lying-in women. Heaven permits the forgetfulness that the world may be peopled, and that folks may take journeys to Provence.
Ibid. (May 31, 1671)

31 True friendship is never serene.
Ibid. (September 10, 1671)

32 Youth is in itself so amiable, that were the soul as perfect as the body, we could not forbear adoring it. Ibid. (October 7, 1671)

33 Luck is always on the side of the big battalions. (*La fortune est toujours pour les gros bataillons.*) Ibid. (December 22, 1673)

34 ... some are content, and others not. There is nothing new in this: it is the world.
Ibid. (February 27, 1679)

35 I am such a libertine when I write that the first turn I take governs my whole letter. It were to be wished that my poor pen, galloping as it does, would gallop at least on a good footing. Ibid. (July 20, 1679)

36 ... it seldom happens, I think, that a man has the civility to die when all the world wishes it. Ibid. (March 1, 1680)

37 I can't think what he [her son, Charles] does with his money.... He finds ways of spending without getting anything in return, of losing without actually gaming, of paying without acquitting his debts. He's a bottomless pit.... His hand is a crucible that melts money. Ibid. (May 27, 1680)

38 ... we must submit to what is bitter, as well as to what is sweet.
Ibid. (June 19, 1680)

39 It is really mortifying to be so corporeal, that we cannot stir a step without dragging this tenement of clay about with us. You will tell me, perhaps, that the imagination travels a great way; that we think, and this is, in reality, the same thing. No, no, my dear; there is a wide difference.

         Ibid. (August 14, 1680)

40 . . . it is not always sorrow that opens the fountains of the eyes; tears flow from many different sensations.

         Ibid. (September 11, 1680)

41 There is no helping it; fate must have its course, and hie away, in a coach with four young horses and no postilion!

         Ibid.

42 . . . a lucky marriage pays for all.

         Ibid.

43 . . . this life is a perpetual chequer-work of good and evil, pleasure and pain. When in possession of what we desire, we are only so much the nearer losing it; and when at a distance from it, we live in expectation of enjoying it again. It is our business, therefore, to take things as God is pleased to send them.   Ibid. (September 22, 1680)

44 All sublunary events are the sport of Providence. . . .   Ibid. (November 8, 1680)

45 I speak what I feel.   Ibid.

46 . . . we grope in the dark, not knowing our way, taking good for evil, and evil for good. . . .   Letter to Count de Bussy (December 18, 1683), op. cit.

47 . . . we are transfused into our children, and . . . feel more keenly for them than for ourselves.   Letter to her daughter (February 27, 1685), op. cit.

48 . . . death interferes everywhere so indiscriminately that there is no building upon anything. . . . Shall we never lay aside the custom of attaching ourselves to these wretched mortals? Ah, it is very imprudent! And yet by what chains are we not riveted.

         Letter to her daughter (June 22, 1689), op. cit.

49 I find that the conditions of life are very hard. . . . I have been dragged against my will to the fatal period when *old age* must be endured; I see it, I have attained it; and I would, at least, contrive not to go beyond it, not to advance in the road of infirmities, pain, loss of memory, *disfigurements*, which are ready to lay hold of me.

         Letter to her daughter (November 30, 1689), op. cit.

50 The fashion of liking Racine will pass like that of coffee. (*La mode d'aimer Racine passera comme la mode du café.*)

         Letter to her daughter (January 29, 1690), op. cit.

420.   Anne-Marie-Louise d'Orléans
(1627–1693)

1 I don't ask for pity. It is something I dislike. I'd much rather be laughed at, for mockery usually reflects envy, and people without merit are seldom envied.   "Self-Portrait," *Mademoiselle's Portrait Gallery*   1657

2 . . . nothing wins me as readily as confidence, because confidence is a mark of respect—and respect is appreciated by anyone of courage and honor.

         Ibid.

3 I would spend my life in solitude rather than submit to the slightest humiliation, even if my fortune were at stake.

         Ibid.

4 . . . self-love is scarcely conducive to piety.

         Ibid.

5 . . . fate has been more lacking in judgment than I, for had it had more sense it would doubtless have treated me better.

         Ibid.

6 Children who are the object of great respect . . . usually become horribly puffed up.   From *Memoirs* (1652–1688), Quoted in *The Grand Mademoiselle*, Francis Steegmuller, tr.   1956

7 Nothing so disfigures a person, to my taste, as the inability to *talk*. . . .
Ibid.

8 . . . there is no doubt that Cupid is French. . . .
Ibid.

9 The sight of a person of my quality exposing himself to danger always does wonders for a population.
Ibid.

10 . . . the people almost always give way willy-nilly to anyone with a little resolution.
Ibid.

11 . . . getting married is a tremendous business. . . .
Ibid.

12 The designs of great princes are like the mysteries of the Holy Faith. It is not up to us to probe into them.
Ibid.

13 I have always had a great aversion for love, even for legitimate love, so unworthy of a noble soul has this passion always seemed to me.
Ibid.

14 Do you think I'm one to get married like damsels in novels? Do you think I'm waiting for some Amadís* to come questing for me on a palfrey, cleaving in twain everyone who crosses his path?
Ibid.

*Amadís de Gaula, eponymous hero of a prose romance of chivalry, possibly Portuguese in origin, dating from late 13th century.

15 . . . passion dies quickly. . . . One is better off to marry rationally: there may be aversion at first, but there will be all the more love later.
Ibid.

16 I'm the least bored person in the world. . . . Even when I daydream my reveries keep me entertained.
Ibid.

17 There is nothing so tiresome as other people's business.
Ibid.

18 . . . continual misfortunes and the griefs they cause, are capable of blunting even the best of memories.
Ibid.

19 It is God who determines our estate: he lets each of us enjoy his own within the limits of our varying dispositions.
Ibid.

20 . . . I had been offered great establishments that would have raised my rank but not increased my happiness. This, I saw now, I could attain only by devoting myself to someone who, in turn, would care for me.
Ibid.

21 I am a *grande dame*: my conduct is governed not by ambition, but by reason.
Ibid.

22 I hope to amuse myself in my old age—if God in his mercy grants me long life—by looking over what I did in my youth: it will give me greater insight into the wickedness of the world and confirm me in my renunciation of it.
Ibid.

23 Though I was born to great rank and wealth, though I have never harmed anyone, God had allowed my life to be afflicted by a thousand scourges. Such an example seems to me a worthy subject of reflection.
Ibid.

421. Dorothy Osborne
(1627–1695)

1 . . . there are certain things that custom has made almost of absolute necessity, and reputation I take to be one of those. . . .
Letter (c.1653), *Letters*,
E. A. Parry, ed.   1914

2 All letters, methinks, should be as free and easy as one's discourse, not studied as an oration, nor made up of hard words like a charm.
Letter to Sir William Temple
(October 1653),
op. cit.

422. Alice Thornton
(1627–1707)

1 Therefore it highly concerned me to enter into this greatest change of my life [marriage] with abundance of fear and caution, not lightly, nor unadvisedly, nor, as I may take my God to witness that knows the secrets of hearts, I did it not to fulfill the lusts of the flesh, but in chastity and singleness of heart, as marrying in the Lord.
The Autobiography of Mrs. Alice Thornton, of East Newton, Co. York 1875

423. Dorothy Berry
(fl. 1630s)

1   Whose Noble Praise
Deserves a Quill pluckt from an Angels wing,
And none to write it but a Crowned King.
Dedicatory poem, Quoted in *A Chaine of Pearle. Or A Memoriall of the peerless Graces, and Heroick Vertues of Queene Elizabeth, of Glorious Memory* by Diana Primrose 1630

2 Shee, Shee* it was, that gave us Golden Daies,
And did the English Name to Heaven raise:
Blest be her Name! blest be her Memory!
That *England* crown'd with such Felicity   Ibid.
*Queen Elizabeth I.

3 . . . some resplendent Star in frosty night
Hast made thy Native Splendor far more bright   Ibid.

424. Diana Primrose
(fl. 1630)

1 . . . Great Eliza, Englands brightest Sun,
The Worlds Renowne and everlasting Lampe,
Admits not here the least Comparison;

Whose Glories, doe the Greatest Princes dampe.   "The Induction,"
A Chaine of Pearle. Or a Memoriall of the peerless Graces, and Heroick Vertues of Queene Elizabeth, of Glorious Memory 1630

2 . . . by these lines so blacke and impolite,
Thy Swan-like lustre shall appeare more white.   Ibid.

3 . . . that Vestall Fire
Still flaming, never would Shee condescend
To Hymen's* Rightes. . . .
     "The Second Pearle. Chastity," op. cit.
*Eponymous god of fruitfulness; also, in Attic legend, representative of happy married life.

4 This Pearle of Prudence then, Wee all should prize
Most highly for it doth indeede comprise
Al Morall Vertues, which are resident
In that blest Soule, where this is president.
     "The Third Pearle. Prudence," op. cit.

5 The golden bridle of Bellerephon*
Is Temperance, by which our passion
And appetite we conquer and subdue.
     Ibid., "The Fourth Pearl. Temperance"
*Greek mythological hero, tamer of Pegasus, from whom he was thrown and lamed as he tried to fly to heaven.

6 Not dazed with fear, not mazed with any chance,
Not with vain hope (as with an empty spoon)
Fed or allured to cast beyond the moon,
Not with rash anger too precipitate,
Not fond to love, nor too, too prone to hate;
Not charmed with parasites' or Siren's songs,
Whose hearts are poisoned, though their sugared tongues
Swear, vow, and promise all fidelity
When they are brewing deepest villainy,
Not led to vain or too profuse expense,
Pretending thereby state magnificence,

Not spending on these momentary pleasures
Her precious time—but deeming her best treasures
Her subjects' love, which she so well preserved.   Ibid.

7 O Golden Age! O blest and happy years!
O music sweeter than that of the Spheres!
When Prince and People mutually agree
In sacred concord and sweet symphony!
                                          Ibid.

8 Among the Vertues Intellectuall,
The Van is lead by that we *Science* call;
A Pearle more precious then the *Aegyptian Queene**   "The Eighth Pearle. Science,"
                                       op. cit.

*Cleopatra.

9 . . . On her Sacred Lips
Angells enthron'd, most Heavenly *Manna* sips.
Then might you see her *Nectar-slewing Veine*
Surround the Hearers; in which sugred Streame,
Shee was able to drowne a World of men,
And drown'd with Sweetnes to revive agen.
                                          Ibid.

10 As Rose and Lillie challenge cheefest place,
For milke-white Lustre, and for Purple Grace:
So Englands Rose and Lillie, had no Peere,
For Princely Bounty shining every-where.
                        "The Tenth Pearle. Bounty,"
                                       op. cit.

425. R. M.
(?–1630?)

1 Women that are chaste when they are trusted, prove often wantons when they are causelesse suspected.   "Live Within Compasse in Chastitie,"
The Mothers Counsell or, Live within Compasse. Being the last Will and Testament to her dearest Daughter.   1630

2 There cannot be a greater clog to man than to be troubled with a wanton woman.
                   "Out of Compasse in Chastitie is Wantonesse,"
                                       op. cit.

3 O it is Temperance, with his golden squire
Between our passions, measures out a mein.
                   "Live Within Compasse in Temperance,"
                                       op. cit.

4 Though men's mindes can cover with bold sterne looks,
Pale women's faces are their owne faults books.   Ibid.

5 A fierce beast and a dangerous foe is an outrageous woman in a commonwealth.
                   "Out of Compasse in Temperance is Madnesse,"
                                       op. cit.

6 She that forsakes her husband because she dislikes his manners, is like her that forsakes the Honey least the Bee might sting her.   Ibid.

7 Heaven made Beauty like itselfe to view,
Not to be lockt up in a smokie mew:
A rosie vertuous cheeke is heavens gold,
Which all men joy to touch, all to behold.
                   "Live Within Compasse in Beautie,"
                                       op. cit.

8 O what is he whose youth can say he loves not,
Or who so old that woman's beauty moves not.   Ibid.

9 The closet of a bad woman's thought is ever open, and the depth of her heart hath a string that stretcheth to her tongue.
                   "Out of Compasse in Beauty is Odiousnesse,"
                                       op. cit.

10 To frivolous questions silence is ever the best answer.   "Live Within Compasse in Humilitie,"
                                       op. cit.

11 When Dogs fall on snarling, Serpents on hissing, and Women on weeping, the first meanes to bite, the second to sting, and the last to deceive.   "Out of Compasse in Humilitie is Pride," op. cit.

426.   Katherine Fowler Philips
(1631–1664)

1   Hence Cupid! with your cheating toys,
Your real griefs, and painted joys,
Your pleasure which itself destroys.
"Against Love,"
St. 1,
*Poems, By the Incomparable
Mrs. K. P.*   1664

2 Who to another does his heart submit,
Makes his own idol, and then worships it.
Ibid., St. 2

3 Beauty is but composure, and we find
Content is but the concord of the mind,
Friendship the unison of well-tuned hearts,
Honour the chorus of the noblest parts.
"To Mr. Henry Lawes,"
op. cit.

4 What built a world may sure repair a state.
Ibid.

5 I did not live until this time
Crowned my felicity,
When I could say without a crime,
I am not thine, but thee.
"To My Excellent Lucasia,* on
Our Friendship,"
St. 1, op. cit.

*Her friend, Anne Owen.

6 No bridgegroom's nor Crown-conqueror's mirth
To mine compar'd can be:
They have but pieces of this earth,
I've all the world in thee.
Ibid., St. 3

7 How soon we curse what erst we did adore.
"A Sea-Voyage From Tenby to
Bristol, Begun September 5,
1652. Sent From Bristol to
Lucasia, September 8, 1652,"
op. cit.

8 Friendship, like heraldry, is hereby known,
Richest when plainest, bravest when alone
Untitled,
op. cit.

9 He who commands himself is more a prince,
Than he who nations keep in awe
Untitled,
op. cit.

10 Religion which true policy befriends,
Designed by God to serve Man's holiest ends,
Is by that old Deceiver's subtle play
Made chief party in its own decay,
And meets that Eagle's destiny, whose breast
Felt the same shaft which his own feathers drest.   "Controversies in Religion,"
op. cit.

11 O what a desperate load of sins had we,
When God must plot for our felicity!
"On II. Corinthians V. 19,"
op. cit.

12 Our changed and mingled souls are grown
To such acquaintance now,
That if each would resume their own,
Alas! we know not how.
We have each other so engrost
That each is in the union lost.
"To Mrs. M. A. at Parting,"
op. cit.

13 There's no such thing as pleasure here,
'T is all a perfect cheat,
Which does but shine and disappear,
Whose charm is but deceit
"Against Pleasure—An Ode,"
St. 1, op. cit.

14 Nay, were our state as we could choose it,
'T would be consumed by fear to lose it.
Ibid., St. 4

15 Th' experienced prince then reason had,
Who said of Pleasure—"It is mad."
Ibid., St. 5

16 It is not brave to be possessed
Of earth, but to despise.
"A Country Life,"
St. 5, op. cit.

17 Opinion is the rate of things.
Ibid., St. 6

18 *Christ* will be King, but I ne'er understood
His Subjects built his Kingdom up with
Blood   "Upon the Double Murther of
King Charles I in Answer to a
Libellous Copy of Rimes by
Vavasor Powell," *Poems.*
*By the most deservedly Admired
Mrs. Katherine Philips, the
Matchless Orinda*...*   1678

*Pseudonym of Katherine Philips.

19 The dying Lion kick'd by every Ass.
Ibid.

20 Slander must follow Treason. . . .
Ibid.

21 If Kingdoms have Good Angels, you* are
ours   "Upon the Princess Royal her
Return into England,"
op. cit.

*Mary, Princess of Orange, later queen of England.

22 O wond'rous Prodigy!* O Race Divine!
Who owe more to your Actions than your
Line,
Your Lives exalt your Father's deathless
Name,
The blush of *England*, and the boast of
Fame.   *Ibid.*

*Charles II.

23 Unhappy Kings, who cannot keep a
Throne,
Nor be so fortunate to fall alone!
"On the 3. of September,
1641,"*
op. cit.

*Date of the defeat of Charles II at the battle of
Worcester.

24 Who would presume upon his Glorious
Birth,

Or quarrel for a spacious share of Earth,
That sees such Diadems become so cheap,
And *Hero's* tumble in a common heap?
Oh give me Virtue then, which sums up all,
And firmly stands when Crowns and Scep-
ters fall.   *Ibid.*

25 The Heart (like *Moses* Bush presumed)
Warm'd and enlightned, not consumed.
"Friendship in Embleme, or the
Seal. To my Dearest Lucasia,"
St. 5, op. cit.

26 They are, and yet they are not, two.
Ibid., St. 6

27 So Friendship from good Angels springs,
To teach the world Heroick things.
Ibid., St. 10

28 Ah, beauteous Blossom, too untimely dead!
Whither? Ah whither is thy sweetness fled?
"In Memory of F. P.* who died
at Acton the 24 of May, 1660, at
Twelve and an Half of Age,"
op. cit.

*Her stepchild, Frances Philips.

29 . . . (woe is me) I thought thee too much
mine.   *Ibid.*

30 Honour's to th' mind as Beauty to the
sense,
The fair result of mixed Excellence.
"To the truly competent Judge
of Honour, Lucasia, upon a
scandalous Libel
made by J. J.,"**
op. cit.

**Col. John Jones, signer of the death warrant of
Charles I.

31 Honour keeps Court at home, and doth not
fear
To be condemn'd abroad, if quitted there.
Ibid.

32 Redeem the poyson'd Age, let it be seen
There's no such freedom as to serve a
Queen.   "To Regina Collier,
on her cruelty to Philaster,"
op. cit.

33 Such horrid Ignorance benights the Times,

That Wit and Honour are become our
Crimes.   "The Prince of Phancy,"*
                                op. cit.

*William Cartwright (1611–1643), poet, playwright,
wit, scholar.

34 'Tis high Wit-Treason to debase thy Coin.
                                Ibid.

35 He's our Original, by whom we see
How much we fail, and what we ought to
be.   "Mr. Francis Finch, the Excellent
                                Palaemon,"
                                op. cit.

36 A Chosen Privacy, a cheap Content,
And all the Peace a Friendship ever lent,
A Rock which civil Nature made a Seat,
A Willow that repulses all the heat
                                "A Revery,"
                                op. cit.

37 He only dies untimely who dies late.
For if 'twere told to Children in the Womb,
To what a Stage of Mischiefs they must
come

· ·
. . . what we call their Birth would count
their Death.   "2 Cor. 5, 19. God was in
                                Christ Reconciling the World to
                                himself,"
                                op. cit.

38 I did but see him, and he dis-appear'd,
I did but pluck the Rose-bud and it fell
                                "Orinda upon little Hector
                                Philips,"*
                                St. 2

*Her son.

39 Tears are my Muse, and sorrow all my Art,
So piercing Groans must be thy Elogy.
                                Ibid., St. 3

40 Too promising, too great a mind
In so small room to be confin'd:
Therefore, as fit in Heavn' to dwell,
He quickly broke the Prison shell.
                                "Epitaph on her son H. P. at St.
                                Syth's Church, where her body
                                also lies Interred,"
                                op. cit.

41 That fierce Disease, which knows not how
to spare
The Young, the Great, the Knowing, or the
Fair.   "On the death of my Lord
                                Rich, only Son to the Earl of
                                Warwick, who dyed of the small
                                Pox, 1664,"
                                op. cit.

42 I'm so entangl'd and so lost a thing
By all the shocks my daily sorrow bring
                                "Orinda to Lucasia parting
                                October, 1661, at London,"
                                op. cit.

43 I meant not all the troubles that I brought.
                                Ibid.

44 Oh pardon me for pouring out my woes
In Rhime now, that I dare not do't in Prose.
                                Ibid.

45 But I can love, and love at such a pitch,
As I dare boast it will ev'n you enrich
                                Ibid., "To my Lady M[argaret]
                                Cavendish, chusing the Name of
                                Polycrite,"
                                op. cit.

46 For kindness is a Mine, when great and
true,
Of Nobler Ore than even *Indians* knew;
'Tis all that Mortals can on Heav'n bestow,
And all that Heav'n can value here below.
                                Ibid.

47 For my sake talk of Graves no more
                                Ibid., "To my Antenor,*
                                March 16, 1661/2,"
                                op. cit.

*Her friend, Philip James.

48 Grief sooner may distract than kill
                                Ibid.

49 Death is as coy a thing as Love.
                                Ibid.

50 Affliction nobly undergone,
More Greatness shews than having none.
                                Ibid.

51 And when our Fortune's most severe,
The less we have, the less we fear.
                                Ibid.

52 Woes have their Ebb as well as Flood
                                        Ibid.

53 Who hath not heard Lucasia's worthy
   Name?   "A Triton to Lucasia going to
              Sea, shortly after the Queens
                                  arrival,"
                                  op. cit.

54 Winds soft as Lovers Vows, Waves smooth
   as Glass.   Ibid.

55 Stout as a Rock, yet soft as melting Snow.
           "Epitaph on my truly honoured
                       Publius Scipio,"*
                                  op. cit.
   *I.e., Philip Skippon (d. 1660), English general.

56 He was above the little Arts of State,
   And scorn'd to sell his Peace to mend his
   Fate   Ibid.

57 And yet so modest, 'twas to him less pain
   To do great things, than hear them told
   again.   Ibid.

58 And if I sigh, it is thy breath is spent.
              "To Mrs. Mary Awbrey,"
                                  op. cit.

59 But we by Love sublim'd so high shall rise,
   To pity Kings and Conquerours despise
                                        Ibid.

60 Friendship's an abstract of this noble flame,
   'Tis love refin'd, and purged from all its
        dross,
   'Tis next to angel's love, if not the same,
   As strong in passion is, though not so gross.
                              "Friendship,"
                                  op. cit.

61 Thick waters show no images of things;
   Friends are each other's mirrors, and
        should be
   Clearer than crystal, or the mountain-
        springs   Ibid.

62 Poets and friends are born to what they are.
                                        Ibid.

63 Since affairs of the State, are already de-
        creed,
        Make room for Affairs, of the Court,
   Employment and Pleasure each other suc-
        ceed,

   Because they each other support.
   Were Princes confin'd
   From slackening their Mind,
   When by Care it is rufled and Curl'd,
   A Crown would appear
   Too heavy to wear
   And no Man would govern the World.
           Untitled, Choise Ayres, Songs,
                    and Dialogues   1675

64 The truth is, I have always had an incorri-
   gible inclination to the vanity of rhyming . . . and therefore did not so much resist
   it as a wise woman would have done.
              Letters from Orinda to
                    Poliarchus*   1705
   *Name used by her husband, James Philips.

65 I find too there are few Friendships in the
   World Marriage-proof. . . .
                                        Ibid.

66 . . . we may generally conclude the Marriage of a Friend to be the Funeral of a
   Friendship. . . .   Ibid.

67 . . . the thing call'd Friendship, without
   which the whole Earth would be but a De-
   sart, and Man still alone, tho' in Company,
   grows sick and languishes, and Love once
   sick, how quickly will it die?
                                        Ibid.

68 I . . . could never govern my Passions by
   the Lessons of the Stoicks, who at best
   rather tell us what we should be, than teach
   us how to be so; they shew the Journey's
   end, but leave us to get thither as we can.
                                        Ibid.

69 . . . the Practice of our Duty, tho' in the
   most difficult Cases, gives us a secret Satisfaction, that surpasses all other earthly
   Pleasures. . . .   Ibid.

70 Waste not in vain the crystal Day,
   But gather your Rose-buds while you may.
                                        Ibid.

71 I now see by Experience that one may love too much, and offend more by a too fond Sincerity, than by a careless Indifferency, provided it be but handsomely varnish'd over with civil Respect.   Letter to Sir Charles, No. XII, *Letters from Orinda to Poliarchus. The Second Edition, with Additions*   1729

427.   Marie-Catherine Desjardins
(1632–1683)

1 Hold your tongues, beautiful lovers, you err to the extreme;
Taking turns a hundred times to say: I love you.
In love, one must speak with elegance.
    "Madrigal,"
tr. Elaine Partnow,
Quoted in *Biography of Distinguished Women*
by Sarah Josepha Hale   1876

2 In our embraces I find all my happiness, and for me there is no more virtue or honor.
(*Dans nos embrassements je mets tout mon bonheur,*
Et je ne connais plus de vertu ni d'honneur)
    Untitled sonnet,
Quoted in *Precious Women*
by Dorothy Backer   1974

3 A sweet languor takes me from my senses, I die away in the arms of my faithful lover, and in this death I rediscover life.
(*Une douce langueur m'ôte le sentiment;*
Je Meurs entre les bras de mon fidèle amant,
Et c'est dans cette mort que je trouve la vie.)
    Ibid.

428.   Kawai Chigetsu-Ni
(1632–1736)

1 Grasshoppers
Chirping in the sleeves

Of a scarecrow.   Untitled haiku,
The Burning Heart: Women Poets of Japan,
Kenneth Rexroth and Ikuko Atsumi, eds. and trs.   1977

429.   Anne Wharton
(1632?–1685)

1 May yours* excel the matchless Sappho's name;
May you have all her wit, without her shame.   "The Temple of Death"   1695
*The English writer Aphra Behn. See 438.

2 Sorrow may make a silent moan,
But joy will be revealed.
    Untitled, St. 2,
Tooke's* Collection of Miscellaneous Poems,
    n.d.
*Probably John Horne Tooke (1736–1812), English politician and philologist.

430.   Mary Dyer
(fl. 1633–d. 1660)

1 In obedience to the will of the Lord I came and in His will I abide faithful to the death.
    Last words on the gallows (June 1, 1660), Boston,
Quoted in
Notable American Women,
Edward T. James, ed.   1971

2 My life not availeth me in comparison of the liberty of the truth.   Carved on monument to Mary Dyer at the Boston Statehouse, n.d.

431.   Catharina Regina von Greiffenberg
(1633–1694)

1 You empress of the stars, the heavens' worthy crown,

The world's great eye, and soul of a all
spreading earth "Spring-Joy Praising God.
Praise of the Sun,"
St. 1, George C. Schoolfield, tr.;
*Anthology of German Poetry
through the Nineteenth Century,*
Alexander Gode and Frederick
Ungar, eds.   1963

2 God's mirror (for naught else can show His
lustre's worth)   Ibid., St. 2

3 You are the king of time, and rule the years
and days.   Ibid., St. 3

4 You mirror-specturm-glance, you many-
colored gleam!
You glitter to and fro, are incomprehensi-
bly clear   "On the Ineffable
Inspiration of the Holy Spirit,"
St. 3,
Geistliche Sonnette, 1662,
Michael Hamburger, tr.;
*The Penguin Book
of Women Poets,*
Carol Cosman, Joan Keefe and
Kathleen Weaver, eds.   1978

5 To us alone did Heaven grant this greatest
good
So that the miracle grew all it could
In pure praise of faith and fame, not in sly
power of the wise.   "Why the
Resurrection was Revealed to
Women,"
St. 2, op. cit.

432.   Marie Madeleine de La Fayette
(1634–1692/93)

1 Splendour and gallantry have never appeared in France with such brilliance as
during the last years of the reign of Henri
II.   *The Princess of Clèves,*
First Part   1678

2 Most mothers think that to keep young
people away from love-making it is enough
never to speak of it in their presence.
Ibid.

3 Ambition and love-making were the soul of
this Court,* and obsessed the minds of men
and women alike.   Ibid.
*The court of Henry II of France.

4 . . . while he was her husband, he did not
cease to be a suitor, because there was always something to hope for beyond mere
possession. . . .   Ibid.

5 "If you judge by appearances in this place,"
replied Madame de Chartres, "you will
often be deceived; what appears on the surface is almost never the truth."
Ibid.

6 "Monsieur de Nemours* thinks," replied
the Prince of Condé,** "that a ball is of all
things the least tolerable for men in love,
both for those who are loved in return and
for those who are not. He says that, if they
are loved, they suffer at being less loved for
several days; that no woman lives who is
not prevented from thinking of her lover by
the cares of her toilette; that these occupy
her mind entirely; that this care in dressing
is for everybody as well as for the person
they love; that when they are actually at the
dance, they wish to attract all who look at
them: that, when they are satisfied with
their beauty, they feel a joy the greater part
of which is not caused by their lover. He
says also that, when a man is not loved, he
suffers still more to see the loved one in public; that, the more people admire her, the
more unhappy he feels at not being loved by
her; that he always fears lest her beauty
should give rise to a love more fortunate
than his—in short, he is of opinion that
there is no suffering equal to that of seeing
the loved one at a ball, unless it be to know
she is there and not be there oneself."
Ibid.

*Jacques de Savoie, duc de Nemours (1531–1585), a
known womanizer, a central character in this pseudo-
historical novel.

**Louis I de Bourbon, prince de Condé (1530–1569),
though physically deformed and weak, renowned for
his wit and courage.

7 " . . . force your husband to take you away. Do not fear that you are taking measures too harsh and too difficult: however terrible they may appear at first, they will be more pleasant in the end than the evils of an illicit love-affair." Ibid.

8 "I wished to wound your pride by letting you see that my love was dying of its own accord. . . . I did not want you to have the pleasure of showing how much I loved you, so as to make yourself appear the more lovable." Ibid., Second Part

9 "I have enjoyed all the pleasures that revenge can give. . . . " Ibid.

10 " . . . it would be impossible for me to be satisfied by your friendship if you were in love. People who are, cannot be trusted— one cannot be sure of their discretion. They are too absent-minded and too absorbed. . . . " Ibid.

11 "I know too much of life to be ignorant of the fact that appreciation of the husband does not prevent a man from falling in love with the wife." Ibid., Third Part

12 "My confession to you was not the result of weakness; and it needs more courage to confess such things than to undertake to hide them." Ibid.

13 "I was wrong in believing there was a man capable of hiding what pleases his vanity." Ibid.

14 "You had forgotten, then, that I loved you to distraction, and that I was your husband? One or the other can drive a man to extremities—how much more so the two together!" Ibid., Fourth Part

15 She spoke with such assurance, and truth convinces so easily, even when it is not probable, that Monsieur de Clèves* was almost assured of her innocence.
Ibid.

*Jacques de Clèves died unmarried in 1564; his marriage and the character of his wife, the Princess of Clèves, are completely fictionalized in the novel.

16 " . . . all who marry Mistresses who love them tremble when they marry them, and have fears with regard to other men when they remember their wives' conduct with themselves. . . . " Ibid.

17 "One reproaches a lover, but can one reproach a husband, when his only fault is that he no longer loves?" Ibid.

18 The necessity of dying, which she saw close at hand, accustomed her to detaching herself from everything. . . . Ibid.

433. Françoise de Maintenon
(1635–1719)

1 Nothing is more adroit than irreproachable conduct. Motto, *Maximes de Mme de Maintenon* 1686

2 Delicacy is to love what grace is to beauty. Ibid.

3 Frankness does not consist in saying a great deal, but in saying everything, and this everything is soon said when one is sincere, because there is no need of a great flourish and because one does not need many words to open the heart. Letter to Madame de Saint-Périer (October 21, 1708), *Lettres sur l'éducation des filles* 1854

4 Do not seek what pleases the intelligence: it is nothing but vanity. *Lettres historiques et édifantes*, Vol. I 1856

5 Renouncing all sensibility to cleverness, the desire to possess it, to exhibit it, to find it in others, discarding the vanity of eloquence, the curiosity to hear those who speak well because they divert our intelligence and stimulate a taste which we should mortify far rather than excite it or even cherish it. Letter to Madame de Berval, op. cit.

6 God gives me grace never to vex anybody. Letter to Madame de Jas (October 15, 1697), op. cit.

7 There is nothing so clever as not to be in the wrong and to bear oneself irreproachably at all times and with all sorts of people.
Letter to Dames de St. Louis, op. cit., Vol. II

8 I have never seen any one who was like me in that respect: I was sensitive to the praises of the King [Louis XIV] and I was just as sensitive to those of a laborer, and there is nothing that I should not have been capable of doing or suffering to get well spoken of.
Remark to Madame Glapion (1707), op. cit.

9 I have been young and beautiful, and I was universally loved; when I was a little older, I passed years in the whirl of wit; I got the favor of the great. Yet I protest to you, my dear child, that all these varied conditions leave a horrible void, a disquiet, a lassitude, a longing to know something different, because none of them is adequate to satisfy us: there is no repose unless one gives oneself to God.
Letter to Madame Glapion (September 1708), op. cit.

10 ... thanks to the goodness of God, I have no passions, that is to say, I love no one to the point of being willing to do anything that God would not approve.
Remark to Madame Glapion (October 1708), op. cit.

11 Behold the fine appointment he makes with me! That man never did love anyone but himself.* (*Voyez le beau rende vous qu'il me donne! Cet homme là n'a jamais aimé que lui-même.*) Remark (September 1, 1715), op. cit.
*Reference to Louis XIV's remark to her, while on his deathbed, "We shall meet again soon."

12 It is true that he [Louis XIV] loved me, and more than he loved any one else; but he loved me only so much as he was capable of loving; for men, when passion does not carry them away, are not very tender in their affection.
Remark to Madame Glapion (October 18, 1716), op. cit.

13 [I wish] to remain an enigma to posterity.
Correspondance générale de Mme de Maintenon, Vol. I, Théophile Lavallée, ed. 1865–1866

14 The longer I live, the more I grow in the opinion that it is useless to pile up wealth.
Letter to Madame de Brinon (April 1683), op. cit., Vol. II

15 Sometimes you have to deceive the King for his own good.
Letter to Bishop of Châlons (August 18, 1695), op. cit., Vol. IV

16 You can't arrange your room as you like, when the King comes to it every day, and you have to perish in symmetry.
Letter to Princess des Ursins (September 18, 1713), Quoted in *Madame de Maintenon, d'après sa correspondance authentique* by A. Geffroy 1887

17 Begin by making them love you, otherwise you will never succeed.
Quoted in *Daughters of Eve* by Gamaliel Bradford 1928

18 I am determined to aid those who aid themselves, and to let the good-for-nothing suffer.
Lettres, Vol. I, Marcel Langlois, ed. 1935–1939

19 [Marriage is] a state that causes the misery of three quarters of the human race.
Letter to Gobelin (August 1, 1674), op. cit.

20 ... the devotion that I look for is merely the same instinct of tidiness that I feel in arranging the furniture at Maintenon.
Letter to Gobelin (March 1675), op. cit.

21 You know that my mania is to make people hear reason.   Letter to Madame de Ventadour (February 1692), op. cit.

22 I see passions of all sorts, treasons, baseness, limitless ambition; on one side horrible desire, on the other people with rage at heart, who seek only to destroy each other; in sum, a thousand evil devices, and often for objects that are utterly trifling.
Remark to Madame Glapion (1708), op. cit., Vol. II

23 If you could see me, you would agree that I do well to keep myself hid: my eyesight is poor, my hearing is worse; nobody can hear me, for my speech has gone with my teeth; my memory goes astray, I no longer recall proper names, I mix up different periods; and misfortune and age together make me weep like all the other old women you have known.   Letter (July 9, 1714), op. cit.

434.   Mary Rowlandson
(c.1635–post-1678)

1 I had often before this said, that if the Indians should come, I should chuse rather to be killed by them then taken alive but when it came to the tryal my mind changed; their glittering weapons so daunted my spirit, that I chose rather to go along with those (as I may say) ravenous Bears, then that moment to end my dayes.
The Soveraignty & Goodness of God, Together, with the Faithfulness of His Promises Displayed; Being a Narrative of the Captivity and Restauration of Mrs. Mary Rowlandson   1682

435.   Rachel Russell
(1636–1723)

1 ... so little we distinguish how, and why we love, to me it argues a prodigious fondness of one's self. ...   Letter to Dr. Fitzwilliam,
Letters   c.1793

2 I was too rich in possessions whilst I possessed him*. ...   Ibid.
*Her husband, Lord William Russell, first Duke of Bedford.

3 But, sure, Doctor, 't is the nature of sorrow to lay hold on all things which give a new ferment to it. ...   Ibid.

4 ... that biggest blessing of loving and being loved by those I loved and respected; on earth no enjoyment certainly to be put in the balance with it.   Letter to the Earl of Galway, op. cit.

5 ... the conversation of friends ... is the nearest approach we can make to heaven while we live in these tabernacles of clay; so it is in a temporal sense also, the most pleasant and the most profitable improvement we can make of the time we are to spend on earth.   Letter to Lady Sunderland, op. cit.

6 ... who would live and not love?
Ibid.

7 Those who have tried the insipidness of [love] would, I believe, never choose it.
Ibid.

8 If I love once, I shall do so ever.
Letter (c.1667), *The Letters of Rachel, Lady Russell*, Lord John Russell, ed.   1853

9 ... I know as certainly as I live that I have been for twelve years as passionate a lover as ever woman was, and hope to be so one twelve years more.   Letter to Lord William Russell (1682), from Stratton, op. cit.

10 However, places are indeed nothing.
> Letter (April 1684),
> from Woburn, op. cit.

11 . . . I know not how to part, with tolerable ease, from the little creature [her son].
> Letter (Summer 1684),
> op. cit.

12 The time seems to be come that you must put anew in practice that submission you have so powerfully both tried yourself and instructed others to. . . .   Letter to
> Tillotson, Dean of Canterbury
> (c.1690),
> op. cit.

13 If your retirement pleases you, indeed, and that you do not deceive yourself, I have nothing to say against it, if your health does not abate, which it certainly will if your mind does not agree perfectly with what your will has chosen; let that be a timely monitor to you. Letter to Dr. Fitzwilliam
> (c.August 1693), from Belvoir,
> op. cit.

14 All common chat is silenced by these bigger matters, since all are judges of all.
> Letter to Lady Roos, her
> daughter (January 1694),
> from Southampton House,
> op. cit.

15 . . . the chiefest blessing on this earth you have—a kind husband and a pretty gentleman. Let that sweeten all other meaner things, as it is your duty it should do; strive to act your part and glory in it; it is a pride I can allow of, but all discontent proceeds from a pride that must be resisted, or a poor mortal can never be happy on earth or prepared to be so in heaven.
> Letter to Lady Roos
> (c.1694), op. cit.

16 I did not know the greatness of my love to his person,* until I could see it no more.
> Letter to Earl of Galway
> (May 1711),
> op. cit.

*Her son, the second Duke of Bedford.

17 The season is exceedingly fine, not much burnt up, but the farmers, for talk's sake, love wishing for what they have not. . . .
> Letter to Lady Roos
> (September 14, 1716),
> op. cit.

18 Consider my beloved, that all the innocent delights of life you may take, and no anxiety of mind with it; but if they shut out religious thoughts and performances, and devour and take up all our time, then indeed we sin; and conscience will sting at some time or other. . . .   Ibid., Letter to her
> children,
> op. cit.

436.   Antoinette Deshoulieres
(1638–1694)

1   It isn't easy for one who thinks
To be honest, and yet play the game;
The desire for gain, a day and night occupation,
     Is a dangerous spur
That goads one towards jeopardy.
> Untitled poem,
> Elaine Partnow, tr.,
> Quoted in *Biography of
> Distinguished Women*
> by Sarah Josepha Hale   1876

2 Alas! little sheep, you are blessed!
You pass through our fields without care,
     without alarm.   From *Les Moutons*
> (1695),
> "Idylle,"
> Elaine Partnow, tr., op. cit.

3 No one is satisfied with his fortune, nor dissatisfied with his intellect. (*Nul n'est content de sa fortune; Ni mécontent de son esprit.*)
> "Epigram," n.d.

437.   Makhfi
(1639–1703)

1 I want to go to the desert

but modesty is chains on my feet.
> Untitled,
> Willis Barnstone, tr.;
> *A Book of Women Poets,*
> Aliki and Willis Barnstone, eds.
> 1980

2 My tears break forth, my will is overridden,
 Reason retreats and resolutions wane;
The stormy bursts of weeping come unbidden,
 Wayward and fitful as the April rain.
> Untitled,
> St. 2, Paul Whalley, tr.;
> *Women Poets of the World,*
> Joanna Bankier and Deirdre
> Lashgari, eds.   1983

3 Upwards and onwards through the sun's dominions
 I soar, a Huma,* to the source of day.
> Ibid., St. 4

*A Persian mythological bird.

438.   Aphra Behn
(1640–1689)

1 Who is't that to women's beauty would submit,
And yet refuse the fetters of their wit?
> Prologue,
> *The Forced*
> *Marriage*   1670/71

2 Women, those charming victors, in whose eyes
Lie all their arts and their artilleries,
Not being contented with the wounds they make
Would by new strategems our lives invade.
Beauty alone goes now at too cheap rates;
And therefore they, like wise and politic states,
Court a new power that may be old supply,
To keep as well as gain the victory:
They'll join the force of wit to beauty now,
And so maintain the right they have in you.
> Ibid.

3 ERMINIA. Ungrateful duty . . .
Who bindest up our virtue too straight,

And on our honour lays too great a weight.
> Ibid.

4 AMINTA. Hang love, for I will never pine
For any man alife;
Nor shall this jolly heart of mine
The thoughts of it receive;
I will not purchase slavery
At such a dangerous rate;
But glory in my liberty,
And laugh at love and fate.
> Ibid.

5 AMINTA. While to inconstancy I bid adieu,
I find variety enough in you.
> Ibid.

6 She's as inconstant as the seas and winds,
Which ne'er are calm but to betray adventurers.   Ibid., Act I, Sc. 1

7 But yet, as tributary kings, we own
It is by you that we possess that throne,
Where had we victors been, we'd reign'd
alone.   Ibid., Epilogue

8 Not serious, nor comic, what is't then?
Th' imperfect issue of a lukewarm brain:
Bait it then as ye please, we'll not defend it,
But he who dis-approve it, let him mend it.
> Prologue,
> *The Amorous Prince*   1671

9 . . . beware of men, for though I myself be one, yet I have the frailties of my sex, and can dissemble too. Trust none of us, for if thou dost, thou art undone. We make vows to all alike we see, and even the best of men . . . is not to be credited in an affair of love.   Ibid.

10 This humour is not à-la-mode. . . .
> Ibid.

11 GOOD, SWEET, HONEYED, SUGAR-CANDIED READER,

Which I think is more than any one has called you yet, I must have a word or two with you before you do advance into the treatise; but 'tis not to beg your pardon for diverting you from your affairs, by such an idle pamphlet as this is, for I presume you have not much to do and therefore are to be obliged to me for keeping you from worse employment. . . .   "An Epistle to the
Reader,"
The Dutch Lover   1673

12 . . . I have heard the most of that which bears the name of learning, and which has abused such quantities of ink and paper, and continually employs so many ignorant, unhappy souls, for ten, twelve, twenty years in a university (who yet poor wretches think they are doing something all the while) as logic, etc. and several other things (that shall be nameless lest I misspell them) are much more absolutely nothing than the errantist play that e'er was writ.
Ibid.

13 (. . . as I would not undervalue poetry, so neither am I altogether of their judgment who believe no wisdom in the world beyond it.)   Ibid.

14 . . . plays were certainly intended for the exercising of men's passions not their understandings. . . .   Ibid.

15 LOVIS. Honour is the child of virtue, and finds an owner everywhere.
Ibid., Act I, Sc. 1

16 LOVIS. Well, go your ways; if marriage do not tame you, you are past all hopes. . . .
Ibid.

17 MARCEL. Only thus much the happier lover I,
Who gather all the sweets of this fair maid
Without the ceremonious tie of marriage;
That tie that does but nauseate the delight. . . .   Ibid., Sc. 2

18 SILVIO. I, like the birds of bravest kind, was hatched
In the hot sunshine of delight; whilst
Thou, Marcel, wert poorly brooded

In the cold nest of wedlock.
Ibid.

19 MARCEL. Oh rage, dull senseless rage, how blind and rude
It makes us.   Ibid., Act II, Sc. 2

20 ALONZO. . . . the natural itch of talking and lying. . . .   Ibid., Sc. 6

21 CARLO. . . . a prudent man speaks least. . . .   Ibid., Act III, Sc. 1

22 ALONZO. What shall I come to? all on the sudden to leave delicious whoring, drinking and fighting, and be condemned to a dull honest wife. Well, if it be my ill fortune, may this curse light on me that has brought me to't: may I love thee even after we are married. . . .   Ibid.

23 SILVIO. . . . he loves most that gives a loose to love.   Ibid., Sc. 4

24 OLINDA. . . . this marrying I do not like: 'tis like going on a long voyage to sea, where after a while even the calms are distasteful, and the storms dangerous: one seldom sees a new object, 'tis still a deal of sea, sea; husband, husband, every day,—till one's quite cloyed with it.   Ibid., Act IV, Sc. 1

25 MARCEL. O, who would be allied unto a woman,
Nature's loose handy-work?
Ibid., Act V, Sc. 1

26 Vows! dost think the gods regard the vows of lovers? They are things made in necessity and ought not to be kept, nor punished when broken.   Ibid.

27 SONG. A many kisses he did give:
And I returned the same
Which made me willing to receive
That which I dare not name.
Ibid.,
"The Willing Mistress"

28 QUEEN. There's a solemnity, methinks, in night,
That does insinuate love into the soul,
And makes the bashful lover more assured.
*Abdelazar; or, the Moor's
Revenge*   1676

182

29 SONG. Make haste, Amyntas, come away,
The sun is up and will not stay;
And O! how very short's a lover's day!
                                    Ibid.

30 SONG. Love in fantastique triumph sat,
Whilst bleeding hearts around him flowed,
For whom fierce pains he did create,
And strange tyranick power he showed.
                                    Ibid.,
                            "Love Armed"

31 I owe a duty where I cannot love.
                            Ibid., Act III, Sc. 3

32 SIR TIMOTHY. The Devil's in her tongue, and
so 'tis in most women's of her age; for when
it has quitted the tail, it repairs to the upper
tier.   *The Town Fop*   1676

33 SHAM. And is it possible you can be tied up
to a wife? Whilst here in London, and free,
you have the whole world to range in, and
like a wanton heifer, eat of every pasture.
                                    Ibid.

34 Sure, I rose the wrong way to-day, I have
had such damn'd ill luck every way.
                            Ibid., Act V, Sc. 1

35 You come bawling in with broken French,
Roaring out oaths aloud, from bench to
bench,
And bellowing bawdy to the orange-wench.
                                Prologue,
                            The Debauchee
                                    1677

36 . . . the disease o' th' age,
That pest, of not being quiet when they're
well,
That restless fever, in the brethren, Zeal;
In public spirits call'd, good o' th' Com-
monweal.
Some for this faction cry, others for that,
That pious nobile [mob] for they know not
what:
So tho' by different ways the fever sees,
In all 'tis one and the same made disease.
                                Prologue,
                            The Rover
                                    1677

37 Come away! Poverty's catching.
                            Ibid., Act I, Sc. 1

38 Variety is the soul of pleasure.
                            Ibid., Act II, Sc. 1, 1.1.

39 See the virtue of a wager, that new philosophical way, lately found out, of deciding
all hard questions.   Ibid., Act III, Sc. 1

40 Money speaks sense in a language all nations understand.   Ibid.

41 One hour of right-down love
Is worth an hour of dully living on.
                            Ibid., Act V, Sc. 1

42 The devil's in't if this will please the nation,
In these our blessed times of reformation.
                                Ibid., Epilogue

43 Conscience: a chief pretence to cozen fools
withal. . . .   Ibid.

44 Constancy, that current coin for fools.
                                    Ibid.

45 Sure he's too much a gentleman to be a
scholar.   *Sir Patient Fancy*   1678

46 He has been on the point of going off these
twenty years.   Ibid.

47 LADY KNOWELL. Can anything that's great
or moving be expressed in filthy English?
                                    Ibid.

48 FANNY. Sir, we shou'd bear with things we
do not love sometimes, 'tis a sort of trial,
sir, a kind of mortification fit for a good
Christian.   Ibid.

49 WHITTMORE. . . . a pox take all tedious
courtship.   Ibid.

50 She's a chick of the old cock.
                            Ibid., Act IV, Sc. 4

51 What has poor woman done, that she must
be debar'd from sense, and sacred poetry?
                                Ibid., Epilogue

52 The Devil take this curset plotting age,
'T has ruin'd all our plots upon the stage;
Suspicions, new elections, jealousies,
Fresh informations, new discoveries,
Do so employ the busy fearful town,

Our honest calling here is useless grown:
Each fool turns politician now, and wears
A formal face, and talks of state-affairs.
Prologue,
The Feigned Curtezans
1679

53 Patience is a flatterer, sir—and an ass, sir.
Ibid., Act III, Sc. 1

54 A brave world, Sir, full of religion, knavery,
and change! We shall shortly see better
days.   *Roundheads,*
Act I, Sc. 1   1682

55 Yet if thou didst but know how little wit
governs this mighty universe.
Ibid., Sc. 2

56 Verily the sin lieth in the scandal.
Ibid., Act III, Sc. 2

57 How the devil rebukes sin!
Ibid., Act V, Sc. 2

58 For 'tis not more to cure the lame & blind,
Then heal an impious, ulcerated mind.
"On Mr. Dryden, Renegade,"
*Poems upon Several
Occasions*   1684

59 'Tis not your saying that you love,
Can ease me of my smart;
Your actions must your words approve,
Or else you break my heart.
"Song,"
op. cit.

60 I saw 'em kindle to desire,
Whilst with soft sighs they blew the fire;
Saw the approaches of their joy,
He growing more fierce, and she less coy,
Saw how they mingled melting rays,
Exchanging love a thousand ways.

For who but a divinity,
Could mingle souls to that degree:
And melt 'em into ecstasy?
"On A Juniper-Tree, Cut Down
To Make Busks,"
op. cit.

61 He oft has fetters worn, and can with ease

Admit 'em or dismiss 'em when he please.
"To My Lady Morland at
Tunbridge" (c. 1670–1674),
op. cit.

62 Write on! and let not after ages say,
The whistle or rude hiss could lay
Thy might sprite of poetry. . . .
Silence will like submission show:
And give advantage to the foe.
"To Edward Howard" (1671),
op. cit.

63 Since Man with that inconstancy was born,
To love the absent, and the present scorn,
Why do we deck, why do we dress
For a short-liv'd happiness?
"To Alexis,"
op. cit.

64 Love does one staple rate on all impose,
Nor leads it to the trader's choice.
"To J. H.,"
op. cit.

65 Let us then love upon the honest square,
Since interest neither have designed,
For the sly gamester, who ne'er plays me
fair,
Must trick for trick expect to find.
Ibid.

66 Who but the learned and dull moral fool
Could gravely have foreseen, man ought to
live by rule?   "The Golden Age,"
St. 7, op. cit.

67 Oh! mischievous usurper of my peace;
Oh! soft intruder on my solitude,
Charming disturber of my ease,
Thou hast been nobly pursued.
"On Desire,"
op. cit.

68 Take back your gold, and give me current
love,
The treasure of your heart, not of your
purse   Ibid.

69 All the desires of mutual love are virtuous
Ibid.

70 For superstition will survive,
Purer religion to perplex.   Ibid.

71 Too often and too fatally we find
    Portion and jointure charm the mind,
The very soul's by interest swayed,
And nobler passion now by fortune is be-
    trayed;
By sad experience this I know,
And sigh, Alas! in vain because 'tis true.
           "To the Earl of Dorset,"
                   op. cit.

72 The soft, unhappy sex.
           "The Wandering Beauty,"
                   op. cit.

73 All I ask, is the privilege for my masculine
part, the poet in me . . . if I must not, because of my sex, have this freedom, I lay
down my quill and you shall hear no more
of me. . . .   Preface,
            The Lucky Chance
                   1686

74 Oh how fatal are forced marriages!
How many ruins one such match pulls on!
                   Ibid.

75 I would pay him in his own coin.
             Ibid., Act I, Sc. 2

76 Too much curiosity lost Paradise.
           Ibid., Act III, Sc. 3

77 Faith, Sir, we are here to-day, and gone to-
morrow.   Ibid., Act IV

78 Madam, 'twas a pious fraud, if it were one.
            Ibid., Act V, Sc. 7

79 Oh, what a dear ravishing thing is the beginning of an Amour!
         The Emperor of the Moon,
           Act I, Sc. 1   1687

80 Of all that writ, he was the wisest bard, who
    spoke this mighty truth—
He that knew all that ever learning writ,
Knew only this—that he knew nothing yet.
               Ibid., Sc. 3

81 Advantages are lawful in love and war.
                   Ibid.

82   Long did the untuned world in
    ign'rance stray,
Producing nothing that was great and gay,

Till taught by thee the true poetic way.
         "On The Death of Edmund
             Waller Esq.,"
           St. 3   1687

83 As love is the most noble and divine passion
of the soul, so it is that to which we may
justly attribute all the real satisfactions of
life; and without it man is unfinished and
unhappy.   *The Fair Jilt*   1688

84 How many idiots has it [love] made wise!
how many fools eloquent! how many home-
bred squires accomplished! how many cowards brave!   Ibid.

85 I will be deaf and blind, and guard my heart
with walls of ice, and make you know, that
when the flames of true devotion are kindled in a heart, it puts out all other fires.
                   Ibid.

86 And though they are all thus naked, if one
lives for ever among them, there is not to be
seen an indecent action, or glance: and being continually used to see one another so
unadorned, so like our first parents before
the fall, it seems as if they had no wishes,
there being nothing to heighten
curiosity. . . .   *Oroonoko, The Royal
                 Slave*   1688

87 "These people represented to me," she said,
"an absolute idea of the first state of innocence, before man knew how to sin: and 'tis
most evident and plain that simple nature is
the most harmless, inoffensive and virtuous
mistress. 'Tis she alone, if she were permitted, that better instructs the world than all
the inventions of man: religion would here
but destroy that tranquility they possess by
ignorance; and laws would tech 'em to
know offences of which now they have no
notion."   Ibid.

88 "And shall we render obedience to such a
degenerate race, who have no one human
virtue left, to distinguish them from the vil-
est creatures?"   Ibid.

89 ... in that country ... where the only crime and sin against a woman, is, to turn her off, to abandon her to want, shame, and misery; such ill morals are only practised in Christian countries, where they prefer the bare name of religion. ...
Ibid.

90 And I have observed, it is a very great error in those who laugh when one says, "A Negro can change colour": for I have seen them as frequently blush, and look pale, and that as visibly as ever I saw in the most beautiful white.
Ibid.

91 ... death, that common revenger of all injuries. ...
Ibid.

92 The captain, who had given the word, ordered his men to bring up these noble slaves in fetters, whom I have spoken of; and having put them, in the other lots, with women and children (which they call pickaninnies) they sold them off, as slaves to several merchants and gentlemen; not putting any two in one lot, because they would separate them far from each other; nor daring to trust them together, lest rage and courage should put them upon contriving some great action, to the ruin of the colony.
Ibid.

93 For when the mind so cruel is grown
As neither love nor hate to own,
The life but dully lingers on.
"To Damon"   1689

94 Love, like Reputation, once fled, never returns more.   *History of the Nun*   1689

95 ... that perfect tranquillity of life, which is nowhere to be found but in retreat, a faithful friend, and a good library. ...
The Lucky Mistake   1689

96 He had a natural aversion to danger, and thought it below a man of wit or common sense to be guilty of that brutal thing called Courage, or Righting. His philosophy told him, "It was safe sleeping in a whole skin."
Ibid.

97 This money certainly is a most devilish thing!   *The Court of the King Bantam*   1696

98 In short, all mankind, had they ever known him, would have universally agreed in this his character, that he was an original; since nothing in humanity was ever so vain, so haughty, so profuse, so fond, and so ridiculously ambitious as Mr. Would-be King.
Ibid.

99 The other sex, by means of a more expensive education to the knowledge of Greek and Roman languages, have a vaster field for their imaginations to rove in, and their capacities thereby enlarged.
"Essay in Defense of the Female Sex"   1696

100 Indeed, indeed, my soul, I know not to what degree I love you; let it suffice I do most passionately, and can have no thought of any other man whilst I have life. No! Reproach me, defame me, lampoon me, curse me and kill me when I do.
Letters   1696

101 That Love, the great instructor of the mind,
That forms anew, and fashions every soul,
Refines the gross defects of humankind.
"Iris to Damon," *The Lover's Watch*   1696

102 ... sighs are the children of lovers, that are born every hour.   Ibid.

103 Love ceases to be a pleasure, when it ceases to be a secret.   "Four O'Clock," op. cit.

104 ... in love we have a thousand foolish things to say, that of themselves bear no great sound, but have a might sense in love; for there is a peculiar eloquence natural alone to a lover, and to be understood by no other creature.   "Eleven O'Clock," op. cit.

105 How greedily his soul drank the strong poison in!   *The Nun, or, the Perjured Beauty*   1696

106 (Ah! how wretched are our sex, in being the unhappy occasion of so many fatal mischiefs, even between the dearest friends!)
Ibid.

107 And often they Languish'd with Joy beyond measure,
All Ravisht with Billing and dying with Pleasure.   "Beneath a Cool Shade"   1697

108 Hymen and priest wait still upon Portion and Jointure; Love and Beauty have their own ceremonies. Marriage is as certain a bane to Love as lending money is to friendship.   (1677), Quoted in *Reconstructing Aphra*
by Angeline Goreau   1980

109   We are forbid all grateful themes,
No ravishing thoughts approach our ear,
The fulsome gingle* of the times,
Is all we are allowed to understand or hear.   Ibid.
*Obsolete form of "jingle."

110 Though love, while soft and flattering, promises nothing but pleasures; yet its consequences are often sad and fatal.
The History of Agnes De Castro,
n.d.

111 It is not enough to be in love, to be happy; since Fortune, who is capricious, and takes delight to trouble the repose of the most elevated and virtuous, has very little respect for passionate and tender hearts, when she designs to produce strange adventures.
Ibid.

112 Nothing is more capable of troubling our reason, and consuming our health, than secret notions of jealousy in solitude.
Ibid.

113 "Love in youth," said old Venerable, "is very fearful of discovery."
The Unfortunate Happy Lady,
n.d.

439.   Joane Hit-him-home
(fl. 1640)

Co-author with Mary Tattlewell. See 440:1.

440.   Mary Tattlewell
(fl. 1640)

1 If you be young men, we wish you modest Maides in marriage; if Batchellours, beautifull Mistresses; if Husbands, handsome wives and good housewifes; if widdowers, wise and wealthy widoes: if young, those that may delight you: if old such as may comfort you.   "The Epistle of the Female Frailty to the Male Gender, in Generall,"
The Women's Sharpe Revenge: or an Answer to Sir Seldome Sober that writ those railing Pamphelets called The Juniper and The Crab-Tree Lectures, etc. Being a sound Reply and a full Confutation of those Bookes: with an Apology in this case for the Defence of us Women,
with Joane Hit-him-home
1640

2 ... what have we women done,
That any one who was a mother's sonne
Should thus affront our sex? Hath he forgot
From whence he came? or doth hee seek to blot
His own conception?   "Epistle to the Reader: Long Megge of Westminster, hearing the abuse, offeres to women to riseth out of her grave and thus speaketh,"
op. cit.

3 ... the corrupt heart discovereth itself by the lewd tongue.   Essay, op. cit.

4 Nature hath bestowed upon us two eares, and two eyes, yet but one tongue; which is an Embleme unto us that though we heare and see much, yet ought wee to speak but little....   Ibid.

5 . . . even fooles being silent have passed for wise men. . . .   Ibid.

6 . . . [as to] the most part of women being lyers, [it] is onely out of their goodnesses to cover the faults and abuses of men.
                                   Ibid.

7 If women be proud (or addicted to pride) it is ten to one to be laid, that it is the men that make them so; for like inchaunters, they do never leave or cease to bewitch & charme poore women with their flatteries.
                                   Ibid.

8 A faire tongue hath been too often the varnish or Embrodery of a false heart.
                                   Ibid.

9 . . . the faults of a weake Woman, are a continuall alarum against her, they are ingraven in brasse. . . .   Ibid.

10 . . . it hath beene the policy of all parents, even from the beginning to curbe us [women] . . . to keep us under, and to make us men's Vassailes even unto all posterity.
                                   Ibid.

11 How . . . comes it to passe, that when a Father hath a numerous issue of Sonnes and Daughters, the sonnes forsooth [are] . . . trained up in the Liberall Arts and Sciences, and there (if they prove not Block-heads) they may in time be book-learned [while] . . . we . . . are set onely to the Needle, to pricke our fingers: or else to the Wheele to spinne a faire thread for our owne undoings.   Ibid.

12 Man is of a dull, earthy, and melancholy aspect, having fallowes in his face, and a very forrest upon his Chin, when our soft and smooth Cheekes are a true representation of a delectable garden of intermixed Roses and Lillies.   Ibid.

13 . . . the man who is married to a peaceable and vertuous wife, being on earth hath attained Heaven, being in want hath arrived to wealth, being in woe is possest of weale, and being in care enjoyeth comfort. . . .
                                   Ibid.

14 . . . he under-went the noble Title of a Captaine, & if I had made triall of him, I doubt not but I might have found him a most desperate Chamber Champion, for he did scent of the Musk-Cat instead of the Musket, he was an Ambergreace gallant.
                                   Ibid.

15 . . . verily he was a dainty purfum'd carpet Captaine, a powdred Potentate, a painted Periwig frizled, frounced, Geometricall curious Glas-gazer, a comb'd curl'd and curried Commander, a resolut profest Chacer or hunter of fashions, and a most stiffe, printed, bristled, beard-starcher.
                                   Ibid.

16 . . . hee never came to me empty mouth'd or handed; for hee was never unprovided of stew'd Anagrams, bak'd Epigrams, sous'd Madrigalls, pickled Round delayes, broyld Sonnets, parboild Elegies, perfum'd poesies for Rings, and a thousand other such foolish flatteries, and knavish devices. . . .
                                   Ibid.

441.   Anna Hume
(fl. 1644)

1 Reader, I have oft been told,
Verses that speak not Love are cold.
                                   "To the Reader,"
                          The Triumphs of Love, Chastity,
                          Death: translated out of
                          Petrarch   1644

2 The fatal hour of her short life drew near,
That doubtful passage which the world doth fear   "The Triumph of Death,"
                          op. cit., Ch. 1

442. Mary Coffyn Starbuck
(1644/45–1717)

1 . . . such who believed once in Christ, were always in Him, without Possibility of falling away; and whom He had once loved, He loved to the End. . . . Quoted in *An Account of the Life of That Ancient Servant of Jesus Christ, John Richardson* by John Richardson 1757

443. Françoise de Grignan
(c.1646-1648–1705)

1 We [women] have not enough reason to use all our strength. [*Nous n'avons pas assez de raison pour employer toute notre force.*] Letter to her mother [Mme. de Sévigné], Quoted in *Letters of Madame de Sévigné to Her Daughter and Her Friends* 1927

444. Nur Jahan
(?–1646)

1 My eyes have one job: to cry. Untitled, Willis Barnstone, tr.; *A Book of Women Poets,* Aliki and Willis Barnstone, eds. 1980

2 Your love turned my body into water. Untitled, Willis Barnstone, tr., op. cit.

3 The key to my locked spirit is your laughing mouth. Ibid.

445. Maria Sibylla Merian
(1647–1717)

1 From my youth I have been interested in insects. First I started with the silkworms in my native Frankfurt am Main. After that . . . I started to collect all the caterpillars I could find in order to observe their changes . . . and I painted them very carefully on parchment. Quoted in "A Surinam Portfolio," *Natural History* December 1962

446. Jeanne-Marie de la Motte Guyon
(1648–1717)

1 But though my wing is closely bound, My heart's at liberty; My prison walls cannot control The flight, the freedom of the soul. "A Prisoner's Song," written while imprisoned at the Castle of Vincennes c.1695–1702

2 It is to be noted that the stream or torrent thus precipitated into the sea does not lose its own nature, though it is so changed and so lost that one knows it no longer. It is always what it was, but its existence is submerged and lost, not in its reality, but in its quality; for it assumes so much the quality of the ocean wave that you can see nothing in it peculiar to itself, and the more it sinks, is buried, and swallowed up, the more it forfeits its own quality to take that of the sea. *Les Torrents spirituelles, Opuscules,* Vol. I 1712

3 All other creatures, celestial and terrestrial, all disappear and vanish, and there is nothing left but God, as he was before the creation. Such a soul sees only God everywhere, and all is God to it, not by reasoning, or even by vision or illumination, but by absolute identity and unity, which making it God by participation destroys totally the vision of itself, and leaves nothing but God everywhere.   Ibid.

4 I have been taught how the angels contemplate.... The soul, raised above all common possibility, admits no distinct view nor object, but is absorbed in the superessential God. It is a condition that surpasses all understanding. I have learned the necessity of admitting no thought, of any nature whatsoever, either good or bad, and that one must be detached from every bond, if one is to enjoy prayer in all its purity.
          Discours chrétiens et spirituels,
          Vol. I   1716

5 There is nothing great, there is nothing holy, there is nothing wise, there is nothing fair, but to depend wholly upon God, like a child who does and can do only what is bidden.   *Lettres chrétiennes et spirituelles,*
          Vol. III   1717–1718

6 O God, what have I done to you that you should load me with souls after this fashion? Have I borne them in my womb that you should seem to wish to make me pay all their debts?   Ibid.

7 I know but one path, but one way, but one road, which is that of continual renouncement, of death, of nothingness. Everybody flies this way and seeks with passion all that makes us live; nobody is willing to be nothing, yet how shall we find what we are all seeking by a road which leads precisely wrong?   Ibid.

8 The soul is no longer either confined or possessed, nor does it possess or even enjoy; it perceives no difference between God and itself, sees nothing, possesses nothing, distinguishes nothing, even in God. God is the soul and the soul is God.
          Ibid., Vol. V

9 God does not destroy the virtues as virtues; but he destroys our proprietorship of these same virtues.   Ibid.

10 My condition in marriage was rather that of a slave than that of a free woman.
          La Vie de Mme J.-M. B. de La
          Mothe Guion, écrite par elle-même
          [Autobiography], Vol. I   1720

11 Let us love without reasoning about it, and we shall find ourselves filled with love before others have found out the reasons that lead to loving.   Ibid.

12 Yet Our Lord, together with all the weakness of childhood, gives me the power of a god over souls; so that with one word I can put them in torment or in peace, according as it may be best for their eternal welfare.
          Ibid., Vol. II

13 There are souls which do not belong to me, to whom I say none of these things. But for those which are given to me, like yours, God, by binding them to me intimately, gives me the knowledge of what is suited to them and of the designs he has for them.
          Letter to François Fénelon,*
          Quoted in
          Fénelon et Madame Guyon
          by Maurice Masson, n.d.
          *French theologian (1651–1715); leader of the Quietist movement.

14 It is an intimacy which cannot be expressed, and unless we should be made of one substance, there could not be anything more near. I had only to think of him [Fénelon] to be brought nearer to God, and when God enfolded me most closely, it seemed to me that with the same arms that enfolded me he also enfolded him.
          Autobiographical fragment,
          op. cit.

447.   Anna Tompson Hayden
(1648?–1720?)

1 For none Can tell who shall be next,
   Yet all may it expect;
   Then surely it Concerneth all,

Their time not to neglect.

"Upon the Death of yt desireable
young virgin, Elizabeth
Tompson, Daughter of Joseph &
Mary Tompson of Bilerika, who
Deceased in Boston out of the
hous of Mr legg, 24 August,
1712, aged 22 years,"
*Handkerchiefs from Paul: Being
Pious and Consolatory Verses of
Puritan Massachusetts,*
Kenneth B. Murdock, ed.
1927

2 Many a time we walk't together
& with discorce have pleasd each other.
(Sum yt have wondred how i could find
Discours with you to pleas your mind.)
"Verses on Benjamin Tompson,
by his sister, Anna Hayden,"
op. cit.

448. Maria Anna Mancini
(1649–1714)

1 You weep, and you are the master! (*Vous
pleurez, et vous êtes le maître!*)
Remark to Louis XIV (c.1658),
in response to being sent away
from Paris,
Memoires, n.d.

449. Nell Gwyn
(1650–1687)

1 Here is a sad slaughter at Windsor, the
young mens taking your Leaves and going
to France, and, although they are none of
my Lovers, yet I am loathe to part with the
men.   Letter to Madam Jennings
(April 14, 1684),
Quoted in
The Story of Nell Gwynn
by Peter Cunningham   1892

2 First, in hope of a joyful resurrection, I do
recommend myself whence I came, my soul
into the hands of Almighty God, and my
body unto the earth. . . . The Will of Nell
Gwyn (July 9, 1687),
Quoted in *Nell Gwyn,
The Story of her Life*
by Lewis Melville   1926

450. Juana Inés de la Cruz
(1651–1695)

1 How many, many days have I explored
The grove; and flower on flower, herb on
herb,
Scented and tasted! Yea, without reward—
My heart a burden that my pains perturb,
My step a draggled vagabond,—to rove
Through Time turned centuries, and
worlds a grove!
"The Divine Narcissus:
The Auto Sacramental,"
St. 3, Roderick Gill, tr.;
The Catholic Anthology,
Thomas Walsh, ed.   1927

2 Stupid men, forever prone
To fix the blame on woman's reason,
When 'tis merely your own treason
That creates her fault alone!
"Redondillas,"
St. 1, Garrett Strange, tr., op. cit.

3 Her resistance you opposed,
Then, all serious, attaint her;
Fickle, light and faithless paint her,
Though 'twas you the role that chose.
Ibid., St. 3

4 Nothing could be funnier
Than the tale of him befouling
His own mirror, and then scowling
When the image was a blur.
Ibid., St. 5

5 The greater evil who is in—
When both in wayward paths are
straying—
The poor sinner for the pain,
Or he that pays her for the sin?
Ibid., St. 9

6 This evening when I spake with thee,
     beloved,
   as in thy face and in thy mien I saw
   that I could not persuade thee with my
     words,
   the longing came for thee to see my heart
                    "This evening when I spake with
                                thee, beloved . . . ,"
                                              St. 1,
                    Anthology of Mexican Poetry,
                         Octavio Paz, ed.; Samuel
                         Beckett, tr.   1958

7 Intimation of the human frame,
   epitome of unavailing grace,
   in whose being nature did unite
   the joyful cradle and the fearsome tomb.
                    "Divine rose, that in a pleasant
                                   garden . . . ,"
                                   St. 2, op. cit.

8 Thus with learned death and ignorant life
   living thou dost deceive and dying teach.
                                   Ibid., St. 4

9 Gentle goldfinch, birdling born to sorrow
                    "Crimson lute that comest in the
                                      dawn . . . ,"
                                   St. 2, op. cit.

10 with thine own voice thou callest on the
     hunter
    that he fail not to strike thee with his shaft.
                                   Ibid., St. 3

11 Oh dreaded destiny and yet pursued!
                                   Ibid., St. 4

12 her lover
    was myrrh a space
    in the bower
    of her white breasts. "Christmas Hymn,"
                                   St. 3, op. cit.

13 But the fair forerunner,
    herald of the bright sun,
    scarce flew her banner in the orient sky,
    calling all the sweet if warlike
    clarions of the birds to arms,
    their featly artless
    sonorous bugles   "First Dream",
                                        op. cit.

14 what time upon our hemisphere the sun

the radiance of his fair golden tresses shed,
with equable diffusion of just light
apportioning to visible things their colours
and still restoring
to outward sense its full efficacy,
committing to surer light
the world illuminated and myself awake.
                                        Ibid.

15 I do not value wealth or riches,
    Wherefore I shall be ever more content
    To bring more richness to my mind
    And not to keep my mind on riches.
                    "En perseguirme, mundo, ¿ qué
                    interesas?" ["Oh World, Why do
                         you thus pursue me?"],
                         St. 2, Muriel Kittel, tr.;
                    *An Anthology of Spanish Poetry,
                    from Garcilaso to García Lorca*,
                         Angel Flores, ed.   1961

16 In my opinion, better far it be
    To destroy vanity within my life
    Than to destroy my life in vanity.
                                   Ibid., St. 4

17 "Diuturna enfermedad de la Esperanza
    . . . " ("Perpetual Infirmity of Hope . . . ")
                                   Title of poem,
                    Muriel Kittel, tr., op. cit.

18 Green embellishment of human life
                    "Esperanza" ["Hope"],
                    St. 1, Kate Flores, tr., op. cit.

19 Lure of the world, senescent lushness,
    Imagination's decrepit verdure,
    Today expected by the happy,
    And by the hapless not before tomorrow.
                                   Ibid., St. 2

20   I
    Keep both my eyes in my two hands,
    And see no more than I can touch.
                                   Ibid., St. 4

21 If from the savage hounds
    the timorous hare in terror flies
    and leaves no trace, that it may live,
    of its light feet,
    so my hope, in doubting and misgiving,

is close pursued by cruel jealousies.
"Que expresan sentimientos de
ausente" ("Verses expressing the
feelings of a lover"),
St. 8, Samuel Beckett, tr., op. cit.

22 that unspeakable boon
no human pen can tell?
—For how should that which overflows the
whole
of sense within the finite be contained?
Ibid., St. 14

23 my hope, although its greenness cost me
dear,
is watered by mine eyes.   Ibid., St. 15

24 On scant foundations
my sad cares raise
with delusive conceits
a mountain of feeling.

And when that proud mass
falls asunder I find
that the arrogant fabric
was poised on a pin. "En que se describe
racionalmente los efectos
irracionales del amor"
("Describes rationally the
irrational effects of love"),
Sts. 7, 8, Samuel Beckett, tr.,
op. cit.

25 when did my careless scrawls deserve
to occupy your thoughtful care?
"En reconocimiento a las
inimitables plumas de la Europa"
("In acknowledgment of the
praises of European writers"),
St. 1, Constance Urdang, tr.,
op. cit.

26 I am not what you think I am;
but over there you've given me
another being in your pens,
and other breath upon your lips,

and, different from what I am,
not what I truly am, but what
you'd prefer to imagine me.
Ibid., Sts. 4, 5

27   Is it

possible for the truth to be
so far dragged down by courtliness?
Ibid., St. 8

28 What magical infusions, brewed
from herbals of the Indians
of my own country, spilled their old
enchantment over all my lines?
Ibid., St. 14

29 knowledge of myself, being
what ugly feet are to the peacock!
Ibid., St. 19

30 You have brought disgrace on me
in making me so famous, for
the light you shed reveals my faults
more clearly, making them stand out.
Ibid., St. 20

31 Everything that you receive
is not measured according to
its actual size, but, rather, that
of the receiving vessel.   Ibid., St. 27

32 I believed, when I entered this convent, I
was escaping from myself, but alas, poor
me, I brought myself with me!
Quoted in
Women in Myth and History
by Violeta Miqueli   1962

33 Thy winning graces all my heart enchain;
It follows as the steel the magnet's test
"Sonnet"(c.1680),
*Some Spanish American
Poets*   1968

34 this in which flattery has undertaken
to extenuate the hideousness of years,
and, vanquishing the outrages of time,
to triumph o'er oblivion and old age,

is an empty artifice of care.
Untitled,
Samuel Beckett, tr.;
*The Penguin Book
of Women Poets,*
Carol Cosman, Joan Keefe and
Kathleen Weaver, eds.   1978

35 Critics: in your sight
no woman can win:
keep you out, and she's too tight;

she's too loose if you get in.
> Verses from "A Satirical Romance,"
> St. 3, Samuel Beckett, tr., op. cit.

36 . . . sorting the reasons to leave you or hold
you,
I find an intangible one to love you,
and many tangible ones to forego you.
> Untitled, Judith Thurman, tr.,
> op. cit.

37 Stay, fleeting shadow of my love. . . .
> "Detente, sombra de mi bien
> esquivo" ("Stay, Fleeting
> Shadow"),
> St. 1,
> *An Anthology of Spanish Poetry,*
> John A. Crow, ed. and tr.
> 1979

38 It matters not you vanish like a ghost
If you are captive in these dreams of mine.
> Ibid., St. 2

39 I offered you the rose my heart was keeping
> "Esta tarde, mi bien, cuando te
> hablaba" ["This Afternoon, My
> Love"],
> op. cit.

40 My shattered heart grew precious in your
sight.   Ibid.

41 What you see here is a colorful illusion,
an art bragging of its beauty and skill
> "She Attempts to Refute the
> Praises That Truth, Which She
> Calls Passion, Inscribed on a
> Portrait of the Poet,"
> Willis Barnstone, tr.;
> *A Book of Women Poets,*
> Aliki and Willis Barnstone,
> eds.   1980

42 Enough, my love. Don't be stiff. Don't let
maddening jealousies and arrogance
haunt you or let your quiet be upset
by foolish shadows: false signs of a man's
presence. . . .   "In Which She Satisfies a
> Fear with the Rhetoric of
> Tears,"
> Aliki and Willis Barnstone, trs.,
> op. cit.

43 You combat her resistance
and then with gravity,
you call frivolity
the fruit of your intents.   "She Proves the
> Inconsistency of the Desires and
> Criticism of Men Who Accuse
> Women of What They
> Themselves Cause,"
> St. 3, Aliki and Willis Barnstone,
> trs., op. cit.

44 You fight us from our birth
with weapons of arrogance.
> Ibid., St. 17

45   In my arms thou wilt not bide,
But fancy builds a prison still for thee!
> Untitled,
> St. 3, Alice Stone Blackwell, tr.;
> *Women Poets of the World,*
> Joanna Bankier and Deirdre
> Lashgari, eds.   1983

451.   Anne Dacier
(1651–1720)

1 Silence is the ornament of women.
> Quoted in *Biography of
> Distinguished Women*
> by Sarah Josepha Hale   1876

2 A woman ought to read and meditate on
the Scriptures, and regulate her conduct by
them, and to keep silence, agreeably to the
command of St. Paul.   Ibid.

3 . . . let her [her granddaughter] conceal her
learning with as much care as she might
crookedness or lameness.   Letter to her
> daughter,
> Quoted in *The Life of Lady
> Mary Wortley Montagu*
> by Robert Halsband   1956

4 History does not tempt only by flattery. It
leads on to the strengthening of the heart
and the fostering of wisdom.
> Quoted in *Madame Dacier,
> Scholar and Humanist,*
> Ch. 3, by Fern Farnham
> 1976

452.   Margaret Godolphin
(1652–1678)

1 When I go into the withdrawing room, let me consider what my calling is: To entertain the Ladies, not to talk foolishly to men: more especially the King [Louis XVI].

Quoted in
The Life of Mrs. Godolphin
by John Evelyn; H. Sampson,
ed.   1939

2 If you speake anything they like, say 'tis borrowed. . . .   Ibid.

3 . . . may the Clock, the Candle, may everything I see, teach and instruct me some thing.   Ibid.

4 My place is fill'd up with Him, who is All in All. I find in him none of that tormenting Passion to which I neede sacrifice myselfe. . . .   Quoted in *John Evelyn and Mrs. Godolphin*,
Ch. 3, by W. G. Hiscock
1951

5 But birds have always the good nature to teach their young ones, and so must you.
Letter to John Evelyn
(October 1673),
op. cit.

6 . . . your prayer is exelent: your motto good and prity: your grammar shall be stiched: for all you laugh I love a good plain honest leter: god keep you.
Letter to John Evelyn,
op. cit.

7 What mean you to make me weepe and to break my heart by your *love* to me? take me and all I have, give me but *your love*, my deare friend tusday* is longed for by me, and nights and days move a tedious pace till I am near you!   Letter to John Evelyn
(c.April 20, 1673),
op. cit., Ch. 4

*Evelyn visited her regularly on Tuesdays.

8 You have not known me long 'tis true, but I protest for all the treasures of the world I would not but have known you: not as other people, who wish to hear you talke of trees and plants, secrets in natuer: and discours with you that they may the beter entertain others: but I love to hear you becaus often 'tis of god—to se you becaus it puts me in mind of the joy the primative christians tooke in seing one another: to read you becaus I often melt into tears out of a sens of your vertu and my own—what shall I call it wretchednes, wickednes, foly, every thing that is ill: I love you for god and som times I thinke I love god for you. . . .
Letter to John Evelyn,
op. cit., Ch. 5

9 The first moment I am tried, I am forgetful of the Creator.*   Letter to John Evelyn,
op. cit., Ch. 8

*Response to being kissed by Godolphin, at that time her suitor.

10 . . . children servants master father mouther, things that though they are blesings yet often they prove otherwis, and the best of them have days in which one thinkes one could live without them. . . .
Letter to John Evelyn
(July 1675),
op. cit.

11 . . . god knows a litle pain maks one forget a long health, and the unkindes of one frind maks one forget the frindship of many for a time, for we by nateur are apter to grine then laugh, the first sound we make is crying, our childhood is scarce any thing els but frowardnes, and so but in a litle more reasonable maner we proceed till we dye, so that unles we had hops of a beter world we wear of all things most miserable, for reason is apter to put fears into the mind wherby it disturbs the man—then hop wherby he may [be] comforted. . . .

Ibid.

12 ... god knows the more one sees of ther church,* the more one finds to dislike in it: I did not imagin the tenth part of the suppersteon [superstition] I find in it: yet still I aprove of ther orders: the monesterys are very holy institutions, if they be abusd that is not ther fault what is not perverted. ...

> Letter to John Evelyn
> (December 13, 1675),
> op. cit., Ch. 9

*Referring to Catholicism in France.

13 Eating is to satisfy the pain of hunger, sleep to eas wearynes, and divertisments are to take of[f] the mind from being too long bent upon things that it can not always atend without great inconveenece [inconvenience] to the facultys of it: then retyerment again is to eas it of thos burthens and stains it has sustaind and contracted by being in company, so that our wholl life is, in my opinion, a search after remedys, which doe often, if not always, exchange rather than cuer a deseas. ...

> Last letter to John Evelyn,
> op. cit., Ch. 11

453.   Anne Collins
(fl. 1653)

1 As in a cabinet or chest
One jewel may exceed the rest.

> Untitled, St. 2,
> *Divine Songs and Meditacions*
> 1653

2 God is the Rock of his elect
In whom his grace is inchoate

> Ibid., St. 3

3 This may learn
Them that mourn,
To put their grief to flight:
The Spring succeedeth Winter,
And day must follow night.

> "Song,"
> St. 1, op. cit.

4 For if they could with patience
Awhile possess the mind,
By inward consolations

They might refreshing find,
To sweeten all their crosses,
That little time they 'dure:
So might they gain by losses,
And sharp would sweet procure.

> Ibid., St. 3

5 Cheerfulness
Doth express
A settled pious mind;
Which is not prone to grudging,
From murmuring refin'd.   Ibid., St. 5

454.   Francisca Gregoria
(1653–1736)

1 Fair plaything of the breeze tonight

> "Envying a Little Bird,"
> *The Catholic Anthology,*
> Thomas Walsh, ed.   1927

2 Would I were with thee in thy flight,
I follow with a lover's sighs
Impatient, where thou cleav'st disguise,
Feeling my body's prison bars
Withhold my spirit from the stars.

> Ibid.

3 ... the more His splendour shows
The more my dismal blindness grows

> Ibid.

455.   Mary Lee
(1656–1710)

1 MALE VOICE. Then blame us not if we our interest mind,
And would have knowledge to ourselves confined,
Since that alone pre-eminence does give,
And robbed of it we should unvalued live.
While you are ignorant, we are secure,
A little pain will your esteem procure.

> *The Ladies' Defence: Or, the*
> *Bride-Woman's Counsellor*
> *Answered: A Poem in a Dialogue*
> *between Sir John Brute, Sir*
> *William Loveall, Melissa, and a*
> *Parson*   1701

2   The restless atoms play. . . .
Of them, composed with wonderous art,
    We are our selves a part,
And on us still they nutriment bestow;
To us they kindly come, from us they
    swiftly go,
And through our veins in purple torrents
    flow.
Vacuity is nowhere found,
Each place is full, with bodies we're encompassed round:
In sounds they're to our ears conveyed,
In fragrant odors they our smell delight,
And in ten thousand curious forms displayed
    They entertain our sight
            "The Offering,"
            Part One, op. cit.

3 Wife and servant are the same
But only differ in the name,
For when that fatal knot is tied,
Which nothing, nothing can divide,
When she the word *obey* has said,
And man by law supreme has made,
Then all that's kind is laid aside,
And nothing left but state and pride.
            "To the Ladies,"
            op. cit.

4 Like mutes signs alone must make,
And never any freedom take,
But still be governed by a nod
And fear her husband as her God.
            Ibid.

5 Value your selves, and men despise,
You must be proud, if you'll be wise.
            Ibid.

6 For what the world admires I'll wish no
    more,
    Nor court that airy nothing of a name;
Such fleeting shadows let the proud adore,
    Let them be suppliants for an empty
    fame.   "The Resolve,"
                    St. 1,
            *Poems on Several
            Occasions*   1703

7 If I've a Soul above the Reach of Fear,
    And which will nothing mean or sordid prize:

A Soul, which cannot be depress'd by Grief,
    Nor too much rais'd by the sublimest
Joy   Ibid., Sts. 4, 5

8 A mind, that triumphs over vice and fate,
    Esteems it mean to court the world for
    praise.   Ibid., St. 6

456.   Mary Morpeth
(fl. 1656)

1 Perfection in a woman's work is rare;
From an untroubled mind should verses
    flow;
My discontent makes mine too muddy
    show;
And hoarse encumbrances of household
    care,
Where these remain, the Muses ne'er repair.   "Til William Drummond, of
                        Hawthornden,"
            Quoted as Prefix to *Poems*
        by William Drummond   1656

457.   Anne Killigrew
(1660–1685)

1 More rich, more noble I will ever hold
The Muse's laurel, than a crown of gold.
            "Upon the Saying That My
        Verses Were Made by Another,"
                St. 2, *Poems*   1686

2 What pleasing raptures filled my ravished
    sense,
    How strong, how sweet, Fame, was thy influence!   Ibid., St. 3

3 I willingly accept Cassandra's fate,
To speak the truth, although believed too
late.   Ibid., St. 6

4 But O, the laurel'd fool that doats on fame,
            Whose hope's applause, whose
            fear's to want a name;
        Who can accept for pay
        Of what he does, what others say
                "The Discontent,"
                St. 2, op. cit.

197

5 And all for praise of fools
                                    Ibid.

6 Too loud, O Fame! thy trumpet is too shrill
                                    Ibid., St. 3

7 Yet after Man from his first Station fell,
And God from *Eden Adam* did expel,
Thou wert no more an Evil, but Relief
                                    "On Death,"
                                    St. 1, op. cit.

8 No subtile Serpents, in the Grave betray,
Worms on the Body there, not Soul do prey
                                    Ibid.

9 Farewel to Unsubstantial Joyes,
Ye Gilded Nothings, Gaudy Toyes
                    "A Farewel to Worldly Joyes,"
                                    op. cit.

10 Believe you then are truly brave and bold,
To beauty when no slave, and less to gold;
When virtue you dare own, nor think it
odd,
Or ungenteel to say, "I fear a God."
                    "Extempore Counsel to a Young
                            Gallant in a Frolic,"
                    Poems by Eminent Ladies, Vol. II
                                    1755

458.   Anne Finch
(1661–c.1720-1722)

1 Give me, O indulgent fate!
Give me yet before I die
A sweet, yet absolute retreat,
'Mongst paths so lost and trees so high
That the world may ne'er invade
Through such windings and such shade
My unshaken liberty.
                    "The Petition for an Absolute Retreat,"
                    Miscellany Poems, Written by a Lady
                            1713; reprint 1928

2 Give me there (since Heaven has shown
It was not good to be alone)
A partner suited to my mind,
Solitary, pleased and kind
                                    Ibid.

3 Let the time of youth be shown,

The time, alas! too soon outgrown
                                    Ibid.

4 Give me, O indulgent Fate!
For all pleasures left behind
Contemplations of the mind.
Let the fair, the gay, the vain
Courtship and applause obtain;
Let the ambitious rule the earth;
Let the giddy fool have mirth;
Give the epicure his dish,
Every one their several wish;
Whilst my transports I employ
On that more extensive joy
                                    Ibid.

5 Thus we poets that have speech,

Unlike what thy forests teach,
If a fluent vein be shown
That's transcendent to our own,
Criticize, reform, or preach,
Or censure what we cannot reach.
                    "To the Nightingale,"
                                    op. cit.

6 . . . I have applied
Sweet mirth, and music, and have tried
A thousand other arts beside,
To drive thee from my darkened breast,
Thou, who has banished all my rest.
                    "To Melancholy,"
                                    op. cit.

7 Trail all your pikes, dispirit every drum,
March in a slow procession from afar,
Ye silent, ye dejected, men of war.
Be still the hautboys, and the flute be dumb!
Display no more, in vain, the lofty banner;
For see where on the bier before ye lies
The pale, the fall'n, the untimely sacrifice
To your mistaken shrine, to your false idol
Honour.   "Trail All Your Pikes,"
                            in toto, op. cit.

8 How gaily is at first begun
Our life's uncertain race!
                    "Life's Progress,"
                                    St. 1, op. cit.

9 The gently-rising hill of Time
                                    Ibid., St. 5

10 But silent Musings urge the Mind to seek

Something, too high for Syllables to speak
                   "A Nocturnal Reverie,"
                   op. cit.

11 ... whilst tyrant man does sleep ...
In such a *Night* let Me abroad remain,
Till Morning breaks, and All's confus'd
again   Ibid.

12 To-morrow and to-morrow cheat our
    youth.
In riper age, to-morrow still we cry,
Not thinking that the present age we die,
Unpractis'd all the good we have design'd:
There's no to-morrow to a willing mind.
                    "No To-Morrow,"
                   op. cit.

13 Nor will in fading silks compose
Faintly the inimitable rose.
                     "The Spleen,"
                   op. cit.

14 Now the Jonquille o'ercomes the feeble
    brain;
We faint beneath the aromatic pain.
                       Ibid.

15 When first upon the stage a play appears
'Tis not the multitude a poet fears,
Who, from example, praise or damn by
    rote,
And give their censure as some members
    vote.
But if in the expecting box or pit
The wretch discerns one true, substantial
    wit,
Tow'rds him his doubtful sight he'll still di-
    rect,
Whose very looks can all his faults detect.
                     "Aristomenes,"
                Prologue, op. cit.

16 But 'twill appear, in spite of all editing,
A woman's way to charm is not by writing.
                       Ibid.

17 He lamented for [Aphra] Behn, o'er that
    place of her birth,
And said amongst women there was none
    on earth
Her superior in fancy, in language, or wit,

Yet owned that a little too loosely she writ.
                       Ibid.,
                 The Introduction

18 To write, to read, or think, or to enquire
Would cloud our beauty, and exhaust our
    time,
And interrupt the conquests of our prime.
                       Ibid.

19 Alas! a woman that attempts the pen,
Such an intruder on the rights of men,
Such a presumptuous creature, is esteemed,
The fault can by no vertue be redeemed.
                       Ibid.

20 Be caution'd them my Muse, and still
    retir'd;
Nor to be dispis'd, aiming to be admir'd.
                       Ibid.

21 How are we fal'n, fal'n, by mistaken rules?
                       Ibid.

459.   Mary II of England
(1662–1694)

1 There is but one command which I wish
him* to obey; and that is, "*Husbands, love
your wives.*" For myself, I shall follow the
injunction, "*Wives, be obedient to your husbands in all things.*" Quoted in *Biography
of Distinguished Women*
by Sarah Josepha Hale   1876

*Her husband, William III (1650–1702), king of Eng-
land (1689–1702).

460.   Kata Szidónia Petröczi
(1662–1708)

1 Hourly I howl the change in my fate.
                     "Swift Floods,"
               St. 1, Laura Schiff, tr.;
           Women Poets of the World,
       Joanna Bankier and Deirdre
            Lashgari, eds.   1983

2 The winds of sadness lay siege
To my forsaken mind, my wounded heart.
                     Ibid., St. 2

461. Elizabeth Bradford
(1663?–1731)

1 For 'tis no humane knowledge gain'd by
   art,
But rather 'tis inspir'd into the heart
By divine means; for true divinity
Hath with this science great affinity
          "To the Reader, in Vindication
                    of this Book,"
              Preface, *War With the Devil*
              by Benjamin Keach   1707

462. Mary de la Rivière Manley
(1663–1724)

1 Orinda,* and the Fair Astrea* gone,
Not one was found to fill the Vacant
   Throne:
Aspiring Man had quite regain'd the Sway,
Again had Taught us humble to Obey;
Till you** (Nature's third start, in favour of
   our Kind)
With stronger Arms, their Empire have dis-
   joyn'd
          Commendatory verses quoted in
              Foreword to *Agnes de Castro*
                    by Catherine
              Cockburn**   1695

*Orinda is Katherine Philips; see 426. Astrea refers to
Aphra Behn; see 438.

2 O! How I long in the Poetick Race,
To loose the Reins, and give their Glory
Chase.   Ibid.

3 No time like the present. *The Lost Lover*,
                    Act IV, Sc. 1   1696

4 What can pay love but love?
                    Ibid., Act V, Sc. 3

5 ALMYNA. But I shou'd much intrude,
shou'd I but tell
The Half of what our Sex have dar'd for
Glory.   *Almyna; or, The Arabian Vow*
                                   1706

6 ALMANZOR. . . . be it not once imagin'd
That Women have not Souls, divine as we.
                    Ibid.

7 . . . he fell martyr to her tongue. A land-
mark for husbands, how they suffer the
growth of authority in that tyrannical un-
ruly member!   "Corinna,"
          *Secret Memoirs and Manners of
          Several Persons of Quality of
          Both Sexes. From the New
          Atalantis, an Island in the
          Mediterranean*   1709

8 Whatever false notion the world or you
may have of virtue, I must confess I should
be very loathe to bind my self to a man for
ever, before I was sure I should like him for
a night. . . .   Ibid.

9 . . . the truly covetous have never enough!
                    Ibid.

10 . . . nothing ought to hinder a man from
enjoying the present, no reflection of the future carry away his relish of the instant,
provided it be innocently employed.
                    "The Cabal,"
                    op. cit.

11 . . . the ill nature of those censurers, who
will have no diversions innocent, but what
themselves advance!   Ibid.

12 . . . mutual love bestows all things in common. . . .   Ibid.

13 . . . that nice unforgiving sex: who arbi-
trarily decide, that woman was only created
(with all her beauty, softness, passions and
complete tenderness) to adorn the husband's reign, perfect his happiness, and
propagate the kind.   Ibid.

14 Time and chance reveal all secrets.
                    Ibid.

15 . . . she still went on in her own Way . . . till
Experience gave her enough of her indiscretion.   *The Adventures of Rivella: or, The
          History of the Author of the
          Atalantis*   1714

16 She must first be in Love with a Man before
she thought fit to reside with him.
                    Ibid.

17 As long as we have Eyes, or Hands, or
Breath,

We'll Look, or Write, or Talk you all to
Death   Prologue,
             *Lucius, the First Christian King
                          of Britain*   1717

463. Marie Jeanne L'Heritier de
             Villandon
             (1664–1734)

1 You care for nothing but loving and joking.
             "Rondeau, to a Young Girl,"
             Elaine Partnow, tr.;
             Quoted in French in *Biography
             of Distinguished Women*
             by Sarah Josepha Hale   1876

464. Anne of England
             (1665–1714)

1 O, my dear brother, how I pity thee!
             Remark to her brother, the
             future King William III, on her
             deathbed (July 20, 1714),
             Quoted in *Biography of
             Distinguished Women*
             by Sarah Josepha Hale   1876

465. Grisell Home
             (1665–1746)

1 When bonny young Johnnie cam' o'er the
        sea,
  He said he saw naething sae lovely as
        me. . . .
             "Warena My Heart Licht I Wad
                              Dee,"
             Scottish Song,
             Mary Carlyle Aitken, ed.
                                     1874

466. Honnamma
             (fl. 1665–1699)

1 Wasn't your mother a woman?
             Untitled,
             Willis Barnstone, tr.;
             A Book of Woman Poets,
             Aliki and Willis Barnstone, eds.
                                     1980

2 Here and in the other world
        happiness
  comes to a person, not a gender.
             Ibid.

467. Henrietta Johnston
             (c.1665–1728/29)

1 . . . reason and conscience startle not.
             Letter to her husband
             (August 1713),
             Quoted in *Henrietta Johnston,
             America's First Pastellist*
             by Margaret Simons
             Middleton   1966

468. Mary Astell
             (1666?–1731)

1 Women are from their very Infancy de-
  barr'd those advantages [of education] with
  the want of which they are afterwards reproached, and nursed up in those vices with
  which will hereafter be upbraided them. So
  partial are Men as to expect Bricks when
  they afford no straw.   *A Serious Proposal
             to the Ladies for the
             Advancement of their True and
             Greatest Interest*   1694

2 For Custom has usurpt such an unaccountable Authority, that she who would endeavor to put a stop to its arbitrary sway,
  and reduce it to Reason, is in a fair way to
  render herself the Butt for all the Fops in
  Town to shoot their impertinent Censures
  at. And tho' a wise woman will not value
  their censure, yet she cares not to be the
  subject of their Discourse.
             Ibid.

3 If she [a mother] do not make the child, all will agree that she have the power to mar him.   Ibid.

4 The poor lady, having passed the prime of her years in gaiety and company . . . and having all this while been so over-careful of her body, that she had no time to improve her mind, which therefore affords her no safe retreat, now she meets with disappointments abroad, and growing every day more and more sensible that the respect which used to be paid her decays as fast as her beauty. . . .   Ibid.

5 . . . quite terrified with the dreadful name of old maid . . . she flies to some dishonourable match as her last, tho' much mistaken Refuge, to the disgrace of her Family, and her own irreparable Ruin.
                                      Ibid.

6 Bold Truths may pass while the Speaker is Incognito, but are seldom endur'd when he is known; few Minds being strong enough to bear what contradicts their Principles and Practices, without recriminating them when they can.   Advertisement for
                          *Reflections Upon
                          Marriage*   1700

7 They only who have felt it know the Misery of being forc'd to marry where they do not love; of being yok'd for life to a disagreeable Person and imperious Temper, where Ignorance and Folly (the ingredients of a Cockscomb, who is the most unsufferable Fool) tyrannizes over wit and Sense.
                          *Reflections Upon
                          Marriage*   1700

8 Marriage . . . notwithstanding all the loose talk of the Town, the Satires of antient, or modern Pretenders to Wit, will never lose its just Esteem from the Wise and Good.
                                      Ibid.

9 . . . Beauty with all the Helps of Art, is of no long Date; the more it is help'd, the sooner it decays. . . .   Ibid.

10 . . . he who only or chiefly chose for Beauty, will in a little Time find the same Reason for another Choice.
                                      Ibid.

11 But Patience and Submission are the only comforts that are left to a poor People, who groan under Tyranny, unless they are Strong enough to break the Yoke, to Depose and Abdicate. . . .
                                      Ibid.

12 And if a Woman can neither Love nor Honour she does ill in promising to Obey, since she is like to have a crooked Rule to regulate her Actions.   Ibid.

13 But how can a Man respect his Wife, when he has a contemptible Opinion of her and her Sex, when from his own elevation he looks down on them as void of Understanding, full of Ignorance and Passion, so that Folly and a Woman are equivalent Terms with him?   Ibid.

14 A woman . . . has been taught to think Preferment the sum total of her Endeavors, the completion of all her Hopes.
                                      Ibid.

15 There is not anything so excellent, but some will carp at it. . . .   Quoted in Preface
                          (December 18, 1724),
                          *Letters of the Right Honourable
                          Lady Mary Wortley
                          Montagu*   1766

469.   Sarah Kemble Knight
(1666–1727)

1 May all that dread the cruel fiend of night
   Keep on, and not at this curs't mansion light.   Untitled (c.1704),
                          The Journal of Madame Knight,
                          Theodore Dwight, Jr., ed.
                                            1825

2 Yet swelling Fears surprise; all dark appears—
   Nothing but Light can disipate those fears.
   My fainting vital can't lend strength to say,

But softly whisper, O I wish 'twere day.
"Thoughts on the Sight of the
Moon,"
op. cit.

3 I ask thy Aid, O Potent Rum!
To charm these wrangling Topers Dum.
Thou hast their Giddy Brains possest—
The man confounded with the Beast—
And I, poor I, can get no rest.
Intoxicate them with thy fumes;
O still their Tongues till morning comes!
"Resentments Composed because
of the Clamor of Town Topers
Outside My Apartment,"
in toto, op. cit.

4 When I reflect, my late fatigues do seem
Only a notion or forgotten Dreem.
"Thoughts on Pausing at a
Cottage near the Paukataug
River,"
op. cit.

470. Mary Griffith Pix
(1666–1720?)

1 By great Rules of Honour all Men know
They must not Arm on a Defenceless Foe.
The Author on her weakness, not her
strength relies,
And from your Justice to your Mercy flies.
Epilogue,
*Ibrahim, the Thirteenth Emperor
of the Turks*   1696

2 The First Time she was grave, as well she
might,
For Women will be damn'd sullen the first
Night;
But faith, they'll quickly mend, so be n't
uneasie:
To Night she's brisk, and trys New Tricks
to please ye.   Prologue,
The Spanish Wives
1696

3 . . . instead of making his life easie with
jolly *Bona-robas* [courtesans], [he] dotes on
a Platonick Mistress, who never allows him
greater favours than to read Plays to her,
kiss her hand, and fetch Heart-breaking
Sighs at her Feet.   *The Innocent
Mistress*   1697

4 APPAMIA. Let me for ever
Warn my Sex, and fright 'em from the
thoughts of
Black Revenge.   *The False Friends;
or, The Fate of Disobedience*
1699

471. Sophia Dorothea of Celle
(1666–1726)

1 . . . my illness only comes from loving you,
and I do not want to be cured of it.
Letter to George I
(c.1689–1694),
Quoted in *Lives of the
Hanoverian Queens of England*
by Alice Drayton
Greenwood   1909

472. Susannah Centlivre
(c.1667–1723)

1 LUDOVICHO. I never strike Bargains in the
Dark.   *The Perjur'd Husband,*
Act I, Sc. 1   1700

2 COUNT BASSINO. O! happy he Who lives secure and free from Love's Alarms. But happier far, who, master of himself, Ranges
abroad without that Clog, a Wife.
Ibid., Sc. 2

3 COUNT BASSINO. Why must his generous
Passion thus be starv'd, And be confin'd to
one alone? The Woman, whom Heaven sent
as a Relief, To ease the Burden of a tedious
Life, And be enjoy'd when summon'd by
Desire, Is now become the Tyrant of our
Fates.   Ibid.

4 ARMANDO. . . . there's more Glory in subduing Our wild Desires, than an embattl'd Foe.   *Ibid.*, Act IV, Sc. 1

5 PLACENTIA. All Arguments are vain, where Love bears Sway.   *Ibid.*, Act V, Sc. 1

6 ARMANDO. Vengeance always treads on Perjury.   *Ibid.*, Sc. 2

7 COLONEL. How do Men labour to fool themselves?   *The Beau's Duel*, Act I, Sc. 1   1702

8 SIR WILLIAM MODE. Well 'tis an unspeakable Happiness we Men of Parts enjoy above the rest of Mankind: By our good Management we make our Access to every Thing we admire, easy and certain: How many thick-skull'd Fellows are content to dream of their Mistresses, while I take a more secure Method, and wake her in the Morning with harmonius music.   *Ibid.*, Act II, Sc. 2

9 OGLE. Why is it not possible to be acquainted without speaking, Gentlemen? Why a Friend of mine lay all night with a Lady, and never saw her Face, nor knows not who she is to this Moment; now I think seeing is of greater Consequence than speaking.   *Ibid.*

10 AMELIA. I have the best Proof in the World of it, ocular Demonstration.   *Ibid.*, Act III, Sc. 1

11 TOPER. Yesterday I carried to wait on a Relation of ours that has a Parrot, and whilst I was discoursing about some private Business, she converted the Bird, and now it talks of nothing but the Light of the Spirit, and the Inward Man.   *Ibid.*

12 SERGEANT. Why truly, Sir, a Camp would be a pleasant Place, did the Fields produce Feather Beds; or if the Streams like those of the Golden Age, did run pure Wine; or if Camp Meals wou'd every Twelve and Seven observe due Hours!   *Ibid.*, Act IV, Sc. 1

13 MRS. PLOTWELL. Virtue, thou shining Jewel of my Sex—Thou precious Thing, that none knows how to value as they ought, while they enjoy it, but like spendthrift Heirs, when they have wasted all their Store, wou'd give the World they cou'd retrieve their lost Estate.   *Ibid.*, Act V, Sc. 1

14 You see gallants 'it has been our Poets' care,
To shew what Beaus in their Perfection are,
By Nature *Cowards, foolish, useless Tools*,
Made *Men* by *Taylors* and by *Women*,
Fools.   *Ibid.*, Epilogue

15 He surest strikes that smiling gives the blow.   *Ibid.*

16 Friendship's a noble name, 'tis love refined.   *The Stolen Heiress*, Act II, Sc. 2   1702

17 Writing is a kind of Lottery in this fickle Age. . . .   Preface, *Love's Contrivance* 1703

18 SELFWILL. . . . whoever marries is a Merchant Adventurer, and Hope is his best friend.   *Ibid.*, Act I, Sc. 1

19 OCTAVIO. No, no, my Friend, gray Hairs and a bridal Bed are ridiculous Companions.   *Ibid.*

20 MARTIN. Look'e Wife, I love you the better for beating you, faith, 'tis all out of pure Love, 'tis indeed, Wife; and such little Quarrels as these do but cement the Passion of Love: Faith, Wife, if I did not beat thee, I shou'd cuckhold thee.   *Ibid.*

21 WIFE. . . . if I am not revenged, I am no Woman.   *Ibid.*

22 OCTAVIO. . . . for I find by the beating of my Pulse, the Motion of my Brain, and the Heavings of my Heart, I am very far gone in that dangerous Distemper call'd Love, and you are the only Physician can save my life.   *Ibid.*, Act III, Sc. 1

23 LUCINDA. Once a Week! I wou'd not for the World bed with you oftener; why 'tis not the Fashion, Sir Toby; and I assure you when I marry I hope to be my own Mistress, and follow my own Inclination, which will carry me to the utmost Pinnacle of the Fashion. Ibid., Act IV, Sc. 1

24 BELLMIE. Words be given to Man to explain his Mind, the Mind is the Picture of Things, as our Words are the Pictures of our Meaning; but these Pictures differ from all other Pictures, insomuch as other Pictures are distinguish'd by their Originals; and the Word keeps in itself the original Being, that it is nothing else than the Mind explained by some exterior Sign or Motion; whence it comes that those who think well talk the better; explain then your Mind by your Words, which is the most intelligible of all the Signs. Ibid., Act V, Sc. 1

25 'Tis the defect of age to rail at the pleasures of youth. *The Basset-Table*, Act I 1705

26 'Tis better never to be named than to be ill spoken of. Ibid.

27 ALPIEW. ... Widows are accountable to none for their Actions.... Ibid.

28 LADY LUCY. You cross the Purpose of the Day and Night; you wake when you should sleep, and make all who have any Dependence on you wake, while you repose. Ibid.

29 LADY LUCY. While in the Breast our Secrets close remain, 'Tis out of Fortune's Power to give us Pain. Ibid.

30 BUCKLE. Love! No! the Devil take me, if ever I shall be infected with that Madness! 'tis enough for one in the Family to fall under the whimsical Circumstances of that Distemper. Ibid., Act II

31 LOVELY. I'm not for Compliments; 'tis a Land Language, I understand it not; Courage, Honesty, and Plain-Dealing Truth, is the Learning of our Element; if you like that I am for ye.

. . . .

SIR RICHARD PLAINMAN. Like it, Sir? why 'tis the only Thing I do like, hang Compliments and Court Breeding, it serves only to make Men a Prey to one another, to encourage Cowardice and ruin Trade.... Ibid., Act IV

32 LADY LUCY. ... nothing melts a Woman's Heart like gold. Ibid.

33 You are our Stars, by you we live or drown. Ibid., Epilogue

34 FAVOURITE. For she that marries a Gamester that plays upon the Square, as the Fool your Master does, can expect nothing but an Alms-House for a jointure. *The Gamester*, Act I 1705

35 HECTOR. Love's Fever is always highest when the Cash is at an Ebb. Ibid.

36 VALERE. ... there's nothing like ready Money to nick Fortune. Ibid., Act III

37 HECTOR. Lying is a thriving Vocation. Ibid.

38 HECTOR. What Business had you to get Children, without you had Cabbage enough to maintain 'em? Ibid.

39 VALERE. ... 'tis the genteelest Way of passing one's time, every Day produces some thing new—Who is happier than a Gamester; who more respected, I mean those that make any Figure in the World? Who more caress'd by Lords and Dukes? or whose Conversation more agreeable.... In short, there is an Air of Magnificence in't,—a Gamester's Hand is the Philosopher's Stone, that turns all it touches into gold. HECTOR. And Gold into Nothing. Ibid.

40 All policy's allowed in war and love.
Love At A Venture,
Act I   1706

41 SIR GEORGE AIRY. . . . a Man that wants Money thinks none can be unhappy that has it. . . .   *The Busy Body,*
Act I   1709

42 CHARLES. . . . Want, the Mistress of Invention, still tempts me on. . . .
Ibid.

43 MIRANDA. Matrimony! ha, ha, ha! what Crimes have you committed against the God of Love that he should revenge 'em so severely to stamp Husband upon your Forehead?   Ibid.

44 ISABINDA. Let me tell you, Sir, Confinement sharpens the Invention, as Want of Sight strengthens the other Senses, and is often more pernicious, than the Recreation innocent Liberty allows.   Ibid., Act II

45 PATCH. . . . it is impossible a Man of Sense should use a Woman ill, endued with Beauty, Wit, and Fortune. It must be the Lady's fault, if she does not wear the unfashionable Name of Wife easy, when nothing but Complacence and Good-humour is requisite on either Side to make them happy.   Ibid., Act V

46 And lash the Vice and Follies of the Age.
Prologue,
The Man's Bewitched; or, The Devil to Do About Her   1709

47 MANAGE. . . . my present Profession is Physick—Now, when my Pockets are full, I cure a Patient in three Days; when they are empty, I keep him three months.
Ibid., Act II

48 DON PERRIERA. . . . sure Cuckoldom is so rank a Scent, that tho' I lived in *England*, where they scarce breathe any other Air, I cou'd distinguish it.   *Mar Plot, or, The Second Part of the Busy Body,*
Act I, Sc. 1   1711

49 CHARLES. . . . if a Man is born to be a Cuckold, 'tis none of his Wife's Fault. . . .
Ibid., Act II, Sc. 1

50 MARPLOT. I had rather fathom the Depth of Man's Thoughts, than his Pocket. . . .
Ibid., Act III, Sc. 1

51 MLLE. JONETON. . . . I see no Reason why one may not alter and change Form and the Manner of Speaking, according to the Company one keeps, as well as the Mode and Fashion of one's Cloathes. . . .
Ibid.

52 FLORELLA. . . . nobody can boast of Honesty till they are try'd. . . .
The Perplex'd Lovers,
Act III, Sc. 1   1712

53 TIMOTHY. . . . I fancy Cowardice is a kind of Ague, and there is nothing like Brandy to cure it.   Ibid., Act IV, Sc. 1

54 Liberty is the idol of the English, under whose banner all the nation lists.
The Wonder: A Woman Keeps a Secret,
Act I, Sc. 1   1714

55 A poor fool indeed is a very scandalous thing.   Ibid.

56 I value not the world a button.
Ibid.

57 DON LOPEZ. There is no Condition of Life without its Cares, and it is the Perfection of a Man to wear 'em as easy as he can. . . .
Ibid.

58 He is as melancholy as an unbrac'd drum.
Ibid., Act II, Sc. 1

59 LISSARDO. Art thou really so foolish to mind what an enrag'd Woman says?
Ibid., Act III

60 COLONEL BRITTON. Hang Law in Love Affairs. . . .   Ibid., Act IV

61 Lord! what Prerogative might we obtain, Could we from Yielding, a few Months, refrain!   Ibid., Epilogue

62   *Keep a Secret,* says a Beau,
And sneers at some ill-natur'd Wit below;
But faith, if we shou'd tell but half we know. . . .   Ibid.

63 Where are the rough brave Britons to be
found
With Hearts of Oak, so much of old renowned?   *The Cruel Gift*   1717

64 LEARCHUS. You mean to prove my Soul,
and 'tis most just;
For many wear the borrow'd mask of
goodnes. . . .   Ibid., Act I

65 MR. SACKBUT. He hated Posterity, you must
know, and wish'd the World were to expire
with himself. . . .
     A Bold Stroke for a Wife,
     Act I, Sc. 1   1718

66 'Tis my opinion every man cheats in his
way, and he is only honest who is not discovered.   *The Artifice,*
     Act V   1724

67 When the glowing of passion's over, and
pinching winter comes, will amorous sighs
supply the want of fire, or kind looks and
kisses keep off hunger?   Ibid.

68 . . . resolve to be merry though the ship
were sinking.   Ibid.

473.   Susanna Wesley
(1668?–1742)

1 Let every one enjoy the present hour.
     Quoted in *The Women of*
     Methodism: Its Three Foundresses . . .
     by Abel Stevens   1866

2 Age and successive troubles are sufficient to
convince any man that it is a much wiser
and safer way to deprecate great afflictions
than to pray for them. . . .
     Ibid.

3 . . . our Lord knew what was in man when
he directed us to pray, "Lead us not into
temptation."   Ibid.

4 . . . the putting children to learn sewing
before they can read perfectly, is the very
reason why so few women can read in a
manner fit to be heard.   Ibid.

5 You did well to correct that fond desire of
dying before me, since you do not know
what work God may have for you to do
before you leave the world.
     Letter to her son, John Wesley,
     op. cit.

6 [To subdue the will of the child] is the only
strong and rational foundation of a religious education, without which both precept and example will be ineffectual. But
when this is thoroughly done, then a child
is capable of being governed by the reason
and piety of its parents till its own understanding comes to maturity, and the principles of religion have taken root in the mind.
     Ibid.

7 Do not advise me, but command me to de-
sist!   Letter to Isaac Taylor,
     op. cit.

8 O sir! O brother! happy, thrice happy are
you; happy is my sister that buried your
children in infancy, secure from temptation, secure from guilt, secure from want or
shame, secure from the loss of friends. Believe me, it is better to mourn ten children
dead than one living, and I have buried
many.   Letter to her brother,
     op. cit.

9 In good earnest, resolve to make religion
the business of your life; for, after all, that is
the one thing that, strictly speaking, is
necessary. All things besides are compara-
tively little to the purposes of life.
     Letter to her son, John Wesley,
     op. cit.

10 God's prescience is no more the effective
cause of the loss of the wicked than our
foreknowledge of the rising of to-morrow's
sun is the cause of its rising.
     Ibid.

11 If I had twenty sons I should rejoice that
they were all so employed, though I should
never see them again. Remark concerning
     her sons, John and Charles,
     called to the colony of Georgia
     as missionaries,
     op.cit.

474. Frances Boothby
(fl. 1669)

1 I'm hither come, but what d'ye think to
   say?
A Womans Pen present you with a Play:
Who smiling told me I'd be sure to see,
That once confirm'd, the House would
   empty be.
Not one yet gone!   Prologue,
        Marcelia; or, The Treacherous
                Friend   1669

2 But still she hopes the Ladies out of Pride
And Honor, will not quit their Sexes
side.   Ibid.

3 You powerful Gods! if I must be
An injur'd offering to Love's deity,
Grant my revenge, this plague on men,
That woman ne'er may love again.
                  "Song,"
             St. 1, op. cit.

4 O let the world no longer govern'd be
By such a blind and childish Deity!
             Ibid., St. 2

475. Marie Thérèse Rodet Geoffrin
(1669–1757)

1 Give and forgive. Quoted in *Biography of
              Distinguished Women*
    by Sarah Josepha Hale   1876

2 We should not let the grass grow on the
path of friendship.   Ibid.

3 Among those advantages which attract for
us the most consideration are good manners, an erect bearing, a dignified demeanour, and to be able to enter a room grace-
fully; we dare not speak ill of a person who
has all these advantages, for they presuppose thoughtfulness, order, and judgment.
                    Ibid.

476. Anne Baynard
(1672–1697)

1 . . . it is a sin to be content with a little
knowledge.   Quoted in *Biography of
              Distinguished Women*
    by Sarah Josepha Hale   1876

2 I could wish that all young persons might
be exhorted to . . . read the great book of
nature, wherein they may see the wisdom
and power of the Creator, in the order of
the universe, and in the production and
preservation of all things.
            From her deathbed,
                 op. cit.

3 That women are capable of such improvements, which will better their judgments
and understandings, is past all doubt,
would they but set about it in earnest, and
spend but half of that time in study and
thinking, which they do in visits, vanity,
and folly. It would introduce a composure
of mind, and lay a solid basis for wisdom
and knowledge, by which they would be
better enabled to serve God, and to help
their neighbours.   Ibid.

477. Mary Davys
(1674–1732)

1 As a Child born of a common Woman, has
many Fathers, so my poor Offspring has
been laid at a great many Doors. . . . I am
proud they think it deserves a better
Author.   Preface,
    *The Northern Heiress; or, The
        Humours of York*   1716

2 If we divide Mankind into several Classes,
we shall meet with as many different Tempers as Faces, only we have the Art of dis-
guising one better than t'other.
    *The Reform'd Coquet; or, the
    Memoirs of Amoranda*   1724

3 The Pedant despises the most elaborate Undertaking, unless it appears in the World with *Greek* and *Latin* Motto's; a Man that would please him, must pore an Age over musty Authors, till his Brains are as worm-eaten as the Books he reads, and his Conversation fit for nobody else. . . .
Ibid.

4 . . . the busy part of our Species, who are so very intent upon getting Money, that they lose the pleasure of spending it.
Ibid.

5 Vanity, which is most Women's Foible, might be overlook'd or wink'd at, would it live alone; but alack! it loves a long Train of Attendants, and calls in Pride, Affectation, Ill-nature, and often Ill-manners too for its Companions.
Ibid.

6 It is the way of the Damn'd, Madam, to desire all Mankind should be in their own miserable State. . . .
Ibid.

7 Is there no such thing as Justice in Man? No Faith in their Oaths and Vows?
Ibid.

8 Madam, *said he,* Observation puts a great many things into our heads. . . .
Ibid.

9 I have often told myself, it is much better never to know a Satisfaction, than lose it as soon as acquainted; since nothing can give a Man a greater Damp than a Reflection upon past Pleasures, when he has no View to their return. "To Berina, November 1,"
Familiar Letters, Betwixt a Gentleman and a Lady 1725

10 How many brave Men, courageous Women, and innocent Children did I see butcher'd, to do God good Service? . . . I went to the *Irish* Rebellion, where I saw more than three hundred thousand Souls muder'd in cold Blood . . . crying, *Nits will become Lice, destroy Root and Branch*: with a thousand other Barbarities, too tedious as well as too dreadful to repeat, beside what has been transacted abroad.
Ibid.,
"To Artander, November 10"

11 . . . I think there is more Reason to bury one Fault in Oblivion, which was the Result of their Concern for the Reformation, than to keep it up with a Spirit of Malice, to foment and heighten those unhappy Feuds which are already begun, and with so much Industry carry'd on.
Ibid.

12 That there have been ill Men in all Ages, no Man in his Senses will deny; and the Cruelty you speak of, as far as we may trust to tradition, is equally certain: but, *Berina,* we have always look'd upon that Person's Principles to be very trifling who accuses another of a Fault, and the very next minute commits it himself. Is it a sufficient Warrant for me to cut a Man's Throat, because I just saw the Fact committed? No, *Berina,* when we renounced *Rome*'s Errors, we renounced her Cruelties too: but these impudent King-killers, with their legal Proceedings forsooth, plainly shew'd the World they had a mixture of both remaining.
Ibid.,
"To Berina, November 13"

13 A Husband! the very Name makes me almost tremble! and I have once more given it under my Hand, that Marriage shall never spoil my Friendship for *Berina*: when it does, I may cease to be.
Ibid.,
"To Berina, November 21"

14 . . . we Women as naturally love Scandal, as you Men do Debauchery; and we can no more keep up Conversation without one, than you can live an Age without t'other.
Ibid., "To Artander, December 10"

15 I cannot say I was ever so glutted with Pleasure in my Life, as to be weary of it, nor properly speaking, can any body say so; because, when once a Man is tir'd of a thing, it is no longer a Pleasure, but retiring from it is; so that a Person who has power to follow his own Inclinations, is always in Pleasure. . . .
Ibid.,
"To Berina, December 26"

16 Of all the Gods, either Heathens or Poets
ever made, there is none so silly as this
blinking God of Love: he makes mere Idiots
of Mankind, and puts them upon such
ridiculous Actions, that one wou'd think we
were made for nothing but to laugh at one
another.   Ibid.,
                        "To Artander, December 29"

17 . . . if you have deceiv'd me as a Friend, I
have little Reason to trust you as a Lover.
                                                  Ibid.,
                          "To Artander, January 3"

18 When once the blind Archer with a random
Shot has hit a Heart, the wounded Fool
grows stupid, sighs and cries, prays, and
begs for Help and Pity, but never offers to
pull out the Dart, which causes all his Pain:
Wou'd but every body keep their Ground,
and stand boldly in their own Defence, how
easily might they baffle the Attempts of a
Boy?   Ibid.,
                          "To Artander, January 8"

19 Oh! what foolish Things are we Mortals—!
resolving against our Fate, which only
laughs at our weak Endeavours, and makes
a Jest of our broken Resolutions.
                                                  Ibid.,
                            "To Berina, January 9"

20 . . . Love, like Edg'd-Tools, shou'd never
be play'd with.   Ibid.,
                         "To Artander, January 12"

21 When Women write, the Criticks, now-a-
days,
Are ready, e'er they see, to damn their
Plays;
Wit, as the Men's Prerogative, they claim,
And with one Voice, the bold Invader
blame.   Prologue,
                        The Self-Rival; A Comedy
                                                   1725

22 And let them consider, that a Woman left
to her own Endeavours for Twenty-seven
Years together, may well be allow'd to
catch at any Opportunity for that Bread,
which they that condemn her would very
probably deny to give her.
                                               Preface,
                             Works, Vol. I   1725

23 I never was so vain, as to think they [her
plays] deserv'd a Place in the first Rank, or
so humble, as to resign them to the last.
                                                  Ibid.

478.   Elizabeth Rowe
(1674–1736/37)

1 The glorious armies of the sky
                                               "Hymn,"
                                                 St. 1,
                   *Poems on Several Occasions by
                             Philomela*   1696

2 Thy numerous Works exalt Thee thus,
  And shall I silent be?
No; rather let me cease to breathe,
  Than cease from praising Thee!
                                         Ibid., St. 8

3 Oh! lead me to some solitary gloom
                                             "Despair,"
                                              op. cit.

4 . . . the studious follies of the great,
The tiresome farce of ceremonious state.
                                                  Ibid.

5 Let me all day upon my lyre complain,
And wind up all its soft harmonious strings
To noble, serious, melancholy things.
                                                  Ibid.

6 Thine is the hope, th' inestimable prise,
The glorious mark on which we fix our eyes!
                                         "On Happiness,"
                                                 St. 1,
                   *Miscellaneous Works in Prose
                            and Verse*   1739

7 A fair delusion, and a pleasing cheat,
A gaudy vision, and a soft deceit
                                         Ibid., St. 2

8 By this thy glorious lineage thou dost prove
Thy high descent; for GOD himself is Love.
"Ode to Love,"
St. 11, op. cit.

479. Rosalba Carriera
(1675–1757)

1 My profession that occupies me so constantly, and a rather cold disposition, have hitherto kept me from thoughts of love and wedlock. . . .   Letter,
Quoted in *Portraits and
Backgrounds*,
Ch. 3, by Evangeline Wilbour
Blashfield   1917

2 This is the age of music, not painting.
Remark, op. cit., Ch. 6

3 No one loves gayety more than I do; I try to have it at home, and to carry it wherever I go. Diversion and amusements are the best and universal remedy for our ills.
Ibid.

4 . . . I think that pleasures should be enjoyed with great sobriety and moderation.
Ibid.

5 You may be sure that I know that there is a world, men, and bread beyond the lagoons [of Venice], but I submit to the will of heaven which has decreed that my journeys shall be only to my easel. I am contented with but little bread, while as to men, believe me there is nothing in the world that I think less of. . . .   Ibid.

6 . . . for three years I have been deprived of my sight. I wish you to learn from my own hand that thanks to the Divine Goodness I have recovered it. I see but as one sees after an operation, that is to say very dimly. Even this is a blessing for one who has had the misfortune to become blind. When I was sightless I cared for nothing, now I want to see everything. . . .
Letter (August 23, 1749),
from Venice,
op. cit., Ch. 7

480. Elizabeth Thomas
(c.1675-1677–1730/31)

1 Ah! strive no more to know what fate
Is pre-ordain'd for thee:
'Tis vain in this my mortal state,
For Heaven's inscrutable decree
Will only be reveal'd in vast Eternity.
"Predestination;
or the Resolution,"
*Miscellany Poems on Several
Subjects*   1722

481. Penelope Aubin
(1679–1731)

1 But alas! all earthly Blessings are deceitful, and true Happiness is never found but in the grave.   *The Life of the Lady Lucy*,
Ch. 1   1726

2 Love and Honour had a sharp contest, but at last Love got the Victory, and the rose.
Ibid., Ch. 2

3 Who can destroy him who the divine Providence thinks fit to spare?   Ibid., Ch. 5

4 This is the vast difference betwixt doing well and ill; that in Vice the Pleasure is always momentary and of no duration, and the Remorse for having done it, sure and lasting; but in doing virtuous Deeds, tho' we may suffer Loss and Pain for some short time, yet we have always a secret Satisfaction within, that supports us under them, and the End brings us Honour and generally Reward, even in this world. . . .
Ibid., Ch. 10

482. Catherine Cockburn
(1679–1749)

1 . . . when a Woman appears in the World under any distinguishing Character, she must expect to be the mark of ill Nature.
Dedication to Princess Anne,
Fatal Friendship   1698

2 O what a Wretch was I, that could not wait

Heav'ns time; the Providence that never
fails
Those who dare trust it, durst I have been
honest,
One day had chang'd the Scene, and made
me happy.   Ibid.

3 ... those little Gallantries, with which
they only think to amuse themselves; but
tho' innocent, too often gain 'em such a
Character of Lightness, as their future Conduct never can efface. *Love at a Loss; or,*
Most Votes Carry It   1700

4 ... We tax our Judgment, when we cease
to love.   Ibid.

5 LESBIA. Hands, and Seals, and Oaths cannot
secure
A mind like Man's unfaithful and impure.
                                    Ibid., Epilogue

6   But who the useful art can teach,
When sliding down a steepy way,
      To stop, before the end we reach?
                              "The Caution,"
                                        St. 3,
                              The Female Wits,
                        Lucyle Hook, ed.   1704

7 Encouraging Indulgence to the Endeavours
of our Sex ... might incite some greater
Geniuses among us to exert themselves, and
change our Emulation of a Neighbouring
Nation's Fopperies, to the commendable
Ambition of Rivalling them in their illustrious Women. . . .   Dedication to Lady
                              Harriot Godolphin,
                              The Revolution of
                              Sweden   1706

8 I ... cou'd never allow my self to think of
any Subject that cou'd not serve either to incite some useful Virtue, or check some dangerous Passion.   Ibid., Preface

9 CHRISTINA. Why do I dread what will en-
flame
The meanest Soldiers Courage? Are our
Souls too
Like their frail Mansions of weaker frame
than Mans?
Or can the force of Custom and Opinion
Effect this difference?   Ibid.

10 CHRISTINA. And we whom Custom bars
this active Valour,
Branding it with Reproach, shrink at th'
Alarm
Of War, but where our Honour's plac'd, we
oft
Have shewn in its Defence a no less Manly
daring.   Ibid.

11 ARWIDE. O wou'd Men emulate thy great
Example,
Renounce all private Ends, give up their
dear
Their warmest Passions, to the publick
Safety;
Each wou'd be happy in the common
Good.   Ibid.

12 ... those restraints, which have our sex
confin'd,
By partial custom, check the soaring mind:
Learning deny'd us, we at random tread
Unbeaten paths, that late to knowledge lead
                        Remarks upon the Principles and
                        Reasoning of Dr. Rutherforth's
                              Essay on the Nature and
                        Obligation of Virtue   1747

13 If some advent'rous genius rare arise,
Who on exalted themes her talent tries,
She fears to give the work, tho' prais'd, a
name,
And flies not more from infamy than fame.
                                           Ibid.

14 A heart whose safety but in flight does lie,
Is too far lost to have the power to fly.
                              "The Vain Advice,"
                                        St. 2,
                        The Works of Mrs. Catharine
                        Cockburn, Theological, Moral,
                        Dramatic, and Poetical,
                        Thomas Birch, ed.   1751

15 Being married in 1708, I bid adieu to the
muses, and so wholly gave myself up to the
cares of a family, and the education of my
children, that I scarce knew, whether there
was any such thing as books, plays, or poems stirring in Great Britain.
                  "Account of the Life of the Author,"
                              op. cit., Vol. I

16 ... when anything is written by a woman, that [men] cannot deny their approbation to, [they] are sure to rob us of the glory of it, by concluding 'tis not her own; or at least, that she had some assistance, which has been said in many instances to my knowledge unjustly.   Ibid., Vol. II

17 You* were our Champion, and the Glory ours.
Well you've maintain'd our equal right in Fame,
To which vain Man had quite engrost the claim   Commendatory verses quoted in *The Royal Mischief* by Mary de la Rivière Manley* 1796

18 Sundays being privileged from the needle, I have found time of late to read three short pamphlets. . . .   Letter to her niece (October 6, 1732), Quoted in *Biography of Distinguished Women* by Sarah Josepha Hale   1876

483. Joan Philips
(fl. 1679–1682)

1 The toy I've long enjoyed, if it may
Be called t'enjoy,
A thing we wish away;

. . . .
'Tis a fantastic ill, a loathed disease,
That can no sex, no age, no person please.
"Maidenhead,"
Female Poems on Several Occasions   1679

2 Thou dull companion of our active years,
That chill'st our warm blood with thy frozen fears,
How is it likely thou shouldst long endure,
When thought itself thy ruin may procure?
Ibid.

3 Though much desired, 'tis but seldom men
Court the vain blessing from a woman's pen.   Ibid.

4 Think me all man: my soul is masculine,

And capable of as great things as thine.
"To Phylocles, Inviting Him to Friendship,"
St. 3, op. cit.

5 We'll mix our souls, you shall be me, I you;
And both so one it shall be hard to say
Which is Phylocles, which Ephelia.
Ibid., St. 6

484. Elizabeth Haddon Estaugh
(1680–1762)

1 I'll venture to say, few, if any, in a married State, ever lived in sweeter Harmony than we did.
Quoted in Introduction to *A Call to the Unfaithful Professors of Truth* by John Estaugh   1744

2 I have received from the Lord a charge to love thee, John Estaugh.   Attributed, Quoted in *Tales of a Wayside Inn* by Henry Wadsworth Longfellow   1863

485.   Elizabeth Elstob
(1683–1756)

1 ... I shou'd think it as Glorious an Employment to instruct Poor Children as to teach the Children of the Greatest Monarch.   Letter to George Ballard (c.1740), Quoted in *A Galaxy of Governesses* by Bea Howe   1954

2 Alas! my acquaintance and interest is reduced to a very narrow compass.
Letter to George Ballard (1750), op. cit.

3 ... you can come into no company of Ladies and or Gentlemen, where you shall not hear an open and Vehement exclamation against Learned Women.
Letter to George Ballard (c.1753), op. cit.

4 The prospect I have of the next age is a melancholy one to me who wish Learning
might flourish to the end of the world, both
in men and women, but I shall not live to
see it.   Ibid.

486.   Eleonora von dem Knesebeck
(fl. 1684–1713)

1 The [British] government must have done a
deed of great injustice since they stop my
mouth, for if they can answer to all the
world for what they have done . . . why am
I not [allowed to] speak? If their judge-
ments are righteous, how should I dare to
speak wrongfully?   (c.1697),
              Quoted in *Lives of the
        Hanoverian Queens of England*
              by Alice Drayton Greenwood
                                        1891

487.   Jane Brereton
(1685–1740)

1 Pope* is the emblem of true wit,
    The sunshine of the mind.
          "On Mr. Nash's Picture at Full
          Length, Between the Busts of Sir
          Isaac Newton and Mr. Pope,"
                                        St. 4,
          Mrs. Jane Brereton's Poems
                                        1744

*The poet Alexander Pope.

2 Nash* represents man in the mass,
    Made up of wrong and right;
Sometimes a knave, sometimes an ass,
    Now blunt, and now polite.
                                   Ibid., St. 5
*British satirist and pamphleteer Thomas Nash
(1567–1601)

3 The picture placed the busts between,
    Adds to the thought much strength,
Wisdom, and Wit are little seen,
    But Folly's at full length.
                                   Ibid., st. 6

4 I scorn this mean fallacious art

By which you'd steal, not win, my heart
                                   "To Damon,"
                                   St. 1, op. cit.

5 If you to love would me incline,
Assert the man, forbear to whine;
Let time and plain sincerity
And faithful love your pleaders be
                                   Ibid., St. 2

6 . . . Cupid's empire won't admit
Nor own, a Salic Law.*   "To Philotinus,"
                                   St. 2, op. cit.

*European law of succession (derived from a 5th-
century Frankish code), prohibiting daughters from
inheriting land and women from succeeding to a
throne.

488.   Mrs. Taylor
(fl. 1685)

1   . . . tears,
Those springs that water Love.
                                        "Song,"
                                        St. 2,
          *Miscellany, Being a Collection of
              Poems by several Hands,*
              Aphra Behn, ed.   1685

2 And those who think themselves secure,
    The soonest are betray'd.
                                   Ibid., St. 4

3 Alas! it does my soul perplex,
    When I his charms recall,
To think he should despise the sex,
    Or what's worse, love them all.
                                        "Song,"
                                        St. 3, op. cit.

489.   Claudine Alexandrine de
Tencin
(1685–1749)

1 Unless God visibly interferes, it is physically impossible that the state [France]
should not fall to pieces.   Quoted in
          Biography of Distinguished Women
              by Sarah Josepha Hale   1876

490. Mary Chandler
(1687–1745)

1 Fatal effects of luxury and ease!
We drink our poison and we eat disease
"Temperance,"
The Female Poets of Great Britain,
Frederic Rowton, ed. 1853

2 All but the human brute: 'tis he alone,
Whose works of darkness fly the rising sun.
Ibid.

491. Jane Barker
(fl. 1688–1715)

1 Happy life . . .
Fearless of twenty-five and all its train,
Of slights and scorns, or being called old
maid. . . .
Ah lovely state how strange it is to see,
What mad conceptions some have made of
thee,
As though thy being was all wretchedness,
Or foul deformity in the ugliest dress.
"A Virgin Life,"
Poetical Recreations 1688

2 Poverty's the certain fate
Which attends a poet's state.
"Poetical Recreations,"
op. cit.

3 I cannot but reflect on this Part of Life as
the Happiest Time we are born to know,
when Youth and Innocence tune all things,
and render them harmonious; our Days
pass in Play and Health, and our Nights in
sound Sleep; our Pillows are not stuff'd
with Cares, nor our waking hours encum-
bred with Passions: We reflect not on what
is past, nor take a Prospect of what is to
come. . . . Thus we pass our happy Days
till Reason begins to bud in our Actions;
then we no sooner know that we have a Being, and rejoice that we are the noblest Part
of the Creation, but Passion takes Root in
our Hearts, and very often outgrows and
smothers our Rational Faculties.
Love Intrigues 1713

4 . . . thus we see that Human Projects are
mere Vapours, carried about with every
Blast of cross Accidents. . . .
Ibid.

5 . . . how difficult it is to draw a Scheme of
Vertuous Politicks, whereby to govern this
little Microcosm; but by that Model of all
Perfection, *Deny thy self, &c.* and that not
only in Deeds, but in the most secret Inten-
tions. . . .
Ibid.

6 . . . in our Youth we commonly dress our
Thoughts in the Mirrour of Self-Flattery,
and expect Heaven, Fortune, and the
World should cajole our Follies, as we do
our own; and lay all Faults upon others,
and all Praise on our selves. . . .
Ibid.

7 . . . as if one shou'd daily wind up a Watch,
and keep it clean, but never set it to the
Hour: By which means the little Machine is
useless, tho' it go never so well. . . .
Ibid.

8 A thousand times I wish'd that some kind
Serpent wou'd creep out of its Hole and
sting me to Death, or that Thunder wou'd
descend, and strike me into the Earth; and
so at once perform my Death, and Funeral!
Ibid.

9 . . . Love is apt to interpret things in its
own Favour. . . . Ibid.

492. Mary Wortley Montagu
(1689–1762)

1 I will not be cheated—nor will I employ
long years of repentance for moments of
joy. Comment to [Alexander] Pope,
Quoted in *History of English Literature*
by Jeremy Collier c.1720

2 But I hate to be cheated, and never will buy
Long years of repentance for moments of
joy. "The Lover: A Ballad," St. 2,
Six Town Ecologues 1747

3 And we meet with champagne and a
chicken at last. Ibid., St. 4

4 From such a dear lover as here I describe,
No danger should fright me, no millions
should bribe;
But till this astonishing creature I know,
As I long have liv'd chaste, I will keep my-
self so.　　　　　　　　　Ibid., St. 6

5 I loath the lewd rake, the dress'd fopling de-
spise:
Before such pursuers the nice virgin flies:
And as Ovid has sweetly in parable told,
We harden like trees, and like rivers grow
cold.　　　　　　　　　Ibid., St. 7

6 In crowded courts I find myself alone,
And pay my worship to a nobler throne.
　　　　　　"In Answer to a Lady who
　　　　　　　　advised Retirement,"
　　　　　　　　　　　St. 1,
　　　　　　　　The London Magazine
　　　　　　　　　　May 1750

7 Pity the madness, and despise the show.
　　　　　　　　　　　　Ibid.

8 Seldom I mark mankind's detested ways
　　　　　　　　　　Ibid., St. 2

9 Nature is seldom in the wrong, custom al-
ways.　　　　Letter to Miss Anne Wortley
　　　　　　　　(August 8, 1709),
　　　　　Letters of the Right Honourable
　　　　　Lady Mary Wortley Montagu
　　　　　　　　　　1767

10 . . . I hate the noise and hurry inseparable
from great estates and titles, and look upon
both as blessings that ought only to be given
to fools, for 'tis only to them that they are
blessings.
　　　　　　Letter to Wortley Montagu,
　　　　　　her husband (March 28, 1710),
　　　　　　　　　　op. cit.

11 . . . I know how to make a man of sense
happy; but then that man must resolve to
contribute something towards it himself.
　　　　　　　　　　　　Ibid.

12 General notions are generally wrong.
　　　　　　　　　　　　Ibid.

13 I believe to travel is the most likely way to
make a solitude agreeable, and not tiresome. . . .
　　　　　　Letter to Mr. Wortley Montagu
　　　　　　　　(August 1712),
　　　　　　　　　　op. cit.

14 'Tis better I should not be yours at all, than,
for a short happiness, involve myself in ages
of misery.　　　　　　　Ibid.

15 I know very well that nobody was ever
tiezed [sic] into a liking: and 'tis perhaps
harder to revive a past one, than to overcome an aversion.
　　　　　　Letter to Mr. Wortley Montagu
　　　　　　　(November 24, 1714),
　　　　　　　　　　op. cit.

16 . . . a man that is ashamed of passions that
are natural and reasonable, is generally
proud of those that [are] shameful and silly.
　　　　　　　　　　　　Ibid.

17 At the age of forty she is very far from being
cold and insensible: her fire may be covered
with ashes, but it is not extinghished.
　　　　　　　Letter to Lady ————
　　　　　　　　(January 13, 1716),
　　　　　　　　　　op. cit.

18 A woman, till five-and-thirty, is only looked
upon as a raw girl, and can possibly make
no noise in the world till about forty. I don't
know what your ladyship may think of this
matter; but 'tis a considerable comfort to
me, to know there is upon earth such a
paradise for old women.
　　　　　　Letter to Lady R[ich], from Vienna
　　　　　　　(September 20, 1716),
　　　　　　　　　　op. cit.

19 . . . if it were the fashion to go naked, the
face would be hardly observed.
　　　　　　　Letter to Lady Rich from
　　　　　　　　Sophia, Turkey (1717),
　　　　　　　　　　op. cit.

20 I live in a place that very well represents the Tower of Babel: my grooms are Arabs; my footmen, French, English and Germans; my nurse, an Armenian; my housemaids, Russians, half a dozen other servants, Greeks; my steward, an Italian; my janizaries, Turks; so that I live in the perpetual hearing of this medley of sounds. . . .
Letter, from Constantinople
(1717),
op. cit.

21 I am patriot enough to take pains to bring this useful invention [smallpox innoculation] into fashion in England; and I should not fail to write to some of our doctors very particularly about it, if I knew any one of them that I thought had virtue enough to destroy such a considerable branch of revenue for the good of mankind.
Letter to Lady Mar [her sister],
from Belgrade (April 1, 1717),
op. cit.

22 . . . I am assured there needs more art to keep a fondness alive in solitude, where it generally preys upon itself.
Letter to Mr. Wortley Montague
(c.1720),
op. cit.

23 . . . to be ever beloved, one must be ever agreeable.   Ibid.

24 A perpetual solitude, in a place where you see nothing to raise your spirits, at length wears them out. . . .   Ibid.

25 The last pleasure that fell in my way was Madame de Sévigné's letters; very pretty they are, but I assert without the least vanity, mine will be full as entertaining forty years hence. I advise you, therefore, to put none of them to the use of waste-paper.
Letter to Lady Mar (1724),
op. cit.

26 I give myself sometimes admirable advice, but I am incapable of taking it.
Letter to Lady Mar (1725),
op. cit.

27 Nobody can deny but religion is a comfort to the distressed, a cordial to the sick, and sometimes a restraint on the wicked; therefore, whoever* would laugh or argue it out of the world, without giving some equivalent for it, ought to be treated as a common enemy.   Letter to Countess of Bute
[her daughter]
(1752),
op. cit.

*Refers to the satirist Jonathan Swift.

28 . . . the knowledge of numbers is one of the chief distinctions between us and the brutes.   Letter to Countess of Bute
(January 28, 1753),
op. cit.

29 It is the common error of builders and parents to follow some plan they think beautiful (and perhaps is so), without considering that nothing is beautiful that is displaced.
Ibid.

30 No entertainment is so cheap as reading, nor any pleasure so lasting.
Ibid.

31 True knowledge consists in knowing things, not words.   Ibid.

32 To say truth, there is no part of the world where our sex is treated with so much contempt as in England. . . . I think it the highest injustice [that] our knowledge must rest concealed, and be as useless to the world as gold in the mine.   Letter (1753),
op. cit.

33 Copiousness of words, however ranged, is always false eloquence, though it will ever impose on some sort of understandings.
Letter to Countess of Bute
(July 20, 1754),
op. cit.

34 Only a mother knows a mother's fondness.
Letter to Countess of Bute
(July 22, 1754),
op. cit.

35 People are never so near playing the fool as when they think themselves wise.
Letter to Countess of Bute (March 1, 1755), op. cit.

36 Civility costs nothing and buys everything.
Letter to Countess of Bute (May 30, 1756), op. cit.

37 We have all our playthings; happy are they who can be contented with those they can obtain.   Letter to Countess of Bute, from Louvère (c.1743–1758), op. cit.

38 . . . valuable books, they are almost as rare as valuable men.   Ibid.

39 . . . it is now eleven years since I have seen my figure in a glass, and the last reflection I saw there was so disagreeable, that I resolved to spare myself the mortification in the future.   Letter, from Venice (c.1758–1761), op. cit.

40 It [her health] is so often impaired that I begin to be as weary of it as mending old lace; when it is patched in one place, it breaks out in another.   Ibid.

41 I enjoy vast delight in the folly of mankind; and, God be praised, that is an inexhaustible source of entertainment.
Letter to Countess of Mar (n.d.), op. cit.

42 This world consists of men, women, and Hervey's.*   Ibid., Letter (n.d.), op. cit.

*John Hervey, English memoir writer (1696–1743).

43 See how that pair of billing doves
With open murmurs own their loves
And, heedless of censorious eyes,
Pursue their unpolluted joys:
No fears of future want molest
The downy quiet of their nest.
"Verses Written in a Garden," Poetical Works   1768

44 Life is too short for any distant aim;

And cold the dull reward of future fame.
"Epistle to the Earl of Burlington," op. cit.

45 Satire should, like a polished razor keen, Wound with a touch that's scarcely felt or seen.   "To the Imitator [Alexander Pope] of the First Satire of Horace," op. cit.

46 While in vain coquets affect to be pursued, And think they're virtuous if not grossly lewd,
Let this great maxim be my virtue's guide: In part she is to blame that has been try'd— He comes too near, that comes to be deny'd.
"The Lady's Resolve," op. cit.

47 Be plain in dress, and sober in your diet; In short, my deary, kiss me! and be quiet.
"In Summary of Lord Lyttleton's Advice to a Lady," op. cit.

48 But the fruit that will fall without shaking, Indeed is too mellow for me.
"To a Lady Making Love; or, Answered, for Lord Hamilton," op. cit.

49 A real marriage bears no resemblance to these marriages of interest or ambition. It is two lovers who live together. A priest may well say certain words, a notary may well sign certain papers—I regard these preparations in the same way that a lover regards the rope ladder that he ties to his mistress's window.   Essay, n.d.

493.   Mary Barber
(1690?–1757)

1 A richer present I design,
A finished form, of work divine,
Surpassing all the power of art;

A thinking head, a grateful heart.
> "On Sending my Son as a
> Present to Dr. [Jonathan] Swift,
> Dean of St. Patrick's,
> on his Birthday,"
> *Poems on Several Occasions*
> 1734

494.   Francisca Josefa del Castillo y Guevara
(1691?–1743)

1 The land grew bright in a single flower—
One great carnation rare....
> "Christmas Carol,"
> St. 1,
> *The Catholic Anthology,*
> Thomas Walsh, ed.   1927

2 "My sin has led me far
As some wild thirsting bee
Beneath Thy meadow star,
Idly forgetting Thee;
But Thou dost call me home; I hear
Thy voice whose sweetness charms mine
ear.   "The Holy Eclogue,"
> St. 6, op. cit.

495.   Martha Corey
(?–1692)

1 Ye are all against me and I cannot help it.*
> Remark (1692),
> Quoted in *Notable American Women,*
> Edward T. James, ed.   1971

*Remark at her trial in Salem, Mass., for witchcraft.

496.   Eliza Haywood
(1693?–1756)

1   Criticks! be dumb to-night—no Skill display;
A dangerous Woman-Poet wrote the Play:
One, who not fears your Fury, tho' prevailing,
More than your Match, in every thing, but Railing.

Give her fair Quarter, and whene'er she tries ye,
Safe in superior Spirit, she defies ye....
> Prologue,
> *A Wife to Be Let*   1723

2 Flattery is a Vice so much in Fashion, and, I am sorry to say, so much encouraged, that there is nothing more difficult than to find a Patron who not expects, nor would be pleased with it....   Dedication,
> *The Rash Resolve*   1724

3 Tho' nothing is more laudible than a Firmness of Resolution, yet there is no one thing more apt to bring us into Misfortunes, than too inconsiderately to form them....
> Ibid., Pt. I

4 ... to renew a Friendship with a Person whose Unworthiness or Baseness has once forfeited it, is to put it in his power a second time to deceive us, and no other than joining in our Destruction.   Ibid.

5 "It is enough—in knowing one, I know the whole deceiving Sex—Nor will I be a second time betray'd—I'll hide me for ever from their Arts, their soothing Flattery, their subtle Insinuations—no more I'll hear, or see, or think of Man—The best is base...."   Ibid.

6 Pity is a prodigeous Alleviator of affliction, the most violent Grief finds some Ease in complaining; but when our Woes are of a nature, as will not admit revealing, they play on our very Vitals, and waste the Spirits with unintermitting Anguish, and seldon fail of bringing on Death or Destruction.
> Ibid., Pt. II

7 How little are the ill judging Multitude capable of chusing for themselves! How far are Wealth and Beauty, the two great Idols of the admiring World, from being real Blessings to the Possessors of them!
> *The Mercenary Lover; or, the*
> *Unfortunate Heiresses*   1726

8 ... but alas! where is the Skill to trace, or Rules to reach the unfathomable Heart of artful Man, practis'd in Wiles, experienc'd in Deceit....   Ibid.

9 The base are always Cowards, the same Meaness of Spirit which makes them the one, inclines them to the other also; they are ever in Fear, and while there remains even the smallest Probability of Danger, Peace is a Stranger to their Minds.
Ibid.

10 The natural Propensity which all People have to listen to any Arguments which may serve to excuse the Errors they commit. . . .
Ibid.

11 *Confidence* alone makes *Love* a Blessing. . . .   Ibid.

12 "I am not without some share of that too common Foible of Humanity, which makes us placè less Value on the things we are in possession of, than those above our reach. . . . "   *The Secret History of the Present Intrigues of the Court of Caramania,*
Pt. I   1727

13 "*Hope* is the most pleasing Passion of the Soul. . . . "   Ibid.

14 . . . the painful *present,* the Fears of the *future,* and those Racks of Thought which are inseperable from a State of uncertainty, made his Mind a perfect Chaos of confus'd Idea's, incapable of Invention, Ease, or Resolution.   Ibid., Pt. II

15 . . . he was too well acquainted with human Nature, not to know that nothing violent is of long continuance, and of all the Passions that invade the Mind, none so short-liv'd as Rage. . . .   Ibid.

16 . . . that Passion, which is often mistaken for Love, and is ordinarily more successful. . . .   Ibid., Pt. III

17 . . . those tender Doubts which are almost inseparable from Love. . . .
Ibid.

18 "Good Heaven," pursu'd he wildly, "why do you suffer that Face still to retain its show of Innocence? Why is it not her Form grown black and horrid, like her polluted Soul? some publick mark of Infamy should appear to warn unwary Gazers from her destructive Charms."   Ibid., Pt. V

19 Blast, blast her charms, some balloon-destroying air!
And turn his love to loathing, but let hers
Know no decrease, that disappointment,
Lovers worst hell, may meet her warmest wishes,
And make her curse the hour in which she wedded.   *Frederick, Duke of Brunswick Lunenburgh*   1729

20 Love's not the effect of reason, or of will,
Few feel that passions force because they choose it
And fewer yet when it becomes their duty.
Ibid.

21 He represented to her, that the greatest Glory of a Monarch was the Liberty of the People, his most valuable Treasures in *their* crowded Coffers, and his securest Guard in their *sincere Affection.*   *Adventures of Eovaii, Princess of Ijaveo*   1736

22 . . . nothing but Liberty was denied her.
"The History of Yximilla,"
op. cit.

23 "Where Kings are invested with so absolute and uncontrollable a Sway as to have the Power of acting in all things according as Ambition prompts," said Eovaai, "I wonder not the Nations under them have good Reason to regret the cruel Necessity of submitting to it."   "The Harangue of Alhahuza to the Populus of Hypotofa,"
op. cit.

24 To endure all the toils and hardships of the field with patience and intrepidity, to be fearless of danger when the duties of his post commanded, is highly laudable and emulative; but to run into them without a call, and when bravery can be of no service, is altogether idle; and courage like all other virtues, degenerates into a vice by being carried to an extreme.
"Effeminacy in the Army,"
The Female Spectator
1744–1746

25 Nature is in itself abhorrent of vice. . . .
"Masquerades, How Prejudicial,"
op. cit.

26 All that can justly be objected against any arguments made use of to prove the reasonableness of a belief in a plurality of worlds is, that to us, that live in this, it is no manner of concern, since there is not a possibility of travelling to them, or of ever becoming acquainted with the inhabitants.
"Flying-Machines, The Impossibility of Their Use,"
op. cit.

27 Could the region of air, indeed, afford any shelter from that all devouring fire which, we are told, shall consume the earth, there might be some little shadow of a hope, that the race of man might be preserved a second time by means no less surprising than the first.   Ibid.

28 Philosophy is the toil which can never tire the persons engaged in it; all its ways are strewed with roses, and the farther you go, the more enchanting objects appear before you and invite you on.   "Study of Philosophy Recommended,"
op. cit.

29 Honour was the only excitement, applause the only end proposed by each bold attemptor. These, alas! of later days, are but empty names; a thousand pounds has more real charm than any that are to be found in glory. Gain, sordid gain, is all that engrosses the heart, and adds transport to success.   "Tennis, a Manly Exercise,"
op. cit.

30 Chance may in a moment destroy all that the utmost care can do. . . .
"Caution Necessary in Parents,"
op. cit.

31 . . . the Avarice and Self-interestedness, which is generally observed in those Women who make Sale of their Beauty, is chiefly owing to Men.   "The Story of the Enchanted Well,"
Memoirs of a Certain Island Adjacent to the Kingdom of Utopia   1775

32 I desire no other Revenge for my abused Sincerity, than that you may, some time or other, find a Woman fair enough to create a real Passion in you; and as insensible of it, as you are of mine.   "The History of Graciana,"
op. cit.

33 . . . many Women, who have little or no sense of Gratitude, have a very quick one of Jealousy. . . .   "The History of the Chevalier Windusius, and the fair, false Wyaria,"
op. cit.

34 She was so exact an Economist, and made so good use of her Time, that she had always an Opportunity of being happy with the Man she lik'd, and never miss'd one with the Man whose Purse was at her devotion.   "The History of Hortensia,"
op. cit.

35 That Generosity and open Candor, which is almost inseparable from good Sense, renders the Person possess'd of it, at once incapable of a base Action himself, or of suspecting it in others.   "The History of Count Orainos, and Madame Del Millmonde,"
op. cit.

36 'Tis kinder far to kill than to forsake.
"Extract from the Tea Table,"
The Female Poets of Great Britain,
Frederic Rowton, ed.   1853

37 Death is a safe, a sure retreat from care.
Ibid.

497.   Charlotte Elizabeth Aissé
(1694/95–1733)

1 The Queen has twin daughters; what a pity there is not a dauphin among them!
> Letter,
> Quoted in *Portraits and Backgrounds,* Ch. 5,
> by Evangeline Wilbour Blashfield
> 1917

2 One must console oneself for the losses of fortune. Far better people than I am are much more to be pitied.   Ibid.

3 We sup wretchedly, we have neither good fish nor good friends.   Ibid.

4 It seems to be a natural human impulse to profit by the weakness of others. I do not know how to use such arts; I know only one: to make life so sweet to him I love that he will find nothing preferable to it.
> Letter,
> op. cit., Ch. 6

5 I am full of faults but I respect and love virtues.   Ibid.

6 . . . I could never love where I could not respect.   Ibid.

7 From the moment that I began to open my eyes to my transgressions, remorse never abandoned me.
> Letter,
> op. cit., Ch. 7

498.   Elizabeth Tollet
(1694–1754)

1 The conscious moon and stars above
Shall guide me with my wandering love.
> "Winter Song,"
> *Poems on Several Occasions.*
> *With Anne Boleyn to King Henry VIII, an Epistle*   1755

2 'Tis vanished all! remains alone
The eyeless scalp of naked bone;
The vacant orbits sunk within;
The jaw that offers at a grin.
Is this the object, then, that claims

The tribute of our youthful flames?
> "On a Death's Head,"
> op. cit.

3 How high does Melancholy swell!
> Ibid.

499.   Ariadne
(fl. 1695)

1 [I] could not conquer the Inclination I had for Scribling from my Childhood. And when our Island enjoyed the Blessing of the incomparable Mrs. [Aphra] Behn, even then I had much ado to keep my Muse from shewing her Impertinence; but, since her death, has claim'd a kind of Privilege; and, in spite of me, broke from her Confinement.
> Preface,
> *She Ventures and He Wins*
> 1695

2 Our Author hopes indeed,
You will not think, though charming Aphra's* dead,
All Wit with her, and with Orinda's** fled.
> Ibid., Prologue

*The playwright Aphra Behn. See 438.
**Pseudonym of the poet Katherine Philips. See 426.

500.   Cornelia Bradford
(1695?–1755)

1 The Punsters are of Opinion, that though we could not Cope with the Rebellion at first, we shall make shift to Wade thro' it at last.*
> From article in *American Weekly Mercury,*
> Quoted in *Andrew Bradford, Colonial Journalist*
> by A. J. DeArmond   1949

*Neither Sir John *Cope* nor Field Marshal George *Wade* was successful in stemming the Jacobite invasion of 1745.

501. Marie Anne du Deffand
(1697–1780)

1 What more can you ask? He [Voltaire] has invented history! (*Que voulez-vous de plus? Il a inventé l'histoire!*).
> Quoted in *L'Esprit dans histoire* by Fournier 1857

2 The distance is nothing: it is only the first step that is difficult.* Letter to Jean Le Rond d'Alembert (July 7, 1763), *Correspondance inédite* 1859
*Refers to the legend that St. Denis, carrying his head in his hands, walked two leagues.

3 I do not know why Diogenes went looking for a man: nothing could happen to him worse than finding one. Ibid.

4 . . . everything seems insupportable to me. This may very well be because I am insupportable myself. Ibid.

5 I hear nothings, I speak nothings, I take interest in nothing and from nothing to nothing I travel gently down the dull way which leads to becoming nothing.
> Ibid.

6 . . . I have a gnawing worm which sleeps no more than I do. . . . Ibid.

7 I remember thinking in my youth that no one was happy but madmen, drunkards, and lovers. Ibid.

8 I am not insensible to natural and rural beauties, but one's soul must be in a very gentle and peaceful mood to get much pleasure from them. Ibid.

9 Let me whisper in your ear that I make precious little account of kings; their protestations, their retractations, their recriminations, their contradictions, I find them of no more moment than the mixing of a breakfast for my cat. Ibid.

10 Everything I read bores me; history, because I am totally incurious; essays, because they are half platitude and half affected originality; novels; because the lovemaking seems sentimental and the study of passion makes me unhappy.
> Ibid.

11 To me music is a noise more importunate than agreeable. Ibid.

12 Faith is a devout belief in what one does not understand. Ibid.

13 Everything that exists is wretched, an angel, an oyster, perhaps even a grain of sand; nothingness, nothingness, what better can we have to pray for? Ibid.

14 One seeks everywhere for something to lean on. One is charmed with the hope of having found it: it turns out to be a dream which harsh facts scatter with a rude awakening.
> Ibid.

15 [I am] a visionary, who watches the clouds and sees lovely things there that fade even as one beholds them. Ibid.

16 I love nothing and that is the true cause of my ennui. Ibid.

17 God is not more incomprehensible than you; but if he is not more just, it is hardly worth while believing in him.
> Ibid.

18 You cannot let go in your letters. You always say just what you want to say.
> Letter to Madame Louise de Choiseul*, op. cit.
*See 563.

19 Vanity ruins more women than love.
> Quoted in *Lettres à Voltaire*, Joseph Trabucco, ed. 1922

20 Women are never stronger than when they arm themselves with their weaknesses.
> Ibid.

21 Write disagreeably, if you like; as the man said of the rack, it will help me to pass an hour or two, at any rate.   Quoted in *Horace Walpole's Correspondence with Madame du Deffand and Wiart,* W. S. Lewis and Warren Hunting, eds.   1939

22 She [Madame de Choiseul] wants to be perfect. That is her defect.   Ibid.

23 It is vexatious that she [Madame de Choiseul] is an angel. I had rather she were a woman.   Ibid.

502. Frïederika Karoline Neuber
(1697–1760)

1 Dear reader, here is something for you to read. To be sure, it is not written by a great, scholarly man. Oh, no! It is by a mere woman whose name you scarcely know and for whose station in life you have to look among the most humble of people, for she is nothing but a comedian. She cannot be responsible for anything but her own art, though she does know enough to understand another artist when he talks about his work. If you should ask her why she writes at all, her answer will be the customary feminine "Because." If any one asks you who helped her, you had better answer, "I don't know"—for it may very well be that she did it all herself.
     Preface to the play *Vorspiel,* Quoted in *Enter the Actress* by Rosamond Gilder   1931

2 For the rest, she submits gladly to the judgment of those who think straight, who speak at the right moment and who know how to keep quiet when necessary. The others may think what they like, speak if they can and keep silent when they have to.
     Ibid.

503. Susanna Wright
(1697–1784)

1 Flowers on thy breast, and round thy head,

With thee their sweets resign,
Nipp'd from their tender stalks, and dead,
Their fate resembles thine
     "On the Death of a Young Girl,"
     St. 11 (1737),
     Women Poets in Pre-Revolutionary America,
     Pattie Cowell, ed.   1981

2 And what are they—a vision all the past,
A bubble on the water's shining face,
What yet remain, till the first transient blast,
Shall leave no more remembrance of their place.   "My Own Birth-Day,"
     St. 2 (August 1, 1761),
     op. cit.

3 Since early reason gave reflection birth.
     Ibid., St. 4

4 One all-disposing God, who gave you birth,
That life sustain'd, which his good pleasure gave,
Then cut you off, from ev'ry claim on earth,
Is the same guardian God, beyond the grave.   Ibid., St. 10

504. Mary Delany
(1700–1788)

1 Hail to the happy times when fancy led
My pensive mind the flow'ry path to tread,
And gave me emulation to presume,
With timid art, to trace fair nature's bloom
     Preface, *Flora, or, Herbal,*
     n.d.

505. Sarah Updike Goddard
(c.1700–1770)

1 . . . [the] mystick art of printing. . . .
     Untitled poem,
     from *Providence Gazette*
     (March 16, 1765),
     Quoted in *William Goddard, Newspaperman,* Ch. 4,
     by Ward L. Miner   1962

2 You can storm a strong fort, or can form a
   blockade,
   Yet ye stand by like dastards; and see me a
   maid.   "The Distressed Maid"
                            (August 30, 1766),
                                      op. cit.

3 Ye learned physicians, whose excellent
   skill,
   Can save, or demolish, can cure, or can kill;
   To a poor forlorn damsel contribute your
   aid,
   Who is sick, very sick of remaining a maid.
                                          Ibid.

4 . . . every one who takes delight in publicly
   or privately taking away any person's *good
   name*, or striving to render him ridiculous,
   are in the gall of bitterness, and in the bonds
   of iniquity, whatever their pretences may be
   for it.   Letter to her son,
                          William Goddard (1765),
                                Ch. 5, op. cit.

5 I heartily wish it was within the reach of my
   faint efforts to convey to you what three-
   score and almost ten years experience has
   taught me, of the mere nothingness of all
   [the political hogwash] you are disputing
   about, and the infinite importance and
   value of what you thereby neglect and
   disregard—a jewel of inestimable value.*
                                          Ibid.

*Their newspaper, the *Providence Gazette.*

506.   Fukuzoyo Chiyo
(c.1701-1703–1775)

1   The dew of the rouge-flower
When it is spilled
         Is simply water.   Untitled haiku,
                            R. H. Blyth, tr.;
                          *The Penguin Book
                            of Women Poets*,
                     Carol Cosman, Joan Keefe and
                     Kathleen Weaver, eds.   1978

2 After a long winter
giving
each other nothing, we collide

with blossoms in our hands.
                                       Untitled,
                            in toto, David Ray, tr.;
                          A Book of Women Poets,
                     Aliki and Willis Barnstone, eds.
                                            1980

507.   Jane Wiseman
(fl. 1701)

1 The Reception it [her play] met with in the
   World, was not kind enough to make me
   Vain, nor yet so ill, to discourage my Pro-
   ceeding.   Dedication,
                        *Antiochus the Great; or, The
                            Fatal Relapse*   1701

2 I'll add to my Diligence, and with more
   eagerness pursue the Chase; and sure
   there's a necessity that all resolv'd like me,
   should meet success at last.
                                          Ibid.

508.   Constantia Grierson
(1706?–1733)

1 And if to wit, our courtship they pretend,
   'Tis the same way that they a cause defend;
   In which they give of lungs a vast expence,
   But little passion, thought, or eloquence
              "To Miss Laetitia Van Lewen
               (Afterwards Mrs. Pilkington), at
                        a Country Assize,"
                     Poems on Several Occasions,
                     Mary Barber, ed.   1734

509.   Mercy Wheeler
(1706–c.1733)

1 Poor, wretched and vile sinners all
   Rank'd with the heathen nation,
   Who unto God ne'er pray nor call,
   For pardon and salvation.
                                       Untitled,
                                    St. 1 (1732),
                          *Women Poets in Pre-
                            Revolutionary America*,
                     Pattie Cowell, ed.   1981

510. Anna Williams
(1706–1783)

1 When Delia strikes the trembling string,
   She charms our list'ning ears;
But when she joins her voice to sing,
   She emulates the spheres.
                    "On A Lady Singing,"
                               St. 1,
                    Quoted in *Biography of*
                    Distinguished Women
        by Sarah Josepha Hale   1876

511. Selina Hastings
(1707–1791)

1 I am well; all is well—well for ever. I see,
wherever I turn my eyes, whether I live or
die, nothing but victory.*
               Quoted in *The Women of*
   Methodism: Its Three Foundresses. . .
             by Abel Stevens   1866
*Remark after a stroke that presaged her death.

2 The coming of the Lord draweth nigh, the
coming of the Lord draweth nigh! The
thought fills my soul with joy unspeakable,
my soul is filled with glory; I am as in the
element of heaven itself. I am encircled in
the arms of love and mercy; I long to be at
home; O, I long to be at home!
                                        Ibid.

3 My work is done; I have nothing to do but
to go to my Father.   Some of her last
                                   words,
                                   op. cit.

512. Jane Colman Turell
(1708–1735)

1 My good fat Bacon, and our homely Bread,
With which my healthful Family is fed.
Milk from the Cow, and Butter newly
   churn'd,

And new fresh Cheese, with Curds and
   Cream just turn'd.   "An Invitation Into
                    the Country, In Imitation of
                               Horace,"
                               St. 4
          Reliquiae Turellae et Lachrymae Pater-
                               nae
                    [*Relics of Turell and Paternal*
                           Tears]   1735

2 O Palestina! our once dear abode
Thou once wert blest with peace, and lov'd
   by God,
But now art desolate, a barren waste,
Thy fruitful fields by thorns and weeds
   defac'd.
               "Psalm CXXXVII. Paraphras'd"
                         (August 5, 1725),
                    Women Poets in Pre-
                    Revolutionary America,
                    Pattie Cowell, ed.   1981

3 Dauntless you undertake th' unequal strife,
And raise dead virtue by your verse to life.
A woman's pen strikes the curs'd serpent's
   head,
And lays the monster gasping, if not dead.
               "On Reading the Warning by
                         Mrs. Singer,"*
                               op. cit.
*Elizabeth Singer Rowe. See 478.

4 . . . no pain is like a bleeding heart.
               "Part of the Fifth Chapter of
          Canticles Paraphras'd From the
                         8th Verse,"
               St. 1 (September 14, 1725),
                               op. cit.

5 His head is wisdom's spacious theatre
                         Ibid., St. 4

6 Come now, fair muse, and fill my empty
   mind
With rich ideas, great and unconfin'd.
                         "To My Muse"
                    (December 29, 1725),
                               op. cit.

7   Thrice in my womb I've found the
           pleasing strife,
In the first struggles of my infant's life:

But O how soon by Heaven I'm call'd to
mourn,
While from my womb a lifeless babe is torn?
Born to the grave ere it has seen the light,
Or with one smile had cheer'd my longing
sight.   "Lines On Childbirth,"
St. 2, op. cit.

8   She's gone! she's gone! I saw her rise
And quickly gain the distant skies.
"Lines On Her Mother's Death,"
St. 1, op. cit.

9 If sinners wrangle, let the saints agree;
The gospel breathes out nought but unity.
"Some Unhappy Affairs of
Medford [Mass.] in the Years
1729 and 1730,"
op. cit.

513.   Mary Washington
(1708–1789)

1 ... George [Washington] will not forget
the lessons I early taught him—he will not
forget *himself*, though he is the subject of so
much praise.   *Recollections and Private
Memoirs of Washington by his
adopted son, George Washington
Parke Curtis, with a Memoir of
the Author, by his
daughter...*   1860

2 I am not surprised at what George has
done, for he was always a very good boy.
Ibid.

514.   Lydia Fish Willis
(1709–1767)

1 The gate is straight,—the way is narrow,—
my heart is hard,—my sins are great,—my
strength is weak,—my faith is so benighted
with doubts, that I am ready to cast all offered good away....

Such languid, faint desires I feel,
Within this wicked, stupid heart,
I should, I would, but that, I will,

I hardly dare (with truth) assert.
"Lines from an Undated Letter
to her Niece,"
*Rachel's Sepulchre; Or, a
Memorial of Mrs. Lydia Willis,
taken Chiefly, from her Letters to
Friends...*   1767?

515.   Sarah Pierpont Edwards
(1710–1758)

1 I seemed to myself to perceive a glow of divine love come down from the heart of
Christ in heaven, into my heart, in a constant stream, like a stream or pencil of
sweet light. At the same time, my heart and
soul all flowed out in love to Christ.
(1738), Quoted in *The Works of
President Edwards,**
Vol. I, Ch. XIV, Sereno E.
Dwight, ed.   1830
*Her husband Jonathan Edwards (1703–1758),
theologian, philosopher, and president of the College
of New Jersey (later Princeton University) from 1757
to his death.

2 My soul remained in a kind of heavenly
elysium.   Ibid.

516.   Sarah Fielding
(1710–1768)

1 "... the height of my distress lies in not
knowing my own mind; if I could once find
that out, I should be easy enough. I am so
divided by the desire of riches on the one
hand, and by my honour and the man I like
on the other, that there is such a struggle in
my mind I am almost distracted."
David Simple   c.1750

2 "I hope to be excused by those gentlemen
who are quite sure they have found one
woman who is a perfect angel, and that all
the rest are perfect devils...."
Ibid.

3 "Whenever I hear a man express an uncommon detestation of any one criminal action, I always suspect he is guilty of it himself . . . or, perhaps, as most men take a great deal of pains to flatter themselves, they continually endeavour, by giving things false names, to impose on their own understandings till at last they prevail so far with their *own good nature*, as to think they are entirely exempt from those very failings they are most addicted to."

Ibid.

4 "A number of figures of men . . . would talk for ever, and say nothing—were always in motion, yet could not properly be said ever to act. They have neither wit nor passions, they are seldom guilty of so many indiscretions as other men; the only thing they can be said to have is pride, and the only way to find that out is by a strut in their gait— something resembling that of the peacock, which shows they are conscious, if they can be said to have any consciousness, of their own dignity."

Ibid.

5 Spatter made no other answer but by uttering the word "fools" with some earnestness; a monosyllable he always chose to pronounce before he went to bed, insomuch as it was thought, by some who knew him, he could not sleep without it.

Ibid.

6 " . . . the praising of people for [what] they don't deserve is the surest way of making them contemptible, and leading others into the thinking of their faults."

Ibid.

7 "I think there is nothing so pleasant as revenge; I would pursue a man who had injured me to the very brink of life. I know it would be impossible for me ever to forgive him; and I would have him live only that I might have the pleasure of seeing him miserable."

Ibid.

8 . . . he had not learned that most useful lesson of reducing his knowledge to practice. . . .

Ibid.

517.   Mary Singleton Copley Pelham
(c.1710–1789)

1 Your fame, my dear son, is sounded by all who are lovers of the art you bid fair to excel in. May God prosper and cause you to succeed in all your undertakings, and enroll your name among the first in your profession. Letter to John Singleton Copley, her son (February 6, 1788), from Boston,

Quoted in *The Domestic and Artistic Life of John Singleton Copley, R.A.,* by Martha Babcock Amory* 1882

*Her granddaughter.

518.   Marie de Beauveau
(1711–1786)

1 Say what you will in two Words and get through.

"Air: Sentir avec ardeur," St. 1, Ezra Pound, tr.; *Confucius to Cummings*; *An Anthology of Poetry,* Ezra Pound and Marcella Spann, eds. 1964

2 Know how to read? you *must* Before you can write.   Ibid., St. 2

3   An idiot Will always Talk a lot.   Ibid.

519.   Catherine Clive
(1711–1785)

1 WILLING. But don't your heart ache when you think of the first night, hey?

The Rehearsal: or, Boys in Petticoats   1753

2 MRS. HAZARD. Oh fie, Miss! that will never do: you speak your words as plain as a parish girl: the audience will never endure you in this kind of singing; if they understand what you say. You must give your words the Italian accent.   Ibid.

3 SURLY. Marry her! I would sooner marry a Woman that had been detected in ten Amours, than one, who, in Defiance to all Advice, and without the Pretence that most People write for, (for every body knows she's a Woman of Fortune) will convince the whole World she's an Ideot [sic].
          Ibid.

4 SIR ALBANY ODELOVE. If men, who are properly graduated in Learning, who have swallow'd the Tincture of a polite Education, who, as I may say, are hand and glove with the Classics, if such Genius's as I'm describing, fail of Success in Dramatical Occurences, or Performances, ('tis the same Sense in the Latin) what must a poor Lady expect, who is ignorant as the Dirt.
          Ibid.

5 Necessity or inclination brings every one to the stage.   Quoted in
          The Life of Mrs. Catherine Clive
          by Percy Fitzgerald   1888

6 ... I have always despised the French Politics, but I never yet heard we were at war with their wit....   Ibid.

7 I know 'tis in vain to Expostulate with people in power....   Letter to the [theater] Managers (February 13, 1768),
          op. cit.

8 I am at present in such health and such spirits, that when I recollect I am an old woman, I am astonished.   Letter to Mr. [David] Garrick,* London (April 14, 1769),
          op. cit.

*English actor and theater manager (1717–1779).

9 ... when they have sank their spirits till they are ill, [they] will find that nothing but submission can give any consolation to inevitable misfortunes.   Letter to Mr. George Colman (April 12, 1771),
          op. cit.

10 I have seen you with your magical hammer in your hand, endeavouring to beat your ideas into the heads of creatures who have none of their own. Letter to Mr. Garrick, from Twickenham (June 23, 1776),
          op. cit.

11 I have seen your lamb turned into a lion: by this your great labour was entertained; they thought they all acted very fine—they did not see you pull the wires.
          Ibid.

12 I send you walnuts which are fine, but pray be moderate in your admiration, for they are dangerous dainties.   Letter to Miss Pope, from Twickenham (October 17, 1784),
          op. cit.

520.   Ho Shuang-ch'ing
(1712–?)

1 The hardest thing in the world
Is to reveal a hidden love.
          To the tune
          "A Watered Silk Dress,"
          The Orchid Boat,
          Women Poets of China,
          Kenneth Rexroth and Ling
          Chung, eds. and trs.   1972

521.   Laetitia Pilkington
(1712–1750/51)

1 Lying is an occupation
     Used by all who mean to rise;
Politicians owe their station
     But to well-concerted lies.

These to lovers give assistance
     To ensnare the fair one's heart;

And the virgin's best resistance
    Yields to this commanding art.

Study this superior science,
    Would you rise in church or state;
Bid to truth a bold defiance,
    'Tis the practice of the great.
                       "Song,"
                       in toto,
     Memoirs of Mrs. Laetitia
Pilkington, written by herself,
Wherein are occasionaly
interspersed all her Poems, with
Anecdotes of several eminent
persons living and dead   1748

522.   Alicia Cockburn
(1713–1794)

1 I've seen the smiling of fortune beguiling,
I've felt all its favours and found its decay;
Sweet was its blessing and kind its caressing,
But now it is fled—it is fled far away.
           "The Flowers of the Forest,"*
                  Scottish Song,
         Mary Carlyle Aitken, ed.
                      1874

*This is a reworking of a much older, anonymous song. (Cf. Jean Elliot, 546:1.) The reference is to the thousands of men led by James IV who were slain at the Battle of Flodden Field (Sept. 9, 1513).

2 The flowers of the forest are withered away.
                  Ibid., refrain

523.   Abigail Colman Dennie
(1715–1745)

1 Yet still my fate permits me this relief,
To write to lovely Delia* all my grief.
To you alone I venture to complain;
From others hourly strive to hide my pain.
       Lines From a Letter to Her
          Sister, Jane Colman
         (March 23, 1733),
      Quoted in *New England*
Historical and Genealogical
      Register, No. 14
                    1860

*Her sister, the poet Jane Colman Turell. See 512.

524.   Mary Monk
(?–1715)

1 O'er this marble drop a tear,
    Here lies fair Rosalind;
All mankind were pleased with her,
    And she with all mankind.
            "Lady of Pleasure,"
    Marinda: Poems and Translations
       on Several Occasions   1716

2 A just applause and an immortal name
Is the true object of the Poet's aim
          "Epistle to Marinda,"
                  op. cit.

3 Say, shouldst thou grieve to see my sorrows end?
Thou know'st a painful pilgrimage I've past;
And shouldst thou grieve that rest is come at last?
Rather rejoice to see me shake off life,
And die as I have liv'd, thy faithful wife.
        "Verses written on her deathbed
           at Bath, to her husband in
                 London,"
                  op. cit.

525.   Elizabeth Carter
(1717–1806)

1 She loves the cool, the silent eve,
Where no false shows of life deceive,
    Beneath the lunar ray.
Here Folly drops each vain disguise,
Nor sports her gaily-colour'd dyes,
    As in the glade of day.
            "Ode to Wisdom,"
                  St. 3,
   Poems Upon Particular Occasions
                    1738

2 But, taught by thy unerring rules,
To shun the fruitless wish of fools,
    To nobler views aspires.
                Ibid., St. 5

3 For Wealth, the smiles of glad content,
　For Power, its amplest, best extent,
　　An empire o'er the mind.
　　　　　　　　　　Ibid., St. 7

4 Thy breath inspires the poet's song,
　The patriot's free unbias'd tongue,
　　The hero's generous strife:
　Thine are retirement's silent joys,
　And all the sweet engaging ties
　　Of still, domestic life.
　　　　　　　　　　Ibid., St. 13

5 Beneath her clear discerning eye,
　The visionary shadows fly
　　Of Folly's painted show:
　She sees, through every fair disguise,
　That all but Virtue's solid joys
　　Is vanity and woe.　Ibid., St. 16

6 Through Nature's ever varying scene,
　By different ways pursued,
　The one eternal end of Heaven
　　Is universal good.　"Lines Written at
　　　　　　　　Midnight during a
　　　　　　　　Thunderstorm,"
　　　　　　　　St. 4, op. cit.

7 When through Creation's vast expanse
　The last dread thunders roll,
　Untune the concord of the spheres,
　　And shake the rising soul
　　　　　　　　　　Ibid., St. 8

8 The true post of honour consists in the discharge of those duties, whatever they happen to be, which arise from that situation in which Providence has fixed us, and which we may be assured is the very situation best calculated for our virtue and happiness.
　　　　　　　Letter to a friend,
　　　　　　Quoted in *Biography of
　　　　　　Distinguished Women*
　　　by Sarah Josepha Hale　1876

9 . . . between reading, working, writing, twirling the globes, and running up and down stairs to see where everybody is and how they do, I seldom want either business or entertainment. Quoted in *A Woman of
　　　　　　　Wit and Wisdom*
　　　by Alice C. C. Gaussen　1906

10 I have nothing to assist me but industry; genius I have none, and I want mightily to know whether one can make any progress without it.　　　　　Ibid.

11 I am sick of people of sense because they can act like fools, and of fools because they cannot talk like people of sense, and of myself for being so absurd as to trouble my head about them.　　　Letter to a friend
　　　　　　　　　　　　(1745),
　　　　　　　　　　　op. cit.

12 Remember that not to be happy is not to be grateful.　　　　　　　Ibid.

13 Do you want employment? Choose it well before you begin, and then pursue it. Do you want amusement? Take the first you meet with that is harmless, and never be attached to any. Are you in a moderate station? Be content, though not affectedly so; be philosophical, but for the most part keep your thoughts to yourself. Are you sleepy? Go to bed.　　　　　　　Ibid.

14 Our great people break through all the sacred authority of law, and lose all sense of what is decent in pursuit of French diversions, and are surrounded by French taylors, French valets, French dancing masters, and French cooks. Our fine ladies disgrace the "human shape divine," and become helpless to themselves and troublesome to all the world besides, with French hoops, and run into indecent extravagance of dress, inconsistent with all rules of sober appearance and good economy.　　　　　　　Ibid.

526.   Maria Theresa
(1717–1780)

1 My son,* as you are the heir to all my worldly possessions, I cannot dispose of them; but my children are still, as they have ever been, my *own*. I bequeath them to you; be to them a father.   Last words
(November 29, 1780),
Quoted in *Biography of Distinguished Women*
by Sarah Josepha Hale   1876

*Joseph II (1741–1790), Holy Roman Emperor, 1765–1790.

2 I want to meet my God awake.
Remark on her deathbed
(November 1780), refusing drugs;
attributed by Thomas Carlyle,
n.d.

527.   Anne Steele
(1717–1778/79)

1 Little monitor, by thee
Let me learn what I should be;
Learn the round of life to fill,
Useful and progressive still.
"To My Watch,"
Poems on Subjects Chiefly Devotional   1760

528.   Mary Draper
(c.1718–1810)

1 He [her son] is wanted and must go. You [her daughter] and I, Kate, have also service to do. Food must be prepared for the hungry; for before to-morrow night, hundreds, I hope thousands, will be on their way to join the continental forces.
Response to a call to arms (1776),
Quoted in *The Women of the American Revolution*
by Elizabeth F. Ellet   1848

529.   Mary Hearne
(fl. c.1719)

1 Love ... generally hurries us on without Consideration. ...   "The Third Day,"
The Lover's Week   1718

2 ... Love and Reason, like a Fever and Ague, took their alternate Turns in my Breast. ...   "The Amours of Calista and Torismond,"
The Female Deserters   1719

3 ... therefore You should not by the vulgar Notion of Marriage make yourself uneasy, since that Ceremony is nothing but a piece of Formality, introduced on purpose to bring Profit to the Church; and I think that Love is much more to be Esteem'd, which has no other Motive but mutual Affection.
Ibid.

530.   Frances Fulke Greville
(1720–1789)

1   Haply some herb or tree,
Sov'reign as juice of western flower,
Conceals a balm for me.
"Prayers for Indifference,"*
St. 4 (1753),
Maxims and Characters   1756
*See Isabella Howard, 536:1, for reply poem.

2 No peace nor ease the heart can know,
Which, like the needle true,
Turns at the touch of joy or woe,
But, turning, trembles too.
Ibid., St. 6

3 O haste to shed the sovereign balm—
My shattered nerves new string:
And for my guest serenely calm,
The nymph Indifference bring.
Ibid.

4 And what of life remains for me
I'll pass in sober ease;
Half pleased, contented will I be,
Content but half to please.
Ibid., last stanza

531. Charlotte Lennox
(1720–1804)

1 We saw, with astonishment, a new sort of city raised in the compass of a few hours: for these people, when they travel, carry with them the materials for building their houses, which consist of the bark of trees, and two or three wooden poles, with some bear skins to lye on: thus a square of ten feet will serve to contain a very large family; and it being now in the middle of summer, their hutts were decorated with the boughs of trees on the outside, to keep out the sun, which (on account of their different verdure) formed a new and beautiful prospect.
The Life of Harriot Stuart,
Vol. I   1751

2 [His library,] . . . in which, unfortunately for her, were great Store of Romances, and, what was still more unfortunate, not in the original *French*, but very bad Translations.
Arabella; or, The Female Quixote,
Vol. I   1752

3 I am not cruel enough to wish his Death; say that I command him to live, if he can live without Hope.   Ibid.

4 "For Heaven's sake, Cousin," replied Arabella, laughing, "how have you spent your Time; and to what Studies have you devoted all your Hours, that you could find none to spare for the Perusal of Books from which all useful Knowledge may be drawn. . . . "   Ibid.

5 The Law has no Power over Heroes; they may kill as many Men as they please without being called to any Account for it; and the more Lives they take away, the greater is their Reputation for Virtue and Glory.
Ibid.

6 " . . . I wish some of our Town Beauties were, if not altogether of your Opinion, yet sufficiently so, as to make it not a Slavery for a Man to be in their Company; for unless one talks of Love to these fair Coquets the whole time one is with them, they are quite displeased, and look upon a Man who can think anything, but themselves, worthy his Thoughts or Observation, with the utmost Contempt."   Ibid.

7 "I will despatch you To-morrow Morning with my Orders to him, to live, or, at least, to proceed no farther in his Design of dying, till he has farther Cause."
Ibid.

8 "Ods-heart! it is pity you are not poor enough to be an Author; you would occupy a Garret in Grub-street, with great Fame to yourself, and Diversion to the Public."
Ibid., Vol. II

9 "Oh! Sir," cried Sir George, "I have Stock enough by me, to set up an Author To-morrow, if I please: I have no less than Five Tragedies, some quite, others almost finished; Three or Four Essays on Virtue, Happiness, etc., Three thousand Lines of an Epic Poem; half a Dozen Epitaphs; a few Acrostics; and a long String of Puns, that would serve to embellish a Daily Paper, if I was disposed to write one."
Ibid.

10 The only Excellence of Falshood . . . is its Resemblance to Truth. . . .
Ibid.

11 When a Crime is to be concealed, it is easy to cover it with an imaginary Word.
Ibid.

12 It is the Fault of the best Fictions, that they teach young Minds to expect strange Adventures and sudden Vicissitudes, and therefore encourage them often to trust to Chance. A long Life may be passed without a single Occurrence that can cause much Surprize, or produce any unexpected Consequence of great Importance; the Order of the World is so established, that all human Affairs proceed in a regular Method, and very little Opportunity is left for Sallies and Hazards, for Assault or Rescue; but the Brave and the Coward, the Sprightly and the Dull, suffer themselves to be carried alike down the Stream of Custom.   Ibid.

13 Oh couldst thou teach the tortur'd Soul to know,
With Patience, each Extream of human Woe   "On reading [Francis] Hutcheson*
on the Passions,"
Poems on Several Occasions
November 4, 1752

*British philosopher and moralist (1694–1746) and author of "An Essay on the Nature and Conduit of the Passions and Affections . . . " (1728)

14 I said before, that the Story of *Juriste* and *Epitia* afforded an affecting Subject for a Play; and it is to be wished, since *Shakespeare* thought proper to found one upon it, that he had left the Fable simple and entire as it was, without loading it with useless Incidents, unnecessary Characters, and absurd and improbable Intrigue.
"The Fable of *Measure for Measure,*"
Shakespear Illustrated; or, the Novels and Histories, On which the Plays of Shakespear Are Founded   1753

15 That *Shakespear* made a wrong Choice of his Subject, since he was resolved to torture it into a Comedy, appears by the low Contrivance, absurd Intrigue, and improbable Incidents, he was obliged to introduce, in order to bring about three or four Weddings, instead of one good Beheading, which was the Consequence naturally expected.   Ibid.

16 Thus did these noble persons accommodate themselves to the manners of those whom they in secret despised; and, for the sake of a few paltry thousands, shewed the utmost solicitude to associate plebean meanness in the honours of a noble ancestry, and to give title, rank, precedence, to one who would disgrace them all.   *Henrietta,*
Vol. II   1758

17 "Madam," replied Mrs.———, "I take care that my servants shall not think me an atheist. They know my principles better: they know that I am a Deist; they have heard me declare that I believe there is an intelligent cause which governs the world by physical rules. As for moral attributes, there is no such thing; it is impious and absurd to suppose it."   Ibid.

18 "Prayer and such like artifices of religion, is foolish: for whatever is, is right."
Ibid.

19 "Whatever is, is best. The law of nature is sufficiently clear; and there is no need of supernatural revelation."   Ibid.

20 MISS AUTUMN. I protest I tremble at the idea, of being one day, what my stepmother is at present. Oh heavens! in the midst of wrinkles and grey hairs, to dream of gentle languishment, vows, ardors!—but there is some comfort yet, fifty and I are at an immense distance. *The Sister*   1759

21 MISS COURTENEY. . . . whatever advances with such rapidity cannot be accounted far distant. . . .   Ibid.

22 . . . unwearied application to reading, her mind became a beautiful store-house of ideas: hence she derived the power and the habit of constant reflection, which at once enlarged her understanding, and confirmed her in the principles of piety and virtue.
Sophia   1762

23 In a word, the savage is subject to none but natural evils. . . .   *Euphemia,*
Vol. III   1790

24 The life of a good man is a continual prayer.
Ibid., Vol. IV

25 The request they [the Mohawks] made, to be permitted to pay their compliments of condolence to the widow and daughters of the Great Chief, as they stile him, show that these untutored savages, have in their minds those natural principles of humanity, which is the foundation of true politeness.
Ibid.

26 "Conversation has been properly stiled the air of the soul; they who value the health and ease of the mind, ought to chuse an element pure and serene for it to breathe in."
Ibid.

532.   Elizabeth Montagu
(1720–1800)

1 Will an intelligent spectator not admire the prodigeous structures of Stone-Henge because he does not know by what law of mechanics they were raised?
An Essay on the Writing and Genius of Shakespeare Compared with Greek and French Dramatic Poets (1769)   1785

2 To judge therefore of Shakespeare by Aristotle's rule is like trying a man by the Laws of one Country who acted under those of another.
Ibid.

3 Shakespeare wrote at a time when learning was tinctured with pedantry, wit was unpolished and mirth ill-bred. The court of Elizabeth spoke a scientific jargon. . . .
Ibid.

4 Shakespeare seemed to have had the art of the Dervish in the Arabian tales who could throw his soul into the body of another man and be at once possessed of his sentiments, adopt his passions and rise to all the functions and feelings of his situation.
Ibid.

5 Vapours and love are two things that seek solitude, but for me, who have neither in my constitution, a crowd is not disagreeable, and I always find myself prompted . . . to go where two or three are gathered together. *The Letters of Mrs. Elizabeth Montagu*
1810–1813

6 Gold is the chief ingredient in the composition of worldly happiness. Living in a cottage on love is certainly the worst diet and the worst habitation one can find out.
Ibid.

7 The town of Newcastle is horrible, like the ways of thrift it is narrow, dark and dirty, some of the streets so steep one is forced to put a dragchain on the wheels. . . .
Ibid.

8 Five months are to pass before I return to the Land of the Living but I can amuse myself in the regions of the dead: if it rains so that I cannot walk in the garden Virgil will carry me into the Elysian fields or Milton into Paradise.   Ibid.

9 Wit is generally satyrical and severe and oftener the cause of mirth than the original effect of it.   Ibid.

10 Do you not admire these lovers of liberty! What do the generality of men mean by a love of liberty but the liberty to be saucy to their superiors, and arrogant to their inferiors, to resist the powers of others over them, and to exert their powers over others.
Letter to Mrs. Scott,
op. cit.

11 If she [Catherine the Great] is not a good woman, she is a great Prince.
Letter to Lord Lyttleton,
op. cit.

12 The man who has only the graces of the drawingroom, and the tone of conversation of any particular set of men is little superior to what a monkey would be who had the articulate talents of a parrot.
Letter to her nephew Matthew
Montagu, Baron Rokeby,
op. cit.

13 Are you not provoked that such an animal call itself a Philosopher? What Pretence can he [Voltaire] have to Philosophy who has not fear of God which is the beginning of Wisdom.   Letter to Mrs. Carter, op. cit.

14 Pompous declamation season'd with moral reflections is surely far from the perfection of dramatik writing, tho' in a nation too much polish'd and refin'd it is to be preferr'd to the natural sallies of passion as fops love essences better than the flowers from where they are extracted.
          Letter to Lord Bath, op. cit.

15 I agreed perfectly with him* that the endeavour to shine in conversation and to lay on for admiration is very paltry.
          Letter to Mrs. William Robinson, her sister-in-law, op. cit.

*The English poet Thomas Gray (1716–1771).

16 . . . there is a much higher character from that of a wit or a poet or a savant, which is that of a rational sociable being, willing to carry on the commerce of life with all the sweetness and condescension, decency and virtue will permit.   Ibid.

17 The great duty of conversation is to follow suit as you do at whist; if the eldest hand plays the deuce of diamonds let not his neighbour cast down the King of Hearts because his hand is full of honours. I do not love to see a man of wit win all the tricks in conversation nor yet to see him sullenly pass. . . .   Ibid.

18 Minds ripen at very different ages.
          Ibid.

19 Madam, As I always acquaint Your Grace with my motions from place to place, I think it's incumbent upon me to let you know I died last Thursday; having that day expected to hear of a certain Dutchess and being disappointed I fell into a vexation and from thence into a chagrin and from that into a melancholy with a complicated et cetera and so expired.   Letter to Duchess of Portland (c.1734), op. cit.

20 I endeavor . . . to be wise when I cannot be merry, easy when I cannot be glad, content with what cannot be mended and patient when there is no redress.   Letter (c.1739), op. cit.

21 The man was laughed at as a blunderer who said in a public business: "We do much for posterity; I would fain see them do something for us."   Letter (January 1, 1742), op. cit.

22 There are but two kinds of people I think myself at liberty to hate and despise, the first is of the class of *soi disant* philosophers who by sophistry would cheat the less acute out of their principles, the only firm basis of moral virtue; the second are witts who ridicule whatsoever things are lovely, whatsoever things are of good report.
          Letter (1768), op. cit.

23 It is surprizing what money I have spent out of a principle of economy; because they are cheap I have bought more shoes than a millipede could wear in VII years. By my caps you would think I had more heads than Hydra.
          Letter to her brother (1776), op. cit.

24 But where there has not subsisted a good form of government and a regular system of Laws and mode of manners the people in general never are of a good character.
          Letter to Mrs. Carter (1777), op. cit.

25 ... that something which marks a poet divine, that lifts him "above the visible diurnal sphere," that gives him visions of worlds unknown, makes him sing like a seraphim, tune his harp to the music of the spheres, and raise enchantments around him. ...   Letter to Sylph Vesey (1777), op. cit.

26 We are become a scoundrel nation worthy to be scorned and fit to be cudgel'd.
Letter (1779), op. cit.

27 The most brilliant persons are not always the happiest or the most esteem'd; more rarely still the best beloved. Too much presumption in their excellencies, too little indulgence to the defects of others if it does not totally destroy our admiration certainly eliminates our affection and it is far better to be beloved than admired.
Letter to Mrs. William Robinson (1785), op. cit.

28 Wit in women is apt to have bad consequences; like a sword without a scabbard, it wounds the wearer and provokes assailants. I am sorry to say the generality of women who have excelled in wit have failed in chastity. ...   (1750), Quoted in
Reconstructing Aphra
by Angeline Goreau   1980

533. Peg Woffington
(1720–1760)

1 I count time by your absence; I have not seen you all morning, and is it not an age since then?   Remark to David Garrick* (1776),
Quoted in *Days of the Dandies*, Ch. 6,
by J. Fitzgerald Molloy, n.d.
*English actor and theater manager (1717–1779).

534. Jeanne Poisson Pompadour
(1721–1764)

1 The King and I have such implicit confidence in you* that we look upon you as a cat, or a dog, and go on talking as if you were not there.   Quoted in
The Memoirs of Louis XV and of Madame de Pompadour
by Mme du Hausset   1802
*Mme du Hausset, her bed-chamber attendant. See 606.

2 What a strange pleasure, to endeavor to fill one's mind with images which one ought to endeavour to banish, especially when one is surrounded by so many sources of happiness! But that is the King's way; he loves to talk about death.   Ibid.

3 I am agitated by the fear of losing the King's heart by ceasing to be attractive to him. Men, you know, set great value on certain things, and I have the misfortune to be a very cold temperament. I, therefore, determined to adopt a heating diet, in order to remedy this defect, and for two days this elixir has been of great service to me, or, at least, I have thought I felt its good effects.
Ibid.

4 I adore that man [the King], I wish so earnestly to be agreeable to him! But, alas! sometimes he says I am a *macreuse.**
Ibid.
*A scoter, a northern sea duck.

5 Ah! here come my kittens;* all that we are about is Greek to them; but their gaiety restores my tranquility, and enables me to attend again to serious affairs.
Ibid.
*Her friends Mmes D'Amblimont and d'Esparbès, members of the court.

6 It is his [Louis XV's] heart I wish to secure; and all those young girls who have no education will not run away with it from me. I should not be equally confident were I to see some fine woman belonging to the Court, or the city, attempt his conquest.
Ibid.

7 Ah! my life is that of the Christian, a perpetual warfare. Ibid.

8 The King likes variety, but he is also bound
by habit; he fears éclat, and detests manoeuvering. Ibid.

9 It is a wolf who makes the sheep reflect.
Ibid.

10 . . . it seems as if a fatality attended
Princes, forcing them to shut their ears,
those of the mind, at least, to the best advice, and especially in the most critical moments. Ibid.

11 After us the deluge! (*Après nous le déluge !*)
Her motto,
op. cit.

12 Wait a moment, monsieur, and we will set
forth together. (*Attendez-moi, monsieur le
curé, nous partirons ensemble.*)
Last words, spoken to the priest,
op. cit.

535. Anna Dorothea Lisiewska-Therbusch
(1721–1782)

1 I would not have dared suggest it to you,
but you have done well, and I thank you.*
Quoted by Denis Diderot in
Diderot Salons,
Vol. III, 1767, Jean Adhémar
and Jean Seznec, eds. 1963

*In response to Diderot's voluntary disrobing for his
portrait bust by her.

536. Isabella Howard
(c.1722–c.1793-1795)

1 "I dare not change a first decree:
She's doomed to please, nor can be free:
Such is the lot of Beauty!"
"Reply by the Countess of C—,"*
St. 11 (c.1753),
The Female Poets of Great Britain,
Frederic Rowton, ed. 1853

*Reply poem to Frances Greville's "Prayers for Indif-
ference." See 530:1–4.

537. Mary Leapor
(1722–1746)

1 Our servile Tongues are taught to cry for
Pardon
Ere the weak Senses know the Use of
Words:
Our little Souls are tortur'd by Advice;
And moral Lectures stun our Infant Years:
Thro' check'd Desires, Threatnings, and
Restraint
The Virgin runs; but ne'er outgrows her
Shackles
They still will fit her, even to hoary Age.
Untitled,
Poems Upon Several Occasions,
Vol. II 1751

2 On the bright walls around her and above,
Were drawn the statutes and the arts of
love:
These taught the silent language of the eye,
The broken whisper, and amusing lie;
The careless glance peculiar to the fair,
And vows of lovers that dissolve in air;
The graceful anger, and the rolling eyes,
The practis'd blush, and counterfeit sur-
prise,
The language proper for pretending swains,
And fine description for imagin'd pains;
The friendly caution, and designing ease,
And all the arts that ruin while they please.
"The Temple of Love—a
Dream,"
St. 3, op. cit.

3 A group of ghastly phantoms stood behind,
Whose task it is to rack the guilty mind;
Wide-mouth'd Reproach with visage rude
and thin,
And hissing Scandal, made a hideous din;
Remorse, that darted from her deadly
wings
Invenom'd arrows and a thousand stings.
Ibid., St. 6

4 I woke, and found old night her course had
run,
And left her empire to the rising sun.
Ibid., last lines

538. Eliza Pinckney
(1722?–1793)

1 [I resolve] to be a good Mother to my children . . . to instill piety, Virtue and true religion into them; to correct their Errors whatever uneasiness it may give myself.
From Letterbook (1739–1762),
Journal and Letters of Eliza Lucas Pinckney,
Harriet R. Holbrook, ed.
1850

2 Be particularly watchful against heat of temper; it makes constant work for repentance and chagrin. Letter to Charles Pinckney* (1761),
op. cit.

*Her husband, a politician and judge.

539. Janet Graham
(1723/24–1805)

1 Alas! my son, you little know
The sorrows that from wedlock flow,
Farewell to every day of ease,
When you have got a wife to please.
"The Wayward Wife,"
Scottish Song,
Mary Carlyle Aitken, ed.
1874

2 Great Hercules and Samson too,
Were stronger men than I or you,
Yet they were baffled by their dears,
And felt the distaff and the shears.
Ibid.

540. Frances Brooke
(1724–1789)

1 . . . the superstition of men is gloomy and ferocious; it lights the fire, and points the dagger of the assassin; whilst that of women takes its color from the sex; is soft, mild, and benevolent; exerts itself in acts of kindness and charity, and seems only substituting the love of God to that of man.
The History of Emily Montague,
Vol. I, Letter V,
1769

2 To be happy in this world, it is necessary not to raise one's ideas too high. . . .
Ibid., Letter XV

3 I think all the moral writers, who have set off with promising to shew us the road to happiness, have obligingly ended with telling us there is no such thing. . . . This fancy of hunting for what one knows is not be found, is really an ingenious way of amusing both one's self and the world: I wish people would either write to some purpose, or be so good as not to write at all.
Ibid.

4 I have said married women are, on my principles, forbidden fruit: I should have explained myself; I mean in England, for my ideas on this head change as soon as I land at Calais. Ibid., Letter XXXVI

5 We have been saying, Lucy, that 'tis the strangest thing in the world people should quarrel about religion, since we undoubtedly all mean the same thing; all good minds in every religion aim at pleasing the Supreme Being; the means we take differ according to where we are born, and the prejudices we imbibe from education; a consideration which ought to inspire us with kindness and indulgence to each other.
Ibid., Letter L

6 . . . coquetry is dangerous to English women, because they have sensibility; it is more suited to the French, who are naturally something of the salamander kind.
Ibid., Vol. II, Letter LXII

7 Parents should chuse our company, but never even pretend to direct our choice. . . .
Ibid., Letter LXV

8 The vulgar of every rank expect happiness where it is not to be found, in the ideal advantages of splendor and dissipation; those who dare to think, those minds who partake of the celestial fire, seek it in the real solid pleasures of nature and soft affection.
Ibid., Letter LXVI

9 . . . this love is the finest cosmetik in the world.
Ibid., Letter XCIII

10 . . . happiness is not to be found in a life of intrigue. . . .
Ibid., Letter XCIX

11 Emily and I, however, differ in our ideas of love: it is the business of her life, the amusement of mine; 'tis the food of her hours, the seasoning of mine.
Or, in other words, she loves like a foolish woman, I like a sensible man: for men, you know, compared to women, love in about the proportion of one to twenty.
Ibid., Letter CXII

12 In my opinion, the man who conveys, and causes to grow, in any country, a grain, a fruit, or even a flower, it never possessed before, deserves more praise than a thousand heroes: he is a benefactor, he is in some degree a creator.
Ibid., Letter CXXI

13 There is sometimes, both in persons and things, an invisible charm, a natural grace, which we cannot define, and which we are therefore obliged to call je ne sais quoi.
It seems to me that this is an effect principally founded on surprise.
Ibid., Vol. III, Letter CXXV

14 Fortune has no power over minds like ours; we possess a treasure to which all she has to give is nothing, the dear exquisite delight of loving, and of being beloved.
Ibid., Letter CXLVI

15 It is a painful consideration, my dear, that the happiness or misery of our lives are generally determined before we are proper judges of either.
Ibid., Letter CLII

16 Restrained by custom, and the ridiculous prejudices of the world, we go with the crowd, and it is late in life before we dare to think.
Ibid.

17 Those virtues which command esteem do not often inspire passion.
Ibid.

18 A marriage where not only esteem, but passion is kept awake, is, I am convinced, the most perfect state of sublunary happiness: but it requires great care to keep this tender plant alive. . . .
Ibid., Letter LXXIII

19 The inebriation, the tumult of passion, will undoubtedly grow less after marriage, that is, after peaceable possession; hopes and fears alone keep it in its first violent state: but, though it subsides, it gives place to a tenderness still more pleasing, to a soft, and, if you will allow the expression, a voluptuous tranquillity: the pleasure does not cease, does not even lessen; it only changes its nature.
Ibid.

20 I love the country: the taste for rural scenes is the taste born with us. After seeking pleasure in vain amongst the works of art, we are forced to come back to the point from whence we set out, and find our enjoyment in the lovely simplicity of nature.
Ibid., Vol. IV, Letter CLXXXII

21 If the Supreme Creator had meant us to be gloomy, he would, it seems to me, have clothed the earth in black, not in that lively green, which is the livery of chearfulness and joy.
Ibid., Letter CXCIV

22 Nothing can be more false than that we are naturally inclined to evil: we are indeed naturally inclined to gratify the selfish passions of every kind; but those passions are not evil in themselves, they only become so from excess.
Ibid., Letter CCIV

23 Certainly, my dear, friendship is a mighty pretty invention, and, next to love, gives of all things the greatest spirit to society.
Ibid., Letter CCX

24 ROSINA. Why should I repine? Heaven, which deprived me of my parents and my fortune, left me health, content, and innocence. Nor is it certain that riches lead to happiness. Do you think the nightingale sings the sweeter for being in a gilded cage?
Rosina: A Comic Opera,
Act I, Sc. 1   1783

25 ROSINA. How small a part of my evils is poverty!   Ibid.

26 MR. BELVILLE. Her mouth, which a smile,
    Devoid of all guile,
        Half opens to view,
    Is the bud of the rose,
    In the mourning that blows,
        Impearl'd with the dew.
            Ibid., "Air," St. 1

27 CHORUS OF REAPERS. What would gilded
                pomp avail
            Should the peasant's
                labour fail?
            Ibid., "Air," St. 4

28 DORCAS. If I must be a trouble to the dear child, I had rather owe my bread to her labour than her shame.   Ibid.

29 PHOEBE. Lads and lasses all advance,
    Carol blithe, and form the dance;
    Trip it lightly while you may
    This is Nature's holiday.
                Ibid.,
            "Air—*Finale,*"
                St. 8

30 RUSTIC. . . . I hate money when it is not my own.   Ibid., Act II, Sc. 1

31 ROSINA. Whoever offends the object of his love is unworthy of obtaining her.
                Ibid.

32 What music celestial! when urging the race
Sweet Echo repeats—"To the chase, to the chase!"   Untitled poem,
        St. 1, *Marian*
            1788

541. Sarah Ryan
(1724?–1768)

1 My merciful God did not leave me to follow my own imaginations, but often checked me by that thought, "Must all men die? Must all have an end? And must I die?"
Quoted in *The Women of Methodism: Its Three Foundresses . . .*
by Abel Stevens   1866

542. Frances Sheridan
(1724–1766)

1 I must take her down a peg or so.
The Dupe,
Act IV, Sc. 4   1760

2 As quick as lightning.   *The Discovery,*
Act I, Sc. 2   1763

3 What taught me silently to bear,
To curb the sigh, to check the tear,
    When sorrow weigh'd me down?

'T was Patience!   "Ode to Patience,"
Sts. 3, 4,
The Female Poets of Great Britain,
Frederic Rowton, ed.   1853

4   . . . Patience! goddess ever calm!
O pour into my breast thy balm,
    That antidote to pain.
            Ibid., St. 6

543. Eva Maria Garrick
(1725–1822)

1 Groans and complaints are very well for those who are to mourn but a little while; but a sorrow that is to last for life will not be violent or romantic.   Quoted by Hannah More in *Biography of Distinguished Women*
by Sarah Josepha Hale   1876

544.   Bridget Fletcher
(1726–1770)

1 God's only son by woman came,
   To take away our shame;
And so thereby, to dignify,
   Also to raise our fame.
                    Hymn XXXVI: St. 1,
              "The Greatest Dignity of a
      Woman, Christ Being Born of One,"
              Hymns and Spiritual Songs
                                   1773

545.   Hester Chapone
(1727–1801)

1 "Love worketh no ill to his neighbour;"
therefore, if you have true benevolence; you
will never do any thing injurious to individuals, or to society. Now, all crimes
whatever are (in their remoter consequences at least, if not immediately and apparently) injurious to the society in which
we live.   "The Two Commandments,"
              *Letters on the Improvement of
                    the Mind*   1773

2 Affectation is so universally acknowledged
to be disgusting, that it is among the faults
which the most intimate friends cannot
venture gravely to reprove in each other; for
to tell your friends that they are habitually
affected, is to tell them they they are habitually disagreeable; which nobody can bear to
hear.   "Affectation,"
          Miscellanies in Prose and Verse
                                   1775

3 The great and irresistible influence which
the choice of our company, as well as the
mode of our own conversation, has on our
habits of thinking and acting, and on the
whole form and colour of our minds, is a
subject too common to be much enlarged
upon; it cannot, however, be too deeply
considered, as it seems the leading circumstance of our lives, and that which may
chiefly determine our character and condition to all eternity.   "A Timely Word,"
                                   op. cit.

4 Awake my soul, from thy forgetful trance!
   The storm calls loud, and Meditation
      wakes,
   How at the sound pale Superstition
      shakes,
   Whilst all her train of frantic Fears ad-
      vance!
   Children of Darkness, hence! fly from
      me!
   And dwell with Guild and Infidelity!
      "Written during a Storm at Midnight,"
                          St. 3 (1749),
                    A Volume of Miscellanies
                                   1775

5 Thou gentle nurse of pleasing woe,
   To thee from crowds, and noise, and show,
      With eager haste I fly;
   Thrice welcome, friendly Solitude,
   O let no busy foot intrude,
      Nor listening ear be nigh!
                        "Ode to Solitude,"
                          St. 1, op. cit.

6 Shall Fancy cheat the precious hour,
   Sacred to Wisdom's awful power,
      And calm Reflection's part?
                          Ibid., St. 5

7 Peace, which when human wishes rise,
   Intense, for aught beneath the skies,
      Can never be secure.
                          Ibid., St. 9

8 . . . Prudence slow, that ever comes too late
                              "To Stella,"
                          St. 3, op. cit.

9 Say, Stella, what is Love, whose tyrant
      pow'r
   Robs Virtue of content and Youth of
      joy?
What nymph or goddess in a fatal hour
   Gave to the world this mischief-
      making boy?   Ibid., St. 4

10 . . . Fate forbids that Peace should dwell
with Love!   Ibid., St. 16

11 I make no scruple to call romances the worst of all species of writing; unnatural representation of the passions, false sentiment, false precepts, false wit, false honour, and false modesty, with a strange heap of improbable, unnatural incidents mixed up with true history.... Letter to Elizabeth Carter (July 31, 1750), *The Works of Mrs. Chapone,* Vol. I 1818

546. Jean Elliot
(1727–1805)

1 I've heard them lilting, at the ewes milking.
Lasses a' lilting, before dawn of day;
But now they are moaning, on ilka green loaning;
The Flowers of the Forest* are a' wede away. "The Flowers of the Forest," *Scottish Song,* Mary Carlyle Aitken, ed. 1874

*The forces of James IV who were slain at Flodden Field (Sept. 9, 1513). See note on Alicia Cockburn, 522:1.

2 The English, for ance, by guile wan the day;
The Flowers of the Forest, that fought aye the
foremost,
The prime of our land, lie cauld in the clay.
Ibid.

547. Hannah Griffitts
(1727–1817)

1 Here fix our trust, though Nature shake,
And frighted, feels her loosen'd tie;
The soul, amidst the general wreck,
"Is safe, in God's immensity."
"The Storm,"
St. 11 (1765),
Women Poets in Pre-Revolutionary America, Pattie Cowell, ed. 1981

2 Where conq'ring palms are by the victor won,
And endless rest insures the warfare done,

Where faith in perfect vision shall be found,
And Death, the tyrant, meet his final wound "To the Memory of Our Valued Friend, Samuel Fothergill, Who Died the 6th Month 1772," St. 5 (1773), op. cit.

3 Then for the sake of Freedom's name,
(Since British wisdom scorns repealing)
Come sacrifice to Patriot fame,
And give up tea by way of healing.
" 'Beware of the Ides of March,' Said the Roman Augur To Julius Caesar," St. 3 (1775), op. cit.

4 Like a Newton, sublimely he soar'd,
To a summit before unattain'd,
New regions of science explor'd,
And the palm of philosophy gain'd.
"Inscription On A Curious Chamberstove In the Form of an Urn, Contriv'd in Such A Manner as to Make the Flame Descend Instead of Rising, Invented By The Celebrated B.F.,"* St. 1 (1776), op. cit.

*Benjamin Franklin; poem also attributed to Jonathan Odell.

5 But words are vain, the powers of harmony
Are useless here, ev'n friendship's soothing voice
Has lost its balm, in woundings like to yours "On the Death of John Roberts and Abraham Carlisle," St. 2 (November 4, 1778), op. cit.

6 Mark you severe, as you have others mark'd,
How will your souls sustain His dread decision,*
Whose laws are justice, and whose words are truth? Ibid., St. 5

*Allusion to Matthew 18:23-35.

548. Sarah Prince Gill
(1728–1771)

1 —Thou, thou art all!
My soul flies up and down in thoughts of
thee,
And finds herself but at the center still!
I AM, thy name! Existence, all thine own!
Creation's nothing to Thee, the great Origi-
nal!   Untitled, St. 1,
*Dying Exercises of Mrs. Deborah
Prince and Devout Meditations of
Mrs. Sarah Gill . . .*   1784

549. Margaret Klopstock
(1728–1758)

1 Love, dear sir, is all what me concerns! and
love shall be all I will tell you in this letter.
Letter to Samuel Richardson*
(March 14, 1758), from
Hamburg,
*Letters from the Dead to the
Living*   post 1758
*The English novelist (1689–1761).

2 I could not speak, I could not play; I
thought I saw nothing but Klopstock.*
Ibid.
*Her husband, the poet Friedrich Gottlieb Klopstock
(1724–1803).

3 I answered, that is was not love, but friendship, as it was what I felt for him; we had
not seen one another enough to love. (As if
love must have more time than friendship.)
Ibid.

4 For it may be that an action displeases us
which would please us, if we knew its true
aim and whole extent.   Ibid.

5 It is long since I made the remark that the
children of geniuses are not geniuses.
Letter to Samuel Richardson
(August 26, 1758),
op. cit.

550. Mercy Otis Warren
(1728–1814)

1 BRUTUS.   . . . hoodwink'd justice
Drops her scales, and totters from her basis.
The Adulateur, Act I, Sc. 1
1773

2 BRUTUS.   The distant branches lop'd,
The root now groans—let not the thought
of *power*,
Ungenerous thought! freeze up the genial
current.   Ibid.

3 RAPATIO. . . . curse the hour that gave me
birth;
That hung me up a meteor in the sky,
Which from its tail, shook pestilence and
ruin.   Ibid., Sc. 2

4 BRUTUS. He who in virtue's cause remains
unmov'd,
And nobly struggles for his country's good:
Shall more than conquer—better days shall
beam,
And happier prospects crowd again the
scene. . . .   Ibid., Act III, Sc. 3

5 RAPATIO. To ride triumphant o'er my na-
tive land,
And revel on its spoils. . . .
Ibid., Act IV, Sc. 2

6 E———R. [sic] Honors, places, pensions—
'Tis all a cheat, a damn'd, a cruel cheat.
Ibid., Act V, Sc. 2

7 CRUSTY CROWBAR. I too am almost sick of
the parade
Of honours purchas'd at the price of peace.
The Group,
Act I, Sc. 1   1775

8 SIMPLE-SAPLING. . . . my ambition beggars
all her babes.   Ibid.

9 HAZELROD. But neither commerce, or my
conjuring rods,
Nor yet mechanics, or new fangled drills,
Or all the Iron-mongers curious arts,
Gave me a competence of shining ore,
Or gratify'd my itching palm for more
Ibid.

10 MONSIEUR. So great the itch I feel for titl'd place
Some honorary post, some small distinction,
To save my name from dark oblivions jaws,
I'll Hazard all, but ne'er give up my place.
Ibid., Act II, Sc. 1

11 BEAU-TRUMPS. There's nought on earth that has such tempting charms As rank and show, and pomp, and glitt'ring dress
Ibid.

12 BEAU-TRUMPS. The social ties that bind the human heart. . . .
Ibid.

13 SECRETARY DUPE. While virtue's banners shroud each warrior's head
Stern Justice binds the helmet on his brow,
And liberty sits perch'd on ev'ry shield.
Ibid., Sc. 3

14 HATEALL. Pho—what's a woman's tears . . . ?
Ibid.

15 HATEALL. I broke her spirits when I'd won her purse*
Ibid.
*His wife's dowry.

16 HATEALL. Then the green Hick'ry, or the willow twig,
Will prove a curse for each rebellious dame
Who dare oppose her lord's superior will.
Ibid.

17 SECRETARY. What shifts, evasions, what delusive tales,
What poor prevarication for rash oaths,
What nightly watchings, and what daily cares
To dress up falshood in some fair disguise
Ibid.

18 But it must be a bold adventurer in the paths of literature, who dreams of fame, in any degree commensurate with the duration of laurels reaped by an hero, who has led the armies of America to glory, victory and independence. Dedication to George Washington, President of the United States of America, *Poems Dramatic and Miscellaneous* 1790

19 AETIUS. Where is the emperor? Does he not awake
From his soft slumbering lethargy of soul?

LEO. Supinely sunk in dreams of wanton bliss,
Ignoble pleasures of a splendid court,
Or peace, or war, or truce, the same to him.
The Sack of Rome,
Act I, Sc. 2, op. cit.

20 VALENTINIAN. I fear no storms but from an injur'd wife
Ibid., Act II, Sc. 1

21 VALENTINIAN. A woman, weaken'd by a sense of wrongs,
With a creative fancy, spreads contagion,
If she names her fears. . . .
Ibid.

22 PLACIDIA. Alas! I fear—I know not what I fear—
Imagination's short of what I dread
From complicated guilt, which stalks abroad.
Oh! Heaven avert the destiny of Rome!
Ibid., Sc. 3

23 VALENTINIAN. Where are his friends?—his num'rous train of clients?
Where the admiring crowds fed by his hand,
And basking in his wealth?

HERACLIUS. Just as the world in ev'ry age have done,
Playing their court where better fortune smiles
Ibid., Sc. 4

24 MAXIMUS. The bird of death that nightly pecks the roof
Ibid., Act III, Sc. 1

25 MAXIMUS. . . . the silent deep abode of guilt
Ibid.

26 MAXIMUS. That dignity the gods themselves inspir'd,
When Rome inflam'd with patriotick zeal,
Long taught the world to tremble and admire,
Lies faint and languid in the wane of fame,
And must expire in luxury's lew'd lap
If not supported by some vigorous arm
Ibid., Sc. 2

27 GAUDENTIUS. Ambition, in a noble, virtu-
ous mind,
Is the first passion that the gods implant,
And soars to glory till it meets the skies
Ibid.

28 MAXIMUS. The wheel of fortune, rapid in its
flight,
Lags not for man, when on its swift routine;
Nor does the goddess ponder unresolv'd:
She wafts at once, and on her lofty car,
Lifts up her puppet—mounts him to the
skies,
Or from the pinnacle, hurls headlong down,
The steep abyss of disappointed hope.
Ibid., Act IV, Sc. 1

29 EDOXIA. This predilection's left to man
alone,
To drink and riot on his brother's blood.
Ibid., Sc. 2

30 EDOXIA. I have no country.
What's life, or empire, or the world to me?
Ibid.

31 GAUDENTIUS. Fate may do much before we
meet again;
She has a busy hand, and swiftly rides
On revolution's wheel. . . .
Ibid., Sc. 5

32 EDOXIA. Enough of life and all life's idle
pomp—
Nor by a tyrant's fiat will I live—
I leave the busy, vain, ambitious world
To cheat itself anew, and o'er and o'er
Tread the same ground their ancesters have
trod,
In chace of thrones, of sceptres, or of
crowns,
'Till all these bubbles break in empty air,
Nor leave a trace of happiness behind.
Ibid., Act V, Sc. 3

33 DON JUAN DE PADILLA. A jealousy for free-
dom kept alive
Precludes the softer passions of the mind.
The Ladies of Castile,
Act I, Sc. 1, op. cit.

34 DON JUAN DE PADILLA. Let freedom be the
mistress of thy heart
Ibid.

35 DON JUAN DE PADILLA. The sword must rescue, or the nation sink
Ibid.

36 DON JUAN DE PADILLA. Tis freedom's
genius, nurs'd from age to age,
Matur'd in schools of liberty and law,
On virtue's page from sire to son convey'd,
E'er since the savage, fierce, barbarian
hords,
Pour'd in. . . .
Ibid.

37 DE HARO. But in the hero ne'er forget the
man.
Ibid., Sc. 2

38 MARIA. Men rail at weakness themselves
create,
And boldly stigmatize the female mind,
As though kind nature's just impartial hand
Had form'd its features in a baser mould
Ibid., Sc. 5

39 MARIA.   . . . fortune's on the wing:
The fickle goddess waves her glossy plume,
And holds an era in the life of man.
Ibid.

40 FRANCIS. Mistaken man!
Ibid.

41 LOUISA. Deception oft beneath a flimsy veil,
Hides human hearts, nor lets man know
himself.
Ibid., Act II, Sc. 2

42 FRANCIS. Description would but beggar
love like mine
Ibid.

43 MARIA. Today the cap of liberty's toss'd
up—
Tomorrow torn and given to the winds,
And all their leaders, by the fickle throng
Are sacrific'd by violence, or fraud.
Ibid., Sc. 4

44 DON JUAN. Most men are brave till courage
has been try'd,
And boast of virtue till their price is
known. . . .
Ibid., Sc. 5

45 DON PEDRO. . . . the bubble freedom—
empty name!—
'Tis all a puff—a visionary dream—
That kindles up this patriotic flame;
'Tis rank self love, conceal'd beneath a
mask
Of public good. The hero's brain inflates—
He cheats himself by the false medium,

Held in virtue's guise, till he believes it just
Ibid.

46 DE HARO. Great souls—form'd in the same etherial mould,
Are ne'er at war—they, different paths
Of glory may pursue, with equal zeal;
Yet not a cruel, or malignant thought,
Or rancorous design, deform the mind.
Ibid., Act III, Sc. 1

47 LOUISA. Man, the vile sport of restless passion, roves
Through sad inquietudes and painful cares,
'Till his ambition sets the world on fire.
Ibid., Sc. 2

48 DON JUAN. So well I know the shifting tide of life,
I'm not appal'd whene'er its ebb runs off,
And leaves man shallow'd on the oozy strand.
Ibid., Sc. 3

49 MARIA. I scorn the feeble soul that cannot brave,
With magnanimity, the storms of life.
Ibid., Sc. 5

50 DON JUAN. To learn to die is an heroic work
Ibid., Act IV, Sc. 2

51 MARIA. Maternal softness weakens my resolve,
And wakes new fears—thou dearest, best of men,
Torn from my side, I'm levell'd with my sex.
The wife—the mother—make me less than woman.
Ibid., Sc. 5

52 FRANCIS. The free born mind mounts upwards with the gods,
And soars and spurns a base, ignoble world.
Ibid., Act V, Sc. 4

53 . . . artful politicians saw the jest,
And laugh'd at virtue as a state machine,
An engine fit the multitude to rein;
With more facility to rule mankind,
They lent their efforts to obscure the mind.
Miscellaneous Poems,
"To Torrismond, a young Gentleman educated in Europe,"
St. 3, op. cit.

54 Some visionary souls have lost their way,
Eccentric wandering 'mid the noon tide ray.
Ibid., St. 6

55 Thus man, frail man, to wide extremes so prone,
Truth's perfect path by him so little known,
That when emerging from the dismal gloom,
Of night and sable, wrap'd in chaos' womb;
Some danc'd and play'd around the boundless shore,
The depths of erudition just skim'd o'er
Ibid., St. 7

56 As *ignis fatuus** floats from lake to bog,
The vapor plays in pestilential fog,
Sparkles and sinks in the dark marshy tomb,
As modern wits in metaphysic fume.
"The Genius of America weeping the absurd follies of the Day,"
St. 16, op. cit.

*Will-o'-the-wisp.

57 'Tis social converse, animates the soul.
"To Fidelio,* Long Absent on the Great Public Cause, Which Agitates All America" (1776),
St. 1, op. cit.

*Pseudonym of James Warren, her husband, who fought in the Revolutionary War.

58 While solitude sits brooding o'er her cares,
She oft accelerates the ills she fears
Ibid.

59 The balm of life, a kind and faithful friend.
Ibid.

60 Each humbler muse at distance may admire,
But none to Shakespeare's fame e'er dare aspire. "To Mrs. Montague,* Author of 'Observations On the Genius and Writings of Shakespeare,' "
St. 2 (July 10, 1790), Plymouth,
op. cit.

*Elizabeth Robinson Montague. See 532.

61 The narrow bounds, prescribed to female life. "Simplicity Primitive,"
St. 2, op. cit.

62   Is there no permanent, no steady pole,
To point us on, and guide the wand'ring
soul?   "To Mr. Adams,"*
St. 3 (October 11, 1773),
Warren-Adams Letters, Vol. II
1917

*John Adams, second president of the United States.

63 The more we search, the more are we deceived?   Ibid., St. 5

64   What is it moves within my soul,
And as the needle to the pole,
Directs me to the final cause,
The central point of nature's laws?
'Tis reason, Lord, which thou hast given
"A Thought On the Inestimable
Blessing of Reason, Occasioned
by its Privation to a Friend of
very superior Talents and Virtues,"
St. 1, (1770),
*Womens Poets in Pre-
Revolutionary America*,
Pattie Cowell, ed.   1981

551.   Catherine II of Russia
(1729–1796)

1 For to tempt and to be tempted are things
very nearly allied, and in spite of the finest
maxims of morality impressed upon the
mind, whenever feeling has anything to do
in the matter, no sooner is it excited than we
have already gone vastly farther than we
are aware of.   *Memoirs*,
A. Herzen, ed. and tr.
1857

2 If you do not fly, there is nothing, it seems
to me, so difficult as to escape from that
which is essentially agreeable. All that can
be said in opposition to it will appear but a
prudery quite out of harmony with the
natural instincts of the human heart.
Ibid.

3 I may be kindly, I am ordinarily gentle, but
in my line of business I am obliged to will
terribly what I will at all.
Letter (August 30, 1774),
*Correspondance avec le Baron F.
M. Grimm (1774–1796)*   1878

4 A great wind is blowing, and that gives you
either imagination or a headache.
Letter (April 29, 1775),
op. cit.

5 I am one of the people who love the why of
things.   Letter (January 20, 1776),
op. cit.

6 In my view he who goes ahead is always the
one who wins.   Letter (August 11, 1778),
op. cit.

7 I would give anything to hear and to love
music, but do the best I can, it is just noise
and nothing more.   Letter (October 1,
1778),
op. cit.

8 Do you know, it is not praise that does me
good, but when men speak ill of me, then,
with a noble assurance I say to myself, as I
smile at them, "let us be revenged by prov-
ing them to be liars."
Letter (December 4, 1793),
op. cit.

9 In my position you have to read when you
want to write and to talk when you would
like to read; you have to laugh when you
feel like crying; twenty things interfere with
twenty others; you have not time for a moment's thought, and nevertheless you have
to be constantly ready to act without allowing yourself to feel lassitude, either of body
or spirit; ill or well, it makes no difference,
everything at once demands that you
should attend to it on the spot.
Letter (August 23, 1794),
op. cit.

10 Reign or die, that is the true device: we would write it on our escutcheon from the very start . . . we must make the world speak of us, we must bear good and bad fortune with an equal glory. Letter (September 5, 1796), op. cit.

11 Your wit makes others witty. (*Votre esprit en donne aux autres.*) Letter to Voltaire, *The Complete Works of Catherine II,* Evdokimov, ed. 1893

12 I praise loudly, I blame softly. Letter, op. cit.

13 Men make love more intensely at twenty, but make love better, however, at thirty. Letter, op. cit.

14 The only way to save our empires from the encroaching of the people is to engage in war, and thus substitute national passions for social aspirations. Letter, op. cit.

15 Above all things, teach him* to be beneficent and then inspire him with the love of truth. That will make him beloved by God and by men. Quoted in *La Jeunesse d'un Tsar* [*The Boyhood of a Czar*] by Dimitri Kobeko 1896

*Her son, Constantine.

16 In an affair so great as that we have been speaking of [the French Revolution] you must be profoundly penetrated with your object, you must will it passionately, you must then communicate your passion to others and act accordingly, without hesitating when your decision is once made, and you must preserve supreme calm in the midst of all agitation, never appearing disturbed or anxious about anything that may occur. "Mémoire sur la Révolution," Quoted in *La France et la Russie au XVIII siècle* by Charles de la Rivière 1909

17 What is certain is that I have never undertaken anything without being intimately persuaded that what I was doing was conforming to the good of my Empire. . . . Letter to Meilhan (June 1791), op. cit.

18 I have labored to procure the good of every individual everywhere, so far as this did not conflict with the good of the whole. Ibid.

19 If Fate had given me in youth a husband whom I could have loved, I should have remained always true to him. The trouble is that my heart would not willingly remain one hour without love. Letter to Prince Potemkin (1774), Quoted in *Memoirs,* Katharine Anthony, ed. and tr. 1925

20 At the age of fourteen she made the three-fold resolution, to please her Consort, [Empress] Elizabeth, and the Nation. Epitaph, written by herself (1789), op. cit.

21 Be assured that I shall . . . either perish or reign. Letter (August 9, 1756), *Correspondence with Sir Charles Hanbury Williams,* Earl of Ilchester and Mrs. Langford-Brooke, eds. and trs. 1928

22 I should tell you that I like to connect everything possible with myself. I thank you for allowing me to do so. Letter (August 12, 1756), op. cit.

23 I have learned long since to view people as they are, and not as I should wish them to be. Letter (August 21, 1756), op. cit.

24 To govern you have to have eyes and hands, and a woman has only ears. Quoted in *Daughters of Eve* by Gamaliel Bradford 1928

552.   Sarah Crosby
(1729–1804)

1 The day after, at church, the Lord showed me that many things which I had thought were sins were only temptations, and also what a little thing it was for him to take the root of sin out of my heart.

> Quoted in *Women of Methodism:*
> *Its Three Foundresses . . .*
> by Abel Stevens   1866

553.   Marguerite Brunet
(1730–1820)

1 Will I then really have no company here, and does the King absolutely insist that I sleep alone?

> Remark upon entering her prison cell,
> Quoted in *Enter the Actress*
> by Rosamond Gilder   1931

2 I am the dean of theatre directors in France. I built the theatre in which the Opéra is housed. The leading actors of the French stage have been my pupils and members of my company.

> Remark, op. cit.

3 . . . these special gala performances are always good for trade.   Ibid.

554.   Elizabeth Cooper
(fl. 1730s)

1 . . . Regularity and Decorum. 'Tis what we Women-Authors, in particular, have been thought greatly deficient in; and I shou'd be concern'd to find it an Objection not to be remov'd.

> Preface,
> *The Rival Widows; or, Fair Libertine*
> 1735

2 BELLAIR. . . . Money is of no Value till 'tis used.   Ibid.

3 BELLAIR. We can talk of Murder, Theft, and Treason, without blushing: and surely there's nothing a-kin to Love that's half so wicked.   Ibid.

555.   Caterina Gabrielli
(1730–1796)

1 I should not be mistress of my own will, and whenever I might have a fancy not to sing, the people would insult, perhaps misuse me: it is better to remain unmolested, were it even in a prison.

> Response to an
> invitation to sing in England,
> Quoted in *Queens of Song*
> by Ellen Creathorne Clayton
> 1865

2 In this case, your majesty has only to engage one of your field-marshals to sing.

> Reply to Catherine the Great's
> response ("None of my field-
> marshals receive so enormous a
> sum!") to Gabrielli's fee of 5,000
> ducats to sing,
> Quoted in *Biography of*
> *Distinguished Women*
> by Sarah Josepha Hale   1876

556.   Sophie de la Briche Houdetot
(1730–1813)

1 Youth, I loved you; those loveliest years, when,
Brief as they were, love was my only occupation.   "Imitation de Marot,"

> Elaine Partnow, tr.
> Quoted in *Biography of*
> *Distinguished Women*
> by Sarah Josepha Hale   1876

557. Mrs. Weddell
(fl. 1730s–1740s)

1 [I cannot] admit of making the People's
Taste the Rule of Writing, [for] it is known
to all who consider the Intention of a
Theatre, That its peculiar Business is to
correct a wrong Taste, instead of complying
with it.   Preface, *The City Farce*   1737

2 ... [they are] a wise People, and fond of
Liberty, who consider all Men as Denizens
of the Earth's plenteous Blessings, nor
think the casual Tincture of the Skin, differ-
ing from the European Hue alienates any
from the indubitable Right they are naturally entitled to, as Fellow Creatures.
Preface, *Incle and Yarico*
1742

3 [Africa] ...
Where the Remembrance of the Multitudes
Borne hence, to Slav'ry, by our Country-
men,
Must make each Man we meet an Enemy.
Ibid.

558. Lucy Terry
(c.1731–c.1822)

1 August 'twas the twenty-fifth
Seventeen hundred forty-six
The Indians did in ambush lay
Some very valient men to slay
"Bars Fight,"*
*The Poetry of the Negro,
1746–1970,*
Langston Hughes and Arna
Bontemps, eds.   1949

*Refers to an Indian raid on Deerfield, Massachusetts
(August 25, 1746).

2 Eunice Allen see the Indians comeing
And hoped to save herself by running
And had not her petticoats stopt her
The awful creatures had not cotched her
And tommyhawked her on the head
And left her on the ground for dead.
Ibid.

559. Martha Washington
(1731–1802)

1 The consciousness of having attempted to
do all the good in his power, and the pleasure of finding his fellow-citizens so well satisfied with the disinterestedness of his conduct, will, doubtless, be some compensation
for the great sacrifices which I know he has
made.   Letter to Mrs. Warren
(December 26, 1789),
Quoted in
Lives of Celebrated Women
by Samuel Griswold
Goodrich   1844

2 ... I have learned too much of the vanity
of human affairs to expect felicity from the
scenes of public life.   Ibid.

3 ... the greater part of our happiness or misery depends on our dispositions, and not
on our circumstances. We carry the seeds of
the one or the other about with us in our
minds wherever we go.   Ibid.

4 It is all over now. I shall soon follow him. I
have no more trials to pass through.*
Remark (1799),
op. cit.

*Referring to the death of her husband, George Wash-
ington.

5 I live a very dull life here ... indeed I think
I am more like a state prisoner than any-
thing else. ...   Letter to a relative,
Quoted in *Martha Washington*
by Anne Hollingsworth
Wharton   1897

6 ... steady as a clock, busy as a bee, and
cheerful as a cricket. ...   Letter to a
friend,
op. cit.

560. Julie-Jeanne-Eléonore de Lespinasse
(1732–1776)

1 There is a certain hour in the day when I wind up my moral machine as I wind my watch. And then, the movement once given, it goes more or less well. . . . What is curious is that no one suspects the effort required to appear what I am thought really to be.   Letter to Condorcet*
(May 4, 1771),
Lettres inédites   1887

*Marquis de Condorcet (1743–1794), French philosopher and politician.

2 . . . people observe very little, and it is fortunate, for there is not much to be gained by seeing more than others do.

Ibid.

3 If you can attain repose and calm, believe that you have seized happiness. Alas! Is there any other? And can there be any when one has made one's existence dependent upon another? Were he a god, the sacrifice would be too great.

Letter (August 23, 1772),
op. cit.

4 . . . as attention is for me a violent state, I was dead that evening after it. My physical machine was worn out from the state of tension that had overcome my spirit.

Letter to Condorcet
(April 5, 1773),
op. cit.

5 I am worn and weary with this voyage that is called life. I have not energy enough to terminate it abruptly, but I see with relief that I am verging toward the end.

Letter to Condorcet (1773),
op. cit.

6 Is it not desolating to see that with a king who desires only the good and a minister who has a passion for it, it is evil that is done and that the great part of the public wishes only evil.   Letter to Condorcet
(May 1775),
op. cit.

7 I knew terror and dread, before I had the power to think or to judge.

Ibid.

8 I do nothing but love, I know nothing but love.   Letter to Guibert* (May 30, 1773),
Lettres   1906

*François-Apollini Guibert, French military reformer (1744–1790).

9 Consider whether it is possible to have a moment of repose when you are trembling for the life of one to whom you would at any moment sacrifice your own.

Letter (July 1, 1773),
op. cit.

10 I cannot read with interest: I am always reading what I feel and not what I see.

Letter (August 8, 1773),
op. cit.

11 Ah! how the mind weakens when one loves.

Ibid.

12 The logic of the heart is absurd.

Letter (August 27, 1774),
op. cit.

13 Paris is the place in the world where one can be poor with the least privation; it is only the tiresome and the foolish who require to be rich.

Letter (September 19, 1774),
op. cit.

14 There is but one thing in the world that does me good, it is music; but it is a good that others would call agony. I wish I might hear ten times a day that air which tears me in pieces and brings back to me with ecstasy all that I regret.

Letter (September 22, 1774),
op. cit.

15 Good God! was there ever so much pride, so much disdain, so much contempt, so much injustice, in a word, the accumulation and mixture of all that has peopled hell and the mad-houses for a thousand centuries? All this was yesterday in my sitting-room, and the walls did not fall in!

Letter (1774),
op. cit.

16 You know that when I hate you, it is because I love you to a point of passion that unhinges my soul. Letter (1774), op. cit.

17 To love and to suffer, heaven and hell, this is what I would seek for myself, this is what I would live to feel, this is the climate in which I would dwell forever, and not in that temperate region which suits the fools and the automatons who are all about us playing and trifling with life. Letter (1775), op. cit.

18 Oh, what pleasures, what delights a soul intoxicated with passion can still feel! My love, I know it, my life depends upon my madness: if I became calm, if I really gave myself up to reason, I could not live twenty-four hours. Letter (1775), op. cit.

19 Oh, heaven! how *terribly* one lives when one is dead to everything except to one object which is the universe for us, and which possesses our faculties to such a point that it is no longer possible to live in any other moment than that in which one is living. Letter (1775), op. cit.

20 Let me say, let me repeat, that I judge nothing, but that I feel everything; and that is why you never hear me say "this is good," "this is bad," but I say a thousand times a day, "I enjoy"; yes, I enjoy, and I shall continue to enjoy so long as I breathe. *Nouvelles lettres* 1920

561. Mary Knowles
(1733–1807)

1 He [Dr. Johnson] gets at the substance of a book directly; he tears out the heart of it. Letter (April 15, 1778), Quoted in *The Life of Samuel Johnson, LL. D.* by James Boswell 1791

562. Mary Masters
(fl. 1733–1755)

1 What if the charms in him I see
Only exist in thought
"To Lucinda," St. 2,
*Poems on Several
Occasions* 1733

2 Love is a mighty god, you know,
That rules with potent sway;
And when he draws his awful bow,
We mortals must obey.
Ibid., St. 6

563. Louise Honorine de Choiseul
(1734–1801)

1 You think I love you from complaisance and ask you to visit me from politeness. I don't. I love you because I love you. Letter to Marie du Deffand, *Correspondance complète de Mme Du Deffand avec la duchesse de Choiseul, l'abbé Barthélemy et M. Craufurt* 1866

2 He* does not mean to go without anything. He lets no pleasure escape him. He is right in thinking that pleasure is a legitimate end, but not every one is satisfied with pleasures that come as easily as his. Some of us cannot get them for merely stooping to pick them up. Ibid.
*Her husband the Duc de Choiseul (1719–1785).

3 You know you love me, but you do not feel it. Ibid.

4 Books help us to endure ignorance and life itself: Life, because the knowledge of past wretchedness helps us to endure the present; ignorance, because history tells us nothing but what we already know. Ibid.

5 Eat little at night, open your windows, drive out often, and look for the good in things and people. . . . You will no longer be sad, or bored, or ill. Ibid.

6 One [gentleman] is charming for the manner that he has and the other for the manner that he has not.
Quoted in
Portraits of Women
by Gamaliel Bradford   1916

7 We were alone and it was raining. This suggested talk of ourselves and, after all, what is there that we know so much about?
Ibid.

8 To love and to please is to be always young.
Ibid.

9 ...it is often the irregularity of our thought that causes the irregularity of our expressions.
Ibid.

10 It is well to love even a dog when you have the opportunity, for fear you should find nothing else worth loving.
Ibid.

11 ...it is a great point gained when we no longer mortify those whom we would have love us.
Ibid.

12 If I have learned anything, I owe it neither to precepts nor to books, but to a few opportune misfortunes. Perhaps the school of misfortunes is the very best.
Ibid.

13 Let us beware of metaphysics applied to simple things.
Ibid.

14 He [Jean-Jacques Rousseau] has always seemed to me to be a charlatan of virtue.
Ibid.

15 He [Voltaire] tells us he is faithful to his enthusiasms; he should have said, to his weaknesses. He has always been cowardly where there was no danger, insolent where there was no motive, and mean where there was no object in being so. All which does not prevent his being the most brilliant mind of the century. We should admire his talent, study his works, profit by his philosophy, and be broadened by his teaching. We should adore him and despise him, as is indeed the case with a good many objects of worship.
Ibid.

16 Gaiety, even when it is habitual, seems to me only an accident. Happiness is the fruit of reason, a tranquil condition, and an enduring one, which knows neither transport nor ecstasy. Perhaps it is a slumber of the soul, death, nothingness.
Ibid.

17 My scepticism has grown so great that it falls over backward and from doubting everything I have become ready to believe everything.
Ibid.

18 We grow old as soon as we cease to love and trust.
Ibid.

19 Good-by, dear child, I wish you good sleep and a good digestion. I don't know anything better to desire for those I love.
Ibid.

564.   Mrs. Pennington
(1734–1759)

1 On glories greater glories rise.
"Ode to Morning," St. 1,
The Female Poets of Great Britain,
Frederic Rowton, ed.   1853

2 But by some unexpected blow
Our giddy follies we shall know,
And mourn them when too late!
Ibid., St. 7

565.   Nancy Hart
(1735?–1830)

1 *Well fooled*, in an opposite course to that of my whig boy; when, if they had not been so lofty minded—but had looked on the ground inside the bars, they would have seen his horse's tracks up to that door, as plain as you can see the tracks on this here floor, and out of t'other door down the path to the swamp. On hoodwinking Tories in search of a Whig,
Quoted in *The Women of the American Revolution*,
Vol. II, by Elizabeth F. Ellet   1848

2 Surrender your damned Tory carcasses to a Whig woman.   On her capture of five Loyalists, op. cit.

566. Caroline Keppel
(1735–?)

1 What's this dull town to me?
    Robin's not near—
He whom I wished to see,
    Wished for to hear;
Where's all the joy and mirth
        Made life a heaven on earth?
O! they're all fled with thee,
    Robin Adair.   "Robin Adair," n.d.

567.   Theodosia De Visme Burr
(1736–1794)

1 Piety teaches resignation. . . . The better I am acquainted with it, the more charms I find.
          Letter to her husband, Aaron Burr (March 6, 1781), *Memoirs of Aaron Burr,* Vol. I, Matthew L. Davis, ed. 1836-1837

2 I am impatient for the evening; for the receipt of your dear letter; for those delightful sensations which your expressions of tenderness alone can excite. Dejected, distracted without them, elated, giddy even to folly with them, my mind, never at medium, claims everything from your partiality.   Ibid., Letter to Aaron Burr (August 1786)

568.   Mary Katherine Goddard
(c.1736-1738–1816)

1 . . . [it is] their duty to inquire into everything that has a tendency to restrain the liberty of the Press. . . .   Letter to the Baltimore Committee of Safety (May/June 1776), Quoted in *William Goddard, Newspaperman,* Ch. 8, by Ward L. Miner   1962

2 The Stoppage of the *Paper-Mill,* near this Town, for the Want of a Supply of Rags, and the enormous Prices demanded at the Stores here for PAPER, constrains us to print the *Maryland Journal* on this dark and poor Sort, which our Readers will, we are persuaded excuse, for one Week at least, when they are assured, that rather than deprive them of *the important Intelligence of the Times,* by the Discontinuance of our *Journal,* we have given from *Forty* to *Fifty Pounds* a Week for the Article of Paper *alone,* an equal Quantity of which, might, formerly, have been purchased for *Eight Dollars*!   Notice in *Maryland Journal* (May 26, 1778), op. cit.

569. Ann Lee
(1736–1784)

1 It is not I that speak, it is Christ who dwells in me.   Quoted in *The Testimony of Christ's Second Appearing* by Benjamin S. Youngs   1808

2 I converse with Christ; I feel him present with me, as sensibly as I feel my hands together.   Ibid.

570. Annis Stockton
(1736–1801)

1 My mind—so late the seat of joy sincere,

Thy absence makes a prey to gloomy care.
"By A Lady in America to Her
Husband in England,"
St. 3, *Pennsylvania Magazine*
June 1775

2 All day in secret sighs I've pour'd my soul,
My downy pillow, us'd to scenes of grief,
Beholds me now in floods of sorrow roll
"An Extempore Ode in a
Sleepless Night by a Lady
Attending on Her Husband* in a
Long and Painful Illness,"
II (December 3, 1780), Morven,
Quoted in *Funeral Sermon on
the Death of the Hon. Richard Stockton*,
Rev. Samuel Stanhope   1781
*Richard Stockton (1730–1781) American politician
and signer of the Declaration of Independence.

3 O death! thou canker-worm of human joy!
Ibid., VII

4 Drop fast my tears, and mitigate my woe:
Unlock your springs, and never cease to
flow:
For worth like his demands this heart-felt
grief,
And drops like these can only yield relief.
"An Elegy Sacred to the
Memory of Richard Stockton,
Esquire,"
St. 2, op. cit.

5 For thee awaits the patriot's shining crown;
The laurel blooms in blest elysian groves,
That twin'd by angel hands shall grace thy
brow. "Addressed to General Washington
in the Year 1777 After the
Battles of Trenton and Princeton,"
Columbian Magazine
January 1787

6 ... future ages shall enroll thy name
In sacred annals of immortal fame.
Ibid.

7 For, oh! I find on earth no charms for me
But what's connected with the thought of
thee!   "Epistle to Mr. S[tockton],"
*Women Poets in Pre-
Revolutionary America*,
Pattie Cowell, ed.   1981

8 Thousands of heroes from his dust shall rise
"On Hearing That General [Dr.
Joseph] Warren Was Killed on
Bunker Hill, the 17th of June,
1775,"
op. cit.

9 For friendship soars above low rules
"To Laura*,"
St. 6,
op. cit.
*The poet Elizabeth Graeme Ferguson. See 571.

571.   Elizabeth Graeme Ferguson
(1737–1801)

1 A transient, rich, and balmy sweet
Is in thy fragrance found;
But soon the flow'r and scent retreat—
Thorns left alone to wound.
"On a Beautiful Damask Rose,
Emblematical of Love and
Wedlock," St. 3,
Columbian Magazine
May 1789

2 Thus over all, self-love presides supreme
"On the Mind's Being Engrossed
By One Subject,"
Columbian Magazine
July 1789

3 Though oft we change through life's swift
gliding stage,
And seek fresh objects at each varying age,
Here we are constant, faithful to one cause,
Our own indulgence as a center draws.
That faithful inmate makes our breast its
home,
From the soft cradle, to the silent tomb.
Ibid.

4 Birth day odes to lords and kings,
Oft are strain'd and stupid things!
Poet laureate's golden lays,

Fulsome hireling's hackney'd praise!
    "An Ode Written on the
Birthday of Mr. Henry Ferguson
By His Wife When They Had
Been Married Two Years, He
    Aged 26 Years,"
St. 1 (March 12, 1774),
*Women Poets in Pre-
Revolutionary America*,
Pattie Cowell, ed.   1981

5 Expression is in feeling lost,
For shallow strains oft babble most.
    Ibid., St. 4

6 One prosperous wind expands each sail.
    Ibid., St. 5

7 Too deep this point, a female pen
Dare not such heights explore;
The subject's left to learned men,
Of philosophic lore! "Upon the Discovery
    of the Planet by Mr. Herschel*
of Bath and By Him Nam'd the
Georgium Sidus in Honor of His
    Britannic Majesty,"
    St. 3, op. cit.
*The English astronomer Sir William Herschel (1738–1822).

8 . . . angel-like he spake, and God-like died.
    "On the Death of Leopold,
Hereditary Prince of Brunswick,
Who was Drowned in the Oder,
April 17, 1785, in Attempting to
Save Some Children Whose
Mother had Left Them on the
    Banks of that River"
(July 5, 1785), Montgomery
    County,
    op. cit.

572.   Margaret Morris
(1737?–1816)

1 A loud knocking at my door brought me to
it. . . . I opened it, and a half a dozen men,
all armed, demanded the key of the empty
house. . . . I put on a very simple look and
exclaimed—"Bless me! I hope you are not
Hessians!"*

"Do we look like Hessians?" asked one
rudely.
    "Indeed, I don't know."
    "Did you never see a Hessian?"
    'No—never in my life; but they are *men*;
and you are men; and may be Hessians for
aught I know!"   From her Journal
    (December 16, 1776),
Quoted in *The Women of the
American Revolution*,
Vol. II, by Elizabeth F.
    Ellet   1848
*German mercenaries hired by the British.

2 . . . there is a god of battle as well as a God
of peace. . . .   Ibid. (December 27, 1776)

3 Being now so rich, we thought it our duty
to hand out a little to the poor around us,
who were mourning for want of salt. . . .
    Ibid. (June 14, 1777)

4 Indeed, it seemed to us as if our little store
was increased by distribution, like the bread
broken by our Saviour to the multitude.
    Ibid.

573.   Suzanne Chardon Necker
(1737–1794)

1 . . . I cannot help thinking that the vows
most women are made to take are very fool-
hardy. I doubt whether they would willingly go to the altar to swear that they will
allow themselves to be broken on the wheel
every nine months.   Quoted in *Mistress to
an Age: A Life of Madame de Staël*
by J. Christopher Herold
    1958

2 Governesses have always one great disad-
vantage; if they are qualified for their calling, they intercept the child's affection for
its mother.   Ibid.

574. Mary Fletcher
(1739-1815)

1 And now that thought, I am brought out of the world, I have nothing to do but to be holy, both in body and spirit, filled me with consolation; thankfulness overflowed my heart; and such a spirit of peace and content flowed into my soul, that all about me seemed a little heaven.   Quoted in
The Women of Methodism:
Its Three Foundresses...
by Abel Stevens   1866

2 I was deeply conscious it [religion] is one of the most delicate subjects in the world, and requires both much wisdom and much love, to extinguish false fire, and yet keep up the true.   Ibid.

3 The Lord treated me as we do a child; he put one thing into my hand to take away another. Remark concerning the death of
her friend, Sarah Ryan,
op. cit.

4 I feel at this moment a more tender affection toward him* than I did at that time [of her marriage], and by faith I now join my hand afresh with his.   Journal entry
(November 12, 1809),
op. cit.
*Her husband, Jean Guillaume de la Flechère; written during her widowhood, on the anniversary of her marriage.

5 It is as if every meeting [of the church] would take away my life; but I will speak to them while I have my breath.
Journal entry
(c.September 1815),
op. cit.

6 O I long that the year fifteen may be the best of all my life.   Journal entry (1815),
op. cit.

575. Madame de Charrière
(1740-?)

1 I would prefer being my lover's laundress and living in a garret to the arid freedom and the good manners of our great families.
Quoted in *Mistress to An Age: A*
Life of Madame de Staël
by J. Christopher Herold
1958

576. Mrs. Hoper
(fl. 1740s)

1 Is playing meaner, than to run in Debt?
Prologue, *Queen Tragedy*
Restores   1749

2 The Stage shall flourish, Tragedy shall thrive,
And Shakespear's Scenes ne'er die whilst They* survive   Ibid.
*Othello, Hamlet, Falstaff and Richard II.

577. Milcah Martha Moore
(1740-1829)

1 Let the Daughters of Liberty nobly arise
"The Female Patriots. Address'd to the Daughters of Liberty in America" (1768),
William and Mary Quarterly
April 1977

578. Clementina Rind
(c.1740-1774)

1 Open to ALL PARTIES, but Influenced by NONE.   Motto,
Quoted in *Virginia Gazette*
(first issue)   May 16, 1766

579. Martha Brewster
(fl. 1741-1757)

1 Pardon her bold Attempt who has reveal'd

Her thoughts to View, more fit to be Con-
ceal'd
Since thus to do was urged Vehemently,
Yet most no doubt will call it Vanity
Introduction,
*Poems on Divers
Subjects*   1757

2 I here presume upon your Clemency,
For rare it is to see a *Female Bard*,
Or that my sex in print have e're appeared
Ibid.

3 Oh!————he————is————gone.
"To the Memory of that worthy
Man Liet. NATHANAEL
BURT of *Springfield*... [who
died] in the Battle of Lake-
George in the Retreat, September
8th, 1753,"
op. cit.

4 There is a wheel within a wheel
"A Farewell to Some of My
Christian Friends at Goshen, in
Lebanon,"
St. 4 (April 5, 1745), op. cit.

5 God meant it all for good; and thus
To us He often shows
A Sampson's riddle; so our thorns
May bear the sweetest rose.
Ibid., St. 11

6 Dear friends, the life is more than meat,
The soul excels the clay;
O labor then for gospel food,
Which never shall decay.
Ibid., St. 14

7 Absent for ever, O that dreadful sound!
"A Funeral Poem, on the Death
of the Reverend Isaac Watts, D. D."*
op. cit.

*English theologian and hymn writer (1674–1748).

8 ... the brittle cords of life. ...
Ibid.

9 O absence! absence! sharper than a thorn
"A Letter to My Daughter Ruby
Bliss,"
op. cit.

580.   Sarah Parsons Moorhead
(fl. 1741/42)

1 ... pray beware,
Least too much terror, prove to some a
snare.
Least stupid scoffers be provok'd to say,
They were by awful curses drove away.
"Lines ... Humbly Dedicated to
the Rev. Gilbert Tennant,"
New England Weekly Journal
March 17, 1741

2 Despise the blest instructions of their
tongue,
Conversion is become the drunkard's song;
God's glorious work, which sweetly did
arise,
By this unguarded sad imprudence dies;
Contention spreads her harpy claws
around,
In every church her hateful stings are
found.   "To the Reverend Mr. James
Davenport on His Departure
from Boston, By Way of a
Dream," St. 1
1742

581.   Hester Lynch Piozzi
(1741–1821)

1 Johnson's conversation was by much too
strong for a person accustomed to obsequi-
ousness and flattery; it was *mustard in a
young child's mouth!* Remark (May 1781),
Quoted in
The Life of Samuel Johnson, LL. D.
by James Boswell   1791

2 It is a maxim here [at Venice], handed
down from generation to generation, that
change breeds more mischief from its novelty than advantage from its utility.
"Observations on a Journey
through Italy,"
*Autobiography, Letters and
Literary Remains,*
Abraham Hayward, ed.   1861

3 The tree of deepest root is found
Least willing still to quit the ground:

'Twas therefore said by ancient sages,
That love of life increased with years
So much, that in our latter stages,
When pain grows sharp and sickness rages,
The greatest love of life appears.

"Three Warnings,"
op. cit.

4 Ah! he was a wise man who said Hope is a
good breakfast but a bad dinner. It shall be
my supper, however, when all's said and
done.   From *Autobiography . . . ,*

Vol. II

5 A physician can sometimes parry the scythe
of death, but has no power over the sand in
the hourglass.   Letter to Fanny Burney*

(November 12, 1781),
op. cit.

*English diarist and novelist. See 615.

6 'Tis never for their wisdom that one loves
the wisest, or for their wit that one loves the
wittiest; 'tis for benevolence and virtue and
honest fondness one loves people; the other
qualities make one proud of loving them,
too.   Letter to Fanny Burney (1781),

op. cit.

582.   Dorcas Richardson
(1741?–1834)

1 I do not doubt that men who can outrage
the feelings of a woman by such threats, are
capable of perpetrating any act of treachery
and inhumanity towards a brave but unfortunate enemy. But conquer or capture my
husband [Captain Richard Richardson], if
you can do so, before you boast the cruelty
you mean to mark your savage triumph!
And let me tell you, meanwhile, that some
of you, it is likely, will be in a condition to
implore *his* mercy, before he will have need
to supplicate, or deign to accept yours.

Remark to the British,
Quoted by Dr. Joseph Johnson in
The Women of the American Revolution
by Elizabeth F. Ellet   1848

583.   Sarah Kirby Trimmer
(1741–1810)

1 Happy would it be for the animal creation,
if every human being . . . consulted the welfare of inferior creatures, and neither
spoiled them by indulgence, nor injured
them by tyranny! Happy would mankind
be . . . by cultivating in their own minds
and those of their own children, the divine
principle of general benevolence.

*Fabulous Histories: or, The
History of the Robins. Designed
for the Instruction of Children,
Respecting Their Treatment of
Animals,* 13th ed., 1821

2 It is by no means desirable to be shut up for
life, let the place of confinement be ever so
splendid. . . .   Op. cit.

3 Every living creature that comes into the
world has something allotted him to perform, therefore he should not stand an idle
spectator of what others are doing.

Op. cit.

584.   Isabella Graham
(1742–1814)

1 Hail! thou state of widowhood,
State of those that mourn to God;
Who from earthly comforts torn,
Only live to pray and mourn.

"Widowhood" (1774),
Life and Writings, n.d.

585.   Anne Home
(1742–1821)

1 'Tis hard to smile when one would weep,
      To speak when one would silent be;
To wake when one would wish to sleep,
      And wake to agony.

"The Lot of Thousands,"
Poems by Mrs. John Hunter
1802

2 My mother bids me bind my hair
With bands of rosy hue,

Tie up my sleeves with ribbons rare,
  And lace my bodice blue.
"For why," she cries, "sit still and weep,
  While others dance and play?"
Alas! I scarce can go or creep
  While Lubin is away.
      "My Mother Bids Me Bind My
               Hair,"
               op. cit.

3 'Tis sad to think the days are gone,
  When those we love were near;
I sit upon this mossy stone,
  And sigh when none can hear.
               Ibid.

4 How heavy falls the foot of Time!
            "To-Morrow,"
            St. 1, op. cit.

5 Man still believes, and is thy slave;
Nor ends the chase but in the grave,
For there *to-morrow* is no more.
            Ibid., St. 4

586. Darcy Maxwell
(1742?–1810)

1 It is seldom that we go beyond our teachers.
      Quoted in *The Women of
Methodism: Its Three Foundresses* . . .
      by Abel Stevens   1866

2 Suffice it to say, I was chosen in the furnace
of affliction. The Lord gave me all I desired
in this world, then took all from me;* but
immediately afterward sweetly drew me to
Himself.   Letter to a friend (c.1776),
      Quoted in *Biography of
Distinguished Women*
      by Sarah Josepha Hale   1876

*She was widowed at nineteen; six weeks later her only
child died.

587. Anna Seward
(1742–1809)

1   O hours! more worth than gold,
By whose blest use we lengthen life, and
  free

From drear decays of age, outline the
old!   Untitled (December 1782),
          Sonnets   1789

2   . . . for thou art gone,
And many a dark, long eve I sigh alone,
In thrill'd remembrance of the vanish'd
  hours,
When storms were dearer than the balmy
  gales,
And the grey barren fields than green lux-
  uriant vales.   "Time Past,"
       St. 4 (January 1773),
            op. cit.

3 . . . in the silent grave, no talk! no music!
No gay surprise, by expected good,
Social, or individual!—no glad step
Of welcome friend, with more intenseness
  listen'd
Than warbled melody! no father's counsel!
No mother's smile! no lover's whisper'd
  vow!
There nothing breathes save the insatiate
  worm   "The Grave of Youth,"
            op. cit.

4 This last and long enduring passion for
Mrs. Thrale* was, however, composed of
cupboard love, Platonic love, and vanity
tickled and gratified.   Letter, *Letters*,
          Vol. II, n.d.

*Allusion to Dr. Samuel Johnson's relationship with
Hester Lynch Piozzi, aka Mrs. Thrale. See 581.

5 My fair cousin, Miss Marten, is completely
buried through the dreary months. . . . She
tells us she weeps for joy at the sight of the
first daisy, and welcomes and talks to and
hails the little blessed harbinger of brighter
days, her days of liberty as well as of peace.
          Letter (1767),
            op. cit.

588.　Anna Letitia Barbauld
(1743–1825)

1 While Genius was thus wasting his strength in eccentric flights, I saw a person of a very different appearance, named Application.

"The Hill of Science,"
Miscellaneous Pieces in Prose
1773

2 Of all the multifarious productions which the efforts of superior genius, or the labours of scholastic industry, have crowded upon the world, none are perused with more insatiable avidity, or disseminated with more universal applause, than the narrations of famed events, descriptions of imaginary scenes, and delineations of ideal characters.

"On Romance,"
op. cit.

3 The most characteristic mark of a great mind is to choose some one important object, and pursue it for life.

"Against Inconsistency in Our
Expectations,"
op. cit.

4 It must be confessed, that men of genius are of all others most inclined to make . . . unreasonable claims . . . their eccentricity and turn for speculation disqualifies them for the business of the world, which is best carried on by men of moderate genius. . . .

Ibid.

5 The awakenings of remorse, virtuous shame and indignation, the glow of moral approbation—if they do not lead to action, grow less and less vivid every time they occur, till at length the mind grows absolutely callous. "An Inquiry Into Those Kinds of Distress Which Excite Agreeable Sensations,"

op. cit.

6 What fair, what amiable creatures were our first parents when they came from the hands of their Maker! They knew neither Pain, nor Sin, the sire of Pain; nor Shame, the daughter of Sin.

"On Evil:—A Rhapsody,"
op. cit.

7 The spirit of greediness and rapacity is nowhere so conspicuous as in lodging houses.

"Letter on Watering Places,"
op. cit.

8 Education, in its largest sense, is a thing of great scope and extent. It includes the whole process by which a human being is formed to be what he is, in habits, principles, and cultivation of every kind. . . . You speak of *beginning* the education of your son. The moment he was able to form an idea his education was already begun. . . .

"On Education,"
op. cit.

9 Education, it is often observed, is an expensive thing. It is so; but the paying for lessons is the smallest part of the cost. If you would go to the price of having your son a worthy man, you must be so yourself. . . .

Ibid.

10 Prejudice is prejudging; that is, judging previously to evidence. It is therefore sufficiently apparent, that no *philosophical belief* can be founded on mere prejudice; because it is the business of philosophy to go deep into the nature and properties of things. . . .

"On Prejudice,"
op. cit.

11 Let us confess a truth, humiliating perhaps to human pride;—a very small part only of the opinions of the coolest philosopher are the result of fair reasoning; the rest are formed by his education, his temperament, by the age in which he lives, by trains of thought directed to a particular track through some accidental association—in short, by *prejudice*.

Ibid.

12 . . . there are negative prejudices as well as positive.

Let parents, therefore, not scruple to use the power God and Nature have put into their hands for the advantage of their off-spring. Let them not fear to impress them with prejudices for whatever is fair and honourable in action—whatever is useful and important in systematic truth. Let such prejudices be wrought into the very texture of the soul. Such truths let them appear to know by intuition. Ibid.

13 Health to my friend, and long unbroken years,
By storms unruffled and unstained by tears
"The Invitation,"
Poems 1773

14 Clouds behind clouds in long succession rise,
And heavy snows oppress the springing green;
The dazzling waste fatigues the aching eyes,
And Fancy droops th' unvaried scene.
"On the Backwardness of the Spring" (1771),
op. cit.

15 If e'er thy breast with freedom glowed,
And spurned a tyrant's chain,
Let not thy strong oppressive force
A free-born mouse detain!
"The Mouse's Petition,"
op. cit.

16 The well-taught philosophic mind
To all compassion gives;
Casts round the world an equal eye,
And feels for all that lives.
Ibid.

17 Forgotten rimes, and college themes,
Worm-eaten plans, and embryo schemes;—
A mass of heterogeneous matter.
A chaos dark, nor land nor water.
"An Inventory of the Furniture in Dr. Priestley's* Study,"
op. cit.
*The English chemist Joseph Priestley (1733–1804).

18 Gay without toil, and lovely without art,

They spring to cheer the sense and glad the heart. "To A Lady With Some Painted Flowers,"
op. cit.

19 For O, not all that Autumn's lap contains,
Nor Summer's ruddiest fruits,
Can ought for thee atone,

Fair Spring! whose simplest promise more delights
Than all their largest wealth. . . .
"Ode to Spring,"
op. cit.

20 Who can resist those dumb beseeching eyes,
Where genuine eloquence persuasive lies?
Those eyes, where language fails, display thy heart
Beyond the pomp of phrase and pride of art. "To A Dog,"
op. cit.

21 We neither laugh alone, nor weep alone,—why then should we pray alone?
Remarks on Mr. Gilbert Wakefield's Enquiry Into the Expediency and Propriety of Public or Social Worship
1792

22 Humanity is shocked to hear prayers for the success of an unjust war; but humanity and Heaven were then offended when the war was engaged in. . . . Ibid.

23 But every act in consequence of our faith, strengthens faith. Ibid.

24 The doctrine that all are vile, and equally merit a state of punishment, is an idea as conciliatory to the profligate, as it is humiliating to the saint; and that is one reason why it has always been a favourite doctrine.
Ibid.

25 And when 'midst fallen London, they survey
The stone where Alexander's* ashes lay,
Shall own with humbled pride the lesson just
By Time's slow finger written in the dust.
"Eighteen Hundred and Eleven," 1811

*Alexander the Great.

26 The talking restless world shall see,
Spite of the world we'll happy be;
But none shall know
How much were so,
Save only Love and we.
"To Mr. Barbauld"
(November 14, 1778),
*The Works of Anna Letitia
Barbauld*, Vol. I
1826

27   . . . still Afric bleeds,
Unchecked, the human traffic still proceeds
"Epistle to William Wilberforce,
Esq."* (1791),
op. cit.

*English abolitionist; the reference is to slavery.

28 Where seasoned tools of Avarice prevail,
A Nation's eloquence, combined, must fail
Ibid.

29 By foreign wealth our British morals
changed,
And Afric's sons, and India's, smile
avenged.   Ibid.

30 Yes, injured Woman! rise, assert thy right!
Woman! too long degraded, scorned, oppr-
est;
O born to rule impartial Laws despite,
Resume they native empire o'er the breast!
"The Right of Woman,"
op. cit.

31 . . . separate rights are lost in mutual love.
Ibid.

32   No line can reach
To thy unfathomed depths. The reasoning
sage
Who can dissect a sunbeam, count the stars,
And measure distant worlds, is here a child,
And, humbled, drops his calculating pain.
"Eternity,"
op. cit.

33   And thou, dread power! bring'st back
in terrors drest,
Th' irrevocable past, to sting the careless
breast.   "Ode to Remorse,"
op. cit.

34 LIFE! I know that what thou art,
But know that thou and I must part;
And when, or how, or where we met,
I own to me's a secret yet.
"Life,"
op. cit.

35 'Tis hard to part when friends are dear,—
Perhaps 't will cost a sigh, a tear;
Then steal away, give little warning,
Choose thine own time;
Say not "Good-night," but in some
brighter clime
Bid me "Good-morning!"
Ibid.

36 When trembling limbs refuse their weight,
And films, slow gathering, dim the sight,
And clouds obscure the mental light,—
'Tis nature's percious boon to die.
"A Thought on Death"
(November 1814),
op. cit.

37 So fades a summer cloud away;
So sinks the gale when storms are o'er;
So gently shuts the eye of day;
So dies a wave along the shore.
"The Death of the Virtuous,"
op. cit.

38 The world has little to bestow
Where two fond hearts in equal love are
joined.   "Delia,"
op. cit.

39   Is there not
A tongue in every star that talks with man,
And wooes him to be wise?
"A Summer Evening's
Meditation,"
l. 48, op. cit.

40 This dead of midnight is the noon of
thought,
And Wisdom mounts her zenith with the
stars.   Ibid., l. 51

41 Society than solitude is worse,
And man to man is still the greatest curse.
"Ovid to His Wife,"
op. cit.

42 Of her scorn the maid repented,

And the shepherd—of his love.
"Leave Me, Simple Shepherd,"
op. cit.

43 Saints have been calm while stretched upon
the rack,
And Guatimozin* smiled on burning coals;
But never yet did housewife notable
Greet with a smile a rainy washing-day.
"Washing-Day,"
op. cit.

*Aztec emperor, tortured by the conquistadors.

44 The sports of children and the toils of men.
Ibid.

45 Earth, air, and sky, and ocean, hath its bub-
bles,
And verse is one of them—this most of all.
Ibid.

46 In short, women I think may be led on by
sentiment to passion; but men must be subdued by passion before they can taste sentiment.   Letter to Dr. Aiken, her brother
(1774),
from Palgrave, Vol. II

47 . . . [as] a father of three children. I would
advise you to make a hero, as you have determined: another a scholar; and for the
third,—send him to us, and we will bring
him up for a Norfolk farmer, which I suspect to be the best business of the three.
Letter to Dr. Aiken
(September 9, 1775),
op. cit.

48 I begin to be giddy with the world of London, and to feel my spirits flag. There are so
many drawbacks, from hairdressers, bad
weather and fatigue, that it requires strong
health greatly to enjoy being abroad.
Letter to Dr. Aiken
January 2, 1784, from London,
op. cit.

49 To *repair* a ruin carries a better sound with
it than to *build* a ruin, as we do in England.
Letter to Dr. Aiken
(February 27, 1786), from
Thoulouse [sic],
op. cit.

50 It would be difficult to determine whether
the age is growing better or worse; for I
think our plays are growing like sermons,
and our sermons like plays.
Letter to Miss E. Belshan
(later Mrs. Kenrick).
(February 17, 1771), from
London,
op. cit.

51 Nobody ought to be too old to improve; I
should be sorry if I was; and I flatter myself
I have already improved considerably by
my travels. First, I can swallow gruel soup,
egg soup, and all manner of soups, without
making faces much. Secondly, I can pretty
well live without tea. . . .   Letter to Miss
Belshan
(October 21, 1785),
from Geneva,
op. cit.

52 One hardly knows whether to be frightened
or diverted on seeing people assembled at a
dinner-table appearing to enjoy extremely
the fare and the company, and saying all the
while, with the most smiling and placid
countenance, that the French are to land in
a fortnight, and that London is to be sacked
and plundered for three days,—and then
they talk of going to watering places.
Letter to Miss Dixon
(later Mrs. Beecroft).
(July 28, 1803), from London,
op. cit.

53 Long may every sweet illusion continue
that promotes happiness, and ill befall the
rough hand that would destroy them!
Ibid.

54 Here dwell the true magicians. Nature is
our servant. Man is our pupil. We change,
we conquer, we create.   "To Miss C.,"
A Legacy for Young Ladies
n.d.

55 "Miserable country!" I explained; "stepchild of nature!"
Ibid.

56 "I rejoice when nature rejoices; and when I am desolate, nature mourns with me."
"The Pine and the Olive,"
op. cit.

57 Finding out riddles is the same kind of exercise to the mind which running and leaping and wrestling and sport are to the body.
"On Riddles,"
op. cit.

58 I often murmur, yet I never weep;
I always lie in bed, yet never sleep;
My mouth is large, and larger than my head,
And much disgorges though it ne'er is fed;
I have no legs or feet, yet swiftly run,
And the more falls I get, move faster on.
Ibid.

59 In foreign languages you have only to learn; but with regard to your own, you have probably to unlearn, and to avoid vulgarisms and provincial barbarisms.
"On Female Studies,
Letter Two,"
op. cit.

60 You must often be content to know a thing is so, without understanding the proof.
Ibid.

61 Between the greater part of those we call the different classes, there is only the difference of less and more. . . .
Ibid.

62 . . . Taste has one great enemy to contend with . . . Fashion—an arbitrary and capricious tyrant, who reigns with the most despotic sway over that department which Taste alone ought to regulate.
Ibid.

63 . . . a forest was never planted.
"On Plants,"
op. cit.

64 How patiently does she support the various burdens laid upon her! We tear her plows and harrows, we crush her with castles and palaces; nay we penetrate her very bowels, and bring to light the veined marble, the pointed crystal, the ponderous ores and sparkling gems, deep hid in darkness the more to excite the industry of man. Yet, torn and harrassed as she might seem to be, our mother Earth is still fresh and young, as if she but now came out of the hands of her Creator.
"Earth,"
op. cit.

65 We can only love what we know. . . .
"On the Uses of History,"
op. cit.

66 The worst slavery is that which we voluntarily impose upon ourselves. . . .
"Fashion,"
op. cit.

67 . . . a friend was never chosen.
"On Friendship,"
op. cit.

68 Friends should consider themselves as the sacred guardians of each other's virtue; and the noblest testimony they can give of their affection is the correction of the faults of those they love.
Ibid.

69 Happy is he to whom, in the maturer season of life, there remains one tried and constant friend. . . .
Ibid.

589.   Hannah Cowley
(1743–1809)

1 GRANGER. Jack Spitter, to be sure, had twelve hundred; the fellow was honest, and would have paid; but he married a fine lady, so died insolvent.   *Who's the Dupe?*,
Act I, Sc. 1   1779

2 DOILEY. No, no; you must mind your P's and Q's* with him, I can tell you.
Ibid., Sc. 2

*Originally abbreviation for "pints and quarts," used in taverns.

3 DOILEY. You've a confounded knack at laughing; and there's nothing so odious in the eyes of a wise man as a great laughter.
Ibid.

4 DOILEY. Well, good fortune never comes in a hurry. . . .
Ibid.

5 GRADUS. The charms of women were never more powerful—never inspired such achievements, as in those immortal periods, when they could neither read nor write.
Ibid., Sc. 3

6 MISS DOILEY. Ay, to be sure; what's reading good for, but to give a stiff embarrassed air?
Ibid.

7 MISS DOILEY. For my part—for my part, if I was a man, I'd study only dancing and bon-mots. With no other learning than these, he may be light and frolicksome as Lady Airy's ponies; but loaded with Greek, philosophy, and mathematics, he's as heavy and dull as a cart-horse.   Ibid.

8 CHARLOTTE. You know very well, the use of language is to express one's likes and dislikes—and a pig will do this as effectually by its squeak, or a hen with her cackle, as you with your Latin and Greek.
Ibid.

9 CHARLOTTE. It is a *moment* that decides the fate of a lover.   Ibid.

10 GRADUS. Beauty is a talisman which works true miracles, and, without a fable, transforms mankind.   Ibid., Act II, Sc. 1

11 GRADUS. . . . a man who knows more than his neighbours is in danger of being shut out of society; or, at best, of being invited to dinner once in a twelvemonth, to be exhibited like an antique bronze, or a porridge-pot from Herculaneum.   Ibid.

12 GRANGER. But what is woman?—Only one of Nature's agreeable blunders.
Ibid.

13 SAVILLE. Five minutes! Zounds! I have been five minutes too late all my life-time!
The Belle's Strategem,
Act I, Sc. 1   c.1780s

14 DORICOURT. Englishmen make the best soldiers, citizens, artizans, and philosophers in the world; but the very worst footmen. . . . A Frenchman neither hears, sees, nor breathes, but as his master directs; and his whole system of conduct is compris'd in one short word, obedience! An Englishman reasons, forms opinions, cogitates, and disputes; he is not the mere creature of your will, but a being conscious of equal importance in the universal scale with yourself, he is therefore your judge, whilst he wears your livery, and decides on your actions with the freedome of a censor.
Ibid., Sc. 2

15 VILLERS. A lady at her toilette is as difficult to be moved as a quaker.   Ibid., Sc. 3

16 FLUTTER. . . . the common events of this little dirty world are not worth talking about, unless you embellish them!
Ibid.

17 VILLERS. Vanity, like murder, will out.
Ibid.

18 MRS. RACKET. 'Tis a good-natured insignificant creature! let in every where, and cared for no where.   Ibid.

19 MISS OGLE. Pray, sir, what do you take a fine lady to be, that you express such fear of her?

SIR GEORGE TOUCHWOOD. A being easily described, madam, as she is seen everywhere but in her own house. She sleeps at home, but she lives all over the town. In her mind every sentiment gives place to the lust of conquest, and the vanity of being particular. The feelings of wife and mother are lost in the whirl of dissipation. If she continues virtuous, 'tis by chance—and, if she preserves her husband from ruin, 'tis by her dexterity at the card table!—Such a woman I take to be a perfect fine lady.
Ibid., Act II, Sc. 1

20 MRS. RACKET. In a word, a fine lady is the life of conversation, the spirit of society, the joy of the public!   Ibid.

21 SIR GEORGE TOUCHWOOD. Heaven and earth! with whom can a man trust his wife in the present state of society? Formerly there were distinctions of character amongst ye; every class of females had its particular description! grandmothers were pious, aunts discreet, old maids censorious! but now, aunts, grandmothers, girls, and maiden gentlewomen, are all the same creature; a wrinkle more or less is the sole difference between ye.   Ibid.

22 SIR GEORGE TOUCHWOOD. And what is the society of which you boast? a mere chaos, in which all distinction of rank is lost in a ridiculous affectation of ease.
                                                     Ibid.

23 SIR GEORGE TOUCHWOOD. Mr. Flutter, you are one of those busy, idle, meddling people, who, from mere vacuity of mind, are the most dangerous inmates in a family . . . and, because you mean no harm, think yourselves excused, though broken friendships, discords, and murders, are the consequences of your indiscretions.
                                                     Ibid.

24 FLUTTER. A fair tug, by Jupiter—between duty and pleasure! Pleasure beats, and off we go.   ￼   Ibid.

25 COURTALL. But 'tis always so; your reserved ladies are like ice, 'egad!—no sooner begin to soften than they melt!   Ibid., Sc. 2

26 MRS. RACKET. Marry first and love will follow.   Ibid., Act III, Sc. 1

27 LETITIA HARDY. (Singing) What is your fortune, my pretty maid?
My face is my fortune, sir, she said.
Then I'll not have you, my pretty maid.
Nobody axed you, sir, she said.
                                                     Ibid.

28 VILLERS. . . . if she is a true woman, her displeasure will rise in proportion to your contrition. . . .   Ibid., Sc. 4

29 LADY FRANCES TOUCHWOOD. Every body about me seem'd happy—but every body seem'd in a hurry to be happy somewhere else.   Ibid.

30 SIR GEORGE TOUCHWOOD. How lively are first impressions on sensible minds!
                                       Ibid., Act IV, Sc. 1

31 FLUTTER. O lord! your wise men are the greatest fools upon earth; they reason about their enjoyments, and analyse their pleasures, whilst the essence escapes.
                                                     Ibid.

32 SIR GEORGE TOUCHWOOD. How can I be such a fool as to be governed by the fear of that ridicule which I despise?
                                                     Ibid.

33 SAVILLE. Goodness will have interest; its home is heaven: on earth 'tis but a wanderer.   Ibid.

34 LETITA HARDY. This moment is worth a whole existence!   Ibid.

35 FLUTTER. "Live to love," was my father's motto: "Live to laugh," is mine.
                                                     Ibid.

36 VILLERS. The charms that helped to catch the husband are generally laid by, one after another, till the lady grows a downright wife, and then runs crying to her mother, because she has transformed her lover into a downright husband.   Ibid., Act V, Sc. 1

37 MRS. RACKET. It requires genius to make a good pun—some men of bright parts can't reach it.   Ibid., Sc. 5

38 LETITIA HARDY. 'Tis plain, in real life,
    from youth to age,
All wear their masks. Here only on the stage,
You see us as we are; here trust your eyes,
Our wish to please cannot be mere disguise.
                                       Ibid., Epilogue

39 Bright star of Genius! torn from life and fame,
My tears, my verse, shall consecrate thy name!   "On the Death of
                                              Chatterton,"*
                                                     St. 1,
                         Dramas and Poems   1813
*The English poet Thomas Chatterton (1752–1770), dubbed The Marvelous Boy by his admirers.

40 Thou haggard Poverty! whose cheerless eye
Makes note of Rapture change to deepest sigh,
Subdued by thee his pen no more obeys,
No more revives the song of ancient days,
Check'd in his flight, his lofty genius cowers,
Locks her faint wings, and yields to thee her powers! Ibid., St. 2

41 Alone, unknown, the Muses' favourite dies,
And with the vulgar dead, unnoted lies! Ibid., St. 4

590.   Eibhlín Dhubh Ní Chonaill
(1743–1790)

1 Till Art O'Leary returns
There will be no end to the grief
That presses down on my heart,
Closed up tight and firm
Like a trunk that is locked
And the key mislaid.   "The Lament for Arthur O'Leary," St. 35, Ellis Dillon, tr.; *The Penguin Book of Women Poets,* Carol Cosman, Joan Keefe and Kathleen Weaver, tr. and eds. 1978

591.   Abigail Adams
(1744–1818)

1 I am more and more convinced that man is a dangerous creature.... Letter to John Adams (November 27, 1775), *Letters of Mrs. Adams* 1840

2 We are no ways dispirited here, we possess a Spirit that will not be conquered. If our Men are all drawn off and we should be attacked, you would find a Race of Amazons in America. Letter to John Adams (1776), op. cit.

3 If perticuliar care and attention is not paid to the Laidies we are determined to foment a Rebelion, and will not hold ourselves bound by any Laws in which we have no voice, or Representation.   Letter to John Adams (March 31, 1776), op. cit.

4 Men of Sense in all Ages abhor those customs which treat us only as the vassals of your Sex. Ibid.

5 I hope in time to have the Reputation of being as good a *Farmeress* as my partner has of being a good Statesman. Letter to John Adams (April 7–11, 1776), from Braintree, op. cit.

6 I stand in need of the constant assistance of my Better half.   Letter to Mercy Otis Warren* (April 13, 1776), from Braintree, op. cit.

*American writer and historian. See 550.

7 Mr. A. has been so long a Statesman that I cannot get him to think enough upon his domestick affairs. Tho I am very willing to releive him from every care in my power, yet I think it has too much the appearance of weilding instead of sharing the Scepter. Letter to Cotton Tufts (March 8, 1785), op. cit.

8 The Boy is a Freeman as much as any of the young Men, and merely because his Face is Black, is he to be denied instruction?... I have not thought it any disgrace to my self to take him into my parlour and teach him both to read and write.   Letter to John Adams (February 13, 1797), from Braintree, Mass., op. cit.

9 It is vain to talk of being above these little decorums—if we live in the world and mean to serve ourselves and it, we must conform to its customs.   Letter to Mrs. John Quincy Adams, Jr. (December 8, 1804), op. cit.

10 [Letter-writing is] a habit, the pleasure of which increases with practise, but becomes urksome by neglect.   Letter to daughter (May 8, 1808), op. cit.

11 [At] the court of St. James* . . . I seldom meet with characters so innofensive as my Hens and chickings, or minds so well improved as my garden.   Letter to Thomas Jefferson (February 26, 1788), Quoted in *The Papers of Thomas Jefferson*, Julian P. Boyd, ed.   1955

*Reference to James Madison, U.S. president, 1809–1817.

12 . . . had nature formed me of the other Sex, I should certainly have been a rover.   Letter to Isaac Smith, Jr. (April 20, 1771), *The Adams Papers*, L. H. Butterfield, ed.   1963

13 The Natural tenderness and Delicacy of our Constitution, added to the many Dangers we are subject to from your Sex, renders it almost impossible for a Single Lady to travel without injury to her character.   Ibid.

14 Education alone I concede Constitutes the difference in Manner.   Ibid.

15 . . . as all Men of Delicacy and Sentiment are averse to Exercising the power they possess, yet as there is a natural propensity in Humane Nature to domination, I thought the most generous plan was to put it out of the power of the Arbitrary and Tyranick to injure us with impunity by Establishing some Laws in our favour upon just and Liberal principles.   Letter to Mercy Otis Warren (April 27, 1776), op. cit.

16 I can not say that I think you very generous to the Ladies, for whilst you are proclaiming peace and good will to Men, Emancipating all Nations, you insist upon retaining an absolute power over Wives.   Letter to John Adams (May 7, 1776), op. cit.

17 . . . we have it in our power not only to free ourselves but to subdue our Masters, and without voilence [sic] throw both your natural and legal authority at our feet. . . .   Ibid.

592.   Sophie Arnould
(1744–1802)

1 We shall be rich as princes. A good fairy has given me a talisman to transform every thing into gold and diamonds at the sound of my voice.   Quoted in *Queens of Song* by Ellen Creathorne Clayton   1865

2 To go to the Opera is to go to the devil; but what matter? It is my destiny.   Ibid.

3 Oh! that was the good time; I was very unhappy. (*Oh! c'était le bon temps; j'étais bien malheureuse.*)   Remark to Claude-Carlomande Rulhière,* *Sophie Arnould; d'après sa correspondance et ses mémoires inédits*, Edmond and Jules de Goncourt, eds.   1884

*French writer and historian (1734–1791).

593. Sarah Bache
(1744–1808)

1 The subject now is Stamp Act, and nothing else is talked of. The Dutch talk of the "Stamp tack," the negroes of the "tamp"—in short, every body has something to say.
Letter to Benjamin Franklin, her
father (c.November 1764),
Quoted in *The Women of the
American Revolution*
by Elizabeth F. Ellet   1848

2 I send you the newspapers; but . . . they do not always speak true. . . .
Letter to Benjamin Franklin
(February 23, 1777),
from Goshen,
op. cit.

3 My spirits, which I have kept up during my being drove about from place to place, much better than most people's I meet with, have been lowered by nothing but the depreciation of the money. . . . It is indeed, as you say, that money is too cheap; for there are so many people that are not used to have it, nor know the proper use of it, that get so much, that they care not whether they give one dollar or a hundred for any thing they want; but to those whose every dollar is the same as a silver one, which is our case, it is particularly hard. . . .
Letter to Benjamin Franklin
(September 4, 1779),
op. cit.

4 When Betsy [her daughter] looks at your picture here, she wishes her grandpapa had teeth, that he might be able to talk to her; and she has frequently tried to tempt you to walk out of the frame with a piece of apple pie, the thing of all others she likes best.
Letter to Benjamin Franklin
(n.d.),
op. cit.

5 In this country there is no rank but rank mutton.   Note to an Englishwoman who ran a school for girls where her daughters attended,
op. cit.

594. Elizabeth Martin
(c.1745–post-1776)

1 Go, boys; fight for your country! fight till death, if you must, but never let your country be dishonored. Were I a man I would go with you.   Remark to her seven sons at
the call to arms,
Quoted in *The Women of the
American Revolution*
by Elizabeth F. Ellet   1848

2 I wish I had fifty.   Reply to a British officer's query regarding her sons
in arms,
op. cit.

3 He could not have died in a nobler cause!
Response to a British officer's
report that he saw her husband's
"brains blown out on the field of
battle,"
op. cit.

595. Hannah More
(1745–1833)

1 I shall have nothing to do but go to Bath and drink like a fish.
Letter to David Garrick,*
Quoted in *Garrick
Correspondence*,
Vol. II   1778
*English actor and theater manager (1717–1779).

2 . . . dost thou know
The cruel tyranny of tenderness?
Percy   1778

3 Honor! O yes, I know him. 'Tis a phantom,
A shadowy figure, wanting bulk and life,
Who, having nothing solid in himself,
Wraps his thin form in Virtue's plundered robe,
And steals her title.   *The Fatal
Falsehood*   1779

4 In grief we know the worst of what we feel,
But who can tell the end of what we fear?
Ibid., Act IV

5   The keen spirit

Ceases* the prompt occasion,—makes the
    thought
Start into instant action, and at once
Plans and performs, resolves and executes!
                        Daniel   1782

*Seizes.

6 Hast thou then liv'd in courts? Hast thou
    grown grey
Beneath the mask a subtle statesman wears
To hide his secret soul, and dost not know
That of all fickle fortune's transient gifts,
Favour is most deceitful?   Ibid., Pt. I

7 No trifle is so small as what obtains,
Save that which loses favour; 'its a breath
Which hangs upon a smile! a look, a word,
A frown, the air-built tower of fortune
    shakes,
And down the unsubstantial fabric falls.
                                    Ibid.

8 All human projects are so faintly fram'd,
So feebly plann'd, so liable to change,
So mix'd with error in their very form,
That mutable and mortal are the same.
                                    Ibid.

9 I've scann'd the actions of his daily life
With all th' industrious malice of a foe;
And nothing meets mine eye but deeds of
    honour.   Ibid.

10   A crown! what is it?
Is it to bear the miseries of a people!
To hear their murmurs, feel their discon-
    tents,
And sink beneath a load of splendid care!
To have your best success ascribed to for-
    tune,
And fortune's failures all ascribed to you!
It is to sit upon a joyless height,
To ev'ry blast of changing fate expos'd!
Too high for hope! too great for happiness.
                                Ibid., Pt. VI

11 No adulation; 'tis the death of virtue;
Who flatters, is of all mankind the lowest
Save he who courts the flattery.
                                    Ibid.

12 Since, how e'er protracted, death will come,
Why fondly study with ingenius pains
To put it off!—To breathe a little longer

Is to defer our fate, but not to shun it.
Small gain! which wisdom with indiff'rent
    eye
Beholds.   *David and Goliath*   1782

13   O jealousy,
That ugliest fiend of hell! thy healthful
    venom
Preys on my vitals, turns the deadly hue
Of my fresh cheek to haggard sallowness,
And drinks my spirit up!   Ibid., Pt. V

14   O war!—what, what art thou?
At once the proof and scorge of man's fall'n
    state!
After the brightest conquest, what appears
Of all thy glories? for the vanquish'd chains!
For the proud victors, what? alas! to reign
O'er desolated nations!   Ibid.

15   O sad estate
Of human wretchedness! so weak is man,
So ignorant and blind, that did not God
Sometimes withhold in mercy what we ask,
We should be ruin'd at our own request.
                        Moses in the Bulrushes,
                                Pt. 1   1782

16 Accept my thoughts for thanks; I have no
    words.   Ibid.

17 Books, the Mind's food, not exercise!
                        "Conversation,"
                        St. 1, *The Bas Bleu*
                        [The Blue Stocking]
                                1784

18 In taste, in learning, wit, or science,
Still kindled souls demand alliance
                                Ibid., St. 2

19 But sparks electric only strike
On souls electrical alike   Ibid.

20 The flash of Intellect expires,
Unless it meet congenial fires
                                    Ibid.

21 And ancient Wit elicits new.
                            Ibid., last line

22 He liked those literary cooks
Who skim the cream of others' books;
And ruin half an author's graces

By plucking *bon-mots* from their places.
Florio 1786

23 Small habits well pursued betimes
May reach the dignity of crime.
Ibid.

24 Of other tyrants short the strife,
But Indolence is King for life.
Ibid.

25 And Pleasure was so coy a prude,
She fled the more, the more pursued. . . .
Ibid.

26 He thought the world to him was known,
Whereas he only knew the *town*.
In men this blunder still you find:
All think their little set—mankind.
Ibid.

27 What lively pleasure to divine
The thought imposed, the printed line!
To feel allusion's artful force,
And trace the image to its source!
Ibid., "Bas Bleu"

28 For you'll ne'er mend your fortunes, nor
help the just cause,
By breaking of windows, or breaking of
laws.   Address at Spa Fields (1817),
Quoted in *The Life of Hannah More*
by H. Thompson 1838

29 I never afford a moment of a healthy day to
cross a *t* or dot an *i*; so that I find the lowest
stage of my understanding may be turned to
some account, and save better days for better things. I have learned also to avoid procrastination, and that idleness which often
attends unbroken health.   Quoted in
Lives of Celebrated Women
by Samuel Griswold Goodrich
1844

30 I have naturally but a small appetite for
grandeur, which is always satisfied, even to
indigestion, before I leave town; and I require a long abstinence to get any relish for
it again.   Ibid.

31 If effect be the best proof of eloquence, then
mine was a good speech. . . .
Ibid.

32 'Tis well—my soul shakes off its load of
care;
'Tis only the obscure is terrible.
Imagination frames events unknown,
In wild fantastic shapes of hideous ruin;
And what it fears creates!
"Belshazzar,"
The Complete Works of Hannah More
1856

33 Fell luxury! more perilous to youth
Then storms or quicksands, poverty or
chains.   Ibid.

34 Yes, thou art ever present, Power Supreme!
Not circumscrib'd by time, nor fixt to
space,
Confin'd to altars, nor to temples bound.
In wealth, in want, in freedom, or in chains,
In dungeons, or on thrones, the faithful find
Thee!   Ibid.

35 While desolation, snatching from the hand
Of time the scythe of ruin, sits aloft,
Or stalks in dreadful majesty abroad.
Ibid.

36 The roses of pleasure seldom last long
enough to adorn the brow of him who
plucks them; for they are the only roses
which do not retain their sweetness after
they have lost their beauty.
"On Dissipation,"
Essays on Various Subjects,
op. cit.

37 That silence is one of the great arts of conversation is allowed by Cicero himself, who
says, there is not only an art, but even an
eloquence in it.   "Thoughts on
Conversation,"
Essays on Various Subjects,
op. cit.

38 If a young lady has that discretion and
modesty, without which all knowledge is
little worth, she will never make an ostenta-
tious parade of it, because she will rather be
intent on acquiring more, than on displaying what she has.   Ibid.

39 To those who know thee not, no words can
paint;

And those who know thee know all words
    are faint.   "Sensibility"
                            Poems,
                            op. cit.

40 Subduing and subdued, the petty strife,
   Which clouds the colour of domestic life;
   The sober comfort, all the peace which
      springs
   From the large aggregate of little things;
   On these small cares of daughter, wife or
      friend,
   The almost sacred joys of home depend.
                             Ibid.

41 Prompt sense of equity! To thee belongs
   The swift redress of unexamined wrongs!
   Eager to serve, the cause perhaps untried,
   But always apt to choose the suffering side!
                             Ibid.

42 Since trifles make the sum of human things,
   And half our misery from our foibles
      spring.   Ibid.

43 If faith produce no works, I see
   That faith is not a living tree.
   Thus faith and works together grow;
   No separate life they e'er can know:
   They're soul and body, hand and heart:
   What God hath joined, let no man part.
                    "Dan and Jane,"
                          op. cit.

44 How short is human life! the very breath
   Which frames my words accelerates my
      death.   "King Hezekiah,"
                          op. cit.

45 O! let th' ungentle spirit learn from hence,
   A small unkindness is a great offence.
   To spread large bounties though we wish in
      vain
   Yet all may shun the guilt of giving pain.
                             Ibid.

46 O thou sad spirit, whose preposterous yoke
   The great deliverer, death, at length has
      broke!
   Release from misery, and escaped from
      care,

Go, meet that mercy man denies thee here.
                          "Slavery,"
                           Poems,
                           op. cit.

596. Stephanie Félicité Genlis
(1746–1830)

1 For which reason, you may observe that the
man whose probity consists in merely obeying the laws, cannot be truly virtuous or estimable; for he will find many opportunities
of doing contemptible and even dishonest
acts, which the laws cannot punish.
                             "Laws,"
                  Tales of the Castle
                           c.1793

2 Hence it is that men act ill, and judge well.
Feeble and corrupted, they give way to
their passions; but when they are cool—
that is to say, when they are uninterested—
they instantly condemn what they have
often been guilty of; they revolt against every thing that is contemptible; they admire
every thing generous, and they are moved
at every thing affecting.   "Virtue,"
                           op. cit.

3 Can any one be a connoisseur in music,
without knowledge of the science?
No; it is absolutely impossible.
                          "Music,"
                           op. cit.

4 And what do people gain, who wish to seem
learned in things they know nothing about?
They impose on nobody, they talk nonsensically, they judge without taste, they are
accused of pedantry by the ignorant, of
folly by the well-informed, and they are
tiresome and disagreeable to both.
                             Ibid.

5 "A philosopher, desirous of praising a princess, who has been dead these fifty years,
could not accomplish his purpose but at the
expense of all the princesses, and all the
women, who have ever existed or do exist;
and that in a single phrase."
"He has been very laconic indeed."

"You shall hear—*Though a woman and a princess*, said he, *she loved learning!*"
"The orator ought to have been answered, that *though a philosopher*, and an academician, he did not, on this occasion, show either much politeness or equity."

"The Two Reputations," op. cit.

6 "He was absent, no doubt; mathematicians are subject to be so, and we might well advise them to calculate more and write less."

Ibid.

7 " . . . do not you think . . . that there never was a less gallant age than the present?"
"This is a sign greatly in your favour; for it proves there is a real competition for superiority between men and women."

Ibid.

8 They [books] support us in solitude. . . . They help us to forget the coarseness of men and things, compose our cares and our passions, and lay our disappointments to sleep.   *Mémoires*   c.1826

597.   Esther De Berdt Reed
(1746–1780)

1 . . . if these great affairs must be brought to a crisis and decided, it had better be in our time than our children's. Letter to Dennis De Berdt, her brother (1775), Quoted in *The Life of Esther De Berdt, Afterwards Esther Reed* by William B. Reed   1853

598.   Frederica de Riedesel
(1746–1808)

1 Britons never retrograde.   Quoted in *The Women of the American Revolution*, Vol. II, by Elizabeth F. Ellet   1848

2 The incessant cannonade during the solemnity; the steady attitude and unaltered voice with which the chaplain officiated, though frequently covered with dust which the shot threw up on all sides of him; the mute but expressive mixture of sensibility and indignation upon every countenance; these objects will remain to the last of life upon the mind of every man who was present.*

Ibid.

*The burial of General Frazer just after the Battle of Saratoga.

3 The want of water continuing to distress us, we could not but be extremely glad to find a soldier's wife so spirited as to fetch some from the river, an occupation from which the boldest might have shrunk, as the Americans shot every one who approached it. They told us afterwards that they spared her on account of her sex.

Ibid.

4 I . . . while driving through the American camp, was gratified to observe that nobody looked at us with disrespect; but on the contrary, greeted us, and seemed touched at the sight of a captive mother with three children.   Ibid.

5 Seizing some maize, I begged our hostess to give me some of it to make a little bread. She replied that she needed it for her black people. "They work for us," she added, "and you come to kill us."

Ibid.

6 The loyalists received us with frank hospitality, from political sympathy; and those of opposite principles gave us a friendly welcome, merely from habit; for in that country it would be considered a crime to behave otherwise towards strangers.

Ibid.

7 It is astonishing how much the frail human creature can endure. . . . *

Ibid.

*Referring to the breakout of a malignant fever in New York in 1780.

599. Susanna Blamire
(1747–1794)

1 And ye shall walk in silk attire,
And siller* ha'e to spare.   "The Siller
Crown,"
*The Poetical Works of Miss
Susanna Blamire, the Muse of
Cumberland*   1842

*Scottish for "silver."

2 When silent time, wi' lightly foot,
Had trod on thirty years,
I sought again my native land
Wi' mony hopes and fears.
"The Nabob,"
St. 1, op. cit.

3 Till soft remembrance threw a veil
Across these een o' mine,
I closed the door, and sobbed aloud,
To think on aul langsyne!
Ibid., St. 4

4 Ye sons to comrades o' my youth,
Forgie an auld man's spleen,
Wha 'midst your gayest scenes still mourns
The days he ance has seen.
When time has passed and seasons fled,
Your hearts will feel like mine;
And aye the sang will maist delight
That minds ye o' langsyne!
Ibid., St. 8

5 I come, I come, my Jamie dear;
And O! wi' what good will
I follow wheresoe'er ye lead!
Ye canna lead to ill. "The Waefu' Heart,"
St. 5, op. cit.

6 Of aw things that is I think thout* is meast
queer,
It brings that that's by-past and sets it down
here.   "Auld Robin Forbes,"
St. 1, op. cit.

*Thought.

7 When the clock had struck eight I expected
him heame,
And wheyles went to meet him as far as
Dumleane;
Of aw hours it telt, eight was dearest to me,

But now when it streykes there's a tear i'
my ee.   Ibid., St. 4

600. Anna Gordon Brown
(1747–1810)

1 O first he sange a merry song,
An then he sang a grave,
An then he peckd his feathers gray,
To her the letter gave.   "The Gay
Goshawk," St. 10,
The English and Scottish Popular Ballads,
Francis James Child, ed.
1898

2 "He, there's a letter frae your love,
He says he sent you three;
He canna wait your love langer,
But for your sake he'll die."
Ibid., St. 11

601. Marie Letitia Bonaparte
(1748–1836)

1 Napoleon has never given me a moment's
pain, not even at the time which is almost
universally woman's hour of suffering.*
Quoted in *Biography of
Distinguished Women*
by Sarah Josepha Hale   1876

*Reference to birth of her son, Napoleon Bonaparte
(1769–1821).

602. Gertrude Elizabeth Mara
(1749–1833)

1 . . . how can you best convey a just notion
of slight variations in the pitch of a note—
by a fixed instrument? No. By the voice?
No. But by sliding the finger up the string
[of a violin] you instantly make the most
minute variations visibly as well as audibly
perceptible.   Quoted in *Queens of Song*
by Ellen Creathorne Clayton
1865

2 When I give a lesson in singing, I sing with my scholars; by so doing they learn in half the time they can if taught in the usual way—by the master merely playing the tune of the song on the piano. People can not teach what they don't know—my scholars have my singing to imitate—those of other masters seldom any thing but the tinkling of a piano. Ibid.

603.　Charlotte Smith
(1749–1806)

1 Queen of the silver bow! "To the Moon,"
　　Elegiac Sonnets and Other
　　　　　　　Essays　1782

2 Sweet poet of the woods. . . .
　　　　"The Departure of the
　　　　　　　Nightingale,"
　　　　　　　op. cit.

3 The gentle bird, who sings of pity best
　　　　　　　Ibid.

4 Another May new buds and flowers shall bring;
Ah! why has happiness—no second Spring?
　　　　"The Close of Spring,"
　　　　　　　op. cit.

5 Though no repose on thy dark breast I find,
I still enjoy thee, cheerless as thou art;
For in thy quiet gloom th' exhausted heart
Is calm, though wretched; hopeless, yet resigned　　　"To Night,"
　　　　　　　op. cit.

6 I sure shall find thee in that heavenly scene
Where care and anguish shall their power resign;
Where hope alike and vain regret shall cease;
And Memory, lost in happiness serene,
Repeat no more—that misery has been mine!　　　"To Tranquillity,"
　　　　　　　op. cit.

7 The cottage garden; most for use designed,

Yet not of beauty destitute
　　　　"English Scenery
　　　　(from Beachy Head),"
　　　　　　　St. 3, op. cit.

8 An early worshipper at Nature's shrine,
I loved her rudest scenes—warrens, and heaths,
And yellow commons, and birch-shaded hollows,
And hedgerows bordering unfrequented lanes,
Bowered with wild roses and the clasping woodbine.　　　Ibid.

9 "Then, jealous Nature, yield the palm to me,
To me thy pride its early triumph owes;
Though *thy* rude workmanship produced the tree,
'Twas *Education* formed the perfect Rose."
　　　　"The Hot-House Rose,"
　　　　　　　St. 7, op. cit.

10 O herald of approaching spring,
Shalt to the pensive wand'rer sing
Thy song of Hope and Fortitude!
　　　　"Ode to the Missel Thrush,"
　　　　　　　St. 6, op. cit.

11 Little inmate, full of mirth,
Chirping on my humble hearth
　　　　　　　"The Cricket,"
　　　　　　　St. 1, op. cit.

12 O happy age! when Hope's unclouded ray
Lights their green path, and prompts their simple mirth,
Ere yet they feel the thorns that lurking lay
To wound the wretched pilgrims of the earth,
Making them rue the hour that gave them birth　　　Untitled, op. cit.

13 The brilliant Glow-worm, like a meteor. . . .　　　"The Glow-worm,"
　　　　　　　op. cit.

14 [He] dreams that fairy lamps illume his bower;
Yet with the morning shudders to behold
His lucid treasure, rayless as the dust:—
So turn the World's bright joys to cold and blank disgust.　　　Ibid.

15 And weary Hope reclines upon the tomb,
And points my wishes to that tranquil
    shore,
Where the pale spectre Care pursues no
    more.   Untitled sonnet, op. cit.

16 Come, summer visitant, attach
To my reed roof your nest of clay,
And let me ear your music catch,
Low twittering underneath the thatch
At the grey dawn of day.
                          "The First Swallow,"
                                    op. cit.

17 But Reason comes at—Thirty-eight.
                          "Thirty-Eight,"
                          St. 4, op. cit.

18 Stripp'd of their gaudy hues by Truth,
We view the glitt'ring toys of youth. . . .
                          Ibid., St. 7

19 With eye more steady we engage
To contemplate approaching age,
And life more justly estimate;
With firmer souls, and stronger powers,
With reason, faith, and friendship ours,
We'll not regret the stealing hours
That lead from Thirty—even to Forty-
    eight.   Ibid., St. 9

20   Thy prospect fair,
Thy sounds of harmony, thy balmy air,
Have power to cure all sadness—but de-
    spair.   "To Spring,"
                          op. cit.

21 Come balmy Sleep! tired nature's soft re-
    sort,
On these sad temples all thy poppies shed;
And bid gay dreams, from Morpheus' airy
    court,
Float in light vision round my aching head!
                          "To Sleep,"
                                    op. cit.

22 And the poor sea boy, in the rudest hour,
Enjoys thee more than he who wears a
    crown.   Ibid.

23 But still thy opiate aid dost thou deny
To calm the anxious breast; to close the
streaming eye.   Ibid.

24 Swift fleet the billowy clouds along the sky,

Earth seems to shudder at the storm aghast;
While only beings as forlorn as I,
Court the chill horrors of the howling blast.
                          "Montalbert,"
                                    op. cit.

25 . . . the moon, mute arbitress of tides
          "Sonnet Written in the Church-
          Yard at Middleton, in Sussex,"
                                    op. cit.

26 The foolish vanity, whence originates so
many strategems. . . .   *Desmond*,
                    Vol. I, Ch. 5   1792

27 He was stretched upon a sopha—with boots
on—a terrier lay on one side of him, and he
occasionally embraced a large hound,
which licked his face and hands, while he
thus addressed it.—"Oh! thou dear
bitchy—thou beautiful bitchy—damme, if I
don't love thee better than my mother or
my sisters."   Ibid.

28 " . . . they [the revolutionists] have made
Paris so insupportable to people of fashion,
that it must, of course, become a mere de-
sart.—Nobody of any elegance of manners
can exist, where tradesmen, attornies, and
mechanics have the *pas*.—The splendour of
that beautiful capital is gone: the glory of
the *noblesse* is vanished for ever."
                                    Ibid.

29 "I am glad that oppression is destroyed;
that the power of injuring the many is taken
from the few. . . . — That these powers are
annihilated, no generous mind can surely
lament."   Ibid.

30 "Our [English] nobility . . . are armed with
no powers to oppress, individually, the inferior order of men; they have no vassals
but those whose service is voluntary; and,
upon the whole, are so different a body of
men from that which was once the nobility
of France, as to admit no very just comparison. . . . "   Ibid.

31 "... if all those who are now raised above us by their names, were to have no other distinction than their merits.—Let me ask you, would the really great, the truly noble among them (and that there are many such nobody is more ready to allow) be less beloved and revered if they were known only by their family names?"

Ibid.

32 "'Tis an uneasy thing," said he, "a very uneasy thing, for a man of probity and principles to look in these days into a newspaper."
Ibid., Ch. 6

33 "My dear Bethel, why should we call folly that which bestows such happiness, since, after all our wisdom, our felicity depends merely on the imagination?"

Ibid.

34 Montfleuri ... said ... "when I meet, as too often I have done, Englishmen of mature judgment and solid abilities, so lost to all right principles as to depreciate, misrepresent, and condemn those exertions by which *we* [the French] have obtained that liberty they affect so sedulously to defend for themselves ... and pretend to blame *us* for throwing off those yokes, which would be intolerable to themselves, and which they have been accustomed to ridicule us for enduring: I even hear them with a mixture of contempt and indignation, and reflect with concern on the power of national prejudice and national jealousy, to darken and pervert the understanding."

Ibid., Ch. 9

35 "He [Henry IV of England] had not been taught, that to be born a king is to be born something more than man."

Ibid.

36 I, who love, you know, every thing ancient, unless it be ancient prejudices....

Ibid., Ch. 10

37 When the imagination soars into those regions, where the planets pursue each its destined course, in the immensity of space—every planet, probably, containing creatures adapted by the Almighty, to the residence he has placed them in; and when we reflect, that the smallest of these is of as much consequence in the universe, as this world of our's; how puerile and ridiculous do those pursuits appear in which we are so anxiously busied; and how insignificant the trifles we toil to obtain, or fear to lose.

Ibid., Ch. 12

38 National hatred, that strange and ridiculous prejudice....
Ibid., Ch. 13

39 "Mr. Verney, you know, is no politician, or if he were, he would hardly deign to converse on that topic with a woman—for of the understandings of all women he has the most contemptible opinion; and says, 'that we are good for nothing but to make a shew while we are young, and to become nurses when we are old.'—I know that more than half the men in the world are of his opinion; and that by them, what some celebrated author has said, is generally allowed to be true—that a woman even of talents is only considered by man with that sort of pleasure with which they contemplate a bird who speaks a few words plainly—I believe it is not exactly the expression, but, however, it is the sense of it; and, I am afraid, is the general sense of the world."

Ibid., Vol. II, Ch. 5

40 Alas! my friend, there appears to be a strange propensity in human nature to torment itself, and as if the physical inconveniencies with which we are surrounded in this world of ours were not enough, we go forth constantly in search of mental and imaginary evils—This is no where so remarkable as among those who are in what we call affluence and prosperity....

Ibid.

41 The awe that the superiority of riches creates, represses the malignity that envy engenders, though with so much difficulty represses it, that it is every moment obliquely appearing. . . .   Ibid., Ch. 9

42 If government be allowed to be for the benefit of the governed, not the governors, surely these complaints should be heard.
                                                    Ibid., Ch. 10

43 In our daily prints, this shocking inequality is not less striking—In one paragraph, we are regaled with an eulogium on the innumerable blessings, the abundant prosperity of our country; in the next, we read the melancholy and mortifying list of numberless unhappy debtors, who, in vain, solicit, from time to time, the mercy of the legislature, and who are left by the powers who *can* relieve them, to linger out their unprofitable lives, and to perish, through penury and disease, in the most loathsome confinements. . . .   Ibid.

44 Were there, indeed, a sure appeal to the mercies of the rich, the calamities of the poor might be less intolerable; but it is too certain, that high affluence and prosperity have a direct tendency to harden the temper.   Ibid.

45 When a man knows, my dear Bethel, that he is acting like a fool, the most usual way is to keep it to himself, and to endeavour to persuade the world that he is actually performing the part of a wise man. . . .
                                                    Ibid., Ch. 16

46 I find, that seven-and-twenty is not the age of reason. . . .   Ibid.

47 "If I had my health . . . I would request his company to the tenant's feast at my own table, and show him, if he is too young a man to remember, what an old English table was when we were too wise to run after foreign gewgaws, and were content with the best of everything, dressed in the English fashion by English people."
                    The Old Manor House   1793

48 . . . a dignified clergyman, of profound erudition, very severe morals, and very formal manners; who was the most orthodox of men, never spoke but in sentences equally learned and indisputable, and held almost all the rest of the world in as low estimation as he considered highly his own family, and, above all, himself.   Ibid.

49 Possessing something of each of their personal perfections, she was considered by her parents a model of loveliness; and her mind was adorned with all money could purchase.   Ibid.

50 Having never heard anything but her own praises, she really believed herself a miracle of knowledge and accomplishments. . . .
                                                    Ibid.

51 Nature appeared to pause, and to ask the turbulent and troubled heart of man whether his silly pursuits were worth the toil he undertook for them?
                                                    Ibid.

52 The great object of Mrs. Winslow's life had been to be accounted a woman of most elegant taste, and the word elegant was incessantly uttered on all the opinions she held, and in all the decisions she gave.
                    The Young Philosopher,
                    Vol. I, Ch. 1   1798

53 The masters of a great school are apt to shew that pupils connected with title and fortune have a more than ordinary share of their regard; yet among boys of the same age there is always established a certain degree of equality. . . .   Ibid., Ch. 3

54 . . . the wantoness of tyranny, that induces men to exercise power merely because they have it. . . .   Ibid.

55 "If my family are ashamed of me, they have only to leave me out of their genealogical table, as an unworthy branch of the tree, bent towards its native earth, and no longer contributing to their splendid insignificance."   Ibid., Ch. 4

56 . . . he had now for some months established his own liberty . . . making it the rule of his life, as well in trivial as on material occasions, never to trench upon the liberty of others, while he guarded against being cheated out of his own. . . .
                 Ibid., Ch. 6

57 "And let me tell you, Mrs. Winslow," said the Doctor, "that you are too apt to fall into these fits of admiration."   Ibid., Ch. 7

58 In proportion as her prejudices were violent, her arguments were weak.
                 Ibid., Ch. 9

59 " . . . really one is quite bored by being obliged to listen for ever to the same set of notions. I . . . should doat excessively upon a dear creature who could amuse one by starting something new."   Ibid., Ch. 10

60 "True," answered Armitage; "there is nothing absurd in loving merit under whatever form, or at whatever age it is found."
                 Ibid., Ch. 12

61 "You can't think how frightful the stories [Gothic novels] are—all about tapestry waving in the wind, a bloody dagger, and voices calling at midnight, howlings in the air, and dark passages, and coffins full of bones, and poor young ladies got among these alarming objects; quite shocking, I'll assure you."
     "Cursed fee fa fum nonsense," cried Malloch, "I heard a very good judge of them there things say so."   Ibid., Vol. II, Ch. 2

62 "These presentiments of evil are often the causes that evil really arrives. . . . "
                 Ibid., Ch. 5

63 "Youth, even when deprived of all viable support—makes a long and often a successful stand against calamity."
                 Ibid., Ch. 6

64 "Traits of disinterestedness and high-minded generosity are those that to the greater part of mankind appear the strangest, because such they are incapable of imitating or comprehending. . . .
                 Ibid., Ch. 12

604.   Anne Barnard
(1750–1825)

1 When the sheep are in the fauld, and a' the kye at hame,
And all the weary world to sleep are gane.
         "Auld Robin Gray"   1771

2 The waes o' my heart fa' in showers frae my e'e,
While my gudeman lies sound by me.
                 Ibid.

3 My father couldna work, and my mother couldna spin;
I toiled day and night, but their bread I couldna win.   Ibid.

4 My father urged me sair—my mother didna speak,
But she looket in my face till my heart was like to break.   Ibid.

5 They gied him my hand, tho' my heart was at sea.   Ibid.

605.   Sophia Burrell
(1750?–1802)

1 Blindfold I should to Myra run,
And swear to love her ever;
Yet when the bandage was undone,
Should only think her clever.

With the full usage of my eyes,
I Chloe should decide for;
But when she talks, I *her* despise,
Whom, dumb, I could have died for!
            "Chloe and Myra,"
                 Sts. 4, 5,
                 Poems
                 1793

2 Cupid and you, 'it is said, are cousins,
(*Au fait** in stealing hearts by dozens,)
                 "To Emma,"
                 op. cit.

*Proficient.

3 And should you be arraign'd in court
For practising this cruel sport,
In spite of all the plaintiff's fury

Your smile would bribe both judge and jury.   *Ibid.*

606.   Madame du Hausset
(fl. 1750–1764)

1 Great people have the bad habit of talking very indiscreetly before their servants.
The Memoirs of Louis XV, and of Madame de Pompadour*
by Mme. du Hausset
(1802)   1910 ed.
*Jeanne Poisson Pompadour. See 534.

2 See what the Court is; all is corruption there, from the highest to the lowest.
Remark to Mme. de Pompadour, op. cit.

607.   Caroline Lucretia Herschel
(1750–1848)

1 Many a half or whole holiday he* was allowed to spend with me was dedicated to making experiments in chemistry, where generally all boxes, tops of tea-canisters, pepper-boxes, teacups, etc., served for the necessary vessels and the sand-tub furnished the matter to be analyzed. I only had to take care to exclude water, which would have produced havoc on my carpet.
Memoir and Correspondence of Caroline Herschel,
Mrs. John Herschel, ed.   1876
*Her nephew, the astronomer Sir John Frederick Herschel (1792-1871).

2 I am now so enured to receiving honours in my old age, that I take them all upon me without blushing.   *Ibid.*

608.   Mary Jones
(fl. 1750)

1 How much of paper's spoil'd! what floods of ink!

And yet how few, how very few, can think!
I. "Extract from an Epistle to Lady Bowyer," St. 1,
Miscellanies in Prose and Verse
1750

2 What's fame to me, who pray and pay my rent?
If my friends know me honest, I'm content.
Ibid., St. 2

3 For what is beauty but a sign?
A face hung out, through which is seen
The nature of the goods within.
II. "To Stella, after the Small-Pox," St. 1, op. cit.

609.   Judith Madan
(fl. 1750)

1 Doubt not to reap, if thou canst bear to plough. "Verses. Written in her brother's Coke upon Littleton,"*
The Female Poets of Great Britain,
Frederic Rowton, ed.   1853
*I.e., a copy of the commentary by the English jurist Sir Edward Coke on the *Tenures* of Sir Thomas Littleton.

610.   Elizabeth Peabody
(1750–?)

1 Lost to virtue, lost to humanity must that person be, who can view without emotion the complicated distress of this injured land. Evil tidings molest our habitations, and wound our peace. Oh, my brother! oppression is enough to make a wise people mad.
Letter to John Adams, her brother-in-law,
Quoted in *The Women of the American Revolution,*
Vol. II, by Elizabeth F. Ellet
1848

611. Caroline Matilda
(1751–1775)

1 O God, keep me innocent; make others great! *Scratched with a diamond on a window of the castle of Frederiksborg, Denmark, n.d.*

612. Jeanne Isabelle Montolieu
(1751–1832)

1 Here lies the child [Voltaire] spoiled by the world which he spoiled. (*Ci gît l'enfant gâté due monde qu'il gâta.*) "Epitaph on Voltaire," n.d.

613. Judith Sargent Murray
(1751–1820)

1 To the absorbing grave I must resign,
All of my first born child that e'er was mine!
"Lines, Occasioned by the Death of an Infant," St. 4,
The Massachusetts Magazine
January 1790

2 Will it be said that the judgment of a male two years old, is more sage than that of a female's of the same age? I believe the reverse is generally observed to be true. But from that period what partiality! how is the one exalted and the other depressed, by the contrary modes of education which are adopted! the one is taught to aspire, and the other is early confined and limited.
"On the Equality of the Sexes,"
The Massachusetts Magazine
March and April 1790

3 . . . every requisite in female economy is easily attained; and, with truth I can add, that when once attained, they require no further *mental attention*. Nay, while we are pursuing the needle, or the superintendency of the family, I repeat, that our minds are at full liberty for reflection; that imagination may exert itself in full vigour; and that if a just foundation early laid, our ideas will then be worthy of rational beings.
Ibid.

4 I know there are those who assert, that as the animal powers of the one sex are superiour, of course their mental faculties also must be stronger; thus attributing strength of mind to the transient organization of this earth born tenement. But if this reasoning is just, man must be content to yield the palm to many of the brute creation. . . .
Ibid.

5 And few there are who that observance pay,
Which truth in honest colors can display.
"Lines to Philenia,"*
St. 2,
The Massachusetts Magazine
April 1790
*Sarah Wentworth Morton. See 644.

6 The multitude but on the surface glide.
Ibid.

7 But that a female note should dare to swell,
To point at pedants, and our follies tell,
Must surely startle male prerogative.
"Valedictory Epilogue to 'Who's the Dupe,' A Farce Which is the Production of the Elegant Pen of Mrs. Cowley* . . . Written by Constantia, in the Spring of 1790, and Spoken by Mr. Allen,"
St. 4,
The Massachusetts Magazine
May 1791
*Hannah Cowley. See 589:1–12.

8 I would be Cesar, or I would be nothing.
The Gleaner,
Vol. I 1798

9 Religion is 'twixt God and my own soul,
Nor saint, nor sage, can boundless thought control. "Lines Prefacing Essay No. XIX. A Sketch of the Gleaner's Religious Sentiment,"
op. cit.

10 I may be accused of enthusiasm, but such is my confidence in the sex, that I expect to see our young women forming a new era in female history. Vol. III, op. cit.

11 Were I at liberty my plans to choose,
My politics, my fashions, and my muse

Should be American. . . . "Lines Prefacing Essay No. XCVI. A Spirit of National Independence Recommended," op. cit.

614.   Ann Eliza Bleecker
(1752–1783)

1 New worlds to find, new systems to explore:
When these appear'd, again I'd urge my flight
Till all creation open'd to my sight.
"On the Immensity of Creation,"
St. 1 (1773), Tomhanick,
The Posthumous Works of Ann Eliza Bleecker, in Prose and Verse,
Margaretta Faugeres, ed.
1793

2 Man how contemptible thou dost appear!
What art thou in this scene?—Alas! no more
Than a small atom to the sandy shore,
A drop of water to a boundless sea,
A single moment to eternity.
Ibid., St. 3

3 The idol of my soul was torn away;
Her spirit fled and left me ghastly clay!
"Written in the Retreat From [John] Burgoyne,"*
St. 3 (October 29, 1777), op. cit.
*British general who surrendered at Saratoga.

4 Then—then my soul rejected all relief,
Comfort I wish'd not for, I lov'd my grief
Ibid., St. 4

5 Nor shall the mollifying hand of time,
Which wipes off common sorrows, cancel mine.   Ibid., St. 5

6 My gods took care of me—not I of them!
"On Reading Dryden's Virgil"
(1778), op. cit.

7 What art thou now, my love!—a few dry bones,

Unconscious of my unavailing moans
"Recollection,"
St. 2 (February 10, 1778),
Tomhanick, op. cit.

8 (Noise ever was an enemy to song.)
"To Miss M. V. W.,"*
St. 1 (January 1780), Tomhanick,
op. cit.
*Margaret Van Wyck, her cousin.

9 But think not I dislike my situation here; on the contrary, I am charmed with the lovely scene the spring opens around me. Alas! the wilderness is within: I muse so long on the dead until I am unfit for the company of the living.   Letter (April 8, 1780), op. cit.

10 . . . Oh leave the city's noxious air.
"To the Same,"
St. 1, op. cit.

11 Plenty sits laughing in each humble cot
Ibid., St. 2

12 Yet soon fair Spring shall give another scene,
And yellow cowslips gild the level green.
"Return to Tomhanick,"
St. 2, op. cit.

13 You've broke th' agreement, Sir, I find;
(Excuse me, I must speak my mind)
It seems in your poetic fit
You mind not jingling, where there's wit
"To Mr. L****,"
op. cit.

14 Indeed, it suits, I must aver,
A *genius* to be singular.   Ibid.

15 Narcissus (as *Ovid* informs us) expir'd,
Consum'd by the flames his own beauty had fir'd "On a great *Coxcomb* recovering from an Indisposition,"
op. cit.

16 Oh! was I but some plant or star,
I might obey him too;
No longer with the Being war,
From whom my breath I drew.
"An Hymn,"
op. cit.

615. Fanny Burney
(1752–1840)

1 ... it is time that she should see something of the world. When young people are too rigidly sequestered from it, their lively and romantic imaginations paint it to them as a paradise of which they have been beguiled. ...
Evelina,
Letter III
1778

2 These people in high life have too much presence of mind, I believe, to *seem* disconcerted or out of humour, however they may feel. ... Ibid., Letter XI

3 "The difference of natural and artificial colour, seems to me very easily discerned; that of Nature is mottled, and varying; that of art, *set*, and *too* smooth; it wants that animation, that glow, that *indescribable something* which, even now that I see it, wholly surpasses all my powers of expression."
Ibid., Letter XX

4 "Do you come to the play without knowing what it is?" "O, yes, Sir, yes, very frequently. I have no time to read play-bills. One merely comes to meet one's friends, and show that one's alive."
Ibid.

5 "What a jabbering they make!" cried Mr. Braughton; "there's no knowing a word they say. Pray what's the reason they can't as well sing [opera] in English?—but I suppose the fine folks would not like it, if they could understand it." Ibid., Letter XXI

6 It's as like ... as two peas are to one another. Ibid.

7 Nothing is so delicate as the reputation of a woman; it is at once the most beautiful and most brittle of all human things.
Ibid., Letter XXX

8 I'm glad the villain got nothing but his labour for his pains. Ibid., Letter XXXIII

9 It seldom happens that a man, though extolled as a saint, is really without blemish; or that another, though reviled as a devil, is really without humanity. Ibid., Letter XXXV

10 Though gentleness and modesty are the peculiar attributes of your sex, yet fortitude and firmness, when occasion demands them, are virtues as noble and as becoming in women as in men: the right line of conduct is the same for both sexes. ...
Ibid., Letter XLIX

11 Concealment, my dear Maris, is the foe of tranquility. ... Ibid., Letter LX

12 Alas, my child!—that innocence, the first, best gift of heaven, should, of all others, be the blindest to its own danger,—the most exposed to treachery,—and the least able to defend itself, in a world where it is little known, less valued, and perpetually deceived! Ibid., Letter LXVII

13 ... *Imagination* took the reins, and *Reason*, slow-paced, though sure-footed, was unequal to a race with so eccentric and flighty a companion. Ibid.

14 ... but this is not an age in which we may trust to appearances, and imprudence is much sooner regretted than repaired.
Ibid.

15 "If Time thought no more of me, than I do of Time, I believe I should bid defiance, for one while, to old age and wrinkles,—for deuce take me if ever I think about it at all."
Ibid., Letter LXXVII

16 I'd do it as soon as say 'Jack Robinson.'
Ibid., Letter LXXXII

17 "Peace to the spirits of my honoured parents, respected be their remains, and immortalized their virtues! may time, while it moulders their frail relics to dust, commit to tradition the record of their goodness! and, oh, may their orphan descendent be influenced through life by the remembrance of their purity, and in death be solaced, that by her it was unsullied!" *Cecilia,*
Bk. I, Ch. 1
1782

18 So short-sighted is selfish cunning, that in aiming no further than at the gratification of the present moment, it obscures the evils of the future, while it impedes the perception of integrity and honour.
Ibid.

19 The resources of pleasure to the possessors of wealth are only to be cut off by the satiety of which they are productive. . . .
Ibid.

20 "The SUPERCILIOUS . . . and . . . the VULNERABLE . . . this they have in common, that at home they think of nothing but dress, abroad, of nothing but admiration, and at everywhere they hold in supreme contempt all but themselves."
Ibid., Ch. 5

21 "But an old woman . . . is a person who has no sense of decency; if once she takes to living, the devil himself can't get rid of her."
Ibid., Ch. 10

22 "How true is it, yet how consistent . . . that while we all desire to live long, we have all a horror of being old!" *Ibid.*, Bk. II, Ch. 3

23 To a heart formed for friendship and affection the charms of solitude are very short-lived. . . . *Ibid.*, Ch. 4

24 "Report is mightily given to magnify."
Ibid.

25 " . . . men seldom risk their lives where an escape is without hope of recompense."
Ibid., Ch. 6

26 "Dancing? Oh, dreadful! How it was ever adopted in a civilized country I cannot find out; 'tis certainly a Barbarian exercise, and of savage origin." *Ibid.*, Bk. III, Ch. 1

27 " . . . childhood is never troubled with foresight. . . . " *Ibid.*, Ch. 2

28 "The Poor, not impoverished by their own Guilt, are Equals of the Affluent, not enriched by their own Virtue."
Ibid., Ch. 3

29 [The shop] Without a master, without that diligent attention to its prosperity which the interest of possession alone can give . . . quickly lost its fame for the excellence of its goods, and, soon after, its customers, from the report of its declension.
Ibid., Ch. 4

30 . . . but though discernment teaches us the folly of others, experience singly can teach us our own! *Ibid.*

31 . . . I have seen too little good come of pride to think of imitating it. . . .
Ibid., Ch. 7

32 " . . . where anything is left to conjecture, opinion interferes, and the judgment is easily warped." *Ibid.*

33 "Nothing is entertaining," answered he, "for two minutes together. Things are so little different one from another, that there is no making pleasure out of any thing."
Ibid., Bk. IV, Ch. 1

34 "Travelling is the ruin of all happiness! There's no looking at a building here, after seeing Italy." *Ibid.*, Ch. 2

35 "A secret idea of fame makes his forebearance of happiness supportable to him. . . . "
Ibid.

36 Always an enemy to solitude, he now found it wholly insupportable, and ran into company of any sort, less from a hope of entertainment, than from a dread of spending half an hour by himself. *Ibid.*, Ch. 9

37 "But if the young are never tired of erring in conduct, neither are the older in erring of judgment. . . . " *Ibid.*, Ch. 11

38 "... where concession is made without pain, it is often made without meaning. For it is not in human nature to project any amendment without a secret repugnance."
Ibid.

39 "Who then at last," thought Cecilia, "are half so much the slaves of the world as the gay and the dissipated? Those who work for hire, have at least their hours of rest; those who labour for subsistence, are at liberty when subsistence is procured; but those who toil to please the vain and the idle, undertake a task which can never be finished, however scrupulously all private peace, and all internal comfort, may be sacrificed in reality to the folly of saving appearances."
Ibid., Ch. 12

40 The shill I, shall I, of Congreve* becomes shilly shally.	Ibid., Bk. V
*William Congreve, Restoration dramatist (1670–1729).

41 "The character of a gamester," said Mr. Monckton, "depends solely upon his luck; his disposition varies with every throw of the dice...."	Ibid., Ch. 1

42 "... what was acquired by industry and labour, should never be dissipated in idleness and vanity."	Ibid., Ch. 4

43 "... he looked around him for any pursuit, and seeing distinction was more easily attained in the road to ruin, he galloped along it, thoughtless of being thrown when he came to the bottom, and sufficiently gratified in showing his horsemanship by the way."	Ibid., Ch. 7

44 "True, very true, ma'am," said he, yawning, "one really lives no where; one does but vegetate, and wish it all at an end."
Ibid., Bk. VII, Ch. 5

45 In the bosom of her respectable family resided Camilla.	*Camilla,*
Bk. I, Ch. 1
1796

46 The historian of human life finds less of difficulty and of intricacy to develop, in its accident and adventures, than the investigator of the human heart in its feelings and its changes.	Ibid.

47 Repose is not more welcome to the worn and to the aged, to the sick and to the unhappy, than danger, difficulty, and toil, to the young and the adventurous. Danger they encounter but as the forerunner of success; difficulty, as the spur of ingenuity; and toil, as the herald of honour.
Ibid.

48 "... there is nothing so pleasant as working the indolent; except, indeed, making the restless keep quiet...." Ibid., Bk. II, Ch. 5

49 "Far from having taken any positive step, I have not yet even formed any resolution."
Ibid., Ch. 13

50 "To give money without inquiry, or further aid, to those who have adopted bad practices, is, to them, but temptation, and to society an injury; but to give them both the council and the means to pursue a right course, is, to them, perhaps, salvation, and to the community, the greatest service."
Ibid.

51 ... youthful felicity's best ailment, the energy of its own animal spirits.
Ibid., Bk. III, Ch. 1

52 "... believe me when I tell you, that the mere simple avowal of preference, which only ultimately binds the man, is frequently what first captivates the woman. If her mind is not previously occupied, it operates with such seductive sway, it so soothes, so flatters, so bewitches her self-complacency, that while she listens, she imperceptibly fancies she participates in sentiments, which, but the minute before, occurred not even to her imagination...."
Ibid., Ch. 2

53 "There is, indeed, no perfidy so unjustifiable, as that which wins but to desert the affections of an innocent female. It is still, if possible, more cowardly than it is cruel. . . . "   Ibid., Ch. 9

54 "Good and evil are much more equally divided in this world than you are yet aware: none possess the first without alloy, nor the second without palliation."
Ibid., Bk. IV, Ch. 5

55 "Look forward, and look inward. Look forward, that you may view the short life of admiration and applause for such attractions from others, and their inutility to their possessor in every moment of solitude and repose; and look inward, that you may learn to value your own peculiar riches, for times of retirement, and for days of infirmity and age!"   Ibid.

56 "I would instil into your bosom—the courage, my Eugenia, of virtue—the courage to pass by, as if unheard, the insolence of the hard-hearted, and ignorance of the vulgar."
Ibid.

57 "Happiness is in your power, though beauty is not; and on that to set too high a value would be pardonable only in a weak and frivolous mind; since, whatever is the involuntary admiration with which it meets, every estimable quality and accomplishment is attainable without it. . . . "
Ibid.

58 "You will live to feel pity for all you now covet and admire. . . . "   Ibid.

59 "In the lowest life, equally with the highest, wherever nature has been kind, sympathy springs spontaneously for whatever is unfortunate, and respect for whatever seems innocent."   Ibid., Ch. 6

60 "The examination of a fine picture . . . is a constant as well as exquisite pleasure; for we look at it with an internal security, for such as it appears to us today, it will appear again tomorrow, and tomorrow, and tomorrow; but in the pleasure given by the examination of a fine face, there is always, to a contemplative mind, some little mixture of pain; an idea of its fragility steals upon our admiration, and blends with it something like solicitude; the consciousness how short a time we can view it perfect, how quickly its brilliance of bloom will be blown, and how ultimately it will be nothing."
Ibid.

61 "To those who are commonly moulded, the gradual growth of decay brings with it gradual endurance, because little is missed from day to day . . . it is not so with the beauty; . . . change manifested by the mirror might patiently be born; but the change manifested in the eyes of every beholder, gives a shock that does violence to every pristine feeling."   Ibid.

62 The artlessness of unadorned truth, however sure in theory of extorting admiration, rarely in practice fails inflicting pain and mortification.   Ibid., Ch. 8

63 " . . . there's no living upon air, however you students may affect to think eating mere gluttony."   Ibid., Bk. V, Ch. 7

64 Reason was never thrown away upon Eugenia. Her mind was a soil which received and naturalized all that was sown in it.
Ibid.

65 As extravagance and good luck, by long custom, go hand-in-hand, he spent as fast as he acquired.   Ibid., Ch. 13

66 "Pho, pho!—but why should it be so vastly hard an incongruity that a man who, by chance, is rich, should do something for a woman who, by chance, is poor? How immensely impertinent is the prejudice that forbids so natural a use of money!"
Ibid., Bk. VI, Ch. 9

67 "After four-and-twenty a man is seldom taken by surprise; at least, not till he is past forty: and then, the fear of being too late, sometimes renovates the eagerness of the first youth." Ibid., Ch. 10

68 " . . . no man is in love when he marries. He may have loved before; I have even heard he has sometimes loved after: but at the time never. There is something in the formalities of the matrimonial preparations that drive away all the little cupidons." Ibid.

69 Perfect satisfaction is seldom loquacious. . . . Ibid., Bk. VII, Ch. 5

70 Sudden joy is sportive, but sudden happiness is awful. Ibid.

71 "Ask half the married women in the nation how they became wives: they will tell you their friends urged them. . . ." Ibid., Bk. VIII, Ch. 6

72 "The object may be different, but [in marriage] neither side is indebted to the other, since each has self, only, in contemplation; and thus, in fact, rich or poor, high or low, whatever be the previous distinction between parties, on the hour of marriage they can begin as equals." Ibid., Ch. 10

73 But what is so hard to judge as the human heart? The fairest observers misconstrue all motives to action, where any received prepossession has found an hypothesis. Ibid., Bk. IX, Ch. 1

74 "Being a lord is no such great feat that even I could learn. Hal might be a lord too, if he could get a title. There is nothing required for it but what any man may have; nobody asks after what he can do, or what he can say. If he's got a good head, it's well; and if he has not, it's all one." Ibid.

75 No animal is more gregarious than a fashionable young man, who, whatever may be his abilities to think, rarely decides, and still less frequently acts for himself. Ibid.

76 "Where intellect is uncultivated, what is man better than a brute, or a woman than an idiot?" Ibid., Ch. 6

77 Whatever there is new and splendid, is sure of a run for at least a season. Ibid., Bk. X, Ch. 3

78 Care is the offspring of disappointment; and sorrow and repentance commonly hang upon its first lessons. Ibid., Ch. 9

79 What, at last, so diversified as man? what so little to be judged by his fellow? Ibid., Ch. 14

80 Indeed, the freedom with which Dr. [Samuel] Johnson condemns whatever he disapproves is astonishing. Diary entry (August 23, 1778), *Diary and Letters of Madame D'Arblay, 1778–1840,* Vol. I, Charlotte Barrett, ed. 1904

81 'Tis best to build no castles in the air. Ibid., Vol. II

82 We are not yet out of the wood. Ibid., Vol. III

83 All the delusive seduction of martial music. . . . Ibid., Vol. VIII (1802)

616. Jeanne Louise Campan
(1752–1822)

1 I have put together all that concerned the domestic life of an unfortunate princess [Marie Antoinette], whose reputation is not yet cleared of the stains it received from the attacks of calumny, and who justly merited a different lot in life, a different place in the opinion of mankind after her fall. Memorandum, Quoted in *The Memoirs of Marie Antoinette,* Jeanne Louise Campan, ed. 1910

2 Her [Marie Antoinette's]* heart was always open to the feelings of compassion, and the recollection of her rank never restrained her sensibility.   Ibid., Ch. 3
*See 626.

3 His [Louis XVI's] heart, in truth, disposed him towards reforms; but his prejudices and fears, and the clamours of pious and privileged persons, intimidated him, and made him abandon plans which his love for the people had suggested.
                    Ibid., Ch. 6

4 The theatre, that convenient and endlessly diverting resource of superficial minds, was the main subject of conversation at Court. It was talked about habitually in the Queen's *boudoir*.   Ibid., Ch. 8

5 Tremble at the moment when your child has to choose between the rugged road of industry and integrity, leading straight to honour and happiness; and the smooth and flowery path which descends, through indolence and pleasure, to the gulf of vice and misery. It is then that the voice of a parent, or of some faithful friend, must direct the right course.   "To Her Only Son,"
                    Familiar Letters to her Friends,
                    n.d.

6 Learn to know the value of money. This is a most essential point. The want of economy leads to the decay of powerful empires, as well as private families. Louis XVI perished on the scaffold for a deficit of fifty millions. There would have been no debt, no assemblies of the people, no revolution, no loss of the sovereign authority, no tragical death, but for this fatal deficit.   Ibid.

7 A man should seek to gain information by travelling; he must encounter and endure misfortune, contend against danger and temptation, and finally temper his mind so as to give it the strength and solidity of the hardest metal.   Ibid.

8 Never neglect to appropriate a certain portion of your time to useful reading; and do not imagine that even half an hour a day, devoted to that object, will be unprofitable. The best way of arranging and employing one's time is by calculation; and I have often reflected that half an hour's reading every day, will be one hundred and eighty hours' reading in the course of the year.
                    Ibid.

9 To be magnetized was then a fashion; nay, it was more, it was absolutely a rage. In the drawing-rooms, nothing was talked of but the brilliant discovery. There was to be no more dying; people's heads were turned, and their imaginations heated in the highest degree.   "Mesmer and his Magnetism,"
                    Private Journal, n.d.

10 I informed his majesty that the daughters of distinguished and wealthy individuals, and those of the humble and obscure, were indiscriminately mingled together in the establishment. If, said I, I were to observe the least pretension on account of the rank or fortune of parents, I should immediately put an end to it. The most perfect equality is preserved; distinction is awarded only to merit and industry.   "The Emperor
                    Alexander's Visit to Madame
                    Campan's School,"
                    op. cit.

11 I have always taught them that *on domestic management depends the preservation or dissipation of their fortunes.*
                    Ibid.

12 Fortune confers rank, but education teaches how to support it properly.
                    Ibid.

617.　Hannah Mather Crocker
(1752–1829)

1 . . . the wise Author of nature has endowed the female mind with equal powers and faculties, and given them the same right of judging and acting for themselves, as he gave to the male sex. *Observations on the Real Rights of Women*　1818

618.　Jemima Wilkinson
(1752–1819)

1 That you do not enquire after news, or the public resorts of any one; and be careful not to spread any *yourselves*, that are not of the LORD. *The Universal Friend's Advice, to Those of the Same Religious Society*　1784

2 Live peaceably with all men as much as possible; in an especial manner do not strive against one another for mastery, but all of you keep your ranks in righteousness, and let not one thrust another [aside].
　　　　　　　　　　　　　　Ibid.

3 It is a Sifting time; Try to be on the Lords side. . . .　Letter to John and Orpha Rose (1789), Quoted in *Pioneer Prophetess* by Herbert A. Wisbey, Jr.　1964

4 Be not Curious to Search into the Secrets of god　Pick not the Lock where he hath allowed no key　he that will be fitting every Cloud may be smitten with a thunder Bolt he that will Be too familiar with gods Secrets may Be overwhelmed with his judgments　　　　　　　　　Sermon, "An Answer to Roxbury People: Dangerous Curiosity," (c.1789), op. cit.

5 . . . thou needest not Ask who Shall Ascend up into heaven for to Search the record of Eternity, thou mayest But Descend down into thine own heart and there read what thou art and what thou Shalt Be . . .
　　　　　　　　　　"Book of Conscience," op. cit.

6 Nothing is So Sure as death and nothing so uncertain as the time when we may be too old to Live　We can never be too young to Die　I will therefore Live Every hour as if I were to die the next—　　　"Death," op. cit.

7 That way the tree inclineth while it groweth that way it pitcheth when it falleth and there it Lieth. . . . So we Lie down to Eternity whether it Be towards heaven or towards hell　Being Once fallen there is no removing　for as in war an Error is death So in death an Error is damnation therefore Live as you intend to die and die as you intend to Live
　　　　"As We Live So we Die," op. cit.

8 . . . I am weary of them that hate peace.
　　　　　Letter to James Parker (1788), op. cit.

9 Ye cannot be my friends except ye do whatsoever ye command you. Quoted in *Notable American Women*, Edward T. James, ed.　1971

619.   Catharine Greene
(1753–1815?)

1 If you expect to be an inhabitant of this country [Georgia], you must not think to sit down with your netting pins; but on the contrary, employ half your time at the toilet, one quarter to paying and receiving visits; the other quarter to scolding servants, with a hard thump every now and then over the head; or singing, dancing, reading, writing, or saying your prayers. The latter is here quite a phenomenon; but you need not tell how you employ your time.

> Letter to Miss Flagg (c.1783),
> Quoted in *The Women of the American Revolution*,
> Vol. II, by Elizabeth F. Ellet
> 1848

620.   Elizabeth Inchbald
(1753–1821)

1 LADY MARY. Beauty in London is so cheap, and consequently so common to the men of fashion, (who are prodigiously fond of novelty) that they absolutely begin to fall in love with the ugly women, by way of change.   *Appearance is against Them,*
> Act I, Sc. 1   1785

2 HUMPHRY. You can't be at a loss for words, while you are courting!—Women will always give you two for your one.
> Ibid., Sc. 2

3 LADY EUSTON. There is as severe a punishment to men of gallantry (as they call themselves) as sword or pistol; laugh at them—that is a ball which cannot miss; and yet kills only their vanity. *I'll Tell You What,*
> Act III, Sc. 1   1786

4 LADY EUSTON. "You are the most beautiful woman I ever saw," said Lord *Bandy* ; "and your Lordship is positively the most lovely of mankind"—"What eyes," cried he; "what hair," cried I; "what lips," continued he; "what teeth," added I; "what a hand and arm," said he; "and what a *leg* and *foot*," said I—"Your Ladyship is jesting," was his Lordship's last reply; and he has never since paid me one compliment.
> Ibid.

5 LADY EUSTON. . . . in regard to your terrible sex, whether as licentious lovers or valiant champions—women, of *real honour*, are not in danger from the one; and, therefore, like me, ought to forego the assistance of the other.   Ibid.

6 MARQUIS. . . . one likes a little preparation before marriage as well as before death.
> *The Widow's Vow,*
> Act II, Sc. 1   1786

7 Woman! by honest emulation fir'd
By sense directed & by wit inspir'd
Sportive, yet elegant; tho' pointed, chaste,
To mend our manners & refine our taste
> Prologue,
> *All on a Summer's Day*
> 1787

8 GOVERNOR MORETON. Oh! a Father's tenderness overcomes his Justice!
> Ibid., Act V, Sc. 1

9 Nations like Individuals catch the flame
> Ibid., Epilogue

10 MARQUIS. . . . love is a general leveller—it makes the king a slave; and inspires the slave with every joy a prince can taste.
> *The Midnight Hour,*
> Act I, Sc. 1   1787

11 GENERAL. . . . a man never looks so ridiculous as when he is caught in his own snare.
> Ibid., Act III, Sc. 1

12 COUNT VALENTIA. Yes, I once loved; I doated upon Merida—but the first time she kindly condescended to declare her passion for *me*, I fell asleep. *The Child of Nature,*
> Act I, Sc. 1   1788

13 AMANTHIS. "There is no retreat into which love cannot penetrate."—What does he mean by love? he has left out a word—there is—*love of virtue*—*love of duty*—but love all alone by itself, means nothing at all—
Ibid., Act II, Sc. 1

14 THIRD LADY. . . . our sex are seldom kind to the woman that is so prosperous, their pity is confined to those that are forsaken—to be forsaken and ugly, are the greatest distresses a woman can have.
The Mogul Tale,
Act I, Sc. 1   1788

15 FANNY. What are pleasures when those that one loves does not partake them with one. . . .   *Ibid.*, Act II, Sc. 1

16 DOCTOR. I am a Doctor—I am a Doctor of music universally known, and acknowledged—master of legerdemain, adept in philosophy, giver of health, prolonger of life, child of the sun, interpreter of stars, and privy councellor to the moon.
MOGUL. What brought you here?
DOCTOR. A Balloon.
MOGUL. What is a Balloon?
DOCTOR. It is a Machine of French invention, founded on English Philosophy, an experiment by air—lighter than air,—a method of Navigation in the Clouds with winds, wanting only another discovery, still in Nubilibus. . . .   *Ibid.*

17 SIR LUKE TREMOR. . . . he is the slave of every great man, and the tyrant of every poor one.   *Such Things Are,*
Act I, Sc. 1   1788

18 MR. TWINEALL. Why, Madam, for instance, when a gentleman is asked a question which is either troublesome or improper to answer, you don't say you *won't* answer it, even though you speak to an inferior—but you say—"really it appears to me e-e-e-e-e—[mutters and shrugs]—that is—mo-mo-mo-mo-mo—[mutters]—if you see the thing—for my part—te-te-te-te—and that's all I can tell about it at *present*."
Ibid.

19 SIR LUKE TREMOR. Oh! I wou'd not be in your coat, fashionable as it is, for all the Sultan's dominions.   *Ibid.*, Act IV, Sc. 2

20 DOCTOR. They have refused to grant me a *diploma*; forbid me to practice as a physician, and all because I do not know a parcel of insignificant words; but exercise my profession according to the rules of *reason* and *nature*.—Is it not natural to die? Then, if a dozen or two of my patient *have* died under my hands, is not that natural?
Animal Magnetism,
Act I, Sc. 1   1789

21 SIR JOHN CLASSICK. It is the fool, who laughs at the faults of wise men, because they are so unlike his own.   *The Married Man,*
Act I, Sc. 2   1789

22 LADY CLASSICK. Oh! when a heart gives itself away, depend upon it, it never reflects upon the cause.   *Ibid.*, Act II, Sc. 1

23 MR. CLASSICK. Improve *human nature*, that is the first great work of a philosopher.
Ibid., Sc. 2

24 BLUNTLY. Why, to say the truth, sir, virtue is a currency that grows scarce in the world now-a-days. . . .   *Next Door Neighbours,*
Act II, Sc. 1   1791

25 SYLVAN. Why do you know, a good natur'd woman is like a good sort of a Man; both of them good for nothing.   *Lovers, No
Conjurors,*
Act I, Sc. 1   1792

26 SIR SAMUEL PREJUDICE. But you'll never get any body to believe you have amended for once caught in a falsehood, and truth ever after is of no avail—nay—I would advise a person once detected to proceed in untruths throughout their lives; for as everybody will after the first detection take all they say for Invention, the only way not to impose upon Society is, to stick to "inaccuracies" to the end of the Chapter.   *Ibid.*, Sc. 2

27 MADAME TICASTIN. What misers are we all of our real pleasures!   *The Massacre,*
Act I, Sc. 1   1792

28 GLANDEVE. That rash, that ignorant tribunal which beheads your foe to day, may hang *you* up to morrow.　　Ibid., Act III, Sc. 1

29 MISS SPINSTER. I have heard your mother say you were always foolishly tenderhearted, and never shewed one of those discriminating passions of envy, hatred, or revenge, to which all her other children were liable.　　*Every One Has his Fault,*
Act I, Sc. 2　　1793

30 MR. HARMONY. Just by saying a few harmless sentences, which, though a species of falsehood and deceit, yet, being soothing and acceptable to the person offended, I have immediately inspired him with lenity and forgiveness; and then, by only repeating the self-same sentences to his opponent, I have known hearts cold and closed to each other, warmed and expanded, as every human creature's ought to be.
Ibid.

31 SIR ROBERT RAMBLE. We none of us endeavour to *be* happy, Sir, but merely to be *thought* so; and for my part, I had rather be in a state of misery, and envied for my supposed happiness, than in a state of happiness, and pitied for my supposed misery.
Ibid., Act II, Sc. 1

32 LORD NORLAND. Great as is the virtue of *mercy, justice* is greater still. *Justice* holds its place among those cardinal virtues which include all the lesser.
Ibid., Act IV, Sc. 1

33 MRS. PLACID. Oh! how I long to see my dear husband, that I may quarrel with him!
Ibid., Act V, Sc. 2

34 LORD PRIORY. I know several women of fashion, who will visit six places of different amusement on the same night, have company at home besides, and yet, for want of something more, they'll be out of spirits. . . .　　*Wives as they Were, and
Maids as they Are,*
Act I, Sc. 1　　1797

35 COTTAGER. Wife, wife, never speak ill of the dead. Say what you please against the living, but not a word against the dead.
COTTAGER'S WIFE. And yet, husband, I believe the dead care the last what is said about them—　　*Lover's Vows,*
Act II, Sc. 1　　1798

36 VERDUN THE BUTLER. Loss of innocence never sounds well except in verse.
Ibid., Act IV, Sc. 2

37 MR. METLAND. No one lives whose contentment is not, at times, crossed by an "if only." Let us hear the tendency of your "if only."　　*The Wise Man of the East,*
Act II, Sc. 2　　1799

38 GIRONE. . . . women's power seldom lasts longer than their complexion.
A Case of Conscience,
Act I, Sc. 1　　1833

39 GIRONE. He is no man who slights a woman for any thing less than another woman.
Ibid.

40 ADRIANA. Yet, beware how you proceed; beware how you raise the storm—it may descend in thunder!　　Ibid., Act II, Sc. 1

41 GIRONE. My Lord, I *do* know, but I am sworn to secrecy; and 'tis so unmanly to tell! But I will lead you to my wife, who knows also; and being a woman, she would unsex herself as much by keeping the secret, as I should by revealing it.
Ibid.

42 SALVADOR. A lover gains instructions when other men are dull: he sees where others are blind; hears when they are inattentive; and receives intelligence from a word, a look, where volumes are required to teach another.　　Ibid., Act III, Sc. 3

43 My present apartment is so small, that I am all over black and blue with thumping my body and limbs against my furniture on every side; but then I have not far to *walk* to reach anything I want, for I can kindle my fire as I lie in bed, and put on my cap as I dine. . . . From her Journal,
Quoted in
English Women of Letters,
Vol. II, by Julia Kavanagh
1863

44 Thank God, I am not like Vivian [her sister]; I can say No—and from that quality may I date my peace of mind, not to be sullied or much disturbed by ten thousand grease spots. I say No to all the vanities of the world. Ibid.

45 . . . Madame de Stael* . . . entreated me to explain to her the motive why I shunned society. "Because," I replied, "I dread the loneliness that will follow." "What? will you feel your solitude more when you return from this company than you did before you came hither?" "Yes." "I should think it would elevate your spirits; why will you feel your loneliness more?" "Because I have no one to tell that I have seen *you*; no one to describe your person to, no one to whom I can repeat the many encomiums you have passed on my 'Simple Story,' no one to enjoy any of your praises but myself."
Ibid.

*Germaine de Staël, see 676.

46 I have so many reflections concerning a *future* world, as well as concerning the *present*, and there are on that awful subject so many books still unread, that I think every moment lost which impedes my gaining information from holy and learned authors.
Letter to Mrs. [Amelia] Opie,*
op. cit.

*See 688.

47 Stunned with the enchantment of that well known tone directed to her, she stood like one just petrified—all vital power was suspended. *Nature and Art*, n.d.

621. Phillis Wheatley
(1753?–1784)

1 'Twas not long since I left my native shore,
The land of errors, and Egyptian gloom:
Father of mercy, 'twas thy gracious hand
Brought me in safety from those dark abodes. "To the University of Cambridge,
in New-England,"
St. 1 (1767),
*Poems on Various Subjects,
Religious and Moral* 1773

2 Suppress the deadly serpent in its egg.
Ye blooming plants of human race divine,
An Ethiop tells you 'tis your greatest foe;
Its transient sweetness turns to endless pain,
And in immense perdition sinks the soul.
Ibid., St. 3

3 Some view our sable race with scornful eye,
"Their colour is a diabolic dye."
Remember, *Christians*, *Negroes* black as Cain,
May be refin'd, and join th' angelic train.
"On Being Brought From Africa
to America"
(c.1768), op. cit.

4 Now here, now there, the roving *Fancy* flies,
Till some lov'd object strikes her wand'ring eyes,
Whose silken fetters all the senses bind,
And soft captivity involves the mind.
"On Imagination,"
St. 3 (c.1770), op. cit.

5 Imagination! who can sing thy force?
Or who describe the swiftness of thy course? Ibid., St. 4

6 O thou the leader of the mental train
Ibid., St. 6

7 Attend my lays, ye ever honor'd nine*
"An Hymn to the Morning,"
St. 1 (c.1772), op. cit.

*The nine Muses.

8 Aurora*, hail and all the thousand dyes,
Which deck thy progress through the vaulted skies Ibid., St. 2

*Goddess of dawn.

9 "But soon arriv'd to heaven's bright port
assign'd,
"New glories rush on my expanding mind!
"A Poem on the Death of
Charles Eliot, Aged 12 Months.
To Mr. S. Eliot,"
St. 2 (September 1, 1772),
Boston, op. cit.

10 No more, America, in mournful strains
Of wrongs, and grievance unredress'd com-
plain,
No longer shalt thou dread the iron chain,
Which wanton Tyranny with lawless hand
Had made, and with it mean t' enslave the
land.
"To the Right Honourable William,
Earl of Dartmouth, His
Majesty's Principal Secretary of
State for North America, &C.,"
St. 2, op. cit.

11 I, young in life, by seeming cruel fate
Was snatch'd from Afric's fancy'd happy
seat:
What pangs excruciating must molest,
What sorrows labor in my parent's breast?
Steel'd was that soul and by no misery
mov'd
That from a father seiz'd his babe belov'd:
Such, such my case. And can I then but
pray
Others may never feel tyrannic sway?
Ibid., St. 3

12 The land of freedom's heaven-defended
race!   "To His Excellency General
Washington,"
St. 3, op. cit.

13 . . . civil and religious liberty . . . are so inseparably united, that there is little or no
enjoyment of one without the other: . . . in
every human breast, God has implanted a
principle, which we call love of freedom; it
is impatient of oppression and pants for
deliverance. . . . How well the cry for liberty, and the reverse disposition, for the exercise of oppressive power over others
agree—I humbly think it does not require
the penetration of a philosopher to determine.   Letter to Rev. Samson Occom
(February 11, 1774)
Boston Post-Boy
March 21, 1774

14 Lo! Freedom comes. "Liberty and Peace,
a Poem" (1784),
The Poems of Phillis Wheatley,
Julian D. Mason, Jr., ed.
1966

15 Descending Peace and power of War con-
founds;
From every tongue celestial Peace resounds
Ibid.

16 So Freedom comes array'd with charms divine,
And in her train Commerce and Plenty
shine.   Ibid.

622.   Jeanne-Marie Roland
(1754–1793)

1 O liberty! what crimes are committed in thy
name!* (O liberté! que de crimes on commêt
dans ton nom!)   Last words before being
guillotined (November 8, 1793),
Quoted in Histoire des Girondins,
Ch. LI, by Alphonse Lamartine
1847

*Words inscribed on front of Statue of Liberty in New
York City; also recorded as: "O Liberty, how you have
been trifled with!" (O Liberté, comme on t'a jouée!)

2 If I remain much longer [at court] I shall soon detest the people I see so much, that I shall not be able to control my hatred. . . . They make me feel their injustice and their absurdity.   Quoted in *Biography of Distinguished Women* by Sarah Josepha Hale   1876

3 I shall soon be there [at the guillotine]; but those who send me there will follow themselves ere long. I go there innocent, but they will go as criminals; and you, who now applaud, will also applaud them.
                    Remark en route to execution (November 8, 1793), op. cit.

4 The more I see of men, the more I admire dogs. (*Plus je vois les hommes, plus j'admire les chiens.*)   Attributed,* n.d.
*Also attributed to Ouida and to Mme. de Sévigné.

623. Frances Thynne
(?–1754)

1 To thee, all glorious, ever-blessed power, I consecrate this silent midnight hour.
                    "A Midnight Hour,"
                    Miscellanies,
                    Dr. Watt, ed., n.d.

624. Anne Grant
(1755–1838)

1 Gem of the heath! whose modest bloom Sheds beauty o'er the lonely moor
                    "On A Sprig of Heath," St. 3,
                    The Highlanders and Other Poems
                    1808

2 . . . I drew that high relish for the sublime simplicity of nature which has ever accompanied me. This has been the means of preserving a certain humble dignity in all the difficulties I have had to struggle through.
                    Memoirs of an American Lady   1808

3 O where, tell me where, is your Highland laddie gone?

He's gone with streaming banners, where noble deeds are done,
And my sad heart will tremble till he comes safely home.
                    "O Where, Tell Me Where,"*
                    Scottish Song,
                    Mary Carlyle Aitken, ed.
                    1874
*Both this and "The Blue Bells of Scotland" by Dorothea Jordan (see 657:1) are variants on an older popular song.

625. Anna Maria Lenngren
(1755–1817)

1 Infirm she was, drank tea of elder-flowers blended,
On twinges of her legs for weather signs depended
                    "The Portraits," St. 1,
                    Anthology of Swedish Lyrics from 1750–1915,
                    C. W. Stork, ed. and tr.   1917

2 'Tis plain to see what pride within her glance reposes,
And mark how nobly curved her nose is!
                    Ibid., St. 2

3 The fairer sex possessed a mind
Of sturdy fabric, like her cloak.
Now all is different in our lives—
Other fabrics, other mores!
Taffetas, indecent stories
                    "Other Fabrics, Other Mores!,"
                    Nadia Christensen and Mariann Tiblin, trs.;
                    The Penguin Book of Women Poets,
                    Carol Cosman, Joan Keefe and Kathleen Weaver, eds.   1978

626. Marie-Antoinette
(1755–1793)

1 Let them eat cake.* (*Qu'ils mangent de la brioche.*)   Quoted in *Confessions* by Jean-Jacques Rousseau
                    1740
*Brioche, or "cake," was equivalent to a round, hard-crusted bread.

2 I cannot consent to be separated from my son. I can feel no enjoyment without my children; with them I can regret nothing.
Remark (January 21, 1793; day of Louis XVI's execution),
Quoted in *Women of Beauty and Heroism*
by Frank B. Goodrich 1858

3 Courage! I have shown it for years; think you I shall lose it at the moment when my sufferings are to end?
Remark (October 16, 1793; on way to guillotine), op. cit.

4 Adieu, once again, my children, I go to join your father. Last words, op. cit.

5 I have seen all, I have heard all, I have forgotten all.
Reply to inquisitors (October 1789),
Quoted in *Biography of Distinguished Women*
by Sarah Josepha Hale 1876

6 I was a queen, and you took away my crown; a wife, and you killed my husband; a mother, and you deprived me of my children. My blood alone remains: take it, but do not make me suffer long.
Remark at the revolutionary tribunal (October 14, 1793), op. cit.

7 History is busy with us. Ibid.

8 Remember that not a grain of poison will be put in use against me. . . . this age possesses calumny, which is a much more convenient instrument of death; and it is by that I shall perish. Quoted in *The Memoirs of Marie Antoinette*,
Ch. 18, Jeanne Louise Campan*, ed. 1910

*See 616.

9 All have contributed to our downfall; the reformers have urged it like mad people, and others through ambition, for the wildest Jacobin seeks wealth and office, and the mob is eager for plunder. There is not one real patriot among all this infamous horde. the emigrant party have their intrigues and schemes; foreigners seek to profit by the dissensions of France; every one has a share in our misfortunes. Ibid., Ch. 22

10 Yes, I will say to them: Frenchmen, they have had the cruelty to persuade you that I do not love France!—I! the mother of a Dauphin who will reign over this noble country!—I! whom Providence has seated upon the most powerful throne of Europe! Of all the daughters of Maria Theresa am I not the one whom fortune has most highly favoured? And ought I not to feel all these advantages? What should I find at Vienna? Nothing but sepulchres! What should I lose in France? Everything which can confer glory! Ibid.

627. Renier Giustina Michiel
(1755–1832)

1 For me ennui is among the worst evils—I can bear pain better. Quoted in *Biography of Distinguished Women*
by Sarah Josepha Hale 1876

2 My deafness is an inestimable advantage in company; for with the stupid and gossiping I shun all communication; their nonsense passes unheeded—but I can employ my trumpet with sensible people, and often gain in that way valuable knowledge. Ibid.

3 The world improves people according to the dispositions they bring into it. Ibid.

4 Time is a better comforter than reflection. Ibid.

628.   Sarah Siddons
(1755–1831)

1 To you, whose fost'ring kindness rear'd my
name,
O'erlooked my faults, but magnified my
fame.   Address to audience
(May 21, 1782), Bath,
Quoted in *Life of Mrs. Siddons*, Vol. I,
by Thomas Campbell   1834

2 I am, as you may observe, acting again: but
how much difficulty to get my money!
Sheridan* is certainly the greatest phenomenon that Nature has produced for
centuries. Our theatre is going on, to the astonishment of everybody. Very few of the
actors are paid, and all are vowing to withdraw themselves: yet still we go on. Sheridan is certainly omnipotent.
Letter to a friend
(November 9, 1796),
op. cit., Vol. II
*Richard Brinsley Sheridan (1751–1816), playwright
especially noted for *The School for Scandal*, and
manager of the Drury Lane Theatre in London.

3 . . . I know, by sad experience, with what
difficulty a mind, weakened by long and
uninterrupted suffering, admits hope, much
less assurance.   Letter to Mrs. FitzHugh
(July 14, 1801),
from Preston, op. cit.

4 Her [Lady Macbeth's] feminine nature, her
delicate structure, it is too evident, are soon
overwhelmed by the enormous pressure of
her crimes. Yet it will be granted, that she
gives proofs of a naturally higher toned
mind than that of Macbeth. . . . Her frailer
frame, and keener feelings, have now sunk
under the struggle—his robust and less sensitive constitution has not only resisted it,
but bears him on to deeper wickedness, and
to experience the fatal fecundity of crime.
Notes on character
(c.1815), op. cit.

5 I pant for retirement and leisure, but am
doomed to inexpressible and almost unsup-
portable hurry.   Letter to Rev. Sedgewick
Whalley (June 21, 1784),
from Dublin,
Quoted in *Journals and
Correspondence of Thomas
Sedgwick Whalley*,
Vol. I, Rev. Hill Wickham, ed.
1863

6 . . . what is charming in the closet often
ceases to be so when it comes into consideration for the stage.   Letter to Rev.
Whalley (September 28, 1785),
op. cit.

7 I beseech you not to give me descriptions of
the country. . . . : all that relates to you is interesting, but I don't care sixpence about
situation, vegetation, or any of the ations.
Letter to Rev. Whalley
(August 11, 1786), op. cit.

8 This woman* is one of those monsters (I
think them) of perfection, who is an angel
before her time, and is so entirely resigned
to the will of heaven, that (to a very mortal
like myself) she appears to be the most pro-
voking piece of still life one ever had the
misfortune to meet.
Letter to Rev. Whalley
(c.1787), op. cit.
*The lead character in a new play by Bertie Greatheed.

9 . . . sorry am I to say I have often observed,
that I have performed worst when I most
ardently wished to do better than ever.
Letter to Rev. Whalley
(July 16, 1781), from Bristol,
Quoted in *The Kembles*,
Vol. I, by Percy
Fitzgerald   1871

10 She is told that the splendid appearance on that night, and the emoluments arising from it, exceed anything ever recorded on a similar account in the annals of the English stage; but she has not the vanity to imagine that this arose from any superiority over many of her predecessors, or some of her contemporaries. She attributes it wholly to that liberality of sentiment which distinguishes the inhabitants of this great metropolis from those of any other in the world.
Statement of gratitude to management of Drury Lane Theatre (December 14, 1782), op. cit.

11 The sea was particularly rough; we were lifted mountains high, and sank again as low in an instant. Good God! how tremendous, how wonderful!   Letter to Rev. Whalley (July 14, 1783), from Cork, op. cit.

12 [I] . . . commenced my study of Lady Macbeth. As the character is very short, I thought I should soon accomplish it. Being then only twenty years of age, I believed, as many others do believe, that little more was necessary than to get the words into my head, for the necessity of discrimination, and the development of character, at that time of my life, had scarcely entered into my imagination.   Recollections (1785), op. cit.

13 I have paid severely for eminence.
Letter to the Rev. and Mrs. Whalley (March 15, 1785), op. cit.

14 A strange capricious master is the public. . . .   Ibid.

15 . . . my spirits are not equal to, or my internal resources are too few, for a life of solitude.   Letter to Lord Harcourt (1787), op. cit.

16 It is so long since I have felt anything like joy, that it appears like a dream to me. . . .
Letter to Elizabeth Inchbald* (1801), op. cit., Vol. II

*See 620.

17 Tho' I have nothing to do I find myself more busy than ever.   Letter to Sir Charles Hotham (September 22, 1788), from Guy's Cliffe, Quoted in *The Hothams* by A. M. W. Stirling   1918

18 In tribute to his* triumphant Genius I cannot but remark his instantaneus decission [sic] on the attitude and expression. In short, it was in the twinkling of an eye.
The Reminiscences of Sarah Kemble Siddons, (1824), William Van Lennep, ed. 1942 reprint
*The painter Sir Thomas Lawrence (1769–1830) with whom she had a long and intense friendship.

19 Alas! How wretched is the being who depends on the stability of public favour!
Ibid.

20 The awful consciousness that one is the sole object of attention to that imense space, lined as it were with human intellect from top to bottom, and on all sides round, may perhaps be imagined but can not be described, and never never to be for- gotten. . . .   Ibid.

21 Alas, why had I enemies, but because to be prosperous is sufficient cause for enmity.
Ibid.

22 . . . customary interruptions [from the audience] are not only gratifying and cheering, but they are also really necessary in order to gain breath and voice to carry one on through some violent exertions; though after all it must be confessed that *Silence* is the most flattering applause an *Actor* can receive.   Comment on audiences in Edinburgh, op. cit.

23 Doctors differ you know and it seems they are very much at odds about poor me, for Sir Lucas Pepys says my Complaint is *Nerves* and Nerves only. Letter to Bedina Wynn (June 2, 1790), Quoted in *Sarah Siddons, Portrait of an Actress*, Ch. 5, by Roger Manvell 1970

24 . . . I believe one half of the world is born for the convenience of the other half. . . . Letter to Hester Lynch Piozzi* (August 27, 1794), op. cit.

*See 581.

25 I shall never begin to live for myself I believe and perhaps I should not like it, were it in my power. Ibid.

26 Oh! I have suffered too much from a husband's unkindness, not to detest the man who treats a creature ill that depends on her husband for all her comforts. Letter to P. Galindo (October 18, 1803), op. cit., Ch. 7

27 . . . the testimony of the wisdom of all ages, from the foundation of the world to this day is childishness and folly, if happiness be anything more than a *name*. . . . No, no, it is the inhabitant of a better world, content, the offspring of moderation, [that] is all we ought to aspire to *here*, and moderation will be our best and surest guide to that happiness to which she will most assuredly conduct us. Letter to Catherine Galindo (1803), op. cit.

28 I fell as if my foot were now on the first round of the Ladder which reaches to another world. Letter to Hester Lynch Piozzi (June 12, 1812), op. cit., Ch. 8

629. Elisabeth Vigée-Lebrun
(1755–1842)

1 I found the painting hung in the salon, and since the woodwork was painted white, which generally kills paintings, he had arranged a large green drapery which surrounded the frame and fell below it. In addition for the evening he had arranged a candelabra with many candles and a reflector in such a way that all the light was directed towards my portrait. It is useless for me to say how touched a painter is by this kind of gallantry. *Souvenirs de Mme. Vigée-Lebrun* (1835–1837) 1869

2 I was so fortunate as to be on very pleasant terms with the Queen [Marie Antoinette].* When she heard that I had something of a voice we rarely had a sitting without singing some duets . . . together, for she was exceedingly fond of music. . . . *Memoirs of Madame Vigée-Lebrun* (1835), Lionel Strachey, tr. 1907

*See 626. Vigée-Lebrun painted several portraits of the queen, beginning in 1779.

3 The women reigned then; the Revolution dethroned them. Ibid.

630. Eliza Wilkinson
(c.1755–?)

1 . . . they [soldiers] really merit every thing, who will fight from principle alone; for from what I could learn, these poor creatures had nothing to protect them, and seldom got their pay; yet with what alacrity will they encounter danger and hardships of every kind! Quoted in *The Women of the American Revolution*, Vol. II, by Elizabeth F. Ellet 1848

2 I heard the horses of the inhuman Britons coming in such a furious manner, that they seemed to tear up the earth, the riders at the same time bellowing out the most horrid curses imaginable—oaths and imprecations which chilled my whole frame. Surely, thought I, such horrid language denotes nothing less than death. . . .
                                        Ibid.

3 They then began to plunder the house of every thing they thought valuable or worth taking. . . . But such despicable figures! Each wretch's bosom stuffed so full, they appeared to be all afflicted with some dropsical disorder. Had a party of rebels (as they call us) appeared, we should have seen their circumference lessen.   Ibid.

4 After asking for the articles I wanted, I saw a broad roll of ribbon, which appeared to be of black and white stripes . . . so I took it, and found that it was narrow black ribbon, carefully wound round a broad white. I returned it to its place on the shelf.
"Madam," said the merchant, "you can buy the black and white too, and tack them in stripes."
"By no means, sir; I would not have them *slightly tacked*, but *firmly united*."*
                                        Ibid.

*Alluding to the thirteen stripes representing the United States.

631.   Henrietta Luxborough
(?–1756)

1 Yon bullfinch, with unvaried tone,
Of cadence harsh, and accent shrill,
Has brighter plumage to atone
For want of harmony and skill.
          "The Bullfinch in Town," St. 2,
A Collection of Poems. By Several Hands,
          Robert Dodsley, ed.   1748

632.   Hester Ann Rogers
(1756–1794)

1 What I suffered is known only to God.
          Quoted in *The Women of
          Methodism: Its Three
          Foundresses . . .*
          by Abel Stevens   1866

633.   Anna Young Smith
(1756–1780?)

1 Blest be this humble strain if it imparts
The dawn of peace to but one pensive breast
          "An Elegy to the Memory of the
          American Volunteers, who Fell
          in the Engagement Between the
          Massachusetts-Bay Militia, and
          the British Troops.
          April 19, 1775,"
          St. 9 (May 2, 1775),
          Philadelphia,
          Pennsylvania Magazine
          June 1775

2 How weak the balm the laurel wreath bestows,
To heal our breasts, when love or friendship falls.   Ibid., St. 10

3 To Thee, Eternal Parent, we resign
Our bleeding cause and on thy wisdom rest;
With grateful hearts we bless thy power divine,
And own resign'd "Whatever is, is best."
                              Ibid., St. 18

4 But should we know as much as they,
They fear their empire would decay;
For they know women heretofore
Gained victories, and envied laurel's war.
And now they fear we'll once again
Ambitious be to reign,
And so invade the territories of the brain.
          *Sylvia's Complaint of her Sex's
                    Unhappiness*   1788

5 *Custom* and *modesty*, much more severe,
Strictly forbid our passion to declare.
If we reveal, then decency's provoked,

If kept, then we are with the secret choked.
Ibid.

6 Say when thou dipp'st thy keenest pen in
    gall,
Why must it still on helpless woman fall?
Why must our "dirt and dullness" fill each
    line,
Our love of "follies, our desire to shine?"
Why are we drawn as a whole race of fools,
Unsway'd alike by sense or virtue's rules?
                    "On Reading Swift's Works"
                        (1774), Philadelphia,
        Universal Asylum & Columbian Magazine
                            September 1790

7 But now, so oft filth chokes thy sprightly
    fire,
We loathe one instant, and the next ad-
    mire—
Even while we laugh, we mourn thy wit's
    abuse,
And while we praise thy talents, scorn their
    use.   Ibid.

8 Teach my unskilled mind to sing
The feelings of my heart.   "An Ode to
                Gratitude, Inscribed to Miss
                Elizabeth Graeme* by her Niece,
                            Anna Young,"
                    Pt. 1 (1770), Philadelphia,
                        *Women Poets in Pre-
                        Revolutionary America*,
                    Pattie Cowell, ed.   1981
*See 571.

9 Bereft of him it is but death to live!
                    "Occasional Verses on the
                Anniversary of the Death of my
                Grand-father, Dr. Thomas
                            Graeme"
                        (1774), op. cit.

10 Oh Sensibility divine!   "Ode to
                            Sensibility,"
                    Pt. 1 (1774), Philadelphia,
                                op. cit.

634. Augusta
(1757–1831)

1 It seems as if nature had allied itself with
humanity to destroy all thoughts of happiness. There are nothing but storms in the atmosphere and amongst men.
            Diary entry (April 2, 1806),
            *In Napoleonic Days, Extracts
            from the private diary of Augusta,
            Duchess of Saxe-Coburg-Saalfeld,
            Queen Victoria's maternal
            grandmother, 1806–1821*,
            H. R. H., the Princess Beatrice,
                ed. and tr.   1941

2 How can his [Napoleon's] conscience be
quite in abeyance, with so many thousands
of lives sacrificed to his insane ambition?
What would I not give to read his inner
thoughts. If he will ever awake from his
mad dream of power, God only knows,
Who has permitted him to become the
scourge of the nations of the earth.
            Diary entry (January 26, 1813),
                            op. cit.

3 Only in England is it possible for the husband of the heiress to the throne to lead the
happy unfettered life of a private gentleman.   Diary entry (December 16, 1816),
                            op. cit.

4 How fast time has gone by, but I should not
care to live over again those long years,
which appear to me now as a dream.
            Diary entry (January 19, 1817),
                            op. cit.

5 When one gets old one is so thankful to be
quiet.   Diary entry (December 19, 1817),
                            op. cit.

635. Georgiana Cavendish
(1757–1806)

1 Where Art and Nature shed profusely
round

Their rival wonders—Italy, farewell!
*Passage of the Mountain of Saint
Gothard*, St. 1
1802

2 Their Liberty requir'd no rites uncouth,
No blood demanded, and no slaves en-
chain'd;
Her rule was gentle, and her voice was
truth,
By social order form'd, by law restrain'd.
Ibid., St. 26

3 Hope of my life! dear children of my heart!
That anxious heart, to each fond feeling
true,
To you still pants each pleasure to impart,
And none—O transport!—reach its home
and you.   *Ibid.*, St. 30

636.   Hannah Webster Foster
(1758/59–1840)

1 An unusual sensation possesses my
breast—a sensation which I once thought
could never pervade it on any occasion
whatever. It is *pleasure*, pleasure, my dear
Lucy, on leaving my paternal roof.
*The Coquette; or, The History of
Eliza Wharton*,
Letter I   1797

2 "The round of fashionable dissipation is
dangerous. A phantom is often pursued,
which leaves its deluded votary the real
form of wretchedness."   *Ibid.*, Letter V

3 Are we not all links in the great chain of society, some more, some less important, but
each upheld by others, throughout the con-
federated whole?   *Ibid.*, Letter XXI

4 In whatever situation we are placed, our
greater or less degree of happiness must be
derived from ourselves. Happiness is in a
great measure the result of our own dispositions and actions.   *Ibid.*

5 Prudence and economy are such necessary,
at least such decent, virtues, that they claim
the attention of every female, whatever be
her station or her property.
Ibid., Letter XL

6 As human life hath many diseases which require medicines, are we not right in selecting the most agreeable and palatable?
Ibid., Letter XLI

7 The Deity is not confined to temples made
with hands.   *Ibid.*

8 If the conviction of any misconduct on your
part gives you pain, dissipate it by the reflection that unerring rectitude is not the lot
of mortals; that few are to be found who
have not deviated, in a greater or less degree, from the maxims of prudence. Our
greatest mistakes may teach lessons which
will be useful through life.
Ibid., Letter XLIII

9 It is by surmounting difficulties, not by
sinking under them, that we discover our
fortitude.   *Ibid.*, Letter LII

10 True courage consists not in flying from the
storms of life, but in braving and steering
through them with prudence.
Ibid.

11 Avoid solitude. It is the bane of a disordered mind, though of great utility to a
healthy one.   *Ibid.*

12 How can that be a diversion which racks
the soul with grief, even though that grief
be imaginary? The introduction of a funeral
solemnity upon the stage is shocking indeed!   *Ibid.*

637.   Elizabeth Hamilton
(1758?–1816)

1 The politician, who measures the interests of his country by her preponderence in the scale of empire, regards all consideration for individual happiness as a weakness; and by the man who thinks riches and happiness synonymous, all that does not directly tend to increase the influx of wealth, is held in contempt.   Preface, *The Cottagers of Glenburnie: A Tale for the Farmer's Ingle-nook*   1808

2 "I had a good mother, who, when I was a little child, taught me to subdue my own proud spirit, and to be tractable and obedient. Many poor people think that their children will learn this time enough, when they go into the world; and that as they will meet with hardships when they grow up, it would be a pity to make them suffer by contradicting them when they are little. But what does a child suffer from the correction of a judicious parent, in comparison of what grown people suffer from their passions?"   Ibid., Ch. 2

3 " . . . let us never allow ourselves to depart from truth; it is the beginning of all iniquity."   Ibid., Ch. 4

4 "Those who wait till evening for sunrise," said Mrs. Mason, "will find that they have lost the day."   Ibid., Ch. 8

5 "The best charm against witchcraft is cleanliness," says she.   Ibid., Ch. 13

6 Of a' roads to happiness ever were tried,
There's nane half so sure as ane's ain fireside.
My ain fireside, my ain fireside,
O there's naught to compare wi' ane's ain
     fireside.   "My Ain Fireside,"
Scottish Song,
Mary Carlyle Aitken, ed.
1874

7 With expectation beating high,
Myself I now desire to spy;
And straight I in a glass surveyed

An antique lady, much decayed
     Untitled,
Quoted in *Biography of
Distinguished Women*
by Sarah Josepha Hale   1876

8 If the mind be thus cramped in early life, (as is generally the fate of my sex,) it is a thousand to one that it remains stationary for ever, never making an attempt to rise above the level of its immediate associates; and even where it has been enabled to expand, it is so much easier to sink to the level of others, than to raise the minds of others to a level with our own, that few in such circumstances do not sink.
     "The Benefits of Society,"
Private Letters, n.d.

9 It is only by the love of reading that the evil resulting from the association with *little* minds can be counteracted.
     Ibid.

10 Of all the privileges enjoyed by the lords of the creation, there is none so estimable as having it in their power to form a society of their own liking.   Ibid.

11 I perfectly agree with you in considering castles in the air as more useful edifices than they are generally allowed to be. It is only plodding matter-of-fact dullness that cannot comprehend their use.
     "Imagination,"
op. cit.

638.   Esther Hayden
(?–1758)

1 I'm sore distress'd, and greatly 'press'd
With filthy Nature, Sin;
I cannot rise to view the Prize
Of happiness within.   Untitled,
*A Short Account of the Life,
Death and Character of Esther
Hayden, the Wife of Samuel
Hayden of Braintree*
[Mass.]   1759

639. Henrietta O'neill
(1758–1793)

1 In early days, when Fancy cheats,
A varied wreath I wove,
Of laughing Spring's luxuriant sweets,
To deck ungrateful love

> "Ode to the Poppy,"
> St. 3,
> Quoted in *Elegaic Sonnets*
> *and Other Essays*,
> Charlotte Smith, ed.   1782

2 Hail, lovely blossom! thou canst ease
The wretched victims of Disease;
Canst close those weary eyes in gentle sleep,
Which never open but to weep;
For oh! thy potent charm
Can agonizing Pain disarm;
Expel imperious Memory from her seat,
And bid the throbbing heart forget to beat.

> Ibid., St. 5

640. Mary Robinson
(1758–1800)

1 Yet when love and hope are vanished,
Restless memory never dies.

> "Stanzas, written between Dover
> & Calais," St. 4,
> *Poems*   1775

2 Power and splendour could not charm me,
I no joy in wealth could see;
Nor could threats nor fears alarm me,
Save the fear of *losing thee*!

> Ibid., St. 12

3 I have wept to see thee weep.

> Ibid., St. 13

4 When with thee, what ills could harm me!
Thou coulds't every pang assuage;
But when absent, what could charm me!
Every moment seemed an age.

> Ibid., St. 14

5 The Snow-drop, Winter's timid child,
Awakes to life, bedew'd with tears.

> "The Snow-Drop,"
> St. 1, op. cit.

641. Jane West
(1758–1852)

1 Great and sudden reverses of fortune are not frequent; yet little disappointments hourly occur, which fall with the greatest severity on those, whose amiable, though dangerous enthusiasm, induces them to expect too much, and to feel too severely.

> Preface,
> *The Advantage of Education; or,*
> *The History of Maria Williams, a*
> *tale for Misses and their*
> *Mammas*, Vol. I
> 1793

2 "Maria, you have read many instances of the fascination of pleasure; but you are too inexperienced to know, that even amongst those to whom rank and fortune allow the frequent indulgence, not all the satiety and distaste that attends repeated enjoyments, are found effectual to stop the desire of inordinate pursuit."   Ibid., Ch. 7

3 " . . . your newly acquired taste for reading, prevents even the hazard of your ever perceiving time to be an intolerable burden."

> Ibid.

4 Oh! gather in life's early prime,
The produce which despises time;
Waste not in pleasure's soothing bowers
Youth's irrecoverable hours

> Ibid., Ch. 13,
> Untitled poem, St. 4

5 Oh! seize the time, with happiest aim
Awake exertion's powerful flame

> Ibid., St. 5

6 Friendship in affectionate bosoms, generally revives with redoubled tenderness, after a little interruption.   Ibid., Ch. 16

7 She found the tears which this sacrifice to virtue and duty cost, far preferable to the most agreeable reveries which a fertile imagination could form, when the passion that gave them birth, could not bear the penetrating glance of the God within the mind.   Ibid., Ch. 17

8 It is in the power of cunning to affect simplicity, but simplicity itself, when it would assume art, finds it too thin a disguise.
                              Ibid., Vol. II, Ch. 1

9 Nothing has contributed to increase the licentiousness which is but too visible in the manners of the world, more than the soothing epithets which folly and levity have made it customary to bestow on immorality.   Ibid., Ch. 3

10 When virtue loses its abhorrence of vice, she dismisses one of her most vigilant guards. Let but self-interest surmount principle, and her ruin is compleat.
                              Ibid.

11 . . . jealousy must be the inseparable companion of love in the breast of a libertine. . . .   Ibid.

12 "A husband claims a kind of proscriptive authority over the friendships of our sex."
                              Ibid., Ch. 9

13 "It is my interest, however, to forbid your having any intercourse with beings so superior to myself, lest it should lead to dangerous comparisons."   Ibid.

14 He was a miserable being, disgusted at the folly of vice, because it was unsuccessful; infatuated by the charms of that virtue, which he could not ruin; and caught in the net which he had spread for the destruction of others.   Ibid., Ch. 13

15 Guilt, even when triumphant, can never know repose; but when to the worm in its own breast, disappointments and misfortunes are added, it will generally fly for relief to that despair, which seals its condemnation.   Ibid.

16 Perfection belongs to no human institution, and I will own that sometimes we *may* be wrong.   *A Gossip's Story,*
                              Vol. I, Ch. 1   1797

17 The spirit of penetration or the ability to discover people's characters by a cursory glance, though arrogated by almost every body, is in reality possessed by very few. Nothing can be more intricate than the human heart, and the discriminating shades which serve to mark variation of character, are generally too minute and confused to write distinct traits upon the countenance. Even words and actions are often deceitful guides. People frequently step out of themselves.   Ibid., Ch. 2

18 There are some secrets which scarcely admit of being disclosed even to ourselves.
                              Ibid., Ch. 8

19 As wise people often defeat their aims by too great caution, cunning also frequently overshoots the mark by too much craft.
                              Ibid., Ch. 11

20 "It is always fortunate for a woman, when she marries a man whose character can in some degree be ascertained, by his having been for some time under his own guidance."   Ibid., Vol. II, Ch. 21

21 Man, lord of all, beneath the reign of time,
Awaits perfection in a nobler clime.
                              Ibid., Ch. 24,
                              "To a Rose Bush"

22 Delicacies are apt to satiate the appetite, and to produce such a whimsical craving after novelty, as to render the coarsest food unpalatable. The most luxurious Epicures sometimes prescribe to themselves abstinence, in order to excite the greater relish for an expected dainty.   Ibid., Ch. 28

23 They beheld his happiness with that sort of good-humoured envy, which warm admiration is apt to inspire, and which, though it desires as fortunate a lot for itself, has no malevolent wish to lessen the felicity of another.   Ibid.

24 "How disgraceful are these baby quarrels! how ridiculous these high theatrical passions, which subject them to the laugh of the neighbourhood! nay, worse, which point out to artful villany, means whereby it may *effectually* undermine domestick happiness." Ibid., Ch. 31

25 Early in life, before his character was formed, or his opinions methodized, Mr. Clermont entered into marriage; with vague, floating ideas of angelick goodness, and consummate bliss. In proportion as his romantick enthusiasm had raised the mortal nymph into a goddess, his cooler, but not more accurate judgment, as the infatuation of love subsided, magnified her errors into indelible offences. Ibid., Ch. 35

26 "I know that she has sufficient greatness of soul to dignify narrow circumstances by cheerful patience. . . ." Ibid., Ch. 38

642. Martha Wilson
(1758–post-1848)

1 . . . let it never be forgotten by you that the reputation established by a boy at school and college, whether it be of merit or demerit, will follow him through life.
Letter to C. S. Stewart, her nephew and adopted son (February 16, 1811), Quoted in *The Women of the American Revolution*, Vol. II, by Elizabeth F. Ellet 1848

2 As to your dress and manners, avoid as you would a pestilence those of a fop. Ibid.

3 . . . nothing affords more pleasure to the good and truly great, while nothing certainly is more prepossessing than a modest youth. Ibid.

4 There is much even in external manner—more than many wise people think; and a gentlemanlike deportment, accompanied by honest candor, strict integrity, and undeviating truth will secure more respect and esteem for you in youth, as well as in after age, than any degree of talent, however brilliant, possibly can without them.
Letter to C. S. Stewart (March/April 1811), op. cit.

5 Press forward, my dear son, in the ways of wisdom—they are ways of pleasantness, and their end is peace. Letter to C. S. Stewart (May 31, 1814), op. cit.

6 Industry is the handmaid of good fortune. . . . Ibid.

7 Acquire, too, a habit of observation on men and manners, without which you can never secure the knowledge of the world essential to success in practical life. Ibid.

8 Man can do much for himself as respects his own improvement, unless self-love so blinds him that he cannot see his own imperfections and weaknesses. Ibid.

9 Some of the most finished characters, in all ages, of which the world can boast, are those who found the greatest difficulty in controlling their natural propensities, but whose persevering efforts caused even bad habits to give place to the most graceful accomplishments. Ibid.

10 The exercise of a little self-denial for the time being will be followed by the pleasure of having achieved the greatest of triumphs—a triumph over one's self. Ibid.

11 Confident that the life of a sincere Christian will ever be your highest honor, on this subject regard neither the smiles nor frowns of the world—neither its fashions nor its favors. Letter to C. S. Stewart (March 20, 1815), op. cit.

643. Agnes Craig
(1759–1841)

1 Talk not of love, it gives me pain,
For love has been my foe;
He bound me with an iron chain,
And plunged me deep in woe.
But friendship's pure and lasting joys,
My heart was formed to prove.
"Talk Not of Love,"
Scottish Song,
Mary Carlyle Aitken, ed.
1874

644. Sarah Wentworth Morton
(1759–1846)

1 When life hung quiv'ring on a single hair
"To Constantia," St. 1,
Massachusetts Magazine
May 1790

2 But timid genius from herself retires,
Conceals her darting rays, and damps her
kindling fires. "Ode Inscribed to Mrs. M.
Warren,"* St. 2,
Massachusetts Magazine
July 1790

*Mercy Otis Warren. See 550.

3 . . . that stagnation of heart, and that pulsa-
tion of brain, which sometimes seems to
precede the most deplorable of human miseries.
My Mind and Its Thoughts 1823

4 To the mere superficial observer, it would
seem that man was sent into this breathing
world for the purpose of enjoyment—
woman for that of trial and of suffering.
"The Sexes,"
op. cit.

5 To man belong professions, dignities,
authorities, and pleasures; for woman,
there remain only duties, domestic virtue,
and perhaps as the result of these, the happiness of tranquil submission.
Ibid.

6 More prized than wealth; than worlds more
dear "Lines to the Breath of Kindness,"
St. 2, op. cit.

7 Expression in its finest utterance lives,
And a new language to creation gives.
"To Mr. [Gilbert] Stuart.* Upon
Seeing Those Portraits Which
were Painted by Him at
Philadelphia, in the Beginning of
the Present Century,"
St. 1, op. cit.

*Famed American portrait painter (1755–1828).

8 Genius is sorrow's child—to want allied—
Consoled by glory, and sustained by pride,
To souls sublime her richest wreath she
owes,
And loves that fame which kindred worth
bestows. Ibid., St. 5

9 So my lost boy, arrayed in fancy's charms,
Just born to mourn—with premature decay
To the cold tyrant stretched his feeble arms,
And struggling sighed his little life away.
"Memento, for My Infant Who
Lived But Eighteen Hours,"
St. 2, op. cit.

10 Did all the Gods of Afric sleep,
Forgetful of their guardian love,
When the white tyrants of the deep
Betrayed him in the palmy grove?
"The African Chief,"
St. 2, op. cit.

11 Let sorrow bathe each blushing cheek,
Bend piteous o'er the tortured slave,
Whose wrongs compassion cannot speak,
Whose only refuge was the grave.
Ibid., St. 15

645. Martha Laurens Ramsay
(1759–1811)

1 . . . the bucks, the fops, the idlers of college. . . . *Letters to her Son at College,*
n.d.

2 ... of all the mean objects in creation, a lazy, poor, proud gentleman, especially if he is a dressy fellow, is the meanest. ...
Ibid.

3 God has given you an excellent understanding. Oh, make use of it for wise purposes; acknowledge it as his gift; and let it regulate your conduct, and harmonize your passions.   Ibid. (June 13, 1810)

4 "Give me thine heart, my son," is the language of Scripture; and where there is any heart worth giving or worth having, I believe it is seldom refused to the authors of our being, the protectors of our infancy. ...   Ibid. (July 18, 1810)

646. Anna Green Winslow
(1759–1780)

1 Stoop down my thoughts, that use to rise,
Converse a while with death;
Think how a gasping mortal lies,
And pants away his breath.
"On the Death of Mr. Stephen March"
(March 14, 1772),
Diary of Anna Green Winslow:
A Boston School Girl of 1771,
Alice Morse Earle, ed.   1895

2 Those golden arts* the vulgar never knew.
"To her Parents"
(March 17, 1772), op. cit.

*Virtues.

647. Mary Wollstonecraft
(1759–1797)

1 ... women, intoxicated by the adoration which men, under the influence of their senses, pay them, do not seek to obtain a durable interest in their hearts, or to become the friends of the fellow creatures who find amusement in their society.
Introduction to 1st ed.,
A Vindication of the Rights of
Women   1792

2 Perhaps the seeds of false-refinement, immorality, and vanity, have ever been shed by the great. Weak, artificial beings, raised above the common wants and defections of their race, in a premature unnatural manner, undermine the very foundation of virtue, and spread corruption through the whole mass of society!   Ibid.

3 ... elegance is inferior to virtue. ...
Ibid.

4 The mind will ever be unstable that has only prejudices to rest on, and the current will run with destructive fury when there are no barriers to break its force.
"The Prevailing Opinion of a
Sexual Character Discussed,"
op. cit.

5 ... till society be differently constituted, much cannot be expected from education.
Ibid.

6 ... it is a farce to call any being virtuous whose virtues do not result from the exercise of his own reason.   Ibid.

7 But in the education of women the cultivation of the understanding is always subordinate to the acquirement of some corporeal accomplishment. ...   Ibid.

8 Standing armies can never consist of resolute robust men; they may be well disciplined machines, but they will seldom contain men under the influence of strong passions, or with very vigorous faculties.
Ibid.

9 ... as blind obedience is ever sought for by power, tyrants and sensualists are in the right when they endeavour to keep women in the dark, because the former only want slaves, and the latter a play-thing.
Ibid.

10 Youth is the season for love in both sexes; but in those days of thoughtless enjoyment provision should be made for the more important years of life, when reflection takes place of sensation.   Ibid.

11 ... the chaste wife, and serious mother, should only consider her power to please as the polish of her virtues, and the affection of her husband as one of the comforts that render her task less difficult, and her life happier. But, whether she be loved or neglected, her first wish should be to make herself respectable. ... Ibid.

12 Fondness is a poor substitute for friendship! Ibid.

13 But when forebearance confounds right and wrong, it ceases to be a virtue. ... Ibid.

14 ... females ... have been stripped of the virtues that should clothe humanity ... their sole ambition is to be fair, to raise emotion instead of inspiring respect; and this ignoble desire, like the servility in absolute monarchies, destroys all strength of character. Ibid.

15 Liberty is the mother of virtue. ... Ibid.

16 The human character has ever been formed by the employments the individual, or class, pursues; and if the faculties are not sharpened by necessity, they must remain obtuse. Ibid.

17 From the respect paid to property flow, as from a poisoned fountain, most of the evils and vices which render this world such a dreary scene to the contemplative mind.
"Of the Pernicious Effects which Arise from the Unnatural Distinctions Established in Society," op. cit.

18 ... love is not to be bought, in any sense of the word; its silken wings are instantly shriveled up when anything beside a return in kind is sought. Ibid.

19 The respect ... which is paid to wealth and mere personal charms, is a true northeast blast that blights the tender blossoms of affection and virtue. Ibid.

20 The preposterous distinctions of rank, which renders civilization a curse by dividing the world between voluptuous tyrants and cunning envious dependents, corrupt, almost equally, every class of people. ... Ibid.

21 But take away natural rights, and duties become null. Ibid.

22 When poverty is more disgraceful than even vice, is not morality cut to the quick? Ibid.

23 It is a melancholy truth—yet such is the blessed effect of civilization!—the most respectable women are the most repressed. ... Ibid.

24 Would man but generously snap our chains, and be content with rational fellowship instead of slavish obedience, they would find us more observant daughters, more affectionate sisters, more faithful wives, more reasonable mothers—in a word, better citizens. We should then love them with true affection, because we should learn to respect ourselves. ... Ibid.

25 Tyrants would have cause to tremble if reason were to become the rule of duty in any of the relations of life, for the light might spread till perfect day appeared.
"Parental Affection," op. cit.

26 Meek wives are, in general, foolish mothers; wanting their children to love them best, and take their part, in secret, against the father, who is held up as a scarecrow. Ibid.

27 But a child, though a pledge of affection, will not enliven it, if both father and mother be content to transfer the charge to hirelings; for they who do their duty by proxy should not murmur if they miss the reward of duty—parental affection produces filial duty. Ibid.

28 And when children are confined to the society of men and women, they very soon acquire that kind of premature manhood which stops the growth of very vigourous power of mind or body.   "On National Education," op. cit.

29 I . . . think schools, as they are now regulated, the hot-beds of vice and folly, and the knowledge of human nature supposedly attained there, merely cunning selfishness.   Ibid.

30 . . . only that education deserves emphatically to be termed cultivation of mind which teaches young people how to begin to think.   Ibid.

31 The imagination should not be allowed to debauch the understanding before it gains strength, or vanity will become the forerunner of vice: for every way of exhibiting the acquirements of a child is injurious to its moral character.   Ibid.

32 If marriage be the cement of society, mankind should all be educated after the same model. . . .   Ibid.

33 In this plan of [co-]education . . . I presuppose that such a degree of equality should be established between the sexes as would shut out gallantry and coquetry, yet allow friendship and love to temper the heart for the discharge of higher duties.   Ibid.

34 Society can only be happy and free in proportion as it is virtuous. . . .   Ibid.

35 . . . it is indolence and vanity—the love of pleasure and the love of sway, that will reign paramount in an empty mind.   Ibid.

36 . . . only by the jostlings of equality can we form a just opinion of ourselves.   Ibid.

37 . . . whatever tends to incapacitate the maternal character, takes woman out of her sphere.   Ibid.

38 You perceive that sorrow has almost made a child of me, and that I want to be soothed to peace.   Letter XII, from Paris (January 1794), *Letters to Imlay**
*Captain Gilbert Imlay, her lover.

39 How I hate this crooked business! This intercourse with the world, which obliges one to see the worst side of human nature!   Ibid., Letter XXX (December 29, 1794)

40 . . . why does one project, successful or abortive, only give place to two others? Is it not sufficient to avoid poverty?   Ibid.

41 . . . if there be a searcher of hearts, mine will not be despised. Ibid., Letter XXXVI (February 10, 1795)

42 Society fatigues me inexpressibly. So much so, that finding fault with everyone, I have only reason enough to discover that the fault is in myself.   Ibid., Letter XXXVII (February 19, 1795)

43 I never wanted but your heart—That gone, you have nothing more to give.   Ibid., Letter LXX, London (November 1795)

44 I begin to love this little creature, and to anticipate his birth as a fresh twist to a knot, which I do not wish to untie.   Letter to William Godwin, her husband (March 1797), Quoted in *Godwin and Mary* by Ralph M. Wardle   1966

648.   Sally Sayward Wood
(1759–1855)

1 Amelia was not a disciple of Mary Woolstonecraft* [sic], she was not a woman of fashion, nor a woman of spirit. She was an oldfashioned wife, and she meant to obey her husband: she meant to do her duty in the strictest sense of the word.   *Amelia; or, the Influence of Virtue*   1802

*See 647.

649. Margaret Shippen Arnold
(1760–1804)

1 Weak woman as I am, I would not wish to prevent what would be deemed necessary to preserve his* honor.   Letter to her father
(June 26, 1792),
Quoted in
"Life of Margaret Shippen"
by Lewis Burd Walker,
*Pennsylvania Magazine of History
and Biography*, Vol. XXV
1901

*Her husband, Benedict Arnold.

2 . . . my ambition has sunk with my fortune.
Letter to E. Burd
(August 15, 1801), op. cit.

3 At one period, when I viewed everything through a false medium, I fancied that nothing but the sacrifice of my life would benefit my children, for that my wretchedness embittered every moment of their lives; and dreadful to say, I was many times on the point of making the sacrifice.
Letter to her father (1801),
op. cit.

4 I have rescued your father's memory from disrespect by paying all his just debts, and his children will now never have the mortification of being reproached with his speculations having injured anybody beyond his own family. . . .
Letter to her sons, Richard and
Henry (August 1803), op. cit.

650. Charlotte Charke
(?–1760)

1 Your two Friends, PRUDENCE and REFLECTION, I am inform'd, have lately ventur'd to pay you a Visit; for which I heartily congratulate you, as nothing can possibly be more joyous to the Heart than the Return of absent Friends, after a long and painful Peregrination.
Dedication,
*A Narrative of the Life of Mrs.
Charlotte Charke*   1755

2 'Tis every Parent's Duty to breed their Children with every Advantage their Fortunes will admit of. . . .   Text, op. cit.

3 . . . there are too many busy Meddlars in the World, who are ever ready to clinch the Nail of Sedition, when once 'tis struck. . . .
Ibid.

4 An excellent Demonstration of the Humanity of those low-lived Wretches! who have no farther Regard to the Persons they employ, but while they are immediately serving 'em; and look upon Players like Pack-horses, though they live by 'em.
Ibid.

5 . . . forced again to . . . find fresh means of Subsistence . . . 'till even the last thread of Invention was worn out.   Ibid.

6 Misfortunes are too apt to wear out Friendship. . . .   Ibid.

7 Power, when invested in the Hands of Knaves or Fools, generally is the Source of Tyrany. . . .   Ibid.

8 . . . I think 'tis Pity to draw Tears FROM THOSE, WHO HAVE SO GENEROUSLY CONTRIBUTED TOWARDS MAKING ME SMILE.   Ibid.

651. Rebecca Franks
(c.1760–1823)

1 I have gloried in my rebel countrymen!
Would to God I, too, had been a patriot!
Remark to General Winfield
Scott (c.1816),
Quoted in *Rebecca Franks: An
American Jewish Belle of the
Last Century*
by Max J. Kohler
1894

652. Anne Douglas Howard
(?–1760)

1 Nothing so like as male and female youth;
Nothing so like as man and woman old
A defence of her sex in answer
to [Alexander] Pope's
"Characters of Women,"
The British Female Poets,
George W. Bethune, ed.   1848

2 Ambitious thoughts the humblest cottage
fill;
For as they can they push their little fame,
And try to leave behind a deathless name.
Ibid.

3 In education all the difference lies;
Woman, if taught, would be as learned and
wise
As haughty man, inspired by arts and rules.
Ibid.

4 Culture improves all fruits, all sorts we find,
Wit, judgment, sense, fruits of the human
mind.   Ibid.

5 Can they on other themes converse or
write,
Than what they hear all day, or dream all
night?   Ibid.

653. Dicey Langston
(1760?–?)

1 Shoot me if you dare! I will not tell you.*
Quoted by the Hon. B. F. Perry
in *The Women
of the American Revolution*,
Vol. II, by Elizabeth F. Ellet
1848

*Response to a Loyalist's demand for intelligence concerning the Whigs; Langston was 16 years old at the time.

2 Pewter bullets, sir, will not kill a Whig. . . .
It is said, sir, that a witch can be shot only
with a silver bullet; and I am sure the Whigs
are more under the protection of Providence. Remark to a Tory captain, op. cit.

654. Mary Slocumb
(1760–1836)

1 Allow me to observe and prophesy, the only
land in these United States which will ever
remain in possession of a British officer, will
measure but six feet by two.
Remark to a British colonel,
Quoted in *Women of the
American Revolution*,
Vol. II, by Elizabeth F. Ellet
1848

2 My husband is not a man who would allow
a duke, or even a king, to have a quiet [titled] seat upon his ground.

Op. cit.

3 "Where is my husband?"
"Where he ought to be, madam; in pursuit
of the enemy. But pray," said he, "how
came you here?"
"Oh, I thought," replied I, "you would
need nurses as well as soldiers. See! I have
already dressed many of these good fellows;
and here is one"—going to Frank and lifting him up with my arm under his head so
that he could drink some more water—
"would have died before any of you men
could have helped him."

"I believe you," said Frank. Just then I looked up, and my husband, as bloody as a butcher, and as muddy as a ditcher, stood before me.
"Why, Mary!" he exclaimed, "What are you doing there? Hugging Frank Cogdell, the greatest reprobate in the army?"
"I don't care," I cried. "Frank is a brave fellow, a good soldier, and a true friend to Congress."   Op. cit.

655. Anne Yearsley
(1760–1806)

1 Earth by the grizzly tyrant desert made,
The feathered warblers quit the leafless shade;
Quit those dear scenes where life and love began,
And, cheerless seek the savage haunts of man.   "Clifton Hill,"
St. 1 (January 1785),
The British Female Poets,
George W. Bethune, ed.   1848

2 Love seeks a milder zone. . . .
Ibid.

3 Go be a bear of Pythagorean name,
From man distinguished by thy hideous frame.   Ibid.

4 All Nature's sweets in joyous circles move
And wake the frozen soul again to love.
Ibid., St. 2

5 With more than needful awe I view the great   "To Stella;* On Her Accusing the Author of Flattery,"
op. cit.
*Pseudonym of Hannah More. See 595.

6 For mine's a stubborn and a savage will
Ibid.

7 The portals of the swelling soul ne'er ope'd
By liberal converse, rude ideas strove
Awhile for vent, but found it not, and died.
Thus rust the mind's best powers.
"A Poem on Mrs. Montague,"*
The Female Poets of Great Britain,
Frederic Rowton, ed.   1853

*Mary Wortley Montague. See 492.

656. Joanna Baillie
(1762–1851)

1 There is a melancholy pleasure
In tales of hapless love;—a treasure
From which the sadden'd bosom borrows
A respite short from present sorrows.
"A Metrical Legend of William Wallace," St. ix,
Fugitive Verses
1790

2 For what a thrilling sympathy,
Did e'er in human bosom vie
With that which stirs the soldier's breast,
When high in god-like worth confest,
Some noble leader gives command,
To combat for his native land?
Ibid., St. xxxix

3 Is it o'er modesty or pride
Which may not open praise abide?
"The Legend of Christopher Columbus,"
St. iv, op. cit.

4 They eyed the wondrous strangers o'er and o'er,—
Those beings of the ocean and the air,
With humble, timid rev'rence; all their store
Of gather'd wealth inviting them to share;
To share what e'er their lowly cabins hold;
Their feather'd crowns, their fruits, their arms, their gold.
Their gold, that fatal gift!—O foul disgrace!
Repaid with cruel wreck of all their harmless race.   Ibid., St. xvii

5 "May the great spirit smooth the tide
"With gentle gales, and be thy guide!"
. . .
He saw them still upon the strand
Tossing their dark arms on the wind.
He saw them like a helpless flock
Who soon must bear the cruel shock
Of savage wolves
. . .
He saw the fate he could not now control.

And groan'd in bitter agony of soul.
                                    Ibid., St. xli

6 O! who shall lightly say that fame
Is nothing but an empty name?
                                    Ibid., St. lix

7 O lovely Sisters! is it true
That they are all inspired by you,
And write by inward magic charm'd,
And high enthusiasm warm'd?
                        "Address to the Muses,"
                                St. xi, op. cit.

8 "Ah! happy is the man whose early lot
Hath made him master of a furnish'd cot;
Who trains the vine that round his window
    grows,
And after setting sun his garden hoes;
Whose wattled pails his own enclosure
    shield,
Who toils not daily in another's field."
                                    "A Reverie,"
                                St. iii, op. cit.

9 "How simple is the lad, and 'reft of skill,
Who thinks with love to fix a woman's
    will!"   "A Disappointment,"
                                St. ii, op. cit.

10 "What hollow sound is that?" approaching
    near,
The roar of many wheels breaks on his ear.
It is the flood of human life in motion!
                                    "London,"
                                St. iii, op. cit.

11 Sweet bud of promise, fresh and fair,
Just moving in the morning air.
The morn of life but just begun,
The sands of time just set to run!
Sweet babe with cheek of pinky hue,
With eyes of soft ethereal blue,
With raven hair like finest down
Of unfledged bird, and scant'ly shown
Beneath the cap of cumbrous lace,
That circles round thy placid face!
Ah, baby! little dost thou know
How many yearning bosoms glow,
How many lips in blessings move,
How many eyes beam looks of love

At sight of thee!
                "To Sophia J. Baillie, an Infant,"
                                in toto, op. cit.

12 Busy work brings after ease;
Ease brings sport and sport brings rest;
For young and old, of all degrees,
The mingled lot is best.   "Rhymes,"
                                St. i, op. cit.

13 But deem not that the Parent of mankind,
Maker of all, hath to one race confined
The gifts His blessed Spirit can bestow
On all Earth's scatter'd nations here below.
                                "Ahalya Baee,"
                                St. iii, op. cit.

14 The learned Sage who loves to muse,
And many a linked thought pursues,
Says to himself, and heaves a sigh
For things to come and things gone by,
"O that our restless chiefs, by misery
    school'd,
Would rule their states as that brave
    woman ruled!"   Ibid., St. xxx

15 GEOFFRY. Some men are born to feat and
    not to fight:
Whose sluggish minds, e'en in fair honours
    field
Still on their dinner turn—
Let such pot-boiling varlets stay at home,
And wield a flesh-hook rather than a
    sword.   Basil,
                            Act I, Sc. 1   1798

16 COUNT ROSINBERG. Such men have been; of
    whom it may be said,
Their spirits conquer'd when their clay was
    cold.   Ibid.

17 What custom hath endeared
We part with sadly, tho we prize it not.
                                    Ibid., Sc. 2

18 COUNT ROSINBERG. 'Faith, ev'ry woman
    hath some witching charm,
If that she be not proud, or captious.
                                       Ibid.

19 VICTORIA. If Love a tyrant be,
How dare his humble chained votaries
To tell such rude and wicked tales of him?

BASIL. Because they most of lovers' ills complain,
Who but affect it as a courtly grace,
Whilst he who feels it is silent.
                                        Ibid., Act II, Sc. 1

20 DUKE. But int'rest, int'rest, man's all-ruling pow'r. . . .   Ibid., Sc. 3

21 COUNTESS OF ALBINI. For she who only finds her self-esteem
In other's admiration, begs in alms;
Depends on others for her daily food,
And is the very servant of her slaves. . . .
                                        Ibid., Sc. 4

22 COUNT ROSINBERG. The brave man is not he who feels no fear,
For that were stupid and irrational;
But he, whose noble soul its fear subdues,
And barely dares the danger nature shrinks from.   Ibid., Act III, Sc. 1

23 GAURIECIO. And he who teaches men to think, though nobly,
Doth raise within their minds a busy judge
To scan his actions.   Ibid., Sc. 2

24 COUNT ROSINBERG. For well thou knowest that flatt'ry ever is
The tickling spice, the pungent seasoning
Which makes this motley dish of monstrous scraps
So pleasing to the dainty lover's taste.
                                        Ibid., Sc. 3

25 SONG. Child, with many a childish wile,
Timid look, and blushing smile,
Downy wings to steal thy way,
Gilded bow, and quiver gay,
Who in thy simple mien would trace
The tyrant of the human race?
                                        Ibid.

26 COUNT ROSINBERG. But woman's grief is like a summer storm,
Short as it violent is. . . . Ibid., Act V, Sc. 3

27 DE MONFORT. Thus, it is true, from the sad years of life,
We sometimes do short hours, yea minutes strike,

Keen, blissful, bright, never to be forgotten. . . .   *De Monfort,*
                    Act I, Sc. 1   1798

28 Thinks't thou there are no serpents in the world
But those that slide along the grassy sod,
And sting the luckless foot that presses them?
There are who in the path of social life
Do bask their spotted skins in Fortune's sun,
And sting the soul.   Ibid., Sc. 2

29 DE MONFORT. That man was never born whose secret soul,
With all its motley treasure of dark thoughts,
Foul fantasies, vain musings, and wild dreams,
Was ever open'd to another's scan.
                                        Ibid.

30 DE MONFORT. To be annihilated,
What all men shrink from; to be dust, be nothing, were bliss to me, compar'd to what I am!   Ibid., Act II, Sc. 2

31 A willing heart adds feather to the heel.
                                        Ibid., Act III, Sc. 2

32 BERNARD. See'st thou that lifeless corpse, those bloody wounds?
See how he lies, who but so shortly since
A living creature was, with all the powers
Of sense, and motion, and humanity!
O! what a heart had he who did this deed!
                                        Ibid., Act V, Sc. 2

33 DE MONFORT. This little term of nature's agony
Will soon be o'er, and what is past is past. . . .   Ibid., Sc. 4

34 1ST MONK. Ay, who knows
What voices mix with the dark midnight winds?   Ibid., Sc. 5

35 JANE DE MONFORT. He died that death which best becomes a man,
Who is with keenest sense of conscious ill
And deep remorse assail'd, a wounded spirit.
A death that kills the noble and the brave,

And only them. He had no other wound.
Ibid., Sc. 6

36 MR. HARWOOD. . . . the more fools speak the more people will despise them. . . .
The Trial,
Act I, Sc. 2 1798

37 HUMPHRY. . . . but I don't know how it is, nothing that we take in hand ever comes to any good; and what provokes me more than all the rest is, that the more pains we take about it the worst it always succeeds.
Ibid., Act II, Sc. 2

38 MR. ROYSTON. O! hang it! I never spare myself: I must work to make others work. . . .
Ibid.

39 COL. HARDY. It is so seldom that a young fellow has any inclination for the company of an old man. . . . Ibid., Act IV, Sc. 1

40 COL. HARDY. Nay, heaven defend us from a violent woman; for that is the devil himself!
Ibid.

41 MR. WITHRINGTON. But these are men whose passions are of such a violent overbearing nature, that love in them may be considered as a disease of the mind; and the object of it claims no more perfection or pre-eminence among women, than chalk, lime, or oatmeal do among dainties, because some diseased stomachs do prefer them to all things. Ibid., Act V, Sc. 1

42 The bliss e'en of a moment still is bliss.
The Beacon,
Act I, Sc. 2 1802

43 ETHWALD. I am as one
Who doth attempt some lofty mountain's height,
And having gain'd what to the upcast eye
The summit's point appear'd, astonish'd sees
Its cloudy top, majestic and enlarg'd,
Towering aloft as distant as before.
Ethwald, Part First,
Act II, Sc. 4 1802

44 ALWY. Ay, vengeance! vengeance! rouse thee like a man! Ibid., Sc. 5

45 ETHWALD. Dull hopeless privacy!
From it my soul recoils: unto my nature
It is the death of death, hard and hateful.
Ibid., Act IV, Sc. 1

46 ALWY. Glory is ever bought by those who earn it
With loss of many lives most dear and precious. Ibid., Sc. 4

47 ETHWALD. For, ah! thou knowest not in how short a space
The soul of man within him may be changed. Ibid., Act V, Sc. 3

48 ETHWALD. He who will not give
Some portion of his ease, his blood, his wealth,
For other's good is a poor frozen churl.
Ethwald, Part Second,
Act I, Sc. 2 1802

49 The tyrant now
Trusts not to men: nightly within his chamber
The watch-dog guards his couch, the only friend
He now dare trust. Ibid., Act V, Sc. 3

50 ROBERT. . . . but when a body is vexed he'll be angry, and when a body is angry, good sooth! he'll e'en bolt out with the first word that comes to him, though he were a saint.
The Second Marriage,
Act I, Sc. 1 1802

51 SIR CRAFTY SUPPLECOAT. Pride is a fault that great men blush not to own: it is the ennobled offspring of self-love; though, it must be confessed, grave and pompous vanity, like a fat plebeian in a rove of office, does very often assume its name.
Ibid., Act II, Sc. 4

52 MORGAN. Every thing in my native country is plesant to me, or at least ought to be so; but I don't know; I return to it again like a dog to a deserted house; he begins to wag his tale at the threshhold, but there is nobody to welcome him in; there is another generation grown up, that knows not me; there is nothing but young people now in the world. Ibid., Act III, Sc. 1

53 SIR CRAFTY SUPPLECOAT. . . . but there have been certain places, time out of mind, which . . . stand up in the great field of honour like finger-posts in a wide-tracked common, saying 'This is the way to such a place:' they who are once possessed of those places, move on to the others, for no earthly reason, that we can perceive, but because they have been placed in the first; and this you will readily allow is no time for innovation.   Ibid., Act IV, Sc. 1

54 MAHOMET. In mortal man
I have no trust; they are all hollow slaves,
Who tremble and detest, and would betray.
Constantine Paleologus,
Act III, Sc. 2   1804

55 RODRIGO. How do men act, when they together stand, on the last perch of this swiftly-sinking wreck?
Do they not bravely give their parting cheer,
And make their last voice loud and boldly sound
Amidst the hollow roarings of the storm?
Ibid., Act V, Sc. 1

56 OTHUS. . . . heaven ofttimes
Success bestows where blessing is denied.
Ibid., Sc. 3

57 WORSHIPTON. Curse your snug comfortable ways of living! my soul abhors the idea of it. I'll pack up all I have in a knapsack first, and join the wild Indians in America.
The Country Inn,
Act V, Sc. 2   1804

58 I would have time turn'd backward in his course,
And what is past ne'er to have been: my self
A thing that no existence ever had.
Canst thou do this for me?
Rayner   1804

59 The mind doth shape itself to its own wants
And can bear all things.   Ibid.

60 Still on it creeps,
Each little moment at another's heels,
Till hours, days, years, and ages are made up

Of such small parts as these, and men look back
Worn and bewilder'd, wondering how it is.
Ibid.

61 RAYNER. . . . I have observ'd
That those who bear misfortunes overmeekly
Do but persuade mankind that they and want are all too fitly match'd to be disjoin'd. . . .   Ibid., Act I, Sc. 1

62 3RD CROWD. I paid half a dollar for a place near the scaffold; and it would have made any body's heart drop blood to have seen him when he lifted up the handkerchief from his eyes, and took his last look of the day-light, and all the living creatures about him.
2ND CROWD. Ay, man, that a human creature should be thus thrust out of the world by human creatures like himself; is it a piteous thing?   Ibid., Act III, Sc. 1

63 RAYNER. To be upon the verge of death is awful;
And awful from that verge to be recall'd.
Ibid., Act V, Sc. 4

64 EARL OF ARGYLL. That day will come,
When in the grave this hoary head of mine,
And many after heads, in death are laid;
And happier men, our sons, shall live to see it.
O may they prize it too with grateful hearts;
And, looking back on these our stormy days
Of other years, pity, admire, and pardon
The fierce, contentious, ill-directed valour
Of gallant fathers, born in darker time!
The Family Legend,
Act V, Sc. 4   1810

65 BALTIMORE. O! hang them, but they won't laugh! I have seen the day, when, if a man made himself ridiculous, the world would laugh at him. But now, everything that is mean, disgusting, and absurd, pleases them but so much the better!   *The Election,*
Act I, Sc. 2   1811

66 TROUBRIDGE. A man may injure in a hundred different ways and provoke no hostile return; but when, added to some petty offences, he varies his voice and gesture, wears his coat and dublet, nay, moves his very hand in a manner that is irksome to us, what mortal is there, pagan, or believer, that can refrain from setting himself in array against him? *Ibid.*

67 Pampered vanity is a better thing perhaps than starved pride. *Ibid., Act II, Sc. 2*

68 CHARLOTTE. There never was any body like me! for always when I wish to behave best, something or other comes across me and I expose myself . . . some devil put it into my head, and I could not help it.
Ibid., Act III, Sc. 1

69 CHARLOTTE. I wish I were with some of the wild people that run in the woods, and know nothing about accomplishments!
Ibid., Sc. 3

70 MRS. BALTIMORE. . . . the pleasing hum of happy unseen life is in the air.
Ibid., Act IV, Sc. 1

71 1ST VOTER. . . . but somehow or other I have a kindness for every thing that pertains to the great salt sea, with all the ships, and the waves roaring, and all that. . . .
Ibid., Sc. 3

72 TROUBRIDGE. There is something in man that always inclines him to the side of the oppressed. *Ibid., Act V, Sc. 2*

73 OSTERLOO. Can there be virtue in penances suffered by the body to do away offences of the soul? If there be!—O if there be, let them channel my body with stripes, and swathe round in one continued girth of wounds! Any thing that can be endured here is mercy compared to the dreadful abiding of what may be hereafter.
The Dream,
Act II, Sc. 3   1812

74 JEROME. Death is but a short though awful pass; as it were a winking of the eyes for a moment. We shut them in this world and open them in the next: and there we open them with such increased vividness of existness, that this life, in comparison, will appear but as a state of slumber and of dreams. *Ibid., Act III, Sc. 1*

75 Priest, spare thy words; I add not to my sins
That of presumption, in pretending now
To offer up to heaven the forc'd repentance
Of some short moments for a life of crime.
Orra   1812

76 ORRA. Dreams I fear not: it is the dreadful waking,
When, in deep midnight stillness, the roused fancy
Takes up th' imperfect shadows of its sleep,
Like a marr'd speech snatch'd from a bungler's mouth,
Shaping their forms distinctively and vivid
To visions horrible:—this is my bane;
It is the dreadful waking that I fear.
Ibid., Act II, Sc. 2

77 ORRA. Can spirit from the tomb, or fiend from Hell,
More hateful, more malignant be than man? *Ibid., Act III, Sc. 2*

78 ORRA. The very air rests thick and heavily,
Where murder has been done.
Ibid.

79 ORRA. He was not all a father's heart could wish;
But oh, he was my son!—my only son.
Ibid.

80 ORRA. A fearful kindredship there is between
The living and the dead—an awful bond!
Ibid., Act IV, Sc. 3

81 CRAFTON. Fy, fy! let no man be on his knees but when he is at his prayers.
The Alienated Manor,
Act V, Sc. 2   1836

82 SANCHO. Me care for te laws when te laws care for me. *Ibid.*

83 ARTINA. Misfortune is not dainty in associates. *The Bride,*
Act I, Sc. 2   1836

84 SAMARKOON. Associates! Solitude, in trackless deserts,
Where locusts, ants, and lizards poorly thrive,—
On the bare summit of a rugged peak,
Where birds of prey in dusky circles wing
The troubled air with clam'rous din,
Were to an honest heart endurable,
Rather than such associates.
Ibid.

85 MISS FRANKLAND. I am no great admirer of poetry,—of what is called sentimental poetry, at least ... but why should such beautiful thoughts be cramped up in such patterned shapes of versification,—all rule and difficulty? I have neither ear for the measure, nor quickness of comprehension for the meaning. *Enthusiasm,*
Act I, Sc. 2   1836

86 CLAUDIEN. Thou precious creature! thy affection gleams
Like sunshine through one solitary loophole,
In a dark firmament of gather'd clouds,
Gilding one spot of ocean, hill, or plain,
With brightness beautiful though circumscribed. *The Homicide,*
Act III, Sc. 1   1836

87 CORDENIUS MARO. Is it madness
To be the humble follower of Him,
Who left the bliss of heaven to be for us
A man on earth, in spotless virtue living,
As man ne'er lived....
That which is reason call'd, and yet has taught you
To worship different gods in every clime,
As dull and wicked as their worshipers,
Compared to it, is poor, confined, and mean.... *The Martyr,*
Act III, Sc. 2   1836

88 CORDENIUS MARO. ... this earth on which we stand
Is but the vestibule to glorious mansions,
Through which a moving crowd for-ever press.... Ibid.

89 SONG. Sweet sleep be with us, one and all!
And if upon its stillness fall
The visions of a busy brain,
We'll have our pleasure o'er again,
To warm the heart, to charm the sight,
Gay dreams to all! good night, good night.
The Phantom   1836

90 DUNARDEN. The times are changed,
And fashion now makes all things dull and spiritless. Ibid., Act I, Sc. 2

91 MALCOLM. Well, freely I confess our mountain matrons
In useful virtues do excel their mates;
And in what earthly region is it otherwise?
Ibid.

92 ROBINAIR. This will be triumph! this will be happiness! yea, that very thing, happiness, which I have been pursuing all my life, and have never yet overtaken.
The Stripling,
Act IV, Sc. 1   1836

93 ANNABELLA. Evil is but evil, and torment is but torment!—I have felt both—I have felt them to extremity—what have I then to fear? *Witchcraft,*
Act I, Sc. 1   1836

94 BLACKBAWLDY. I understand you weel enough: but will witches speak the truth, when the de'il is their teacher?
Ibid., Act II, Sc. 4

95 VIOLET. A creature so stricken with sorrow and disgrace has nothing to do in this world but to wait, in humble patience, till God in His mercy shall take her out of it.
Ibid., Act V, Sc. 2

96 Words of affection, howso'er express'd,
The latest spoken still are deem'd the best.
"Address to Miss Agnes Baillie
on Her Birthday,"
ll.125–126, n.d.

97 ... Some still a thought,
And clip it round the edge, and challenge him
Whose 'twas to swear to it. To serve things thus
Is as foul witches to cut up old moons

Into new stars. *Festus*, n.d.

98 Why Mammon sits before a million hearths
Where God is bolted out from every house.
Ibid.

99 Some souls lose all things but the love of
beauty;
And by that love they are redeemable.
For in love and beauty they acknowledge
good,
And good is God. Ibid.

100 The beautiful are never desolate;
But some one always loves them.
Ibid.

101 Her cheek had the pale pearly pink
Of the sea-shells, the world's sweetest tint,
as though
She lived, one half might deem, on rose's
sopp'd
In silver dew. Ibid.

102 Look on the bee upon the wing 'mong flow-
ers
—How brave, how bright his life. Then
mark him hiv'd,
Cramp'd, cringing in his self-built, social
cell.
Thus is it in the world-hive: most where
men
Lie deep in cities as in drifts.
Ibid.

103 Kind was she, and my friends were free
But poverty parts good company.
"Poverty Parts Good Company,"
n.d.

657. Dorothea Jordan
(1762–1816)

1 'Oh where, and Oh! where is your Highland
laddie gone?'
'He's gone to fight the French, for King
George upon the throne,
And it's Oh! in my heart, how I wish him
safe at home!' "The Blue Bells of
Scotland,"*

*Both this and "O Where, Tell Me Where" by Anne
Grant (see 624:3) are variants on an older popular
song.

658. Mrs. Lyon
(1762–1840)

1 Yet the doctors they do a' agree,
That whiskey's no the drink for me.
Saul! quoth Neil, 'twill spoil my glee,
Should they part me and whiskey, O.
"Neil Gow's Farewell to Whiskey,"
Scottish Song,
Mary Carlyle Aitken, ed.
1874

659. Susanna Haswell Rowson
(1762–1824)

1 FETNAH. Nature made us [women] equal to
them, and gave us the power to render ourselves superior. *Slaves in Algiers, or a
Struggle for Freedom* 1794

2 To raise the fall'n—to pity and forgive,
This is our noblest, best prerogative.
By these, pursuing nature's gentle plan,
We hold—in silken chains—the lordly ty-
rant man. Ibid., Epilogue

3 Nay, start not, gentle sirs; indeed, 'tis true,
Poor woman has her rights as well as you;
And if she's wise, she will assert them too.
"Rights of Women,"
Miscellaneous Poems 1804

4 . . . what is she fit for, but an upper servant
"Women As They Are," op. cit.

660. Helen Maria Williams
(1762–1827)

1 While Thee I seek, protecting Power,
Be my vain wishes stilled;
And may this consecrated hour
With better hopes be filled.
"Trust in Providence," St. 1,
*An Ode to Peace and Other
Poems* 1782–1788

2 In ev'ry joy that crowns my days,
   In ev'ry pain I bear,
   My heart shall find delight in praise,
   Or seek relief in prayer.   Ibid., St. 4

3 No riches from his scanty store
   My lover could impart;
   He gave a boon I valued more,
   He gave me all his heart.   "Song,"
                                    St. 1, op. cit.

4 The night is dark, the waters deep,
   Yet soft the billows roll;
   Alas! at every breeze I weep,
   The storm is in my soul.   Ibid., St. 5

5 As o'er thy work the seasons roll,
   And soothe, with change of bliss, the soul,
   Oh never may their smiling train
   Pass o'er the human scene in vain!
                                    "A Paraphrase,"
                                    St. 2, op. cit.

6 O ever skell'd to wear the form we love!
   To bid the shapes of fear and grief depart;
   Come, gentle Hope! with one gay smile
   remove
   The lasting sadness of an aching heart.
                                    "Sonnet to Hope,"
                                    Poems, moral, elegant and
                                    pathetic: viz. Essay on Man, by
                                    Pope . . . And Original Sonnets by
                                    Helen Maria Williams   1796

7 Meek twilight! haste to shroud the solar
   ray,
   And bring the hour my pensive spirit loves
                                    "Sonnet to Twilight,"
                                    op. cit.

8 O come! repass the stormy wave,
   O toil for gold no more!
   Our love a dearer pleasure gave
   On Evan's* peaceful shore.
                                    "Song,"
                                    St. 7, op. cit.
   *A small river near the poet's home.

9 Thy light can visionary thoughts impart,
   And lead the Muse to soothe a suffering
   heart.   "Sonnet to the Moon,"
                                    op. cit.

661. Josephine
(1763–1814)

1 Trust to me, ladies, and do not envy a splendor which does not constitute happiness.
                    Quoted in *Lives of Celebrated Women*
                    by Samuel Griswold Goodrich
                                                1844

2 . . . patience and goodness will ever in the end conciliate the goodwill of others.
                    Letter to her children (1794),
                                                op. cit.

3 Socrates, when condemned, philosophized with his disciples; a mother, on the point of undergoing a similar fate, may discourse with her children.   Ibid.

662. Anne Willing Bingham
(1764–1801)

1 The women of France interfere in the politics of the Country, and often give a decided Turn to the Fate of Empires.
                    Letter to Thomas Jefferson
                    (c.1783–1786),
                    Quoted in *The Papers of*
                    Thomas Jefferson,
                    Vol. XI, Julian P. Boyd, ed.
                                                1955

663. Elizabeth Phillipine Marie Hélène
(1764–1794)

1 I am Elizabeth of France, the aunt of your king [Louis XVII].   In answer to request for her identity at her tribunal
                    (May 10, 1794),
                    Quoted in *Biography of*
                    Distinguished Women
                    by Sarah Josepha Hale   1876

664.   Catherine Rilliet-Huber
(1764–?)

1 All I can say is that she [Germaine de
Staël*] is as lively and brilliant as ever—
which proves the advantage of organizing
one's heart in a system of multiple hiding
places.   Letter to Henri Meister
(November 13, 1810),
Quoted in *Mistress to an Age: A
Life of Madame de Staël*
by J. Christopher Herold
1958

*See 676.

665.   Juliana Krudener
(1764–1824)

1 Stay quiet; refuse nothing; flowers grow
only because they tranquilly allow the sun's
rays to reach them. You must do the same.
Remark to Germaine de Staël*,
Quoted in *Mistress to an Age: A
Life of Madame de Staël*
by J. Christopher Herold
1958

*See 676.

666.   Mary Anne Lamb
(1764–1847)

1 Who, that e'er could understand
The rare structure of a hand,
With its branching fingers fine,
Work itself of hands divine,
Strong, yet delicately knit,
For ten thousand uses fit   "Cleanliness,"
Poetry for Children   1809

2 All-endearing Cleanliness,
Virtue next to Godliness,
Easiest, cheapest, needfullest duty,
To the body health and beauty;
Who that's human would refuse it,
When a little water does it?
Ibid.

3 This rose-tree is not made to bear
The violet blue, nor lily fair,
Nor the sweet mignonette:

And if this tree were discontent,
Or wish'd to change its natural bent,
It all in vain would fret.   "Envy,"
St. 2, op. cit.

4 Now, abject, stooping, old, and wan,
Neglected is the beggar man.
"The Beggar Man,"
St. 2, op. cit.

5 Whatever she taught them beside,
In his turn every bird of them said,
Tho' the nest-making art he ne'er tried,
He had just such a thought in his head.
"The Magpie's Nest,"
III, St. 1, op. cit.

6 There's not a more productive source
Of waste of time to the young mind
Than dress. . . .   "Time Spent in Dress,"
St. 2, op. cit.

7 The house is full enough of sorrow;
Little baby, don't be cross.
"Nursing,"
St. 2, op. cit.

8 "A wicked action fear to do,
When you are by yourself; for tho'
You think you can conceal it,
A little bird that's in the air
The hidden trespass shall declare
And openly reveal it."
"The Boy and the Skylark,"
I, St. 1, op. cit.

9 But best resolves will sometimes sleep
Ibid., St. 4

10 His conscience slept a day or two,
As it is very apt to do   Ibid., St. 5

11 "When once he feels his conscience stirr'd,
That voice within him is the *bird*
That moves him to confession."
Ibid., II, St. 6

12 An infant is a selfish sprite
"The Broken Doll,"
St. 1, op. cit.

13 Reproof a parent's province is;
A sister's discipline is this;
By studied kindness to effect

A little brother's young respect.
> Ibid., St. 3

14 Puss-in-corners, hide-and-seek,
Sports for girls and punies weak!
Bate-the-bear he now may play at,
Leap-frog, football, sport away at;
Show his skill and strength at cricket—
Mark his distance, pitch his wicket
> "Going Into Breeches,"
> St. 2, op. cit.

15 My writing, all misshap'd, uneven as my
mind,
Within this narrow space can hardly be
confin'd.   "Written in the First Leaf of a
> Child's Memorandum-Book,"
> op. cit.

16 And every day I will set down in order due
How that day wasted is. . . .
> Ibid.

17 A tiger is. Observe how sleek
And glossy smooth his coat: no streak
On satin ever match'd the pride
Of that which marks his furry hide.
> "The Beasts in the Tower,"*
> I, St. 3, op. cit.

*I.e., the cages in a zoo.

18 This place, methinks, resembleth well
The world itself in which we dwell.
Perils and snares on every ground,
Like these wild beasts, beset us round.
> Ibid., II, St. 2

19 Through the house what busy joy
Just because the infant boy
Has a tiny tooth to show!
I have got a double row,
All as white, and all as small;
Yet no one cares for mine at all.
> "The First Tooth,"
> Sister, op. cit.

20 A child is fed with milk and praise.
> Ibid., Brother

21 Shut these odious books up, brother—
They have made you quite another
Thing from what you used to be;

Once you liked to play with me. . . .
> "The Sister's Expostulation on
> the Brother's Learning Latin,"
> op. cit.

22 Know ye not, each thing we prize
Does from small beginnings rise?
> "The Brother's Reply,"
> I, op. cit.

23 All the poets with their wit,
All the grave historians writ,
Who the lives and actions show
Of men famous long ago   Ibid.

24 But an unlearned eye may view
Nature's rare sights, and love them too.
> "The Rainbow,"
> op. cit.

25 *Thus ignorance a kind heart narrows.*
> "The Rook and the Sparrows,"
> op. cit.

26 . . . when distress
Does on poor human nature press,
We need not be too strict in seeing
The failings of a fellow-being.
> Ibid.

27 He struck his milk-white hand against a
nail,
Sees his own blood, and feels his courage
fail.
Ah! where is now that boasted valour flown
> "Feigned Courage,"
> op. cit.

28 O happy town-bred girl, in fine chaise going
For the first time to see the green grass
growing!   "The First Sight of Green
> Fields,"
> op. cit.

29 "For gold could Memory be bought,
What treasures would she not be worth!"
> "Memory,"
> St. 1, op. cit.

30 "The only substitute for me
Was ever found, is call'd a pen"
> Ibid., St. 6

31 High-born Helen, plainly telling
Stories of thy cold disdain;

I starve, I die, now you comply,
And I no longer can complain.
"Helen,"
St. 2 (Summer 1800),
Quoted in *John Woodvil, A Tragedy
by Charles Lamb* (1802),
with Poems Attached   1818

32 Mother
"Play with the bride-maids, and be glad,
    my boy,
For thou shalt be a second father's joy."
Child
"One father fondled me upon his knee.
One father is enough, alone, for me."
"Dialogue Between a Mother
and Child,"
Sts. 4, 5 (1804),
Quoted in *Works*
by Charles Lamb   1818

33 Once on a charger there was laid,
And brought before a royal maid,
As price of attitude and grace,
A guiltless head, a holy face.
"Salome,"*
St. 1 (1808/09), op. cit.

*See 41.

34 Honey and locusts were his* food,
And he was most severely good.
Ibid., St. 3

*John the Baptist.

35 A cruel triumph, wicked pride,
That for your sport a saint had died.
Ibid., St. 5

36 A child's a plaything for an hour.
"Parental Recollections," op. cit.

37 Thou straggler into loving arms,
Young climber up of knees,
When I forget thy thousand ways,
Then life and all shall cease.
"A Child,"
St. 3, op. cit.

38 Those spirits of Youth, which Age so ill can
    miss   "In Miss Westwood's Album"
(May 17, 1828),
The Works of Charles and Mary Lamb,
Vol. V, E. V. Lucas, ed.
1903

39 Till mirthful malice tempts us to exclaim
'Gainst the dear Thief, who robb'd you of
your *Name*.   Ibid.

40 . . . I cannot enter into your feelings, and
views of things, *your ways not being my
ways*, why should I tell you what I would do
in your situation. So child take thy own
ways and God prosper thee in them.
Letter to Sarah Stoddart
(September 21, 1803),
The Letters of Charles and Mary Lamb,
Vol. II, 1801–1809,
Edwin W. Marrs, Jr., ed.
1976

41 One thing my advising spirit must say—use
as little *Secresy* as possible. . . .
Ibid.

42 My Aunt & my Mother were wholly unlike
you and your sister, yet in some degree
theirs is the secret history I believe of all sis-
ters-in-law. . . .   Ibid.

43 . . . I do not expect or want you to be otherwise than you are, I love you for the good
that is in you, and look for no change.
Ibid.

44 . . . by secrecy I mean you both want the
habit of telling each other at the moment
everything that happens,—where you go—
and what you do—that free communication
of letters and opinions, just as they arise, as
Charles [her brother] and I do, and which is
after all the only groundwork of
friendship. . . .   Ibid.

45 It is a pleasant thing for a friend to put into
one's hand a letter just fresh from the post.
Ibid.

46 . . . I never have the power of altering or
amending anything I have once laid aside
with dissatisfaction.   Letter to Dorothy
Wordsworth (May 7, 1805),
op. cit.

47 All I can gather from your clear, & I have no doubt, faithful history of Maltese politics, is, that . . . your sister in law is pretty much like what all sister's in law have been since the first happy invention of the happy marriage state. Letter to Sarah Stoddart (early November 1805), op. cit.

48 You would laugh, or you would cry, perhaps both, to see us [Lamb and her brother Charles] sit together looking at each other with long and rueful faces, & saying how do you do? & then we fall a crying & say we will be better on the morrow—he says we are like tooth ach [sic] & his friend gum bile, which though a kind of ease, is but an uneasy kind of ease, a comfort of rather an uncomfortable sort. Ibid.

49 . . . I have lost all self confidence in my own actions & one cause of my low spirits is that I never feel satisfied with any thing I do—a perception of not being in a sane state perpetually haunts me. Letter to Sarah Stoddart (November 9–14, 1805), op. cit.

50 Writing plays, novels, poems, and all manner of such-like vapouring and vapourish schemes are floating in my head. . . .
Letter to Sarah Stoddart (February 20–22, 1806), op. cit.

51 It is well enough when one is talking to a friend to hedge in a odd word by way of counsel now, & then, but there is something mighty irksome, in its staring upon one in a letter where one ought only to see kind words, & friendly remimbrances [sic]—.
Ibid.

52 . . . I have been just looking in the pint perter pot which I find quite empty, and yet I am still very dry, if you was with me, we would have a glass of brandy & water, but it is quite impossible to drink brandy & water by oneself therefore I must wait with patience till the kettle boils.
Letter to Sarah Stoddart (March 14, 1806), op. cit.

53 It is but being once thourowly [sic] convinced one is wrong, to make one resolve to do so no more. . . . Ibid.

54 Our love for each other* has been the torment of our lives hitherto. I am most seriously intending to bend the whole force of my mind to counteract this, and I think I see some prospect of success.
Ibid.

*Referring to her brother Charles Lamb.

55 I have known many single men I should have liked in my life (if it had suited them) for a husband: but very few husbands have I ever wished was mine which is rather against the state [of marriage] in general [so] that one is never disposed to envy wives their good husbands, So much for marrying—but however get married if you can.
Letter to Sarah Stoddart (May 30–June 2, 1806), op. cit.

56 . . . [the] truth is my poor mind is so weak that I never dare trust my own judgement in anything, What I think one hour a fit of low spirits makes me unthink the next.
Letter to Dorothy Wordsworth (August 29, 1806), op. cit.

57 I have read your silly very silly letter & between laughing & crying I hardly know how to answer it. You are too serious & too kind a vast deal, for we are not much used to either seriousness or kindness from our present friends and therefore your letter has put me into a greater hurry of spirits that your pleasant Segar [sic] did last night for believe me your two odd faces amused me much more than the mighty transgression [of smoking] vexed me.
Letter to [Samuel Taylor] Coleridge (September 1806), op. cit.

58 If you fancy a very young man, and he likes an elderly gentlewoman, if he likes a learned & accomplished lady, and you like a not very learned youth who may need a little polishing which probably he will never acquire; it is all very well & God bless you both together & may you both be very long in the same mind.   Letter to Sarah Stoddart (October 23, 1806), op. cit.

59 . . . disappointed authors must not complain of actors. . . .   Letter to Mrs. Clarkson (December 23, 1806), op. cit.

60 You know I make a pretence not to interfere, but like all old maids I feel a mighty solicitude about the event of love stories. Letter to Sarah Stoddart (November 28, 1807), op. cit.

61 . . . you must begin the world with ready money. . . .   Letter to Sarah Stoddart (December 21?, 1807), op. cit.

62 You ought to begin the world with a good stock of health & spirits; it is quite as necessary as ready money at first setting out. Ibid.

63 Nurse is now established in Paradise alias the Incurable ward*.   Letter to Sarah Stoddart Hazlitt (November 7, 1809), op. cit., Vol. III, 1809–1817 1978

*Reference to her death.

64 . . . he [Coleridge] offered to write to you, but as I found it was to be done *Tomorrow*, and as I am pretty well acquainted with his to-morrows, I thought good to let you know his determination *to-day*. Letter to Mary Matilda Betham (March 6, 1811), op. cit.

65 We had the lock forced and let poor puss out from behind a panel of the wainscot, and she lived with us from that time, for we were in gratitude bound to keep her as she had introduced us to four untenanted, unowned rooms, and by degrees we have taken possession of these unclaimed apartments—First putting up lines to dry our clothes—then moving my brother's bed into one of these, more commodious than his own rooms—and last winter my brother being unable to pursue a work he had begun, owing to the kind interruptions of friends who were more at leisure than himself, I persuaded him that he might write at his ease in one of these rooms, as he could not ere hear the door knock, or hear himself denied to be at home, which was sure to make him call out and convict the poor maid in a fib. Here I said he might be almost really not at home.   Letter to Barbara Betham (November 2, 1814), op. cit.

66 I know that you have many judicious friends, but I have so often known my brother spy out errors in a manuscript, which has passed through many judicious hands, that I shall not be easy if you do not permit him to look yours carefully through with you. . . . Should you feel nervous at the idea of meeting Charles in the capacity of a *severe censor* give me a line and I will come to you any where and convince you in five minutes that he is even timid, stammers and can scarcely speak for modesty and fear of giving pain when he finds himself placed in that kind of office.   Letter to Mary Matilda Betham (May 4?, 1815), op. cit.

67 He* says he never saw a man so happy in *three wives* as Mr. [William] Wordsworth is.   Letter to Sarah Hutchinson (November 1816), op. cit.

*Henry Crabb Robinson (1775-1867), English diarist and journalist.

667. Ann Radcliffe
(1764–1823)

1 At first a small line of inconceivable splendour emerged on the horizon, which, quickly expanding, the sun appeared in all of his glory, unveiling the whole face of nature, vivifying every colour of the landscape, and sprinkling the dewy earth with glittering light. The low and gentle responses of the birds, awakened by the morning ray, now broke the silence of the hour, their soft warbling rising by degrees till they swelled the chorus of universal gladness. *The Romance of the Forest* 1791

2 Fate sits on these dark battlements, and frowns;
And as the portals open to receive me,
Her voice, in sullen echoes, through the courts,
Tells of a nameless deed. Motto,
The Mysteries of Udolpho 1794

3 Lightnings, that show the vast and foamy deep,
The rending thunders, as they onward roll.
"The Mariner,"
St. 9, op. cit.

4 But hark! what shriek of death comes in the gale,
And in the distant ray what glimmering sail
Bends to the storm?—Now sinks the note of fear!
Ah! wretched mariners!—no more shall day
Unclose his cheering eye to light ye on your way! "Shipwreck,"
op. cit.

5 As they glided on, the grander features of the city [Venice] appeared more distinctly; its terraces crowned with airy yet majestic fabrics, touched, as they now were, with the splendour of the setting sun, appeared as if they had been called up from the ocean by the wand of an enchanter, rather than reared by mortal hands. Ibid.

6 . . . the whole edifice was invested with the solemn duskiness of evening. Silent, lonely, and sublime, it seemed to stand the sovereign of the scene, and to frown defiance on all who dared to invade its solitary reign.
Ibid.

7 "Oh! useful may it be to have shown that, though the vicious can sometimes pour infliction upon the good, their power is transient and their punishment certain; and that innocence, though oppressed by injustice, shall, supported by patience, finally triumph over misfortune." Ibid.

8 "We in Italy are not so apt to despair. . . ."
The Italian 1797

9 . . . the sea, trembling with a long line of radiance, and showing in the clear distance the sails of vessels stealing in every direction along its surface. . . .
Ibid.

10 "From my mind the illusion which gave spirit to the colouring of nature is fading fast. . . ." *Gaston de Blondeville* 1826

11 Then let me stand amidst thy glooms profound
On some wild woody steep, and hear the breeze "Night,"
St. 8, *Poems* 1834

12 So falls o'er Grief the dew of pity's tear
Dimming her lonely visions of despair.
"Sonnet,"
op. cit.

668. Sun Yün-fêng
(1764–1814)

1 Under the waning moon
In the dawn—
A frosty bell. "Starting At Dawn,"
The Orchid Boat,
Women Poets of China,
Kenneth Rexroth and Ling
Chung, eds. and trs. 1972

2 Along the shore the willows

Wait for their Spring green.
　　　　　"On the Road Through Chang-te,"
　　　　　　　　　　　op. cit.

3 I pause above a stream and envy the fisher-
　　man
Who sits there in solitude and leisure,
Thinking his own elegant thoughts.
　　　　　"Travelling in the Mountains,"
　　　　　　　　　　　op. cit.

4 I am bound on a journey without end,
And can not bear the song of the cuckoo.
　　　　　"The Trail Up Wu Gorge,"
　　　　　　　　　　　op. cit.

669.　Catherine Marie Fanshawe
(1765–1834)

1 'Twas whisper'd in heaven, 'twas mutter'd
　　in hell,
And echo caught faintly the sound as it fell;
On the confines of earth 'twas permitted to
　　rest,
And the depths of the ocean its presence
　　confess'd.　　　"Enigma: The Letter H,"
　　　　　　　　　　　Memorials　　　1865

2 At their speed behold advancing
Modern men and women dancing;
Step and dress alike express
Above, below from heel to toe,
Male and female awkwardness.
　　　　　"The Abrogation of the Birth-
　　　　　　　　　Night Ball,"
　　　　　　　　　　　op. cit.

670.　Emma Hamilton
(1765–1815)

1 When she [her daughter] comes and looks
in my face and calls me "mother," indead
[sic] I then truly am a mother. . . .
　　　　　Letter to Charles Greville
　　　　　　　　　(June 1774),
　　　　　Quoted in *Memoirs of Emma,
　　　　　Lady Hamilton*　　　1815

671.　Ho Xuan Huong
(fl. 1765–1799)

1 I am like a jackfruit on the tree.
To taste you must plug me quick, while
　　fresh:
the skin rough, the pulp thick, yes,
but oh, I warn you against touching—
the rich juice will gush and stain your
　　hands.　　　　"The Jackfruit," in toto,
　　　　　*A Thousand Years of Vietnamese
　　　　　　　　　　　Poetry*,
　　　　　Nguyen Ngoc Bich, ed. and tr.
　　　　　　　　　　　1975

2 Pray hard: you too can be a Superior
And squat, proud, on a lotus.
　　　　　"A Buddhist Priest,"
　　　　　Nguyen Ngoc Bich and Burton
　　　　　Raffel, trs., op. cit.

672.　Nancy Storace
(1765–1815)

1 I have as good a right to show the power of
my *bomba** as any body else.
　　　　　Quoted in *Queens of Song*
　　　　　　by Ellen Creathorne
　　　　　　　　Clayton　　　1865

*Tremolo.

673.　Barbara Frietschie
(1766–1862)

1 "Shoot, if you must, this old gray head
But spare your country's flag"
　　　　　Attributed, Quoted by John
　　Greenleaf Whittier in "Barbara Fritchie,"
　　　Atlantic Monthly　　October 1863

674.　Carolina Nairne
(1766–1845)

1 The Laird o' Cockpen, he's proud an' he's
　　great,

His mind is ta'en up wi' things o' the
State....   "The Laird o' Cockpen,"
St. 1, *Lays from Strathearn*
1846

2 A penniless lass wi' a lang pedigree.
Ibid., St. 2

3 Will ye no come back again?
Better lo'ed ye canna be,
Will ye no come back again?
"Bonnie Charlie's* now awa',"**
Life and Songs   1869

*The reference here and in quotations 12–14 is to
Charles Edward Stuart, aka "Bonnie Prince Charlie"
or The Young Pretender (1720–1788).

**Also attributed to the Scottish poet James Hogg
(1770–1835).

4 Wha'll buy my caller* herrin'?
They're bonnie fish and halesome farin';
Wha'll buy my caller herrin',
New drawn frae the Forth?
"Caller Herrin',"
op. cit.

*Fresh.

5 Oh, ye may ca' them vulgar farin',
Wives and mithers maist despairin',
Ca' them lives o' men.   Ibid.

6 Gude nicht, and joy be wi' you a'.
"Gude Nicht,"
op. cit.

7 Wi' a hundred pipers an' a', an' a',
Wi' a hundred pipers an' a', an' a',
We'll up an' gie them a blaw, a blaw,
Wi' a hundred pipers an' a', an' a'.
"The Hundred Pipers,"
op. cit.

8 I'm wearin' awa'
To the land o' the leal*.
"The Land o' the Leal,"
op. cit.

*Heaven (literally, "loyal" or "faithful").

9 There's nae sorrow there, John,
There's neither cauld nor care, John,
The day is aye fair
In the land o' the leal.   Ibid.

10 O, we're a' noddin', nid, nid, noddin':

O, we're noddin' at our house at hame.
"We're a' Noddin',"
op. cit.

11 Now a' are gane! we meet nae mair, aneath
the Rowan tree,
But hallowed thoughts around thee twine o'
hame and infancy.   "The Rowan
Tree,"
Scottish Song,
Mary Carlyle Aitken, ed.
1874

12 O, Charlie is my darling,
My darling, my darling;
Charlie is my darling,
The young Chevalier.   "Charlie Is My
Darling,"
op. cit.

13 His right these hills; his right these plains;
O'er Hieland hearts secure he reigns;
What lads e'er did our lads will do;
Were I a laddie, I'd follow him too.
"He's Owre the Hills,"
op. cit.

14 Then here's a health to Charlie's cause,
An' be't complete and early,
His very name my heart's blood warms,—
To arms for royal Charlie!
"Wha'll Be King But Charlie,"
op. cit.

675.   Nancy Dennis Sproat
(1766–1826)

1 How pleasant is Saturday night,
When I've tried all the week to be good,
Not spoken a word that is bad,
And obliged every one that I could.
"How Pleasant is Saturday
Night," n.d.

676. Germaine de Staël
(1766–1817)

1 Young girls never depend on themselves. Everything around them conspires to shield their hearts from the impression of the senses. *Lettres sur les ouvrages et le caractère de J.-J. Rousseau [Letters on the Works and Character of J.-J. Rousseau]* 1788

2 . . . wait until a woman is married . . . one no longer seeks to exalt their minds with romantic notions but to soil their hearts with cold jests on everything they have been taught to respect. Ibid.

3 . . . inventiveness is childish, practice sublime. *Réflexions sur la paix intérieure [Reflections on Internal Peace]* 1795

4 If France crumbles, Europe must crumble. . . . Even America would feel a shock against which neither water nor space can cushion it. Ibid.

5 . . . the destiny of France must be decided by the French. . . . Ibid.

6 All their resolutions have followed events instead of forestalling them. Nobody was willing to yield what he could not help losing. Ibid.

7 Condemned to be famous without being known, I feel a need to let the world judge me by my writings. Preface (July 1, 1796), *De l'influence des passions sur le bonheur des individus et des nations [A Treatise on the Influence of the Passions upon the Happiness of Individuals and of Nations]* 1796

8 It is obvious that the most despotic forms of social organization would be suitable for inert men who are satisfied with the station fate has placed them in, and that the most abstract form of democratic theory would be practicable among sages guided only by their reason. The only problem is to what degree it is possible to excite or to contain the passions without endangering public happiness. Ibid.

9 Love is the whole history of a woman's life, it is but an episode in a man's. Ibid.

10 This unshakable calm in so young a heart [Napoleon's], far from reassuring me, fills me with terror. *Jan de Witt* 1797

11 From his [Napoleon's] earliest years he has coveted power; before his mind was formed, artifice took hold of it and strangled the nascent voice of nature. Ibid.

12 Intellect does not attain its full force unless it attacks power. *De la littérature considérée dans ses rapports avec les institutions sociales [The Influence of Literature upon Society]* 1800

13 [Literature has] ceased to be a mere art; it [has] become a means to an end, a weapon in the service of the spirit of man. Ibid.

14 . . . the tyranny of ridicule. . . . Ibid.

15 It [aristocratic society] laughs at all those who see the earnestness of life and who still believe in true feelings and in serious thought. . . . It soils the hope of youth. Ibid.

16 There is a certain kind of sensibility which increases in proportion with the world of ideas. Ibid.

17 Every time a new nation, America or Russia for instance, advances toward civilization, the human race perfects itself; every time an inferior class emerges from enslavement and degradation, the human race again perfects itself. Ibid.

18 One of the causes of the destruction of empires in antiquity was the ignorance of several important scientific discoveries. These discoveries have placed nations as well as individuals on a footing of greater equality. The decadence of empires is no more in the natural order of things than is the decadence of literature and science.

             Ibid.

19 The life of famous men was more glorious in antiquity; the life of obscure men is happier with the moderns.   Ibid.

20 Happy the land where the writers are sad, the merchants satisfied, the rich melancholic, and the populace content.

             Ibid.

21 From the severity with which philosophy, liberty, and reason have been censured, one might conclude that prejudices, servility, and lies never did humanity any harm.

             Ibid.

22 Scientific progress makes moral progress a necessity; for if man's power is increased, the checks that restrain him from abusing it must be strengthened.   Ibid.

23 Why should it not be possible some day to compile tables that would contain the answer to all questions of a political nature based on statistical knowledge, on positive facts gathered for every country?

             Ibid.

24 Morality must guide calculation, and calculation must guide politics.

             Ibid.

25 . . . if a man had only his personal interest to guide his conduct, even if this guide were never to deceive him . . . the source of all generous actions would dry up in his heart.

             Ibid.

26 . . . it is not true that self-interest is the most powerful motive of human conduct; pride, vanity, and fury easily make men sacrifice their interests.   Ibid.

27 The entire social order . . . is arrayed against a woman who wants to rise to a man's reputation.   Ibid.

28 There can be no passion in a woman's heart unless she feels for the object of her love an admiring respect not unmixed with fear, and a deference bordering on submissiveness.   Preface,
          Delphine   1802

29 In our century, it is not love that corrupts morality, but the contempt of all principles which has its cause in the contempt of feelings.   Ibid.

30 Between God and love, I recognize no mediator but my conscience.

           Text, op. cit.

31 Egoism is permissible to a feeling heart; whoever centers his existence in love may, without remorse, detach himself from the rest of the world.   Ibid.

32 For a long time I made conversation with him, in front of him, for him.

             Ibid.

33 "Follow me, let this instant decide our lives! There are decisions that must be made in the heat of passion, without giving bitter reflections the time to revive!"

             Ibid.

34 Nobody knows better than I do how to put indolence to use: I make use of it to undo quite naturally the activity of others.

             Ibid.

35 I was, and I still am convinced that women, being the victims of all social institutions, are destined to misery if they make the least concession to their feelings and if, in any way whatever, they lose control of themselves.   Ibid.

36 . . . nobody can ever be influenced in a sense contrary to his character.

             Ibid.

37 "Delphine, nothing is more indelicate than to reproach people for favors one has done them."   Ibid.

38 "Ingratitude is a big word that is much abused. I help you because I like you; when I stop liking you, I leave you. Whatever is done in life is done either for gain or for pleasure: I don't know what gratitude has to do with either."   Ibid.

39 When intimacy has reached the point where one finds happiness in childlike games, in standing jokes, in innumerable small details whose meaning is known only to you two, then the heart is captive in a thousand ties, and a single word, a gesture, the most fleeting allusion to such sweet memories would suffice to recall it from the end of the world.   Ibid.

40 A man must know how to defy opinion; a woman how to submit to it.
                        Ibid.

41 I believe that [it is] useful and compatible with the strictest morality to show how, with a superior soul, one can commit more errors than a mediocre person could, unless the power of passion is matched by that of reason; and how, with a generous and sensible heart, one is apt to become guilty of many sins if one does not submit to the most rigid morality.   "Reflections of the Moral Aim of Delphine," op. cit., 2nd ed.

42 Kindness and generosity . . . form the true morality of human actions.
                        Ibid.

43 She liked to make others' lives as drab as possible, perhaps so as not to feel too much regret at the dissolution of her own.
                        Corinne, or Italy   1807

44 It looks as if people, in the present state of society, had almost no use for the simple gift of life.   Ibid.

45 The most beautiful landscapes in the world, if they evoke no memory, if they bear no trace of a remarkable event, are uninteresting compared to historic landscapes.
                        Ibid.

46 A person who suffers is likely to convince himself that he is guilty, for violent sorrows bring disorder even into one's conscience.
                        Ibid.

47 There is in this country [Italy] a bizarre mixture of naïveté and corruption, of dissimulation and frankness, of good nature and vindictiveness, of weakness and energy, which explains this general rule: that all the good qualities spring from the fact that nothing is ever done here to satisfy one's vanity, and all the bad qualities from the fact that a great deal is done to serve one's interests—love, ambition, or money.
                        Ibid.

48 Fate persecutes the exalted souls, the poets whose creative power springs from their capacity for suffering and love.
                        Ibid.

49 . . . duty means to sacrifice whatever talent one has, and intellect is a sin that must be atoned for by leading exactly the life of those who have none.   Ibid.

50 . . . weakness and irresolution. . . . These defects are never noticed by him who has them, and with every changing circumstance they take on a new disguise in his eyes; at one moment, prudence makes it advisable to postpone a decision and to prolong an ambiguous situation; another time, it is sensibility or delicacy; almost never does one realize that it is one's own character which attributes the same kind of difficulty to all circumstances.
                        Ibid.

51 Love, supreme power of the heart, mysterious enthusiasm that encloses in itself all poetry, all heroism, all religion!
                        Ibid.

52 To understand all makes one very indulgent.   Ibid.

53 The sight of such a monument is like a continuous and stationary music.
                        Ibid.

54 ... words [in France] are not merely, as they are in all other countries, a means to communicate ideas, feelings, and needs, but an instrument one likes to play and which revives the spirit, just as does music in some nations, and strong liquors in others.
De l'Allemagne [Germany] 1810

55 Of all composers, Mozart probably has shown the greatest ingenuity in marrying music and words. ... This witty alliance of musician and poet also gives a kind of pleasure—but a pleasure that originates in the mind, and this kind of pleasure does not belong to the marvelous sphere of the arts.
Ibid.

56 The spirit of the Germans seems to have no communication with their character: the one cannot tolerate any limits; the other submits to every yoke.
Ibid.

57 Could I keep his love forever, I who have known the fires of the marriage bed? He needs the love of a heart that has beaten for no one but him. *Sapho* [Sappho] 1811

58 Love is above the laws, above the opinion of men; it is the truth, the flame, the pure element, the primary idea of the moral world.
Zulma, and Other Tales 1813

59 ... one could fear the worst or hope for the best, depending on whether or not one served the interests of the man [Napoleon] who dared make himself, and himself alone, the purpose of the entire human race.
Mémoires sur la vie privée de mon père [Memoirs of the Private Life of My Father] 1818

60 ... the confidence of youth ... relies on its own strength to attain all its desires.
Ibid.

61 Magnificence is the characteristic of everything one sees in Russia. *Dix années d'exil [Ten Years of Exile]* 1821

62 It is the characteristic of this nation [Russia] to fear neither fatigue nor physical pain; they are at the same time patient and active, gay and melancholy.
Ibid.

63 ... only superior beings possess mutually opposed qualities.
Ibid.

64 A Russian's desire ... is capable of blowing up a city; fury and ruse possess them in turn when they want to accomplish whatever they have resolved upon, be it good or evil.
Ibid.

65 In every way, there is something gigantic about this people [Russians]: ordinary dimensions have no application whatever to it. I do not mean by this that true greatness and stability are never met with; but their boldness, their imaginativeness knows no bounds. With them everything is colossal rather than well-proportioned, audacious rather than well-considered, and if they do not attain their goals, it is because they exceed them.
Ibid.

66 In the great crisis in which Russia found herself when I crossed her, one could not but admire the vigor and resignation which that nation manifested in its resistance and its sacrifices, and in the face of such virtues one scarcely dared to notice what one might have blamed at other times.
Ibid.

67 Oh, nothing can equal the emotion that a woman feels when she has the happiness of hearing the name of one beloved repeated by a whole people. Quoted in *Lives of Celebrated Women* by Samuel Griswold Goodrich 1844

68 The question is not what I want, but what I think.
Ibid.

69 The phantom of *ennui* forever pursues me.
Ibid.

70 Life resembles Gobelin tapestry; you do not see the canvas on the right side; but when you turn it, the threads are visible.
Ibid.

71 The mystery of existence is the connection between our faults and our misfortunes.
Ibid.

72 Women of France, I appeal to you; your empire is over, if ferocity continues to reign; your destiny is ended, if your tears do not prevail.
Remark (c.1795),
Quoted in *Women of Beauty and Heroism*
by Frank B. Goodrich   1858

73 If this Old World of ours is to be nothing but a single man [Napoleon], what is the use of staying here?
Letter to Thomas Jefferson (April 25, 1807),
Revue de Littérature Comparée   1922

74 It is better to be united at a distance.
Letter to Adrien de Mun (September 1796),
from Coppet,
Revue de Paris   December 1923

75 The universe is in France; outside it, there is nothing.
Letter to Chevalier François de Pange (c.March 1796),
Madame de Staël et François de Pange: lettres et documents inédits,
Jean de Pange, ed.   1925

76 In a word, give me back the past, which is my only future!
Letter to de Pange (c.May 1796),
from Coppet, op. cit.

77 The greatest happiness is to transform one's feelings into actions. . . .   Ibid.

78 Is it not the beginning of the story which is the most beautiful time for a woman? And you want to deprive me of my reign so soon? Yours will come only too soon.
Letter to Graf Moritz O'Donnell von Tyrconnel (c.1807),
Madame de Staël et Maurice O'Donnell, 1805–1816, d'après des lettres inédites,
Jean Mistler, ed.   1926

79 By trying to clip my wings, you prevent me from feeling and exalting your own distinction.
Letter to O'Donnell (c.May 1807),
from Vienna, op. cit.

80 There are people whose characters cannot be judged from their behavior in society. . . .   Ibid.

81 There is no reality on this earth except religion and the power of love; all the rest is even more fugitive than life itself.
Letter to O'Donnell (September 22, 1808),
from Coppet, op. cit.

82 What I love about noise is that it camouflages life.
Letter to Eric Staël von Holstein,
Revue des Deux Mondes
June/July 1932

83 Money alone determines your entire life, political as well as private.
Letter to Benjamin Constant* (April 1815),
from Coppet,
Lettres à un ami,
Jean Mistler, ed.   1949
*French writer (1767–1830), Mme. de Staël's lover.

84 I never was able to believe in the existence of next year except as in a metaphysical notion.
Quoted in *Mistress to an Age: A Life of Madame de Staël*
by J. Christopher Herold   1958

85 The pursuit of politics is religion, morality, and poetry all in one.   Ibid.

86 Those gentlemen [Lafayette and Sylvain Bailly*, mayor of Paris] are like the rainbow; they always appear after the storm is over.   Ibid.
*French astronomer and politician (1736–1793), guillotined.

87 Genius has no sex!   Ibid.

88 Sir, I understand everything that deserves to be understood; what I don't understand is nothing.   Ibid.

89 There is a kind of physical pleasure in resisting an iniquitous power.
Ibid.

90 If one hour's work is enough to govern France, four minutes is all that is needed for Italy. There is no nation more easily frightened; even its poetic imagination predisposes it to fear, and they look upon power as on an image that fills them with terror.
Ibid. (1804)

91 There are only two distinct classes of people on this earth: those who espouse enthusiasm and those who despise it.
Ibid.

92 I have no doubt that America shall inherit the civilization of Europe.
Ibid. (c.1810)

93 I shall have to conquer myself once more, despite everything. Ibid.
(September 27, 1810), near Blois

94 Life teaches much, but to all thinking persons it brings ever closer the will of God—not because their faculties decline, but on the contrary, because they increase.
Last will (preamble, dated
October 12, 1816),
Coppet, op. cit.

95 I have always been the same, lively and sad, I have loved God, my father, and liberty.... Spoken to François René de Chateaubriand (c.Spring 1817), Paris, op. cit.

96 You [America] are the vanguard of the human race. You are the world's future.
Spoken to George Ticknow*
(c.Spring 1817), op. cit.
*American author and teacher of languages (1791–1871).

97 The circulation of ideas is, of all kinds of commerce, the one whose benefits are most certain.... "The Spirit of Translation," op. cit.

98 One must, so long as there is any life left, back up the character of one's life.
Letter to a friend, op. cit.

99 It is a terrible ordeal for all one's feelings to have to look at each other face to face. One needs company to be bright, company to be in love, company for everything.... As soon as one is two, one needs to be many more. Letter to a friend (c.1796), op. cit.

100 One must, in one's life, make a choice between boredom and suffering.
Letter to Claude Hochet
(Summer 1800), op. cit.

101 What matters in a character is not whether one holds this or that opinion: what matters is how proudly one upholds it.
Letter to Hochet (c.May 1802),
op. cit.

102 ... I have a woman's fears, but they cannot make me into a hypocrite or a slave.
Letter to Charles de Lacretelle
(c.May 1802), op. cit.

103 There is nothing more clumsy, nothing more smoke-filled in the moral as in the physical sense, than German men.
Letter to de Lacretelle (c.Nov./
Dec. 1803), op. cit.

104 All this [acclaim] gives me release from pain but no real pleasure. Pleasure would be love, or Paris, or power. I need one of these three things in order to exalt my heart, my mind, or my activity. Letter to Jacques Necker [her father]
(c.March 1804),
from Weimar?, op. cit.

105 Society in the large cities of Germany imitates Paris, and Paris in German loses a great deal in translation. Letter to Joseph Bonaparte [King of Naples and Spain] (March 1804),
from Berlin, op. cit.

106 The thinkers are soaring in the empyrean, and on earth you find only grenadiers.
Letter to F. H. Jacobi
(March 1804),
from Berlin, op. cit.

107 In every respect they are two very remarkable men*. If they had been able to be remarkable without trying to be extraordinary, they would have been more remarkable still.   Letter to Johann von Müller (c.October 1804), from Coppet, op. cit.

*The German writers and brothers August Wilhelm (1767–1845) and Friedrich (1772–1829) von Schlegel.

108 What attracts me in this city [Rome] is a mystery that does not reveal itself on first acquaintance, a sensation of the South that is completely unknown to those who have not been there, a certain sympathy between nature and man that cannot be imagined anywhere else—and a noble and calm image of death in the tombs and the traces of great men.   Letter to Claude Hochet (c.February 1805), from Rome, op. cit.

109 . . . what better things has this earth than to think and to feel?   Letter to Duque Pedro de Souza e Holstein (c.June 1805), from Florence, op. cit.

110 In matters of the heart, nothing is true except the improbable.   Letter to her cousin Juliette Récamier (October 5, 1810), from Fossé, op. cit.

111 I must keep on rowing, not until I reach port but until I reach my grave.   Letter to Albertine Necker de Saussure [her daughter] (July 1814), from Coppet, op. cit.

112 . . . the third epoch of . . . enthusiasms— first liberty, then religion, now ambition.   Letter to Juliette Récamier (1816), from Coppet, op. cit.

113 How much past there is in a life, however brief it be.   Letter to Récamier (c.February 1816), op. cit.

114 I would gladly give half of the wit with which I am credited for half of the beauty you possess.   Ibid.

115 . . . I have always made it a point to adopt the opinions of the man whom I prefer.   Letter to Adolf Ludvig Ribbing (c.1794), *Lettres à Ribbing*, Simone Balaye, ed.   1960

677. Betty Zane
(1766?–1831?)

1 You have not one man to spare.*   Quoted in *Chronicles of Border Warfare* by Alexander S. Withers 1831

*Attributed remark as she volunteered to run a dangerous mission.

678. Maria Edgeworth
(1767–1849)

1 Possessed, as are all the fair daughters of Eve, of an hereditary propensity, transmitted to them undiminished through succeeding generations, to be "soon moved with the slightest touch of blame"; very little precept and practice will confirm them in the habit, and instruct them in all the maxims, of self-justification.

Candid pupil, you will readily accede to a first and sentimental axiom—that a lady can do no wrong.   *An Essay on the Noble Science of Self-Justification* (1787) 1795

2 Right and wrong, if we go to the foundation of things, are, as causists tell us, really words of very dubious signification, perpetually varying with custom and fashion, and to be adjusted ultimately by no other standards than opinion and force.   Ibid.

3 Obtain power, then, by all means; power is the law of man; make it yours.   Ibid.

4 . . . therefore friends should quarrel to strengthen their attachment, and offend each other for the pleasure of being reconciled. Ibid.

5 When one illusion vanishes, another shall appear, and, still leading me forward towards an horizon that retreats as I advance, the happy prospect of futurity shall vanish only with my existence.
Letters of Julia and Caroline
(1787), Letter I
1795

6 Man is to be held only by the *slightest* chains; with the idea that he can break them at pleasure, he submits to them in sport. . . . Ibid.

7 The moment the prize of glory is to be won by other means, do not millions sacrifice their fortunes, their peace, their health, their lives, for *fame*? Ibid., Letter II

8 Despair is either madness or folly; it obtains, it deserves nothing from mankind but pity; and pity, though it be akin to love, has yet a secret affinity to contempt. In strong minds, despair is an acute disease; the prelude to great exertion. In weak minds, it is a chronic distemper, followed by incurable indolence. Ibid., Letter IV

9 The tendency of any particular mode of education is not always perceived before it is too late to change the habits or the character of the people. *Mademoiselle Panache* 1795

10 "Pleasing for a moment," said Helen, smiling, "is of some consequence; for, if we take care of the moments, the years will take care of themselves, you know."
Ibid.

11 A man who marries a showy entertaining coquette, and expects she will make him a charming companion for life, commits as absurd a blunder as that of the famous nobleman who, delighted with the wit and humour of Punch at a puppet-show, bought Punch, and ordered him to be sent home for his private amusement. Ibid.

12 The following words were written . . . over the chimneypiece in his uncle's spacious kitchen—"Waste not, want not."
The Parent's Assistant 1796

13 After having worked like horses, don't set about to fight like dogs. Ibid.

14 "Oppressed, degraded, enslaved,—must our unfortunate sex for ever submit to sacrifice their right, their pleasures, their *will*, at the altar of public opinion. . . . "
Angelina,
Ch. 1, c.1799

15 The unaffected language of real feeling and benevolence is easily understood and is never ridiculous. . . . Ibid., Ch. 3

16 "It is useful, I allow," replied Madame du Rosier, "to know by heart the names of the English kings and Roman emperors, and to remember the dates of their reigns, otherwise we should be obliged, whenever we wanted them, to search in the book in which they are to be found, and that wastes time." *The Good French Governess* c.1799

17 " . . . even poor asses are not obstinate when they are well treated."
Ibid.

18 ALEFTSON. There's the student so crabbed and wonderful wise,
With his plus and his minus, his *x*'s and *y*'s;
Pale at midnight he pours o'er his magical spells—
What is he, my friends, but a fool without bells? *The Knap-Sack*,
Act 1 c.1799

19 I've a great fancy to see my own funeral afore I die. *Castle Rackrent*,
Ch. 1 1800

20 And all the young ladies said . . . that to be sure a love-match was the only thing for happiness, where the parties could anyway afford it. Ibid.

21 Nothing for nothing. Ibid.

22 He . . . was very ill-used by the Government about a place that was promised him and never given, after his supporting them against his conscience very honourably, and being greatly abused for it, which hurt him greatly, he having the name of a great patriot in the country before.

Ibid.

23 "It is quite fitting that charity should *begin* at home," said Wright; "but then it should not *end* at home; for those that help nobody will find none to help them in time of need."

The Will,
Ch. 2   1800

24 How success changes the opinion of men!

Ibid., Ch. 4

25 "What can be more advantageous than a partnership between prudence and justice on the one side, and generosity and abilities on the other?"   Ibid.

26 Come when you're called;
And do as you're bid;
Shut the door after you;
And you'll never be chid.

The Contrast,
Ch. 1   1801

27 Business was his aversion; pleasure was his business.   Ibid., Ch. 2

28 "It is a bitter thing to think of a good son who is dead; but it is worse, perhaps, to think of a bad son who is alive."

Ibid., Ch. 3

29 All work and no play makes Jack a dull boy,
All play and no work makes Jack a mere toy.   *Harry and Lucy*   1801

30 Artificial manners vanish the moment the natural passions are touched.

Almeria   1802

31 Few people have such strength of mind as to be indifferent to the opinions of numbers, even considered merely as numbers; hence those who live in crowds in fact surrender the power of thinking for themselves, either in trifles or matters of consequence.

Ibid.

32 There are political advocates for luxury, who assert, perhaps justly, that the extravagance of individuals increases the wealth of nations. But even upon this system, those who by false hopes excite the industrious to exertion, without paying them their just wages, commit not only the most cruel private injustice, but the most important public injury. The permanence of industry in any state must be proportioned to the certainty of its reward.   *The Dun*   1802

33 What mortal, what fashionable mortal, is there who has not, in the midst of a formidable circle, been reduced to the embarrassment of having nothing to say? Who is there that has not felt those oppressive fits of silence which ensue after the weather, and the fashions, and the politics, and the scandal, and all the commonplace topics of the day have been utterly exhausted? Who is there that, at such a time, has not tried in vain to call up an idea, and found that *none would come when they did call.* . . .

Introduction,
Essay on Irish Bulls   1802

34 . . . we cannot make the propensity to laughter the criterion of what is ridiculous in another. . . .   Ibid.

35 When Paddy heard an English gentleman speaking of the fine echo at the lake of Killarney, which repeats the sound forty times, he very promptly observed, "Faith, that's nothing at all to the echo in my father's garden, in the county of Galway: if you say to it, 'how do you do, Paddy Blake?' it will answer, 'pretty well, I thank you, sir.'"

Ibid., Ch. 1

36 Bishop Wilkins prophesied that the time would come when gentlemen, when they were to go on a journey, would call for their wings as regularly as they call for their boots.   Ibid., Ch. 2

37 "Never laugh when the laugh can be turned against you," should be the maxim of those who find their chief pleasure in making others ridiculous.   Ibid., Ch. 3

38 Our Irish blunders are never blunders of the heart. Ibid., Ch. 4

39 "... fancying a roving life would agree with me best, I quit the place, taking nothing with me, but resolved to walk the world, and just trust to the charity of good Christians, or die, as it should please God. How I have lived so long He only knows, and His will be done." Ibid., Ch. 9

40 The Irish nation, from the highest to the lowest, in daily conversation about the ordinary affairs of life, employ a superfluity of wit and metaphor which would be astonishing and unintelligible to a majority of the respectable body of English yeomen. Ibid., Ch. 10

41 Those who are animated by hope can perform what would seem impossibilities to those who are under the depressing influence of fear. *The Grateful Negro* 1802

42 "The law, in our case, seems to make the right; and the very reverse ought to be done—the right should make the law." Ibid.

43 "Then I am of opinion," answered the vizier, "that people are often led to believe others fortunate, or unfortunate, merely because they only know the general outline of their histories; and are ignorant of the incidents and events in which they have shown prudence or imprudence."
Murad the Unlucky,
Ch. 1 1802

44 Few men are so miserable as not to like to talk of their misfortunes, where they have, or where they think they have, any chance of obtaining compassion. Ibid.

45 In her cold fits of ill-humour, this lady was prone to degrade, as monsters below the standard of humanity, those whom, in the warmth of her enthusiasm, she had exalted to the state of angelic perfection.
Emilie de Coulanges 1803

46 "I wish I could forget it—I am always doomed to be obliged to those whom I cannot love." Ibid.

47 "See what it is to live shut up with old folks! You catch all their ways, and grow old and wise before your time."
"The danger of growing wise before my time does not alarm me much. . . ."
The Manufacturers,
Ch. 1 1803

48 "Those who have lived in a house with spoiled children must have a lively recollection of the degree of torment they can inflict upon all who are within sight or hearing." Ibid.

49 Children were pretty things at three years old; but began to be great plagues at six, and were quite intolerable at ten. Ibid.

50 The facility with which I learned my lessons encouraged me to put off learning them till the last moment; and this habit of procrastinating, which was begun in presumption, ended in disgrace.
To-Morrow,
Ch. 1 1803

51 The notes, written in pencil, were almost effaced, and, when I had smoothed the crumpled scraps, I could make nothing of them. It was with the utmost difficulty I could read even those that were written in ink; they were so villainously scrawled and so terribly blotted. When I had made out the words, I was often at a loss for the sense; because I had trusted so much to the excellence of my memory, that my notes were never either sufficiently full or accurate. Ideas which I had thought could never be effaced from my mind were now totally forgotten, and I could not comprehend my own mysterious elliptical hints and memorandums. I remember spending two hours in trying to make out what the following words could mean: *Hoy—alla—hoya;—hoya, hoya,—hoy—waudihoya.*
Ibid., Ch. 2

52 I cannot account for my folly; the power of habit is imperceptible to those who submit passively to its tyranny. Ibid.

53 I was ever searching for some *short cut* to the temple of Fame, instead of following the beaten road. Ibid., Ch. 3

54 But what is kindness, what is affection, what are the best resolutions, opposed to all-powerful habit? Ibid., Ch. 4

55 I now attempted too much: I expected to repair by bustle the effects of procrastination. Ibid.

56 ... when driven to the necessity of explaining, I found that I did not myself understand what I meant. Ibid.

57 What a misfortune it is to be born a woman! ... Why seek for knowledge, which can prove only that our wretchedness is irremediable? If a ray of light break in upon us, it is but to make darkness more visible; to show us the now limits, the Gothic structure, the impenetrable barriers of our prison. *Leonora,* Letter I 1805

58 With me the heart is no longer touched when the imagination ceases to be charmed. Ibid., Letter XI

59 Take courage, my beloved daughter; take courage. Have a just confidence in yourself and in your husband. For a moment he may be fascinated by the arts of an unprincipled woman; for a moment she may triumph over his senses and his imagination; but of his esteem, his affection, his heart, she cannot rob you. Ibid., Letter XXVII

60 A wife who has sense enough to abstain from all reproaches, direct or indirect, by word or look, may reclaim her husband's affections: the bird escapes from his cage, but returns to his nest. Ibid.

61 ... some metaphysicians would seek the moral sense inherently in the heart, others would place it intuitively in the brain, all would confine it to the soul; now in my opinion it resides primarily and principally in the nerves, and varies with their variations. Hence the difficulty of making the moral sense a universal guide of action, since it not only differs in many individuals, but in the same persons at different periods of their existence, or (as I have often experienced) at different hours of the day. Ibid., Letter XXXIX

62 She has a sort of morbid sensibility, which is more alive to pain than pleasure, more susceptible of jealousy than of love. Ibid., Letter LXXIX

63 Mine is not that species of weak or abject affection which can exist under the sense of ill-treatment and injustice.... Ibid., Letter XCIV

64 I think I could, much better, bear the total loss, the death of him I have loved, than endure to feel that he had survived both my affection and esteem.... Ibid.

65 There are some people who cannot be perfectly happy till they know the *rationale* of their happiness. Ibid., Letter CXII

66 In most sudden accidents, and in all domestic misfortune, female resolution and presence of mind are indispensably requisite to safety, health, and life often depends upon the fortitude of women. *Madame De Fleury,* Ch. 1 1805

67 It is not so easy to do good as those who have never attempted it may imagine.... Ibid., Ch. 2

68 Those who fall cannot be destitute; and those who rise cannot be ridiculous or contemptible, if they have been prepared for their fortune by proper education. Ibid., Ch. 16

69 Among the higher classes, whether in the wealthy or the fashionable world, who is unacquainted with *ennui*?

Ennui (1804),
Ch. 1 1809

70 As a highwayman knows that he must come to the gallows at last, and acts accordingly, so a fashionably extravagant youth knows that, sooner or later, he must come to matrimony. Ibid., Ch. 2

71 We resist the efforts made by those who, we think, exert authority or employ artifice to change our determinations; while the perverse mind insensibly yields to those who appear not to have power, or reason, or address sufficient to obtain a victory.

Ibid., Ch. 3

72 Persons not habituated to reason often argue absurdly, because from particular instances they deduce general conclusions, and extend the result of their limited experience of individuals indiscriminently to whole classes. Ibid., Ch. 7

73 "How virtuous we shall be when we have no name for vice!" Ibid., Ch. 10

74 . . . the number of cursory travellers who expose their own ignorance by the attempt to ridicule local customs, of which they have not inquired the cause or discovered the utility. Ibid., Ch. 14

75 There was something in the contemplation of the sea and of the tides . . . a grand operation of nature, accompanied with a sort of vast monopoly of motion and sound which lulled me into reveries. Ibid.

76 "Will you forgive me for convincing you that when a man has sufficient strength of mind to rely upon himself, and sufficient energy to exert his abilities, he becomes independent of common report and vulgar opinion?" Ibid., Ch. 20

77 " . . . sometimes the very faults of parents produce a tendency to opposite virtues in their children . . . " *Manoeuvring*,
Ch. 1 1809

78 " . . . I am convinced that more unpleasant feelings are created in families, by these false delicacies, and managements, and hints, and go-between friends by courtesy, than ever would have been caused by the parties speaking directly to one another, and telling the plain truth about their thoughts and wishes." Ibid., Ch. 11

79 " . . . confidence is the best proof of love. . . . " Ibid., Ch. 16

80 "Yes, and you *cawn't* conceive the *peens* she *teeks* to talk of the *teebles* and *cheers*, and to thank Q, and with so much *teeste* to speak pure English." *The Absentee*,
Ch. 1 1812

81 Well! some people talk of morality, and some of religion, but give me a little snug property. Ibid., Ch. 2

82 People usually revenge themselves for having admired too much, by afterward despising and depreciating without mercy—in all great assemblies the perception of ridicule is quickly caught, and quickly too revealed.

Ibid., Ch. 3

83 "Ay, there's the thing! The body pays for the mind—but those who have feeling minds, pain and pleasure altogether computed, have the advantage; or at least they think so; for they would not change with those who have them not, were they to gain by the bargain the most robust body that the most selfish cockscomb, or the heaviest dunce extant ever boasted."

Ibid., Ch. 15

84 "I believe in the rational, but not in the magical power of education."

Vivian,
Ch. 1 1812

85 "My mother took too much, a great deal too much, care of me; she over-educated, over-instructed, over-dosed me with premature lessons of prudence: she was so afraid that I should ever do a foolish thing, or not say a wise one, that she prompted my every word, and guided my every action. So I grew up, seeing with her eyes, hearing with her ears, and judging with her understanding, till, at length, it was found out that I had no eyes, or understanding of my own."   Ibid.

86 What the evils of a contested election are can be fully known only to those by whom they have been personally experienced.
Ibid., Ch. 2

87 "Ah, woman! woman for ever! always talking us out of our senses! and which of the best of us would not wish it to be so? 'Oh! let me, let me be deceived!' is the cream of philosophy, epicurean and stoic. . . . ."
Ibid., Ch. 8

88 A Frenchman, it will be allowed, can contrive to say more, and to tell more of his private history in a given time, than can be accomplished by a person of any other nation.
Patronage,
Ch. 1   1814

89 "Fortune's wheel never stands still—the highest point is therefore the most perilous."   Ibid., Ch. 2

90 "The heart only can understand the heart—who, in modern times, can describe the human heart?"   Ibid., Ch. 5

91 Whenever the honours of professions, civil, military, or ecclesiastical, are bestowed by favour, not earned by merit—whenever the places of trust and dignity in a state are to be gained by intrigue and solicitation—there is an end of generous emulation, and consequently of exertion. Talents and integrity, in losing their reward of glory, lose their vigour, and often their very existence."   Ibid., Ch. 8

92 "Those young men who are brought up to expect patronage in any profession . . . are apt to depend upon it too much . . . and consequently neglect to acquire knowledge."   Ibid.

93 "A friend's helping hand is no bad thing . . . in that hard and slippery ascent."
Ibid.

94 Beauties are always curious about beauties, and wits about wits.   Ibid., Ch. 16

95 From dictionaries and extracts, abridgements and *beauties* of various authors, here, and there, and everywhere, she picked up shining scraps, and often by an ostentation of superficial knowledge succeeded in appearing in conversation to possess a vast extent of literature, and to be deeply skilled in matters of science, of which she knew nothing, and for which she had no taste.
Ibid.

96 "Of all men, I think a dissipated clergyman is the most contemptible."
Ibid., Ch. 19

97 Alarmed successively by every fashionable medical terror of the day, she dosed her children with every specific which was publicly advertised or privately recommended. No creatures of their age had taken such quantities of Ching's lozenges, Godbold's elixir, or Dixon's anti-billious pills. The consequence was, that the dangers, which had at first been imaginary, became real: these little victims of domestic medicine never had a day's health: they looked, and were, more dead than alive.
Ibid., Ch. 20

98 These favourable accidents happen to many men who are not able to make use of them, and thus the general complaint is preferred or want of good fortune, or of opportunity for talents to distinguish themselves.
Ibid.

344

99 We must be content to begin at the beginning, if we would learn the history of our own mind; we must condescend to be even as little children, if we would discover or recollect those small causes which early influenced the imagination, and afterward become strong habits, prejudices, and passions. *Harrington,*
Ch. 1   1817

100 When the mind is full of any one subject, that subject seems to recur with extraordinary frequency—it appears to pursue or to meet us at every turn: in every conversation that we hear, in every book we open, in every newspaper we take up, the reigning idea occurs; and then we are surprised, and exclaim at these wonderful coincidences.
Ibid., Ch. 4

101 An orator is the worse person to tell a plain fact. . . .   Ibid., Ch. 10

102 Enthusiasm, fancying itself raised above the reach of ridicule, is always incensed when it feels that it is not safe from its shaft.
Ibid., Ch. 12

103 "How can we better celebrate our joy—how can we better fill the measures of our happiness, than by the forgiveness of our enemies?"   Ibid., Ch. 19

104 It is the peculiar misfortune or punishment of misplaced, and yet more unseasonable, passions, that in their distresses they obtain no sympathy; and while the passion is in all its consequences tragic to the sufferer, in all its exhibitions it is ludicrous to the spectator.   *Ormond,*
Ch. 1   1817

105 " . . . in your vocabulary, that's only a good job where you pocket money and do nothing; now my good jobs never bring me in a farthing, and give me a great deal to do into the bargain."   Ibid., Ch. 6

106 " . . . marrying merely to be married, to manage her own affairs, and have her own way—so childish!—or marrying merely to get an establishment—so base! How women, and such young creatures, *can* bring themselves to make these venal matches. . . . "   Ibid., Ch. 11

107 After a certain age, if one lives in the world, one can't be astonished—that's a lost pleasure.   Ibid., Ch. 15

108 There are people who can go on very smoothly with those whose principles and characters they despise and dislike. There are people who, provided they live in *company*, are happy, and care but little of what the company is composed.
Ibid., Ch. 23

109 A bore is a biped, but not always *unplumed.*
Thoughts On Bores   1826

110 But there has arisen in the land men who set at naught the decrees of nature, who undertake to make artificial memories, not only equal but superior to the best natural memory, and who, at the shortest notice, engage to supply the brainless with brains.
Ibid.

111 The everlasting quotation-lover dotes on the husks of learning. He is the infant-reciting bore in second childishness.
Ibid.

112 The bore is usually considered a harmless creature, or of that class of irrational bipeds who hurt only themselves.
Ibid.

113 His [Sir Walter Scott's] morality is not in purple patches, ostentatiously obtrusive, but woven in through the very texture of the stuff.   *Helen,*
Vol. I, Ch. 12   1834

679. Rachel Robards Jackson
(1767–1828)

1 Pensacola [Florida] is a perfect plain. . . .
There is something in it so exhilarating, so
pure, so wholesome, it enlivens the whole
system. All the houses look in ruins, old as
time. . . . The inhabitants all speak Spanish
and French. Some speak four or five languages. Such a mixed multitude you, or any
of us, never had an idea of. There are fewer
white people than any other.
> Quoted in *Dames and Daughters*
> *of the Young Republic*
> by Geraldine Brooks   1901

2 Believe me, this country [Florida] has been
greatly overrated. One acre of our fine
Tennessee land is worth a thousand here.
> Letter to friends, op. cit.

3 To tell you of this city [Washington, D.C.],
I would not do justice to the subject. The
extravagance is in dressing and running to
parties; but I must say they regard the Sab-
bath and attend preaching, for there are
churches of every denomination and able
ministers of the gospel.   Letter to friend,
> op. cit.

4 Oh, my dear friend, how shall I get through
this bustle! There are not less than from fifty
to one hundred persons calling in a day.
> Ibid.

680. Caroline Amelia Elizabeth
(1768–1821)

1 I find him* very fat and not half as handsome as his portrait.
> Recorded by Lord Malmesbury,
> Quoted in *Caroline the Unhappy Queen*,
> Ch. 1, by Lord Russell of
> Liverpool   1967

*Her future husband, King George IV.

2 Judge what it is to have a drunken husband
on one's wedding day and one who spent
the greater part of his bridal night under the
grate where he fell and where I left him. If
anybody were to say to me at this moment,
will you live your life all over again or be
killed, I would choose death, for you know
sooner or later we must all die, but live a life
of wretchedness twice over—oh, *mein Gott*,
no!   As told to Lady Charlotte Bury, her
> lady-in-waiting, op. cit.

3 There is a point beyond which a guiltless
woman cannot with safety carry her forbearance. If her honour is invaded the defence of her reputation is no longer a matter
of choice and it signifies not whether the attack is made openly, manfully and directly,
or by secret insinuation and by holding
such conduct towards her as countenances
all the suspicions that malice can suggest.
> Op. cit., Ch. 3

4 . . . my dear, Punch's wife is nobody when
Punch is present.   Recorded by Lady
> Charlotte Bury,
> op. cit., Ch. 3

5 The wasp leaves his sting in the wound and
so do I.   Recorded by a friend,
> op. cit., Ch. 4

6 Oh no, my dear Mr. Brougham, I shall not
recover and I am much better dead for I be
tired of this life.   Recorded by Henry
> Brougham (August 3, 1821),
> op. cit., Ch. 7

681. Charlotte Corday
(1768/9–1793)

1 I have done my task, let others do theirs.
> Reply during interrogation at
> Abbaye Prison,
> Paris (July 13, 1793),
> Quoted in *Biography of*
> *Distinguished Women*
> by Sarah Josepha Hale   1876

2 I considered that so many brave men need not come to Paris for the head of one man [Jean Paul Marat]. He deserved not so much honour: the hand of a woman was enough. . . .   Letter to Barbaroux, from Abbaye Prison, op. cit.

3 In Paris they cannot understand how a useless woman [Corday], whose longest life could have been of no good, could sacrifice herself to save her country.
                                        Ibid.

4 Forgive me, my dear father, for having disposed of my existence without your permission. I have avenged many innocent victims. I have warded away many disasters. The people, undeceived, will one day rejoice at having been delivered from a tyrant.
                    Letter to her father, on eve of her execution, op. cit.

5 . . . now that he [Marat] is dead, the rest [of the Jacobins] may fear.   Ibid.

6 I have killed one man [Marat] to save a hundred thousand. I was a republican long before the Revolution, and have never failed in energy . . . that feeling which induces us to cast aside selfish considerations, and sacrifice ourselves for our country.
                                        Ibid.

7 The monster takes me for an assassin!
                                        Ibid.

8 . . . we do not execute well that which we have not ourselves conceived.
                        Remark at her trial (July 17, 1793), op. cit.

9 This toilet of death, though performed by rude hands, leads to immortality.
                    Remark upon leaving Abbaye Prison for execution, op. cit.

682.   Dolley Madison
(1768–1849)

1 I would rather fight with my hands than my tongue.   *Memoirs and Letters of Dolley Madison*   1886

2 My poor boy [her son]! Forgive his eccentricities, for his heart is right.
                                        Ibid.

3 You know, I usually like the routs* all too well.   Letter to Anna Cutts (July 31, 1805), op. cit.
*Social gatherings.

4 You may imagine me the very shadow of my husband.*   Letter to Mr. and Mrs. Barlow (1811), op. cit.
*James Madison (1751–1836), fourth president of the United States (1809–1817).

5 How the crowd jostles!   Quoted in *Dames and Daughters of the Young Republic* by Geraldine Brooks   1901

6 The profusion of my table is the result of the prosperity of my country, and I shall continue to prefer Virginia liberality to European elegance.   Retort to the wife of a foreign minister, op. cit.

683.   Maria-Louisa Rose Petigny
(1768–?)

1 How enviable, thy destiny,
Blessed, nimble butterly!
To live out a stable life,
Then change yourself so.   "Le Papillon," St. 1, tr. by Elaine Partnow; *Idylles*, n.d.

684.   Madame Necker de Saussure
(1768?–1847)

1 . . . there are so many causes of excitement in early life, personal affections and the desire to win the love and esteem of others occupy the mind so fully, that the young rarely press steadily onward to the most elevated mark.   Quoted in *Biography of Distinguished Women* by Sarah Josepha Hale   1876

685.   Melesina Trench
(1768–1827)

1 A fat, fair, and fifty card-playing resident of
the Crescent.   (February 18, 1816),
                              Letters   c.1820

686.   Susannah Farnum Copley
(fl. 1769–d. 1836)

1 It was his* own inclination and persevering
industry that brought him forward in the
art of painting, for he had no instructor.
               Letter, Quoted in *The Domestic
                   and Artistic Life of John
                      Singleton Copley, R.A.*,
                     Ch. 1, by Martha Babcock
                             Amory**   1882

*Her husband, the artist John Singleton Copley
(1738–1815).
**Copley's granddaughter.

2 . . . there is a ray of light let in upon us
from a hope that peace may take place; but
everything with regard to public affairs is at
present in a very uncertain state.
                    Letter to Elizabeth Clarke
                        Greene, her daughter
                             (April 6, 1801),
                        from London, op. cit.

3 I tell [your father] I don't know what might
be the effect if our comfort, as well as our
delight, was not so interwoven with the
arts, which it is mortifying to know do not
find a place among the other refinements of
our native country [the United States]. . . .
                     Letter to her daughter
                 (June 1, 1801), op. cit., Ch. 11

4 What a delightful change when peace succeeds to war and its terrible consequences,
and our information consists of French
fashions instead of the sad details of battles!
                     Letter to her daughter
                 (January 8, 1802), op. cit., Ch.
                                              12

5 In the prospect of another long and distressing war, perhaps your father may think
it the best measure [to go back to America],
as those who are engaged in the arts first
feel the distresses that war occasions. . . .
                        Letter to her daughter
                   (July 30, 1803), op. cit., Ch. 13

6 . . . but we find the law, as well as many
other pursuits, requires much perseverance
and patience to obtain the object; it is well
for us that we do not always foresee the degree that is necessary. . . .
                        Letter to her daughter
                      (March 15, 1805), op. cit.

7 My brother tells me that he may visit Boston by a turnpike road, and that such a
work is talked of. I wish that all the important changes which the present wonder-
working age presents to us were of the like
utility; but alas! as to those that are political
we can only await the event: human calculation is inadequate to conjecture what may
take place. . . .   Letter to her daughter
                      (September 1, 1806), op. cit.,
                                          Ch. 14

8 Pray kiss dear little Copley [her grandson]
for me, as well as the rest. Is he to be the
great painter in some future day? Thus the
mind wanders into futurity for those that
are coming on to the stage of life. . . .
                        Letter to her daughter
                        (June 27, 1812), op. cit.

9 The picture (or drawing) room is our dining
apartment, where the monuments of my departed husband's exertions remain at present; wherever they may be eventually assigned they will keep up his memory in the
world, but on the heart where it is engraved
they will produce a variety of sensations.
                        Letter to her daughter
                     (April 17, 1817), op. cit., Ch. 16

10 A happy calm prevails after great apprehension of the reverse.   Letter to her
                       daughter (March 22, 1821),
                                        op. cit.

687. Anne Brunton Merry
(1769–1808)

1 This is the second public attack of Mr. Hodgkinson within a short space of time—the subjects females. Surely the people of your city must think of him as he deserves, and feel that all his assertions are indelicate, inhuman, and unmanly. Letter to William
Dunlap, critic (c.July 1801),
Quoted in *History of The
American Theatre*,
Vol. II, by William
Dunlap   1833

2 Before this time you must have seen by the papers that I have bound myself a slave for four years.*   Letter to William Dunlap
(May 30, 1803), op. cit.

*Allusion to a four-year lease for the Chestnut Street Theatre in Philadelphia.

3 The business of the Theatre has been and is very, very bad indeed.   Letter to Mrs.
Thackerson,
Quoted in *The Career of Mrs.
Anne Brunton Merry in the
American Theatre*
by Gresdna Ann Doty   1971

688. Amelia Opie
(1769–1853)

1 No wonder, then, that when convinced her father was really dead she fell into a state of stupefaction, from which she never recovered; and at the same time was borne to the same grave the father and daughter.
*The Father and the
Daughter*   1801

2 Thy love, thy fate, dear youth, to share,
Must ever be thy happy lot;
But thou may'st grant this humble prayer,
Forget me not! forget me not!
"Go, Youth Beloved," St. 1,
(1802),
*The Warrior's Return & Other
Poems*   1808

3 But oh! if grief thy steps attend,
If want, if sickness be thy lot,

And thou require a soothing friend,
Forget me not, forget me not!
Ibid., St. 2

4 No rest but the grave for the Pilgrim of Love.   "The Pilgrim of Love,"
1.6, op. cit.

5 "What is an orphan boy?" I cried,
As in her face I look'd, and smiled;
My mother through her tears replied,
'You'll know too soon, ill-fated child!' "
"The Orphan Boy's Tale,"
St. 4, op. cit.

6 I know you false, I know you vain,
Yet still I cannot break my chain
"Song,"
St. 1, op. cit.

7 Yet still enchant and still deceive me,
Do all things, fatal fair, but leave me.
Ibid.

8 . . . this *wilderness* of pleasure. . . .
Quoted in *English Women of
Letters*,
Vol. II, by Julia
Kavanagh   1863

9 Knowing, at the time of our marriage, that my most favourite amusement was writing, he did not check my ambition to become an author; on the contrary, he encouraged it, and our only quarrel was, not that I wrote too much, but that I did not write more and better.   Ibid., Journal entry

10 It usually takes some time for the husband and wife to know each other's humours and habits, and to find what surrender of their own they can make with the least reluctance for their mutual good.
"Two Years of Wedded Life,"
A Wife's Duty

11 . . . I fear it is too true that men soon learn to slight what they are sure of possessing.
Ibid.

12 Had I been an artful woman, and could I have condescended to make him doubtful of the extent of my love, by a few woman's subterfuges; could I have feigned a desire to return to the world, instead of owning, as I did, that all my enjoyment was comprised in home and him, I do think that I might have been, for a much longer period, the happiest of wives; but then I should have been, in my own eyes, despicable as a woman; and I was always tenacious of my own esteem.   Ibid.

689.   Anne Newport Royall
(1769–1854)

1 The most childlike simplicity and goodness appeared in the sunshine of his [John Adams']* countenance which when speaking or listening became extremely animated, but when left to itself, subsided into unclouded serenity.   *Sketches of History, Life and Manners in the United States* 1826

*(1735–1826), second president of the United States (1797–1801).

2 Let them be bucktails or cowtails, the nether end of any animal fits them well.
The Black Book; or, A Continuation of Travels in the United States, Vol. 1   1828

3 . . . the evangelical-tractical-biblical-Sabbath School-prayer meeting—good, honest, pious, sound Presbyterians of Capitol Hill. Remarking on witness at her trial (November 28, 1817), *Mrs. Royall's Pennsylvania; or, Travels Continued in the United States,* Vol. II   1829

4 Cards subject you to bad company and bad hours. What is worse?   *Letters from Alabama,* Letter I   1830

5 At length I have reached the state of Tennessee, the land of Heroes. I have been in the state about three hours, and already I seem to tread on sacred ground.
Letter VII
(December 15, 1817)   op. cit.

6 Hitherto I have only learned mankind in theory—but I am now studying him in practice. One learns more in a day, by mixing with mankind, than he can in an age shut up in a closet.   Ibid., Letter XIII
(December 22, 1817)

7 I never but once in life heard a sermon to please me. . . .   Ibid.

8 But this preacher (as he is called) poured out a torrent of nonsense. The men groaned—the young ladies cried—the louder the preacher bawled, the louder they cried—at last they screamed!—Did you ever hear wolves howl? It was more like their howling than any thing else I can name. Is *this* religion?   Ibid.

9 There could not exist a greater evidence of unbounded avarice and ambition which distinguishes the Christian world, than the one that lay before me. There was a time when the owners of this beauteous country flattered themselves that *distance* alone would screen them from the intrusion of the whites. Vain hope!   Letter XXIII
(January 12, 1818)   op. cit.

10 You want every-day things, common-life, living-manners, evening-chat, and have I not done so? Not every thing to be sure, for I see and hear many things, that, of heavens! . . . would not look very seemingly on paper.   Letter XXXI
(January 30, 1818)   op. cit.

11 . . . true to their nature, the people, or rabble, rather always think the greatest fool the wisest man. They have proved it in this instance, by their selecting him [a local politician] to make laws for them. Alas, for my country! all your citizens want is rope.
Letter XLIV
(June 2, 1821)   op. cit.

12 The United States Bank not a political machine! It is a despot. It is the rack. It is the inquisition. It is a monster of corruption.
Quoted by Lucille Griffith, ed., in "Anne Royall, Tireless Traveler and Common Nuisance,"
Anne Royall's Letters from Alabama 1969

690. Martha Bratton
(fl. 1770s–d. 1816)

1 It was I who did it.* Let the consequence be what it will, I glory in having prevented the mischief contemplated by the cruel enemies of my country. Quoted in *The Women of the American Revolution*, Vol. II, by Elizabeth F. Ellet 1848

*Setting fire to a cache of ammunition to prevent its falling into the hands of the British.

691. Anna Elliott
(fl. 1770s)

1 [It is called] the rebel flower . . . because it always flourishes most when trampled upon. Remark to a British soldier, Quoted in *The Women of the American Revolution*, Vol. II, by Elizabeth F. Ellet 1848

2 Let not oppression shake your fortitude, nor the hope of a gentler treatment cause you for a moment to swerve from strict duty. Remark to her father, Thomas Ferguson, on his removal as a prisoner of war, op. cit. 1848

3 Better times are in store for us; the bravery of the Americans, and the friendly aid of France, will yet achieve the deliverance of our country from oppression. We shall meet again, my father, and meet with joy.
Ibid.

692. Mrs. Daniel Hall
(fl. 1770s–1780s)

1 What is it you wish to look for? [Treason, came the reply.] Then you may be saved the trouble of search, for you may find enough of it at my tongue's end. Upon handing over the key of her trunk to a British officer, Quoted in *The Women of the American Revolution*, Vol. II, by Elizabeth F. Ellet 1848

693. Margaret Holford
(fl. 1770s)

1 'T is man's pride,
His highest, worthiest, noblest boast,
The privilege he prizes most,
To stand by helpless woman's side.
"Margaret of Anjou,"
Fanny and Selina, Gresford Vale and Other Poems 1798

694. Mary(?) Scott
(fl. 1770s)

1 Owl, that lov'st the cloudy sky,
Sure, thy notes are harmony!
"The Owl,"
St. 1,
The Female Poets of Great Britain,
Frederic Rowton, ed. 1853

695. Mrs. Richard Shubrick
(fl. 1770s–1780s)

1 To men of honor, the chamber of a lady should be sacred as a sanctuary!
Remark to British soldiers hunting for an American hiding in her bedroom, Quoted in *The Women of the American Revolution*, Vol. II, by Elizabeth F. Ellet 1848

696.   Mary Wordsworth
(1770–1859)

1 O My William! it is not in my power to tell thee how I have been affected by this dearest of all letters—it was so unexpected—so new a thing to see the breathing of thy inmost heart upon paper that I was quite overpowered. . . .   Letter to William Wordsworth, her husband (August 1, 1810), from Grasmere, *The Love Letters of William and Mary Wordsworth*, Beth Darlington, ed.   1982

2 . . . I am SORRY for what causes in me such pious & exulting gladness—that you cannot fully enjoy your absence from me. . . .   Ibid.

3 We have more butterflies this year than I think I ever saw, or this study is a room more fitted to attract them than any other I ever sate in. . . . Yesterday one was flying about . . . & D.* followed it steadily with her eyes for a long time & said, "Mother do you wish you was a Butterfly, I do"—when I asked her why? she could only answer "that then she could do whatever she had a mind—" Truly I think she has a good deal of the Butterfly in her if such are its powers.   Ibid.

*Their daughter, Dora.

4 . . . I had hoped for a letter—another heart feeding letter. . . . Ibid. (August 14, 1810)

5 It is truly wonderful to see what an effect being much in the air has upon this child [Dora] she is always a merry creature, but when she is much out of doors she seems to be almost crazy with happiness. . . .
                                Ibid.

6 —tis true I am losing my teeth & my hair is becoming grey—these, the two great ornaments my Youth had to boast of, (my hair especially I prized, because thou once ventured to speak in admiration of it) I must own are *upon the wain*—else I think I am as good as ever. . . .   Ibid.

7 Only one thing that time has robbed me of had I to regret—& that is, the very great weakness of my eyes & this I feel most painfully when looking at the Country. . . .
                        Ibid. (May 13–14, 1812)

8 Bad as this is, it is some satisfaction to think this act* could only be done by a Lunatic— We were fearful that it was some dreadful Plot which might now be raging, the first act only being gone through—Alas for this Country [England], Who have we now—I fear a shadow pated Creature** to take his Place. . . .   Ibid

*The assassination of Prime Minister Spencer Perceval (1762–1812) in the House of Commons.

**Robert Banks Jenkinson (1770–1828), second earl of Liverpool; Tory statesman and prime minister (1812–1827).

9 Yet I *do* not regret that this separation has been, for it is worth no small sacrifice to be thus assured, that instead of weakening, our union has strengthened—a hundred fold strengthened those yearnings towards each other. . . . Oh William I can not tell thee how I love thee, & thou not desire it—but feel it, O feel it in the fullness of thy soul & *believe* that I am the happiest of Wives & of Mothers & of all Women the most blessed. . . . I am the most grateful—not only to thee but to every thing that breathes & to the Great God the giver of all good. . . .   Ibid. (May 23, 1812)

697.   Maria Falconar
(1771–?)

1 Once Superstition, in a fatal hour,
O'er Europe rais'd the sceptre of her power;
She reign'd triumphant minister of death,
And Peace and Pleasure faded in her breath;
Deep in monastic solitude entomb'd,
The bud of beauty wither'd ere it bloom'd
        Untitled, *Poems, by Maria and Harriet Falconar**   1788

*See 706.

2 Thus Superstition could not fix her sway

In heaven, but look'd on earth to seize her
prey   Ibid.

698. Margaretta Van Wyck Faugères
(1771–1801)

1 *There*, wrapt in musings deep, and steadfast gaze,
In solemn rapture hath she past the night.
"Winter,"
Essays in Prose and Verse
1795

2 How feels the soul just stepping from its barque,
Upon those boundless shores, dreary and dark,
Where ends all space and time, a stranger there?   "Night,"
op. cit.

3 Let the candid decide which the chaplet should wear,
The *charms* which *destroy*, or the *charms* which *repair*. "The following Lines were occasioned by Mr. Robertson's refusing to paint for one Lady, and immediately after taking another lady's likeness" (1793), op. cit.

4 "When I am gone—ah! who will care for thee?" "Elegy to Miss Anna Dundass," op. cit.

699. Elizabeth Holland
(1771–1845)

1 Your poetry is bad enough, so pray be sparing of your prose.
Remark to Samuel Rogers,*
Quoted in *Portraits of Women*
by Gamaliel Bradford   1916
*English poet (1763–1855) known for his wit.

2 I am sorry to hear you are going to publish a poem. Can't you suppress it?
Remark to Lord Porchester, op. cit.

3 The old Marchesa was also delightful, not to the eye, for she was hideous, nor to the ear, for she squalled, nor to the nose, for she was an Italian; yet, from her unbounded desire of pleasing, the *tout ensemble* created more agreeable sensations than many more accomplished could have inspired.
From her Journal, op. cit.

4 Ah, me! what can please or cheer one who has no hope of happiness in life? Solitude and amusement from external objects is all I hope for; home is the abyss of misery!
Ibid.

5 Oh! my beloved friend, how hast thou by becoming mine endeared the every day occurences of life! Letter to her husband, Lord Holland, op. cit.

6 There is a sensation in a mother's breast at the loss of an infant that partakes of the feeling of instinct. It is a species of savage despair.   Ibid.

7 Oh, God! chance, nature, or whatever thou art. . . .   Ibid.

8 A long acquaintance is with me a passport to affection.   Ibid.

9 . . . as nobody can do more mischief to a woman than a woman, so perhaps might one reverse the maxim and say nobody can do more good.   Ibid.

700. Rachel Levin Varnhagen
(1771–1833)

1 My whole day is a feast of doing good!
Letters, n.d.

701. Dorothy Wordsworth
(1771–1855)

1 I sat a long time upon a stone at the margin of the lake, and after a flood of tears my heart was easier.* *The Grasmere Journal*
(May 14, 1800)   1889
*After departure of her brothers William and John.

2 . . . our favorite birch tree. It was yielding to the gusty wind with all its tender twigs, the sun shone upon it and it glanced in the wind like a flying sunshiny tower. It was a tree in shape with stem and branches but it was like a Spirit of water. . . . The other birch trees that were near it looked bright and chearful, but it was a creature by its own self among them.   Ibid.
(November 24, 1801)

3 The half dead sound of the near sheep-bell in the hollow of the sloping coombe, exquisitely soothing.   *The Alfoxden Journal*   1897

4 At once the clouds seemed to cleave asunder, and left the moon in the centre of a black-blue vault. She sailed along, followed by multitudes of stars, small, and bright, and sharp.   Ibid.

5 I found a strawberry blossom in a rock. I uprooted it rashly and felt as if I had been committing an outrage, so I planted it again.   Ibid.

6 All the heavens seemed in one perpetual motion when the rain ceased; the moon appearing, now half veiled, and now retired behind heavy clouds, the stars still moving, the road very dirty.   Ibid. (January 31, 1798)

7 I never saw such a union of earth, sea and sky.   Ibid. (February 3, 1798)

8 One only leaf upon the top of a tree—the sole remaining leaf—danced round and round like a rag blown by the wind.
Ibid. (March 7, 1798)

9 . . . interesting groups of human creatures, the young frisking and dancing in the sun, the elder quietly drinking in the life and soul of the sun and air.   Ibid.
(March 10, 1798)

702. Mary Tighe
(1772–1810)

1 There as she sought repose, her sorrowing heart

Recall'd her absent love with bitter sighs;
Regret had deeply fix'd the poison'd dart,
Which ever rankling in her bosom lies
          *Psyche, or the Legend of
          Love*   1795–1805

2 Oh! how impatience gains upon the soul,
When the long promised hour of joy draws near!
How slow the tardy moments seem to roll!
What specters rise of inconsistent fear!
To the fond doubting heart its hopes appear
Too brightly fair, too sweet to realize;
All seem but day-dreams of delight too dear!   Ibid.

3 Vain schemer! think not to prolong thy joy!
But cherish while it lasts the heavenly boon.
          Ibid.

4 Change is the lot of all.   Ibid.

5 In pleasing e'er may I rather rove,
With blind reliance on the hand so dear,
Then let cold prudence from my eyes remove
Those sweet delusions, where no doubt, nor fear,
Nor foul disloyalty, nor cruel change appear.   Ibid.

6 To love the tender heart hath ever fled,
As on its mother's breast the infant throws
Its sobbing face, and there in sleep forgets its woe.   Ibid.

7 Oh! have you never known the silent charm
That undisturb'd retirement yields the soul
          Ibid.

8 Oh! who the exquisite delights can tell,
The joy which mutual confidence imparts?
          Ibid.

9 While cheated memory to the past returns,
And, from the present leads my shivering heart
Back to those scenes from which it wept to part.   "Sonnet,"
          The British Female Poets,
George W. Bethune, ed.   1848

10 Yes, gentle Time, thy gradual, healing hand

Hath stolen from sorrow's grasp the en- ve-
nomed dart;
Submitting to thy skill, my passive heart
"To Time,"
op. cit.

11 Sorrow and I shall part; and these faint
throes
Are but the remnant of severer woes.
Ibid.

12 Who can speak a mother's anguish
"Hagar in the Desert,"
St. 2, op. cit.

13 Odours of Spring, my sense ye charm
With fragrance premature;
And, 'mid these days of dark alarm,
Almost to hope allure. "On Receiving a
Branch of Mezereon which
Flowered at Woodstock,"
St. 1 (December 1800), op. cit.

14 Look up, my soul, through prospects dark,
And bid thy terrors rest;
Forget, forego thy earthly part,
Thine heavenly being trust:—
Ah, vain attempt! my coward heart
Still shuddering clings to dust.
Ibid., St. 4

15 The careless eye can find no grace,
No beauty in the scaly folds,
Nor see within the dark embrace
What latent loveliness it hold.
Yet in that bulb, those sapless scales,
The lily wraps her silver vest.
"The Lily,"
Sts. 2, 3,
The Female Poets of Great Britain,
Frederic Rowton, ed. 1853

16 And thou, O virgin Queen of Spring!
Shalt from thy dark and lowly bed,
Bursting thy green sheath's silken string,
Unveil thy charms, and perfume shed;
Unfold thy robes of purest white,
Unsullied from their darksome grave
Ibid., Sts. 8, 9

703. Harriet Auber
(1773–1862)

1 And His that gentle voice we hear,
Soft as the breath of even,
That checks each fault, that calms each
fear,
And speaks of heaven. "Our Blest
Redeemer, ere He breathed,"
Spirit of the Psalms 1829

704. Sophie Cottin
(1773–1807)

1 We have resisted a little while, and we think
we have done wonders; because we estimate
the merit of our resistance, not by its duration, but by the difficulty it has cost us.
Quoted in *Biography of
Distinguished Women*
by Sarah Josepha Hale 1876

2 It is in affliction that the imagination ele-
vates itself to the great thoughts of eternity
and supreme justice, and that it takes us out
of ourselves, to seek a remedy for our pains.
Ibid.

3 But still, amidst the horror and gloom of an
eternal winter, nature displays some of her
grandest spectacles.... "The Exiles and
their Home,"
Elizabeth, or the Exile of Siberia,
n.d.

4 "I have nothing left to give: the blessing of
my parents is the only recompense I have to
offer for your kindness; it is the only treasure I possess." "The Mite given in
Charity,"
op. cit.

705.   Mary Moody Emerson
(1774–1863)

1 Rose before light every morn; . . . commented on the Scriptures; . . . touched Shakespeare,—washed, carded, cleaned house, baked.   Diary entry (1805), Quoted in *Notable American Women*, Edward T. James, ed.   1971

2 Scorn trifles, lift your aims; do what you are afraid to do.   Remark to Ralph Waldo Emerson, op. cit.

3 Alive with God is enough—'tis rapture. Diary entry (later years), op. cit.

706.   Harriet Falconar
(1774–?)

1 Shall Britain view, unmov'd, sad Afric's shore
Delug'd so oft in streams of purple gore!
            Untitled, St. 2,
            *Poems, by Maria and Harriet Falconar**   1788
*See 697.

2 Britain, where science, peace, and plenty smile,
Virtue's bright seat, and freedom's favour'd isle!   Ibid.

3 When Truth, perplex'd in error's thorny maze,
Threw o'er the world obscur'd and darken'd rays,
Then Newton rose, unveil'd the beauteous maid:
He spoke, and nature stood at once displayed.   Ibid.

707.   Cecile Renard
(c.1774–1794)

1 I wanted to see how a tyrant looks.
            Reply at inquiry on her attempted assassination of Robespierre (1794),
            Quoted in *Biography of Distinguished Women*
            by Sarah Josepha Hale   1876

2 We have five hundred tyrants, [but] I prefer one king.   Ibid.

708.   Elizabeth Seton
(1774–1821)

1 Afflictions are the steps to heaven.
            Quoted in *Notable American Women*,
            Edward T. James, ed.   1971

709.   Louisa Catherine Adams
(1775–1852)

1 That open front where wisdom sits
That Eye which speaks the soul
That brow which study gently knits
That soft attemper'd whole. . . .
            "On the Portrait of my Husband"* (1816),
            Quoted in *Portraits of John Quincy Adams and His Wife*,
            Ch.2, by Andrew Oliver   1970
*The portrait of John Quincy Adams (1767–1848), sixth president of the United States (1825–1829), by Charles Robert Leslie, English painter (1794–1859).

2 Go flatter'd image tell the tale
Of years long past away;
Of faded youth, of sorrows wail,
Of times too sure decay. . . .
            "To my Sons with my Portrait by Stewart,*
            (December 18, 1825), op. cit., Ch. 3

3 I saw my portrait at the exhibition. . . . Nobody likes it and Stewart* is quite vexed. It looks very much as I looked, like a woman who was just attacked by the first chill of death and the features stiffning into torpor. The hair is as white as the face and the fine lilac bows in the Cap seem to mock the general frigidity of the half Corps. It speaks too much of inward suffering and a half broken heart to be an agreeable remembrancer. *Mais n'import* [but it doesn't matter]. . . .
Letter to her sons, op. cit.

*Gilbert Stuart, famed American portrait painter (1755–1828).

710. Jane Austen
(1775–1817)

1 "Beware of the insipid Vanities and idle Dissipations of the Metropolis of England; Beware of the unmeaning Luxuries of Bath and of the stinking fish of South Hampton."
Love and Friendship, Letter Fourth
1790

2 She was nothing more than a mere good-tempered, civil and obliging young woman; as such we could scarcely dislike her—she was only an Object of Contempt—.
Letter Thirteenth, op. cit.

3 Beware of fainting-fits . . . though at the time they may be refreshing and agreable, yet believe me they will in the end, if too often repeated and at improper seasons, prove destructive to your Constitution.
Letter Fourteenth, op. cit.

4 She is probably by this time as tired of me, as I am of her; but as she is too polite and I am too civil to say so, our letters are still as frequent and affectionate as ever, and our Attachment as firm and sincere as when it first commenced. *Lesley Castle*,
Letter the Fourth   1792

5 "Well, but (he continued) tho' they [the Misses Lesley] may be above the common size, their figures are perfectly elegant; and as to their faces, their Eyes are beautiful." "I never can think such tremendous, knock-me-down figures in the least degree elegant, and as for their eyes, they are so tall that I never could strain my neck enough to look at them."   Letter the Sixth, op. cit.

6 It is very hard that a pretty woman is never to be told she is so by any one of her own sex without that person's being suspected to be either her determined Enemy, or her professed Toadeater.   Letter the Ninth,
op. cit.

7 It is to be supposed that Henry was married since he had certainly four sons, but it is not in my power to inform the reader who was his wife. Be this as it may, he did not live for ever, but falling ill, his son the Prince of Whales came and took away the crown; whereupon the king made a long speech, for which I must refer the Reader to Shakespear's Plays, and the Prince made a still longer.   *The History of England*,
"Henry the Fourth"   1793?

8 The Crimes and Cruelties of this Prince, were too numerous to be mentioned . . . and nothing can be said in his vindication, but what his abolishing Religious Houses and leaving them to the ruinous depredations of time has been of infinite use to the landscape of England in general. . . .
"Henry the Eighth", op. cit.

9 It was the peculiar misfortune of this Woman to have bad Ministers—Since wicked as she herself was, she could not have committed such extensive mischeif, had not these vile and abandoned Men connived at and encouraged her in her crimes.
"Elizabeth", op. cit.

10 An annuity is a very serious business.
Sense and Sensibility,
Pt. I, Ch. 2   1811

11 "Only conceive how comfortable they will be. Five hundred a year! I am sure I cannot imagine how they will spend half of it."
   Ibid.

12 "I am afraid," replied Elinor, "that the pleasantness of an employment does not always evince its propriety."
   Ibid., Ch. 13

13 Lady Middleton . . . exerted herself to ask Mr. Palmer if there was any news in the paper.
   "No, none at all," he replied, and read on.
   Ibid., Ch. 19

14 The less said the better. Ibid., Pt. II, Ch. 5

15 On every formal visit a child ought to be of the party, by way of provision for discourse.
   Ibid., Ch. 6

16 "It is not time or opportunity that is to determine intimacy; it is disposition alone. Seven years would be insufficient to make some people acquainted with each other, and seven days are more than enough for others."
   Ibid., Ch. 12

17 Like half the rest of the world, if more than half there be that is clever and good, Marianne, with excellent abilities and an excellent disposition, was neither reasonable nor candid. She expected from other people the same opinions and feelings as her own, and she judged of their motives by the immediate affect of their actions on herself.
   Ibid., Ch. 31

18 "A man who has nothing to do with his own time has no conscience in his intrusion on that of others."
   Ibid.

19 Every qualification is raised at times by the circumstances of the moment, to more than its real value; and she was sometimes worried down by officious condolence to rate good breeding as more indispensable to comfort than good nature.
   Ibid., Ch. 32

20 He had just compunction enough for having done nothing for his sisters himself, to be exceedingly anxious that everybody else should do a great deal.   Ibid., Ch. 33

21 . . . though a very few hours spent in the hard labour of incessant talking will dispatch more subjects than can really be in common between any two rational creatures, yet with lovers it is different. Between *them* no subject is finished, no communication is even made, till it has been made at least twenty times over.   Ibid., Ch. 49

22 It is a truth universally acknowledged, that a single man in possession of a good fortune, must be in want of a wife.
   Pride and Prejudice,
   Ch. 1 (first sentence)   1813

23 She* was a woman of mean understanding, little information, and uncertain temper.
   Ibid.
   *Mrs. Bennet, the heroine's mother.

24 "Kitty has no discretion in her coughs," said her father: "she times them ill."
   "I do not cough for my own amusement," replied Kitty fretfully.   Ibid., Ch. 2

25 "Pride . . . is a very common failing, I believe. By all that I have ever read, I am convinced that it is very common indeed; that human nature is particularly prone to it, and that there are very few of us who do not cherish a feeling of self-complacency on the score of some quality or the other, real or imaginary. Vanity and pride are different things, though the words are often used synonymously. A person may be proud without being vain. Pride relates more to our opinion of ourselves, vanity to what we would have others think of us.
   Ibid., Ch. 5

26 A lady's imagination is very rapid; it jumps from admiration to love, from love to matrimony in a moment.   Ibid., Ch. 6

27 "There is so much of gratitude or vanity in almost every attachment, that it is not safe to leave any to itself."   Ibid.

28 "Happiness in marriage is entirely a matter of chance. If the dispositions of the parties are ever so well known to each other or ever so similar beforehand, it does not advance their felicity in the least. They always continue to grow sufficiently unlike afterwards to have their share of vexation; and it is better to know as little as possible of the defects of the person with whom you are to pass your life." Ibid.

29 How can you contrive to write so even? Ibid., Ch. 10

30 " . . . you are really proud of your defects in writing, because you consider them as proceeding from a rapidity of thought and carelessness of execution, which, if not estimable, you think at least highly interesting. The power of doing anything with quickness is always much prized by the possessor, and often without any attention to the imperfection of the performance." Ibid.

31 Mr. Collins had only to change from Jane to Elizabeth—and it was soon done—done while Mrs. Bennet was stirring the fire. Ibid., Ch. 15

32 "You have delighted us long enough." Ibid., Ch. 18

33 "It is particularly incumbent on those who never change their opinion, to be secure of judging properly at first." Ibid.

34 "An unhappy alternative is before you, Elizabeth. From this day you must be a stranger to one of your parents.—Your mother will never see you again if you do *not* marry Mr. Collins, and I will never see you again if you *do*." Ibid., Ch. 20

35 Nobody is on my side, nobody takes part with me: I am cruelly used, nobody feels for my poor nerves. Ibid.

36 Without thinking highly either of men or of matrimony, marriage had always been her object; it was the only honourable provision for well-educated young women of small fortune, and however uncertain of giving happiness, must be their pleasantest preservative from want. Ibid., Ch. 22

37 "The more I see of the world, the more am I dissatisfied with it; and every day confirms my belief of the inconsistency of all human characters, and of the little dependence that can be placed on the appearance of either merit or sense." Ibid., Ch. 24

38 "Is not general incivility the very essence of love?" Ibid., Ch. 25

39 "Pray, my dear aunt, what is the difference in matrimonial affairs, between the mercenary and the prudent move? Where does discretion end, and avarice begin?" Ibid., Ch. 27

40 "Adieu to disappointment and spleen. What are men to rocks and mountains?" Ibid.

41 . . . where other powers of entertainment are wanting, the true philosopher will derive benefit from such as are given. Ibid., Ch. 42

42 Mrs Bennet was restored to her usual querulous serenity. Ibid.

43 "Unhappy as the event must be for Lydia, we may draw from it this useful lesson: that loss of virtue in a female is irretrievable; that one false step involves her in endless ruin; that her reputation is no less brittle than it is beautiful; and that she cannot be too much guarded in her behavior towards the undeserving of the other sex." Ibid., Ch. 47

44 "You ought certainly to forgive them as a Christian, but never admit them in your sight, or allow their names to be mentioned in your hearing." Ibid., Ch. 57

45 For what do we live, but to make sport for our neighbours, and laugh at them in our turn? Ibid.

46 I have been a selfish being all my life, in practice, though not in principle.
Ibid., Ch. 58

47 Those who do not complain are never pitied.
Ibid.

48 Think only of the past as its remembrance gives you pleasure.
Ibid.

49 "I pay very little regard," said Mrs. Grant, "to what any young person says on the subject of marriage. If they profess a disinclination for it, I only set it down that they have not yet seen the right person."
Mansfield Park,
Ch. 4　　1814

50 "An engaged woman is always more agreeable than a disengaged. She is satisfied with herself. Her cares are over, and she feels that she may exert all her powers of pleasing without suspicion. All is safe with a lady engaged; no harm can be done."
Ibid., Ch. 5

51 " . . . there is not one in a hundred of either sex who is not taken in when they marry. Look where I will, I see that it *is* so; and I feel that it *must* be so, when I consider that it is, of all transactions, the one in which people expect most from others, and are least honest themselves."
Ibid.

52 "What strange creatures brothers are! You would not write to each other but upon the most urgent necessity in the world; and when obliged to take up a pen to say that such a horse is ill, or such a relation dead, it is done in the fewest possible words. You have but one style among you. I know it perfectly. Henry, who is in every other respect exactly what a brother should be . . . has never yet turned the page in a letter; and very often it is nothing more than—'Dear Mary, I am just arrived. Bath seems full and everything as usual. Yours sincerely.' That is the true manly style; that is a complete brother's letter."
Ibid., Ch. 6

53 "Those who see quickly, will resolve quickly, and act quickly. . . . "
Ibid.

54 "Selfishness must always be forgiven, you know, because there is no hope of a cure."
Ibid., Ch. 7

55 "At any rate, it is safer to leave people to their own devices on such subjects [as religion]. Everybody likes to go their own way—to choose their own time and manner of devotion. The obligation of attendance, the formality, the restraint, the length of time—altogether it is a formidable thing, and what nobody likes; and if the good people who used to kneel and gape in that gallery could have foreseen that the time would ever come when men and women might lie another ten minutes in bed when they woke with a headache, without danger of reprobation because chapel was missed, they would have jumped with joy and envy."
Ibid., Ch. 9

56 " . . . it will, I believe, be everywhere found, that as the clergy are, or are not what they ought to be, so are the rest of the nation."
Ibid.

57 "Oh! do not attack me with your watch. A watch is always too fast or too slow. I cannot be dictated to by a watch."
Ibid.

58 . . . that favouring *something* which everybody who shuts their eyes while they look, or their understandings while they reason, feels the comfort of.
Ibid., Ch. 11

59 "Indolence and love of ease; a want of all laudable ambition, of taste for good company, or of inclination to take the trouble of being agreeable, which makes men clergymen. A clergyman has nothing to do but be slovenly and selfish; read the newspaper, watch the weather, and quarrel with his wife. His curate does all the work, and the business of his own life is to dine."
Ibid.

60 "Here's harmony!" said she; "here's repose! Here's what may leave all painting and all music behind, and what poetry can only attempt to describe! Here's what may tranquillise every care, and lift the heart to rapture! When I look out on such a night as this, I feel as if there could be neither wickedness nor sorrow in the world; and there certainly would be less of both if the sublimity of Nature were more attended to, and people were carried more out of themselves by contemplating such a scene." Ibid.

61 "I am perfectly persuaded that the tempers had better be unlike: I mean unlike in the flow of the spirits, in the manners, in the inclination for much or little company, in the propensity to talk or to be silent, to be grave or to be gay. Some opposition here is, I am thoroughly convinced, friendly to matrimonial happiness. I exclude extremes, of course; and a very close resemblance in all those points would be the likeliest way to produce an extreme. A counter action, gentle and continual, is the best safeguard of manners and conduct." Ibid., Ch. 35

62 "Let him have all the perfections in the world, I think it ought not to be set down as certain that a man must be acceptable to every woman who he happens to like himself." Ibid.

63 "Good-humoured, unaffected girls will not do for a man who has been used to sensible women. They are two distinct orders of being." Ibid.

64 Let other pens dwell on guilt and misery. Ibid., Ch. 48

65 An egg boiled very soft is not unwholesome. *Emma,* Ch. 3 1815

66 "If I lay it down as a general rule, Harriet, that if a woman *doubts* as to whether she should accept a man or not, she certainly ought to refuse him. If she can hesitate as to 'Yes,' she ought to say 'No,' directly." Ibid., Ch. 7

67 "Vanity working on a weak head produces every sort of mischief." Ibid., Ch. 8

68 One half of the world cannot understand the pleasures of the other. Ibid., Ch. 9

69 A basin of nice smooth gruel, thin, but not too thin. Ibid., Ch. 12

70 With men he can be rational and unaffected, but when he has ladies to please, every feature works. Ibid., Ch. 13

71 It was a delightful visit—perfect, in being much too short. Ibid.

72 The youth and cheerfulness of mourning are in happy analogy, and of powerful operation; and if the distress be not poignant enough to keep the eyes unclosed, they will be sure to open to sensations of softened pain and brighter hope. Ibid., Ch. 16

73 . . . but a sanguine temper, for ever expecting more good than occurs, does not always pay for its hopes by any proportion of depression. It soon flies over the present failure, and begins to hope again. Ibid., Ch. 18

74 "There is one thing, Emma, which a man can always do, if he chooses, and that is, his duty; not by manoeuvring and finessing, but by vigour and resolution." Ibid.

75 Nobody who has not been in the interior of a family can say what the difficulties of any individual of that family may be. Ibid.

76 My mother's deafness is very trifling, you see, just nothing at all. By only raising my voice, and saying anything two or three times over, she is sure to hear. Ibid., Ch. 19

77 "But, my dear sir," cried Mr. Weston, "if Emma comes away early, it will be breaking up the party." "And no great harm if it does," said Mr. Woodhouse. "The sooner every party breaks up the better." Ibid., Ch. 25

78 "I do not know whether it ought to be so, but certainly silly things do cease to be silly if they are done by sensible people in an impudent way. Wickedness is always wickedness, but follyness is not always folly. It depends upon the character of those who handle it."   Ibid., Ch. 26

79 "Open the windows! But, surely Mr. Churchill, nobody would think of opening the windows at Randall's. Nobody could be so imprudent."   Ibid., Ch. 29

80 "Young ladies should take care of themselves. Young ladies are delicate plants. They should take care of their health and their complexion. My dear, did you change your stockings?"   Ibid., Ch. 34

81 Business, you know, may bring money, but friendship hardly ever does.
                    Ibid.

82 "The post-office is a wonderful establishment!" said she. "The regularity and dispatch of it! If one thinks of all that it has to do, and all that it does so well, it is really astonishing!"
"It is certainly very well regulated."
"So seldom that any negligence or blunder appears! So seldom that a letter, among the thousands that are constantly passing about the kingdom, is even carried wrong—and not one in a million, I suppose, actually lost! And when one considers the variety of hands, and of bad hands too, that are to be deciphered, it increases the wonder."
                    Ibid.

83 "One cannot have too large a party. A large party secures its own amusement."
                    Ibid., Ch. 42

84 "But after all the punishment that misconduct can bring, it is still not less misconduct. Pain is no expiation."
                    Ibid., Ch. 48

85 "A man would always wish to give a woman a better home than the one he takes her from; and he that can do it, where there is no doubt of *her* regard, must, I think, be the happiest of mortals."   Ibid., Ch. 49

86 What did she say? Just what she ought, of course. A lady always does.
                    Ibid.

87 Seldom, very seldom, does complete truth belong to any human disclosure. Seldom can it happen that something is not a little disguised, or a little mistaken; but where, as in this case, though the conduct is mistaken, the feelings are not, it may not be very material.   Ibid.

88 "It is very difficult for the prosperous to be humble."   Ibid., Ch. 50

89 "To look *almost* pretty is an acquisition of higher delight to a girl who has been looking plain the first fifteen years of her life than a beauty from her cradle can ever receive."   *Northanger Abbey*,
                    Ch. 1   1818

90 "Not keep a journal! How are your absent cousins to understand the tenor of life in Bath without one? How are the civilities and compliments of everyday to be related as they ought to be unless noted down every evening in a journal? How are your various dresses to be remembered, and the particular state of your complexion, and curl of your hair to be described in all their diversities, without having constant recourse to a journal? My dear madam, I am not so ignorant of young ladies' ways as you wish to believe me. It is this delightful habit of journalizing which largely contributes to form the easy style of writing for which ladies are so generally celebrated. Everybody allows that the talent of writing agreeable letters is peculiarly female. Nature may have done something, but I am sure it is essentially assisted by the practice of keeping a journal."
                    Ibid., Ch. 3

91 "And what are you reading, Miss—?" "Oh! it is only a novel!" replies the young lady: while she lays down her book with affected indifference, or momentary shame.—"It is only Cecilia, or Camilla, or Belinda:" or, in short, only some work in which the most thorough knowledge of human nature, the happiest delineation of its varieties, the liveliest effusions of wit and humour are conveyed to the world in the best chosen language. Ibid., Ch. 5

92 But are they all horrid, are you sure they are all horrid? Ibid., Ch. 6

93 Oh, Lord! not I; I never read much; I have something else to do. Ibid., Ch. 7

94 " . . . I am sure of *this*, that if everybody was to drink their bottle a day, there would be not half the disorders in the world there are now. It would be a famous good thing for us all." Ibid., Ch. 9

95 She knew not how to reconcile two such very different accounts of the same thing; for she had not been brought up . . . to know to how many idle assertions and impudent falsehoods the excess of vanity will lead. Her own family were plain matter-of-fact people, who seldom aimed at wit of any kind; her father at the utmost being contented with a pun, and her mother with a proverb; they were not in the habit, therefore, of telling lies to increase their importance, or of asserting at one moment what they would contradict the next. Ibid.

96 "Very true," said Henry, "and this is a very nice day; and we are taking a very nice walk; and you are two very nice ladies. Oh! it is a very nice word, indeed! . . . every commendation on every subject is comprised in that one word." Ibid., Ch. 14

97 "I read [history] a little as a duty; but it tells me nothing that does not either vex or weary me. The quarrels of popes and kings, with wars and pestilences in every page; the men also good for nothing, and hardly any women at all, it is very tiresome; and yet I often think it odd that it should be so dull, for a great deal of it must be invention." Ibid.

98 "At this rate, I shall not pity the writers of history any longer . . . labouring only for the torment of little boys and girls, always struck me as a hard fate; and though I know it is all very right and necessary, I have wondered at the person's courage who could sit down and do it." Ibid.

99 Where people wish to attach, they should always be ignorant. To come with a well informed mind, is to come with an inability of administering to the vanity of others, which a sensible person would always wish to avoid. Ibid.

100 "Dear Miss Morland, Consider the dreadful nature of the suspicions you have entertained. What have you been judging from? Remember the country and the age in which we live. Remember that we are English: that we are Christians." Ibid., Ch. 24

101 "But your mind is warped by an innate principle of general integrity, and, therefore, not accessible to the cruel reasonings of family partiality, or a desire for revenge." Ibid., Ch. 27

102 How quick come the reasons for approving what we like! *Persuasion,* Ch. 2 1818

103 "In fact, as I have long been convinced, though every profession is necessary and honourable in its turn, it is only the lot of those who are not obliged to follow any, who can live in a regular way, in the country, choosing their own hours, following their own pursuits, and living on their own property, without the torment of trying for more; it is only *their* lot, I say, to hold the blessings of health and a good appearance to the utmost: I know no other set of men but what lose something of their personableness when they cease to be quite young."
Ibid., Ch. 3

104 She had been forced into prudence in her youth, she learned romance as she grew older: the natural sequence of an unnatural beginning.   Ibid., Ch. 4

105 "If there is anything disagreeable going on men are always sure to get out of it. . . ."
Ibid., Ch. 7

106 "It is the worst evil of too yielding and indecisive a character that no influence over it can be depended on. You are never sure of a good impression being durable; everybody may sway it. Let those who would be happy be firm."   Ibid., Ch. 10

107 Everybody has their taste in noises as well as in other matters; and sounds are quite innoxious or most distressing, by their sort rather than their quantity.
Ibid., Ch. 14

108 "My idea of good company, Mr. Elliot, is a company of clever, well-informed people, who have a great deal of conversation; that is what I call good company."
"You are mistaken," said he, gently, "that is not good company; that is the best."
Ibid., Ch. 16

109 Warmth and enthusiasm did captivate her still. She felt that she could so much more depend upon the sincerity of those who sometimes looked or said a careless or a hasty thing, than of those whose presence of mind never varied, whose tongue never slipped.   Ibid., Ch. 17

110 My sore throats are always worse than anyone's.   Ibid., Ch. 18

111 "No, no, it is not man's nature. I will allow it to be more man's nature than woman's to be inconstant and forget those they do love, or have loved. I believe the reverse. I believe in a true analogy between our bodily frames and our mental; and that as our bodies are the strongest, so are our feelings; capable of bearing most rough usage, and riding out the heaviest weather."   Ibid., Ch. 23

112 "Man is more robust than woman, but he is not longer lived; which exactly explains my view of the nature of their attachments."
Ibid.

113 " . . . I do not think I ever opened a book in my life which had not something to say upon woman's inconstancy. Songs and proverbs all talk of woman's fickleness. But, perhaps, you will say, these were all written by men."
"Perhaps I shall. Yes, yes, if you please, no reference to examples in books . . . the pen has been in their hands. I will not allow books to prove anything."
Ibid.

114 What dreadful hot weather we have! It keeps me in a continual state of inelegance.
Letter to her sister Cassandra
(September 18, 1796),
Jane Austen's Letters,
R. W. Chapman, ed.   1932

115 I do not want people to be very agreeable, as it saves me the trouble of liking them a great deal.   Letter to Cassandra
(December 24, 1798), op. cit.

711. Mary Martha Sherwood
(1775–1851)

1 " . . . fishes are certainly very inferior creatures to birds or beasts. There is no one of this class which has the least regard or care for its young ones, and many of them are even so unnatural as to feed upon their offspring." *The History of Henry Milner,*
Part First, Ch. 10,
from *The Works of Mrs. Sherwood,* Vol. I
1856

2 "The book of Nature, my dear Henry, is full of holy lessons, ever new and ever varied; and to learn to discover these lessons should be the work of good education; for there are many persons who are exceedingly wise and clever in worldly matters, and yet with respect to spiritual things are wholly blind and dark, and are as unable to look on divine light as the bats and moles to contemplate the glory of the sun's rays at midday." Ibid., Ch. 16

3 " . . . it is the very nature of sin to prevent man from meditating on spiritual things. . . . " Ibid., Part Second, Ch. 11

4 "We are getting too fine in this country, Lord H———; too fine in our habits. I doubt much whether our intellectual advancement bears a due proportion with the refinements of our habits. If that is the case, as I apprehend, there will be a reaction by-and-by—a reaction in which all that is mere tinsel in the state of society will be reduced to non-entity, and nothing will remain but that which is solid and real."
Ibid., Part Third, Ch. 2

5 "Where the habits are simple, and the mind truly elevated, then is society in the best state. . . . " Ibid.

6 "Whether I speak or not, time runs on, death and eternity approach. I do not see why it should be a matter of politeness to throw dust in each other's eyes. . . . "
"The History of Little Henry and his Bearer,"
op. cit., Vol. III

7 "Because," I said, "although I am poor, yet I fear my God, and I will never take any money but such as I can get in an honest manner. Did God see fit, he could make me richer in one day than I should become were I for a long life to use every wicked means. . . . " "The History of Susan Gray,"
op. cit.

8 "You do not know how desperately wicked the world is, and what hard trials are in the way of young men, ay, and of young women too, when they go out into it: it is next to an impossible thing for a young man to mix with his fellow-creatures, if it be but at a village-wake, without falling into sin."
"The History of Lucy Clare,"
op. cit.

9 O, how little do children know what parents sometimes endure for their sake!
"The Hedge of Thorns,"
op. cit.

10 They who have never been on board large vessels can form no idea of the dismal abodes which lie in the depths of their hulls; abodes without light, against whose hollow sides the green waves of the raging ocean continually dash themselves—abodes which are never refreshed by the pure air of heaven; but which are constantly filled with noxious smells, and an insufferable marine odour. "The Recaptured Negro,"
op. cit.

11 . . . it has been one of the chief arts of Satan to cause himself to be represented in the most burlesque point of view by the false church, in order that he may not be known in his true character, wherein he often appears as an angel of light, and acts, or rather influences his people to act, with much attention to worldly wisdom, and what is called expediency. "Victoria,"
op. cit., Vol. VIII

12 "And why not?" returned the *fakeer;* "I can read books and men too, and I tell you that the latter is a much more profitable branch of study than the former."

Arzoomund,
Ch. 5, op. cit.

13 "To speak the plain truth, all religions seem alike to me, one mass of absurdities and lies—... I know that there is a God, but I know no more of him; and I believe that all those are liars who pretend to know more than I do."   Ibid.

14 "I have seen the world, and lived with all sorts of men, and have thrown away all prejudices."   Ibid.

15 But Mrs. Timmins overlooked all these things, in consideration of her rare and undeviating honesty; "For," as the good old servant would often say to her lady, "I can hire a seamstress to sew linen; I can call in a neighbour to converse with me; I can get a clever cook and clean housemaid for money; but where, my lady, is the servant to be met with to whom I can give my keys, and be sure not to be robbed, or into hands I can put a purse of untold gold and have a faithful account of every penny?"

"Joan; or, Trustworthy,"
op. cit.

16 ... there is much difference of opinion concerning what may justly be called admirable in the female character, some making the fashions of the world, and others the principles of the Christian religion, the test of true excellence....   *The Lady of the Manor; being a Series of Conversations on the Subject of Confirmation intended for the use of the Middle and Higher Ranks of Young Female,*
Vol. I, Ch. 1,
Introductory, op. cit., Vol. IX

17 Humility becomes our fallen nature....
Ibid., Ch. 2

18 "It is commonly said, by the profane and thoughtless, that youth is the time for pleasure, and for the enjoyment of life. We will not now stay to decide whether what the world calls pleasure is the same thing with the true enjoyment of life...."
Ibid.

19 ... but the spirits of youth are buoyant, and the sense of shame from natural causes soon passes away.   Ibid., Ch. 3

20 And now poor Maria saw her happiness passing gradually from her, earthly cares were rapidly consuming that tender love which had so lately subsisted between herself and her husband.   Ibid., Ch. 5

21 "... whatever station the child may occupy, humility must be enforced, and enforced upon Christian principles. All education, however otherwise excellent, which fails in this point, has, in my opinion, a pernicious tendency; and, humanly speaking, can only produce, at the best, a species of worldly morality, or a mere profession of religion...."   Ibid., Ch. 7

22 "Children are not taught to consider that every thing they possess or enjoy is more than they deserve; and that were they dealt with according to their merits, their portion would be endless misery."
"Hence when they grow up—wanting true humility, they consider themselves entitled to many pleasures and distinctions, which they never can enjoy, because their inordinate desires have overstepped the boundaries of their actual possession and privileges."   Ibid.

23 "Nay, supposing that we possessed faculties capable of forming an opinion of the divine government of the universe," continued the lady of the manor, "we still want that knowledge of facts without which no judgment can be formed on any, even the commonest, subject in ordinary life."
Ibid., Ch. 10

24 "If, therefore," proceeded she, "it would be utterly impossible to make a child of four years old form a proper judgment of a speech in parliament, how, I ask, can we be supposed able to reason justly upon what is proper in the government of the universe?"
            Ibid.

25 "But inasmuch as no human teacher is able to separate the wheat from the tares, the rulers of the Church are compelled to let them all grow together until the harvest, allowing the latter to enjoy all the privileges of cultivation and protection in common with the former."   Ibid., Ch. 11

26 ... for what is the zest of argument when the antagonist is not allowed to answer?
        The Monk of Climiés,
        Ch. 5, op. cit., Vol. XIV

27 But, blessed be God! the spirit of Antichrist has been robbed of its power in this our own country; the infidel may revile the Church of England, and be ungrateful for what our reformers did, but he that sees popery only in England, where its worst features are concealed from observation, can never sufficiently appreciate the deliverance which was wrought for us when the papal authority was thrust out of this land.
           Ibid., Ch. 12

28 "I don't see much use in troubling one's self about being very great in these times; if all the great people of the world fall into the dust one after another, as you say they do, papa, and their very names are forgotten, as to be sure they are—only a very few, such as I have at the end of my Dictionary—and if I was to work and strive ever so hard, it might still be a chance whether the people would choose to place mine along with the rest...."   "The Roman Baths,"
             op. cit.

29 "... my father has lived abroad till he has lost his judgment...." *The History of*
          John Marten,
       Ch. 1, op. cit., Vol. XVI

30 "... happiness cannot fail to proceed from submission to the will of God, if not just at first, yet certainly in the progress of time."
            Ibid.

31 ... a dirty exterior is a great enemy to beauty of all descriptions.
          Ibid., Ch. 13

32 " 'No man can change the heart, or enlighten the mind of another.' "
"But he may instruct the head of any one possessing his due share of natural intellect," replied Mansfield, "and there certainly must be a defect somewhere, when a minister, after forty years, leaves his congregation without head-knowledge, ignorant, as you say, as heathen Greeks."
          Ibid., Ch. 16

712. Sydney Owenson Morgan
(c.1776-83–1859)

1 Religious enthusiasm never gave to the fancied form of the first of the patriarchs a countenance of more holy expression or divine resignation; a figure more touching by its dignified simplicity, or an air more beneficently mild—more meekly good.
    The Wild Irish Girl 1805

2 Slowly departing, I rose my eyes to the Castle of Innismore, sighed and almost wished I had been born the lord of these ruins, the prince of this isolated little territory, the adored chieftain of these affectionate and natural people.   Ibid.

3 ... he listened to those strains which had once spoke to the heart of the father, the patriot, and the man—breathed from the chords of his country's emblem—breathed in the pathos of his country's music—breathed from the lips of his apparently inspired daughter!   Ibid.

4 ... this child of genius and of passion.
            Ibid.

5 There can be no individual happiness but that which harmonizes with the happiness of society—there may be virtue without felicity, but there can be no felicity without virtue. . . .   *Ida of Athens*   1808

6 Literary fiction, whether directed to the purpose of transient amusement, or adopted as an indirect medium of instruction, has always in its most genuine form exhibited a mirror of the times in which it is composed; reflecting morals, customs, manners, peculiarity of character, and prevalence of opinion. Thus, perhaps, after all, it forms the best history of nations. . . .
Preface, *O'Donnell: A National Tale,*
Vol. I   1813

7 The vexations of life are not always to be estimated by their dignity; and there is, perhaps, no annoyance more perplexing than the cross accidents of a journey, sharpened by the accumulated evils arising out of time, place, season, and weather.
Ibid., Ch. 8

8 . . . the ring was all that remained to him of the earlier and most brilliant period of his existence, when full of hope and joy, his light and gallant spirit had received no impression from time, but such as love and glory gave, when new to life, and flushed with passion, he feared no change, and suspected no illusion. . . .   Ibid., Vol. II, Ch. 4

9 He stood, indeed, at the head of that class of apathetic men of gallantry, *qui se laissent aimer* [who allow themselves to be loved]; and who . . . if they sometimes commit the feelings of the objects they select, never risk their own; who lounge away their mornings in boudoirs, their evenings in assembly rooms; . . . and plot, manoever [sic], and intrigue, according to the interests and the views of that heartless vanity in which "they live and breathe, and have their being," less anxious to be loved than to be adulated—to awaken a sentiment than to expose a triumph; they demand *obvious* attentions, rather than *hidden devotion*; nor seek . . . the exclusiveness of friendship, nor the tenderness of passion.
Ibid., Vol. III, Ch. 1

10 "That you are an Irishman, *genuine* and thorough bred, there can be no doubt; with your porcupine spirit, rising before it is assailed, and throwing its quill before it receives a wound. . . . "   Ibid., Ch. 3

11 "I have done a little; that is, I have *undone* everything; but, for the present, I shall not have time to complete anything."
Ibid.

12 " . . . as is usual among the semi-barbarous, improvement is resisted as innovation; . . . the old muddling system must go on for ever in the same old muddling way."
Ibid.

13 "And so, Mr. M'Rory, you are really such a superstitious blockhead as to believe in purgatory, are you?" "I believe, sir, in what my people believed before me; and what more does your honour, and the likes of you, do more than that? But, in truth, in respect of purgatory, sir, myself is noways particular; only, bad as it is, sure you, your honour, may go farther and faire worse for all that."
Ibid.

14 " . . . if foreigners won't understand one another, who do they expect will, I wonder."   *Florence Macarthy: An Irish Tale,*
Vol. I, Ch. 1   1819

15 "There is," said the Commodore, "a mixture of indolence and laboriousness in these miserable people that is singular; they have neither the activity of savages nor the industry of civilization. They want energy for the one, and motive for the other.
Ibid., Ch. 4

16 "With your missions and missionaries, conversions and perversions, have you left a tinpenny in my pocket to give to my own poor in New-Town Mount Crawley? And pray, what's gone of my one pound note that went to make christians of the black negroes? Never saw a single soul of them set foot in a church yet, barring Mrs. Casey's little black boy, that carries her prayer-book to early service. And I'd trouble you for my eleven and fourpence halfpenny, Miss Crawley, that you made me give to get King Pomarre, of the Otaheitee Islands, to let himself be baptised. . . . And 'bove all, where's my sixteen and threepence, carried off by your "*angel without wings,*" for "*lighting up* the *dark* villages;" and my eloquent *surtout*, that was stolen out of the hall in Merrion Square, by your converted Jew, that was waiting for your "*guide to the Land of Promise?* " I wish you had given the Devil his *Jew*, and left me my great coat; that's all, Miss Crawley."
Ibid., Vol. II, Ch. 2

17 "Oh! *par exemple*, for fine men," said Lady Dunore, throwing herself into an arm chair, "I think they are really quite extinct with us altogether." Ibid., Vol. III, Ch. 3

18 "South America," he observed, "is well known to us in the Spanish histories of its early discoverers, when Spain invaded it under the Simoniacal pretext of *religion*; letting loose, at the same time, *bloodhounds and apostles*, while they opened its mineral veins and exterminated its population . . . almost [depriving] these great regions of a place in the history of nations. . . ." Ibid.

19 "Temporary measures of expediency have nothing to do with general views," replied young Crawley to Mr. Daly's observation. "What is wisdom *to-day* in the conduct of a government may be madness *to-morrow.*"
Ibid.

20 She had made herself necessary to the amusement of those so difficult to amuse, and she consequently assumed an overweening importance, which never fails to succeed with indolence or mediocrity in all ranks. Ibid., Vol. IV, Ch. 3

21 "You have no idea how I hate to have people hanged." Ibid.

22 "I have stolen inspiration from the eye of beauty, and sung the charms of woman and the omnipotent power of love."
The Novice of St. Dominick,
Vol. I, Ch. 1   1823

23 "The world," said the Lady Magdelaine, "is not only buried in the profound ignorance of the middle ages, but immersed in the atheistical darkness of antiquity!"
Ibid., Ch. 3

24 For him let *Time's* protracting pow'rs
Still spare existence, drooping flow'rs,
And wreaths of joyless years entwine,
But, Oh! *One* raptur'd *hour* be mine!
Ibid., Ch. 4,
"Ode to a Butterfly"

25 "Such is thy power, oh sweet affection of the heart!" sighed Imogen: "oppressed by tyranny, despoiled by the licentious rapine of warfare, driven to the last outline of misery, to herd with the beast of the field and bird of the air. . . . " Ibid., Ch. 11

26 "You are right, madam; the soul is of no sect, no party: it is, as you say, our passions and our prejudices, which give rise to our religious and political distinctions."
Ibid., Vol. II, Ch. 12

27 "Seek not to imitate, but to improve, even to perfection, the excellences of thy nature. . . . " Ibid., Ch. 14

28 "All," said he mentally, "sweet child of nature, is pleasing to thee, because all is new: O youth, what a season of delight is thine."
Ibid., Ch. 19

29 "It is a sorry truth, my sweet young friends, that this life is but probationary to another scene of trial and suffering. . . . "
Ibid., Vol. III, Ch. 23

30 "Dreadful to the soul is that moment when the lingering light of hope is finally extinguished, and all its sweet energies of fond expectations are buried in the gloom of despondency."
Ibid., Ch. 24

31 Love in a heart which receives its every motion from the sphere of affectionate feeling, to which the existence of lively and powerful sentiments is an indispensible necessity,—love in such a heart is not to be vanquished even by the influence of reason.
Ibid., Vol. IV, Ch. 31

32 It is under the pressure of great and sudden exigencies that the faculties of a strong and comprehensive mind awaken to a full sense of their own power.
Ibid., Ch. 35

33 "You see, madam, your wine is like the nepenthe of Helen, for it gives the cares as well as the senses of your guests to oblivion."
Ibid., Ch. 40

34 "For," says O'Brien, who worships his new found sister as a thing enskied, "with woman and music, Abbé, dear, you might proselytize all Ireland, far better than by all the peynals [sic] and all the persecutions that ever were invented:" and wonders that the government never hit upon it.
The O'Briens and the O'Flahertys,
Vol. I, Ch. 1   1827

35 But to disunite, to undermine, to sap, to slander, and to villify, were always practicable in Ireland. Corruption, the old medium, was again resorted to. Religion, the old state engine of English policy, was again brought into play. Ridicule, under many forms, launched by the witty and the profligate, the hireling satirist and the pensioned buffoon, was set to work to raise "that dread laugh," against which even virtue is not always proof.
Ibid., Ch. 3

36 It is an awful thing to hear some great public bell at some unwonted hour solemnly toll the toxin of alarm, the announce of some public calamity or private misfortune, of death, of fire, of insurrection.
Ibid., Vol. II, Ch. 2

37 "A heart that never resisted woman, nor flinched from man. . . . "   Ibid., Ch. 3

38 "Beauty is the staple commodity of the country, and superior to any fabric which foreign policy would impose on us. But it is the old fashion of Ireland to neglect its native produce, and to give the preference to whatever comes marked with the stamp of a distant market."   Ibid., Vol. IV, Ch. 3

39 "Fate has always been upheld by sacrifice; and who so fit to make it as woman?"
Ibid., Ch. 4

40 "She* was a chosen instrument to forward a system, injurious alike to the liberties and happiness of mankind. . . . "
Ibid.
*St. Teresa of Genoa.

41 "To be born an Irishman is a dark destiny at the best. . . . "   Ibid.

42 "Here [Ireland] genius is the object of suspicion to dull rulers, and of insult to petty underlings; and all that bends not—falls."
Ibid.

43 The social group
At closing eve, that circled round the fire;
Sweet hour, that fondly knits each human tie—

Unites the children, mother, friend, and sire! Untitled,
Quoted in *English Women of Letters,*
Vol. II, by Julia Kavanagh
1863

713. Adelaide O'Keeffe
(1776–1855?)

1 The butterfly, an idle thing,
Nor honey makes, nor yet can sing.
"The Butterfly," n.d.

714. Jane Porter
(1776–1850)

1 Such, thought she, O Sun, art thou!—The resplendent image of the Giver of All Good. Thy cheering beams, like His All-cheering Spirit, pervades the very soul, and drives thence the despondency of cold and darkness. *Life of Sir William Wallace; or, The Scottish Chiefs* [a novel]
1810

2 "In your prayers, sometimes remember the most desolate of men!" Ibid.

3 As I am a knight, I am sworn to defend the cause of right; and where shall I so justly find it as on the side of bleeding, wasted Scotland? Ibid.

4 "I march at your command no more," replied the veteran; "the moment you perpetrated this bloody deed, you became unworthy of the name of man; and I should disgrace my own manhood were I ever again to obey the word of such a monster." Ibid., Ch. 3

5 "The cruel are generally false." Ibid.

6 "I have nothing now that binds me to life but my country; and henceforth she shall be to me as mistress, wife, and child." Ibid., Ch. 5

7 "Nothing is perilous to me," replied he, with a heroic smile, "that is to serve my country." Ibid., Ch. 9

8 "No country is wretched, sweet lady," returned the knight, "till by a dastardly acquiescence it consents to its own slavery." Ibid.

9 "You would teach confidence to Despair herself. . . ." Ibid.

10 "We must go forward; but resolution, not rashness, must be the principle of our proceeding. . . ." Ibid., Ch. 10

11 "For shame, Murray!" was the reply of Wallace; "they are dead, and our enemies no more. They are men like ourselves; and shall we deny them a place in that earth whence we all sprung?" Ibid., Ch. 13

12 "I should be insensible to all your charms, were I even vile enough to see no evil in trampling upon your husband's rights. Yes, were virtue lost to me, still memory would speak; still would she urge that the chaste and last kiss imprinted by my wife on these lips, should live there in unblemished sanctity, till I again meet her angel embraces in the world to come!" Ibid., Ch. 16

13 ". . . these wounds speak more eloquently than a thousand tongues the gallantry with which you maintained the sword that fate compelled you to surrender. . . ." Ibid., Ch. 22

14 "Better for a brave people so to perish," replied Wallace, "than to exist in dishonour." Ibid., Ch. 28

15 "I am not such a slave," cried Wallace, "as to prefer what men might call aggrandizement before the higher destiny of preserving to my country its liberties untrammelled." Ibid.

16 "Earthly crowns are dross to him who looks for a heavenly one." Ibid., Ch. 33

17 "You may bind me with a hair," said he; "I contend no more." Ibid., Ch. 37

18 "You are like a bad mirror that, from radical defect, always gives false reflections."
Thaddeus of Warsaw,
Vol. II, Ch. 17   1835

19 "The man who dares to be virtuous and great, and appears so, arms the self-love of all common characters against him."
Ibid., Ch. 22

20 "Possessed of all the softness of thy sex, dearest girl," added he still more affectionately, "nature has not alloyed it with one particle of weakness."   Ibid., Ch. 25

21 If to love tenderly, to be devoted, life and soul, to one being, be weakness, Mary felt that she was the weakest of the weak. . . .
Ibid.

22 "Efaith, I cannot help thinking, that if we spend half of our days in pleasure, and the other in lolling off its fatigues, we shall have passed through life more to our shame than our profit!"   Ibid., Ch. 27

23 "O no; that is a chameleon in man's clothing. He breathes air, he eats air, he emits air; and a most pestilential breath it is; only observe how he is pouring nonsense into the ear of yonder sable statue."*
Ibid.

*Referring to a woman dressed in black.

24 " . . . my friend; my brother! you are the last cord that binds me to the world."
Ibid., Ch. 29

25 There is an omnipresence in thought, or a velocity producing nearly the same effects which brings within the short space of a few minutes, the images of many foregoing years.   Ibid.

26 That sickness which is the consequence of mental pain, usually vanishes with its cause.   Ibid., Ch. 33

715.   Hester Lucy Stanhope
(1776–1839)

1 At twenty my complexion was like alabaster, and at five paces distant the sharpest eyes could not discover my pearl necklace from my skin.   Quoted in *Little Memoirs of the Nineteenth Century,* Pt. I, by George Paston   1902

2 If you were to take every feature in my face, and lay them one by one on the table, there is not a single one that would bear examination. The only thing is that, put together and lighted up, they look well enough. It is homogeneous ugliness, and nothing more.
Ibid.

3 At Athens I saw nothing in him [Lord Byron] but a well-bred man, like many others: for as for poetry, it is easy enough to write verses; and as for the thoughts, who knows where he got them? Many a one picks up some old book that nobody knows anything about, and gets his ideas out of it.
Ibid.

4 The granddaughter of Chatham, the niece of the illustrious [William, first Earl of Chatham] Pitt [herself], feels herself blush that she was born in England—that England who has made her accursed gold the counterpoise to justice; that England who puts weeping humanity in irons, who has employed the valour of her troops, destined for the defence of her national honour, as the instrument to enslave a freeborn people; and who has exposed to ridicule and humiliation a monarch [Louis XVIII] who might have gained the goodwill of his subjects if those intriguing English had left him to stand or fall upon his own merits.
Letter to Marquis [later Duke] of Buckingham, her cousin (April 1816), op. cit.

5 . . . I shall go on making sublime and philosophical discoveries, and employing myself in deep, abstract studies.   Letter to Dr. Meryon (1827), op. cit., Pt. II

6 I am reckoned here [Syria] the first politician in the world, and by some a sort of prophet.   Letter to Dr. Meryon (1836), op. cit.

7 Nobody is such a fool as to moider [waste] away his time in the slipslop conversation of a pack of women.   Remark, op. cit.

8 My roses are my jewels, the sun and moon my clocks, fruit and water my food and drink. I see in your face that you are a thorough epicure; how will you endure to spend a week with me?   Remark, op. cit.

716. Anna Chamber
(?–1777)

1 But modern quacks have lost the art,
And reach of life the sacred seat;
They know not how its pulses beat,
Yet take their fee and write their bill,
In barb'rous prose resolved to kill.
"To the Duchess of Leeds, who, being ill, desired a copy of my verses to cure her," *Poems, printed at Strawberry Hill* 1764

717. Mary Brunton
(1778–1818)

1 . . . —"Let them persecute me, and I will be a martyr." "You may be so now, to-day, every day," returned Mrs. Douglas. "It was not at the stake that these holy men began their self-denial. They had before taken up their cross daily; and whenever, from a regard to duty, you resign anything that is pleasing or valuable to you, you are for the time a little martyr."
"Sketch of the Heroine," *Self-Control* 1811

2 . . . little acquainted with other minds, deeply studious of her own, she concluded that all mankind were like herself engaged in a constant endeavour after excellence. . . .   Ibid.

3 The passion which we do not conquer will, in time, reconcile us to any means that can aid its gratification.   "The Lover and his Declaration," op. cit.

4 He forgot that solitude is delightful to the innocent alone.   Ibid.

5 I am here as a soldier who strives in an enemy's land; as one who must run—must wrestle—must strain every nerve, exert every power, nor once shrink from the struggle, till the prize is my own.
"Laura Refuses Colonel Hargrave," op. cit.

6 "It is the guilty should kneel," said Laura, turning away, "but not to their fellow-mortals. Rise, sir; this homage to me is but mockery."   Ibid.

7 To me, through every season, dearest,
In every scene—by day, by night,
Thou present to my mind appearest
A quenchless star—for ever bright!
My solitary, sole delight!
Alone—in grove—by shore—at sea,
I think of thee!   "Stanzas for Music," St. 4, *The Works of Mary Brunton* 1820

718. Margaret Hodson
(1778–1852)

1 How wilt thou marvel then to hear,
That gossip tales and baby fear,
Sleep's flimsy shades—night's mockeries,
With magic film delude my eyes,
Till to my heart the future seems
Crowded with sanguine forms, a scene of ghastly dreams. "The Dream of Graeme," *Wallace; or The Fight at Falkirk; a Metrical Romance* 1809

2 No! this is not the land of Memory
"On Memory; Written at Aix-la-Chapelle," St. 1, *Poems* 1811

3 But Memory from Fancy turns away,
  She hath wealth of her own to guard;
  And whisperings come to her ear which say
  Sweeter things than the song of the bard.
  They are solemn and low, and none can
     hear
  The whispers which come to Memory's ear!
                       Ibid., St. 3

4 For there's dearer dust in Memory's land
  Than the ore of rich Peru.
                       Ibid., St. 7

5 But she is calm:—a peace profound
  On the unruffled surface rests;
  Yet is that breast in iron bound,
  And fill'd with rude and sullen guests;
  No female weakness harbour'd there,
  Relentings soft, nor shrinking fear,
  Within its centre deep abide:
  The stern resolve, the purpose dire,
  And grim revenge's quenchless fire,
  The intrepid thought, cold, thawless pride,
  And fortitude in torture tried,—
  These are its gentlest inmates now
          Margaret of Anjou: A Poem in
                 Ten Cantos, 1st canto
                         1816

6 No more to conquer than we fought,
  That thought, that cheering thought was
     chill'd,
  And now the prize for which we sought
  Was death upon the hostile field!
                     Ibid., 4th canto

7 "Bright success
  May only for a while sustain Man's feeble
  spirit!"   Ibid.

8 And sounds without a name,—so drear,
  So full of wonder and of fear,
  As seldom come to those who walk this
  middle sphere!   Ibid., 7th canto

9 Strong spirits, tremble in my chain,
  And tread my circle,—now let all,
  Mute and unseen, attend my call,
  And all within, around, and over
  The magic ringlet, closely hover!—
                         Ibid.

10 "Let me Fate's awful page explore!
  Leaf after leaf would I unfold,

E'en to the final word!—till *all* the tale be
told!"   Ibid.

11 And, hark! the signal!—Now begin,
   Of those who lose and those who win,
   The strife, the shout, the mortal din!
   Behold!—they meet!—they clash!—they
     close!—
   They mix!—Sworn friends and deadly foes,
   In one dire mass, one struggling host,
   All order and distinction lost,
   Roll headlong, guideless, blind, like waves
     together toss'd!   Ibid.

12 Oh, holy father! if indeed
   To mutter'd prayer, or counted bead,
   The distant powers of heaven give heed,
   I know not:—But 't is now too late
   By humbleness to conquer fate!
                   Ibid., 10th canto

13 " 'T is strange
   How memory fails with fortune's change!"
                          Ibid.

14 "Monsters! A mother's curse lie strong
   And heavy on you! May the tongue,
   The ceaseless tongue which well I ween
   Live in the murderer's murky breast,
   With goading whispers, fell and keen,
   Make havoc of your rest!"
                         Ibid.

719.   Ann Murry
(fl. 1778–1799)

1 Mark but the hist'ry of a modern day,
  Composed of nonsense, foppery, and play.
                 "A Familiar Epistle,"
         Poems on Various Subjects
                         1779

720.   Angelica Catalani
(1779–1848)

1 For when God has given to a mortal so extraordinary a talent as I possess, people ought to applaud and honour it as a miracle: it is profane to depreciate the gifts of Heaven!   Quoted in *Queens of Song* by Ellen Creathorne Clayton 1865

721.   Elizabeth Fry
(1780–1845)

1 Does capital punishment tend to the security of the people?
By no means. It hardens the hearts of men, and makes the loss of life appear light to them; and it renders life insecure, inasmuch as the law holds out that property is of greater value than life. From her Journal, Quoted in *Biography of Distinguished Women* by Sarah Josepha Hale   1876

2 Punishment is not for revenge, but to lessen crime and reform the criminal.
Ibid.

722.   Hannah Farnham Lee
(1780–1865)

1 Astronomers tell us of countless worlds;— if we look within our own precincts we shall find an equal multiplication; every class of society talks of *the world*, and every class means something different.
Elinor Fulton, Ch. 1   1837

2 "I never could bear people that are always striving to rise."   Ibid.

3 "We are often accused of being only a money-making people. Let us not justify this character, by gaining money for charity through traffic and barter."
"I don't care how we get it," said Mrs. Smith; "if we only get it, that is the point."

"*I do*," said Mrs. Watson. "I want charity to be a mutual benefit, to bless those who give and those who receive, to be a school for our children."   Ibid., Ch. 2

4 Every one thinks it necessary to assume the *appearance* of truth. How much contrivance, manoeuvering, and waste of words would they save themselves, by adopting the *reality*!   Ibid.

5 Jane had fallen into the error that many people do, of thinking *age* is *experience*; that passing through a certain number of those events that crowd round our path, is experience; whereas, it is not born of time, but of thought, of investigation. Like all other treasures of mind, we find it within. The fountain of wisdom lies deep in our own hearts, and it is there we must seek for it.   Ibid., Ch. 3

6 The experience that does not form our characters is worthless; for, while we are acquiring it, the opportunity of using it is gone.   Ibid.

7 Invention, it is true, is a rare gift; but we must remember that it is born of *thought*.
Ibid.

8 "No, here as everywhere, the radical causes of disease among the poor are dirt, humidity, and intemperance. Now, you know, the only elixir for this is moral improvement; everywhere it is the *elixir vitae*."
Ibid., Ch. 5

9 "If people would only take a proper stand, and act from principle, this class [servants] would find its level, and the odious system of liberty and equal rights be done away."
Ibid., Ch. 6

10 "Well, I must confess," said Mrs. Reed, "I am no radical; I do not wish to level all orders of society."
"Neither do I," replied Mrs. Davenport; "but I must say, that I wish all orders of society to feel that there is a mutual bond between them. . . . "   Ibid.

11 No one can have any high degree of virtue, without self-respect; it is the twin-sister of virtue. Ibid., Ch. 8

12 Domestics must be taught to feel the responsibility of their situation; that they are members of the family in which they live; to feel that the domestic roof is their *sanctuary.* Ibid.

13 Liberty has set her foot on our shore, and she is now not to be restricted in her walks. Ibid.

14 We have arrived at that period when there is no putting a padlock on the human mind; every one is contending for his rights, every one ready to strike for them. Ibid.

15 I believe no hands were made to be idle," said Ellen. Ibid., Ch. 9

16 "Our good and bad depend much on circumstances." Ibid.

17 A man's conscience begins life with him; if he does not keep friends with it, he is continually at warfare with this principle within. Ibid., Ch. 10

18 Though the human mind can never stagnate for want of motives, yet all nature has its seasons of rest. Ibid., Ch. 11

19 "What is a new bonnet, or a new pelisse [fur piece], to the pleasure of feeling there is something in reserve that you may call your own! Blessings on the Savings Bank! It is truly, to those who resolutely deposit their earnings there, the purse of Fortunatus. . . ." Ibid.

20 . . . is there no exterminating the shoots of vanity where it has once taken root? Ibid.

21 It is in vain to talk of the "rights of women," as long as they are obliged to confess the supremacy of the other sex in so many different ways. What spinster is there who has a few thousands, that is not obliged to call upon some kind brother, nephew, or friend, to transact her affairs? It matters not what the capacity of her mind may be for business; her education, or rather her want of business education, makes her a child in these affairs. Ibid., Ch. 12

22 Fireside occupation is one of the rights of women that men may envy. Ibid., Ch. 13

23 What are talents, genius, or good temper, without high and resolute principle? Ibid., Ch. 15

24 Away with division of interests! our fathers fought for one and the same cause; they have given us this land [the United States] for our inheritance, and we are children of one family. Let us have confidence in each other; let us realize, that our hearts are mutually warmed by the same vital stream that flows from the Creator; that we have humane and benevolent purposes, and that it is the duty of all to unite cordially and sincerely in carrying those purposes into execution. Ibid.

25 There is something in benevolent purpose, as well as in industry, that cheers and supports the mind. "Beginning Life," *Three Experiments of Living* c.1838

26 Well may British travellers scoff, when they come amongst us, and see our own native Americans adopting the most frivolous parts of civilized life,—its feathers and gewgaws,—our habits and customs made up of awkward imitations of English and French, our weak attempts at aristocracy. . . . "The Reward," op. cit.

27 Let us ... with true independence, adopt the good of every nation,—their arts and improvements,—their noble and liberal institutions,—their literature,—and the grace and real refinement of their manners; but let us strive to retain our simplicity, our sense of what is consistent with our own glorious calling, and above all, the honesty and wisdom of living within our income, whatever it may be. Ibid.

28 "I begin now to see that we must have motives that do not depend on the praise or censure of this world,—motives that must have nothing to do with it."
"Living Beyond the Means," op. cit.

29 A mere compilation of facts presents only the skeleton of History; we do but little for her if we cannot invest her with life, clothe her in the habiliments of her day, and enable her to call forth the sympathies of succeeding generations. Preface, *The Huguenots in France and America*, Vol. I 1843

30 Unless history can be converted to moral uses, it is only "a little book got by heart." Ibid.

31 He [John Calvin], who had so loudly declaimed against the tyranny of Rome, was doomed to prove how dangerous an instrument is power in the hands of a human being. Ibid., Ch. 3

32 Few men had filled a wider sphere in his native kingdom [than the Duke of Guise*]; it was his fate to live in troubled times.
Ibid., Ch. 8
*François de Lorraine (1519–1563).

33 It is amusing to observe in every age the ingenuity of dress in changing the human figure. Ibid., Ch. 13

34 Time had robbed her [Catherine de Medici] of her personal charms, and that scourge of the human race, the gout, was racking her bones and sinews. Ibid., Ch. 17

35 Who hears the name of Catharine de Medici, that does not connect with it emotions such as few other women have excited? With strong powers of mind, with great personal beauty, she seems to have wanted *a heart*. Her principles were never guided by her affections, her errors were never those of weakness, her vices never proceeded from self-gratification, nor her virtues benevolence. Ibid.

36 She [Catherine de Medici] has been termed a monster of cruelty; but she was merely indifferent about human life. . . . Her love for the fine arts never seems to have softened or moulded her mind. . . . Ibid.

37 . . . while her [Catherine de Bourbon's] eye was fixed on heaven, her heart wandered to earth. Ibid., Ch. 18

38 It is greatly to be regretted, that the modern passion for *journalizing* did not take hold of a few; we might have gained most interesting facts from private memoirs.
Ibid., Vol. II, Ch. 29

39 It is those in whom the power of virtue is formed and matured, that are truly great. It matters not how many millions a man may command, the next day may strip him of all; but the *undying principle* of duty is his own, and can only be surrendered by his will. Ibid.

40 Although we have, in the present time, troubles in business and pecuniary losses, like those set forth by the afflicted Gabriel, yet we have none of so appalling a nature, as to require us to take up arms, and march into a wilderness among savages, for nightly yells around the cabins of the early settlers even the howling of the tempest was often mistaken, and was the frequent cause of momentary thrills of alarm.
Ibid., Ch. 30

41 There are principles implanted in the breast that cannot be wholly eradicated. God does not leave himself without witnesses in the heart of every human being.
Ibid., Ch. 31

377

42 Even under an absolute monarchy men will have an instinctive sense of justice.
Ibid., Ch. 33

43 A new intellectual development took place.* Every man felt, that he had a right *to think*; and those, who had no materials for thought, found it easy to pull down the old fabrics, overgrown with ivy and nightshade; but they could not rebuild, and this work remained for the new philosophers.
Ibid., Ch. 35
*During the reign of Louis XV.

44 Miserable France! more respectable in its sanguinary robes, dyed with the blood of the revolution, than basely sleeping in the poisonous and corrupted air of the court [of Louis XV]. . . .
Ibid., Ch. 36

45 The roughest weep when a pet dog dies; and are no tears shed for a monarch?
Ibid.

46 Trifling circumstances are exciting in still life. *The Log-Cabin; or, the World Before You,*
Part First   1844

47 " . . . keep your money if you can, but remember it hath wings. . . . "
Ibid.

48 We sin often from ignorance and thoughtlessness; and I have now lived long enough to see that a word spoken in season is never to be neglected; it often sinks deep into the heart; let no one be discouraged at the apparent improbability of beneficial counsel or even reproof,—try it at least, for a few seeds when sown will spring up even in barren ground.
Ibid.

49 . . . but I was going among *men*, not wild animals; I had confidence in them,—I considered them as beings made in the image of God, endowed with reason and feeling,—and, however perverted or debased they might be, still honest, benevolent, and kindhearted endeavours would make their way amongst them.
Ibid., Part Second

50 There is nothing old tolerated in this new world [America].
Ibid.

51 The habits of civilized life do something for us, they habituate us to cleanliness and personal neatness, which becomes essential to our moral dignity.
Ibid.

52 . . . but has not my whole life been made up of trifles?
Ibid.

53 Causes are often disproportioned to effects.
Ibid.

54 "The school may do much; but alas for the child where the instructor is not assisted by the influences of home!"
Ibid.

55 There is no more effective way of instruction than familiar conversation, and how much does this lighten the task of an intelligent and benevolent teacher! He may gather lessons from all, and everything around him, for nature is continually furnishing him with materials.
Ibid.

56 Surely we ought to prize those friends on whose principles and opinions we may constantly rely—of whom we may say in all emergencies, "I know what they would think."
Ibid.

57 Let not a man receive favours from, or intimately frequent the society of a *female* candidate, who dreads an entanglement.
Ibid., Part Third

58 God has made man to be a brother to man, if we will only place confidence in each other.
Ibid.

59 "The first time I see you I said you was *green*, and now I say you are green by name and green by nature."
Ibid.

60 . . . a good nurse is of more importance than a physician.
Ibid.

61 How many stoop to the low arts of fraud, who would spurn at the idea of becoming a day-labourer and earning an honest competency in a land abounding with the luxuries of life! Does not every public print teem with accounts of forgeries and frauds? Is there no way of removing these plague-spots? Is there no way of showing youth the dread perspective—a blasted name, exiles from all that makes life valuable, skulking from honourable men, and, almost invariably, at last doomed to *day labour* in a penitentiary! Ibid.

723. Mary Somerville
(1780–1872)

1 And who shall declare the time allotted to the human race, when the generation of the most insignificant insect existed for unnumbered ages? Yet man is also to vanish in the everchanging course of events. The earth is to be burnt up, and the elements to melt with fervent heat—to be again reduced to chaos—possibly to be renovated and adorned for other races of beings. These stupendous changes may be but cycles in those great laws of the universe, where all is variable but the laws themselves and He who ordained them.
"God and His Works,"
Physical Geography   1848

2 ... no circumstance in the natural world is more inexplicable than the diversity of form and colour in the human race.
"Varieties of the Human Race,"
op. cit.

3 Poetry of the highest stamp has fled before the utilitarian spirit of the age, yet there is as much talent in the world, and imagination too, at the present time, as ever there was at any period, though directed to different objects; but, what is of more importance, there is a constant increase of liberal sentiment and disinterested benevolence.
"Benevolence,"
op. cit.

4 ... one of the greatest improvements in education is that teachers are now fitted for their duties by being taught the art of teaching. Ibid.

5 The moral disposition of the age appears in the refinement of conversation.
"Influence of Christianity,"
op. cit.

6 Selfishness and evil passions may possibly ever be found in the human breast; but the progress of the race will consist in the increasing power of public opinion, the collective voice of mankind, regulated by the Christian principles of morality and justice. Ibid.

724. Frances Milton Trollope
(1780–1863)

1 The frightful manner of feeding with their knives, till the whole blade seemed to enter into the mouth; and the still more frightful manner of cleaning the teeth afterwards with a pocket-knife. *Domestic Manners of the Americans*, Ch. 3
1832

2 The poor creatures ... seated themselves on the "anxious benches."
Ibid., Ch. 8

3 She was not one of the idle gossipers who delight in chattering about their own concerns to every one who will listen ... rightly considering, that when such matters are unceasingly discussed, they may be exceedingly likely to prevent people's minding their own business, while devoting an undue share of attention to that of others. *The Life and Adventures of Michael Armstrong, the Factory Boy,*
Ch. 1
1839

4 "Is not amusement the very soul of life?"
Ibid., Ch. 6

5 Sir Matthew, too, forgot for an instant, that every movement made within that crowded [factory] chamber, not having for its object the transmutation of human life into gold, was a positive loss to him. . . .
Ibid., Ch. 8

6 "I tell you what, Mr. Parsons, an overlooker is not worth his salt if he does not continually keep it in his head, that the more the machinery is improved the faster must the brats move to follow it. And . . . I will be much obliged to any man who will tell me how I am to help being undersold in the market, if I don't contrive to make my machinery go as fast, and as long too, as the best of 'em." Ibid., Ch. 13

7 "That's nonsense, Michael," said Fanny. "They can't keep us here for ever. When we die, we are sure to get away from them."
Ibid., Ch. 17

8 "Times are altered with me now, nurse Tremlett," replied Mary; "I have left off living for myself, and I feel my temper improving already by it." Ibid., Ch. 22

9 It is the vast, the beautiful, the elaborate machinery by which they were surrounded that called forth all their attention, and all their wonder. The uniform ceaseless movement, sublime in its sturdy strength and unrelenting activity, drew every eye and rapt the observer's mind in boundless admiration of the marvelous power of science! No wonder that along every line a score of noiseless children toiled, thought of, after the admirable machine. Strangers do not visit factories to look at them; it is the triumphant perfection of British mechanism which they come to see, it is of that they speak, of that they think, of that they boast when they leave the life-consuming process behind them. Ibid.

725.   Lucy Aiken
(1781–1864)

1 Their kindness cheer'd his drooping soul;
And slowly down his wrinkled cheek

The big round tears were seen to roll,
And told the thanks he could not speak.
The children, too, began to sigh,
And all their merry chat was o'er;
And yet they felt, they knew not why,
More glad than they had done before.
"The Beggar Man,"
Sts. 9, 10,
The Female Poets of Great Britain,
Frederic Rowton, ed.
1853

2 And often o'er the level waste
The stifling hot winds fly;
Down falls the swain with trembling haste,
The gasping cattle die.
Shepherd people on the plain
Pitch their tents and wander free;
Wealthy cities they disdain,
Poor,—yet blest with liberty.
"Arabia,"
St. 3, op. cit.

3 That life may not be prolonged beyond the power of usefulness, is one of the most natural, and apparently of the most reasonable wishes man can form for the future. . . .
"Memoirs"
(of her father, Dr. Aiken),
Quoted in *Biography of Distinguished Women*
by Sarah Josepha Hale   1876

726.   Janet Colquhoun
(1781–1846)

1 This day I am thirty years old. Let me now bid a cheerful adieu to my youth. My young days are now surely over, and why should I regret them? Were I never to grow old I might be always here, and might never bid farewell to sin and sorrow.
Diary entry (April 17, 1811),
Quoted in *A Memoir of Lady Colquhoun*, Ch. 2,
by James Hamilton,
D. D.   1851

2 The world? it is nothing to me; its pomps, its pleasures, its vanities,—all nothing, nothing.   Diary entry (July 19, 1816), op. cit.

3 *My book** came out last week. I have prayed to be kept out of sight, and to be honored as an instrument in the hand of God. Who knows what good may be done? I have also prayed to be kept humble if it should meet with any approbation, and I am not sensible of any elation regarding it.   Diary entry (March 2, 1823), op. cit., Ch. 4

*Thoughts on the Religious Profession and Defective Practice in Scotland.

4 I feel something within me that lives for God, that delights in God, that cannot exist without God, that must be derived from God.   Diary entry (September 8, 1844), op. cit., Ch. 6

727.   Anna Jane Vardill
(1781–1852)

1 Behold this ruin! 'Twas a skull
One of ethereal spirit full!
This narrow cell was Life's retreat;
This place was Thought's mysterious seat!
What beauteous pictures fill'd that spot,
What dreams of pleasure, long forgot!
Nor Love, nor Joy, nor Hope, nor Fear,
Has left one trace, one record here.
     "Lines to a Skull,"
European Magazine
November 1816

728.   Susan Edmonstone Ferrier
(1782–1854)

1 "There's no talking to a young woman now about marriage, but she is all in a blaze about hearts, and darts. . . . "
     Marriage,
     Ch. 1   1818

2 "People's tastes alter according to circumstances."   Ibid., Ch. 3

3 . . . petty ills; like a troup of locusts, making up by their number and their stings what they want in magnitude.
     Ibid., Ch. 6

4 Mortified pride in discovering the fallacy of our own judgment. . . .   Ibid.

5 . . . money . . . They knew it essential to life, and concluded that it would come some way or other; either from the east or west, north or south.   Ibid., Ch. 19

6 . . . as . . . the surface was covered with flowers . . . who would have thought of analysing the soil?   Ibid., Ch. 28

7 Experience *cannot* be imparted. We may render the youthful mind prematurely cautious, or meanly suspicious; but the experience of a pure and enlightened mind is the result of observation, matured by time.
     Ibid., Ch. 35

8 In every season of life grief brings its own peculiar antidote along with it.
     Ibid., Ch. 36

9 "Think of me as a creature with too many faults of her own to presume to mettle with those of others. . . . "   Ibid., Ch. 39

10 The real evils of life, of which we so loudly complain, are few in number, compared to the daily, hourly pangs we inflict on one another.   Ibid.

11 There are some people who, furious themselves at opposition, cannot understand the possibility of others being equally firm and decided in a gentle manner.
     Ibid., Ch. 52

12 "Yet, alas! our time here is so short that it matters little whether it be spent in joy or grief, provided it be spent in innocence and virtue."   Ibid., Ch. 61

13 For, oh! the unutterable anguish that heart must endure which lavishes all its best affections on a creature mutable and perishable as itself, from which a thousand accidents may separate or estrange it, and from whom death must one day divide it! Yet there is something so amiable, so exaulting, in the fervour of a pure and generous attachment, that few have been able to resist its overwhelming influence. . . .
Ibid., Ch. 65

14 There are plenty of fools in the world; but if they had not been sent for some wise purpose, they wouldn't have been here; and since they are here they have as good a right to have elbow-room in the world as the wisest.   Ibid., Ch. 68

15 Even the dark uncertain future becomes a bright field of promise to the eye of pride, which, like Banquo's bloody ghost, can smile even upon the dim perspective of posthumous greatness.   *The Inheritance*,
Ch. 1   1824

16 The natural wish of every human being, the weakest as well as the wisest, seems to be, to leave some memorial of themselves to posterity—something, if but to tell how their fathers thought or fought, at least to show how they talked or walked.
Ibid.

17 "Oh, how easy it must be to be good when one has the power of doing good!"
Ibid., Ch. 4

18 There are people, it is well known, who have no feelings, and there are others who have not time to feel; then, alas! there are many whose misfortune it is to have feeling and leisure, and who have time to be nervous, have time to be discontented, have time to be unhappy, have time to feel ill-used by the world, have time to weary of pleasure in every shape; to weary of men, women, and children; to weary of books, grave and witty; to weary of authors, and even of authoresses. . . .   Ibid., Ch. 10

19 "Music!" reiterated Miss Pratt; "fiddlesticks! . . . now you have music in all shapes, and such contrivances!—there's musical glasses, and musical clocks, and musical snuff-boxes, and now they've got musical workboxes."*   Ibid., Ch. 15
*I.e., sewing kits.

20 . . . there is sometimes no surer way of creating an interest in one party than by exciting a prejudice in another.
Ibid., Ch. 22

21 . . . it was upon the bodies of their children that they lavished their chief care and tenderness, for, as to the immortal interests of their souls, or the cultivation of their minds, or the improvement of their tempers, these were but little attended to, at least in comparison of their health and personal appearance.   Ibid., Ch. 27

22 Ah! what will not the heart endure e'er it will voluntarily surrender the hoarded treasure of its love to the cold dictates of reason or the stern voice of duty!
Ibid., Ch. 33

23 To speak with a pen is the art of letter-writing, and even a confused, vulgar, natural letter, flowing direct from the brain, or, it may be, from the heart, of one of uncultivated intellect, is more pleasing than the most studied and elaborate performance from the same source.   Ibid., Ch. 36

24 . . . it is not the first stroke of grief, however heavy it may fall, that can at once crush the native buoyance of youthful spirit; it is the continuance of misery which renders its weight insupportable. . . .
Ibid., Ch. 43

25 "The profane and licentious works of Lord B.* will live only in the minds of the profane and impure, and will soon be classed amongst worthless dross, while all that is fine in his works will be culled by the lovers of virtue, as the bee gathers honey from even the noxious plant, and leaves the poison to perish with the stalk; so shall it be with Burns,** so shall it be with More."***
Ibid., Ch. 45

*Lord Byron (1788–1824), English poet.
**Robert Burns (1759–1796), Scottish poet.
***Henry More (1614–1687), English poet and philosopher.

26 " . . . the synagogin', the tabernaclin', the psalmin' that goes on in this hoose, that's enough to break the spirits o' ony young creature." Ibid., Ch. 46

27 The king of Terrors gives to other attributes their power of terrifying: the thunder's roar, the lightning's flash, the billow's roar, the earthquake's shock—all derive their dread sublimity from Death. All are but the instruments of his resistless sway.
Ibid., Ch. 56

28 The want of a will is a desideratum which invariably causes disappointment to many an expectant. Ibid., Ch. 58

29 "Why must I be accounted rebellious, undutiful, because I cannot see as you see, and think as you think?" Ibid.

30 "A smokey house and a scolding wife have, indeed, always been looked upon as the *ne plus ultra* of human misery; but that is only amongst the rich." Ibid., Ch. 65

31 " . . . passion without passion is an anomaly I cannot comprehend." Ibid., Ch. 72

32 . . . lovers, it is well known, carry the art of tautology to its utmost perfection, and even the most impatient of them can both bear to hear and repeat the same things time without number, till the sound becomes the echo to the sense or the nonsense previously uttered. Ibid.

33 "I am for everything starting into full-blown perfection at once."
Ibid., Ch. 79

34 " . . . make me then, what you will, only, pray don't make me a fine lady."
Ibid., Ch. 80

35 " . . . there is no doctor like meat and drink. . . ." Ibid., Ch. 98

36 "Which of all the gifts a liberal Creator has endowed you with would you exchange for those empty distinctions which one creature bestows upon another? Would you exchange your beauty for rank, your talents for wealth, your greatness of mind for extended power; for all of them would you exchange your immortal soul?"
Ibid., Ch. 101

37 . . . the sickness of hope deferred crept like poison through her veins.
Ibid., Ch. 102

38 But who can count the beatings of the lonely heart? Ibid.

39 The indulgence of her grief had now become a sort of strange unnatural luxury to her. . . . Ibid., Ch. 104

40 "He only who made the heart can judge it, for He only knows what have been its trials." Ibid.

41 To crown the whole, she set up for being a sensible woman, and talked maudlin nonsense by the yard; for she was one of those who would ask if the sea produced corn, rather than hold her tongue.
"A Bustling Wife,"
Destiny, or the Chief's Daughter 1831

42 "It was the saying, sir, of one of the wisest judges who ever sat upon the Scottish bench, that a *poor* clergy made a *pure* clergy—a maxim which deserves to be engraven in letters of gold on every manse in Scotland." Ibid.

43 The next day was Sunday—day of rest to the poor and the toil-worn—of weariness to the rich and the idle. "Sunday,"
op. cit.

44 Never more, did it seem, could her heart awaken to the love of aught that life could bestow. The idol her imagination had fashioned had fallen; but even while it lay in slivers at her feet, still her fond, credulous heart had unconsciously hovered amid the broken fragments, in the vain hope that the image it had so adored might again rise, to receive the homage of a still enslaved soul.
"Disappointed Love," op. cit.

45 ... what heir of immortality would wish to remain the dupe of this world's enchantments?   Ibid.

46 ... from the first dawn of consciousness, it was a parent's love that beamed upon our hearts, and awakened all their best and holiest sympathies. Friends may meet as strangers—the tenderest bands of love, even wedded love, may be broken—but 'tis God himself who has formed that one indissoluble bond which neither human power nor human frailty ever can dissolve.
Ibid.

47 It is not those who have been born and bred in affluence who can all at once comprehend the nature of absolute poverty—those who have been accustomed to will their every gratification can ill conceive the privations of want—the shifts and expedients of fallen fortune—the difficulty which the mind has to contract its desires, and the habits of self-indulgence and luxury which have to be overcome or annihilated; in short, no things differ more than abstract and actual poverty.   "Sudden Poverty," op. cit.

48 ... could affections, once so blighted as hers had been, ever again revive, and own a second spring?   "Second Love," op. cit.

49 Alas! how short-sighted or sometimes even second-sighted mortals!   Destiny, Ch. 1   (later ed.)

50 Whence it is that two persons who seem to have been born only to hate each other, should, under any circumstances, ever fancy that they actually love each other, is a phenomenon which even philosophers may have encountered, but which they certainly have not yet explained.   Ibid., Ch. 2

51 "... the best education a poor man can give his son is to make him know and feel betimes that he is the son of a poor man."
Ibid., Ch. 15

52 "I am no friend to a premature knowledge of the world; it comes soon enough to most of us."   Ibid.

53 Winter days and stormy nights and summer suns rolled on, and still all was silence. To the watchfulness of expectation now succeeded the feverishness of apprehension, and then came that awful stillness, the oppressive weight of time which we have loaded with our own dread presentiments—when all nature seems to be wrapped in silence and in gloom, when every object seems to proclaim the downfall of our hopes, when the gayest scenes only move us to tears, when the gladdest tones only sound as the death-knell of our happiness.   Ibid., Ch. 28

54 Alas! how does our startled fancy recoil from the first dread thought, and seek to cheat itself, by conjuring up, and enthroning anew, that image in our hearts which our reason sternly tells us is no more. No more! the being all life and motion, and strength and beauty ... is that being indeed gone from the face of this bright earth for ever? Still, still would we seek the living among the dead!   Ibid.

55 "I hope I may never turn into a fashionable; for I think one had better be merry and happy, even though it should not be the fashion, than be mournful and genteel...."
Ibid., Ch. 41

56 "... I do assure you, it is a very tiresome thing to be trained up to be a person of consequence...."   Ibid., Ch. 47

57 "The human mind has often been compared to a musical instrument; perhaps most minds may be capable of giving a variety of tones, but it is not every one who has the power of calling them forth . . . [and] it is not every hand that can touch the right chords, or every ear that can appreciate their excellence."   Ibid., Ch. 50

58 " . . . the stomach requires to be amused as well as the mind."   Ibid., Ch. 55

59 All who have perceptions must be aware there is a difference between England and Scotland, and that all the powers of steam and locomotion have not yet brought them to assimilate.   Ibid., Ch. 70

60 No generous impulse ever led her beyond the strict line of duty. . . .
Ibid., Ch. 71

61 "Oh, my darling, beware of hasty judgments; they ill become us, poor, ignorant, sinful creatures that we are."
Ibid., Ch. 78

62 " . . . there's no face like the face that loves us."   Ibid.

63 . . . dauntless as is the heart of woman on great and heroic occasions, still, in the coarser occurences of this working-day world, she is ill qualified by nature or education for taking a part. . . .
Ibid.

64 There is no surer mark of a selfish character than that of shrinking from the truth.
Ibid., Ch. 89

65 " . . . Pepys'* . . . sentiments are those felt by all vain and vulgar minds to this day; and it must be the very truth and universality of their application which gives his diary its chief interest."   Ibid.
*Samuel Pepys (1633–1703), English diarist.

66 "In the mind of Cowper,* awfully and mysteriously as it was occasionally eclipsed, still shone with a divine light, which has awakened and exhaulted the hearts of thousands of his fellow-creatures. . . ."
Ibid.

*William Cowper, English poet (1731–1800) who suffered periodic mental breakdowns.

67 " . . . time and eternity are but different periods of the same state. . . . "
Ibid.

729. Ann Taylor
(1782–1866)

1 Who ran to help me when I fell,
And would some pretty story tell,
Or kiss the place to make it well?
My mother.
"My Mother," St. 6,
Original Poems for Infant Minds   1804

2 Thank you, pretty cow, that made
Plesant milk to soak my bread.
"The Cow,"
op. cit.

3 In vain you told her not to touch,
Her trick of meddling grew so much.
"Meddlesome Matty,"
op. cit.

4 Oh, how very thankful I always should be,
That I have kind parents to watch over me,
Who teach me from wickedness ever to flee!
"Poor Children,"
op. cit., with Jane Taylor

5 He went about, he was so kind,
To cure poor people who were blind;
And many who were sick and lame,
He pitied them and did the same.
"About Jesus Christ,"
op. cit.,
with Jane Taylor

6 'Tis a *credit* to any good girl to be neat,
But quite a disgrace to be *fine*.
"Neatness,"
op. cit.,
with Jane Taylor

7 For a good-natured girl is loved best in the main,

If her dress is but decent, though ever so
plain. "Finery,"
op. cit.,
with Jane Taylor

8 So, while their bodies moulder here,
Their souls with God himself shall dwell,—
But always recollect, my dear,
That wicked people go to hell.
"About Dying,"
op. cit.,
with Jane Taylor

9 Two good little chidren, named Mary and
Ann,
Both haply live, as good girls always can;
And though they are not either sullen or
mute,
They seldom or never are heard to dispute.
"The Good-Natured Girls,"
op. cit., with Jane Taylor

10 Twinkle, twinkle, little star,
How I wonder what you are,
Up above the world so high,
Like a diamond in the sky!
"The Star," St. 1,
Rhymes for the Nursery 1806

11 And willful waste, depend upon 't,
Brings, almost always, woeful want!
"The Pin," St. 6,
Hymns for Infant Minds
1810

12 Oh, that it were my chief delight
To do the things I ought!
Then let me try with all my might
To mind what I am taught.
"For a Very Little Child,"
op. cit., with Jane Taylor

730. Theodosia Burr Alston
(1783–1813)

1 I exert myself to the utmost, feeling none of
that pride so common to my sex, of being
weak and ill. Letter to her father, Aaron
Burr* (March 17, 1802),
Quoted in *Memoirs of Aaron
Burr*, Vol. II,
Matthew L. Davis, ed.
1836–1837

*(1756–1836), third vice president of the United States
(1801–1805).

2 Novel-reading has, I find, not only the ill effect of rendering people romantic, which,
thanks to my father on earth, I am long
past, but they really furnish no occupation
to the mind. A series of events follow so
rapidly, and are interwoven with remarks
so commonplace and so spun out, that there
is nothing left to reflect upon.
Letter to her father
(October 21, 1803), op. cit.

3 What a charming thing a bustle is! Oh,
dear, delightful confusion! It gives a circulation to the blood, an activity to the mind,
and a spring to the spirits.
Letter to her father
(December 1803), op. cit.

4 You know, I love to convict you of an error,
as some philosophers seek for spots in the
sun. Letter to her father
(February 1, 1809),
Quoted in *The Private Journal of
Aaron Burr*, Vol. I,
Matthew L. Davis, ed.
1838

5 Indeed, I witness your extraordinary fortitude with new wonder at every new misfortune. Often, after reflecting on this subject,
you appear to me so superior, so elevated
above other men; I contemplate you with
such strange mixture of humility, admiration, reverence, love and pride, that very little superstition would be necessary to make
me worship you as a superior being. . . . I
had rather not live than not be the daughter
of such a man. Letter to her father
(August 1, 1809), op. cit.

6 Alas! my dear father, I do live, but how does it happen? Of what am I formed that Live, and why? . . . You talk of consolation. Ah! you know not what you have lost. I think Omnipotence could give me no equivalent for my boy; no, none—none.
>Letter to her father on the death of her son (August 12, 1812), op. cit., Vol. II

731. Amelia
(1783–1810)

1 Unthinking, idle, wild, and young,
I laugh'd and danc'd and talk'd and sung.
>"Youth," n.d.

732. Jane Taylor
(1783–1824)
(See also Ann Taylor, 729:4–9, 12)

1 He minded not his friends' advice
But followed his own wishes.
>"The Little Fisherman,"
>*Original Poems for Infant Minds*   1804

2 Every heart to heaven aspires.
>"Hymn,"
>op. cit.

3 Though man a thinking being is defined,
Few use the grand prerogative of mind.
How few think justly of the thinking few!
How many never think, who think they do!
>"Prejudice, or, Essay on Morals and Manners,"
>St. 45, op. cit.

4 How pleasant it is, at the end of the day,
No follies to have to repent;
But reflect on the past, and be able to say,
That my time has been properly spent.
>"The Way to be Happy,"
>*Rhymes for the Nursery*   1806

5 I like little Pussy, her coat is so warm;
And if I don't hurt her she'll do me no harm.
>"I Like Little Pussy,"
>St. 1, op. cit.

733. Mary Austin Holley
(1784–1846)

1 How hard it is to be poor.
>*Texas: Observations Historical, Geographical and Descriptive*
>1833

2 It is truly in Texas, "Man never is, but always to be—blest." You are put off—put off—forever.
>Ibid.

3 Taste does not spring up in the wilderness, nor in prairies, nor in log cabins!
>Quoted in *Letters of an Early American Traveller: Mary Austin Holley*
>by Mattie Austin Hatcher
>1933

734. Bettina von Arnim
(1785–1859)

1 . . . I shall flutter joyfully my life long in the air, and no one will know whence the joy comes; it is only because I know that, when I come to him,* he will be alone with me, and forget his laurels.
>Letter to Frau Rath [Goethe's mother] (March 15, 1807), Quoted in *Correspondence Between Goethe and a Young Girl*   1835

*Johann Wolfgang von Goethe (1749–1832), German poet, dramatist, novelist.

2 A purple sky my mind, a warm love-dew my words, the soul must come forth like a bride from her chamber, without evil, and avow herself.   Various letters to Goethe,
>op. cit.

3 Without trust, the mind's lot is a hard one; it grows slowly and needily, like a hot plant betwixt rocks: thus am I—thus was I till today. . . .
>Ibid.

4 Talent strikes conviction, but genius does not convince; to whom it is imparted, it gives forebodings of the immeasurable and infinite, while talent sets certain limits, and so because it is understood, is also maintained.   Ibid.

5 . . . every art is the body of music, which is the soul of every art: and so is music, too, the soul of love. . . .   Ibid.

6 Love expresses nothing through itself, but that it is sunk in harmony. Love is fluid; it flows in its own element, and that element is harmony.   Ibid.

7 . . . for no other am I born; am I not the bee which flies forth, bringing home to you the nectar of each flower?   Ibid.

8 Like a new-born babe, must I nurse this love between us; beautiful butterflies balance themselves upon the flowers which I have planted about its cradle, golden fables adorn its dreams, I joke and play with it, I try every stratagem in its favour. But you rule it without trouble, by the noble harmony of your mind—with you there is no need of tender expressions or protestations. While I take care of each moment of the present, a power of blessing goes forth from you, which reaches beyond all sense and above all the world.   Ibid.

9 All which spiritually lays claim on man, here goes to the senses; therefore is it that through them he feels himself moved to all things.   Ibid.

10 All *learning* in art is only, that we may lay the foundation of self-dependence within us, and that it may remain our conquest.   Ibid.

11 O yes! the ascending from out of unconscious life into revelation,—that is music!   Ibid.

12 Art is the hallowing sensual nature, and that is all I know about it. What is beloved shall serve to love: spirit is the beloved child of God,—chosen by God for the service of sensual nature, this is art; intuition of the spirit into the senses is art. What you feel becomes thought, and what you think, what you strive to invent, that becomes sensual feeling. What men compile in arts; what they produce in it; how they force their way through it; what they do more or less, that would be submitted to many contradictions, but yet it is ever a spelling of the Divine. Let it be.   Ibid.

13 But this breaking forth of the mind to light, is it not art? This inner man asking for light, to have by the finger of God loosened his tongue; untied his hearing; awakened all senses to receive and to spend: and is love here not the only master, and we its disciples in every work which we form by its inspiration?   Ibid.

14 Works of art, however, are those which alone are called art, through which we think to perceive and enjoy art; but as far as the producing of God in heart and mind overpowers the idea we make to ourselves of him and his laws, which, in temporal life, are of value, even so does art overpower men's valuing of it. They who fancy to understand it will perform no more than what is ruled by understanding; but when senses are submitted to its spirit, he has revelation.   Ibid.

15 Whoever is come to something in art, did forget his craftiness, his load of experience, became shipwreck, and despair led him to land on the right shore.   Ibid.

16 In music, producing is, itself, a wandering of the divine idea, which enlightens the mind without object, and man, himself, is conception.   Ibid.

17 To inhale the divine spirit is to engenerate, to produce; to exhale the divine breath is to breed and nourish the mind. . . .   Ibid.

18 Body is art, art is the sensual nature engenerated into the life of the spirit.
Ibid.

19 Man cannot invent, only feel himself, only conceive, learn what the genius of love speaks to him, how it nourishes itself in him, and how it teaches him by itself. Without transforming its perceptions of divine love into the language of knowledge, there is no invention. Ibid.

735. Caroline Lamb
(1785–1828)

1 Then, for the first time, Camioli beheld, in one comprehensive view, the universal plan of nature—unnumbered systems performing their various but distinct courses, unclouded by mists, and unbounded by horizon—endless variety in infinite space!
Glenarvon,
Vol. I, Ch. 1   1816

2 " . . . may the God of Mercy avert from you the heaviest of all my calamities, the power of looking into futurity." Ibid.

3 Where are they who claim kindred with the unfortunate? Ibid.

4 It is the common failing of an ambitious mind to over-rate itself. . . .
Ibid., Ch. 2

5 He had so long and so frenquently been informed that he was heir of the immense possessions now belonging to his uncle, that he was overpowered by the sense of his greatness. . . . Ibid.

6 From that hour he courted her with unremitting assiduity: he was the slave of every new caprice, which long indulgence of every selfish feeling could awaken. But the promised hour of his happiness was delayed; and his passion thus continually fed by hope, and yet disappointed, overcame in his bosom every feeling of humanity, till he no longer cherished a thought that did not tend to facilitate the immediate gratification of his wishes.
Ibid., Ch. 4

7 It is said there is no happiness, and no love to be compared to that which is felt for the first time. Most persons erroneously think so; but love like other arts requires experience, and terror and ignorance, on its first approach, prevent our feeling it as strongly as at a later period. Ibid., Ch. 11

8 . . . . for the sins of children rise up in judgment against their parents.
Ibid., Ch. 20

9 Time which passes swiftly and thoughtlessly for the rich and the gay, treads ever with leaden foot, for those who are miserable and deserted. Ibid., Ch. 21

10 " . . . she is in love with ruin: it stalks about in every possible shape, and in every shape, she hails it:—woe is it; victim of prosperity, luxury and self indulgence."
Ibid., Ch. 28

11 "Something within seems to warn me, and to say that, if I wander from virtue like her, nothing will check my course—all the barriers, that others fear to overstep, are nothing before me. God preserve me from sin!"
Ibid., Vol. II, Ch. 3

12 Love's blighted flower, can never bloom again. Ibid., Ch. 17

13 "Think of me, for I am jealous even of thy dreams." Ibid.

14 "I had rather be the cause of her laughter, than of her tears." Ibid., Ch. 24

15 But, when the flame [of love] is unsupported by ... pure feelings, it rages and consumes us, burns up and destroys every noble hope, perverts the mind, and fills with craft and falsehood every avenue to the heart.   Ibid., Vol. III, Ch. 72

16 And can'st thou bid my heart forget
What once it lov'd so well
                              Ibid., Ch. 73,
                                   "Song"

17 Hope nothing from the miserable: a broken heart is a sepulchre in which the ruin of every thing that is noble and fair is enshrined.
                                   Ibid., Ch. 81

18 That which causes the tragic end of a woman's life, is often but a moment of amusement and folly in the history of a man.   Ibid.

19 Women, like toys, are sought after, and trifled with, and then thrown by with every varying caprice.   Ibid.

20 "Nature formed me fierce, and your authority was not strong enough to curb and conquer me."   Ibid., Ch. 94

21 "When they tell me I am base, I acknowledge it: pride leads me to confess what others dare not; but I think them more base who delight in telling me of my faults: and when I see around me hypocrisy and all the petty arts of fashionable vice, I too can blush for others, and smile in triumph at those who would trample on me."
                                   Ibid.

22 " ... my mind is a world in itself, which I have peopled with my own creatures."
                                   Ibid.

23 "It is virtue that women prize [in men]? Is it honour and renown they worship? Throw but the dazzling light of genius upon baseness, and corruption, and every crime will be to them but an additional charm."
                                   Ibid., Ch. 98

24 "Bid him repent, but he shall not hear you. Bid him amend, but like you he shall delay till it is too late. Then, neither his arts, nor talents, nor his possessions, shall save him, nor friends, though leagued together more than ten thousand strong; for the axe of justice must fall. God is just; and the spirit of evil infatuates before he destroys."
                              Ibid., Ch. 106, last lines

25 [My husband] ... called me prudish—said I was strait-laced,—amused himself with instructing me in things I need never have heard or known, and the disgust I at first felt for the world's wickedness I till then had never heard of, in a very short time gave way to a general laxity of principles which, little by little, unperceived of you all has been undermining the few virtues I ever possessed.   Letter to Lady Melbourne, her
                                   mother-in-law,
                         Quoted in the Introduction
                              by James L. Ruff
                         to Glenarvon: Facsimile
                         Reproduction   1972

26 Mad, bad, and dangerous to know.*
                              Journal, n.d.
   *Her description of her lover, Lord Byron.

736.   María Augustín
(1786–1857)

1 Death or victory!*   Speech at siege of
                         Zaragoza (June 2, 1808),
                    Quoted in Women of Beauty and Her-
                                   oism
                              by Frank B. Goodrich
                                   1858
   *Cry that led the Spanish resistance to Napoleon's assault.

737.   Marceline Desbordes-Valmore
(1786–1859)

1 Searching with light the tranquil heart's seclusion,

Making us quail before the unknown
morrow. . . . "Presentiment,"
Elegies and Romances
St. 1   1842

2   For I was drunk with a most innocent
gladness,
Life glowed with vivid hues; I had a throng
Of mates who shared my mood of
merry madness,
The dance, the flowers, the laughter, and
the song.   Ibid., St. 3

3   "Has any seen a little child astray among
the crowd?
The mother has been seeking it, and weeping long and loud."   "The Lost
Child,"
1., St. 1 (refrain), op. cit.

4   Sure, her long madness was God's blessing
Ibid., 2., St. 3

5   "I see the earth. I have lost heaven!"
Ibid., St. 8

6   . . . guilty one!—but pale,
Fled, plunged adown the hillside at that
word,
And vanished like some dark and evil bird
Ibid., St. 10

7   It seems that we were born for misery,
And when we are too happy, can but die.
Ibid.

8   Thou who art free as air, beautiful Spring!
Hark to his chains, and let thy blos-
soms fall!
"The First Imprisonment of Bé-
ranger,"*
St. 1, op. cit.

*Pierre-Jean de Béranger (1780–1857), French poet,
songwriter, and political activist.

9   His merry heart proclaims him innocent;
A sweet soul breathes in his melodious
rhyme   Ibid., St. 2

10   Such was his crime, O judges of the land!
He freely gave out of his poor posses-
sions;
He strove to lighten lonely sorrow, and
His tears of sympathy ye made trans-
gressions.   Ibid., St. 6

11   But God said "Seek!" and this man glory
found;
"Sing!" and the laws divine he
straightway chanted.   Ibid., St. 8

12   Thanks, noisy rumor! Not alone of ill,
But now of sweetest good thy voice
hath spoken   Ibid., St. 11

13   For still the mother-soul attends the child
"Flowers at the Cross,"
St. 3, op. cit.

14   Oft in a flower love's secret hidden lies.
Ibid., St. 4

15   Heart for heart,—could there be
A sweeter guaranty?   "What Hast Thou
Done with These?,"
St. 1, op. cit.

16   Like a poor, hapless child,
Mother-forsaken;
Like a poor hapless child
Unguarded in the wild. . . .
Ibid., St. 5

17   "I love the child just falling asleep;
Give him a golden dream to keep!"
"Lullaby,"
St. 4, op. cit.

18   "And the child who storms and sighs and
cries,
Cannot enter my Paradise!"
Ibid., St. 17

19   "We climb the rock, we watch, we hark,
And now the lightning rends the dark!
And now we see a floating deck,
And one who kneels upon the wreck!"
"The Sailor's Return,"
St. 4, op. cit.

20   "What?—find my vanished Eden?"
"A Woman's Dream,"
St. 1, op. cit.

21   "Back to thy vernal happiness
Fly like a bird on pionions fleet
Ibid., St. 2

22   "Have then thy wish! Thy steps retrace!
Flowers, perfume, song, be thine once
more!
Yet shall time lead thee to the place

Of tears as surely as before."
Ibid., St. 4

23 Shall I never play again in my mother's gar-
den-close?   "Tristesse,"
St. 1, op. cit.

24 And when I murmur fondly of idle times
like those,
Why does my voice in weeping die
away?   Ibid.

25 . . . the early, downy fruits that above the
cradle grow!   Ibid., St. 2

26 For hast thou never gazed upon the mock-
ing flame
Of a memory very sore till thy cheeks
were burning red?   Ibid., St. 4

27   Ah, when the soul is young,
It is lightly filled with joy, and the taste is
yet unknown
Of the morsel steeped in tears, with honey
overstrown,
That leaves a bitter savor on the
tongue.   Ibid., St. 10

28 . . . the deep, mysterious well,—an urn set
in the wild,
That held, methought, the ashes of the
departed sun?
Its wave became a mirror to every passing
child.
It is turbid now, alas!—and all things are
defiled:
In this, that water and my life are one.
Ibid., St. 16

29 Where grew my caged soul, and my spirits
worked like wine   Ibid., St. 17

30 So suddenly set free, I was pale with rapture
sweet;
Methought that heaven had opened
and earth had grown more wide.
Ibid., St. 18

31 He [her father] was like God, and I was satisfied.   Ibid.

32 But the rose waits not the winter, as we
know.   Ibid., St. 20

33 Why are our joys remembered more bitter
than our woes?   Ibid., St. 21

34 And, in the depth of my despair,
I knelt and murmured dreamily,
Because I had not breath for prayer:
My God, my Father, art thou there?
Or hast thou quite forgotten me?"
"To Alphonse de Lamartine,"
St. 3, op. cit.

35 "I wonder who will take the oar
When my poor bark at last is found"
Ibid., St. 6

36 But nothing lasts. The storm passed on,
The wild birds with it. . . .
Ibid., St. 8

37 A sacred pity seems to flow
Around my desolated life.
Ibid., St. 14

38 Only a woman, with no higher
Or deeper lore than love and tears!
Whose heart has been her only lyre
Ibid., St. 17

39 "The world where you are queen was ever
harsh to me"   Untitled poem, St. 1,
Quoted in *Memoirs of Madame
Desbordes-Valmore*,
Ch. 1, by C. A. Sainte-Beuve;
Harriet W. Preston, tr.   1872

40 In the vain shows where wit doth win ap-
plause,
Hushed lies the heart, and hidden:
To please becomes the first of laws;
To love is aye forbidden.
Ibid., St. 2

41 "O strange caprice of the unstable crowd!"
Ibid., St. 3

42 "The scattered lights of fame!"
Ibid., St. 4

43 A summer without thee?—Oh, night of
starless gloom!—   "Parted,"
St. 1 (c.1834), op. cit.

44 Do not show living water to one who cannot drink;
The writing of a friend is a likeness
passing true.

Do not write.   Ibid., St. 3

45 And hope hath never been betrayed
By that farewell of thine.
                    "To the sun,"
                    St. 1, op. cit., Ch. 2

46 ... money demoralizes even the giver.
                    Remark, op. cit.

47 We must make our lives as we sew,—stitch
by stitch.   Ibid.

48   God will gather like bruised flowers
The souls of babes and women who to
him
Are fled,—the air with outraged souls
is dim,
On earth men wade in blood,—Merciful
Powers!   "Lyons,"
                    St. 2 (1834), op. cit., Ch. 3

49 So our dead lie all torn with cruel balls,
Awaiting coffins, crosses, and remorse.
                    Ibid., St. 3

50 Are we* not like the two volumes of one
book?   Letter, op. cit., Ch. 4
*Referring to her friend, Pauline Duchambge, com-
poser, with whom Valmore frequently collaborated on
songs.

51 ... like all men of great literary talent, he
[Alexandre Dumas père] is not to be cultivated. He belongs to the world,—to all
worlds.   Remark to her son, Hippolyte
                    (1833), op. cit.

52 I am condemned to a feverish unrest.
                    Letter to M. Antoine de Latour
                    (October 15, 1836), op. cit.

53 I never see a denizen of that literary world
which forms taste and purifies language. I
am my own sole judge, and I know nothing,
so where is my security?
                    Letter to de Latour
                    (February 7, 1837), op. cit.

54 I am climbing, as best I may, to the goal of
an existence in which I speak very much
oftener to God than to the world.
                    Ibid.

55 All the miseries of Lyons are added to my
own,—twenty or thirty thousand workmen
begging daily for a little bread, a little fire, a
garment, lest they die. Can you realize,
monsieur, this universal and insurmounta-
ble despair which appeals to one in God's
name, and makes one ashamed of daring to
have food and fire and two garments, when
these poor creatures have none? I see it all,
and it paralyzes me.   Ibid.

56 Mark whatever is *repugnant* to you in the
verses which I have just written for you. I
do not see clearly. A little light, if you
please!   Letter to de Latour
                    (November 20, 1837), op. cit.

57 What a happy place this world is to one
who possesses the faculty of admiration, at
once the humblest and the proudest of all!
                    Letter to her son
                    (October 21, 1840), op. cit.

58 I meant to have done some work here
[Brussels] in my solitude, but it is like the
solitude of Paris. Hobgoblins come in by
the key-hole.   Letter to her son
                    (October 26, 1840), op. cit.

59 ... the more I read, the farther I penetrate
into the shadows which have hidden our
great lights from me, the less I dare to write:
I am smitten with terror,—I am like a glow-
worm in the sun.   Ibid.

60 Women who do not need the permanent
valor of men, can always have strength
from above.   Letter to Hippolyte and
                    Undine, her son and daughter
                    (November 1, 1840), op. cit.

61 It is certainly true that housekeeping cares
bring with them a thousand endearing com-
pensations. They are a woman's peculiar
joy, and women are apt to be light-hearted.
                    Ibid.

62 Something great is concealed by what we
suffer, and the more we pay in advance, the
more richly will he reward us for having
sought and trusted him in the midst of our
trials.   Letter to her brother, Felix
                    Desbordes (January 14, 1843),
                    op. cit.

63 ... the light and transient character of this world's friendships.   *Ibid.*

64 ... if I were not poor, you would not be so.   *Ibid.*

65 In these days the rich will come and tell you their troubles with such utter candor, such bitter bewailings, that you are compelled to pity them more than you do yourself.
Letter to Pauline Duchambge
(February 10, 1843), op. cit.

66 An attack of hope is the same for us as an attack of fever.   *Ibid.*

67 Obstacles of many kinds seem to contradict that word *always.*   Letter to her brother
(April 14, 1843), op. cit.

68 Worldly possessions fade away, but this refuge remains immutable.   *Ibid.*

69 If we believe in a just and compassionate Judge, nothing can humiliate us.
Ibid.

70 Nothing is very clear in my memory, except that we were very happy, and very unhappy....   *Ibid.*

71 I know by sad experience that these sensitive young souls need either happiness or the dream of it, and that they should be fed, from the first, on unalterable indulgence.
Letter to M. Richard
(August 22, 1847), op. cit.

72 But politics poison the mind.
Letter to her brother
(September 28, 1847), op. cit.

73 To gain in strength and elevation of mind, day by day; to shame, or at least to soften, those who have despised us, and render them glad to have been our allies and old friends,—there is something in all this which may yet sanctify life.
Ibid.

74 It is easier to resign one's self to indigence if one thrills at the sight of trees and sunshine, and the pleasant daylight, and surely hopes to see again those whose loss one mourns.
Letter to her brother
(October 26, 1847), op. cit.

75 ... what are grace and wit and wisdom in times like these?   Letter to her brother
(January 12, 1848), op. cit.

76 For myself, I work like a day laborer, and only pause to cry, to love, to pray.
Letter to M. Richard
(December 24, 1849), op. cit.

77 Life certainly is a warfare for all of us.
Letter to M. Richard
(February 25, 1850), op. cit.

78 Yes, God is in every place,—particularly here where the silence is unbroken by the sound of literary or political wrangling.
Letter to her son (October 1852),
op. cit.

79 To write what I think, is to betray myself. To write any thing else is to deceive....
Letter to Mme. Derains
(October 4, 1852), op. cit.

80 This world of ours grows dizzy.
Letter to her niece, Camille
(March 26, 1854), op. cit.

81 ... another existence swallowed up in the fearful rush of what is called civilization, but is very like chaos.   *Ibid.*

82 The last result of misfortune is to sow seeds of discord in families which happiness would have united. When it becomes necessary for each member to work hard in order to escape absolute indigence, the wings of the soul are folded, and soaring is postponed to a future day. Letter to her niece
(September 6, 1854), op. cit.

83 ... the sum and substance of volumes that I feel ... will remain unwritten, like seeds put away in closets, which dry up and are never sown.   Letter to Mme. Derains
(c.September 1854), op. cit.

84 To lodge on the second floor! High privilege of the moderately ambitious! Can I never aspire to that?   *Ibid.*

85 The rich are no worse than we, but they are utterly unable to understand how one can want for the humblest necessities of life.
> Letter to her sister, Cecile
> (November 9, 1854), op. cit.

86 This is an iron age. Grief, luxury, poverty, make men wild. For hearts warm as ours, it is cold.   Ibid.

87 My tears keep all alive.   Ibid.

88 The Indian lies down in the bottom of his canoe when a storm bursts upon the deep. But I,—I cannot lie still; I must try to find a ray of light somewhere, that none but I may know how deep the waters are.
> Letter to Pauline Duchambge
> (December 27, 1855), op. cit.

89 And what a hard stepmother is life. . . .
> Ibid.

90 You say, my dear and true friend, that poetry is my consolation. On the contrary, it torments me, as with a bitter irony. I am like the Indian who sings at the stake.
> Letter to Duchambge (January
> 15, 1856), op. cit.

91 . . . my life is love. And still it rains, and the clouds are so dark!   Letter to Mme.
> Derains (May 11, 1856), op. cit.

92 Are we not always young?
> Letter to Pauline Duchambge
> (January 5, 1857), op. cit.

93 Life may become wearisome, but it does not end.   Ibid.

94 The afflicted ought to understand one another, and better on Sundays than on other days,—*mon Dieu*!   Letter to
> Duchambge (April 1857), op. cit.

95 Ah, how many stabs are concealed by the smiles and sweet "goodmornings" of the world!   Ibid.

96 There are times when one cannot lift a blade of grass without finding a serpent under it.   Letter to Duchambge
> (May 11, 1857), op. cit.

97   I stayed the fleeting visions at my will

Until they failed—ah, mother, I could weep!—
And vanished. Only one dream haunts me still. . . .   *Idyls*, "The Roses,"
> St. 3, op. cit.

98   And our joy, when we meet,
From joy remembered a new bliss will gain.
> "Parting at Night," St. 3, op. cit.

99 And yet, 'tis ever sad to say good-night.
> I cannot choose but dream of thy return.
> Let us ere long that sorry word unlearn!
The lips of love pronounce it not aright.
> Ibid., St. 4

100   "Flowers o' the home," says he,
"Are daughters." "Mother and Maiden,"
> St. 15, op. cit.

101 And one hears best, methinks, when one hears blindly   Ibid., St. 17

102 Their fragrance fills my gown this evening, still;
That is all that remains of their fragrant souvenir.   "The Roses of Sa'adi,"
> St. 3, tr. by Elaine Partnow;
> *Les poètes maudits*,
> Paul Verlaine, ed.   1884

738.   Caroline Anne Southey
(1786–1854)

1 Sleep, little baby! sleep!
> Not in thy cradle bed,
Not on thy mother's breast
> "To A Dying Infant," St. 1,
> *Solitary Hours, and Other Poems*
> 1826

2 Mount up, immortal essence!
> Young spirit! hence—depart!
And is *this* Death? Dread thing!
> Ibid., St. 8

3 And then to lie and weep,
> And think the livelong night
(Feeding thine own distress
With accurate greediness)

Of every past delight.
Ibid., St. 13

4 (Time brings such wondrous easing)
Ibid., St. 16

5 She dwelt alone, a cloistered nun,
In solitude and shade.
"The Primrose,"
St. 5, op. cit.

6 Balmy freshness! heavenly air,
Cool, oh! cool this burning brow
"Aura Veni,"
St. 1, op. cit.

7 O Grave! we come.   "The Last Journey,"
St. 1, op. cit.

8 Bear not the form we love
Fast from our sight—
Let the air breathe on him,
And the sun leave on him
Last looks of light.   Ibid., St. 8

9 I never cast a flower away,
The gift of one who cared for me—
A little flower—a faded flower—
But is was done reluctantly.
"I Never Cast a Flower Away,"
St. 1, op. cit.

10 You must love—*not my faults*—but in *spite*
of them, me,
For the very caprices that vex ye;
Nay, the more should you chance (as it's
likely) to see
'T is my special delight to perplex ye.
"The Threat,"
St. 6, op. cit.

11 But I have drunk enough of life
(The cup assign'd to me
Dash'd with a little sweet at best,
So scantily, so scantily)
"To Death,"
St. 4, op. cit.

12   O, Death!
Come quietly—come lovingly,
And shut mine eyes, and steal my breath
Then willingly, oh! willingly,
I'll go away with thee.
Ibid., St. 6

13 Pale flowers!—pale, perishing flowers!
I woo your gentle breath;
I leave the summer rose
For younger, blither brows.
Tell me of change and death.
"Autumn Flowers,"
St. 7,
*Autumn Flowers, and Other
Poems*   1844

14 Oh, change! oh, wondrous change—
Burst are the prison bars—
This moment there, so low,
So agonized, and now
Beyond the stars!   "The Pauper's
Deathbed,"
St. 6, op. cit.

15 Alas! unconscious little one, thou 'lt never
know that best,
That holiest home of all the earth, a living
mother's breast. "The Dying Mother
to her Infant,"
St. 7, op. cit.

16 This weak, weak head! this foolish heart!
they'll cheat me to the last:
I've been a dreamer all my life, and now
that life is past!   Ibid., St. 11

17 I've heard that little infants converse by
smiles and signs
With the guardian band of angels that
round about them shines,
Unseen by grosser senses; belovëd one! doest thou
Smile so upon thy heavenly friends, and
commune with them now?
Ibid., St. 14

18 Come, Death! and make me to my child at
least in spirit known.
Ibid., St. 15

19 River! river! brimming river!
Broad, and deep, and *still* as Time;
Seeming *still*, yet still in motion,
Tending onward to the ocean,
Just like mortal prime.
"The River,"
St. 3, op. cit.

20 How happily, how happily, the flowers die
away!

Oh, could we but return to earth as easily as they! "The Death of the Flowers," St. 1, op. cit.

21 Set thy sails warily,
Tempest will come;
Steer thy course steadily;
Christian, steer home!
"Mariner's Hymn,"
Poetical Works 1867

739. Eliza Lee Follen
(1787–1860)

1 The night comes on,
And sleep upon this little world of ours,
Spreads out her sheltering, healing wings;
and man—
The heaven-inspired soul of this fair earth,
The bold interpreter of nature's voice,
Giving a language even to the stars—
Unconscious of the throbbings of his
heart,—
Is still "Winter Scenes in the Country,"
St. 1, *Poems* 1839

740. Eliza Leslie
(1787–1858)

1 On one thing, however, the old people were agreed—which was, that it was not to hurry matters. "The Red Box, or, Scenes at the General Wayne,"
Pencil Sketches; or, Outlines of Character and Manners 1837

2 "The truth is," pursued Mr. Culpepper, "I am travelling for my health, and therefore I am taking cross-roads, and stopping at out of the way places. For there is no health to be got by staying in cities, and putting up at crowded hotels, and accepting invitations to dinner-parties and tea-parties, or in doing any thing else that is called fashionable." Ibid.

3 "I have no patience," said he, "with such fellows. To think that full-grown men—men that have hands to work and get their own living, should humble themselves to the dust, and submit to be treated as lackeys by an old uncle, (or indeed by any body,) merely because he happens to be rich, and they expect to get his money when he sees proper to die, which may not be these twenty years, for it is plain that nothing ails him. 'I'd rather be a dog and bay the moon,' as I once heard an actor say in the Philadelphia playhouse." Ibid.

4 Servility and integrity rarely go together. Ibid.

5 Habit is second nature. Ibid.

6 When masks are only of gauze it is not worth while to wear them. Ibid.

7 "However, there is but one rule on these occasions—crape and bombazine, and every thing of the best. Nothing, you know, is more disreputable than mean mourning."
"Constance Allerton; or, the Mourning Suits,"
op. cit.

8 "Certainly every body ought to feel on these occasions; but you know it is impossible to devote every moment between this and the funeral to tears and sobs. One cannot be crying all the time—nobody ever does." Ibid.

9 "Duty requires of us no sacrifice by which neither the living nor the dead can be benefited." Ibid.

10 "Excuse me, but innovations on established customs ought only to be attempted by people of note—by persons so far up in society that they may feel at liberty to do any out-of-the-way thing with impunity." Ibid.

11 . . . she had always found occupation to be one of the best medicines for an afflicted mind. . . . Ibid.

12 . . . she knew that it is only in the eyes of the vulgar-minded and the foolish, that a woman is degraded by exerting her ingenuity or her talents as a means of support.
Ibid.

13 "Certainly," said Harriet Darnel, "it is right and proper to wish for peace; but still, to say the truth, war-time is a very amusing time. Everything will seem so flat when it is over." "The Officers. A Story of the Last War," op. cit.

14 "I have no fancy for respectable young men," said Harriet, in a low voice.
Ibid.

15 "Well," said Mrs. Darnel, "I wish for a thousand reasons that this war was over. Setting aside all more important considerations, the inconvenience it causes in our domestic concerns is too incessant to be trifling. We are not yet prepared to live comfortably without the aid of foreign importations." Ibid.

16 "Oh! you don't know us at all," replied Tinsley. "We are so used to the ague that when it quits us we feel as if we were parting with an old friend. As for me I fit against it for awhile, and then gave up; finding that all the remedies, except mint-juleps, were worse than the disease." Ibid.

17 Kindred spirits soon understand each other. Ibid.

18 "There is no better cure for folly, and particularly for romantic folly, than a good burlesque. . . . " "The Serenades," op. cit.

19 It is true that as soon as a song becomes popular it ceases to be fashionable; but is not its popularity an evidence of its merit, or at least of its possessing melody and originality, and of its sounds being such as give pleasure to the general ear? Whoever heard a dull and insipid tune played or sung in the streets, or whistled by the boys?
Ibid.

20 "The pleasure of listening to delightful notes, with delightful words, uttered with taste and feeling by an accomplished and intellectual singer, is one of the most perfect that can fall to the lot of beings who are unable to hear the music of the spheres and the songs of Paradise." Ibid.

21 He missed, it is true, the hawthorn hedges of England; those beautiful walls of verdure whose only fault is that their impervious foliage shuts out from view the fields they inclose; while the open fences of America allow the stranger to regale his eye, and satisfy his curiosity with a free prospect of the country through which he is travelling.
"The Old Farm House," op. cit.

22 There is considerable variety in American ghosts. In Europe these phantoms are nearly all of the same stamp. . . .
Ibid.

23 "Why, Pharaoh—my old fellow!" exclaimed Lindsay, "Is this really yourself?"
"Can't say, masser," replied Pharaoh. "All people's much the same—Best not be too personal—But I b'lieve I'm he."
Ibid.

24 "And the Newman girls mix up their talk with all sorts of French words that sound very ugly to me. Instead of 'good night' they say bone swear [bon soir]; and a 'trifle' they call a bag-tail [bagatelle]; and they are always talking about having a Gennessee Squaw [je ne sais quoi]; though what they mean by that I cannot imagine; for, I am sure I never saw any such thing in this part of the country." Ibid.

25 " . . . you Americans always know more of every thing than you ought to. I don't wonder so few of you look plump and ruddy. You all wear yourselves out with headwork." "That Gentleman," op. cit.

26 What American, when returning to his native country, and almost in view of its shores, is not reminded of that night, when Columbus stood on the prow of the Santa Maria, and watched in breathless silence with his impatient companions, for the first glimpse of the long wished-for land—that memorable night, which gave a new impulse to the world already known, and to that which was about to be discovered.
Ibid.

27 " . . . there's a considerable difference between doing without a thing of your own accord, and being made to do without it."
"Chase Loring. A Story of the Revolution," op. cit.

28 "Nobody but an Englishman can mistake a white man for an Indian, however well disguised." Ibid.

29 "Well," remarked Aunt Rhoda, "I'm no tory—but it does seem to me very strange that any christian people could go in cold blood, and set regularly about destroying anything eatable or drinkable; I raley can't see how the country is to be bettered by it. But every body now-a-days seems to have got their heads full of wild, unnateral notions." Ibid.

30 "As I've said before, I don't see how the nation could be hurt or liberty put down by just one old woman, more or less, taking a cup of tea* when she was all but pining away for it." Ibid.

31 "Aunt Rhoda," observed Tudor, "a cause* that is sanctioned by the approval of so many wise and pious men cannot fail to prosper." Ibid.

32 "When the boys chopp'd away,
Soon the tea dropp'd away,
Then they all hopp'd away,
And nobody stopp'd the way."*
Ibid.

*References to Boston Tea Party.

33 . . . with the young and impetuous, imaginary injuries often wound more deeply than real ones. Ibid.

34 "Oh!" cried Annis, "I never could understand why boys think they must always do whatever they are dared."
Ibid.

35 Our anticipations cannot keep pace with the realities that are continually overtaking them. . . .
Quoted in
Godey's Lady's Book
November 1845

36 Albert Colesbury, of Philadephia, fell in love with Catherine Branchely, of New York, at a quarter past ten o'clock, while dancing opposite to her on the evening of his arrival at Ballston Springs. . . .
"Love at First Sight,"
Kitty's Relations, and other pencil sketches 1847

37 "Love at first sight is certainly a most amusing thing," remarked Mrs. Seabright, "at least to the by-standers." Ibid.

38 "Some goes by coffee-grounds, which is low and vulgar; and some goes by the lines on the parms of your hands, which is nothing but plexity and puzzledem; and some goes by the stars and planipos [planets], which is too far off to be certain. But cards is the only true things, as all the best judges can scratify [certify]." "The Fortune-Teller,"
Leonilla Lynmore, and Mr. and Mrs. Woodbridge, or A lesson for young wives 1847

39 "Horne Tooke, my boy," said Mr. Bloxham, "you are certainly sharp enough to understand that when we are at an inn, and a public table, where we pay all the same eat or no eat, it is advisable to indulge ourselves with everything that is to be had; so as to be quite sure of getting the worth of our money." "The English Radical and the American Citizen,"
The Maid of Canal Street, and the Bloxhams 1851

40 "There's something in the air of this country that is not fit for English children. It makes them rude, and saucy, and unbiddable, from the moment they set their feet on the land of liberty, as you call it."

Ibid.

741. Mary Russell Mitford
(1787–1855)

1 JULIAN. A sick man is as wayward as a child. . . .   *Julian,*
Act I, Sc. 1   1823

2 JULIAN. I have been
Sick, brainsick, heartsick, mad I thought—
I feared—
It was a foretaste of the pains of hell
To be so mad and yet retain the sense
Of that which made me so.

Ibid., Act II, Sc. 1

3 COUNT D'ALBA. . . . I'm not
An over-believer in man's excellence:
I know that in this slippery path of life
The firmest foot may fall. . . .

Ibid., Act III, Sc. 1

4 COUNT D'ALBA. If I were not weary
Of a world that sweats under a load of fools,—
Old creaking vanes that turn as the wind changes,—
Lords, I'd defy ye!   *Ibid.,* Act V, Sc. 1

5 Cheerfulness is, perhaps, the word that best describes the impression conveyed by the more frequented streets of Belford. . . . It is neither more nor less than an honest English borough, fifty good miles from "the deep, deep sea," and happily free from the slightest suspicion of any Spa, chalybeate, or saline.   "The Town,"
Belford Regis; or, Sketches of a Country Town,
Vol. I   1835

6 Of all living objects, children, out of doors, seem to me the most interesting to a lover of nature. . . . Within doors . . . I am one of the many persons who like children in their places,—that is to say, anyplace where I am not. But out of doors there is no such limitation: from the gypsy urchins under a hedge, to the little lords and ladies in a ducal demesne, they are charming to look at, to watch, and to listen to. Dogs are less amusing, flowers are less beautiful, trees themselves are less picturesque.

"The Carpenter's Daughter,"
op. cit.

7 Nothing in the whole routine of country life seems to me more capricious and unaccountable than the choice of a country beauty.   "Belles of the Ball-Room,"
op. cit.

8 The grave equals all men. . . .
No. III, op. cit., Vol. II

9 RIENZI. Whichever wheel turn round, we shall be crushed
Between the millstones. That's our destiny,—
The destiny we earn.   *Rienzi,*
Act I, Sc. 1   1857

10 RIENZI. . . . give thanks
To the all-gracious power that smoothed the way
For woman's tender feet. She but looks on,
And waits and prays for the good cause, whilst man
Fights, struggles, triumphs, dies.

Ibid.

11 COLONNA. The fool's grown wise—
A grievous change.   *Ibid.,* Act II, Sc. 1

12 COLONNA. Joined! by what tie?
RIENZI. By hatred—
By danger—the two hands that tightest grasp
Each other—the two cords that soonest knit
A fast and stubborn tie: your true love knot
Is nothing to it. Faugh! the supple touch
Of pliant interest, or the dust of time,
Or the pin-point of temper, loose, or rot,

Or snap love's silken band. Fear and old
hate,
They are sure weavers—they work for the
storm,
The whirlwind, and the rocking surge; their
knot
Endures till death. Ibid.

13 LADY COLONNA. Now ye have clothed death
In the brave guise of war, and made him
gay
And lovely as a bridegroom. . . .
Ibid., Act IV, Sc. 3

14 I have discovered that our great favourite,
Miss [Jane] Austen,* is my country-
woman . . . with whom mamma before her
marriage was acquainted. Mamma says
that she was then the prettiest, silliest, most
affected, husband-hunting butterfly she
ever remembers. Letter to Sir William
Elford (April 3, 1815),
Quoted in *Life of Mary Russell Mitford*,
Vol. I, Rev. A. G. L'Estrange, ed.
1870

*See 710.

15 There is a thrilling awfulness, an intense
feeling of simple power in that naked co-
lourless beauty which falls on the earth, like
the thoughts of death—death pure, and
glorious, and smiling—but still death.
Sculpture has always had the same effect on
my imagination, and painting never. Colour is life. "Walks in the Country:
Frost and Thaw,"
Our Village 1892

16 Last year, in spite of the love which we are
now pleased to profess towards that ardent
luminary, not one of the sun's numerous
admirers had courage to look him in the
face: there was no bearing the world till he
had said "good-night" to it.
"The Hard Summer,"
op. cit.

742. Emma Hart Willard
(1787–1870)

1 Rocked in the cradle of the deep

I lay me down in peace to sleep;
Secure I rest upon the wave,
For Thou, O Lord! hast power to save.
"The Ocean Hymn,"
St. 1, written at sea July 14,
1831

2 In Ocean's cave, still safe with Thee,
The germ of immortality Ibid., St. 2

3 Take care of health. Would you enjoy life?
Take care of health; for without it, existence
is, for every purpose of enjoyment, worse
than a blank. "Care of Health.—To
Young Ladies."
*A Treatise for the Motive Powers
which Produce the Circulation of
the Blood* 1846

4 The human mind will wander to future
times. Address on behalf of the Greek
Normal School, n.d.

5 . . . what if the good we undertake be for
the distant and the future? when our souls
are free, no longer bound to a clod that
gravitates to the earth, these things *will* be
neither *distant* nor *future*.
Ibid.

6 In the regions where immortal spirits hold
blessed communion, we may . . . look down
with joy upon the good which is maturing
upon the earth—the souls that are ripening
for heaven. Ibid.

7 In searching for the fundamental principles
of the science of teaching, I find few axioms
as indisputable as is the first principles of
mathematics. One of these is this, HE IS
THE BEST TEACHER WHO MAKES
THE BEST USE OF HIS OWN TIME
AND THAT OF HIS PUPILS. *For* TIME
*is all that is given by God in which to do the
work of Improvement.* "How to Teach,"
Address to the Columbian
Association, n.d.

8 He is not necessarily the best teacher who performs the most labour; makes his pupils work the hardest, and bustle the most. A hundred cents of copper, though they make more clatter and fill more space, have only a tenth of the value of one eagle of gold.
Ibid.

9 The voice of conscience residing in his heart is as the voice of God; and if you invariably interpret that voice with correctness and truth, the child will submit and obey you naturally and affectionately. But if your government is unjust or capricious, if you punish one day, what you pass over or approve another, the dissatisfied child will naturally rebel. "What to Teach,"
op. cit.

10 Reason and religion teach us that we too are primary existences, that it is for us to move in the orbit of our duty around the holy center of perfection, the companions not the satellites of men. Inscribed beneath her bust in the Hall of Fame of Great American, Bronx, New York

743. Sarah Josepha Hale
(1788–1879)

1 We all are children in our strife to cease
Each petty pleasure, as it lures the sight *The Genius of Oblivion and Other Poems* 1823

2 And ever those, who would enjoyment gain
Must find it in the purpose they pursue.
Ibid.

3 What matter though the scorn of fools be given
If the path follow'd lead us on to heaven!
Ibid.

4 Ay, justice, who evades her?
Ibid.

5 O wondrous power! how little understood,
Entrusted to the mother's mind alone
To fashion genius, form the soul for good,

Inspire a West*, or train a Washington!
Ibid.
*The American painter Benjamin West (1738–1820).

6 And bards and prophets tune their mystic lyres
While listening to the music of the waves!
Ibid.

7 A century hence, when our country boasts its tens of millions of inhabitants . . . this unpretending book may be a reference describing faithfully the age when to be industrious was to be respectable.
Preface,
Northwood, A Tale of New England 1828

8 The great error of those who would sever the Union, rather than see a slave within its borders, is that they forget the master is their brother as well as the servant. . . .
Ibid. (5th edition, 1852)

9 . . . there is a period when nations as well as individuals quit their minority. . . .
Text, op. cit.

10 The nations of Europe will band against her [Great Britain], for she has trampled them down in her day of triumph; and she has the light of freedom which tyrants hate. The nations will gather against her and she will be sore beset.
And then will America remember. . . .
Ibid.

11 Those who tread a devious path may possibly retrace their steps, or by a circuitous route finally reach the goal; but those who never stir, how can they win the race!
Ibid.

12 You may easily tell a rich Yankee farmer—he is always pleading poverty.
Ibid.

13 In this age of innovation perhaps no experiment will have an influence more important on the character and happiness of our society than the granting to females the advantages of a systematic and thorough education. The honour of this triumph, in favour of intellect over long established prejudice, belongs to the men of America.
Editorial,
The Ladies' Magazine
January 1828*
*First issue of first woman's magazine in the United States.

14 There is no influence so powerful as that of the mother, but next in rank in efficacy is that of schoolmaster. Ibid.

15 Victoria's reign will be one of the longest in English annals. . . .
She may so stamp her influence on the period in which she flourishes that history shall speak of it as her own. . . .
It will be the Victorian, as a former one now is the Elizabethan age . . . *
Editorial,
The Ladies' Magazine
February 1829
*Predicted two years before Victoria ascended the throne.

16 She was a weak woman—too highly elated in prosperity, too easily depressed by adversity—not considering that *both* are situations of trial. . . . "Walter Wilson,"
Sketches of American Character 1829

17 . . . just the disposition for a woman, a wife; a spirit that can accommodate itself to the wishes and humours of those on whom it is dependent for happiness, and yet retain sufficient firmness to act with decision when circumstances shall require its exertion.
Ibid.

18 "One of those tempers, so difficult to manage, and so well worth the attempt of managing." Ibid.

19 How much of personal convenience, of private pique, of selfishness, envy, anger or ambition, would be found to mingle in the motives of the patriot and the politician!
"The Soldier of the Revolution,"
op. cit.

20 Party spirit was then, and always will be, wherever indulged, the bane of society and good neighbourhood. Ibid.

21 Without this self-approving voice within us, the applause of shouting millions is idle, empty praise. "Weddings and Funerals,"
op. cit.

22 Death is called the king of terrors—but may he not often be the angel of consolation? How much of mortal sorrow is spared or ended when he drops his sable curtain, and closes the drama of human life!
Ibid.

23 Thirty years make little alteration in the appearance of nature. It is on man and his works that the characters of time are impressed. "Ann Ellsworth,"
op. cit.

24 It is necessary that *all* our people should be instructed, as universal education is the main pillar that must eventually support the temple of our liberty. "The Village Schoolmistress,"
op. cit.

25 When the soul is most innocent, that is in youth, the passions are most ardent.
Ibid.

26 But in a country where there is no privileged class, genius and industry may attain the highest honors. . . . "The Poor Scholar,"
op. cit.

27 Why cannot reason and education free the mind from the dominion of prejudice?
Ibid.

28 In short she was always of the opinion that those amusements, which were inconvenient or unsuitable for her, were either very vulgar or very sinful. "The Springs,"
op. cit.

29 ... Americans ... are remarking, reasoning, scheming. ... They are like travellers who are looking forward with earnestness to the next stage in their journey, and feel quite unprepared to rest or enjoy themselves by the way.   Ibid.

30 There is no standard, there can be none of personal beauty; the feelings of the heart have more influence than rules of taste in our estimation of the human face; yet there are countenances so peculiarly fascinating, that criticism and comparison are out of the question.   "Prejudices," op. cit.

31 A Yankee (I speak of the common minded,) calculates his generosity and sympathy, as methodically as his income; and to waste either, on an unprofitable, or undeserving object, would be foolish, if not wicked.   Ibid.

32 ... though we may be excessively annoyed by the prejudice of others, we shall never be quite wretched if we do not yield ourselves to the guidance of our own.   Ibid.

33 Democracies have been, and governments called, *free*; but the spirit of independence and the consciousness of unalienable rights, were never before transfused into the minds of a whole people. ... The feeling of equality which they proudly cherish does not proceed from an ignorance of their station, but from the knowledge of their rights; and it is this knowledge which will render it so exceedingly difficult for any tyrant ever to triumph over the liberties of our country.   "The Apparition," op. cit.

34 So far as the human mind can shake off selfishness and act from a sacred regard to truth, justice and duty, so far will men not only be virtuous, but fearless in virtue.   Ibid.

35 ... of all kinds of knowledge, I consider antiquarian lore as the most unwomanly. It must be gained by so much research, and explained by such learned terms, and defended by so many arguments, in the Sir Pertinax style of obstinacy, that, heaven defend me from ever meeting with that anomaly in our species—an antiquarian without a beard.   "William Forbes," op. cit.

36 There is something in the decay of nature that awakens thought, even in the most trifling mind.   "A Winter in the Country," op. cit.

37 ... this tenaciousness of the human mind to maintain and uphold what it has received as a truth, and defend it as truth, even after convinced that it is not true. ...   Ibid.

38 Mary had a little lamb,
    Its fleece was white as snow,
And everywhere that Mary went
    The lamb was sure to go.

It followed her to school one day,
    Which was against the rule.
It made the children laugh and play
    To see a lamb at school.

"What makes the lamb love Mary so?"
    The eager children cry.
"Oh, Mary loves the lamb, you know,"
    The teacher did reply.
                                    "Mary's Little Lamb," in toto, *Poems for Our Children*   1830

39 O, beautiful rainbow, all woven of light!
There's not in thy tissue one shadow of night;
Heaven surely is open when thou dost appear,
And bending above thee, the angels draw near,
And sing—"the rainbow! the rainbow!
The smile of God is here."
                                    "Beautiful Rainbow," op. cit.

40 O, give to us, daily,
    Our portion of bread!

It is from thy bounty
That all must be fed.
"Prayer,"
op. cit.

41 We need not power or splendor;
Wide hall or lordly dome;
The good, the true, the tender,
These form the wealth of home.
"Home,"
op. cit.

42 The Hand,—what wondrous Wisdom
plann'd
This instrument so near divine!
How impotent, without the Hand,
Proud Reason's light would shine!
"The Hand and Its Work,"
op. cit.

43 Though Mind Aladdin's lamp might be,
His Geni was the Hand.   Ibid.

44 I consider every attempt to induce women
to think they have a just right to participate
in the public duties of government as injurious to their best interests and derogatory to
their character. Our empire is purer, more
excellent and spiritual. . . .
Editorial,
*The Ladies' Magazine and
Literary Gazette*   February
1832

45 There is a deep moral influence in these
periodical seasons of rejoicing, in which
whole communities participate. They bring
out, and together, as it were, the best sympathies in our natures. *Traits of American
Life*   1835

46 What in the rising man was industry and
economy, becomes in the rich man par-
simony and avarice.   Ibid.

47 Any man who has money may obtain the
reputation of taste by the mere purchasing
of the works of art.   Ibid.

48 Political controversies are never entered
into with any wish to gain knowledge, but
only a triumph for the party.
Ibid.

49 Americans have two ardent passions; the
love of liberty and the love of distinction.
Ibid.

50 Few individuals enter into public life who
would not be wealthier and happier as private citizens—but then they would not be
known, would not see their names in the
newspaper, except for raising a curious calf,
or a mammoth cabbage.   Ibid.

51 There is small danger of being starved in
our land of plenty; but the danger of being
stuffed is imminent.   Ibid.

52 . . . rouse all your energies for the work
that is before you. In a country and age distinguished by such mighty privileges, it requires warm hearts, strong minds and liberal minds to devise, and dare, and do.
"The Lloyds,"
op. cit.

53 There can be no education without leisure,
and without leisure education is worthless.
*Godey's Lady's Book
(passim)*   1837-1877

54 . . . the progress of female improvement.
Ibid., Motto (passim)

55 The barbarous custom of wresting from
women whatever she possesses, whether by
inheritance, donation or her own industry,
and conferring it all upon the man she marries, to be used at his discretion and will,
perhaps waste it on his wicked indulgences,
without allowing her any control or redress,
is such a monstrous perversion of *justice* by
law, that we might well marvel how it could
obtain in a Christian community.
"The Rights of Married
Women,"
Godey's Lady's Book (May 1837)

56 In all our mental pursuits, it seemed the aim
of my husband to enlighten my reason,
strengthen my judgment, and give me confidence in my own powers of mind, which he
estimated more highly than I did.
The Ladies Wreath   1837

57 I have had dreams of greatness, glorious
dreams   *Ormond Grosvenor*   1838

58 I never see a wounded enemy,
Or hear of a foe slain on the battle-field,
But I bethink me of his pleasant home,
And how his mother and his sisters watch
For one who nevermore returns. Poor
souls!
I've often wept to think how they must
weep.   Ibid.

59 . . . man in blessing others finds his highest
fame!   Ibid.

60 If each might have dominion of himself,
And each would govern wisely, and thus
show
Truth, courage, knowledge, power, benevo-
lence,
And all the princely soul in private vir-
tues,—
Then each would be a prince, a Hero—
greater—
He would be man in likeness of his Maker!
                                               Ibid.

61 There's no power
In ancestry to make the foolish wise.
                                               Ibid.

62 Hence man's best riches must be gain'd—
not given;
His noblest name deserv'd, and not deriv'd.
                                               Ibid.

63 There is no impossibility to him
Who stands prepar'd to conquer every haz-
ard:
The fearful are the failing.
                                               Ibid.

64 Shout *freedom*! and the talismanic word
Will open all the treasures of the soul—
And war for these is just, and wise, and
holy:
But cry *revenge*! and a dark host of pas-
sions,
Fell as the fierce hyena, sweeps along,
And makes e'en victory a sound of terror,—
For what is gain'd that we can turn to
good?   Ibid.

65 The temple of our purest thoughts is—
silence!   Ibid.

66 Why he, when war's stern strength is on his
soul,
Will stalk in apathy o'er slaughter'd
friends,
Counting the dead and dying, as their loss
Was all computed in the numbers slain.
                                               Ibid.

67 Nothing can be more absurd in theory and
vile in practise than the attempt in common
parlance "to break the temper" and "to
crush the will" . . . while of all debasing, de-
grading influences the worst is bodily fear.
                                       Editorial,
                            Godey's Lady's Book
                                  February 1844

68 'T is best to make the Law our friend
                            Harry Guy   1848

69 . . . to books the heart must turn
When with unspoken thoughts we yearn,
And gather from the silent page
The just reproof, the counsel sage,
The consolation kind and true
That soothes and heals the wounded heart.
                      *Three Hours: or, The Vigil of
                      Love and Other Poems*   1848

70 Bathing our renovated sight
In the free Gospel's glorious light,
We marvel it was ever night.
                                               Ibid.

71 And how is it with the little children of our
American cities in general? . . . the public
squares are very neatly kept, and there the
children may have the freedom of the gravel
walk . . . but they must be careful not to set
their little weary, dusty feet on the green,
soft grass!   Editorial,
                            Godey's Lady's Book
                                       May 1849

72 . . . rights are liable to be perverted to
wrongs when we are incapable of rightly exercising them.   Editorial,
                            Godey's Lady's Book
                                   January 1850

73 As some deep valley, made dark and un-wholesome from the dark shade of the over-hanging trees, leaps into beauty and freshness when the sun's rays fall unobst-ructed upon it, so great an entire transfor-mation did happiness produce in Keziah [hero of the novel]. *Liberia,* Ch. 1   1853

74 There is nowhere a more sympathetic or imitative race than the African.... *Ibid.,* Ch. 2

75 "I belong to you all the same, mas'r; and if you ever want me, speak the word, and I come from the farmost ends of the arth [sic]; but I's burn to be free, mas'r; I allers know'd it. Some niggers born for slaves—heaps on 'em fit for nothin' else; but this chile ain't one of them ar people." *Ibid.*

76 "You talk to me about educating my chil-dren; but what's the use of it.... The more they know the wuss it will be for 'em; for they won't keep company with their own color, and white folks won't associate with them, and thar they are shut up by them-selves... and they won't be any thing but just what I am, a nigger that every body de-spises." *Ibid.,* Ch. 3

77 "... it's might hard for a man like me, that could be as good as any body, if his skin were a shade or two lighter, to be kept down so all the time, and not get drunk or wicked." *Ibid.*

78 "... what's de good of strong arms when de heart is a coward's?" *Ibid.,* Ch. 5

79 While a slave, as long as she was treated like one, she had rebelled almost to death... while... the more she was al-lowed to consider the service one of free will, the more heartily was it performed. *Ibid.*

80 "What a wonderful continent is the rounded, smooth-shored Africa, known from the earliest dawn of time, yet so unk-nown; the granary of nations, yet sterile and fruitless as the sea; swarming with life, yet dazzling the eyes with its vast track of glit-tering sands!... the mother of civiliza-tion—the grey-haired Africa." *Ibid.,* Ch. 7

81 "Africa... is the home... of the mysteri-ous Negro races yet lying dormant in the germ, destined, perhaps, to rule this earth when our proud Anglo-Saxon blood is as corrupt as that of the descendents of Homer or Perricles [sic]." *Ibid.*

82 The belief in witchcraft was and is univer-sal, where the spirit of Christianity has not shed its blessed light. *Ibid.,* Ch. 9

83 Liberia has outlived the doubts of the weak-hearted, the sneers of the disbelieving, the open opposition of its foes, and is now a great and triumphant reality. *Ibid.*

84 If men cannot cope with women in the medical profession let them take an humble occupation in which they can. Editorial, *Godey's Lady's Book* January 1853

85 Every young woman in our land should be qualified by some accomplishment which she may teach, or some art or profession she can follow, to support herself creditably, should the necessity occur. Editorial, *Godey's Lady's Book* March 1854

86 For ourselves our spirits fall with the first rising of steam in the kitchen, and only re-turn to natural temperature when the clothes are folded in the ironing basket. We rejoice that a better day is at hand*.... Editorial, *Godey's Lady's Book* April 1854

*Refers to the invention of the first washing machine.

87 Lambs skip and bound, kittens and puppies seem wild with the joy of life; and little children naturally run, leap, dance and shout in the exhuberance of that capacity for happiness which the young human heart feels as instinctively as the flower buds open to the sun. To repress their natural joyousness, not to direct and train it for good, seems to be the object of most parents. So the merry little children are ... subjected to a routine of ... quiet until this painful lesson is impressed—that to be active is to be very naughty.   Editorial,
Godey's Lady's Book
October 1857

88 Growing old! growing old! Do they say it of me?
Do they hint my fine fancies are faded and fled?
That my garden of life, like the winter-swept tree,
Is frozen and dying, or fallen and dead?
"Growing Old"
[written on her 70th birthday],
Godey's Lady's Book
October 24, 1858

89 ... the whole process of home-making, housekeeping and cooking, which ever has been woman's special province, should be looked on as an art and a profession. ...
Editorial,
Godey's Lady's Book
c.1859

90 The most welcome guest in society will ever be the one to whose mind everything is a suggestion, and whose words suggest something to everybody.   "Manners,"
Godey's Lady's Book
c.1868

91 We again repeat that we will not accept any stories where runaway horses or upsetting of boats is necessary to the denouement.
"To Writers,"
Godey's Lady's Book
October 1868

92 The profession of teacher requires ... as thorough and special training as that of any of the other intellectual professions. The great majority of our teachers are deficient in this training ... the complaint on this head is indeed universal, and it is coupled with another complaint of the inadequate salaries almost every where paid to teachers, but more especially in rural districts.
Editorial,
Godey's Lady's Book
December 1868

93 What has made this nation great? Not its heroes but its households.
Editorial,
Godey's Lady's Book
July 1869

94 And now, having reached my ninetieth year, I must bid farewell to my countrywomen, with the hope that this work of half a century may be blessed to the furtherance of their happiness and usefulness in their Divinely appointed sphere. New avenues for higher culture and for good works are opening before them, which fifty years ago were unknown. That they may improve these opportunities, and be faithful to their high vocation, is my heartfelt prayer.
Editorial,
Godey's Lady's Book
December 1877

95 Every century has its pecular tide of thought.   *Woman's Record*   1877

96 ... 't is man's highest glory to be good!
"Constantia", n.d.

97 The meaner creatures never feel control,
By glowing instinct guided to the goal;
Each sense is fed, each faculty employ'd,—
And all their record is—a life enjoy'd.
Ibid.

744. Marguerite Blessington
(1789–1849)

1 "Och! Jim, and is this the way you keep the Bible oath you took over to Father Cahill last Easther Sunday, that you would not dhrink a dhrop in any sheban-house for a year and a day? . . . "
"I did not dhrink a dhrop in the sheban-house, for I put my head clean out of the window while I was dhrinking, so my oath is safe. . . . " *The Repealers,* Ch. 1   1833

2 "How is it, Jim dear, that I, who love you betther than ever I loved myself, and you, who say you love me—that we, who have but one heart, can have two minds?"
Ibid.

3 "Liberty, Grace a-vourneen, is just what like we imagine of the grand ould times in Ireland; it's something that we don't quite rightly understand, but which, we believe, must be all the finer for that."
Ibid.

4 "Why liberty, cuishlamachree, manes to do every thing we like ourselves, and hinder everyone else from doing it."
Ibid., Ch. 2

5 "Isn't it enough for poor ignorant people like us to do our duty, and follow our own religion, without troubling ourselves about the religion of others?"   Ibid.

6 "Sure there's different roads from this to Dungarvan—some thinks one road pleasanter, and some think another; wouldn't it be mighty foolish to quarrel for this?—and sure isn't it twice worse to thry to interfere with people for choosing the road they like best to heaven?"   Ibid.

7 "Though I maintain that a similarity of *tastes* is highly conducive to happiness, a too great assimilation of feeling is apt to mar it."   Ibid., Ch. 19

8 "Each is afraid of wounding the other; hence, one half their lives passes in refined and delicate understandings, and other half in concealments, or *éclaircissements* [explanations] of them."   Ibid.

9 Those are indeed fortunate who find, when sorrow assails them, that friendship administers an anodyne; and as this good fortune becomes more rare, it is, like all rarities, enjoyed still more poignantly.
Ibid., Ch. 23

10 " . . . I see no chance of our ever having this poor ould, throubled counthry happy, unless some plain, honest-spoken people will take the pains to show the poor people what fools and tools they're made of to sarve the interests of a few men who are puffed up by ambition, and who would give up the counthry clear and clane to sarve their own ends."   Ibid., Ch. 27

11 "Imagination, which is the eldorado of the poet and of the novel-writer, often proves the most pernicious gift to the individuals who compose the talkers instead of the writers in society."   Ibid., Ch. 40

12 "It is not the crime, but its consequences that you all dread."   Ibid., Ch. 41

13 "Virtue, like a portionless beauty, has more admirers than followers: and politeness, like love, is only approved when one's self is the object. . . . "   Ibid., Ch. 42

14 Politeness, that cementer of friendship and soother of enmities, is nowhere so much required, and so frequently outraged, as in family circles. . . .   Ibid., Ch. 57

15 Friends can see defects with the naked eye, however weak that organ may be; but too frequently require magnifying glasses to discover good qualities.   Ibid.

16 Forbearance towards errors and defects, and a just appreciation of good qualities, joined to mildness and good breeding, is what we would inculcate, as the surest means of preserving domestic harmony, and of promoting domestic affection.
Ibid.

17 Happy are they who misfortune awakens to a sense of their errors! Even the best must own that patience and resignation are the pillars of human peace on earth. . . .
　　　　　　　　　　　　Ibid., Ch. 60

18 There is a peculiar lightness in the air in Ireland, which . . . brings healing on its wings to the over-excited mind, as well as to the exhausted body. . . .　　Ibid., Ch. 62

19 " . . . he who would remain honest ought to keep away want."　　　　Ibid., Ch. 63

20 "I live in the world and am of it; you pass through it, as on a forced march—your person in it, but your thoughts engaged in some Utopian speculation for bettering mankind. . . . "　　The Two Friends,
　　　　　　　　　　　Ch. 1　　1835

21 " . . . chance, the very worst guardian a man can choose for his personal comfort."
　　　　　　　　　　　　Ibid.

22 This beauty, which had enabled her to reign despotically over his heart, she looked on with much the same feelings with which despotic sovereigns regard the divine right of kings, knowing that its basis is founded on the weakness of their subjects.
　　　　　　　　　　　　Ibid., Ch. 7

23 . . . the impropriety, or sinfulness of an action had never been taken into consideration, and her conscience had so long slumbered, that its powers had become inert and its whispers silenced.
　　What will the world think of it? was the only question that ever suggested itself to her mind. . . .　　Ibid., Ch. 17

4 It is shocking to reflect to how many meannesses—nay, crimes—vanity may urge its votaries. . . .　　　　　Ibid.

25 "My spaniel Dido is not more submissive," said Scamper; "for though I try Lady Janet by contradicting flatly to-day, what I maintained yesterday, it is all the same to her; she never has any opinion but mine: this is what I call the only solid foundation to build matrimonial happiness upon; and so I have made up my mind to marry."
　　　　　　　　　　　　Ibid., Ch. 28

26 Much as he loved France, he was not sorry to leave it at the present moment, when the people, intoxicated with the triumph they had gained, thought more of displaying than of using it soberly, to secure to themselves those rights, in the hope of obtaining which they had upset one monarchy, and erected another.　　　　Ibid., Ch. 41

27 . . . she endured pangs of humiliated pride, known only to the proud but guilty mind—which, conscious of meriting reprobation, shrinks from its infliction, and receives with anger, instead of penitence, the punishment induced by misconduct.　　Ibid., Ch. 43

28 "This is always the way with you men; let a woman only be handsome, and you are already to pity her, whatsoever her transgressions may have been."　　Ibid., Ch. 45

29 She had thought of, and lived but for society, unmindful that it casts from its bosom the unhappy and the erring, as a vigourous constitution repels contagious diseases.　　　　　　Ibid., Ch. 48

30 . . . many are they who think of little else than of Elderly Gentlemen; but alas! these are young *wives* impatient of act the part of young *widows*; heirs in a hurry to come into possession; holders of post obits;* expectant legatees; and *faithful* servants anxious to render the last duties to their dear masters, and to receive the meed of their *disinterested* services.　　The Confessions of an
　　　　　　　Elderly Gentleman　　1836

*A bond payable after a person's death.

31 This is an autobiographical-loving age. . . .
　　　　　　　　　　　　Ibid.

32 . . . it is better to die young than to outlive *all* one loved, and *all* that rendered one lovable. Ibid.

33 How absurd it is to see a red-faced, fat-paunched sexagenarian weeping! Ibid.

34 . . . I looked forward to proposing to enter a state in which the whole happiness or misery of life depends on the selection of the object with whom it is to be shared.
"My Second Love,"
op. cit.

35 "Half your sex run after a woman, *not* because you individually admire her, but because it gratifies your inordinate *amour propre*, to appear preferred by one, who has a train of adorers. . . . " "My Third Love,"
op. cit.

36 "Attracted by the beauty of a woman, as they are by that of a horse, a picture, a statue, or any other object, the possession of which is likely to excite the envy of their acquaintances . . . the heartless voluptuary of modern days turns from the beauty he has won, to seek, *not* a fairer, but a newer, face. . . . Ibid.

37 . . . the grief that I thought indestructible, passed away, like all other things in this sublunary world, fading day by day, until nothing of it was left but a tender melancholy, like the softened feeling that a summer's twilight produces on the mind. . . .
"My Fourth Love,"
op. cit.

38 Women like to inspire *hopeless* passions; for, even the most mundane of the sweet sex, always retain some portion of the pristine romance of their characters: just as flowers, though withered and faded, still retain some faint remnant of their native perfume. Ibid.

39 Love is, I think, like fever; one severe attack leaves the patient subject to relapses through youth; and each succeeding one renders him more weakened, and, consequently, more exposed to future assaults.
Ibid.

40 HERMIONE. But, ah! so fleetly do their lives pass,
That even when their bloom the richest glows,
I, looking forward to its swift decay,
Feel a strange sadness as I gaze on them,
And thoughts of death come o'er me.
Flowers of Loveliness,
"Roses" 1836–1841?

41 HELENA. . . . is't not strange
That what awakens only joy in me,
Should fill thy soul with images of gloom?
Ibid.

42 O! more than garden blossom nursed,
I lov'd it—for my hand was first
To find it there! "Lillies of the Valley"

43 Flowers and children—emblems meet,
Of all things innocent and sweet.
Ibid.,
"Daisies"

44 'Tis folly to grieve
For the friends we leave; new lands—new friends we'll find,
Then away! away!
Is burthen gay;
Let us leave all care behind.
Ibid.,
"Forget-me-not"

45 Oft I see her when I sleep,
And her kiss feel on my brow;
But when morning comes, I weep,
Just as you do, Sister, now.
Ibid.,
"Snow-Drop"

46 . . . this bright and constant flower enamoured of the sun. . . . Ibid.,
"Sun-flower"

47 Happiness is a rare plant, that seldom takes root on earth: few ever enjoyed it, except for a brief period; the search after it is rarely rewarded by the discovery. But, there is an admirable substitute for it, which all may hope to attain, as its attainment depends wholly on self—and that is, a contented spirit. *The Victims of Society,* "Lady Mary Howard to Lady Augusta Vernon"   1837

48 Injurious as are the examples of bad conduct, the impunity which too frequently attends the perpetration is still more fatally pernicious.   Ibid., "Lord Delaward to Lady Delaward"

49 It is a sad thing to look at happiness only through another's eyes.   Ibid., "The Countess of Anandale to the Countess of Delaward"

50 . . . we [the French] believe that the people who support the ills of life with the most cheerfulness, and forget them with the greatest facility, are the happiest, and, consequently, the wisest. *You* [the English] are above this happiness, and *we* are superior to the *ennui* which sends half your nation wandering into every clime; as if locomotion could relieve a malady that arises in the discontented mind. . . . Ibid., "The Marquise Le Villeroi to Miss Montressor"

51 . . . in France or Italy . . . women, in losing one virtue, are not necessarily exposed to the loss of all. There, our sex are saved from the necessity of hypocrisy; and are not compelled to pull down the reputations of their contemporaries, in order to erect on the ruins a pedestal for the elevation of their own.   Ibid., "Miss Montressor to La Marquise Le Villeroi"

52 You ask me whether English husbands are, in general, bons et aimables? Pas du tout, ma chère; tout au contraire. They are, as far as I can judge from the specimens I have seen, the most selfish beings imaginable. Ibid.

53 He, or she, who can boast of wealth, no matter how obtained, is sure of being well-received in society; though such persons may be illiterate, ill-mannered, and not immaculate in reputation.   Ibid.

54 How dreadful, how appalling it is, to be so conscious of one's crimes! to tremble at their consequences, and to loathe one's baseness, yet be compelled, by force of circumstances, to persevere in the career of guilt!   Ibid.

55 . . . through what a fearful ordeal does the virtue of a woman pass—that virtue which should never be questioned—when it is subjected to the odious, the defiling publicity of a judicial investigation!   Ibid., "The Countess of Delaward to the Earl of Delaward"

56 It is the motive, and not the results, that constitutes the crime.   Ibid., "La Marquise Le Villeroi to Miss Montressor"

57 . . . with a good fortune, a brilliant position, and a weak, indulgent husband, what more could she desire?   Ibid.

58 How soothing is affection! and how do those who, like me, know little of this sweetener of life, turn, with awakened tenderness, to him who administers the cordial!   Ibid., "The Countess of Anandale to La Marquise Le Villeroi"

59 Let him go: from the right he will never depart:—
He may fall, but he never will yield. "The Cairngohrm," *Gems of Beauty*   1837–1838

60 A mother's love! O holy, boundless thing! Fountain whose waters never cease to spring.   Ibid., "Affection"

61 Not for herself those tears—they ceased to flow
For her own cares and sorrows long ago:
They fall for thee, poor babe, her link to life—

The one last treasure of the widowed wife.
Ibid.,
"Pity"

62 Dreams—all dreams—yet who could say
Flatterer, thy false music stay?
Who could break thy wand? not I—
Cheat me, dear one, till I die!
Ibid.,
"Hope"

63 Spirit of bright and gladsome mien!
Ibid.,
"Cheerfulness"

64 O cruel Sleep!
Time was, thou stoop'st thy wing to close
mine eyes
As gentle as mild twilight shuts up flowers
Ibid.,
"Remorse"

65 How can I bear this soleless, senseless joy,
And know my hand is powerless to inflict
On them a wound as painful and as deep
As that which eats, like fire, into my heart!
Ibid.,
"Envy"

66 People seem to lose all respect for the past;
events succeed each other with such
velocity that the most remarkable one of a
few years gone by, is no more remembered
than if centuries had closed over it.
*The Confessions of an Elderly
Lady* 1838

67 ... modern historians are all would-be
philosophers; who, instead of relating facts
as they occurred, give us their version, or
rather perversions of them, always colored
by their political prejudices, or distorted to
establish some theory, and rendered obscure by cumbrous attempts to trace effect
from cause. Ibid.

68 ... if those only wrote, who were sure of
being read, we should have fewer authors;
and the shelves of libraries would not groan
beneath the weight of dusty tomes more
voluminous than luminous.
Ibid.

69 The ephemeral fancies young ladies dignify
with the appellation of love, no more resemble the real sentiment, than do the imaginary maladies resemble those for which
they are mistaken: but the effects of both
are equally dangerous. Ibid.

70 There is no magician like Love. . . .
Ibid.

71 How prone are we to blame others, when
we ourselves only are in fault.
Ibid.

72 People are always willing to follow advice
when it accords with their own wishes. . . .
Ibid.

73 Time, that omnipotent effacer of *eternal*
passions. . . . Ibid.

74 I encouraged rather than attempted to subdue my grief; for an oblivion of it appeared
to me nothing short of an insult to the memory of the dead. Ibid.

75 Tears fell from my eyes—yes, weak and
foolish as it now appears to me, I wept for
my departed youth; and for that beauty of
which the faithful mirror too plainly assured me, no remnant existed.
Ibid.

76 If mine was no longer a figure or face to
captivate the young and unthinking, it
might satisfy the less scrupulous taste of the
elderly and reflecting. Ibid.

77 Novels and comedies end generally in a
marriage, because, after that event, it is sup-
posed that nothing remains to be told.
"The Honey-Moon,"
*The Works of Lady
Blessington* 1838

78 Passion—possession—what a history is
comprised in these two words! But how
often might its moral be conveyed in a
third—indifference! Ibid.

79 They perceived that the love, unceasing and ecstatic, of which they had dreamt before their union, was a chimera existing only in imagination; and they awoke, with sobered feelings, to seek content in rational affection, instead of indulging in romantic expectations that never falls to the lot of human beings: each acknowledging, with a sigh, that even in a marriage of love, the brilliant anticipations of imagination are never realised; that disappointment awaits poor mortals even in that brightest portion of existence—The Honey-Moon.
Ibid.

80 Love-matches are made by people who are content, for a month of honey, to condemn themselves to a life of vinegar.
Commonplace Book, n.d.

81 When the sun shines on you, you see your friends. Friends are the thermometers by which one may judge the temperature of our fortunes.   Ibid.

82 Religion converts despair, which destroys, into resignation, which submits.
Ibid.

745.   Charlotte Elliott
(1789–1871)

1 Just as I am, without one plea
But that Thy blood was she for me,
And that Thou bidd'st me come to Thee,
O Lamb of God, I come!
"Just As I Am,"
Invalid's Hymn Book   1834

2 "Christian! seek not yet repose,"
Hear thy guardian angel say;
Thou art in the midst of foes—
"Watch and pray."   "Christian! Seek
Not Yet Repose,"
Morning and Evening Hymns   c.1840

746.   Hannah Flagg Gould
(1789–1865)

1 He went to the windows of those who slept,
And over each pane, like a fairy, crept;
Wherever he breathed, wherever he stepped,
By the light of the morn, were seen
Most beautiful things. . . .
"The Frost,"
Poems   1832

2 O Thou, who in thy hand dost hold
The winds and waves that wake or sleep,
Thy tender arms of mercy fold
Around the seamen on the deep.
"Changes on the Deep,"
op. cit.

747.   Ann Hasseltine Judson
(1789–1826)

1 We conversed much on death and the probability of our finding an early grave. The subject was solemn and affecting, yet secretly pleasing and consoling.
Quoted in *Memoir of Mrs. Ann H. Judson, Late Missionary to Burma* by James D. Knowles
1829

2 Either I have been made, through the mercy of God, a partaker of divine grace, or I have been fatally deceiving myself, and building upon a sandy foundation. Either I have, in sincerity and truth, renounced the vanities of this world, and entered the narrow path which leads to life, or I have been refraining from them for a time only, to turn again and relish them more than ever. God grant that the latter may never be my unhappy case!   Journal entry
(December 22, 1806), op. cit.

3 I find more real enjoyment in contrition for sin, excited by a view of the adorable moral perfections of God, than in all earthly joys.
Ibid.

4 I am a creature of God, and He has an undoubted right to do with me as seemeth good in His sight. Journal entry (October 1810), op. cit.

5 O America! my native land, must I leave thee! Journal entry (February 1812), op. cit.

748. Catharine Maria Sedgwick
(1789–1867)

1 "Well," said Debby, "contentment is a good thing and a rare; but I guess it dwells most where people would least expect to find it." "The Opinions of a Yankee Spinster," *Redwood* 1824

2 "There is some pure gold mixed with all this glitter; some here that seem to have as pure hearts and just minds as if they had never stood in the dazzling sunshine of fortune." Ibid.

3 "... contentment is a modest, prudent spirit; and ... for the most part she avoids the high places of the earth, where the sun burns and the tempests beat, and leads her favourites along quiet vales and to sequestered fountains." Ibid.

4 She knows not—no one knows—how to look upon the troubled and vanishing dream of this life, till the light of another falls upon it. "Thoughts of a Dying Mother," op. cit.

5 He who should embody and manifest the virtues taught in Christ's sermon on the Mount, would, though he had never seen a drawingroom, nor even heard of the artificial usages of society, commend himself to all nations, the most refined as well as the most simple. "True Politeness," op. cit.

6 "I must say, I think there is a useless and senseless outcry against rich men. It comes from the ignorant, unobserving, and unreflecting. We must remember that in our country there are no fixed classes: the poor family of this generation is the rich family of the next; and more than that, the poor of to-day are the rich of to-morrow, and the rich of to-day the poor of to-morrow. The prizes are open to all, and they fall without favour." "Mr. Aikin's Philosophy," *The Poor Rich Man and the Rich Poor Man* 1836

7 "... money is the representative of power—the means of extended usefulness, and we all have dreams of the wonderful good we should do if we had these means in our hands. But this I do know; that, if we are conscious of employing, and *employing well*, the means we have, we ought not to crave more." Ibid.

8 I had a good education. I do not mean as to learning; that is only one part of it; I was taught to use my faculties. But, first and best of all, I early learned to seek the favour of God and the approval of conscience. "The Poor Rich Man's Blessing," op. cit.

9 The fountains are with the rich, but they are no better than a stagnant pool till they flow in streams to the labouring people. "His Advice to his Children," op. cit.

10 If there were none of these hateful rich people, who, think you, would build hospitals and provide asylums for orphans, and for the deaf and dumb, and the blind? Ibid.

11 "If parents are civil and kind to one another, if children never hear from them profane or coarse language, they will as naturally grow up well-behaved, as that candle took the form of the mould it was run in." "His Remarks on Manners," op. cit.

749.   Eliza Townsend
(1789–1854)

1   Thou!—source and support of all
That is or seen or felt; thyself unseen,
Unfelt, unknown—alas, unknowable!
                    "The Incomprehensibility of
                                    God," St. 1,
                    The Female Poets of America,
                    Rufus Griswold, ed.   1849

2   . . . let that come now,
Which soon or late must come. For light
like this
Who would not dare to die?
                                            Ibid.

750.   Harriette Wilson
(1789–1846)

1 I shall not say why and how I became, at
the age of fifteen, the mistress of the Earl of
Craven.   *Memoirs,*
                    n.d. (first sentence)

751.   Ann Eliza Bray
(1790–1883)

1 Never fear spoiling children by making
them too happy. Happiness is the atmosphere in which all good affections
grow . . . unhappiness—the chilling pressure which produces . . . "the mind's green
and yellow sickness"—ill temper.
                    Attributed, n.d.

752.   Mary Cole
(fl. 1790s)

1 If all the writers upon Cookery had acknowledged from whence they took their
receipts, as I do, they would have acted
with more candour by the public. Their
vanity to pass for Authors, instead of Com-
pilers, has not added to their reputation.
                    *The Lady's Complete
                    Guide*   1791

753.   Louisa Macartney Crawford
(1790–1858)

1 Kathleen Mavourneen; what, slumbering
    still?
Oh, hast thou forgotten how soon we must
    sever?
O hast thou forgotten this day we must
    part?
It may be for years, and it may be for ever!
Oh, why art thou silent, thou voice of my
    heart? "Kathleen Mavourneen," n.d.

754.   Eleanor Anne Franklin
(c.1790-1797–1825)

1 Oh! could I pour his deep clear tones along,
And steal his accents as I steal his song!
        Coeur de Lion, * an Epic Poem in
                    Sixteen Cantos*   1822
    *Richard I (the Lion-Heart), 1157–1199.

2 "Frown, frown, Clorinda—I would prize
        Thy smile o'er all that arms might
            gain;
O'er wealth and fame. . . ."
                                            Ibid.

3   "Thine icy heart I well can bear,
But not the love that others share."
                                            Ibid.

4 "The widow'd dove can never rest,
The felon kite has robb'd her nest;
With wing untir'd she seeks her mate,
To share or change his dreadful fate."
                                            Ibid.

755. Hannah Godwin
(fl. 1790s)

1 Good sense without vanity, a penetrating judgment without a disposition to satire, with about as much religion as my William likes, struck me with a wish that she [Miss Gay] was my Williams' wife.
> Letter to William Godwin, her brother, Quoted in *William Godwin: His Friends and Contemporaries* by C. K. Paul   1876

756. Rahel Levin
(fl. 1790s–1810s)

1 Poor woman [Germaine de Staël*], she has seen nothing, heard nothing, understood nothing. Quoted in *Mistress to an Age: A Life of Madame de Staël* by J. Christopher Herold   1958

*See 676.

757. Rahel Morpurgo
(1790–1871)

1 A woman's fancies lightly roam, and weave Themselves into a fairy web.
> Sonnet, *Ugab Rachel [The Harp of Rachel]*, I. Castiglione, ed.   1890

2 I will try but this once more
If I still have the power to sing—
> Untitled, op. cit.

3 Wherever you go, you will hear all around: The wisdom of woman to the distaff is bound.   Untitled, St. 4, op. cit.

4 Lament no more, with sleep no more be dumb!
Let men of understanding now arise
And teach us by their calculations wise
How long till our redemption's star shall come.   "Fear not the portents of heaven" (1859), op. cit.

5 What joy upon the honoured sire must come
When showing forth the wisdom of his child!
Lo, she is fair and pure and undefiled—
Thanks, thanks to her, the gladness of his home!   Untitled (1859), op. cit.

6 Yesterday the Spirit of Song passed over me, after being separated from me these two years.   Journal entry (1863), op. cit.

7 Better to die—to rest in shadows folded,
Than thus to grope amid the depths in vain!
"And here also I have done nothing that they should put me into the dungeon"
(aka "the Dark Valley"), St. 1 (1867), op. cit.

8 The winds are blowing through your lofty places,
And who, ah! who can say how sweet they are?   Ibid., St. 3

9 I will tell thee an idea that has come into mind that "oil from the flinty rock"* is *petroleum*, and there is nothing new under the sun.   Letter to Isaac Luzzatto (1869), op. cit.

*From Deuteronomy 32:13.

10 Woe! my knowledge is weak,
My wound is desperate.   Last Poem (1871), op. cit.

758. Charlotte Elizabeth Tonna
(1790–1846)

1 When we name the infliction of a wrong, we imply the existence of a right. Therefore, if we undertake to discuss the wrongs of women, we may be expected to set out by plainly defining what are the rights of women.   *The Wrongs of Women*, P. I, "Milliners and Dress-makers," Ch. 1   1833–1834

2 "Why, it seems every man as gets his wages is expected to lay out a shilling in drink, at the tap where they wait for the money. 'Tis all of a piece with the rest of the robbery plan; but a man can't help himself—he must do like the rest."   Ibid., P. II, "The Forsaken Home," Ch. 3

3 . . . it is all a matter of talk—by clock, or by hour-glass, as the progress of either may be interpreted by superior authority, the poor must labour on to the stipulated moment of release.   Ibid., P. III, "The Little Pin-headers," Ch. 3

4 There is no presumption in taking God at his word: not to do so, is very impertinent. . . .   Personal Recollections, Letter I   1841

5 "See what a stoop she has already; depend on it, this girl will be both a dwarf and a cripple if we don't put her into stays."
"My child may be a cripple, ma'am, if such is God's will; but she shall be one of his making, not our's."   Ibid., Letter II

6 There can be no doubt that the hand which first encloses the waist of a girl in these cruel contrivances [stays], supplying her with a fictitious support, where the hand of God has placed bones and muscles that ought to be brought into vigorous action, that hand lays the foundation of bitter suffering. . . .   Ibid.

7 The love that grew with us from our cradles never knew diminution from time or distance. Other ties were formed, but they did not supersede or weaken this. Death tore away all that was mortal and perishable, but this tie he could not sunder.   Ibid., Letter III

8 How very much do they err who consider the absence of order and method as implying greater liberty or removing a sense of restraint!   Ibid., Letter IV

9 . . . the want of punctuality is a want of honest principle; for however people may think themselves authorised to rob God and themselves of their own time, they can plead no right to lay a violent hand on the time and duties of their neighbour.   Ibid.

10 "And how do you feel when you have got absolution?" "I feel all right; and I go out and begin again." "And how do you know that God has really pardoned you?" "He doesn't pardon me directly; only the priest does. He [the priest] confesses my sins to the bishop, and the bishop confesses them to the pope, and the pope sees the Virgin Mary every Saturday night, and tells her to speak to God about it." Ibid., Letter VIII

11 Nothing rights a boy of ten or twelve years like putting him on his manhood. . . .   Ibid., Letter XIV

12 We "give place to the Devil" daily; and nothing more effectually helps him to lead us into this breach of a positive command, than our readiness to forget his continual presence, either personally or by his active ministers; and perhaps to leave out of sight the fact of his very existence.   Principalities and Powers in Heavenly Places, Sec. II   1842

13 . . . the danger that besets the path of such as are bent on acquiring knowledge apart from godliness. They have a master at hand, ready and able to teach them as much as human understanding may grasp, and sure to clothe with every attraction the bait which he has found to be so efficacious in bringing souls into his net; but the price of his lesson is such, that the man who strikes that bargain is bankrupt forever.   Ibid., Sec. VII

14 Fast flies the ship before the tempest's ire, While reeling to and fro the hapless crew

Gaze on the wild abyss, and shudder at the
view.   *Osric, A Missionary Tale,*
Canto I, St. 1,
from *The Works of Charlotte
Elizabeth,* Vol. I
1844

15 There's music in thy motion: such as creeps
O'er the charmed spirit when the billow
sleeps   *Miscellaneous Poems,*
"The Swan,"
St. 3, op. cit.

16 A story of despair
Imprints the leaf.   "The Rose,"
St. 2, op. cit.

17 The snare is before thee, the pang and the
sorrow,
The breath of the syren, the voice of
the rod,
The crime of to-day, the despair of to-
morrow,
And all that can sever the soul from its
God.   "To J. W. B.,"
St. 2 (1825), op. cit.

18 Who that has seen the sun's uprising, when
his first bright beam comes sparkling over
the billows on a clear autumnal morning,
but has felt a thrill of gladness at his heart—
an involuntary, perhaps an unconscious as-
cription of praise to the Creator, who has so
framed him that all his innate perverseness
cannot bar the entrance of that thrill?
Helen Fleetwood,
Ch. 1, op. cit.

19 "He must be sworn. Boy, do you know the
nature of an oath?"
The wretched child answered by repeating some of the most common and blas-
phemous modes of execration, which, to
Richard's great horror, drew forth a peal of
laughter, some on the bench more than
smiling.
"Pho!" said the presiding magistrate,
angrily, "Do you know, sir, what will
become of those who take a false oath?"
"I have heard some say that it is bad to
swear, sir."   Ibid., Ch. 14

20 "It seems to me that the harvest is not a
miracle worked in spite of us, but a merciful
gift bestowed where we honestly labour for
it."
"You surprise me, young man: you
seem to make the growth of religion in the
soul a work of the creature, not of the Creator."
"No, sir; all the creatures that ever
lived could not make one grain of wheat to
take root downwards or to spring upwards."   Ibid., Ch. 17

21 "The weight seemed to be not only on my
head, but all over me; and then the sicken-
ing smell and the whirring noise—I'll tell
you what, the first few days in a factory
would make me ill, and when I got over
that, I should become stupid."
Ibid., Ch. 19

22 Truth is a very aggressive principle; it does
not stand still to be attacked, but marches
on, under the conduct of faith, to assail the
enemy, to make conquests, and to recover
what falsehood has stolen, or violence
wrested away. *Second Causes; or, Up and
be Doing,*
Ch. 7, op. cit.

23 Still vigilance and [the Duke of] Wellington
are one   *Poems,*
"A Sketch,"
St. 3, op. cit.

24 Scorning the rude world's idle toys,
Its faithless vows and treacherous joys. . . .
Posthumous and Other Poems,
"After a Tempest,"
St. 3, op. cit.

25 I ask not summer days and sunny skies,
Nor flow'rs in life's cold wilderness to
bloom   "The Paschal Moon,"
St. 12 (c.1826), op. cit.

26 Bridegroom of the weeping spouse!
Listen to her longing vows,
Listen to her widowed moan,
Listen to creation's groan
"Signs of the Times,"
St. 2 (1828), op. cit.

27 "The drowsy world lies dead around,

But thou, upon the turret's height,
Art watching yet—What of the night?"
"The Watchman,"
St. 1, op. cit.

28 "What seest thou watchman? look
around:"
—I see a world in madness drowned;
A drunken world that will not wake,
Till the last wrathful vial break,
And on their pillow pour a flood,
A tempest-stream of flame and blood.
Ibid., St. 3

29 A self-sold, suicidal world
Ibid., St. 4

30 Man, the proud sleeper, will not wake.
Ibid.

31 And, snow-like, still dost thou descend
Where grace her silent work hath done,
Subdue with noiseless force, and blend
Opposing natures into one.
"Christmas,"
St. 2 (December 24, 1829),
op. cit.

32 Humbly rejoicing we watch for the morn-
ing,
Morning of triumph, and rescue, and
praise—
Day-star of life, with thy lustre adorning,
Bid the wide universe bask in thy blaze.
"Easter Vigil,"
St. 7 (April 15, 1838), op. cit.

33 Oh let me share the joy of those,
Who journeyed from afar
Through wondering friends and angry foes,
To follow Bethlehem's star;
Who, when the world was dark and cold
And mocked their anxious care,
Looked up rejoicing to behold
The star of promise there.
"The Star of Bethlehem,"
St. 1, op. cit.

34 Look upon thy negro brother—
Be one moment *bound with him,*
Slave, in flesh and spirit weary—
Ponder what thy need would be—
Ponder deep the touching query

That thy brother asks of thee!
"Anti-Slavery Album,"
No. I, op. cit.

35 Erin mavourneen! Oh, when wilt thou rise
From the torpor of death that has bound
thee!
The veil of delusion is cast o'er thine eyes,
Thy children are weeping around thee.
"Erin Mavourneen,"
St. 1, op. cit.

36 Thou lov'st me, my sweet one, and would'st
not be free
From a yoke that has never borne rudely on
thee.
Ah, pleasant the empire of those to confess,
Whose wrath is a whisper, their rule a ca-
ress.
"To a Horse; written in America,"
St. 2,
The Female Poets of Great Britain,
Frederic Rowton, ed.
1853

37 How precious these moments? fair Free-
dom expands
Her pinions of light o'er the desolate lands
Ibid., St. 4

38 Haste to set thy people free;
Come; creation groans for thee!
"The Millennium,"
St. 4, op. cit.

759.   Eliza Ware Farrar
(1791–1870)

1 The queen* and princesses were all such
common-looking people that they upset my
childish notions of royalty.
Recollections of Seventy Years,
Ch. 2   1865

*Queen Charlotte (1744–1818), consort of George III
of England.

2 . . . Sir William Ellis . . . was at the head of the great lunatic asylum for paupers at Handwell near London. . . . No strait-waistcoats, no strapping patients into beds or chairs, no punishments of any kind were used,—nothing but the personal influence of Sir William and Lady Ellis; and their power over all under their care was extraordinary. Even persons in the height of an attack of mania yielded to it. Part of their system was to keep the patients as fully and as happily employed as was possible, and the whole establishment was like a great school of industry.   Ibid., Ch. 38

760. Anne Marsh
(1791–1874)

1 To say nothing of that brief but despotic sway which every woman possesses over the man in love with her—a power immense, unaccountable, invaluable; but in general so evanescent as but to make a brilliant episode in the tale of life—how almost immeasurable is the influence exercised by wives, sisters, friends, and, most of all, by mothers!   "Woman's Influence,"
Angela   1848

2 He enters life an ill-trained steed; and the best that can be hoped for him is, that the severe lash of disappointment, contradiction, and suffering, will, during the course of his career, supply the omissions of his youth, and train him at last, through much enduring, to that point from which a good education would have started him.
     Ibid.

3 The abundance of every thing around was so great, that . . . over-ripe fruit strewed the ground unheeded, while peas and bean-stalks, still loaded, were blackening and yellowing in the sun; and vegetables running on all sides to waste.

This prodigality of wealth was, however, the only thing that at all militated, to the judicious eye, against the pleasure afforded by the spectacle of these fine, well-ordered gardens.   "An English Garden,"
*Mordaunt Hall; or, A September
Night*   1849

4 Oh, vice is a hideous thing.
A hideous, dark mystery—the mystery of iniquity! Its secret springs are hidden from our view. . . .   "Sin and its
Consequences,"
op. cit.

5 But we are selfish, careless, unreflecting, blinded by inclination and passion, or by that darkness worse than death which attends upon the slothful indifference to questions of right and wrong.   Ibid.

6 A man should be forced to look steadily into the gulf of despair—or far, far, far worse—of degradation and moral ruin into which, for the gratification of the idlest vanity or licentious passion, he plunges a young, innocent, trusting creature, whose only error, it may be, was to love him too well.   "Seduction,"
op. cit.

7 He shall render a heavier account . . . because he is great, and gifted, and wise, and powerful, and fitted to guide a state and rule the interests of a nation—he shall be the less forgiven, because in the plenitude of his powers he has chosen to step aside to crush a poor little insect in its humble path—he shall be the less forgiven, because the wider the knowledge, and the higher the intellect, and the larger the observation, so much the greater is the power of estimating the claims and appreciating the sufferings of whatever breathes; and that thoughtless cruelty which we lament and pardon in the untutored child, is odious, is execrable in the man!   Ibid.

8 Nothing can compensate to any child the simple fact meeting us at the outset, that of belonging to parents not legally and inseparably united.

This is no evil created, as some have perhaps been led to think, by the artificial arrangements and conventions of man in society; its source is in nature—in that nature, the Author of which made marriage coeval with the creation of man; healthfully to rear the precious plant wherein lies the hidden germ of eternity, requires the element of home—and marriage is the foundation of the home.   "Illegitimacy,"
op. cit.

9 Wherever or howsoever the sacredness of marriage is not reverenced, depend upon it, *there* the man will ever be found imperfectly developed.   Ibid.

10 Her life had been like a confused skein of delicate and valuable thread, tangled for want of careful development.
"A Sad Spectacle,"
The Wilmingtons   1850

11 Forbear to sigh, for sighs are weakness, but brace up the feeble knees, and endeavour to amend.   Ibid.

12 She was ready to make every personal sacrifice to duty herself, but she was too fond to impose her own notions of duty upon others.   "A Narrow Mind,"
op. cit.

761.   Sarah Martin
(1791–1843)

1 I knew also that it sometimes seemed good in His sight to try the faith and patience of His servants, by bestowing upon them very limited means of support; as in the case of Naomi and Ruth; of the widow of Zarephath and Elijah; and my mind, in the contemplation of such trials, seemed exalted by more than human energy; for I had counted the cost; and my mind was made up.
Article in *Edinburgh Review*   1847

2   —"I seem to lie
So near the heavenly portals bright,
I catch the streaming rays that fly

From eternity's own light."
Ibid.

762.   Margaret Mercer
(1791–1846)

1 *Conversation is to works what the flower is to the fruit.* A godly conversation shelters and cherishes the new-born spirit of virtue, as the flower does the fruit from the cold, chill atmosphere, of a heartless world; and the beauty of holiness expanding in conversation, gives rational anticipation of noble-minded principles ripening into the richest fruits of good works.   *Ethics,* n.d.

2 ... I confess that the 'unidea-ed chatter of females' is past my endurance; they are very capable of better things, but what of that? Is it not yet more annoying that they will do nothing better?   Quoted in *Memoirs* by Caspar Morris, M.D., n.d.

3 No—if I cannot do good where there is so much to do, I never was and never will be a votary of folly.   Ibid.

4 ... *those very things that are most painful prove how much there is to do* ; and where there is much to do, steady laborious efforts to do good will doubtless be blessed, although we may in mercy be denied the luxury of seeing our work under the sun prosper.   Ibid.

5 I never knew how to be thankful to my parents, above all to my God, for a good education, until I came to look into the state of young ladies generally.
Ibid.

763.   Lydia Howard Sigourney
(1791–1865)

1 "I was a worm till I won my wings"
"Butterfly on a Child's Grave,"
St. 2, *Poems*   1834

2 Why shall we weakly mourn for those
Who dwell in perfect rest?
Bound for a few sad, fleeting years

A thorn-clad path to tread,
Oh! for the *living* spare those tears
Ye lavish on the *dead*.
"Hebrew Dirge,"
op. cit.

3 Fair boy! the wanderings of thy way,
It is not mine to trace,
Through buoyant youth's exulting day,
Or manhood's bolder race
"The Second Birth-Day,"
op. cit.

4 And sweet 'twas to see their light footsteps
advance
Like the wing of the breeze through the
maze of the dance. "Flora's Party,"
op. cit.

5 To evil habit's earliest wile
Lend neither ear, nor glance, nor smile—
Choke the dark fountain ere it flows,
Nor e'en admit the camel's nose.
"The Camel's Nose,"
St. 4, op. cit.

6 Courage, World-finder! "Columbus,"
op. cit.

7 Not on the outer world
For inward joy depend;
Enjoy the luxury of thought,
Make thine own self friend
"Know Thyself,"
op. cit.

8 The axe rang sharply 'mid those forest
shades,
Which from creation toward the sky had
tower'd
In unshorn beauty. There, with vigorous
arm,
Walked a bold emigrant, and by his side
His little son, with question and response
Beguil'd the time. "The Emigrant,"
op. cit.

9 Flow on forever, in thy glorious robe
Of terror and of beauty. "Niagara," St. 1,
Zinzendorff, and Other
Poems 1836

10 God hath set

His rainbow on thy forehead. . . .
Ibid.

11 Empress of Earth's most polish'd clime!
"The Tomb of Josephine,"*
St. 1, op. cit.

*See 661.

12 No wrath he breath'd, no conflict sought,
To no dark ambush drew,
But simply *to the Old World brought,*
The welcome of the New.
"The Indian's Welcome to the
Pilgrim Fathers,"
St. 3, op. cit.

13 But who shall heed thy children's wail,
Swept from their native land?
Ibid., St. 4

14 *Death is the test of life.*—All else is vain.
"The Test of Life,"
St. 1, op. cit.

15 Bid the long-prisoned mind attain
A sphere of dazzling day,
Bid her unpinion'd foot
The cliffs of knowledge climb,
And search for Wisdom's sacred root
That mocks the blight of time.
"Female Education,"
St. 3, op. cit.

16 They, perchance,
Did look on woman as a worthless thing,
A cloistered gem, a briefly-fading flower,
Remembering not that she had kingly
power
O'er the young soul. "Establishment of a
Female College in New-Grenada,
South America,"
St. 1, op. cit.

17 The harp of prophecy was hush'd
"It is Finish'd,"
St. 1, op. cit.

18 The way of wicknedness is hard
"Prisoner's Evening Hymn,"*
St. 3, op. cit.

*Written for the female prisoners in the Connecticut
State Prison.

19 The mind has past away, and who could
call

Its wing from out the sky?
    "The Daughter,"
    St. 4, op. cit.

20 She was a mate for angels.
    Ibid., St. 8

21 —Oh woman, oft misconstrued!
    Ibid.

22 Hope spreads her wing of plumage fair,
Rebuilds her castle bas'd on air
    "The Soap Bubble,"
    op. cit.

23 These were the seeds our mother sowed,—
Let them bear perfect fruit.
    "Filial Grief,"
    St. 4, op. cit.

24 "Where lingers life when breath is o'er,
When light and motion part?"
    "Trouble Not Yourselves, for
    His Life is in Him,"
    St. 1, op. cit.

25 Death's shafts are ever busy.
    "Death of Mr. Oliver D.
    Cooke,"
    St. 1, op. cit.

26 From the haunts
Of living men thine image may not fleet
Noteless away.   Ibid., St. 3

27 History came,
Sublimely soaring on her wing of light
    "Death of Wilberforce,"*
    St. 1, op. cit.
*William Wilberforce, English politician, philanthropist, abolitionist; d. July 29, 1833.

28 It was the evening of the day of God,
And silence reigned around.
    "On Reading the Description of
    Pompeii, in the 'Remains of the
    Rev. E. D. Griffin,' "
    St. 1, op. cit.

29 Revere thyself! for thou art wonderful
Even in thy passiveness. Hail, heir of
  Heaven!
Immortal mind! that when the body sleeps
Doth roam with unseal'd eye, on tireless
  wing,

Where Memory hath no chart, and Reason
  finds
No pole-star for her compass. Guest divine!
    "Dreams,"
    St. 1, op. cit.

30 —See, life is but a dream. Awake! Awake!
Break off the trance of vanity. . . .
    Ibid., St. 4

31 Cold world!—the teachings of thy guile
Awhile from these young hearts restrain   "Hinder Them Not,"
    St. 4, op. cit.

32 Like wild flowers among the dells, or clefts
of the rock, they [poems] sprang up wherever the path of life chanced to lead.
    Preface, *Select Poems* 1841

33   Hail, hallow'd morn!
That binds a yoke on Vice.
    "Sabbath Morning,"
    St. 3, op. cit.

34   His thrifty mate, solicitous to bear
An equal burden in the yoke of care.
    "Connecticut River,"
    St. 5, op. cit.

35 With ruthless haste he bound
The silken fringes of those curtaining lids
For ever.   "Death of an Infant,"
    St. 2 (Winter 1824), op. cit.

36   But there beamed a smile
So fixed, so holy, from that cherub brow,
Death gazed—and left it here.—
 He dare not steal
The signet ring of Heaven.
    Ibid., St. 4

37   O Man! so prodigal of pride and praise,
Thy works survive thee—dead machines
 perform
  Their revolution, while thy scythe-
 shorn days
 Yield thee a powerless prisoner to the
 worm—   "The Ancient Family
    Clock,"
    St. 10, op. cit.

38 Would they had swept cleaner!—
Here's a littering shred

Of linen left behind—a vile reproach
To all good housewifery.   "To a Shred of
                                                    Linen,"
                                        St. 1, op. cit.

39   Perchance his thought,
(For men have deeper minds than
women—sure!)
Is calculating what a thrifty wife
The maid will make. . . .   Ibid.

40   In majesty and mystery, go down
Into the paper-mill, and from its jaws
Stainless and smooth, emerge.—
Happy shall be
The renovation, if on thy fair page
Wisdom and truth, their hallow'd linea-
ments
Trace for posterity.   Ibid., St. 5

41   Thither I went,
And bade my spirit taste that lonely fount,
For which it long had thirsted 'mid the
          strife
And fever of the world.   "Solitude,"
                                        St. 2, op. cit.

42   Thou hast not left thyself in this wide world
Without a witness.   Ibid., St. 3

43   Art thou a friend?   "Thought,"
                                        St. 2, op. cit.

44   —I fear thee. Thou'rt a subtle husbandman,
Sowing thy little seed, of good or ill,
In the moist, unsunn'd surface of the heart.
                                                    Ibid.

45   I saw a cradle at a cottage door,
Where the fair mother, with her cheerful
          wheel,
Carolled so sweet a song, that the young
          bird,
Which, timid, near the threshold sought for
          seeds,
Paused on its lifted foot, and raised its head,
As if to listen.   "A Cottage Scene,"
                                        St. 1, op. cit.

46   Memory, with traitor-tread
          Methinks, doth steal away
          Treasures that the mind had laid

Up for a wintry day.
                    "Barzillai the Gileadite,"*
                                        St. 4, op. cit.
*Aged and wealthy citizen of the city of Gilead, who
befriended David when he fled from Absalom (2 Samuel 17: 27–29; 19:32).

47   And yield the torn world to the angel of
peace.   "The War Spirit,"
                                        St. 5, op. cit.

48   Come thou to life's feast
With dove-eyed meekness, and bland
          charity,
And thou shalt find even Winter's rugged
          blast
The minstrel teacher of thy well-tuned soul
                                        "Winter,"
                                        St. 4, op. cit.

49   Oh man! whose wrinkling labor is for heirs
Thou knowest not who. . . .
                                        "Benevolence,"
                                        St. 4, op. cit.

50   This is the parting place; this narrow house
                                        "The Tomb,"
                                        St. 1, op. cit.

51   "Oh, speak no ill of poetry,
          For 'tis a holy thing."
                                        "Poetry,"
                                        St. 1, op. cit.

52   Alas! how vain
The wreath that Fame would bind
          around our tomb. . . .
                              "The Dying Philosopher,"
                                        St. 4, op. cit.

53   Thou who hast toiled to earn
The fickle praise of far posterity,
Come, weigh it at the grave's brink, here
          with me,
If thou canst weigh a dream.
                                                    Ibid.

54   Lo! with swift wing I mount above your
          spheres,
To see the Invisible, to know the Unknown,
To love the Uncreated! Earth, farewell!
                                        Ibid., St. 5

55   Ye say they all have passed away,

That noble race and brave
"Indian Names,"
St. 1, op. cit.

56 But their name is on your waters,
Ye may not wash it out.
Ibid.

57   Prosperity, alas!
Is often but another name for pride
"Mistakes,"
St. 3, op. cit.

58 Long hast thou slept unnoted.
"The Mother of Washington,"*
St. 1, op. cit.

*Mary Washington. See 513.

59 And say to mothers what a holy charge
Is theirs—with what a kingly power their
love
Might rule the fountains of the new-born
mind.   Ibid., St. 5

60 Such sleep as toil alone may know
"The Western Home," St. 3,
Poems   1854

61 . . . woman's deathless constancy
Ibid., St. 6

62 For, like a child that's tired of play,
In unsuspicious dreams the quiet hamlet
lay.   Ibid., St. 31

63   Ambition in his noble heart
Hath found a flaw, and, entering, built
A nest for birds unclean.
Ibid., St. 47

64 For thou* dost teach us from the dead
A lesson that all pride should tame;
That genius high and morals base
Mar the great Giver's plan,
And, like a comet's flaming race,
Make visible the deep disgrace
Of His best gifts to man.
Ibid., St. 52

*Aaron Burr (1756–1836), third vice president of the
United States (1801–1805).

65   For fashion, or for thirst of gold.
The venal hand may diamonds link,
In velvet pile the foot may sink
The lips from jewelled chalice drink,

Yet every nerve to joy be dead,
And all the life of feeling fled
In the heart's palsied atrophy.
Ibid., St. 53

66 Make friends of potent Memory,
O young man, in thy prime
"Memory,"
St. 3, op. cit.

67 Man's warfare on the tree is terrible.
"Fallen Forests,"
St. 1, op. cit.

68   Ill fares it with a land
Where lust of gold, and wayward passions
fill
The place of righteous law.
"Micah and the Levite,"
St. 12, op. cit.

69 There is a ceaseless shaft that speeds
Unerring through the air,
A sleepless archer all unseen,
Yet active everywhere.
"The Destroyer,"
St. 1, op. cit.

70 They say that the cell of the poet should be
Like the breast of the shell that remembers
the sea   "The Muse,"
St. 1, op. cit.

71 But wilt thou list to cadences that dwell
In hermit places and in noiseless hearts?
"Listen,"
St. 1, op. cit.

72 Nature hath secret lore for those who lean
Upon her breast, with leisure in their soul
Ibid., St. 2

73   In the land where shadows reign,
Hast thou met the flocking ghosts of those
Who at thy nod were slain?
"Return of Napoleon,"
St. 14 (December 15, 1840),
op. cit.

74 Language is slow. "Unspoken Language,"
St. 1, op. cit.

75   He who would acquire
The speech of many lands, must make the
lamp

His friend at midnight, while his fellows
sleep,
Bartering to dusty lexicons and tomes
The hour-glass of his life.
                                    Ibid., St. 3

76   Yet there's a lore,
Simple and sure, that asks no discipline
Of weary years,—the language of the soul,
Told through the eye.   Ibid., St. 4

77 Think'st thou to be conceal'd, thou little
thought!
          That in the curtain'd chamber of the
          soul
Dost wrap thyself so close, and dream to do
A hidden work?   "No Concealment,"
                                    St. 3, op. cit.

78   Then up went the thrush with a trumpet call,
And the martins came forth from their cells
on the wall,
And the owlets peep'd out from their secret
bower,
And the swallows conversed on the old
church-tower,
And the council of blackbirds was long and
loud,
Chattering and flying from tree to cloud.
          "Birds of Passage," St. 6, op. cit.

79 Scholar, and child of rhyme,
This is thy holiday. No vexing fear
Of interruption, and no idler's foot
Shall mar thy revery.   "Storm Sails,"
                                    St. 5, op. cit.

80 We dream, but they awake
                    "The Holy Dead,"
                                    St. 4, op. cit.

81 . . . the few who by example teach,
Making a text-book of their own strong
heart
And blameless life.   "The Ivy," St. 4

82 No old nobility have we,
          No tyrant king to ride us;
Our sages in the capitol
          Enact the laws that guide us.
          Hail, brothers, hail!

Let nought on earth divide us.
                    "The Thriving Family,"
                                    St. 2, op. cit.

83 For every quarrel cuts a thread
          That healthful Love has spun.
                                    Ibid., St. 3

84 . . . that monitor sublime,
Teaching truths that power and prime
          Shrink to learn.
                    "Clock at Versailles,"
                                    St. 7, op. cit.

85 The influence which is most truly valuable
is that of mind over mind.
                    "Power of a Mother,"
                    Letters to Mothers, n.d.

86 Admitting that it is the profession of our
sex to teach, we perceive the mother to be
first in point of precedence, in degree of
power, in the faculty of teaching, and in the
department allotted. For in point of precedence she is next to the Creator; in power
over her pupil, limitless and without com-
petitor; in faculty of teaching, endowed
with the prerogative of a transforming love;
while the glorious department allotted is a
newly quickened soul and its immortal destiny.   Ibid.

87 This, then, is the patriotism of woman; not
to thunder in senates, or to usurp dominion,
or to seek the clarion-blast of fame, but
faithfully to teach by precept and example
that wisdom, integrity, and peace which are
the glory of a nation.
                    "Woman's Patriotism,"
                                    op. cit.

88 . . . it is important that young females
should possess some employment by which
they might obtain a livelihood in case they
should be reduced to the necessity of supporting themselves. "Sketch of a Family,"
                                    op. cit.

764. Virginie Ancelot
(1792–1875)

1 *"There are no longer any women*! no, my
dear, Count, there are no longer any
women," mournfully exclaimed the March-
ioness de Fontenay-Mareuil. . . . "
Gabrielle,
Ch. 1   1840

2 The ardent expressions of youth always unfold wholly or in part their ideas, plans,
hopes, sorrows, and pleasures. They have
so much to say that they speak often without knowing it, and altogether . . .
Ibid.

3 . . . two old people . . . would naturally be
silent if they had not resolved to
converse. . . . Sometimes, even when on the
point of speaking, if they look at each other,
they are silent; for they see those whitened
locks, those furrowed brows, those traces of
time and grief imprinted upon their countenances.   Ibid.

4 "Saloons* exist no longer; conversation has
ceased; good taste has disappeared with it,
and mind has lost all its influences."
Ibid.

*Salons.

765. Sarah Moore Grimké
(1792–1873)

1 In this sublime description of the creation
of man, (which is a generic term including
man and woman,) there is not a particle of
difference intimated as existing between
them. They were both made in the image of
God; dominion was given to both over every other creature, but not over each other.
Created in perfect equality, they were expected to exercise the vice regence intrusted
to them by their Maker, in harmony and
love. . . .   Letter to Mary S. Parker,
President of Boston Female
Anti-Slavery Society,
Amesbury (July 11, 1837),
*Letters on the Equality of the
Sexes, and the Condition of
Woman*   1838

2 . . . Adam's ready acquiescence with his
wife's proposal, does not savor much of that
superiority *in strength of mind*, which is arrogated by man.
Letter to Mary S. Parker,
from Newburyport
(July 17, 1837), op. cit.

3 The lust of dominion was probably the first
effect of the fall; and as there was no other
intelligent being over whom to exercise it,
woman was the first victim of this unhal-
lowed passion.   Letter, op. cit.

4 . . . the false translation of some passages
[of the New Testament] by the MEN who
did that work, and against the perverted in-
terpretation by the MEN who undertook to
write commentaries thereon. I am inclined
to think, when we [women] are admitted to
the honor of studying Greek and Hebrew,
we shall produce some various readings of
the Bible a little different from those we
now have.   Letter, from Haverhill
(July 17, 1837), op. cit.

5 Ah! how many of my sex feel . . . that what
they have leaned upon has proved a broken
reed at best, and oft a spear.
Ibid.

6 In most families, it is considered a matter of far more consequence to call a girl off from making a pie, or a pudding, than to interrupt her whilst engaged in her studies.
Letter, from Brookline
(1837), op. cit.

7 There is another way in which the general opinion, that women are inferior to men, is manifested. . . . I allude to the disproportionate value set on the time and labor of men and women. Ibid.

8 Our southern cities are whelmed beneath a tide of pollution; the virtue of female slaves is wholly at the mercy of irresponsible tyrants, and women are bought and sold in our slave markets, to gratify the brutal lust of those who bear the name of Christians. Ibid.

9 Woman, instead of being elevated by her union with man, which might be expected from an alliance with a superior being, is in reality lowered. She generally loses her individuality, her independent character, her moral being. She becomes absorbed into him, and henceforth is looked at, and acts through the medium of her husband.
Letter, from Brookline
(September 1837), op. cit.

10 They [women] are early taught that to appear to yield, is the only way to govern. Ibid.

11 Brute force, the law of violence, rules to a great extent in the poor man's domicile; and woman is little more than his drudge. Ibid.

12 We cannot push Abolitionism forward . . . *until* we take up the stumbling block [women's rights] out of the road.
Quoted in *Letters of Theodore Dwight Weld,* * Angelina Grimké Weld** and Sarah Grimké, 1822–1844,*
Vol. I, Gilbert H. Barnes and Dwight L. Dumond, eds.
1934

*American abolitionist (1803–1895).

**American abolitionist and feminist (1805–1879). See *The Quotable Woman: 1800–1981,* Contributor 18.

766. Harriet Grote
(1792–1878)

1 Politics and theology are the only two really great subjects. Letter to Lord Rosebery*
(September 16, 1880),
Quoted in *Life of Gladstone*
by John Morley Morly,
Bk. VIII, Ch. 1 1903
*Archibald Philip Primrose, fifth earl of Rosebery (1847–1929), English statesman.

767. Anne Isabella Milbanke
(1792–1860)

1 Yes! Farewell—farewell forever!
Thou thyself has fixed our doom,
Bade hope's fairest blossoms wither,
Ne'er again for me to bloom.
"Fare Thee Well"
(to Lord Byron)
c.January 1816

768. Caroline Symonds
(1792–1803)

1 Simple flow'ret! child of May!
Though hid from the broad gaze of day,
Doom'd in the shade thy sweets to shed,
Unnotic'd droops thy languid head;
Still nature's darling thou'lt remain
"The Harebell,"
The Female Poets of Great Britain, Frederic Rowton, ed.
1853

2 She planted, she lov'd it, she water'd its head,
And its bloom every rival defied;
But alas! what was beauty or virtue, soon fled,
In Spring they both blossom'd and died. "The Faded Rose, which grew on the tomb of Zelida,"
St. 4, op. cit.

3 And since my dear Zelida's torn from my
    arms,
There is nothing I love, but despair.
                            Ibid., St. 5

4 Scarce had thy velvet lips imbib'd the dew,
    And nature hail'd thee, infant queen of
        May;
    Scarce saw thy opening bloom the
        sun's broad ray,
And on the air its tender fragrance threw;
When the north wind enamour'd of thee
    grew,
And from his chilling kiss, thy charms
    decay   "The Blighted Rosebud,"*
                            op. cit.

*Inscribed on the tomb of the writer, who died at the
age of eleven.

769.   Sarah Taylor Austin
(1793–1867)

1 It is the peculiar and invaluable privilege of
a translator, as such, to have no opinions,
and this is precisely what renders the somewhat toilsome business of translating attractive to one who has a profound sense of
the difficulty of forming mature and coher-
ent opinions, and of the presumption of putting forth crude and incongruous ones. . . .
                    Translator's Preface,
            *England in 1835: being a series
            of Letters written to friends in
                    Germany . . . ,*
            by Frederick von Raumer
                            1836

770.   Felicia Dorothea Hemans
(1793–1835)

1 We will give the names of our fearless race
To each bright river whose course we trace.
                    "Song of Emigration,"
                        Works   1839

2 The stately homes of England!
    How beautiful they stand,
    Amidst their tall ancestral trees,

O'er all the pleasant land!
                "The Homes of England," St. 1,
                            op. cit.

3 The breaking waves dash'd high
    On a stern and rock-bound coast,
And the woods, against a stormy sky,
    Their giant branches toss'd.
                "The Landing of the Pilgrim
                    Fathers in New England,"
                        St. 1, op. cit.

4   . . . A band of exiles moored their bark
On the wild New England shore.
                            Ibid., St. 2

5 Ay, call it holy ground,
    The soil where first they trod!
They have left unstained what there they
    found—
    Freedom to worship God!
                            Ibid., St. 10

6 The boy stood on the burning deck,
    Whence all but he had fled.
                        "Casabianca,"
                        St. 1, op. cit.

7 The flames rolled on; he would not go
    Without his father's word.
                            Ibid., St. 3

8   Leaves have their time to fall,
And flowers to wither at the north-wind's
    breath,
    And stars to set—but all,
Thou hast *all* seasons for thine own, O
Death!   "The Hour of Death,"
                        St. 1, op. cit.

9 In the busy haunts of men
                "Tale of the Secret Tribunal,"
                    Pt. I, 1. 203, op. cit.

10 I, too, shepherd, in Arcadia dwelt.
                            "Song,"
                            op. cit.

11 "Passing away" is written on the world and
    all the world contains.
                        "Passing Away,"
                            op. cit.

12 In the music-land of dreams.
"The Sleeper,"
op. cit.

13 Go, stranger! track the deep,
Free, free, the white sail spread!
Wave may not foam, nor wild wind sweep,
Where rest not England's dead.
"England's Dead,"
op. cit.

14 Have ye left the greenwood lone,
Are your steps for ever gone?
Fairy King and Elfin Queen,
Come ye to the sylvan scene,
From your dim and distant shore,
Never more? "Fairy Song,"
op. cit.

15 They speak of hope to the fainting heart,
With a voice of promise they come and
part,
They sleep in dust through the wintry
hours,
They break forth in glory—bring flowers,
bright flowers! "Bring Flowers,"
op. cit.

16 Life's best balm—forgetfullness.
"The Caravan in the Desert,"
op. cit.

17 There smiles no Paradise on earth so fair
But guilt will raise avenging phantoms
there. "The Abencerrage,"
Canto I, 1.33, op. cit.

18 I hear thee speak of the better land
"The Better Land,"
op. cit.

19 Dreams cannot picture a world so fair—
Sorrow and death may not enter there;
Time doth not breathe on its fadeless
bloom,
For beyond the clouds, and beyond the
tomb,
It is there, it is there, my child!
Ibid.

20 Dust, to its narrow house beneath!
Soul, to its place on high!
They that have seen thy look in death

No more may fear to die.
"Dirge,"
op. cit.

21 Home of the Arts! where glory's faded smile
Sheds lingering light o'er many a moulder-
ing pile. "Restoration of the
Works of Art to Italy,"
op. cit.

22 Oh! what a crowded world one moment
may contain. "The Last Constantine,"
op. cit.

23 There is strength,
And a fierce instinct, even in common
souls,
To bear up manhood with a stormy joy
When red swords meet in lightning.
"The Siege of Valencia,"
op. cit.

24 There is none,
In all this cold and hollow world, no fount
Of deep, strong, deathless love, save that
within
A mother's heart! Ibid.

25 We endow
Those whom we love, in our fond,
passionate blindness,
With power upon our souls too absolute
To be a mortal's trust. Ibid.

26 They grew in beauty side by side,
They fill'd one home with glee;—
Their graves are severed far and wide
By mount, and stream, and sea.
"The Graves of a Household,"
op. cit.

27 Oh, lightly, lightly tread!
A holy thing is sleep
"The Sleeper,"
op. cit.

28 Talk not of grief till thou hast seen the tears
of warlike men! "Bernardo del Carpio,"
l. 26, op. cit.

29 Oh! call my brother back to me!
I cannot play alone;
The summer comes with flower and bee—

Where is my brother gone?
       "The Child's First Grief,"
            St. 1, op. cit.

30 Is *all* that we see or seem
But a dream within a dream?
      "A Dream Within a Dream,"
          last lines, op. cit.

31 Thou hast a charmed cup, O Fame
A draught that mantles high,
And seems to lift this earthly frame
Above mortality.
Away! to me—a woman—bring sweet waters from affection's spring!
           Untitled, op. cit.

32 Thou art like night, O sickness! deeply stilling
           Untitled, op. cit.

771. Lucretia Mott
(1793–1880)

1 Let woman then go on—not asking as favour, but claiming as right, the removal of all the hindrances to her elevation in the scale of being—let her receive encouragement for the proper cultivation of all her powers, so that she may enter profitably into the active business of life; employing her own hands in ministering to her necessities, strengthening her physical being by proper exercise and observance of the laws of health. *Discourse on Women*   1850

2 Then, in the marriage union, the independence of the husband and wife will be equal, their dependence mutual, and their obligations reciprocal.   Ibid.

3 Look at the heads of those [Quaker] women; they can mingle with men; they are not triflers; they have intelligent subjects of conversation.
      Women's Rights Convention,
          Proceedings   1853

4 Learning, while at school, that the charge for the education of girls was the same as that for boys, and that, when they became teachers, women received only half as much as men for their services, the injustice of this distinction was so apparent, that I resolved to claim for my sex all that an impartial Creator had bestowed, which, by custom and a perverted application of the Scriptures, had been wrested from woman.
      Letter, Quoted in *Biography of*
           Distinguished Women
      by Sarah Josepha Hale   1876

5 The cause of Peace has had a share of my efforts, taking the ultra non-resistance ground—that a Christian cannot consistently uphold, and actively support, a government based on the sword, or whose ultimate resort is to the destroying weapon.
           Ibid.

6 ... systems by which the rich are made richer, and the poor poorer, should find no favour among people professing to "fear God and hate covetousness."
           Ibid.

7 I ask no courtesy at your hands on account of my sex.   Quoted in *Lucretia Mott*
      by Otelia Cromwell   1958

8 I grew up so thoroughly imbued with women's rights that it was the most important question of my life from a very early day.   Ibid.

9 It is not Christianity, but priestcraft that has subjected woman as we find her. The Church and State have been united, and it is well for us to see it so. Speech, Woman's
      Rights Convention, Philadelphia
           (1854),
      Quoted in *Feminism, The*
          Essential Writings
      by Miriam Schneir   1972

10 Such dupes are men to custom that even servitude, the worst of ills, comes to be thought a good, till down sire to son it is kept and guarded as a sacred thing.
           Ibid.

11 The veneration of man has been misdirected, the pulpit has been prostituted, the Bible has been ill-used.

Ibid.

12 We too often bind ourselves by authorities rather than by the truth.   Ibid.

13 Truth for authority, not authority for truth.

Motto, Quoted in
The Peerless Leader
by Hibben, n.d.

772. Almira Lincoln Phelps
(1793–1884)

1 Novels and poetry are, indeed, the flowers of literature; they afford opportunity for the display of genius, and are pleasant companions for an idle or heavy hour.

"Works of Fiction,"
*Female Student, or Fireside
Friend*   c.1832

2 For yet, alas! the real ills of life
Claim the full vigour of a mind prepared,
Prepared for patient, long, laborious strife,
Its guide *experience*, and *truth* its guard.

Ibid.

3 As sure as there is a future state of existence, so there is a moral influence to be exerted by every human being according to the measure of his abilities.

"Moral Influence,"
op. cit.

4 To discharge aright the duties of life requires not only that the intellect shall be enlightened, but that heart shall be purified.

"Education,"
op. cit.

5 Most of the distinguished men of our country have made their own fortunes; most of them began life knowing that they could hope for no aid or patronage, but must rely solely upon the energies of their own minds and the blessing of God.

"Energy of Mind,"
op. cit.

6 What a pledge for virtuous conduct is the character of a mother!

"The Mother's Hopes,"
The Mother's Journal   1838

7 So, in the physical world mankind are prone to seek an explanation of *uncommon* phenomena only, while the ordinary changes of nature, which are in themselves equally wonderful, are disregarded.

"An Infant's First Ideas,"
op. cit.

8 How often are the beauties of nature unheeded by man, who, musing on past ills, brooding over the possible calamities of the future, building castles in the air, or wrapped up in his own self-love and self-importance, forgets to look abroad, or looks with a vacant stare.

"The Child and Nature,"
op. cit.

9 I have preferred a life of usefulness, to exercise the talents which God has given me, to one of indolence. Quoted in *Almira Hart
Lincoln Phelps:
Her Life and Work*
by Emma Lydia Bolzau   1936

10 The universe, how vast! exceeding far
The bounds of human thought; millions of
suns,
With their attendant worlds moving
around
Some common centre, gravitation strange!
Beyond the power of finite minds to scan!

"The Wonders of Nature,"
St. 1, *Poems*, n.d.

11 Each opening bud, and care-perfected seed,
Is as a page, where we may read of God.

Ibid., St. 3

773. Sarah Alden Ripley
(1793–1867)

1 What a vista! A whole new language!*

Quoted in *Notable American Women*,
Edward T. James, ed.   1971

*Reaction to Cervantes' *Don Quixote*.

2 I have not your faith to console me . . . yet my will, I trust, is resigned where light is wanting.   Letter to her sister-in-law, op. cit.

3 The sun looks brighter . . . as the evening of life draws near.   Ibid.

774.   Catherine Spalding
(1793–1858)

1 My heart still clings to the orphans.
Quoted in *Notable American Women*, Edward T. James, ed.   1971

775.   Caroline Gilman
(1794–1888)

1 Change! Sameness! What a perpetual chime those words ring on the ear of memory!
Recollections of a Southern Matron, Ch. 1
1837

2 I thank thee, Heaven, that all I love are here!—that stranger-dust mingles not with mine! The tumult of the city rolls not across this sanctuary; careless curiosity treads not on these secluded graves; nor does the idler cull the blossoms that affection has planted, or that time, with unsparing hand, has hung in graceful wreaths or clustered beauty around.   Ibid.

3 One clear idea is too precious a treasure to lose.   Ibid., Ch. 3

4 I know how the mind rushes back, in such moments, to infancy, when those stiffened hands were wrapped around us in twining love; when that bosom was the pillow of our first sorrows; when those ears, now insensible and soundless, heard our whispered confidence; when those eyes, now curtained by uplifted lids, watched our every motion. I know the pang that runs through the heart, and I can fancy the shrieking voice within which says, "Thou mightst have done more for thy mother's happiness, for her who loved thee so!"   Ibid.

5 Oh, dark, dark moment, when the fear of death is roused without its hopes, and we see the gloom of the grave untinged by the dawn of salvation.   Ibid.

6 There is no moral object so beautiful to me than a conscientious young man!
Ibid., Ch. 7

7 "Intellectual women are the most modest inquirers after truth, and accomplished women often the most scrupulous observers of social duty."   Ibid.

8 I must ask indulgence of general readers for mingling so much of the peculiarities of negroes with my details. Surrounded with them from infancy, they form a part of the landscape of a southern woman's life; take them away, and the picture would lose half its reality. They watch our cradles; they are the companions of our sports; it is they who aid our bridal decorations, and they wrap us in our shroud.   Ibid., Ch. 14

9 His strong and ardent mind was realizing its dependence. God was receiving the tribute which, sooner or later, awaits his power from every heart.   Ibid.

10 What a blessed thing to childhood is the fresh air and light of heaven! . . . What a blessed thing to *all* is it to enjoy that light, and bathe in that air, whatever may be their deprivation!   Ibid., Ch. 16

11 Go, youthful visionary, enjoy thy flitting happiness! No cold philosophy shall trammel the power, which a kind Providence has given thee, of happy creations . . . reality will come full soon. . . .
Ibid.

12 Correct pronunciation is equally important with distinct emphasis.   Ibid., Ch. 18

13 Death had little to do to crush her shattered frame; . . . and the throbbings of one of the softest hearts that ever ached under the burden of earth's woes were still.
Ibid., Ch. 22

14 ...it is death—there is its stillness—its shroud—its fixed and pale repose; the voice tells not its wants—the eye knows not. We bend over the stiffened form, and turn away, and come not again, for it is death; perchance we lift the bloodless hand, or smooth the straying hair, but only once, for it is death, and we are chilled.

         Ibid., Ch. 23

15 ... convert schools into places for *teaching* instead of *recitation* .... If the system continue as it is, the name of *teacher* should be changed to *lesson-hearer.*   *Ibid.*, Ch. 28

16 ... sitting down to *one* plate, that loneliest of all positions....   *Ibid.*, Ch. 35

17 To repress a harsh answer, to confess a fault, and to stop (right or wrong) in the midst of self-defence, in gentle submission, sometimes requires a struggle like life and death; but these *three* efforts are the golden threads with which domestic happiness is woven; once begin the fabric with this woof, and trials shall not break or sorrow tarnish it.   *Ibid.*

18 Men are not often unreasonable; their difficulties lie in not understanding the moral and physical structure of our sex. They often wound through ignorance, and are surprised at having offended. How clear is it, then, that woman loses by petulance and recrimination! Her first study must be self-control, almost to hypocrisy.

        Ibid.

19 Space for the sunflower,
  Bright with yellow glow
    To court the sky.
       "To the Ursulines,"
    Verses of a Life-Time   1849

20 You must know I've resolved and agreed
  My books from room not to lend,
  But you may sit by my fire and read.
      "One Good Turn Deserves
          Another,"
           op. cit.

776.   Anna Brownell Jameson
(1794–1860)

1 I have heard young artists say, that they have been forced on a dissipated life merely as a means of "getting on in the world" as the phrase is.... The men who talk thus are doomed; they will either creep through life in mediocrity and dependence to the grave; or, at the best, if they have parts as well as cunning and assurance, they may make themselves the fashion, and make their fortune; they may be clever portrait painters and bustmakers, but when they attempt to soar into the ideal department of their art, they move the laughter of Gods and men; to them higher, holier fountains of inspiration are thenceforth sealed.

         "Artists,"
   Visits and Sketches at Home and
       Abroad; With Tales and
         Miscellanies   1834

2 To think of the situations of these women!... steeped in excitement from childhood, their nerves for ever in a state of terror between severe application and maddening flattery; cast on the world without chart or compass—with energies misdirected, passions uncontrolled, and all the inflammable and imaginative part of their being cultivated to excess as part of their profession—of their material!

     "Women Artists—Singers—
         Actresses, &C.,"
          op. cit.

3 In what respect is a female gambler worse than a male? The case is more pitiable—more rare—therefore, perhaps, more shocking; but why more hateful?

        "Female Gambler,"
          op. cit.

4 It is this cold impervious pride which is the perdition of us English, and of England.

         "English Pride,"
          op. cit.

5 ... that indescribable air of high pretension, so elegantly impassive—so self-possessed—which some people call *l'air distingué*, but which, as extremes meet, I would rather call the refinement of vulgarity—the polish we see bestowed on debased material—the plating over the steel—the stucco over the brick-work!

Ibid.

6 Conversation may be compared to a lyre with seven chords—philosophy, art, poetry, politics, love, scandal, and the weather. "Conversation," op. cit.

7 Truth is the golden chain which links the terrestrial with the celestial, which sets the seal of heaven on the things of this earth, and stamps them with immortality.

The Loves of the Poets c.1835

8 The true purpose of education is to cherish and unfold the seed of immortality already sown within us; to develop, to their fullest extent, the capacities of every kind with which the God who made us has endowed us. "Education," *Winter Studies and Summer Rambles* 1842

9 The human soul, be it man's or woman's, is not, I suppose, an empty bottle, into which you shall pour and cram just what you like, and as you like; nor a plot of waste soil, in which you shall sow what you like; but a divine, a living germ planted by an Almighty hand, which you may, indeed, render more or less productive, or train to this or that form—no more. Ibid.

10 Piety in art—poetry in art—Puseyism* in art—let us be careful how we confound them. "The House of Titan," *Memoirs and Essays Illustrative of Art, Literature, and Social Mores* 1846

*Edward Bouverie Pusey (1800–1882), English clergyman, active in the Oxford Movement and propounder of the Real Presence doctrine.

11 He that seeks popularity in art closes the door on his own genius: as he must needs paint for other minds, and not for his own. "Washington Allston,"* op. cit.

*American painter (1779–1843).

12 Reputation being essentially contemporaneous, is always at the mercy of the Envious and the Ignorant. But Fame, whose very birth is *posthumous*, and which is only *known to exist by the echo of its footsteps through congenial minds*, can neither be increased nor diminished by any degree of willfulness. Ibid.

13 The only competition worthy a wise man is with himself. Ibid.

14 Reputation is but a synonym of popularity: dependent on suffrage, to be increased or diminished at the will of the voters.

Ibid.

15 A man may be as much a fool from the want of sensibility as the want of sense. *Detached Thoughts*, n.d.

16 As the rolling stone gathers no moss, so the roving heart gathers no affections. "Sternberg's Novels," *Studies*, n.d.

777. Maria Brooks
(1795–1845)

1 My ills are my desert, my good thy gift. "Hymn," St. 3, *Judith, Esther and Other Poems* 1820

2 Oh, moon of flowers! oh, moon of flowers!*
In scenes afar were passed those hours,
Which still with fond regret I see,
And wish my heart could change like thee!
"The Moon of Flowers," St. 3, op. cit.

*May is referred to as "the moon of flowers" by some North American Indians.

3 An eagle rests upon the wind's sweet breath;

Feels he the charm? woos he the scene
beneath?
He eyes the sun; nerves his dark wing again.
"To Niagara,"
St. 6, op. cit.

4 "Niagara! wonder of this western world,
And half the world beside! hail,
beauteous queen
Of cataracts!" Ibid., St. 7

5 Day, in melting purple dying.
"Song,"
St. 1, op. cit.

6 Save thy toiling, spare thy treasure:
All I ask is friendship's pleasure;
Let the shining ore lie darkling,
Bring no gem in lustre sparkling:
Gifts and gold are naught to me,
I would only look on thee!
Ibid., St. 3

7 Looks are its food, its nectar sighs,
Its couch the lips, its throne the eyes,
The soul its breath: and so possest,
Heaven's raptures reign in mortal breast,
Fratello del mio cor. "Friendship,"
St. 2, op. cit.

8 Was this sweet wilderness,
This distant world, then visited by you?
Canto First,
"Grove of Acadias,"
IV, St. 2,
*Zóphiël; or the Bride of
Seven* 1825

9 . . . whisper my trembling muse!
Ibid., V, St. 1

10 Man, thing of heaven and earth, why,
thou wert made,

Ev'n spirits knew not! yet they loved to
sport
With thy mysterious mind; and lent
their powers,
The good to benefit, the ill to hurt.
Dark fiends assailed thee, in thy dangerous hours Ibid., VII, Sts. 3, 4

11 Who would not brave a fiend to share an angel's smile? Ibid., VIII, St. 1

12 Where passion is not found, no virtue ever
dwelt. Ibid., X, St. 1

13 . . . innate Pride, that queen of noble minds
Ibid., XIII, St. 2

14 "The bird that sweetest sings can least endure the storm." Ibid., XIV, St. 1

15 But thou,* too bright and pure for mortal
touch,
Art like those brilliant things we never taste
Or see, unless with Fancy's lip and eye,
When maddened by her mystic spells, we
waste
Life on a thought, and rob reality.
Ibid., XX, Sts. 1, 2
*The passionflower.

16 . . . Reverie,
Sweet mother of the muses, heart and soul
are thine! Ibid., XXII, St. 1

17 "Distrust my wisdom; but regard my
truth!" Ibid., XXV, St. 1

18 "Man found thee, death: but Death and
dull decay,
Baffling, by aid of thee, his mastery
proves;
By mighty works he swells his narrow day,
And reigns, for ages, in the world he
loves." Ibid., LII, St. 7

19 "He who would gain
A fond, full heart, in love's soft surgery
skill'd,
Should seek it when 'tis sore; allay its pain
With balm by pity prest: 'tis all his
own so heal'd." Ibid., LX, St. 2

20 Nature upon her children oft bestows
The quick, untaught perception; and
while art
O'ertasks himself with guile, loves to dis-
close
The dark thought in the eye, to warn
the o'er-trusting heart.
Ibid., XCII, St. 1

21 He who beheld her hand forgot her face;
Yet in that face was all beside forgot
Ibid., Canto Second,
"Death of Altheëtor,"
LI, St. 1

22 When light, love, music, beauty, all dis-
pense
   Their wild comingling charms, who
   shall control
The gushing torrent of attracted sense,
   And keep the forms of memory and of
   soul?   Ibid., LVI, St. 1

23 He saw what fever raged, and knew its balm
                          Ibid., XCIV, St. 2

24 His warm devoted soul no terror knows,
   And truth and love lend fervour to his
   song.   Ibid., XCVII, St. 1

25 'Tis now the hour of mirth, the hour of love,
   The hour of melancholy: Night, as
   vain
Of her full beauty, seems to pause above,
   That all may look upon her ere it
   wane.   Ibid., Canto Third,
                          "Palace of Gnomes,"
                          I, St. 1

26 He'd hear a tale of bliss, and not aspire
   To taste himself; 'twas meet for his
   compeer.   Ibid., XIII, St. 1

27 Soul, I would rein thee in
                          Ibid., XXXII, St. 1

28 Soul, what a mystery thou art! not one
   Admires, or loves, or worships virtue
   more
Than I; but passion hurls me on, till torn
By keen remorse, I cool, to curse me
   and deplore.   Ibid., XXXIII, St. 1

29 Is there a heart that ever loved in vain,
   Tho years have thrown their veil o'er
   all most dear,
That lives not each sensation o'er again
   In sympathy with sounds like those
   that mingle here?   Ibid., CVII, St. 1

30 How can I longer bear my weary doom?
   Alas! what have I gain'd for all I lost?
                          Ibid., CIX, St. 4

31 "Pain had a joy, for suffering could but
   wring
   Love from my soul. . . . "
                          Canto Fourth,
                          "The Storm,"
                          XLVI, St. 1

32 . . . cold ambition mimicks love so well,
   That half the sons of heaven looked on deceived   Ibid., XLVIII, St. 2

33 How beauteous art thou, O thou morning
   sun?—
   The old man, feebly tottering forth,
   admires
As much thy beauty, now life's dream is
   done,
   As when he moved exulting in his fires.
                          Ibid., Canto Fifth,
                          "Zameïa," I, St. 1

34 How thrills the kiss, when feeling's voice is
   mute!   Ibid., III, St. 1

35   "Women may be
Enthrall'd by love, and often will forsake
   All other gods for love's idolatry."
                          Ibid., XXII, St. 3

36   "If evil things can give
Dreams such as mine, let me turn foe to
   good,
   And make a God of Evil while I live!"
                          Ibid., XXIV, St. 1

37   "Tis not given
   To son of mortal (though he even may
   be
O'erwatch'd and well-beloved by those in
   heaven)
   To know what beings sway his destiny
                          Ibid., XXIX, St. 1

38 And love and hope are twins. . . .
                          Ibid., XCVI, St. 1

39 "The frailest hope is better than despair"
                          Ibid., CII, St. 1

40 Alas! unless her Meles* come to crown
   With fruit, hope's blossoms cannot
      long endure!   Ibid., CXIII, St. 1
*Lover of Zameïa (eponymous/heroine of Canto
Fifth).

41 But thousand evil things there are that hate
   To look on happiness
                          Ibid., Canto Sixth,
                          "Bridal of Helon,"
                          IV, St. 1

42 So many a soul o'er life's drear desert far-
ing,
   Love's pure congenial spring un-
     found—unquaff'd—
Suffers—recoils—then, thirsty and despair-
ing
   Of what it would, descends and sips
     the nearest draught.
                        Ibid., St. 3

43 What—where is heaven? (earth's sweetest
   lips exclaim;)
   In all the holiest seers have writ or
     said,
   Blurred are the pictures given:
   We know not what is heaven,
   Save by those views, mysteriously
     spread,
When the soul looks afar by light of her
   own flame.   *Ode to the Departed*,
                     St. 3   1844

44 Wild fears of dark annihilation, go!
   Be warm, ye veins, now blackening
     with despair!
   Years o'er thee have revolved,
   My first-born—thou 'rt dissolved—
   All—every tint—save a few ringlets
     fair—
Still, if thou didst not live, how could I love
   thee so?   *Ibid.*, St. 7

45 Heaven's hands, howe'er profuse, no
atom's loss allow.   *Ibid.*, St. 24

778.   Frances Manwaring Caulkins
(1795–1869)

1 The divine command to "remember the
days of old, and consider the years of many
generations," so often repeated in varying
terms in Holy Writ, is an imperative argument for the preservation of memorials of
the past. The hand of God is seen in the history of towns as well as in that of nations.
The purest and noblest love of the olden
time is that which draws from its annals,
motives of gratitude and thanksgiving for
the past—counsels and warnings for the future.   Preface, *History of New London,*
              Connecticut   1852

2 The tendency of man among savages, without the watch of his equals and the check of
society, is to degenerate; to decline from the
standard of morals, and gradually to relin-
quish all Christian observances.
                         Ibid., Ch. 6

3 Many excellent men in that day, were believers in impressions, impulses and ecsta-
cies. Imagination was trusted more than
judgment, and transports of feeling were
valued beyond the decisions of reason. Such
a state of things naturally tends to destroy
the equilibrium of the character. Despair,
melancholy, mania, are but a step distant
from the religious enthusiast.
                      Ibid., Ch. 26

779.   Rebecca Cox Jackson
(1795–1871)

1 And I felt, that I was dependent on the
Lord every moment for instruction or I
would fall into temptation. And this spirit
of secret and continual prayer was my wall
of defense.   From her Autobiography
                        (1830–1832),
             in *Gift of Powers, The Writings*
              of Rebecca Jackson, Black
             Visionary, Shaker Eldress,
            Jean McMahon Humez, ed.
                           1981

2 She [Sister A. B.] was jealous, and where
that rules, confusion reigns.
                            Ibid.

3 Yet when I would think how she [Sister A. B.] had stopped the progressive work of God in our little meeting with a wicked heart and by a lying tongue, I *would* think hard of her, and I knowed that I could not do it without sinning against God. He showed me at the beginning that I must love and pray for my enemies, and that vengeance belongs to God. So I knowed all power both in Heaven, earth, and in Hell belonged to God, so I entreated the Lord in prayer, fasting and crying, that if He would give me power over that feeling at all times, I would be willing to suffer all manner of persecution. Ibid.

4 I always believed that if the Lord had a work for His children to do, He was able to make it as plain as the light.
Ibid. (1833–1836)

5 Jesus, the seed of the woman, is the manhood in which the seed of God dwells. Which seed is called the Godhead dwelling in manhood. Ibid. (1844–1851)

6 The fear of God is the beginning of Wisdom. . . . Ibid.

7 The ministers of Christ are as busy in the spirit world, preaching the Gospel of full salvation to souls out of the body, as the ministers of Antichrist are here, preaching for money and marrying and giving in marriage, in this great day of God Almighty, wherein He is judging both the quick and the dead, in time and in eternity. Rebecca Jackson. Ibid., Last entry (June 4, 1864)

780.   Frances Wright
(1795–1852)

1 . . . the road to the senate house shall lead through streets adorned with temples and palaces . . . the rulers of the republic . . . shall roll in chariots . . . through a sumptuous metropolis, rich in arts and bankrupt in virtue. *Views of Society & Manners in America* 1821

2 The prejudices still to be found in Europe . . . which would confine . . . female conversation to the last new publication, new bonnet, and *pas seul* [nothing else] are entirely unknown here. The women are assuming their place as thinking beings. . . .
Ibid.

3 It is not as of yore. Eve puts not forth her hand to gather the fair fruit of knowledge. The wily serpent now hath better learned his lesson; and, to secure his reign in the garden, beguileth her *not* to eat.
Course of Popular Lectures 1829

4 As if truth could be of less importance to the young than to the old; or as if the sex which in all ages has ruled the destinies of the world, could be less worth enlightening than that which only follows its lead!
Ibid.

5 . . . whenever we establish our own pretensions upon the sacrificed rights of others, we do in fact impeach our own liberties, and lower ourselves in the scale of being!
Ibid.

6 . . . women, wherever placed, however high or low in the scale of cultivation, hold the destinies of humankind.
Ibid.

7 Let them not imagine that they know aught of the delights which intercourse with the other sex can give, until they have felt the sympathy of mind with mind, and heart with heart; until they bring into that intercourse every affection, every talent, every confidence, every refinement, every respect.
Ibid.

8 Jealousies, envying, suspicions, reserves, deceptions—these are the fruits of inequality. Ibid.

9 Let us enquire—not if a mother be a wife, or a father a husband, but if parents can supply, to the creatures they have brought into being, all things requisite to make existence a blessing.   (1828), Quoted in *Frances Wright, Free Enquirer* by A. J. G. Perkins and Theresa Wolfson   1939

10 Co-operation has well nigh killed us all.   Ibid.

11 The girl who can her fault deny
Will always at the end be winner;
'Tis she who does for pardon cry
That's held the sinner.
      "The Complaisant Swan," n.d.

781.   Sophia Smith
(1796–1870)

1 It is my opinion that by the higher and more thoroughly Christian education of women, what are called their "wrongs" will be redressed, their wages will be adjusted, their weight of influence in reforming the evils of society will be greatly increased; as teachers, as writers, as mothers, as members of society, their power for good will be incalculably enlarged.   *Last Will and Testament of Miss Sophia Smith, Late of Hatfield, Massachusetts* 1871

782.   Annette Elizabeth von Droste-Hülshoff
(1797–1848)

1 A silence fiercer than the thunder's blare
Moved through the starless highways of the air.
No breath of life was stirred on all the earth. . . .   "Gethsemane," St. 1, *The Catholic Anthology,* Thomas Walsh, ed.   1927

2 The sun still sailed the blue; a lily stalk
Greeted the Saviour on the dewy grass,
From out its chaliced pearl the Angel came
To strengthen him.   Ibid., St. 5

3 At night, when heavenly peace is flying
Above the world that sorrow mars,
Ah, think not of my grave with sighing!
For then I greet you from the stars.
     "Last Words,"
St. 3, op. cit.

4 So still the pond in morning's gray,
A quiet conscience is not clearer.
     "The Pond" ("*Der Weiher*"),
Herman Salinger, tr.;
An Anthology of German Poetry from Hölderlin to Rilke,
Angel Flores, ed.   1960

5 The first star rises overhead
Beyond the reaching tree,
And seems to pause, as though to shed
Astronomy.   "The House in the Heath"
("*Das Haus in der Heide*"),
St. 7, James Edward Tobin, tr.,
op. cit.

6 O spirit free, entrancing youth,
Here at the very railing, I
Would wrestle, hip to hip, against
Your hold; become alive—or die.
     "On the Tower" ("*Am Turme*"),
St. 1, James Edward Tobin, tr.,
op. cit.

7 If heaven listened to my plea,
Made me a man, even though small!
Instead, I sit here—delicate,
Polite, precise, well-mannered child.
Dreams shake my loosened hair—the wind
Lone listener to my spirit wild.
     Ibid., St. 4

8 When you look back at me with surprise,
Out of the misty orbs of your eyes,
Like comets, each a vanishing bubble,
With features in which, passing strange,
Two souls around each other range
Like spies, then whispering words we exchange—
Phantom, you are not my double!
     "The Reflection in the Mirror"
("*Das Spiegelbild*"),
St. 1, Herman Salinger, tr.,
op. cit.

9 Up toward the ruling throne of your brow,

Where thoughts like humble servants bow
Ibid., St. 3

10 This much is sure: you are not I
Ibid., St. 5

11 If you eluded the mirror's band,
Phantom, if you set foot on land,
I'd only tremble slightly, and—
I think for you, for you I'd weep.
Ibid., St. 6

12 Now nearly all's asleep that lives and breathes;
The final doors of bedrooms slowly creak
"Sleepless Night"
("*Durchwachte Nacht*"),
St. 2, Herman Salinger, tr.,
op. cit.

13 O slumber-waking strange, are you the certain
Curse of delicate nerves or yet their blessing?
Ibid., St. 4

14 And—hark! the clock hands wake in fright!
It is midnight.
Ibid., St. 5

15 ... dreams release the soul's love urge
Ibid., St. 6

16 How terrified I was,—O image dear,
Where have you gone, dissolving with the dark!
Unwelcome gray of dawning trickles near.
Ibid., St. 12

17 Up flames from orient lands—the sun's bright blood!
Ibid., St. 13

18 And glacierlike the lands of dream now shrink
And vanish on horizon's burning brink.
Ibid.

19 ... all the ghosts within your breast
(Dead love, dead pleasure, and dead time)
"In the Grass" ("*Im Grase*"),
St. 2, James Edward Tobin, tr.,
op. cit.

20   ... Heaven, grant to me
One gift: for every bird's bright voice
A spirit matching the blue, free,

Limitless sky which is its choice.
Ibid., St. 4

21 O Moon, to me thou art a late-come friend
"Moonrise" ("*Mondesaufgang*"),
St. 6, Herman Salinger, tr.,
op. cit.

22 No sun art thou that blinds and that inspires,
And bleeding ends after a life in fires—
Thou art what to the ailing singer his poem,
Distant, but oh! the mild, mild light of home.
Ibid.

23 The year is at its close,
A spindle ravels thinning thread;
One strand is left, a single hour.
And time, a glowing, pulsing rose,
Will crumble as a final flower,
Dusty and dead.
"The Last Day of the Year"
("*Am letzten Tage des Jahres*"),
St. 1, James Edward Tobin, tr.,
op. cit.

24   Minutes, like rivers, shake
The city walls, each house, each gate.
Ibid., St. 2

25   I have known the rough
Split of trees' breaking bark,
And always will.
Ibid., St. 7

26 The year is dead!   Ibid., St. 9, last line

783. Emily Eden
(1797–1869)

1 As she had no hope of raising herself to the rank of a beauty, her only chance was bringing others down to her own level.
The Semi-Attached Couple,
Pt. I, Ch. 1   1830

2 People may go on talking for ever of the jealousies of pretty women; but for real genuine, hard-working envy, there is nothing like an ugly woman with a taste for admiration.
Ibid.

3 Some thought him too attentive to his prayers for a man in love, and some thought him too attentive to Lady Helen for a man in church. . . .   Ibid., Ch. 2

4 "You will soon see how naturally one acquires a distaste for any ill-judging individual who presumes not to like one's husband."   Ibid., Ch. 3

5 What could be more absurd than to assemble a crowd to witness a man and a woman promising to love each other for the rest of their lives, when we know what human creatures are,—men so thoroughly selfish and unprincipled, women so vain and frivolous?   Ibid., Ch. 7

6 "I said myself the other day, that one never hears anything new till it is old. . . ."
Ibid., Ch. 17

7 There is nothing like a good handsome flood of tears when those atrocious attacks on our good name or good looks are detected. The whirl of resentful thoughts, the angry resolves, the crimson cheeks, the burning eyes, the swelling heart, and the twitching fingers—all these moral and physical symptoms of injured innocence are instantly alleviated by a hardy cry.
Ibid., Ch. 18

8 "Oh, impossible," said Lady Portmore; "it would kill any of the young men of the present day to attempt such a walk; it must be four miles at least, or two, or some immense distance. No, I daresay, a cab is rather an extravagance; but I own I think it an absolute necessity."   Ibid., Ch. 26

9 "I admire your papers beyond all that I see in England. We think much in our country [Italy] of your liberty of the press; but it far passed my hopes. It is the greatest of benefits to a stranger: it lets him at once into secrets of society."   Ibid., Ch. 30

10 Above all, there was a miserable presentiment of coming evil—that expectation of ill which quickens the hearing, blinds the sight, and seems to clench the heart with a grasp, that tightens at every strange sound, at every sudden silence.   Ibid., Ch. 41

11 There is nothing so catching as re- finement. . . .   Ibid., Ch. 48

12 "I often think, my dear, that it is a great pity you are so imaginative, and still a greater pity that you are so fastidious. You would be happier if you were as dull and as matter-of-fact as I am."   *The Semi-Detached House,* Ch. 1
c.1860s

13 "Now is that so like the Post Office?" she said. "Letters that are of no consequence are always delivered directly, but when Arthur writes to me, they send his letters all over England."   Ibid., Ch. 5

14 Now there was nothing in the world pleased Lord Chesterton so much as a small confidence. He liked to feel that he had in his possession an actual secret: something that was made clear in black and white to *him,* and remained a blank to the rest of the world.   Ibid., Ch. 8

15 "I was not meant to live in all this money-making turmoil. It distracts me."
Ibid., Ch. 13

16 It had never come into their minds to analyze life. They took it as it came, and to them it came happily. . . .
Ibid., Ch. 16

17 At last, there came the joyful whisper, "a fine boy," perhaps the only moment of a fine boy's existence in which his presence is more agreeable than his absence.
Ibid., Ch. 18

18 Chance, the Spaniel, is the only individual amongst us whose happiness has been actually improved by the voyage.
Diary entry (1835),
Journals and Correspondence
1862

784. Kamamalu
(1797?–1824)

1 O! heaven; O! earth; O! mountains; O! sea; O! my counsellors and my subjects, farewell! O! thou land for which my father suffered, the object of toil which my father sought. We now leave thy soil; I follow thy command; I will never disregard thy voice; I will walk by the command which thou hast given me.   Farewell address to her people upon her departure to England* (November 27, 1823), Quoted in *Biography of Distinguished Women* by Sarah Josepha Hale   1876

*She died in England, never returning to her native land.

785. Mary Lyon
(1797–1849)

1 Its grand object [Mt. Holyoke Female Seminary] is to furnish the greatest possible number of female teachers, of high literary qualifications, and of benevolent, self-denying zeal.   Quoted in *Biography of Distinguished Women* by Sarah Josepha Hale   1876

2 There is nothing in the universe that I fear but that I shall not know all my duty, or shall fail to do it.*   Quoted in *Eminent Missionary Women* by Mrs. J. T. Gracey   1898

*Inscribed on her monument at Mt. Holyoke College, which she founded, in Hadley, Massachussetts.

3 When you choose your fields of labor go where nobody else is willing to go.   Ibid.

4 Oh, how immensely important is this work of preparing the daughters of the land to be good mothers!   Letter to her mother, from Ipswich (May 12, 1834), Quoted in *Mary Lyon through Her Letters*, Marion Lansing, ed.   1937

5 During the past year my heart has so yearned over the adult female youth in the common walks of life, that it has sometimes seemed as if there was a fire, shut up in my bones.   Quoted in *Notable American Women*, Edward T. James, ed.   1971

786. Penina Moïse
(1797–1880)

1 Lay no flowers on my grave. They are for those who live in the sun, and I have always lived in the shadow.   Last words, Quoted in *Notable American Women*, Edward T. James, ed.   1971

787. Madame Pfeiffer
(1797–post-1852)

1 A small affair would it have been for me to sail around the world, as many have done; it is my land journeys that render my tour a great undertaking, and invest it with interest.   Quoted in *Biography of Distinguished Women* by Sarah Josepha Hale   1876

2 Never betray fear.   Motto, op. cit.

788. Therese Albertine Louise Robinson
(1797—post-1852)

1 Not the untamed passion of the human heart, which, bursting out into a flame, spreading ruinously, destroys all barriers; not the unbridled force, which, in wild outbreaks of savage roughness, crushes under foot tender blossoms, lovely flowers,—not these constitute the greatest, the truest evil of the world; it is cold, creeping *egotism*, heartless *selfishness*; which, with its attendants, treachery, deceit, and hypocrisy, easily bears away the palm, because it knows what it is doing, while passion, in blind fury, shatters its own weapons.
"Selfishness,"
Life's Discipline; a Tale of the Annals of Hungary 1851

2 Losing her faith in the moral worth of the man she loves, a woman loses all the *happiness* of love. "Loving Unworthily," op. cit.

3 Love is dead. We are cured,—but are we happy? Ibid.

4 If it *is* true that constant change and the charm of novelty, the ceaseless rolling on of events around us, the attraction of the beautiful which we discover in a new, strange world, can at last strengthen and heal the most deeply wounded heart, as long as it is *grief* which has enfeebled it; this is not so when *guilt* has weighed it down: the sting of conscience cannot be withdrawn with all the exertion of our will: we cannot escape that pursuing monitress even in the most impetuous whirl of changing events and experiences! "Grief and Guilt," op. cit.

789. Mary Shelley
(1797–1851)

1 ... the most humble novelist, who seeks to confer or receive amusement from his labours, may, without presumption, apply to prose fiction a licence, or rather a rule, from the adoption of which so many exquisite combinations of human feelings have resulted in the highest specimens of poetry.
Preface (September 1817),
Frankenstein (or, the Modern Prometheus) 1818

2 ... my dreams were all my own; I accounted for them to nobody; they were my refuge when annoyed—my dearest pleasure when free. Ibid., Introduction (1831 edition)

3 I felt that blank incapability of invention which is the greatest misery of authorship, when dull Nothing replies to our anxious invocations. Ibid.

4 Invention, it must be humbly admitted, does not consist in creating out of voice, but out of chaos. ... Ibid.

5 "I agree with you," replied the stranger; "we are unfashioned creatures, but half made up, if one wiser, better, dearer than ourselves—such a friend ought to be—do not lend his aid to perfectionate our weak and faulty natures." Ibid., Letter 4, To Mrs. Saville, England

6 The world was to me a secret which I desired to divine. Ibid., Ch. 2

7 To examine the causes of life, we must first have recourse to death. Ibid., Ch. 4

8 Learn from me, if not by my precepts, at least by my example, how dangerous is the acquirement of knowledge, and how much happier that man is who believes his native town to be the world, than he who aspires to become greater than his nature will allow. Ibid.

9 A human being in perfection ought always to preserve a calm and peaceful mind, and never to allow passion or a transitory desire to disturb his tranquillity. I do not think that the pursuit of knowledge is an exception to this rule. If the study to which you apply yourself has a tendency to weaken your affections, and to destroy your taste for those simple pleasures in which no alloy can possibly mix, then that study is certainly unlawful, that is to say, not befitting the human mind. If this rule were always observed; if no man allowed any pursuit whatsoever to interfere with the tranquillity of his domestic affections, Greece had not been enslaved; Caesar would have spared his country; America would have been discovered more gradually; and the empires of Mexico and Peru had not been destroyed.
Ibid.

10 I beheld the wretch—the miserable monster whom I had created.   Ibid., Ch. 5

11 "Alas! Victor, when falsehood can look so like the truth, who can assure themselves of a certain happiness?"   Ibid., Ch. 9

12 "I expected this reception," said the daemon. "All men hate the wretched; how, then must I be hated, who am miserable beyond all living things! Yet you, my creator, detest and spurn me, thy creature, to whom thou art bound by ties only dissoluble by the annihilation of one of us."
Ibid., Ch. 10

13 "Of what a strange nature is knowledge! It clings to the mind, when it has once seized on it, like a lichen on the rock."
Ibid., Ch. 13

14 "Accursed creator! Why did you form a monster so hideous that even *you* turned from me in disgust? God, in pity, made man beautiful and alluring, after his own image, but my form is a filthy type of yours, more horrid even from the very resemblance. Satan had his companions, fellow-devils, to admire and encourage him; but I am solitary and abhorred."   Ibid., Ch. 15

15 His conversation was marked by its happy abundance.   Preface,
Collected Edition of Shelley   1839

16 Mrs. Shelley was choosing a school for her son,* and asked the advice of this lady, who gave for advice—to use her own words to me—"Just the sort of banality, you know, one does come out with: 'Oh, send him somewhere where they will teach him to think for himself!' " . . . Mrs. Shelley answered: "Teach him to think for himself? Oh, my God, teach him rather to think like other people!"   Quoted in *Essays in Criticism, Second Series; Shelley* by Matthew Arnold   1888

*Percy Bysshe Shelley (1792–1822), English poet and husband of Mary Wollstonecraft.

790.   Sojourner Truth
(c.1797–1883)

1 Ef women want any rights more'n dey got, why don't dey jes' *take 'em*, and not be talkin' about it.   Comment   c.1863

2 I . . . can't read a book but I can read de people.   Address, Tremont Temple, Boston, Massachusetts January 1, 1871

3 It is the mind that makes the body.
Interview, Battle Creek, Michigan   c.1877

4 Religion without humanity is a poor human stuff.   Ibid.

5 I'm a self-made woman.
Comment   c.1879

6 Wall, childern, whar dar is so much racket dar must be somethin' out o' kilter.
Speech, The Akron, Ohio, Convention (1851), Quoted in *History of Woman Suffrage*, Vol. I, by Elizabeth Cady Stanton, Susan B. Anthony and Mathilda J. Gage   1881

7 Dat man ober dar say dat womin needs to be helped into carriages, and lifted ober ditches, and to hab de best place everywhar. Nobody eber helps me into carriages, or ober mud-puddles, or gibs me any best place! And a'n't I a woman? Look at me! Look at my arm! I have ploughed, and planted, and gathered into barns, and no man could hear me! And a'n't I a woman? I could work as much and eat as much as a man—when I could get it—and bear de lash as well! And a'n't I a woman? I have borne thirteen chilern, and seen 'em mos' all sold off to slavery, and when I cried out with my mother's grief, none but Jesus heard me! And a'n't I a woman?

Ibid.

8 If my cup won't hold but a pint, and yours holds a quart, wouldn't ye be mean not to let me have my little half-measure full?

Ibid.

9 Den dat little man in black dar,* he say women can't have as much rights as men, 'cause Christ wan't a woman! . . . Whar did your Christ come from? From God and a woman! Man had notin' to do wid Him.

Ibid.

*A clergyman in the audience.

10 If de fust woman God ever made was strong enough to turn the world upside down all alone, dese women togedder ought to be able to turn it back, and get it right side up again!

Ibid.

11 I know that it feels a kind o' hissin' and ticklin' like to see a colored woman get up and tell you about things, and Woman's Rights. We have all been thrown down so low that nobody thought we'd ever get up again; but we have been long enough trodden now; we will come up again, and now I am here.

Speech, The Mob Convention, Broadway Tabernacle, New York City (September 8, 1853), op. cit.

12 Jesus says: "What I say to one, I say to all—watch!" I'm a-watchin'. Ibid.

13 I come from another field—the country of the slave. Speech, Annual Meeting of Equal Rights Convention, New York City (May 9, 1867), op. cit., Vol. II

14 There is a great stir about colored men getting their rights, but not a word about the colored women; and if colored men get their rights, and not colored women theirs, you see the colored men will be masters over the women, and it will be just as bad as it was before. So I am for keeping the thing going while things are stirring; because if we wait till it is still, it will take a great while to get it going again.

Ibid.

15 I have been forty years a slave and forty years free, and would be here forty years more to have equal rights for all.

Ibid.

16 I know that it is hard for one who has held the reins for so long to give up; it cuts like a knife. It will feel all the better when it closes up again. Ibid.

17 Truth burns up error.

Comment c.1882

791. Eliza Vestris
(1797–1856)

1 . . . I left you with unfeigned regret and returned to you with unbounded joy, and though it must be confessed that the mode in which you manifested your regret at my absence was more calculated to feed my vanity than my treasury, your kindness since my return has left the latter nothing to complain of. Farewell address at Olympic Theatre, London (May 31, 1839), Quoted in *Madame Vestris and Her Times*, Ch. 20, by Charles E. Pearce 1923

2 Some kind friends have already prophesied that I shall not succeed there.* My only answer is, that nine years ago they said I should never succeed *here*.

Ibid.

*The Theatre Royal, Covent Garden, to which she was later granted a lease—the first woman of the English stage to have been granted one.

3 Before you here a 'venturous woman bends—
A warrior woman, who in strife embarks,
The first of all dramatic Joan-of-Arcs!
Cheer on the enterprize thus dared by me,
The first that ever led a company;
What though until this very hour and age,
A Lessee lady never owned a stage,
I'm that *Belle Sauvage*—only rather quieter—
Like Mrs. Nelson, turn'd a stage proprietor.

Composed for her Olympic Theatre, London, debut (January 3, 1831), Quoted in *Enter the Actress* by Rosamond Gilder   1931

792.   Katharine Augusta Ware
(1797–1843)

1 I've looked on thee as thou wert calmly sleeping,
And wished—Oh, couldst thou ever be as blest
As now, when haply all thy cause of weeping
Is for a truant bird, or faded rose!

"A New-Year Wish, to a child aged five years," St. 1, *The Power of the Passions, and Other Poems*   1842

2 In youth time flies upon a silken wing.

Ibid., St. 2

793.   Louisa Caroline Tuthill
(1798/99–1879)

1 Never ring for a servant unless it is absolutely necessary; consider whether you have a right to make even your own waiting-maid take forty steps to save yourself one.

"Behaviour to Servants," *The Young Lady's Home*, n.d.

2 Human nature resents the imperative mood, but yields a ready acquiescence to gentle entreaty.   Ibid.

3 A cumbrous set of rules and maxims hung about one, like the charms which the gree-gree man* sells to the poor African, will not ward off the evils, nor furnish an antidote to the trials of life.   "Home Habits," op. cit.

*Voodoo witch.

4 The Well-spring of affection is in your own hearts; let it not be a sealed fountain. . . .

Ibid.

5 Woman owes her present elevation of character and condition to Christianity; in all countries where its benign holy influences is unfelt, she is still an unintellectual, a degraded being; and just in proportion to its purity and its power over a people is her domestic happiness.   "Christianity," op. cit.

794. Catharine Crowe
(c.1799/1800–1876)

1 The great proportion of us live for this world alone, and think very little of the next . . . whilst . . . what is generally called the religious world, is so engrossed by its struggles for power or money, or by its sectarian disputes and enmities, and so narrowed and circumscribed by dogmatic orthodoxies, that it has neither inclination nor liberty to turn back or look around, and endeavour to gather up, from past records and present observation, such hints as are now and again dropt in our path, to give us an intimation of what the truth may be.

*The Night-Side of
Nature*   1848

2 A great many things have been pronounced untrue and absurd, and even impossible, by the highest authorities in the age in which they lived, which have afterwards, and, indeed, within a very short period, been found to be both possible and true.

Ibid.

3 As I have said before, à priori conclusions are perfectly worthless . . . inasmuch as they deceive the timid and the ignorant, and that very numerous class which pins its faith on authority, and never ventures to think for itself, by an assumption of wisdom and knowledge, which, if examined and analyzed, would very frequently prove to be nothing more respectable than obstinate prejudice and rash assertion.

Ibid.

795. Catherine Gore
(1799–1861)

1 "Trust me, there are severer pangs in the world than arise from the rumpling of the rose-leaf!"   "The Female Spendthrift,"
Abednego, the Money-Lender,
n.d.

2 She submitted, therefore,—rendered docile by the iron pressure of necessity.

Ibid.

3 "So long as you enjoy luxuries which you do not and cannot pay for, you are shining at the cost of your coach-makers, jewellers, milliners, money-lenders—the abject obligee of humble tradesmen."

Ibid.

4 Waterton, the naturalist . . . asserts that whenever he countered an alligator *tête-à-tête*, in the wilderness, he used to leap on his back, and ride the beast to death. This feat, so much discredited by the stay-at-home critics, was an act of neither bravery nor braggartry—but of necessity. Either the man or the alligator must have had the upper hand. *Il a fallu opter* [He had to choose].

Just so are we situated with regard to the world. Either we must leap upon its back, strike our spur into its panting sides, and, in spite of its scaly defences, compel it to obey our glowing will, or the animal will mangle us with its ferocious jaws, leaving us expiring in the dust. "How to Manage the World,"
Modern Chivalry, n.d.

5 There is neither courage nor energy left in the world to engender a great reputation.

Ibid.

6 The moment insignificance and monotony become the normal state of a society, yawns are out of place.   "Society,"
op. cit.

7 For the egöist has so far the advantage over every other species of devotee, that his idol is ever present.   Ibid.

8 Thanks to the march of civilization, privacy has been exploded among us, and individuality effaced. People feel in thousands, and think in tens of thousands. No quiet nook of earth remaining for the modern Cincinnatus* to cultivate his own carrots and opinions, where humours may expand into excrescence, or originality let grow its beard!   *Self,* n.d.

*Legendary Roman hero, political leader and farmer (fl. 460 B.C.).

796. Mary Howitt
(1799–1888)

1 "Will you walk into my parlor?" said a Spider to a Fly;
"'Tis the prettiest little parlor that ever you
did spy." "The Spider and the Fly,"
Poems   c.1822–1831

2 Buttercups and daisies,
Oh, the pretty flowers;
Coming ere the spring time,
To tell of sunny hours.
"Buttercups and Daisies,"
op. cit.

3 Old England is our home and Englishmen
are we,
Our tongue is known in every clime, our
flag on every sea.   "Old England is
Our Home,"
op. cit.

4 Then take me on your knee, mother;
And listen, mother of mine.
A hundred fairies danced last night,
And the harpers they were nine.
"The Fairies of the Caldon
Low," St. 5,
op. cit.

5 Heart's ease! one could look for half a day
Upon this flower, and shape in fancy out
Full twenty different tales of love and sor-
row,
That gave this gentle name.
"Heart's Ease,"
op. cit.

6 Yes! in the poor man's garden grow,
Far more than herbs and flowers,
Kind thoughts, contentment, peace of
mind,
And joy for weary hours.
"The Poor Man's Garden,"
op. cit.

7 Not a rainbow shines to cheer us;
Ah! the sun comes never near us.
"The Wet Summer,"
op. cit.

8 Make beauty a familiar guest
Untitled,
Ballads and Other Poems
1847

9 Oh! poverty is a weary thing, 't is full of
grief and pain,
It boweth down the heart of man, and
dulls his cunning brain:
It maketh even the little child with
heavy sighs complain!
"The Sale of the Pet Lamb,"
St. 1, op. cit.

10 Hunger, and cold, and weariness, these are
a frightful three,
But another curse there is beside, that
darkens poverty;
It may not have one thing *to love*, how
small soe'er it be!   Ibid., St. 6

11 Sixteen summers had she seen,
A rose-bud just unsealing
"Tibbie Inglis, or the Scholar's
Wooing," St. 2,
The British Female Poets,
George W. Bethune, ed.   1848

12 Oh life! what after-joy hast thou
Like love's first certain gladness!
Ibid., St. 23

13 For our sufficient happiness
Great charm from woe could borrow.
Ibid., St. 25

14 "My mother is dead, and my father loves
His dogs far more than me;
No one would miss me if I went:
Oh, let me go with thee!"
"The Boy of Heaven,"
St. 15, op. cit.

15 "There are waters deep and wide to pass;
And who hath a load of sin,
Like the heavy rock that will not float,
Is tumbled headlong in."
Ibid., St. 19

16 Snatches of delicious song,
Full of old love-sadness!
"Beatrice. A Lover's Lay,"
St. 9, op. cit.

17 I know thy arts, my Beatrice,

So lovely, so beguiling,
The mockery of thy merry wit,
The witchery of thy smiling.

I know thee for a siren strong,
That smites all hearts with blindness,
And I might tremble for myself,
But for thy loving-kindness.
        Ibid., Sts. 18, 19

18 The clock is on the stroke of six,
The father's work is done;
Sweep up the hearth, and mend the fire,
And put the kettle on.
        "Father Is Coming,"
        St. 1, op. cit.

19 She was nurtured for her fate;
Beautiful she was, and vain;
Like a child of sinful Cain,
She was born a reprobate.
        "Judgment,"
        St. 1, op. cit.

20 I am young, alas! so young;
And the world has been my foe;
And by hardship, wrong, and woe,
Hath my bleeding heart been stung.
        "The Heart of the Outcast,"
        St. 1, op. cit.

21 No one but the sinner knows
What it means to be forgiven,
    God of love!   *Ibid.*, St. 2

22 Ye must run your simple race,
Never know the stir and strife
Of a loftier, nobler life   "Village
        Children,"
    St. 1, op. cit.

23 Ye are neither deep nor wise;
Ye shall ne'er philosophize.
        Ibid.

24 Simple ones, and full of gladness,
Ye shall school my spirit's sadness.
Never-ending joy ye find
In your own contented mind;
Sending not your spirits out
Searching wearily about
For ideal things, that lie
Nowhere underneath the sky.
        Ibid., St. 2

25 Children, though untaught ye be,
Thus ye shall be guides to me.
        Ibid., St. 3

26 Awake, and breathe the living air
Of our celestial clime!
Awake to love which knows no change,
Thou, who hast done with time!
        "Rejoicing in Heaven,"
        St. 3, op. cit.

27 My heart o'erfloweth to mine eyes,
And a prayer is on my tongue,
When I see the poor man's children,
The toiling, though the young
        Untitled,
        The Female Poets of Great
        Britain, Frederic Rowton, ed.
        1853

28 Their lives can know no passing joy,
Dwindled and dwarfed are girl and boy,
And even in childhood old;
With hollow eye and anxious air,
As if a heavy grasping care
Their spirits did infold.
        "Pauper Orphans,"
        St. 3, op. cit.

29 Oh, hapless heirs of want and woe!
        Ibid., St. 5

30 I love the fields, the woods, the streams,
The wild flowers fresh and sweet,
And Yet I love, no less than these,
The crowded city street
        "A City Street,"
        St. 1, op. cit.

31 For life's severest contrasts meet
For ever in the city street.
        Ibid., St. 3

32 When Nature reigns in her deepest rest,
Pure thoughts of heaven come unrepress'd.
        "Thoughts of Heaven,"
        St. 2, op. cit.

33 They come as we gaze on the midnight sky
When the star-gemm'd vault looks dark
and high,
And the soul, on the wings of thought sublime,

Soars from the dim world, and the bounds
of time.   Ibid., St. 3

34   How beautiful they stand,
Those ancient altars of our native land!
                    "English Churches,"
                    St. 1, op. cit.

35   Our lives are all turmoil;
Our souls are in a weary strife and toil,
Grasping and straining—tasking nerve and
brain,
—Both day and night for gain!
We have grown worldly: have made gold
our god   Ibid., St. 3

36 For visions come not to polluted eyes!
                    Ibid.

37 Thou gavest light and darkness; life and
death;
Thou gavest good and ill,
Twin powers, to be
Companions of its mortal devious path;
Yet left the human will
Unlimited and free!   "The Seven
                    Temptations,"
                    St. 1, op. cit.

38 For Truth is God, and He shall make you
free!
Evil is but of Time;—Good, of Eternity!
                    Ibid., St. 2

39 Oh! what had death to do with one like
thee . . . ?   "The Lost One," St. 3

40   Life's journey speedeth on;
Yet for a little while we walk in shade;
Anon, by death the cloud is all dis-
persed;
Then o'er the hills the eternal day doth
burst.   Ibid., St. 5

41 Eloquent the children's faces—
Poverty's lean look, which saith,
Save us! save us! woe surrounds us;
Little knowledge sore confounds us:
Life is but a lingering death!
Give us light amid our darkness;
Let us know the good from ill;
Hate us not for all our blindness;
Love us, lead us, show us kindness—

You can make us what you will.
                    "The Children,"
                    Sts. 2, 3,
        Birds and Flowers; or, Lays and
        Lyrics of Rural Life   1873

42 Let us take our proper station;
We, the rising generation,
Let us stamp the age as ours!
                    Ibid., St. 5

43 How pleasant the life of a bird must be,
Flitting about in a leafy tree;
And away through the air what joy to go,
And to look on the green bright earth be-
low.   "Birds in Summer,"
                    St. 3, op. cit.

44   . . . joys are spread,
Profusely, like the summer flowers
that lie
In the green path, beneath your gamesome
tread!   "Mountain Children,"
                    St. 10, op. cit.

45 And think of angels' voices
When the bird's songs he hears
                    Untitled, op. cit.

797. Ann Holbrook
(fl. c.1800s)

1 An actress can never make her children
comfortable. . . . The mother returning
with harassed frame and agitated mind,
from the varying passions she has been
pourtraying [sic], instead of imparting
healthful nourishment to her child, fills it
with bile and fever, to say nothing of dragging them long journies, at all seasons of the
year. *The Dramatist, or Memoires of the
Stage*   1809

798. Elizabeth Wallbridge
(?–1801)

1 But when I consider what a high calling, what honor and dignity God has conferred upon me, to be called his child, to be born of his Spirit, made an heir of glory, and joint heir with Christ; how humble and circumspect should I be in all my ways, as a dutiful and loving child to an affectionate and loving Father! When I seriously consider these things it fills me with love and gratitude to God, and I do not wish for any higher station, nor envy the rich. I rather pity them if they are not good as well as great.

> Quoted in *The Women of Methodism: Its Three Foundresses...*
> by Abel Stevens   1866

799. Maria de Fleury
(fl. 1804)

1 Thou soft-flowing Keedron,* by thy silver
     stream
Our Saviour at midnight, when Cynthia's
     pale beam
Shone bright on the waters, would often-
     times stray,
And lose in thy murmurs the toils of the
     day.   "Thou Soft-Flowing
           Keedron"   1804

*The brook Cedron (Kidron) near the Mount of Olives; cf John 18:1.

800. Sarah Catherine Martin
(fl. 1805)

1 Old Mother Hubbard
Went to the cupboard,
To get her poor dog a bone;
But when she came there
The cupboard was bare,
And so the poor dog had none.

> "The Comic Adventures of Old
> Mother Hubbard"   1805

801. Elizabeth Trefusis
(fl. 1808)

1 Thus the vain man, with subtle feigning,
     Pursues, o'ertakes poor woman's
           heart;
But soon his hapless prize disdaining,
     She dies!—the victim of his art.

> "The Boy and Butterfly,"
> *Poems and Tales*   1808

2   With my babe on my breast,
     With my babe on my breast,
My heart's lord shall be happy! and I—be at
     rest!   "Eudora's Lamentation over
           her Dead Child,"

> II, *The Female Poets of Great
> Britain*,
> Frederic Rowton, ed.
> 1853

3 "She merited better, but fate has its way"

> Ibid., III

802. Mrs. Henry Rolls
(fl. 1815–1825)

1 There is a sigh—that half supprest,
     Seems scarce to heave the bosom fair;
It rises from the spotless breast,
     The first fair dawn of tender care.

> "Sighs," St. 1,
> *The Female Poets of Great Britain*,
> Frederic Rowton, ed.
> 1853

2 Whence is that sad, that transient smile
     That dawns upon the lip of woe;
That checks the deep-drawn sigh awhile,
     And stays the tear that starts to flow?
'T is but a veil cast o'er the heart,
     When youth's gay dreams have pass'd
           away
When joy's faint lingering rays depart,
     And the last gleams of hope decay!

> "Smiles,"
> Sts. 7, 8, op. cit.

3 Fill high the bowl! 't is perhaps the last
     In which we hail our father's fame;
Oh, when 't is by our children pass'd,

May added glories gild their name!
                    "The Warrior's Song,"
                    St. 4, op. cit.

803.   Dorothea Primrose Campbell
(fl. 1816)

1 The winds of heaven are hushed and mild
As the breath of slumbering child
                    "Moonlight,"
                    Poems   1816

2 "The land of Cakes,"* has oft been sung
In many a poet's strain
                    "Address to Zetland
                    [the Shetlands],"
                    St. 1, op. cit.

3 I dreamed not that a fairer spot
On earth's broad bosom lay;
Nor ever wished my wand'ring feet
Beyond its bounds to stray.
                    Ibid., St. 4

804.   Mme. de Launay
(fl. 1820s)

1 We have at Porte-Saint-Martin a *troupe* of
English comedians. Apparently they are
not very good, but is that any reason why
they should be flayed alive?
            Letter to Marceline Desbordes-
                Valmore (August 6, 1822),*
            Quoted in *Memoirs of Madame
                    Desbordes-Valmore*
            by C. A. Sainte-Beuve, Harriet
                W. Preston, tr.   1872
*See 737.

2 Oh, how the Parisian is changed!
                    Ibid.

3 Leave to others their savage humor; but do
you, Frenchmen, keep your shining qualities.   Ibid.

4 I forgive the *nonchalance* which you assume about receiving a pension. . . . It flatters both the vanity and the purse.
            Letter to Desbordes-Valmore
            (November 1, 1826), op. cit.

5 Our King's [Charles X of France] heart is
the home of every virtue.   Ibid.

Biographical Index

Biographical Index

Every contributor is listed alphabetically using the letter-by-letter method, and her contributor number given (these numbers will be found in page headings throughout the Quotations section). If a woman is well known by a name other than the one used at the head of her entry in the Quotations section, that name is cross-indexed here. All co-authors are listed except "as told to" authors.

Brief biographical information is given for each woman in the following order: full name (those parts of her name not used at the head of her quotations are in brackets) and any hereditary or honorary title she is known to have held; lifespan; nationality, and–if different–country of residence (e.g., "Am./Fr." indicates a woman was born in the United States but lived most of her life in France); profession(s); any other names by which she is known, and alternate spellings; her family relationship to other well-known persons, along with biographical data on them (names of relatives followed by asterisks indicate those relatives are contributors in this book), and the name(s) of her husband(s); any awards or honors she is known to have received, and any "firsts" or outstanding achievements for which she is responsible.

Abbreviations (other than nationalities, which should be clear) are m., mother; w., wife; s., sister; d., daughter; mar., married name; grandd., granddaughter; grandm., grandmother; all other relationships are spelled out in full. If there was more than one husband or married name, the order in which such marriages occurred are indicated parenthetically, e.g., w. Smith (1) and Browne (2). Other terms include: aka, also known as; and asa, also spelled as.

A word about the alphabetization of names: many women nobles, women of the Middle Ages, and all the Japanese women are alphabetized by first names (or what appears to the contemporary Western eye as a "first" name).

A

Abel of Beth-maacah, Woman of (fl. c.1040–970 B.C.)   26
  Is. peacemaker

Abergavenny, [Lady] Frances (fl. 1580s)   351
  Eng. poet; asa Bergavenny, aka Elizabeth Fane, Frances Manners; m. Lady Marie Fane

Abigail (fl. c.990 B.C.)   22
  Judean; w. Naval (1) and David (2), m. Chileah

Abutsu (?–c.1283)   211
  Jap. nun, poet

Adams, Abigail (1744–1818)   591
  Am. letter writer, feminist; née Smith; w. John Adams (2nd U.S. pres.), m. John Quincy Adams (6th U.S. pres.), m-in-law Louisa Catherine Adams,* s. Elizabeth Peabody*

Adams, Louisa Catherine (1775–1852)   709
  Eng./Am. first lady; née Johnson; w. John Quincy Adams (6th U.S. pres.), d-in-law Abigail Adams,* grandm. Henry Adams

Adelwip (*see* Hadewijch)

Agnes the Martyr (fl. 1500–1535)   273
  Eng. Protestant martyr

Agostina (*see* Augustín, Maria)

Agreda, María de (1602–1664/65)   388
  Sp. abbess, essayist, philosopher, mystic; née María Fernandez Coronel, aka Sister María de Jesus

Agrippina the Younger (15–59)   81
  Rom. empress; d. Agrippina the Elder, s. Emperor Caligula, w. Gneus Dominitus (1) and Emperor Claudius (2), m. Nero

Aiken, Lucy (1781–1864)   725
  Eng. poet, historian, letter writer; niece of Anna Letitia Barbauld*

'Aisha bint Ahmad al-Qurtubiyya (fl. 965–999)   152
  Arabic/Sp. poet

Aissé, Charlotte Elizabeth (1694/95–1733)   497
  Circassian/Fr. letter writer, beauty

Akazome Emon (fl. 11th cen.)   157
  Jap. poet, lady-in-waiting; d. Taira no Kanemore (poet)

Akhyaliyya, Laila (fl. 665–699)   114
  Arabic poet

Alais (fl. c.12th cen.)   165
  Fr. *trobairitz*, nun?

Alamanda (fl. 1165–1199)   185
  Fr. *trobairitz*

Albrecht of Johannsdorf, Mistress of (fl. 13th cen.)   193
  Ger.

Albret, Jeanne d' (1528–1572)   303
  Fr. queen of Navarre; d. Marguerite of Navarre,* m. Henry IV of France and Charlotte de Bourbon

Alden, Priscilla (1602?–pre 1687)   387
  Eng./Am. pilgrim; née Mullins, w. John Alden; related to Sarah Alden Ripley*

Aldrude (fl. 1172)   188
  Ital. noble; aka countess de Bertinora

Al-Khansa (575–646)   108
  Arabic poet; née Tumadir bint Amr ibn al Harith ibn al Sharid; aka Tumadir al-Khansa; m. 'Amra (poet), related to Zuhair ibn Abu Sulma (poet)

Almucs de Castelnau (c.1140–?)   179
  Provençal *trobairitz*, patron of troubadours

Alston, Theodosia Burr (1783–1813)   730
  Am. social leader; d. Aaron Burr and Theodosia De Visme Burr,* w. Joseph Alston (governor of South Carolina),

(Il Moro), duke of Milan; great aunt of Anne d'Este*

Este, Isabella d' (1474–1530) 252
Ital. art patron, letter writer; aka marquise of Mantua; d. Ercole I, duke of Ferrara and Leonora of Aragon, s. Beatrice d'Este,* w. Francesco Gonzaga (marquis of Mantua), s.-in-law Elisabetta Gonzaga,* s.-in-law Lucrezia Borgia,* great aunt Anne d'Este

Esther (c.519–465 B.C.) 37
Is./Persian queen; aka Hadassah; d. Abihail, cousin and adopted d. Mordecai, second w. Ahaseurus, king of Persia (aka Xerxes I)

Eve (first generation antediluvian period) 1
w. Adam; m. Cain, Abel, and Seth (ancestor of Christ), grandm. Enoch (child of Cain); first woman

F

Falconar, Harriet (1774–?) 706
Eng. poet; s. Maria Falconar*

Falconar, Maria (1771–?) 697
Eng. poet; s. Harriet Falconar*

Fane, Elizabeth (see Abergavenny [Lady] Frances)

Fanshawe, [Lady] Ann (1625–1680) 417
Eng. author; née Harrison; w. Sir Richard Fanshawe (diplomat and author)

Fanshawe, Catherine Maria (1765–1834) 669
Eng. poet, painter

Farnese, Giulia (c.1476–?) 255
Ital. noble; reputed to have been the mistress of Pope Alexander VI

Farrar, Eliza Ware (1791–1870) 759
Fr./Am. author; née Elizabeth Rotch, aka Mrs. John Farrar

Faugères, Margaretta Van Wyck (1771–1801) 698
Am. poet, essayist; née Bleecker; d. Ann Eliza Bleecker*

Fedele, Cassandra (fl. 1473–1503) 248
Ital. scholar; w. Johannes Maria Mapellus

Ferguson, Elizabeth Graeme (1737–1801) 571
Am. translator, poet, letter writer, diarist, salonist; aunt of Anna Young Smith*

Ferrier, Susan Edmonstone (1782–1854) 728
Scot. novelist; aka Mary Ferrier

Fielding, Sarah (1710–1768) 516
Eng. author

Finch, Anne (1661–1720/22) 458
Eng. poet, translator, literary critic, feminist; née Kingsmill, aka countess of Winchelsea, Ardelia, Flavia

Fletcher, Bridget (1726–1770) 544
Am. hymnist; née Richardson

Fletcher, Mary (1739–1815) 574
Eng. philanthropist, née Bosanquet (asa Basquet)

Fleury, Maria de (fl. 1804) 799
Am. essayist, poet

Follen, Eliza Lee (1787–1860) 739
Ger./Am. poet, author; née Cabott

Foster, Hannah Webster (1758/59–1840) 636
Am. novelist

Fradonnet, Catherine (1547–1587) 320
Fr. poet, playwright; aka with her mother as Les Dames Des Roches; d. Madeleine Fradonnet*

Fradonnet, Madeleine (c.1520–1587) 292
Fr. poet; née Neveu, aka with her daughter as Les Dames Des Roches; w. André Fradonnet (1) and François Eboissard (2), m. Catherine Fradonnet*

Franco, Veronica (1546–1591) 319
Ital. poet, courtesan; founder of hospice for "fallen women"; friend of Tintoretto

Franklin, Eleanor Anne (1790/97–1825) 754
Eng. poet; née Porden

Franks, Rebecca (c.1760–1823) 651
Am./Eng. social figure; aka Lady Johnson

Frietschie, Barbara (1766–1862) 673
Am. patriot; née Hauer, asa Frietchie; subject of John Greenleaf Whittier's poem "Barbara Fritchie"

Fry, Elizabeth (1780–1845) 721
Eng. social and prison reformer

I

Inchbald, Elizabeth (1753–1821)   620
  Eng. playwright, translator, author;
  née Simpson
Irwin, Viscountess (*see* Howard, Anne)
Isabella (c.1180–?)   189
  Romanian?, Ital.? *trobairitz*; friend of
  Elias Cairel (troubadour)
Isabella I (1451–1504)   243
  Sp. queen of Castile and Leon; d. John
  II of Castile and Isabella of Portugal,
  w. Ferdinand II, king of Aragon (aka
  Ferdinand V, king of Castile), m. Cath-
  erine of Aragon*
Isaure, Clemence (1464–1515/16)   246
  Fr. poet, nun; asa Clemenza, aka The
  Sappho of Toulouse, The Queen of Po-
  etry; sponsored the *Jeux Floreaux* (i.e.,
  Floral Games), annual May 1 poetry
  contest
Ise, Lady (875?–938?)   142
  Jap. poet; d. Fujiwara no Tsugukage
  (governor of Ise), mistress of Emperor
  Uda, m. Prince Katsura, Lady Nakat-
  sukasa*
Iselda (fl. c.12th cen.)   168
  Fr. *trobairitz*, nun?
Ise Tayu (11th cen.)   158
  Jap. poet
Iseut de Capio (c.1140–?)   182
  Provençal *trobairitz*
Ishikawa, Lady (fl. 780–800)   135
  Jap. poet
Ita, Saint (480–570)   102
  Ir. nun, poet; asa Ite, Ida, Ide, Ytha,
  Idea, Itha, aka The Brigid of the Mun-
  ster; foster m. St. Brendan, The
  Navigator (484–577)
Iwa no Hime (?–347)   95
  Jap. empress, poet, w. Emperor Nin-
  toku
Izumi Shikibu, [Lady] (974–c.1030)   155
  Jap. courtier, poet, diarist; née Oe
  Shikibu; d. Ō-e no Masamune, lord of
  Echizen; w. Fujiwara no Yasumasa,
  lord of Tango, (1) and Tachibana no
  Michisada, lord of Izumi, (2), mistress
  of Prince Tametaka and his brother,
  Prince Atsumichi, m. Ko-Shikibu no
  Naishi (poetess)

J

Jackson, Rachel Robards (1767–1828)   679
  Am. first lady; née Donelson, w. Lewis
  Robards (1) and Andrew Jackson (2)
  (7th U.S. president)
Jackson, Rebecca Cox (1795–1871)   779
  Am. Shaker religious leader; aka
  Mother Jackson
Jael (fl. 1070 B.C.)   13
  Kenite; w. Heber; killed Sisera, captain
  of Jabin's army, and saved Israel from
  Jabin's oppression
Jahan, Nur (?–1646)   444
  Ind. poet, empress; w. Emperor Jehan-
  gir
Jameson, Anna Brownell (1794–1860)   776
  Ir./Eng. author, art critic; née Mur-
  phy; d. Denis Murphy (miniature
  painter, ?–1842)
Jars, Marie de (1565–1645)   341
  Fr. writer, feminist; aka Demoiselle de
  Gournay; adopt. d. Michel de Mon-
  taigne (French essayist, 1533–1592)
Jeanne of Navarre (1271–1307/09?)   210
  Fr. patroness of arts and letters; w.
  Phillip V, d. Mahout d'Artois;*
  founded College of Navarre
Jefimija (c.1348–c.1405)   217
  Serbian princess, poet; née Jelena; d.
  Vojihna (ruler of province of Drama),
  w. Uglješa Mrnjavcević
Jephthah the Gileadite, Daughter of (fl.
1140 B.C.)   14
  Hebr./Gilead; d. Jephthah (9th judge
  of Israel)
Jevgenija (c.1353–1405)   218
  Serbian poet, princess; née Milica Hre-
  beljanovic; d. Prince Vratko, w. Prince
  Lazar
Jezebel (fl. c.874–853 B.C.)   31
  Tyrian queen; w. Ahab, d.-in-law Omri
  (king of Israel, c.884–872 B.C.)
Joan of Arc, [Saint] (1412–1431)   231
  Fr. heroine, patriot, martyr; aka The
  Maid of Orléans; led battles that turned
  the tide of the Hundred Years War;
  saw Charles VII crowned; burned at
  the stake for heresy
Job, Wife of (c.8th cen. B.C.)   39
  Edomite (from Mt. Seir)

Gabriel Piozzi (2); friend of Dr. Samuel Johnson

Pix, Mary Griffith (1666–1720?)   470
Eng. playwright, novelist

Plotina, Pompeia (c.80–122)   86
Roman empress; w. Emperor Trajan, m. Emperor Adrian

Pocahontas (1595/96–1616/17)   375
Am. Indian princess, heroine; aka Matoaka (i.e., Snowfeather), Rebecca (Christian name), the Nonpareil of Virginia; d. chief Powhatan, w. (?) Kocoum (1) and John Rolfe (2); first American Christian convert, legendary savior of Capt. John Smith of Jamestown

Poisson, Jeanne Antoinette (see Pompadour, Jeanne Poisson)

Poitiers, Diane de (1499–1566)   271
Fr. royal mistress; aka comtesse de Brézé, duchesse de Valentinois; w. Louis de Brézé, comte de Maulevrier (grand seneschal of Normandy), mistress of Henry II of France

Pompadour, [Madame] Jeanne [Antoinette] Poisson (1721–1764)   534
Fr. salonist, art and literary patron; aka marquise de Pompadour, Mme Pompadour; d. François Poisson (equerry to the duke of Orléans), w. Lenormand d'Étoiles, mistress of Louis XV of France

Porcia (?–42 B.C.)   77
Rom. noble; d. Marcus Porcius Cato (Roman patriot, stoic philosopher), w. Decimus Junius Brutus (Roman general, member of the conspiracy to assassinate Julius Ceasar)

Porter, Jane (1776–1850)   714
Eng. novelist; s. Anna Maria Porter (English novelist) and Sir Robert Ker Porter (English artist and traveler)

Praxilla (fl. 451 B.C.)   60
Gr. poet

Prest, Wife of (?–1558)   331
Eng. religious martyr

Primrose, [Lady] Diana (fl. 1630s)   424
Eng. poet; poss. pseud. of Lady Anne Clifford

Prince, Lucy Terry (see Terry, Lucy)

Prostitute of Jerusalem, mother of the dead child (fl. c.950 B.C.)   29
Is.

Prostitute of Jerusalem, mother of the living child (fl. c.950 B.C.)   28
Is.

Pulcheria, Aelia (399–453)   98
Byzantine empress, scholar; d. Emperor Arcadius, s. Emperor Theodosius II, w. General Marcian; canonized and still recognized as a saint by the Greek Orthodox church

Q

Qernertoq (c.900–1400)   146
Eskimo poet

R

Rabi'a bint Isma'il of Syria (?–755)   133
Arabic poet

Rabi'a of Balkh (10th cen.)   145
Iranian poet; d. Ka'b, king of Balkh

Rabi'a the Mystic (712–801)   130
Basra (Iraq) poet, Sufi mystic, Muslim saint; aka Rabi'a al-Adawiyya, "that woman on fire with love"

Rachel (?–1732 B.C.)   7
Hittite; d. Leban, s. Leah,* 2nd w. Jacob, m. Joseph, m. Benjamin, niece of Abraham; mother of two of the twelve tribes of Israel

Radcliffe, Ann (1764–1823)   667
Eng. poet, novelist; née Ward; w. William Radcliffe (editor of the *English Chronicle*)

Radegunda [Saint] (c.518–587)   106
Thuringian/Merovingian nun, princess; w. Chlotar I (asa Clotaire)

Raleigh, Elizabeth (fl. 1601)   386
Eng. noble; d. Sir Nicholas Throckmorton (1515–1571), w. Sir Walter Raleigh

Ramsay, Martha Laurens (1759–1811)   645
Am. letter writer

Rebekah (fl. 18th cen. B.C.)   5
Mesopotamian; d. Bethuel (son of Nahor), s. Laban, w. Isaac, m. Esau and Jacob

Staël, [Anne Louise] Germaine de (1766–1817) 676
   Fr. novelist, literary critic, feminist; d. Jacques Necker (minister of finance of Louis XVI) and Suzanne Chardon Necker,* w. Baron Eric Magnus de Staël de Holstein (1), mistress and w. Lieutenant John Rocca (2), m. (by Vicomte Louis de Narbonne-Lara) Auguste and Albert, cousin Mme Necker de Saussure*

Stampa, Gaspara (1523–1554) 299
   Ital. poet, courtesan, signer; s. Baldassare Stampa (poet, singer), Cassandra Stampa (poet, singer)

Stanhope, [Lady] Hester Lucy (1776–1839) 715
   Eng./Syrian traveler, astrologer; aka White Queen of the Desert; d. Charles, 3rd earl of Stanhope (inventor)

Starbuck, Mary Coffyn (1644/45–1717) 442
   Am. Quaker minister; aka The Great Woman

Steele, Anne (1717–1778/89) 527
   Eng. poet, hymnist; pseud. Theodosia

Stewardess of the Empress Kōka [Mon-in no Bettō] (12th cen.) 172
   Jap. poet; d. Fujiwara no Toshitaka

Stockton, Annis (1736–1801) 570
   Am. poet; née Boudinot, pseud. Emilia (asa Amelia)

Storace, Nancy (1765–1815) 672
   Eng. singer; née Anna Selina Storace

Strozzi, Alessandra de'Machingi (1406–1471) 230
   Ital. letter writer; m. Lorenzo, Filippo and Matteo

Stuart, Mary (see Mary Queen of Scots)

Stubbes, Katherine (1571–1591/92) 348
   Eng. householder; w. Philip Stubbes

Sullam, Sarah Copia (1592–1641) 371
   Ital. poet

Sulpicia (fl. 63 B.C.–A.D. 14) 75
   Rom. poet; niece and ward of Messala

Sulpicia (fl. 80–99) 87
   Rom. poet; aka the Roman Sappho

Sumangala, Mother of (c.3rd–1st cen. B.C.) 67
   Ind. (Pali) poet

Sun Tao-hsüan (fl. 1100–1135) 174
   Chin. poet

Sun Yün-fêng (1764–1814) 668
   Chin. poet; w. Ch'en, the scholar

Suo [Lady] (fl. 1035–1065) 161
   Jap. poet, lady-in-waiting to Emperor Go-Reizei; d. Taira no Tsugunaka (governor of Suo)

Susanna (c.587–538 B.C.) 40
   Jewish; d. Hilkiah, w. Joakim

Sutcliffe, Ann (fl. 1600–1630) 384
   Eng. religious writer; w. John Sutcliffe (groom to His Majesty's Privy Chamber)

Sylvia (see Smith, Anna Young)

Symonds, Caroline (1792–1803) 768
   Eng. poet

T

Tamar (fl. c.990 B.C.) 24
   Hebr. princess; d. David and Maacah, s. Absalom, half-s. Amnon

T'ang Wan [Lady] (c.12th cen.) 173
   Chin. poet; w. Lu Yu (poet)

Tattlewell, Mary (fl. 1640) 440
   Eng. author; pseud. only

Taylor, Ann (1782–1866) 729
   Eng. poet; aka Mrs. Gilbert; s. Jane Taylor*; inventor, with her sister Jane, of the "awful warning" school of poetry

Taylor, Jane (1783–1824) 732
   Eng. poet; s. Ann Taylor*; inventor, with her sister Ann, of the "awful warning" school of poetry

Taylor, Mrs. (fl. 1685) 488
   Eng. poet

Tekoa, Woman of (fl. c.940 B.C.) 25
   Biblical

Telesilla (5th cen. B.C.) 58
   Gr. poet, military leader, heroine

Temple, Countess (see Chamber, Anna)

Tencin, Claudine Alexandrine [Guerin] de (1685–1749) 489
   Fr. salonist, author

Teresa of Avila, [Saint] (1515–1582) 286
   Sp. nun, poet; née Teresa de Cepeda y Ahumada, asa Theresa, aka St. Teresa of Jesus; founded nine convents, re-

Subject Index

Subject Index

The numbers preceding the colons are contributor numbers; guides to these numbers are found at the top of each page in the Quotations section. The numbers following the colons refer to the specific quotations. Semicolons separate contributor numbers.

Entries are in the form of nouns, present participles, or proper names. Where the use of a noun might be confusing, due to the amorphous nature of the English language, "the" has been added for clarification (e.g., "the mind"), or the plural form to distinguish the editor's use of a word (e.g., "appearances" rather than "appearance").

In subclassifications the symbol ~ is used to replace the main word; its placement before or after the subentry aids in creating a whole phrase. For example, "marriage laws" is listed as "marriage, ~ law," whereas "true love" is listed as "love, true ~."

Where there are two words in a main entry with a slash between them, they appear alphabetically; several such couplings have been made when too few quotations under the related subjects warrant separate listings—as in "speeches/speech making."

Extensive cross-referencing is used to aid the reader in locating pertinent quotations.

For a statement on the purpose and style of the Subject Index, please see the Editor's Preface.

A

abandonment, 141:2; 496:36; 620:14

Abelard, Peter, 164:16, 19

ability, 376:19

Abolitionism (*also see* slavery), 765:12

abortion, 214:19

absence, 160:2; 304:6; 533:1; 570:1; 579:3, 9; 599:7

absentmindedness, 156:25; 596:6

absolution (*also see* forgiveness, divine), 416:1; 758:10

absurdity, 656:65

abuse, 265:14

acceptance, 367:2; 588:60; 666:43; 744:17; ∼ of self, 666:3

accomplishment (*also see* achievement), 656:69; 681:1

accusation, 537:3; 551:12; 744:71

achievement, 303:12; 412:32; 641:5; 642:10; 678:41; illusion of ∼, 656:43

acquaintance, wordless ∼, 472:9

acquiescence, 136:8

acting, 628:6, 9, 12, 22; great ∼, 628:10

action, 23:1; 676:3, 77; inadequate ∼, 712:11; need for ∼, 333:1; 588:5

activeness, 215:4; 339:22

activity, 740:11; crowded with ∼, 628:17; 730:5; lack of ∼, 257:1

actor/actress (*also see* performer; theater), 519:2; 576:1; 628:20; 650:4; children of ∼, 797:1; employment for ∼, 628:2

Adam and Eve (*also see* Eve), 344:8, 9; 376:5, 6; 588:6; 765:2

Adams, John, 591:5, 7; 689:1; John Quincy, 709:1; Louisa Catherine, 709:3

adaptability, 472:51; 710:41; 743:17

adaptation, 531:14

admiration, 156:5; 532:1; 603:57; 641:23; 655:5; 678:82; 737:57; desire for ∼, 458:20;

532:15; need for ∼, 656:21; object of ∼, 532:27; written ∼, 424:2

adultery (*also see* faithlessness; infidelity), 69:1; 170:1; 184:8; 279:3; 432:7; 472:48, 49; 540:4

adulthood, threshhold of ∼, 616:5

advantage, 395:8; 438:81; 656:53; lost ∼, 678:98

adventure, 359:2

adversity (*also see* hardship; life, struggle of; obstacle; trouble), 87:3; 291:2; 325:7; 337:13; 391:1; 398:29; 420:23; 641:26; 666:26; 717:5; 743:16; 796:20; overcoming ∼, 636:9; 656:33

advice, 492:26; 666:40; 744:72; beneficial ∼, 722:48; ignoring ∼, 732:1; mother's ∼, 585:2; ∼ to child, 38:2; woman's ∼, 274:2

advisor, 309:35; 317:11; bad ∼, 710:9; need of ∼, 789:5

Aeneas, 196:1

affectation (*also see* fop; pretense), 545:2

affection, 492:22; 647:12; 656:86; 678:63; 699:8; 728:48; 744:58; 770:31; 793:4; 802:1; lack of ∼, 492:15; ∼ of men, 433:12; waning ∼, 678:58; words of ∼, 656:96

affliction, 268:4; 309:53; 438:48; 446:6; 473:2; 586:2; 708:1; bearing ∼, 426:50; 531:13; changing ∼, 286:31; understanding ∼, 737:94

Africa, 557:3; 588:27, 29; 621:1, 11; 644:10; 743:80, 81; depradation of ∼, 706:1

African, 743:74

afterlife, 155:3; 262:4; 286:21; 337:15; 698:2; 712:29; 737:74; 763:54

Age (*also see* century; era; times), Elizabethan ∼, 532:3; Golden ∼, 424:7; Modern ∼, 719:1; Victorian ∼, 743:15

age/aging (*also see* men, older; old age; people, old; women, aging; women, older), 155:2; 201:3; 271:4; 340:1; 418:5; 473:2; 603:19; 615:15, 61; 722:34; 726:1; 743:88; 773:3;

England, 236:1; 317:10; 423:2; 424:10; 426:22; 532:26; 546:2; 588:49; 696:8; 706:2; 710:1; 715:4; 728:59; 796:3; enmity of ∼, 309:40; 743:10; government in ∼, 486:1; houses in ∼, 770:2; ∼ in relation to Africa, 706:1; ∼ in relation to France, 231:9; 482:7; 657:1; ∼ in relation to United States, 547:3; 740:40; mores in ∼, 472:48; 540:4; 588:29; religion in ∼, 711:27; royalty in ∼, 634:3; women in ∼, 492:32

English, the, 472:54, 63; 598:1; 603:47; 710:100; ∼ aristocracy, 603:30; ∼ character, 744:50; 776:4; ∼ countryside, 740:21; ∼ industry, 724:9; ∼ landscape, 710:8; ∼men, 589:14; 740:28; ∼ women, 540:6

Enheduanna, 48:8

enigma, 433:13; 669:1

enjoyment, 560:20; 743:2

enlightenment, 216:14; 293:8; 734:13, 14; 748:4; 749:2; 763:15; path to ∼, 263:9; search for ∼, 737:88

enslavement, personal ∼, 300:20

enthusiasm, 676:91; 678:102

environment, natural ∼, 204:5

envy (*also see* jealousy), 66:1; 139:3; 148:17; 164:13; 184:5; 216:6; 358:6; 420:1; 458:5; 603:41; 641:23; 661:1; 666:3; 744:65; 783:2; lack of ∼, 620:19

epitaph, 309:60; 524:1; 763:1

equality, 647:36; 676:18; 790:15; ∼ for women, 344:10; ∼ of man and woman, 376:6; 394:1; 412:39; 617:1; 659:1; 765:1; 780:7; racial ∼, 557:2; sexual ∼, 186:1, 2, 3; 596:7

era (*also see* Age; century; times), decadent ∼, 472:46

Eros, 55:17

error (*also see* mistake), 293:6; 641:16; 676:41; honest ∼, 406:6; human ∼, 615:37

escape, 58:1

escapism, 229:2; 450:32

essay, 501:10

Esther, 317:19

eternity, 588:32; 728:67; 761:2; 796:40

ethics, 341:10

eulogy, 361:2; 399:3; inadequacy of ∼, 399:4

Europe, 697:1; 743:10

European, ∼ women, 780:2

evasion, polite ∼, 620:18

Eve (*also see* Adam and Eve), 349:2; 401:3; 404:4; 780:3; 790:10

Evelyn, John, 452:8

evening, 763:28

evidence, lack of ∼, 309:2

evil (*also see* bad/badness; evildoing; good and evil; wickedness), 184:18; 195:2; 214:16; 412:13; 418:12; 419:8; 477:12; 492:8; 560:6; 615:9; 656:93; 735:24; 777:36; 788:1; avoiding ∼, 265:34; gains of ∼, 283:4; imaginary ∼, 603:40, 62; portraying ∼, 395:37; suppress ∼, 621:2; withstanding ∼, 418:10

evildoing, 615:8; 667:7

exaggeration, 419:2; 589:16; 676:65

excellence, 398:14; 426:30; 453:1; 468:15; 676:107; 711:16; 741:3; desire for ∼, 628:9; 712:27; pursuit of ∼, 717:2

excuse, 496:10; weak ∼, 219:1

execution (*also see* burning, ∼ at the stake; decapitation), 712:21; facing ∼, 622:3; 626:3; 661:3; 681:9; mass ∼, 308:1; ∼ of husband, 336:5; public ∼, 656:62

exemplar, 424:6; 426:35; 452:8; 656:38; 666:5; 748:11; 763:81

exercise, 382:2; 588:57; physical ∼, 758:6

exhaustion (*also see* fatigue; weariness), 272:1

exile, 550:30; 712:25

exodus, ∼ from Egypt, 10:1

expectation, 286:20; 297:5; 641:1; 702:2; romantic ∼, 744:79

experience, 243:9; 462:15; 676:3; 722:5, 6; 728:7; firsthand ∼, 156:4; lessons of ∼, 760:2

expertise, lack of ∼, 270:4

exploitation, 497:4

exploration (*also see* search), 763:6; ∼ of life, 614:1

exposé, 245:1

expression, futility of ∼, 450:22

extravagance, 615:65

extremism, 419:17

extroversion/extrovert, 300:14

eyes, 309:48; 325:15; 339:16; 361:7; 444:1; 450:20; 588:20; 763:76; 782:8; expressive ∼, 262:5; lustful ∼, 148:9

eyesight, losing one's ∼, 696:7

eyewitness, 472:10

F

face, human (*also see* complexion; eyes; mouth), 148:6; 412:7; 440:12; 492:19; 589:27; 615:60; 709:1; 715:2; 728:62; 743:30; 777:21 brow of ~, 782:9; coloring of ~, 656:101; expression of ~, 425:4; 689:1; vulnerability of ~, 309:22

factionalism, 338:3; 438:36

factory, 724:5, 6, 9; 758:21

fad, health ~, 616:9

failure (*also see* defeat), 458:21; 656:37; 743:63; halt ~, 482:6

faint, 147:1; 710:3

fairy, 770:14; 796:4

faith (*also see* belief; conviction; religion), 268:3; 291:9; 347:2, 3; 357:1; 501:12; 595:43; act of ~, 588:23; ancestral ~, 712:13; ~ in man, 184:30; 599:5; lack of ~, 224:9; 773:2; loss of ~, 788:2

faithfulness, 89:1

faithlessness (*also see* adultery; infidelity), 156:56

Fall, the (biblical), 457:7; 765:3

falseness (*also see* deception; duplicity; lie/lying), 189:2; 220:4; 365:1; 531:10; 550:17; 620:26; 789:11

fame, 265:19; 302:10; 325:11; 344:2; 412:33; 450:30; 457:2, 4, 6; 492:44; 517:1; 570:6; 608:2; 615:35; 628:13; 656:6; 676:7; 678:7; 737:42; 770:31; 776:12; emptiness of ~, 763:52; ephemerality of, 278:2; 455:6; ~ of loved one, 676:67; pursuit of ~, 184:26; 395:14; 412:17; 678:53; women and ~, 482:13, 17

familiarity, 339:23

family (*also see* love, familial), 265:1; 712:43; black sheep of ~, 603:55; chosen ~, 375:2; death in ~, 770:26; difficulties of ~ life, 452:10; 678:78; 710:75; 737:82; 744:14; ~ life, 744:16; ~ partiality, 710:101; surviving ~, 714:24; ~ ties, 758:7

farmer, 435:17; 540:12; 588:47; woman ~, 591:5; Yankee ~, 743:12

fashion (*also see* clothing), 252:4; 588:62; 615:77; 656:90; 666:6; 722:33; passing ~, 419:50; slave to ~, 588:66; 589:19; 615:75; 636:2; 728:55

fastidiousness, 783:12

fasting, 31:3

fate (*also see* destiny; fortune), 279:13; 419:41, 44; 420:5; 462:14; 472:33; 480:1; 491:4; 550:31; 667:2; 676:48; 718:10; 777:30; 801:3; acceptance of ~, 169:1; conquer ~, 718:12; shared ~, 279:16

father (*also see* parents), 620:8; 666:32; 730:7; 737:31; 757:5; 796:18; abusive ~, 350:5; death of ~, 336:4; 688:1; ~ in relation to offspring, 763:8; obligation to ~, 34:1; symbolic ~, 375:1

fatigue (*also see* exhaustion; weariness), 469:4

fault (*also see* shortcoming), 477:11; 497:5; 728:9; accepting one's ~s, 738:10; deny ~, 780:11; overcoming a ~, 286:26; revealing a ~, 450:30

faultfinding (*also see* criticism), 284:3; 404:9; 491:6; 516:3; 647:42; 730:6; 735:21; 744:15

faultlessness, 678:1

favor, 75:3; 339:20; 676:37; conditional ~, 364:2

favoritism, 318:1; 595:6, 7; 678:91; ~ in schools, 616:10

fear (*also see* dread), 238:3; 252:10; 263:10; 397:1; 418:16; 469:2; 496:14; 545:4; 550:22; 560:7; 580:1; 595:4; 741:12; disguise ~, 787:2; influence of ~, 678:41; unfounded ~, 686:10

feelings (*also see* emotion; heart; love; passion; sentiment), 214:8; 407:7; 615:46; 676:109, 110; 728:18; 737:83; barometer of ~, 219:3; deadened ~, 782:19; delicacy of ~, 450:24; dread of ~, 224:13; excited ~, 551:1; expressing ~, 419:45; 450:22; 478:5; 523:1; 571:5; 633:8; 678:15; hurt ~, 162:17; inexpressible ~, 777:34; injured ~, 361:1; 783:7; lack of ~, 64:1; 145:1; 200:7; mask ~, 220:13; 664:1; suppressed ~, 563:3; turbulence of ~, 419:27; understanding ~, 615:73; unfounded ~, 156:21; volatile ~, 162:12

Ferdinand V, King of Aragon, 243:13

fertility, 6:3

festivity, 260:3; 540:29; attending ~, 395:18

feud, 477:11

fickleness (*also see* love, fickle), 184:27; 395:19; 744:69; ~ of women, 265:41; 710:113

fiction (*also see* book; literature; novel; writing), 156:51; 531:12; 588:2; 712:6; tenets of ~, 395:2

fidelity, 270:3; 293:10

cism of ~, 545:2; 678:4; 789:5; faithful ~, 225:2; 398:33; 438:95; 550:59; 588:69; 678:93; 688:3; longing for ~, 426:58; 737:44; 744:44; lost ~, 171:2; mistreatment of ~, 55:11; obligation to ~, 148:14; 588:68; respect of ~, 608:2; 722:56; sharing with ~, 148:13; unreliable ~, 214:2; 477:17; 496:4; 497:3; 550:23; wishes for ~, 588:13

friendship (*also see* companionship), 309:31; 358:15; 419:31; 426:3, 8, 27, 60; 472:16; 540:23; 549:3; 570:9; 641:6; 643:1; 650:6; 710:81; 777:6, 7; basis for ~, 666:44; ~ between men and women (*also see* relationships, ~ between men and women), 374:3; 647:33; 734:1; ~ between women (*also see* woman/women, ~ in relation to women), 55:9; 219:2; 307:1; 438:106; 477:13; 563:1; 737:50; breach in ~, 225:2; ~ curtailed, 641:13; devoted ~, 426:5, 6, 12; 446:13, 14; 452:8; 483:5; 734:7; frustrations of ~, 220:13; ~ grown apart, 156:6; 426:67; 475:2; 710:4; lasting ~, 341:2; limits of ~, 180:4; mistrust in ~, 432:10; rewards of ~, 699:5; 744:9; spark of ~, 595:19; 740:17; transient ~, 737:63

frivolity, 399:10; 425:10

frost, 746:1

fruit, 156:4; overripe ~, 492:48; ripe ~, 169:2; 671:1

fulfillment, 61:2; 302:14; fear of ~, 426:14; search for ~, 265:21; 450:1; wish ~, 97:1

funeral (*also see* burial), 678:19; ~ in wartime, 598:2

future, the (*also see* tomorrow), 676:84; 686:7; 718:1; 728:15; 742:4, 5; foretelling ~, 740:38; preparation for ~, 409:7; ~ prospects, 678:5; seeing ~, 718:10; 735:2

future, seeing the (*also see* foreknowledge; tomorrow)

G

gaiety, 563:16

gallantry, 482:3; lack of ~, 596:7

gambler/gambling (*also see* card playing; wager), 472:39; 615:41; honest ~, 472:34; woman ~, 776:3

game, ~ of cards, 685:1

garden, 300:11; 450:1; 591:11; 603:7; 760:3; poor man's ~, 796:6

gardening, 744:42

garlic, 253:2

Garrick, David, 519:10

gazelle, 169:1

generalization, 678:72

generation, new ~, 796:42

generosity (*also see* bounty), 164:15; 279:9; 358:14; 475:1; 496:35; 603:64; 676:25, 42; calculated ~, 743:31

genius (*also see* greatness), 588:1, 3, 4; 614:14; 644:8; 676:87; 712:42; 734:4; 735:23; 743:26; death of ~, 589:39; offspring of ~, 549:5; timid ~, 644:2; woman ~, 482:13

genocide, 37:7; 477:10; ~ of American Indian, 656:4

gentleman (*also see* man/men), 438:45

gentleness, 286:35

George III, King of England, 657:1

George IV, King of England, 680:1

German/Germany, 676:56; ~ men, 676:103; society in ~, 676:105

Gethsemane, 782:1

ghost, 740:22; 782:16; ~ story, 603:61

girl (*also see* child/children), 729:7; conditioning of ~ (*also see* woman/women, conditioning of), 342:11; 440:11; 473:4; 537:1; 613:2; 637:8; 676:1; 785:4; good ~, 729:9; physical development of ~, 758:5, 6

glance, 269:4; 462:17

glory, 61:2; 286:36; 358:14; 395:30; 423:3; 564:1; 656:46; 737:11; 743:96; desire for ~, 224:6; hollow ~, 633:2; risks for ~, 462:5

gluttony, 214:11

goal (*also see* purpose; pursuit), 412:16; 737:54; distant ~, 492:44; elusive ~, 550:56; 656:43

God* (*also see* absolution; forgiveness, divine; Holy Ghost; Jesus Christ; religion), 15:1; 33:2; 130:1; 137:10; 148:30; 163:7; 164:6, 18; 194:2; 204:3, 13; 231:8; 257:3; 264:6; 265:4; 275:2; 276:1, 3; 282:1; 286:23, 38, 40, 44; 288:5; 290:10; 299:5; 302:3, 8; 311:3; 325:9; 337:2, 3, 7; 357:6, 7; 378:3, 11; 385:1; 410:2; 418:19; 426:4; 452:4; 453:2; 454:3; 478:8; 501:17; 548:1; 623:1; 703:1; 705:3; 711:13; 726:4; 728:40; 749:1; 763:69; 772:11; 796:38; alone with ~, 130:2; 291:4; 412:26; belief in ~, 261:1; commune with

I

Indian, ~ ambush, 558:1, 2; depredation of ~, 689:9; 763:13; ~ encampment, 531:1; ~ in relation to white man, 656:4, 5; 763:12; Mohawk ~, 531:25; North American ~, 434:1; 722:40; 737:88, 90; 763:55, 56

indifference, 202:5; 426:71; 501:21; 530:3; 744:78

indirectness, 678:78

indiscretion, 462:15

individual (*also see* humankind; people), dangerous ~, 419:12; 735:26; delightful ~, 699:3; insignifance of ~, 202:5

individuality (*also see* distinction), 795:8; lack of ~, 532:12

indolence, 349:5; 401:8; 418:5; 595:24; 676:34; ~ in children, 156:39; preventing ~, 615:48

indulgence, 345:2; 615:42; 735:6; 737:71; over-~, 540:22; self-~, 735:10

industriousness, 583:3

industry (*also see* diligence; labor; work, hard),

inequality, 780:8; social ~, 603:43

infant, 90:1; 156:31; 656:11; 666:12; 737:25; birth of ~ (*also see* childbirth), 228:3; crying ~, 666:7; death of ~, 289:1, 2; 398:25; 473:8; 512:7; 613:1; 644:9; 699:6; 737:48; 738:1; 763:35, 36; 801:2; fat ~, 153:6; smiling ~, 738:17; teething ~, 666:19

infatuation, 562:1; 777:22

infection, 419:19

infertility (*also see* barrenness), 6:1

infidelity (*also see* adultery; faithlessness), 156:56; 219:4; 265:1; 413:2; 438:33; marital ~, 678:59; rationalization for ~, 156:66

inflation, 593:3

inflexibility (*also see* unyielding), 710:33

influence, 676:36; 711:32; ~ of peers, 711:8; ~ thought, 96:4

information, ~ leak, 156:53

ingenuousness, 246:2

ingratitude, 339:21; 358:13; 376:14; 525:12; 650:8; 676:38

inheritance (*also see* legacy), ~ for women, 6:5; 11:1; ~ rights of women, 243:11

iniquity (*also see* sin/sinner; vice), 291:11

initiative, 551:6

injury, imaginary ~, 740:33

injustice, bearing ~, 216:32

innocence, 55:1; 417:1; 438:86, 87; 496:18; 615:12; 667:7; 737:9; 743:25; loss of ~, 620:36; maintain ~, 611:1

innocuousness, 438:109

insanity (*also see* madness; mental illness; mind, disease of the), fear of ~, 666:49

insect, 445:1

insensibility, 156:28

inseparability, 164:20; 184:28; 426:26

insight (*also see* perceptivness), 367:4; 790:2; quick ~, 710:53

insignificance, 795:6

insomnia (*also see* sleeplessness), 139:11

inspiration, 395:25; 712:22; artistic ~, 295:1; cause of ~, 744:38

instinct, 309:34; 743:97; trusting ~, 777:20

instruction, 452:3; heavenly ~, 231:3; ~ to children (*also see* child rearing), 226:10

insult, 596:5; ignore ~, 265:52

intangibility, 115:1

integrity (*also see* principle), 39:1; 40:1; 216:32; 260:6; 332:5; 426:56; 596:1; 678:113; 710:101; 740:4

intellect, 309:34; 595:20; 676:12, 49; uncultivated ~, 615:76

intellectual, 589:11; woman ~, 248:3

intelligence (*also see* mind, the; woman/women, intelligence of), 265:31; 433:4; 436:3; 711:2; 728:7; extreme ~, 532:27; ~ of men, 613:4; purpose of ~, 214:11

intention, good ~, 412:13; 666:64

interests, limited ~, 485:2

intimacy, 676:39; 710:16; invitation to ~, 13:1; lack of ~, 666:44; yearning for ~, 135:1

intolerance, 501:4

intrigue, 540:10; political ~, 438:52

introspection (*also see* self-examination), 339:6; 737:1; 763:7; lack of ~, 284:4

invention, 324:5; 472:42; 676:3; 722:7; 789:4

invincibility, 481:3

Ireland, 712:42; 744:3, 10, 18; beauty of ~, 712:38; religion in ~, 712:34; strife in ~, 712:35

Irish, the, 678:38, 40; ~man, 712:10, 41; ~ Rebellion, 477:10

irreligiousness, 509:1

isolation, artistic ~, 737:53

isolationism, 260:12

La Fontaine, Jean de, 419:18
lamb, 743:38
Lamb, Charles, 666:44, 65, 66
landscape, 676:45
language, 341:11; 492:20; 763:74; ~ barriers,
  260:2; English ~, 438:47; French ~,
  676:54; Irish ~, 678:40; learning ~,
  588:59; 763:75; limitations of ~, 438:47;
  pretentious ~, 678:80; 740:24; purpose of
  ~, 589:8
largesse, 330:2
lasciviousness (*also see* lust), 265:8
lateness, 589:13; 758:9
laughter (*also see* mirth), 3:2; 226:4; 444:3;
  588:21; 589:3, 35; 678:34, 37; object of ~,
  656:65; 735:14
laundry, 588:43
law, 472:60; 678:42; 686:6; 743:68; corrupting
  influence of ~, 438:87; obeying ~, 596:1;
  Salic ~, 282:2; 487:6; trust in ~, 305:2;
  656:82; women and ~, 591:15
lawlessness, 763:68
Lawrence, Sir Thomas, 628:18
lawyer, mercenary ~, 343:3; 399:2
Lazar Hrebeljanovic, Prince of Serbia, 218:3
Lazarus, 401:2
leader (*also see* head of state; ruler), 74:1;
  550:43; 647:2; concerns of ~, 309:14; death
  of ~, 108:1; hypocrisy of ~, 744:10; loved
  ~, 309:7; tools of ~, 81:1
leadership, good ~, 758:36; necessity of ~,
  309:12; rewards of ~, 559:1
learning, 156:58; 339:2; 342:1; 409:9; 438:12;
  485:4; 563:12; 589:7; ~ denied, 482:12;
  prejudice against ~, 156:1; purpose of ~,
  220:2
legacy (*also see* inheritance), 263:1
legend, 156:50
leisure (*also see* pleasure; relaxation), 337:13;
  628:5; 743:53; life of ~, 710:103
lessee, 687:2
letters, 153:13; 162:2; 164:10; 274:1; 298:1;
  421:2; 452:6; 492:25; 523:1; 666:45; 730:2;
  ~ from brothers, 710:52; love ~, 549:1;
  567:2; 696:1, 4; newsy ~, 689:10; personal
  ~, 274:7; privacy of ~, 274:6; undelivered
  ~, 153:1; uplifting ~, 666:57; writing of
  ~, 153:10, 11; 287:3; 419:35; 501:18;
  591:10; 710:90; 728:23
liberalism, 723:3

liberation (*also see* freedom; rights), women's
  ~, 344:10
Liberia, 743:83
liberty (*also see* freedom), 290:7; 446:1; 458:1;
  472:54; 532:10; 550:43; 603:56; 622:1;
  635:2; 647:15; 676:112; 722:13; 737:30;
  744:3, 4; civil ~, 621:13; denial of ~,
  496:22; fight for ~, 82:1, 2, 3; preserving
  ~, 714:15
library, 419:16; 438:95; 531:2; 744:68
lie/lying (*also see* deception; falseness), 62:2;
  282:3; 331:2; 337:6; 438:20; 440:6; 472:37;
  521:1; 620:26; 710:95; response to ~, 403:1
life, 96:10; 155:4; 257:2; 269:11; 275:1; 286:21,
  36; 339:10, 14; 560:5; 588:34; 618:7; 676:44,
  70, 111; 737:5, 47, 93; 738:11; 763:30;
  783:16; beginning of ~, 458:8; Christian
  ~, 642:11; civilized ~, 722:51; contemplative ~, 204:7; cycles of ~, 136:4; 156:55;
  452:13; 579:4; 723:1; 763:37; difficulties of
  ~, 283:2; 297:3; 378:14; 382:11; 426:37;
  534:7; 666:18; 738:21; 760:10; 793:3; duration of ~, 418:10; 492:44; 587:1; 588:35;
  595:44; 615:22; 725:3; 728:12; 738:16; essence of ~, 163:16; 737:91; failed ~,
  300:18; fear of ~, 263:15; ~ force, 163:7,
  11; 269:7; 656:70; 789:7; goals of ~, 139:6;
  good ~, 214:15; 226:3; 334:1; 588:13; injustice of ~, 279:6; inner ~ (*also see* consciousness), 139:16; 615:55; 656:29; 763:7;
  insignificance of ~, 603:37; 614:2; last moment of ~, 418:13; lessons of ~, 309:4;
  398:28; 450:8; 452:3; 676:94; 689:6; 722:55;
  love of ~, 156:57; 581:3; 702:14; 711:18;
  743:97; mastering ~, 795:4; meaningless-
  ness of ~, 418:2; 433:9; 550:32; 615:45;
  714:22; meaning of ~, 94:1; miracle of ~,
  38:1; 258:2; 758:20; mystery of ~, 676:71;
  772:7; 777:10; observation of ~, 38:2; or-
  derly ~, 216:12; 531:12; path of ~, 214:4;
  272:2; 279:10; 395:8; 446:7; 741:3; 743:11;
  763:3; priorities in ~, 269:10; purpose of
  ~, 656:88; 712:29; 737:73; sacrifice of ~,
  308:1; simple ~, 796:22, 24; spiritual ~
  (*also see* religion; religious life; spirit),
  269:9; 302:7; 331:4; 579:6; struggles of ~,
  162:3; 214:1; 291:9; 300:8; 302:7; 404:2;
  419:49; 550:49; 711:8; 718:11; 737:77, 89;
  763:2, 31; 772:2; transience of ~, 216:14,
  29; 262:1; 278:2; 299:5; 302:8; 339:11, 12,

15; 384:2; 399:8; 418:6; 438:77; 770:11; 796:40; understanding ~, 96:1; unhappy ~, 263:16; 317:9; 416:3; 656:95; 676:43; 680:2; 737:28; 757:7; 796:35; unpredictability of ~, 311:2; 550:48; 579:8; 615:46; 644:1

light, 55:31

lily, 702:15, 16; 782:2

limitations (*also see* restraint), 676:79; awareness of ~, 265:24; surpass one's ~, 395:25

lips, 118:1

liquor (*also see* drugs; drunkenness), 244:2; 469:3; 490:1; 658:1; 710:94; 728:35; 758:2; abstain from ~, 744:1

listening, 737:101; 763:71

literature (*also see* book; fiction; novel; reading), giants of ~, 737:51; masterpieces of ~, 773:1; 18th century ~, 676:13

livelihood (*also see* annuity; money), lack of ~, 615:63; seeking a ~, 650:5

Liverpool, Robert Banks Jenkinson, 2nd Earl of, 696:8

locality, indifference toward ~, 435:10

lodgings, 588:7

London, England, 588:25, 48

loneliness (*also see* aloneness), 91:2; 136:3; 150:2; 162:14; 419:15; 620:45; 728:38; 775:16; 777:42

longevity, 156:52

longing, 125:5; 157:2; 160:2, 5; 172:1; 259:5; 319:3; 426:58; 438:102; 620:37

Lord (*see* God)

Lorraine, François de, duc de Guise, 722:32

loss, 156:65; 181:6; pain of ~, 409:18; 777:30

lost, the, 29912; 615:82; 737:3, 35

Louis XIV, King of France, 433:11, 12

Louis XV, King of France, 534:2, 6, 8

Louis XVI, King of France, 616:3, 6

Louis XVII, King of France, 663:1

love (*also see* attachment, emotional; heart; life, love of; lovemaking; lover), 53:2; 55:17, 18, 19, 26, 42; 75:5; 125:6; 134:1; 155:5; 156:48; 163:8; 173:1; 176:1; 181:2, 8; 183:1; 184:10, 15; 204:2, 4, 14; 206:5, 6, 7, 8, 9; 222:1; 265:7; 275:1; 277:2; 286:11, 34; 293:5; 299:1, 3, 7; 300:10, 16, 21; 302:4; 319:2; 361:6, 9, 10, 11; 395:10; 412:14; 426:2, 59; 435:1, 6, 7; 438:23, 31, 41, 64, 81, 83, 84, 101, 103, 108; 444:2; 450:37; 462:4; 472:5, 35, 40; 474:4; 477:16, 20; 478:8; 481:2; 491:9; 496:11, 17, 20; 497:6; 498:1;

529:1, 2; 540:9, 11, 14; 545:9; 549:1, 3; 550:42; 554:3; 560:8, 11, 12, 17; 562:2; 563:8; 588:65; 589:35; 620:10, 13, 22; 647:18; 655:2; 656:19; 676:9, 31, 51, 58, 81, 104; 688:4; 710:38; 728:13, 22, 50; 734:6, 13; 744:39, 70; 777:38; anatomy of ~, 395:24; ~ at first sight, 277:1; 395:22; 740:36, 37; aversion to ~, 420:13; 425:8; avowal of ~, 141:2; 155:6; 200:6; 266:1; 271:3; 435:9; 438:26, 59; 615:52; comfort of ~, 702:6; constant ~, 120:4; 178:1; 200:5; 263:4; constrictions of ~, 438:4; 472:2; 758:36; cure for ~, 293:3; 471:1; desire for ~, 293:13; 551:19; 777:42; despotic ~, 744:22; difficulties of ~, 139:13, 15; 180:1; 181:5, 9; 221:2; 303:2; 532:6; 545:10; divine, 734:19; embrace of ~, 392:1; 427:3; end of ~, 55:13; 155:7; 220:18; 395:38; 407:13; 426:67; 438:94; 472:67; 482:4; 588:42; 640:1; 678:64; 735:16, 18; 788:3; excessive ~, 181:1; 426:71; false ~, 259:6; 265:27; 299:8; 300:20; 395:16; 403:6; 440:8; 639:1; 688:6; 735:15; 744:62; 777:32; familial ~, 339:1; 646:2; 666:54; fickle ~, 144:1; 184:17, 27; 265:41; 293:4; 395:5; 450:45; 710:31; first ~, 127:1; 796:12; fleeting ~, 95:1; 492:14; foolish ~, 75:3; 472:30; 620:12; 744:69; forbidden ~, 200:1; futility of ~, 299:11; 604:5; 744:80; game of ~ (*also see* courtship), 200:2; 265:15; 303:11; 319:5; 426:1; 438:65, 85; 470:3; 531:6; 537:2; 666:31; 735:6; 738:10; 744:36; great ~, 406:2; 426:45; 435:16; 696:9; illicit ~, 432:11; 438:17; incapacity for ~, 184:6; 204:7; 401:6; 433:12; 501:16; incapacity to ~, 563:18; indiscriminate ~, 199:1; 407:12; long-lasting ~, 156:69; 435:8; 712:31; lost ~, 116:1; 134:3; 142:1; 171:2; 228:1; 450:38; 566:1; 647:43; 688:2; 698:4; maintain ~, 676:57; men and ~, 167:1; ~ and money, 180:3; 184:16; mutual ~, 435:4; 438:69; 462:12; 529:3; 588:31, 38; 737:15; 744:2; nature of ~, 181:10; 184:13; new ~, 181:13; 438:79; 519:1; 676:78; object of ~, 55:21, 33; 299:2, 6; 300:13; 325:12; 406:5; 433:17; 438:5; 492:23; 532:27; 563:10; 605:3; 620:1; 676:28; 717:7; 744:34; 796:10; obsessive ~, 74:3; 406:4; 419:29; 549:2; 656:41; ~ of humankind, 216:16; 265:20; ~ of men, 418:7; ~ of

military (*also see* army; soldier; war), ~ honors, 550:7

Milton, John, 532:8

mind, the (*also see* intelligence; reason; thinking), 184:20; 194:1; 250:4; 341:14; 407:2; 450:15; 472:24; 525:3; 722:18; 728:57; 735:22; 743:37, 43; childlike ~, 55:1; cultivation of ~, 286:32; 532:18; 550:52; 615:64; 652:4; 737:73; 772:4; empty ~, 647:35; feminine ~, 412:23; 550:38; 617:1; 625:3; flexibility of ~, 656:59; health of ~, 531:26; impious ~, 438:58; influence of ~, 763:85; ~ in relation to body, 678:83; 790:3; limitations of ~, 637:8; 652:5; 655:7; masculine ~, 407:11; 763:39; power of ~, 712:32; resiliance of ~, 309:22; strength of ~, 341:13; troubled ~, 173:2; undeveloped ~, 468:4

ministration, 268:8; 654:3

minutes (*also see* moment; time), 782:24

Mira Bai, 269:7

miracle, witness to ~, 44:2

mirror, 492:39; 637:7; bad ~, 714:18; reflection in ~, 782:8, 11

mirth (*also see* cheerfulness; laughter), 412:3, 4, 5

misandry, 455:5; 496:5

misanthropy, 472:65

misery (*also see* wretchedness), 156:40; 220:22; 279:6; 416:3; 437:2; 452:11; 477:6; 540:15; 559:3; 644:3; 737:7; end of ~, 291:7; 603:6; release from ~, 740:11

misfortune, 137:8; 258:3; 259:2; 420:18; 519:9; 650:6; 656:83; 678:44; 737:82; 760:2; handling ~, 656:61; lessons of ~, 563:12; 744:17

misogyny, 184:19; 220:16; 376:13, 15; 398:17; 403:7; 440:2; 468:13; 488:3; 603:39; 633:6

missionary, 473:11

mist, morning ~, 95:1

mistake (*also see* error), 358:1; 550:40; 636:8; 678:38

mistress, 346:1; 395:19; 432:16; 470:3; 472:8; 750:1; ~ in relation to wife, 288:13

mistrust, 325:6; 656:49; ~ of government, 156:13; ~ of men, 403:6; 438:9; ~ of women, 309:37

mockery, 37:3; 265:40; 286:7; 420:1; 620:3; 633:7

modesty, 342:2; 426:57; 437:1; 452:2; 589:25; ~ in youth, 642:3

molestation, 148:12

moment (*also see* minutes; time), 770:22; great ~, 589:34

monarch/monarchy, 236:2; 309:12; 412:35; 496:21; 551:10, 21

monestary, 452:12

money (*also see* gold; livelihood; wealth), 225:2; 244:1; 286:9; 438:40, 97; 472:36, 50; 540:30; 554:2; 666:61; 676:83; 710:11; 722:47; 728:5; 743:47; acquisition of ~, 477:4; 678:105; 772:5; 783:15; evil of ~, 656:98; friendship and ~, 438:108; lack of ~, 230:4; 593:3; love and ~ (*also see* marriage, economics of), 472:35; 660:8; 678:20; 710:81; love of ~, 216:1; 472:41; 550:9; 637:1; ~ management, 374:2; power of ~, 748:7; saving ~, 722:19; spending ~, 252:2; 419:37; 589:1; 758:2; value of ~, 616:6; women and ~, 616:11; 722:21

monogamy, 472:3

monotheism, 288:5

monotony, 158:1; 795:6

monster (*also see* grotesque), 789:10, 14

month (*see specific months*)

monument, 676:53

moon, 156:38; 244:1; 285:2; 603:25; 782:21, 22; crescent ~, 603:1; light of ~, 660:9

moralist, 438:66; 462:11

morality, 482:8; 676:24, 41; 723:5; 772:4; decaying ~, 260:11; 676:29; 763:64; sense of ~, 678:61; upholding ~, 560:1; 772:3

morbidness, 678:62

More, Henry, 728:25

mores (*also see* custom), changing ~, 625:3

morning (*also see* day), 352:1; 710:72

Morpheus, 603:21

mortality, 283:3

Moses, 8:1; 426:25

mother/motherhood (*also see* parents), 81:5; 90:2; 165:2; 349:4; 412:29, 30; 466:1; 492:34; 670:1; 702:12; 729:1; 763:45; 772:6; comforting ~, 702:6; death of ~, 512:8; 526:1; 661:3; 737:13, 23; 738:15, 18; 744:45; 763:23; 775:4; desire for ~, 412:22; expectant ~, 647:44; illness of ~, 758:35; inadequacies of ~, 647:26; influence of ~, 743:5, 14; 760:1; 763:59, 86; ~ in relation to offspring, 5:3; 28:1; 230:5; 238:1; 260:13;

P

pacifism (*also see* war, opposition to), 771:5; ~ of women, 288:10

pain (*also see* suffering), 77:1; 109:1; 215:6; 418:12; 419:8; 452:11; 588:6; 757:10; 795:1; cause ~, 280:4; 680:5; eternal ~, 294:1; great ~, 656:93; inflict ~, 728:10

painting (*also see* art; portrait), 372:5; 479:5; 741:15; great ~, 628:18; 686:9; setting for ~, 629:1

Palestine, 512:2

pantheism, 215:2; 269:7

Papacy, decrees of ~, 264:2

paper, page of ~, 763:40

paradise (*also see* Eden; heaven), 231:3; 265:47; 515:2; 666:63; 770:18, 19; earthly ~, 378:2; lost ~, 438:76; path to ~, 109:1

parasite (*also see* sycophancy)

parents (*also see* father; mother; motherhood), 324:3; 398:30; 452:5; 492:29; 666:13; 704:4; 728:46; 729:4; 748:11; 780:9; death of ~, 615:17; dependent ~, 540:28; 604:3; ~ in relation to offspring, 311:5; 342:3; 419:47; 540:7; 588:12; 604:4; 647:27; 650:2; 678:77; 711:9; step-~, 153:5

Paris, France, 560:13; 603:28; 676:104, 105; 737:58

Parisian, 804:2

parricide (*also see* patricide), 81:4

parrot, talking ~, 472:11

parting (*also see* departure; separation), 72:1; 125:4; 238:4; 271:2; 274:2; 291:6; 435:11; 674:3, 6; 712:2; 737:45, 99; 767:1; bitter ~, 299:9; ~ from homeland, 317:1; 784:1; sadness of ~, 156:9, 10

partnership, good ~, 678:25

party, 682:3; big ~, 710:83; ~ over, 710:77

party (celebration) (*see* ball, social; festivity)

passion (*also see* desire; emotion; feelings), 160:4; 298:4; 420:15; 491:3; 496:16; 588:46; 712:26; 743:25; 744:78; 788:1; ashamed of ~, 492:16; harnessing ~, 339:8; 472:4; 540:19; inspire ~, 540:17; lack of ~, 777:12; misplaced ~, 678:104; rewards of ~, 560:18; uncontrolled ~, 596:2; 637:2; 717:3; 777:28; undying ~, 744:73; unfulfilled ~, 136:7

passivity, 156:14

past, the (*also see* time, past), 409:5; 676:76, 113; 702:9; 710:48; 744:66 forgetting ~, 260:8; 656:58; remembering ~, 55:9; 409:14; 599:4; scorn of ~, 156:29

pastime, 361:8; 367:6

paternalism (*also see* protectiveness), 710:80; 790:7; resist ~, 771:7

patience, 216:11; 224:11; 286:40; 302:14; 438:53; 453:4; 532:20; 542:3, 4; 744:17

patricide, 350:5

patriot, 651:1; 653:1; 656:2; 673:1; 674:13; 681:6; 690:1; 712:3; 714:6, 7, 15; motives of ~, 743:19; woman ~, 577:1; 681:3; 763:87

patriotism, 550:4, 26; 626:10

patronage, 678:92

Paul, Saint, 79:1; 268:1; 286:39

peace, 214:26; 216:33, 34; 259:2; 288:4; 389:3; 545:7; 618:8; 621:15; 686:4; 763:47; consequences of ~, 87:4; disturbing ~, 268:8; fighting for ~, 303:6; god of ~, 572:2; inner ~ (*also see* tranquility), 263:12; 419:27; price of ~, 550:7; world ~, 789:9

pedantry, 477:3; 596:4; 678:95

pedigree, 674:2

pen, 666:30

penance, 656:73

penitance, true ~, 164:3

Pensacola, Florida, 679:1

people (*also see* humankind; individual; masses, the), 722:49; characteristics of ~, 712:15; complexity of ~, 641:17; connection of ~, 636:3; dichotomy of ~ (*also see* dichotomy, ~ of human beings), inconsistencies of ~, 710:37; interesting ~, 156:59; old ~ (*also see* age/aging; old age), 740:1; 764:3; 777:33; primitive ~, 438:86, 87; 531:23, 25; 778:2; understanding ~, 220:10; weakness of ~, 286:30; 689:11

Pepys, Samuel, 728:65

perception, 190:7

perceptiveness (*also see* insight), 220:10; 309:48; 641:17; lack of ~, 378:8

Perceval, Spencer, 696:8

perfection, 216:15; 299:8; 501:22; 641:16, 21; 710:109; 728:33; portrayal of ~, 399:3; 628:8

performer (*also see* actor/actress), 555:1; salary of, 555:2

perjury, 141:1

W

pendent ~, 152:1; 737:60; influence of ~, 550:21; 678:87; 760:1; 763:16; 781:1; ~ in relation to God (*also see* God, ~ in relation to women), 20:1; 42:2; ~ in relation to men (*also see* relationships, ~ between men and women), 77:1; 136:6; 139:5; 184:11; 265:18, 36; 293:13; 365:2; 404:4; 406:1, 4; 412:28; 418:7; 440:6; 479:5; 482:3; 531:6; 589:28; 615:52; 620:5; 676:28, 115; 710:66; 735:23; 742:10; 765:5; 788:2; ~ in relation to women (*also see* friendship, ~ between women), 620:14; 699:9; 710:6; 744:51; 783:1; intellectual ~, 399:5; 485:3; 775:7; intelligence of ~, 220:1, 2, 3; 342:1; 376:18; 399:11; 412:23; 438:2; 451:3; 492:32; 613:3; limitations imposed upon ~, 438:109; 482:12; 550:61; 591:12, 13; 647:9; 652:5; 659:4; 710:43; objectification of ~, 260:9; 402:5; old ~, 159:1; older ~ (*also see* age/aging; old age; people, old; women, aging), 492:18; 519:8; 615:21; 637:7; 744:76; oppression of ~, 232:1; 365:1; 394:1; 395:26; 412:9, 38; 438:51, 73; 455:1; 588:30; 591:4, 16; 633:5; 647:24; 676:27; 678:14, 57; 765:3; 780:3; potential of ~, 613:10; power of ~, 33:4; 412:28; 591:17; 620:38; 633:4; 790:10; progress of ~, 743:54, 94; 771:1; repressed ~, 139:2; 647:23; 782:7; rights of ~ (*see* rights, women's ~); role of ~ (*also see* housewife; wife), 61:2; 67:1; 220:2; 226:5; 399:14; 450:35; 451:2; 452:1; 458:18; 462:13; 466:1; 472:3; 550:51; 589:21; 644:5; 647:11, 37; 659:2; 737:61; 741:10; 757:3; 763:86, 87; 765:6; self-made ~, 790:5; ~ soldiers, 59:1; strength of ~, 220:9; 482:10; 501:20; 678:66; 718:5; 730:3; 790:7; struggles of ~ (*also see* rights, women's ~), 676:35, 102; symbols of ~, 302:2; ~ talk, 762:2; unmarried ~ (*also see* singleness, spinster), 505:2, 3; weakness of ~, 358:1; 399:22; 404:9; 438:32; 440:9; 743:16; work and ~ (*also see* housework), 743:85; 763:88; working ~ (*also see* ~, career ~), 137:8; 477:22; 740:12; young ~, 339:4; 710:2, 80; 785:5

womb, 90:2

woods, 419:13, 14

words, 398:8; 472:24; fads in ~, 440:16; flattering ~, 379:1; 438:75; hard ~, 148:28; last ~, 259:12; 260:14; 286:2; 464:1; 511:3;

534:12; 622:1; 626:4; 757:10; 782:3; 786:1; poetry of ~, 678:40; power of ~, 358:12; 400:1; 676:54; printed ~, 595:27; usefulness of ~, 390:1

Wordsworth, William ~, 666:67

work (*also see* labor; livelihood), 588:44; 609:1; 656:12, 38; 710:12; 743:52; conditions of ~, 235:1; demands of ~, 647:40; evaluation of ~, 477:23; 603:51; hard ~ (*also see* diligence; industry), 678:13, 29; honest ~, 540:28; 722:61; man's ~, 383:1; value of ~, 678:105; woman's ~, 292:2

worker, exploitation of ~, 540:27; struggles of ~, 339:11

work place, writer's ~, 588:17; 666:65

works, good ~, 762:1; ~ of man, 763:37

world (*also see* earth; universe), 148:21; 404:2; 410:2; 737:80; 789:6; another ~, 496:26; 777:8; blindness of ~, 758:28, 29; destruction of ~, 286:1; dissatisfaction with ~, 710:37; new ~, 740:26; 763:12; renunciation of ~, 420:22; 550:32, 52; 726:2; 747:2; 758:24

worldliness (*also see* fleshliness; materialism), 214:3, 12, 23; 215:3; 327:1; 366:1; 384:3; 391:5; 414:1; 426:16; 481:1; 744:20; 796:35; throw off ~, 263:5; 398:3

worry (*also see* anxiety), 280:2; 560:9; 615:78

worship (*also see* prayer), 130:1; place of ~, 636:7; right to ~ in own way, 710:55

worth/worthiness, 184:26; 744:15; consequences of ~, 184:5; measure of ~, 172:2; 742:8

wren, 246:1

wretchedness (*also see* misery), 378:6; 501:13; 595:15; hatred of ~, 789:12; ~ of women, 438:106

writer (*also see* author; novelist; playwright; poet; writing), 470:1; 477:1; 540:3; 744:11; ambition of ~, 550:18, 60; male ~, 710:113; ~'s block, 789:3; woman ~, 148:2; 292:2; 412:9; 458:16, 19; 462:1; 482:16; 483:3; 499:1; 502:1; 554:1; 571:7; 579:2; 613:7; 688:9; 710:90

writing (*also see* diary; fiction; letters, writing of; novel; poetry; stage play), 48:7; 148:4; 153:12; 286:8; 378:15; 406:3; 412:20; 438:62; 450:22; 462:17; 472:17; 608:1; 666:30; 710:64; 737:79, 83; appreciation of ~, 450:25; bad ~, 402:7; children ~,